THE BOY FROM CLEARWATER

BOOK 2

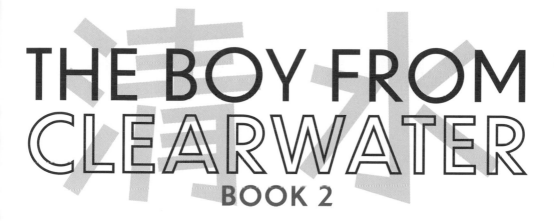

THE BOY FROM CLEARWATER

BOOK 2

YU PEI-YUN · ZHOU JIAN-XIN

TRANSLATION BY LIN KING

LEVINE QUERIDO

Montclair | Amsterdam | Hoboken

This is an Em Querido book
Published by Levine Querido

LEVINE QUERIDO

Levine Querido
www.levinequerido.com · info@levinequerido.com

Levine Querido is distributed by Chronicle Books

Library of Congress Control Number: 2023931856

Hardcover ISBN: 978-1-64614-372-6
Paperback ISBN: 978-164614-373-3

MIX
Paper | Supporting responsible forestry
FSC™ C016779

Printed in India
Published May 2024
First Printing
The text type was set in Sequentialist BB.

COLOR KEY FOR

SPOKEN LANGUAGES

To highlight the diversity of languages in Taiwan during this time period—including Hoklo Taiwanese, Mandarin Chinese, and Japanese—the color-coding system below is used to show which language the characters are speaking.

The gold tones correspond to Part 1, while Part 2 is coded in red tones.

HOKLO TAIWANESE

ENGLISH

PART 1

MANDARIN CHINESE

JAPANESE

PART 2

MANDARIN CHINESE

JAPANESE

NOTE FROM THE TRANSLATOR

The three main languages used in these books—Taiwanese Hoklo, Mandarin Chinese, and Japanese—all share similar written characters with very different pronunciations and romanization systems. The town 清水, for example, is pronounced "Tshing-tsui" in Taiwanese, "Chingshui" in Mandarin, and "Kiyomizu" in Japanese, all of which mean "clear water," hence the translation of the title *The Boy from Clearwater*.

Accordingly, some characters have names in multiple languages throughout the story. The main character, 蔡焜霖, is referred to by both his Taiwanese name, Tshua Khun-lim, and his Mandarin name, Tsai Kun-lin. Throughout the book, Mandarin is not necessarily romanized using the now-common Pinyin system, but also the Wade-Giles and other systems befitting the time periods and regions.

PART 3

THE ERA OF PRINCE MAGAZINE

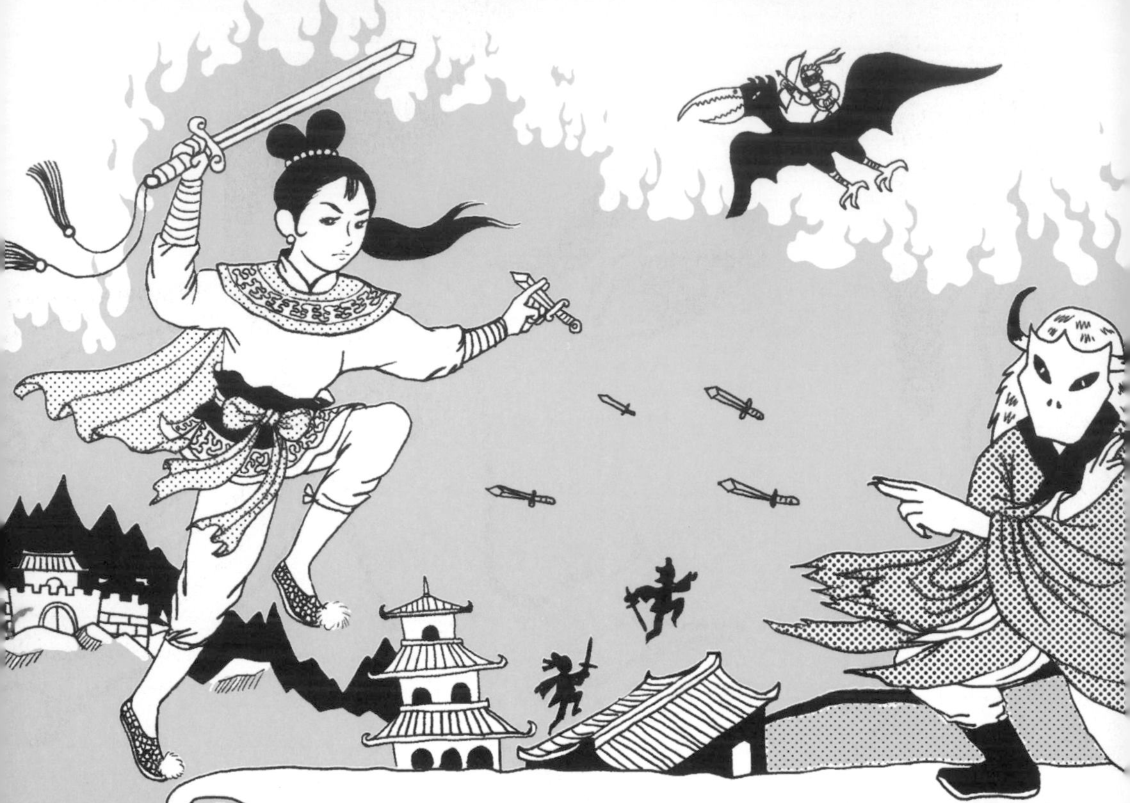

Tensions in the Taiwan Strait eased in the early 1960s. Taiwan, or the Republic of China (ROC), was able to noticeably improve its economy with the backing of the United States and through policies such as replacing agriculture with industry as its main sector and establishing export processing zones to encourage international business. This economic growth was accompanied by the rise of popular culture, including film, music, Taiwanese opera, and potehi—glove puppet television dramas. In 1962, the government founded Taiwan's first television station.

During this time, manhua comics serialized in children's periodicals became the primary source of entertainment for Taiwanese children. Among these, martial-arts-hero epics were most popular. Different publishers began launching their own manhua magazines and standalone manhua publications; they also began investing in cultivating many young manhua artists, setting the stage for the golden age of Taiwanese manhua.

However, despite this new vitality coursing through Taiwanese society, cultural outputs continued to be severely affected by government intervention. Creators were pressured to promote a "renaissance of Chinese culture" through their content and encourage the use of Mandarin Chinese, thereby suppressing Taiwan's local cultures and languages. Ideological control remained stringent, subjecting all books, periodicals, music, films, and television programming to review and censorship. Manhua, which targeted young audiences, was of course likewise strictly monitored.

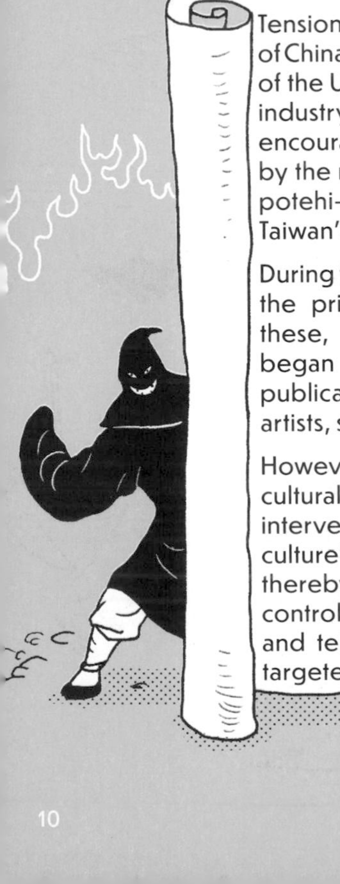

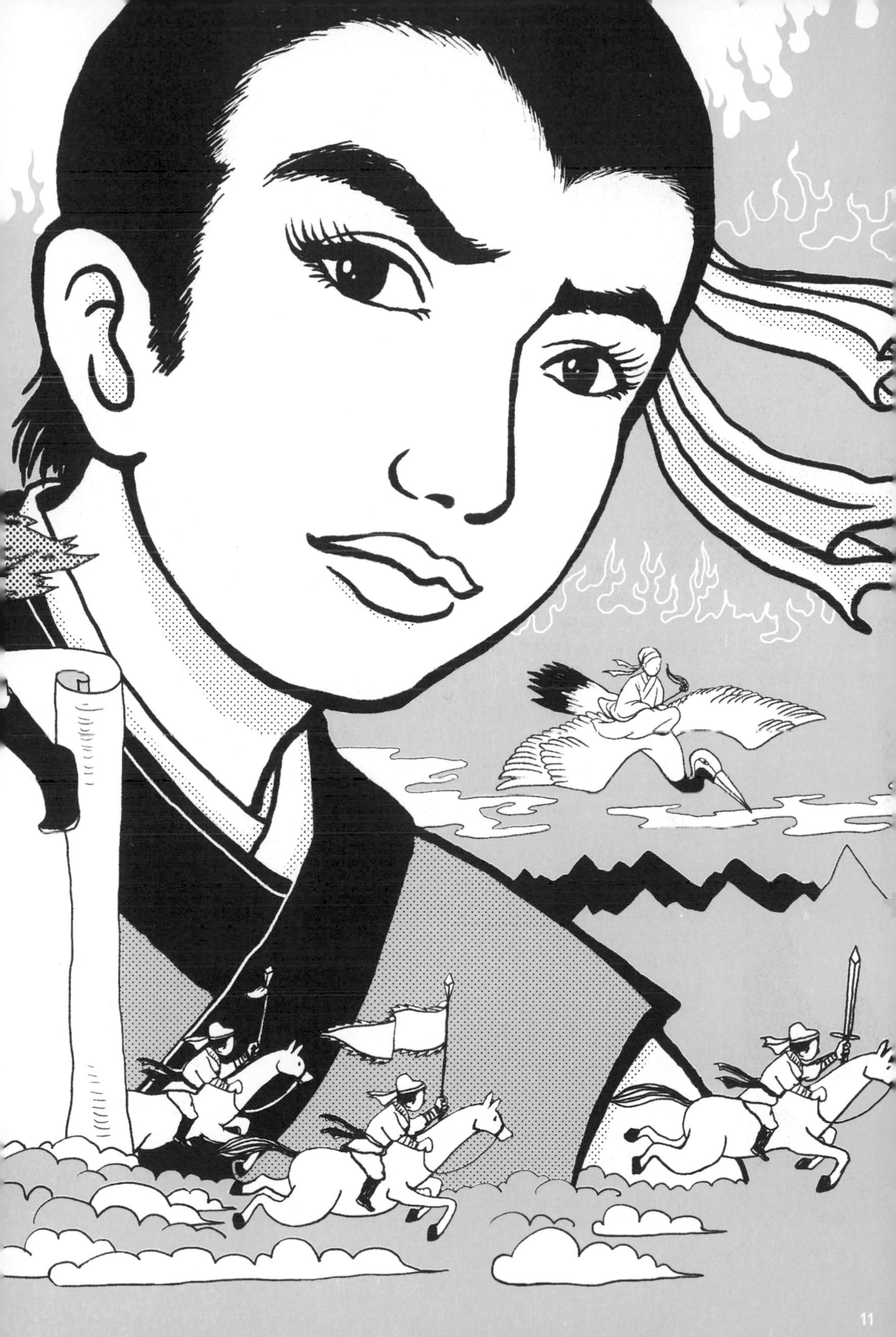

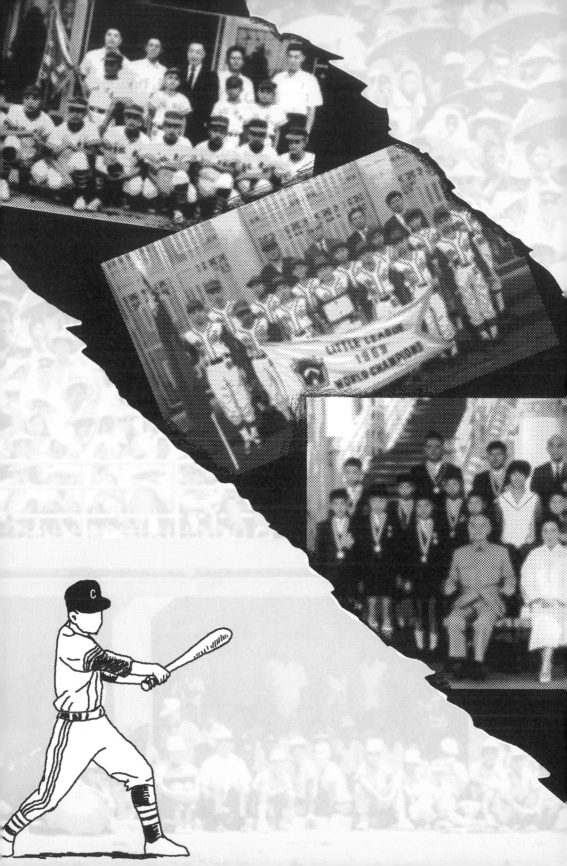

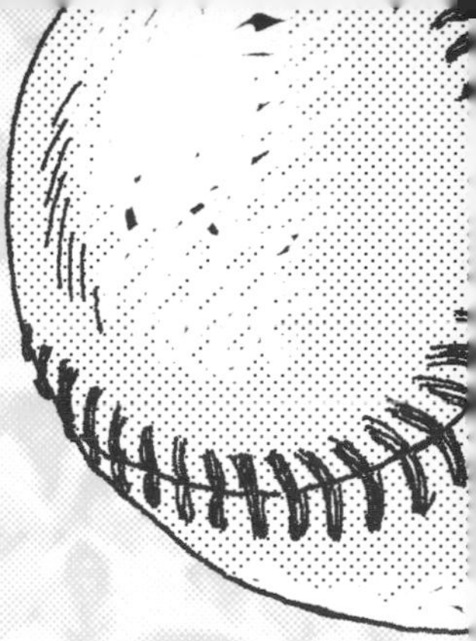

The second half of the 1960s saw the United States and the Soviet Union locked in the Cold War, with one regional conflict after another in a period of worldwide unrest: the Cuban Missile Crisis brought humankind to the brink of nuclear war; the Vietnam War showed no sign of resolution; independence movements in colonized African countries grew; the Arab-Israeli conflict erupted in the Middle East. Meanwhile, the People's Republic of China (PRC), which had only been recognized by a few European countries upon its founding, began to stabilize domestically and expand its diplomatic network overseas. The Taiwan-based ROC's international status gradually came under threat, and its future grew increasingly precarious.

In 1968, the Little League Baseball team Red Leaves, hailing from rural Taitung in eastern Taiwan, defeated the visiting all-star team from Japan, an event that spawned "The Legend of the Red Leaves." The following year, the Golden Dragons team from Taichung won the Little League World Series in the United States, rousing the spirits of Taiwanese citizens. International youth baseball became far more than a sport—it was regarded as a demonstration of national strength, and the young players as national heroes.

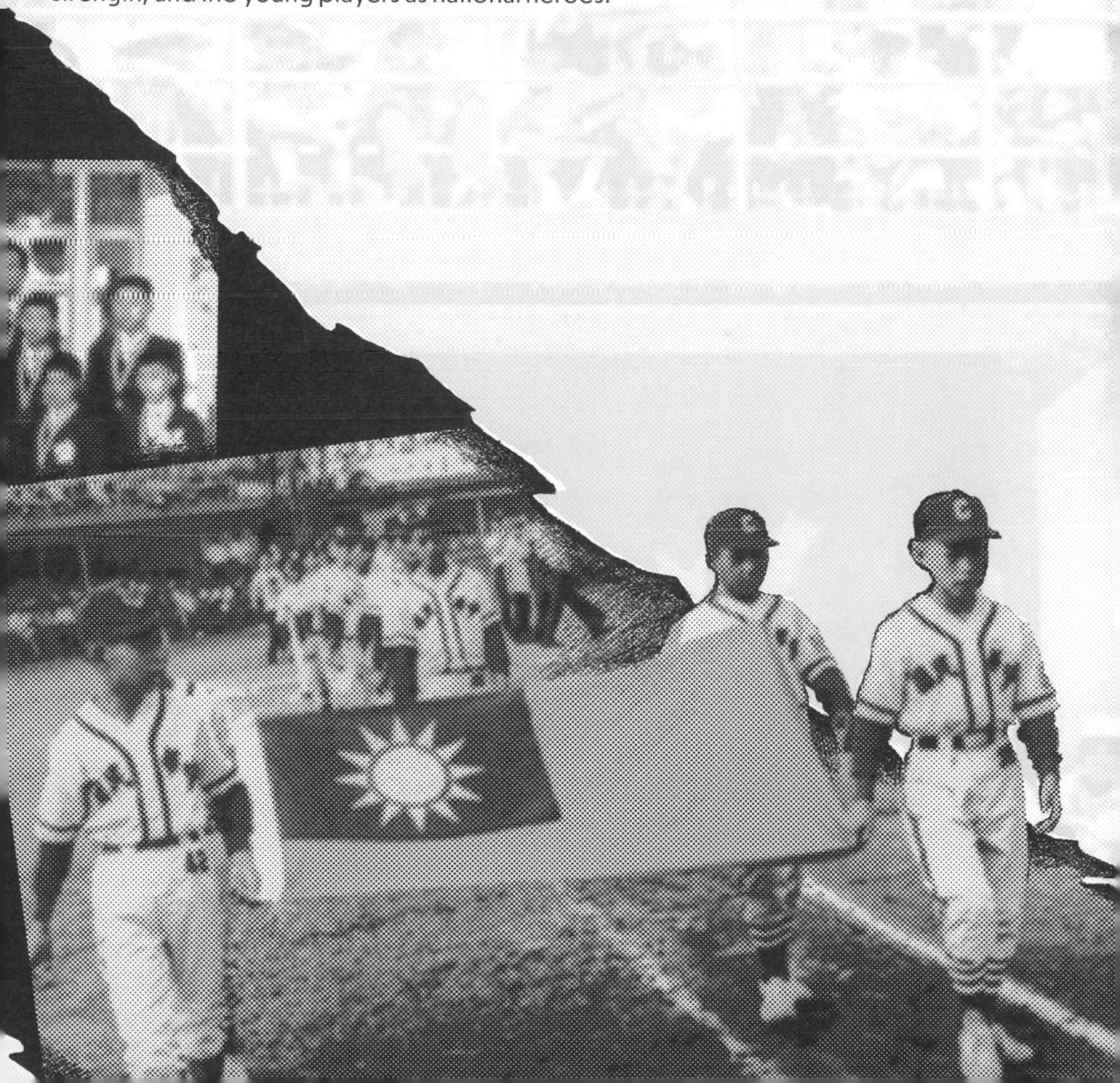

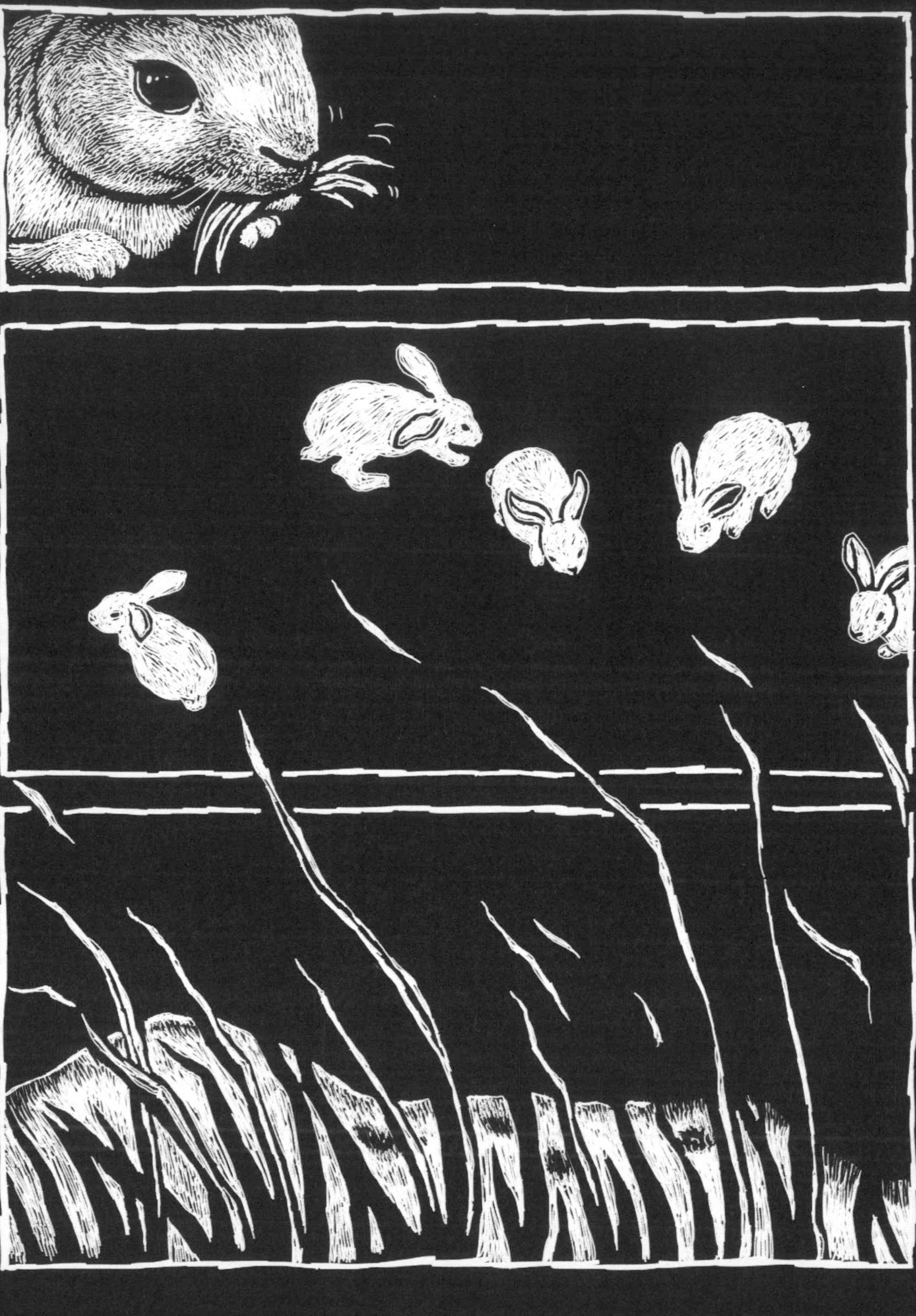

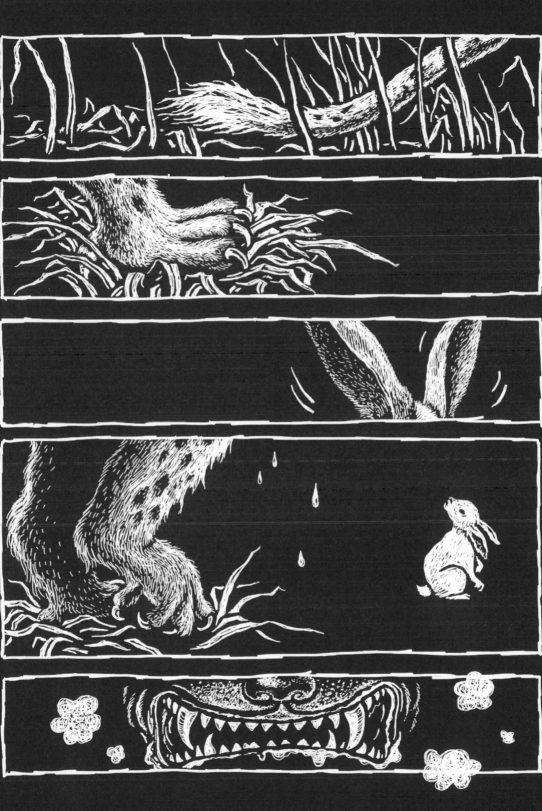

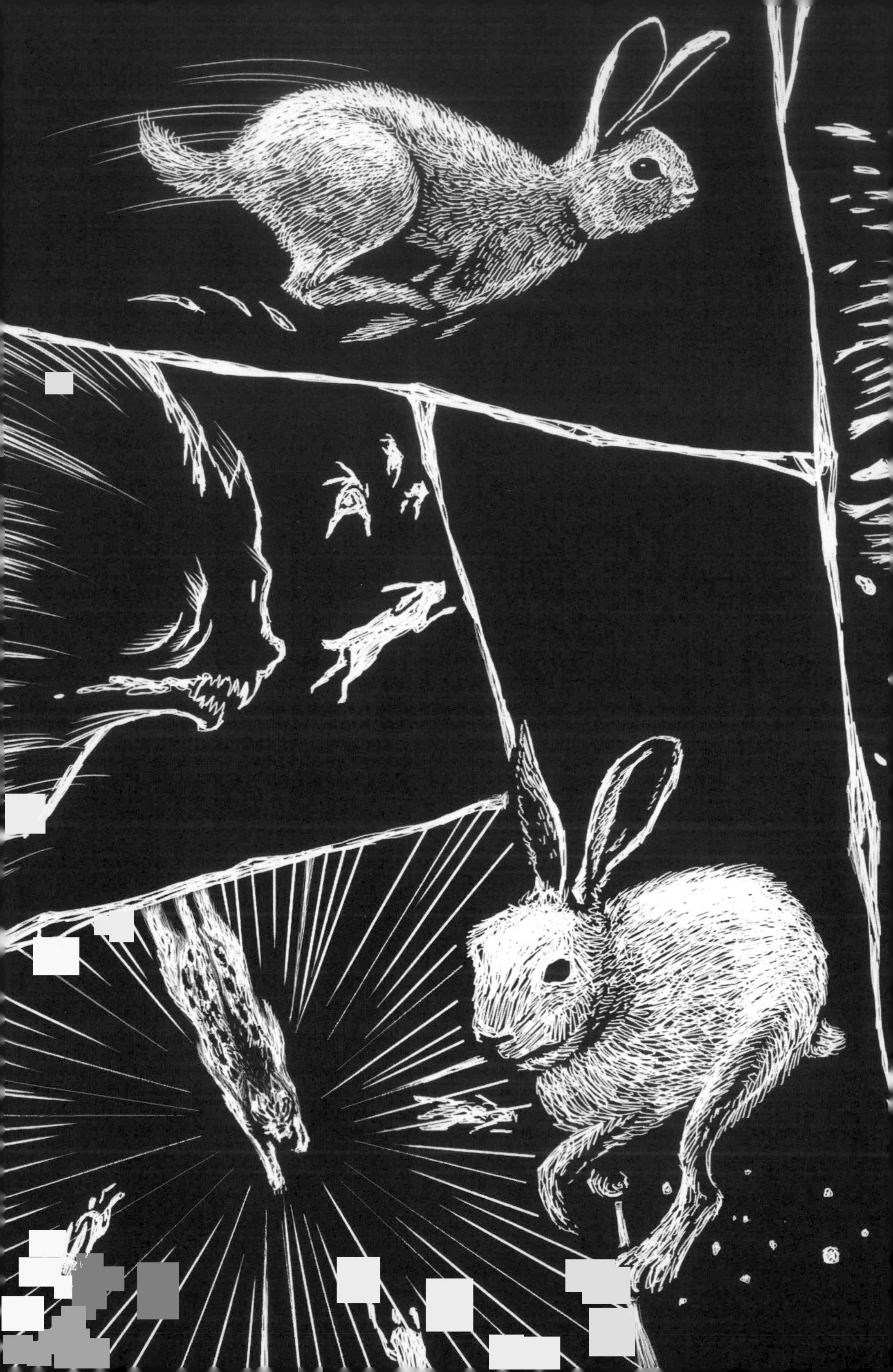

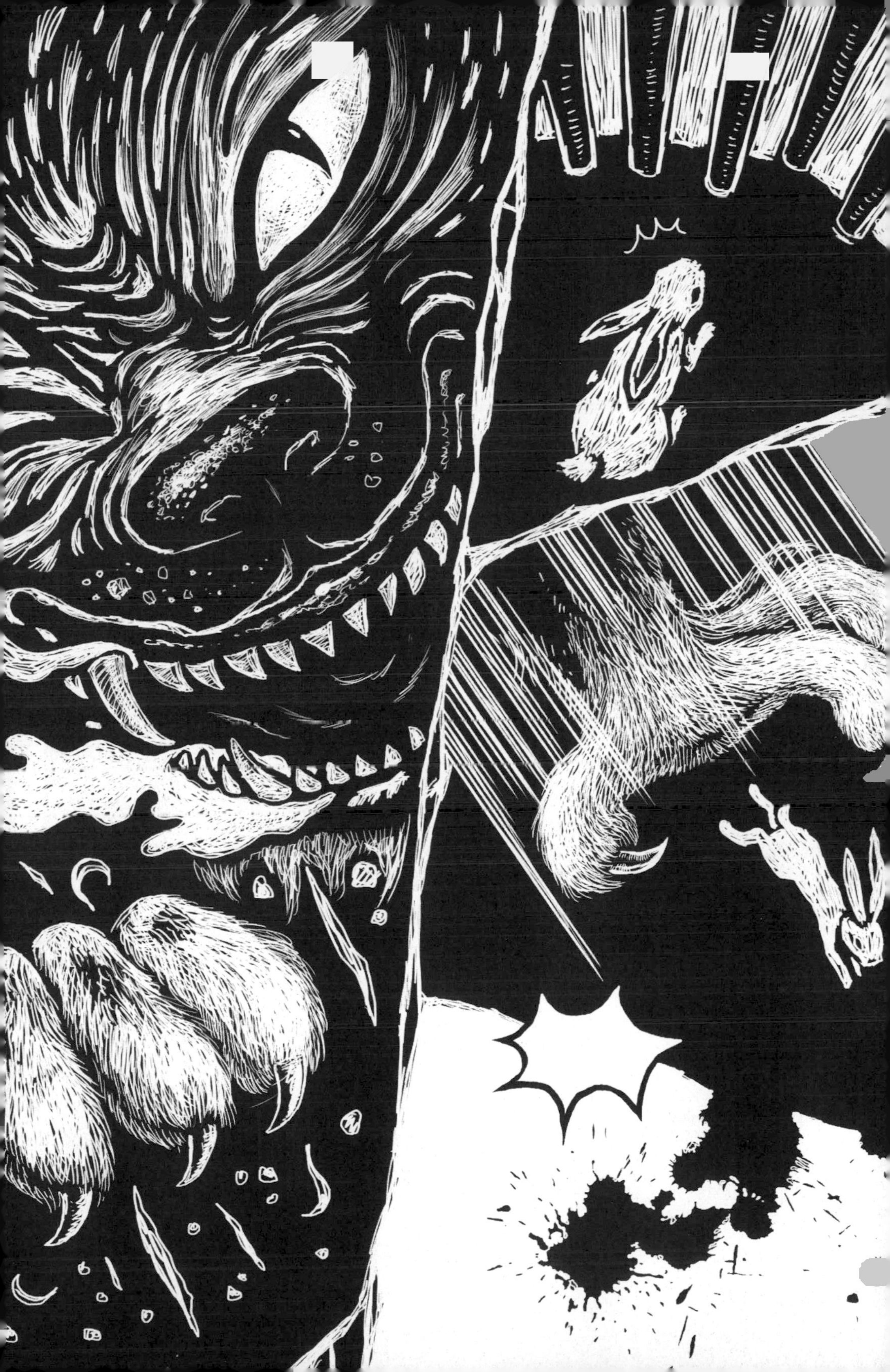

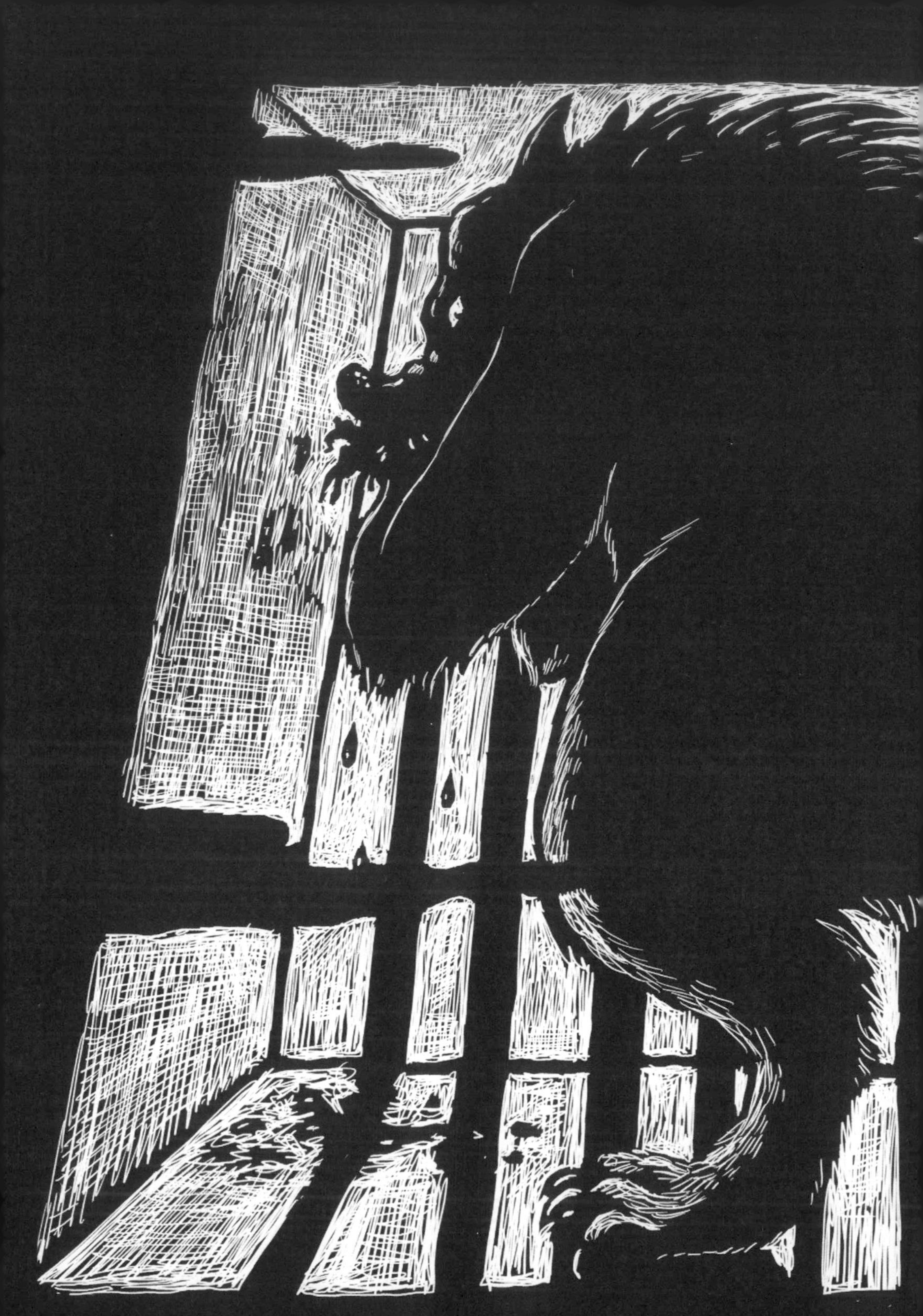

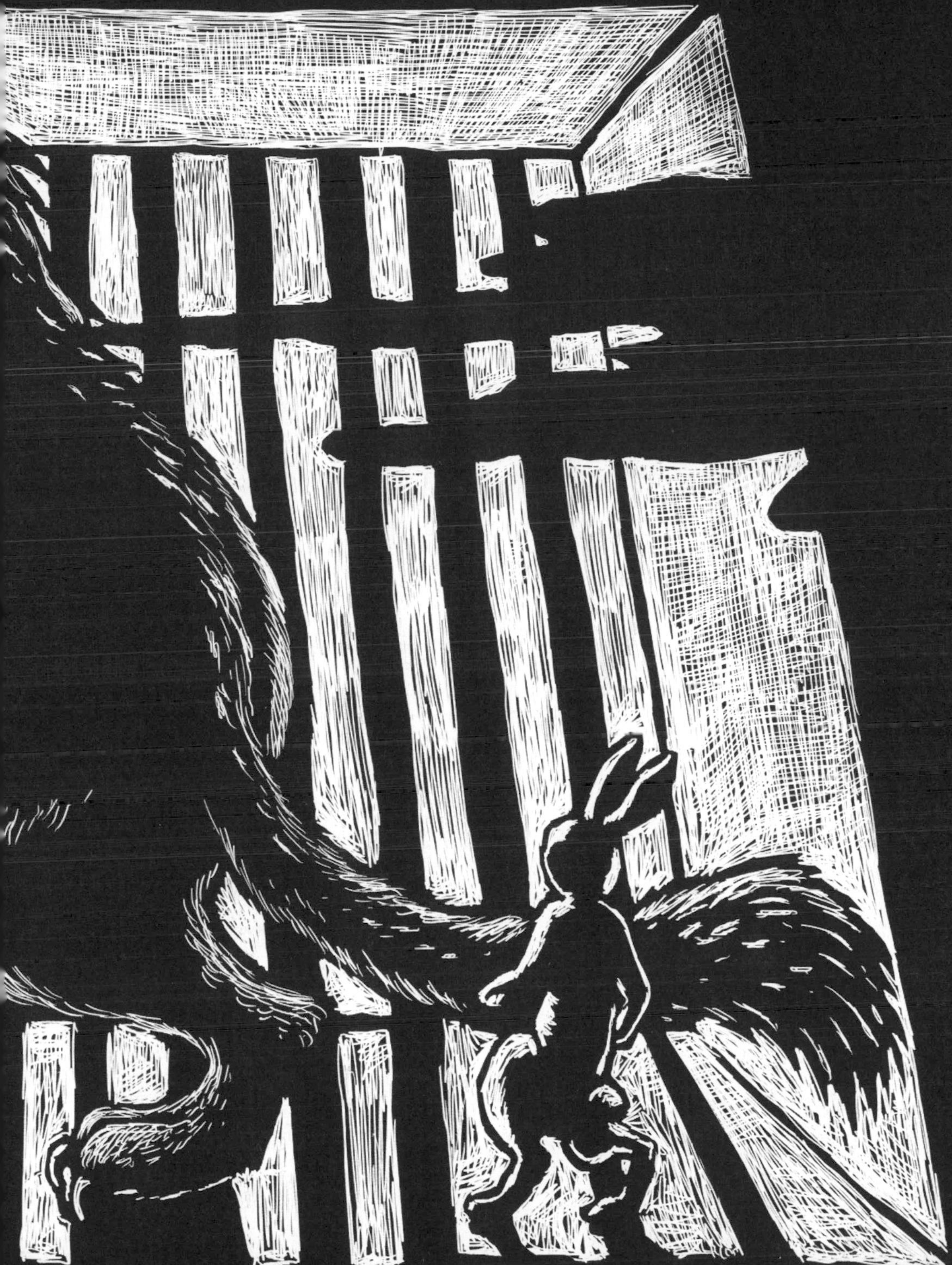

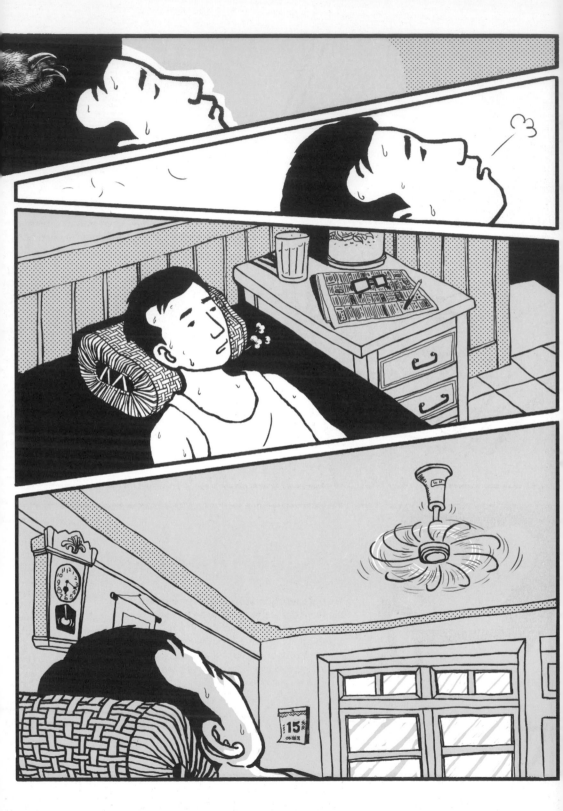

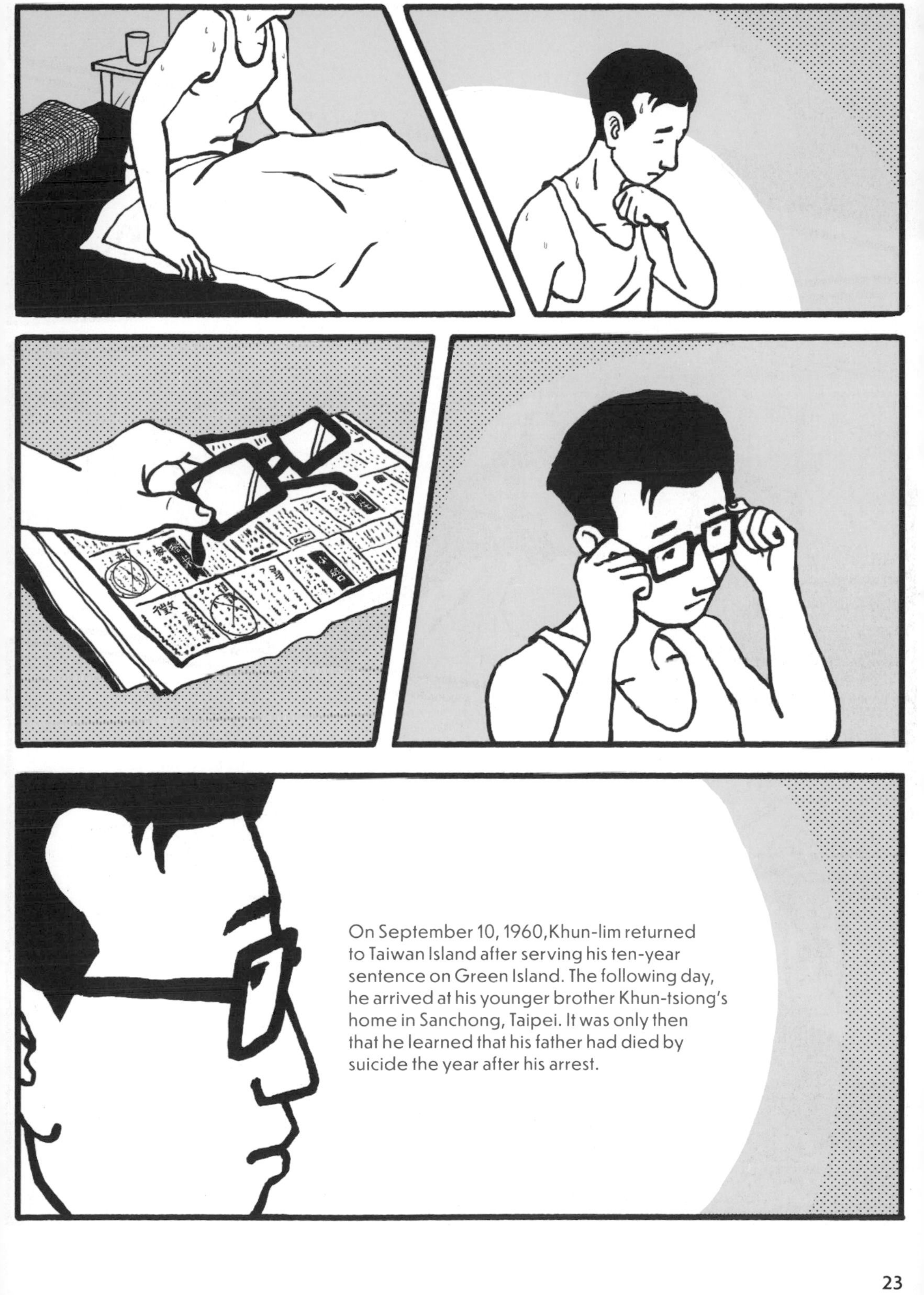
On September 10, 1960, Khun-lim returned to Taiwan Island after serving his ten-year sentence on Green Island. The following day, he arrived at his younger brother Khun-tsiong's home in Sanchong, Taipei. It was only then that he learned that his father had died by suicide the year after his arrest.

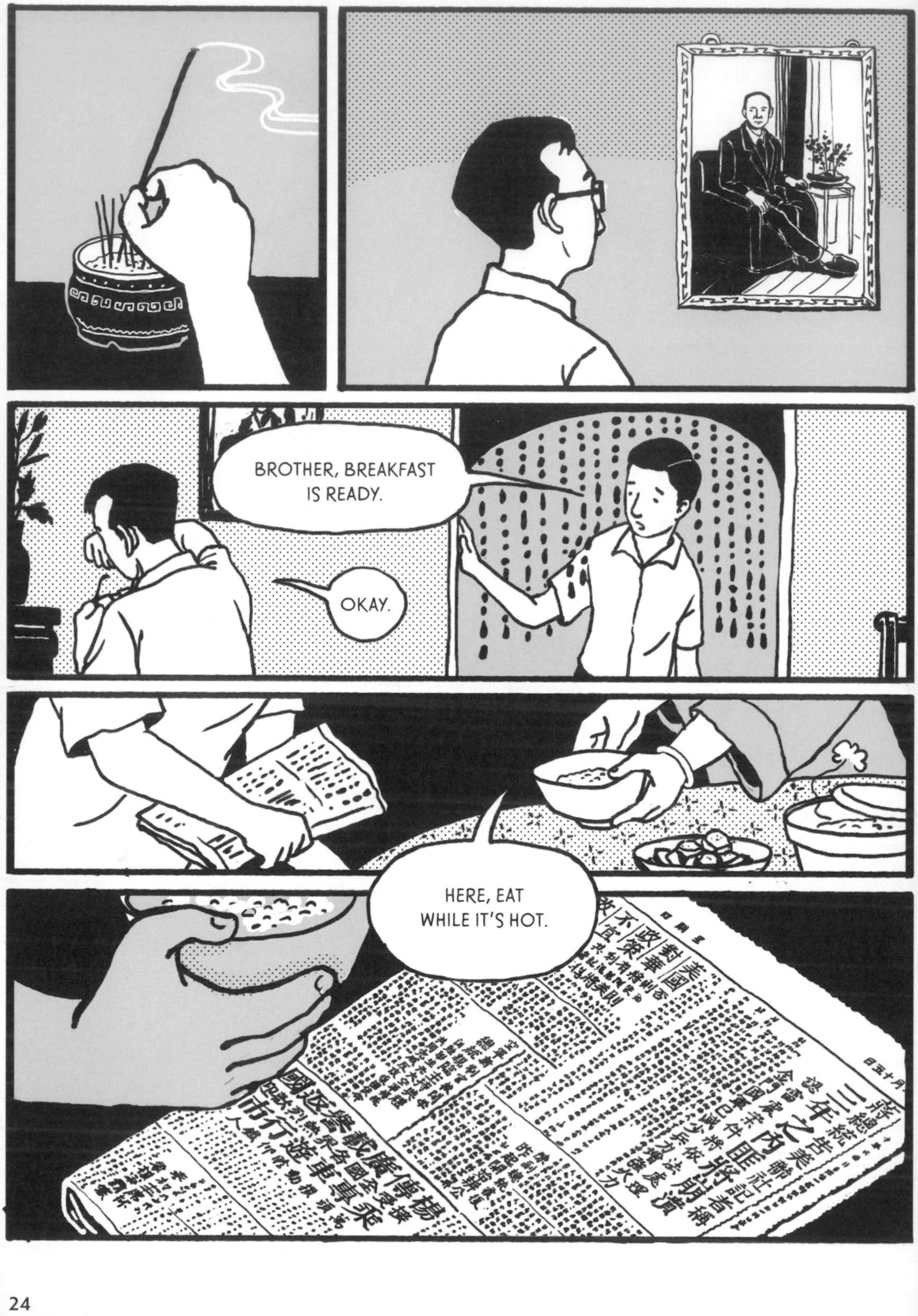
BROTHER, BREAKFAST IS READY.
OKAY.
HERE, EAT WHILE IT'S HOT.

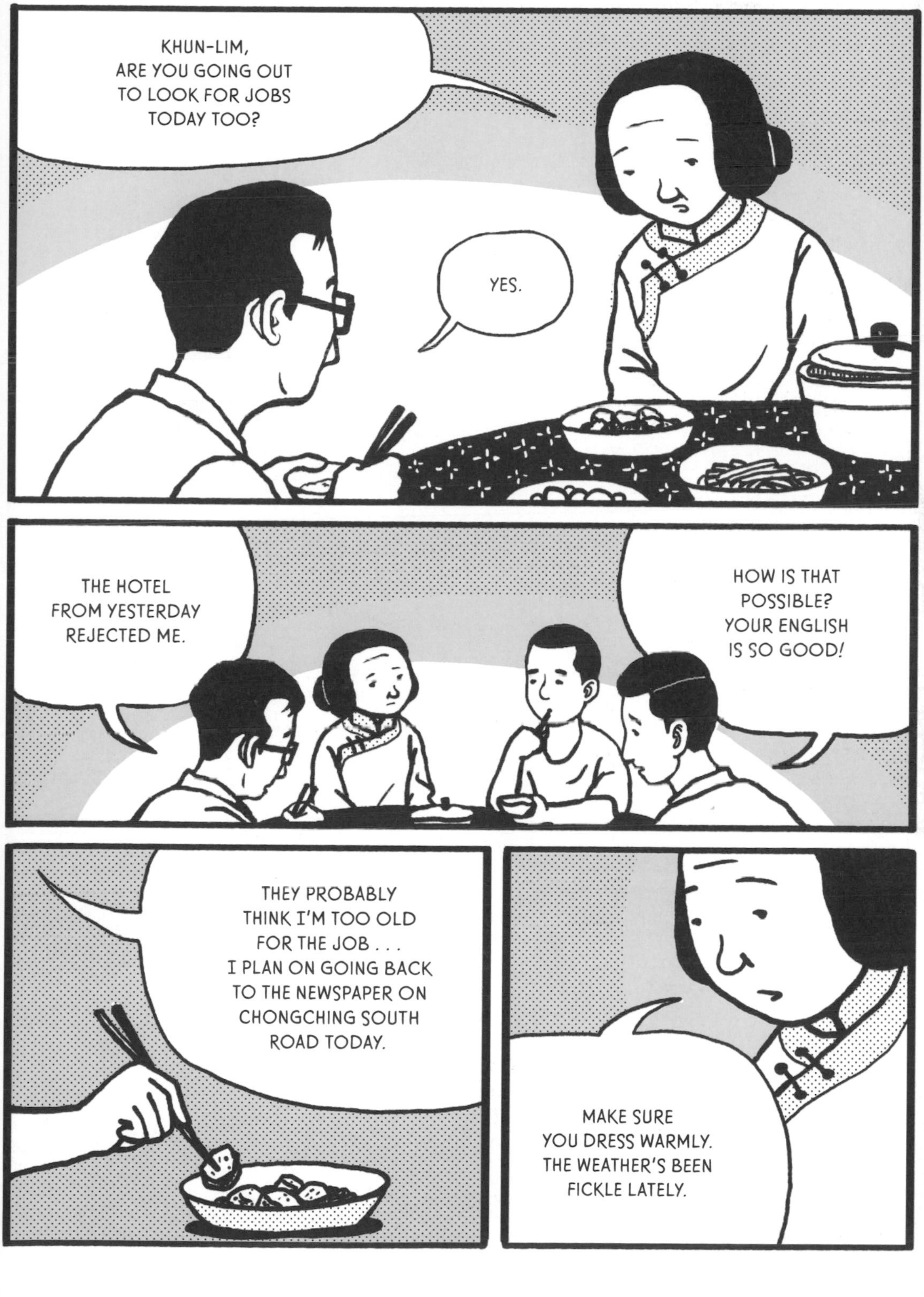
KHUN-LIM, ARE YOU GOING OUT TO LOOK FOR JOBS TODAY TOO?
YES.
THE HOTEL FROM YESTERDAY REJECTED ME.
HOW IS THAT POSSIBLE? YOUR ENGLISH IS SO GOOD!
THEY PROBABLY THINK I'M TOO OLD FOR THE JOB . . . I PLAN ON GOING BACK TO THE NEWSPAPER ON CHONGCHING SOUTH ROAD TODAY.
MAKE SURE YOU DRESS WARMLY. THE WEATHER'S BEEN FICKLE LATELY.

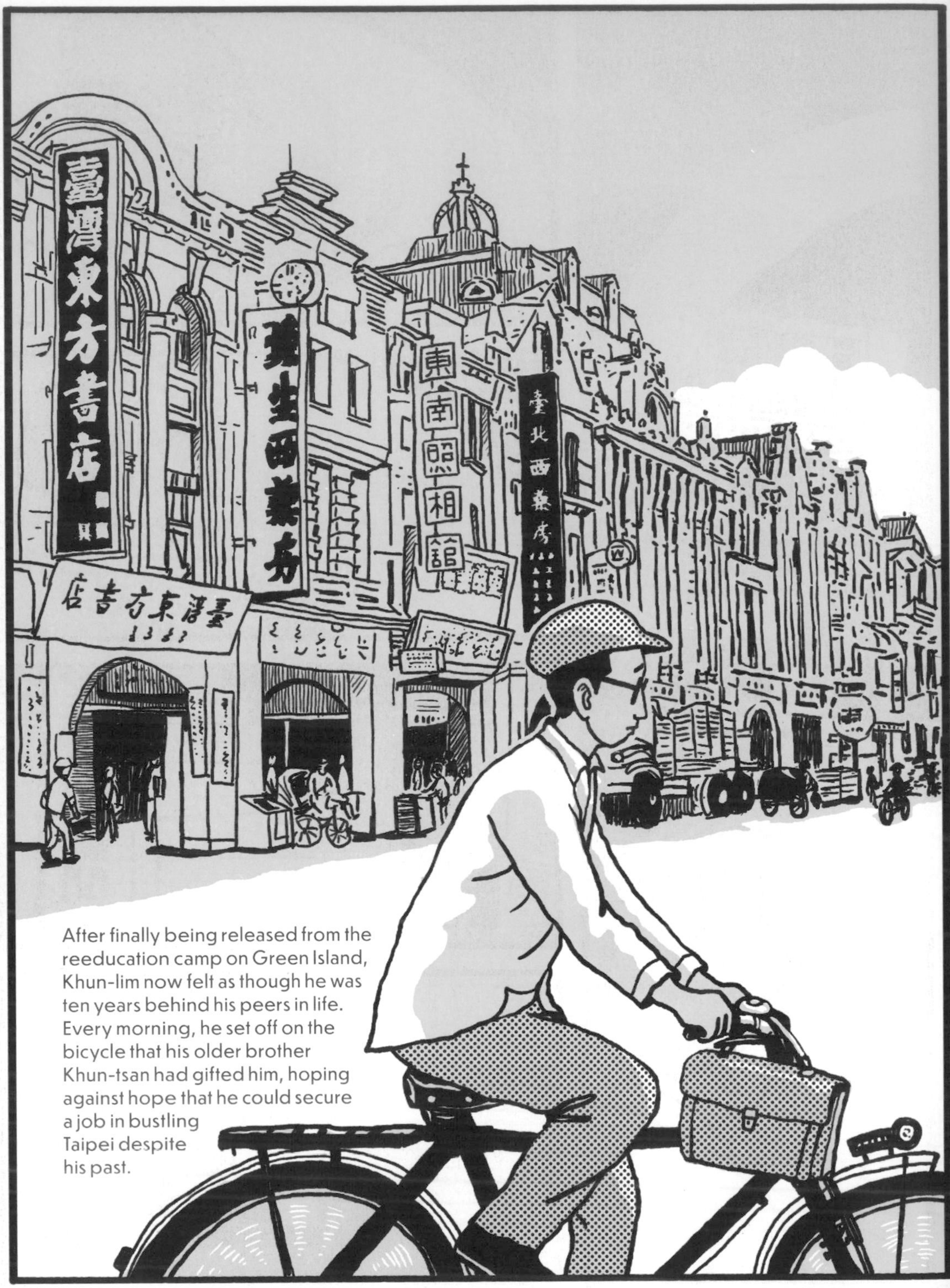
臺灣東方書店
東南照相館
臺北西藥房
After finally being released from the reeducation camp on Green Island, Khun-lim now felt as though he was ten years behind his peers in life. Every morning, he set off on the bicycle that his older brother Khun-tsan had gifted him, hoping against hope that he could secure a job in bustling Taipei despite his past.

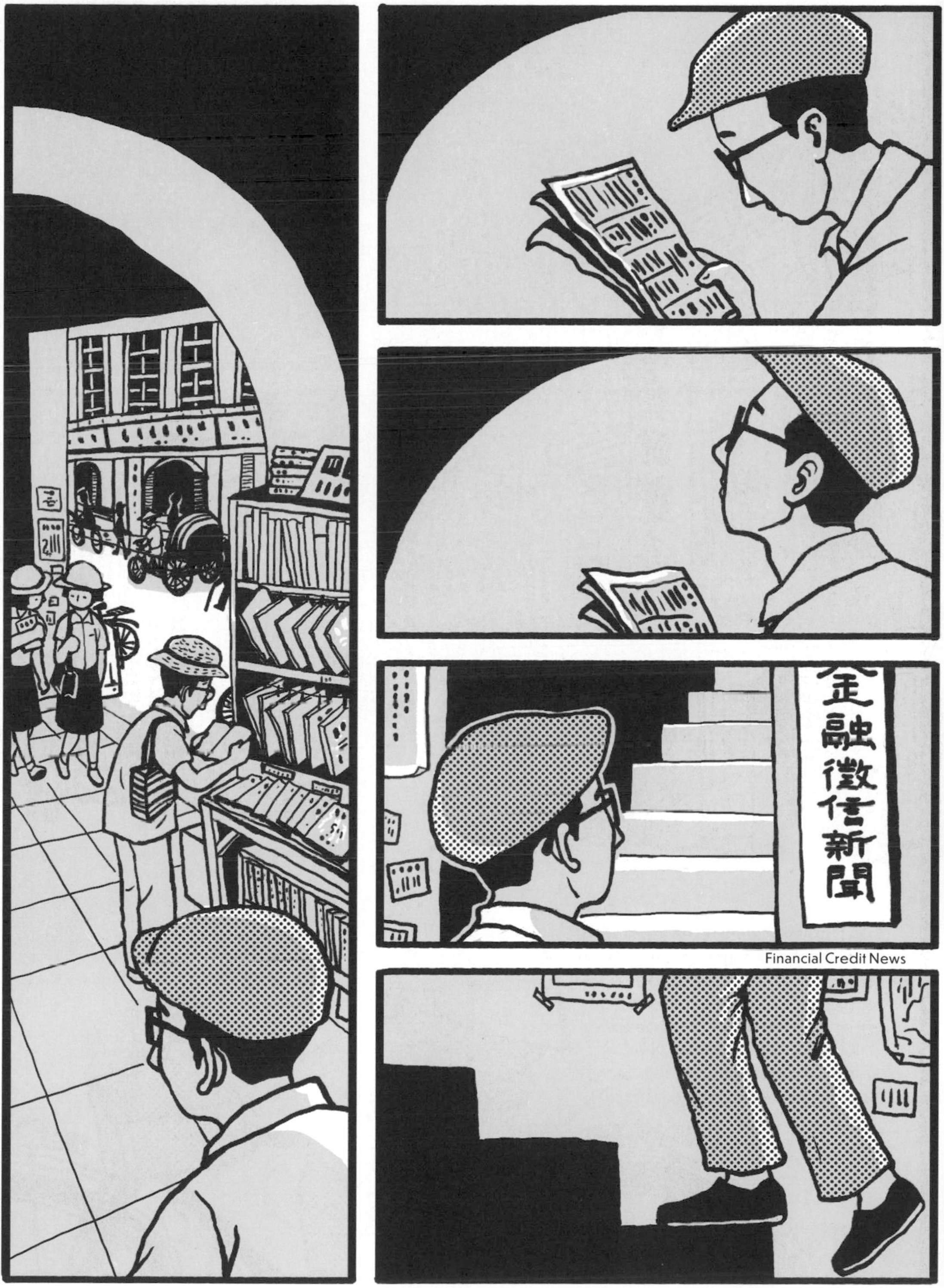
金融徵信新聞
Financial Credit News

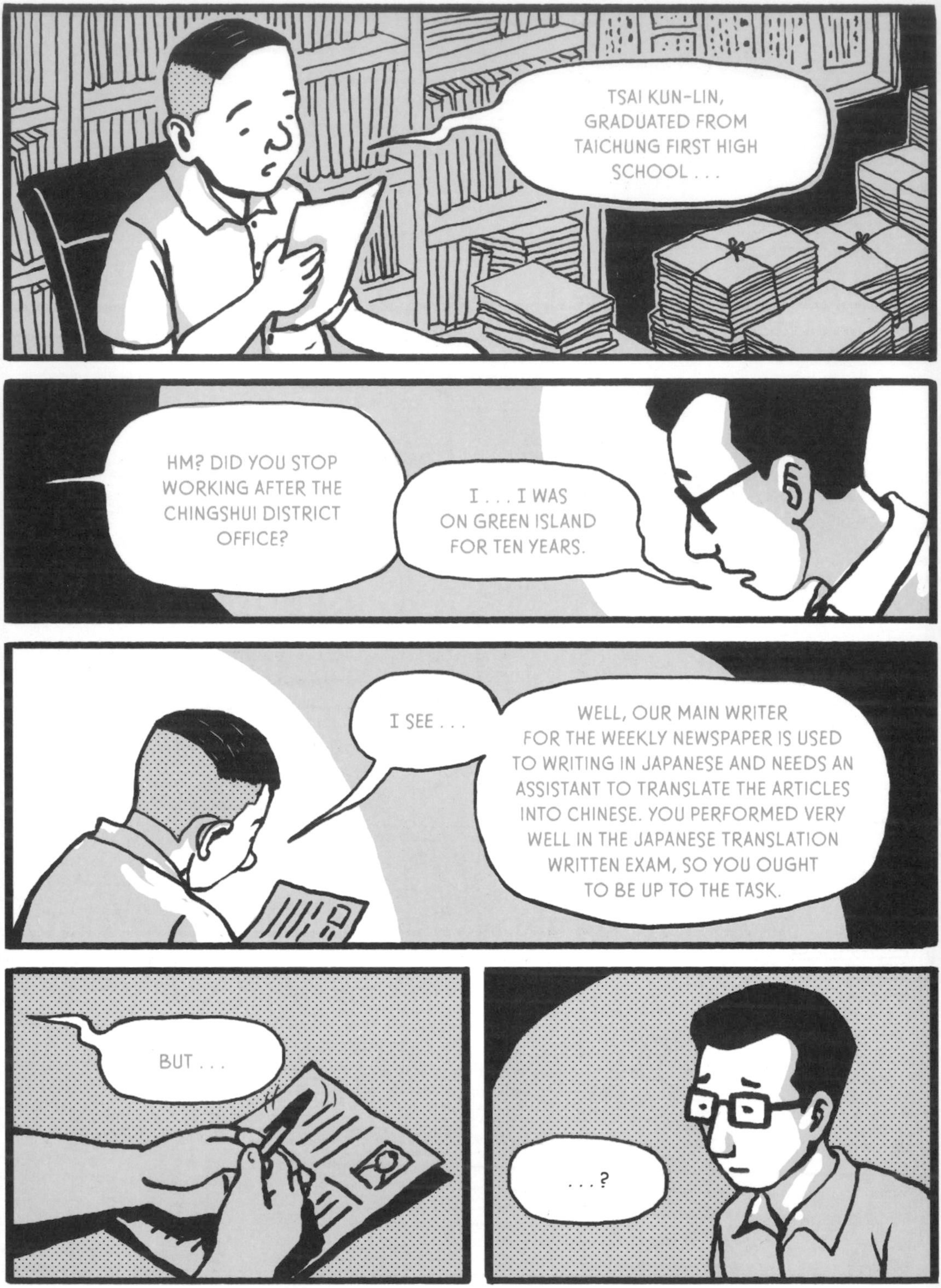
TSAI KUN-LIN, GRADUATED FROM TAICHUNG FIRST HIGH SCHOOL . . .
HM? DID YOU STOP WORKING AFTER THE CHINGSHUI DISTRICT OFFICE?
I . . . I WAS ON GREEN ISLAND FOR TEN YEARS.
I SEE . . .
WELL, OUR MAIN WRITER FOR THE WEEKLY NEWSPAPER IS USED TO WRITING IN JAPANESE AND NEEDS AN ASSISTANT TO TRANSLATE THE ARTICLES INTO CHINESE. YOU PERFORMED VERY WELL IN THE JAPANESE TRANSLATION WRITTEN EXAM, SO YOU OUGHT TO BE UP TO THE TASK.
BUT . . .
. . . ?

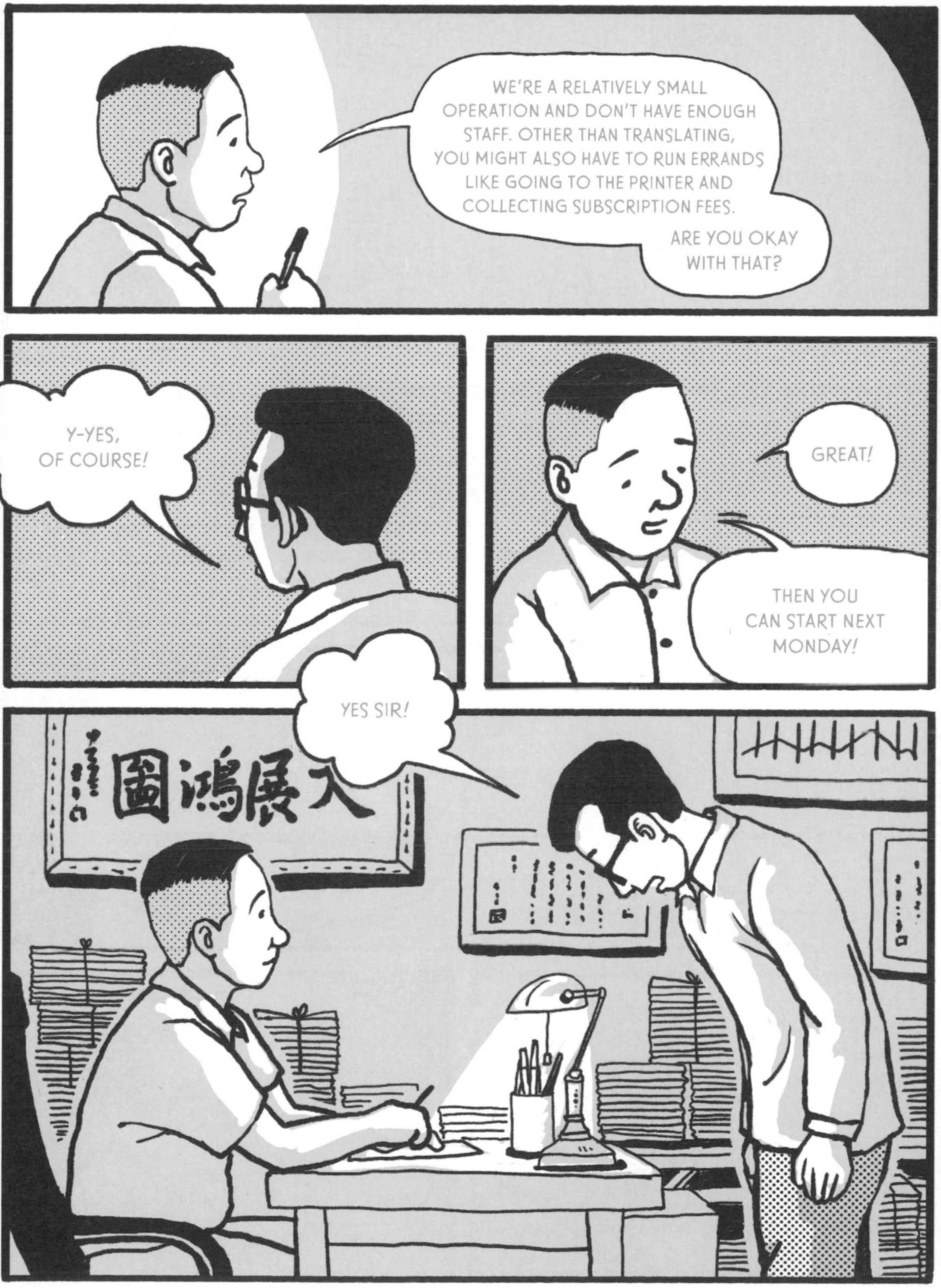
WE'RE A RELATIVELY SMALL OPERATION AND DON'T HAVE ENOUGH STAFF. OTHER THAN TRANSLATING, YOU MIGHT ALSO HAVE TO RUN ERRANDS LIKE GOING TO THE PRINTER AND COLLECTING SUBSCRIPTION FEES.
ARE YOU OKAY WITH THAT?
Y-YES, OF COURSE!
GREAT!
THEN YOU CAN START NEXT MONDAY!
YES SIR!

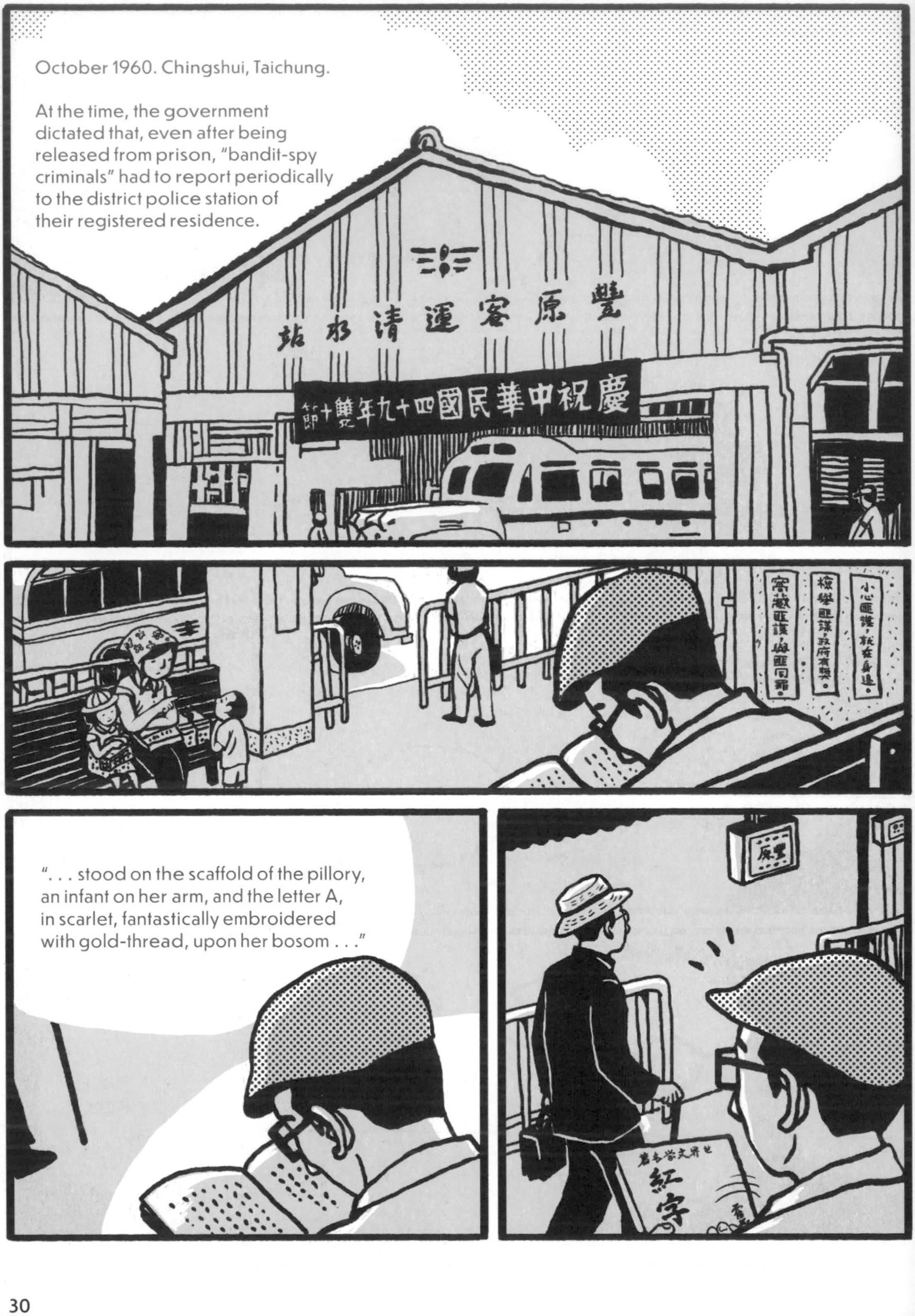
October 1960. Chingshui, Taichung.
At the time, the government dictated that, even after being released from prison, "bandit-spy criminals" had to report periodically to the district police station of their registered residence.
豐原客運清水站
慶祝中華民國四十九年雙十節
小心匪諜，就在身邊。
檢舉匪諜，政府有獎。
窩藏匪諜，與匪同罪。
". . . stood on the scaffold of the pillory, an infant on her arm, and the letter A, in scarlet, fantastically embroidered with gold-thread, upon her bosom . . ."
豐原
世界文学名著
紅字

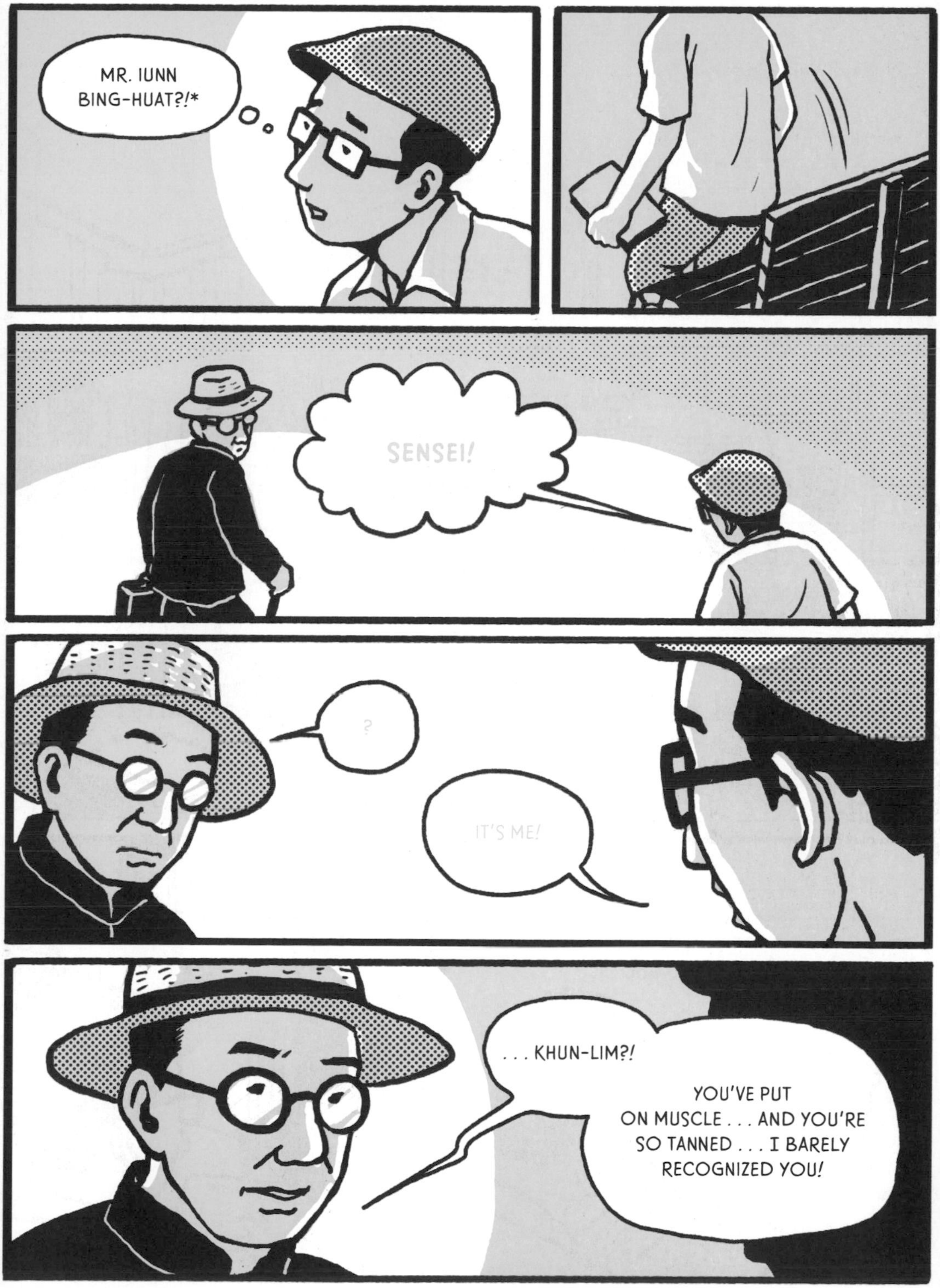
MR. IUNN BING-HUAT?!*
SENSEI!
?
IT'S ME!
. . . KHUN-LIM?!
YOU'VE PUT ON MUSCLE . . . AND YOU'RE SO TANNED . . . I BARELY RECOGNIZED YOU!

*Mr. Kiyomizu, Khun-lim's former teacher, is also known by his Taiwanese name Iunn Bing-huat and his Mandarin name Yang Ming-fa.

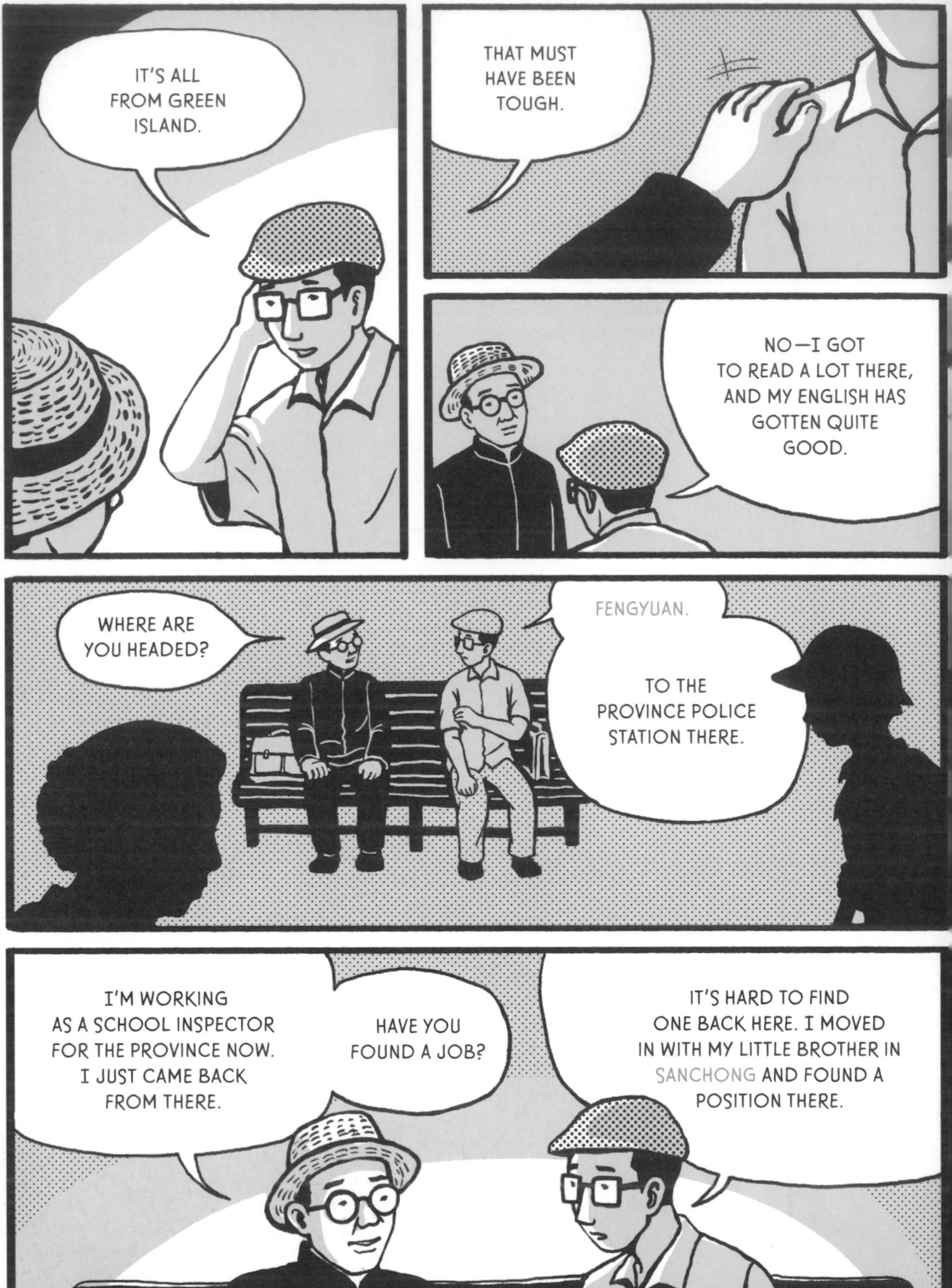
IT'S ALL FROM GREEN ISLAND.
THAT MUST HAVE BEEN TOUGH.
NO—I GOT TO READ A LOT THERE, AND MY ENGLISH HAS GOTTEN QUITE GOOD.
WHERE ARE YOU HEADED?
FENGYUAN.
TO THE PROVINCE POLICE STATION THERE.
I'M WORKING AS A SCHOOL INSPECTOR FOR THE PROVINCE NOW. I JUST CAME BACK FROM THERE.
HAVE YOU FOUND A JOB?
IT'S HARD TO FIND ONE BACK HERE. I MOVED IN WITH MY LITTLE BROTHER IN SANCHONG AND FOUND A POSITION THERE.

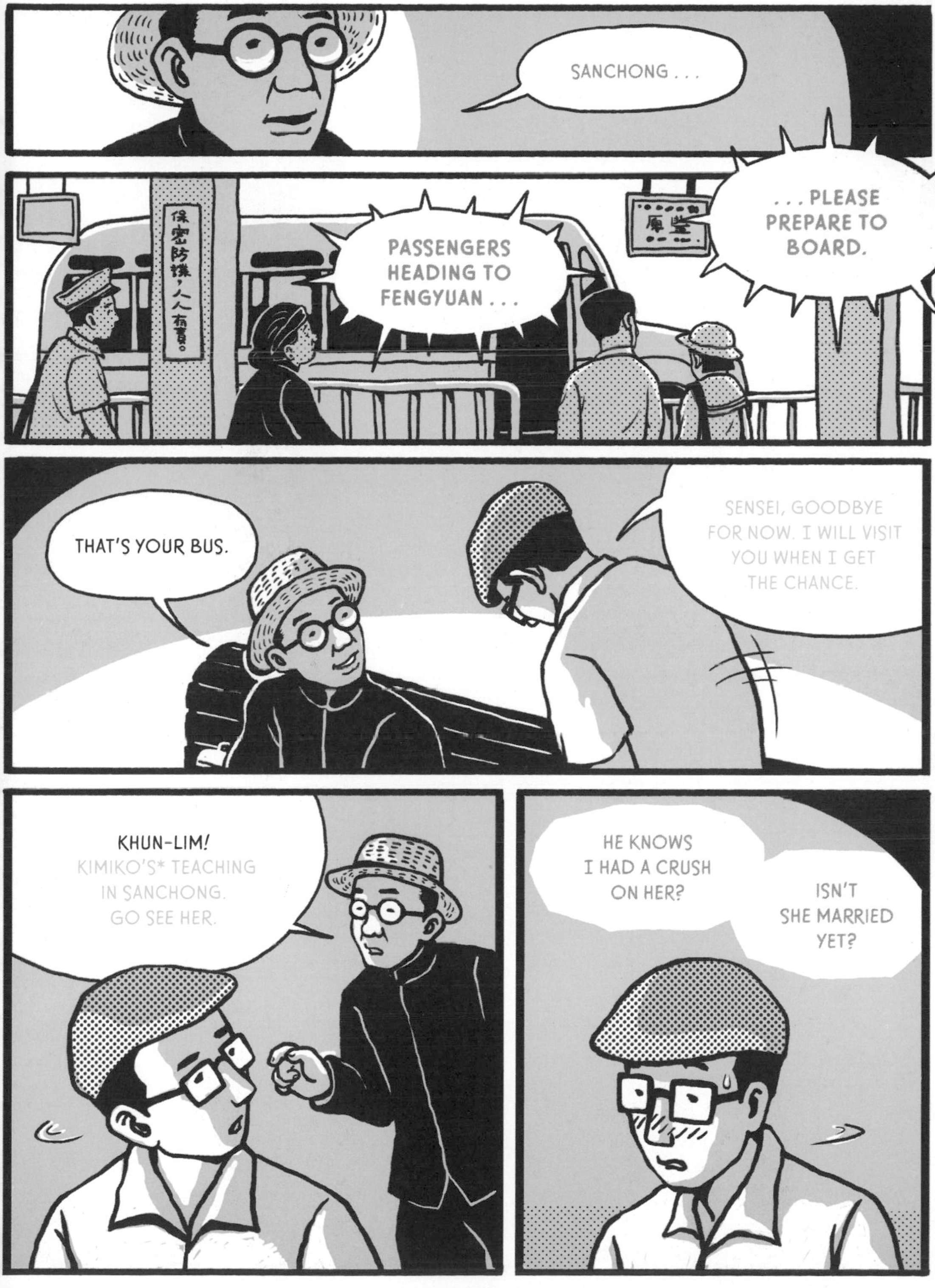
SANCHONG . . .
保密防諜，人人有責。
PASSENGERS HEADING TO FENGYUAN . . .
. . . PLEASE PREPARE TO BOARD.
THAT'S YOUR BUS.
SENSEI, GOODBYE FOR NOW. I WILL VISIT YOU WHEN I GET THE CHANCE.
KHUN-LIM! KIMIKO'S* TEACHING IN SANCHONG. GO SEE HER.
HE KNOWS I HAD A CRUSH ON HER?
ISN'T SHE MARRIED YET?

*Kiyomizu Kimiko is the Japanese name of Iunn Pik-ju, Mr. Iunn Bing-huat's daughter. Her family and friends continued calling her Kimiko after Japanese rule ended.

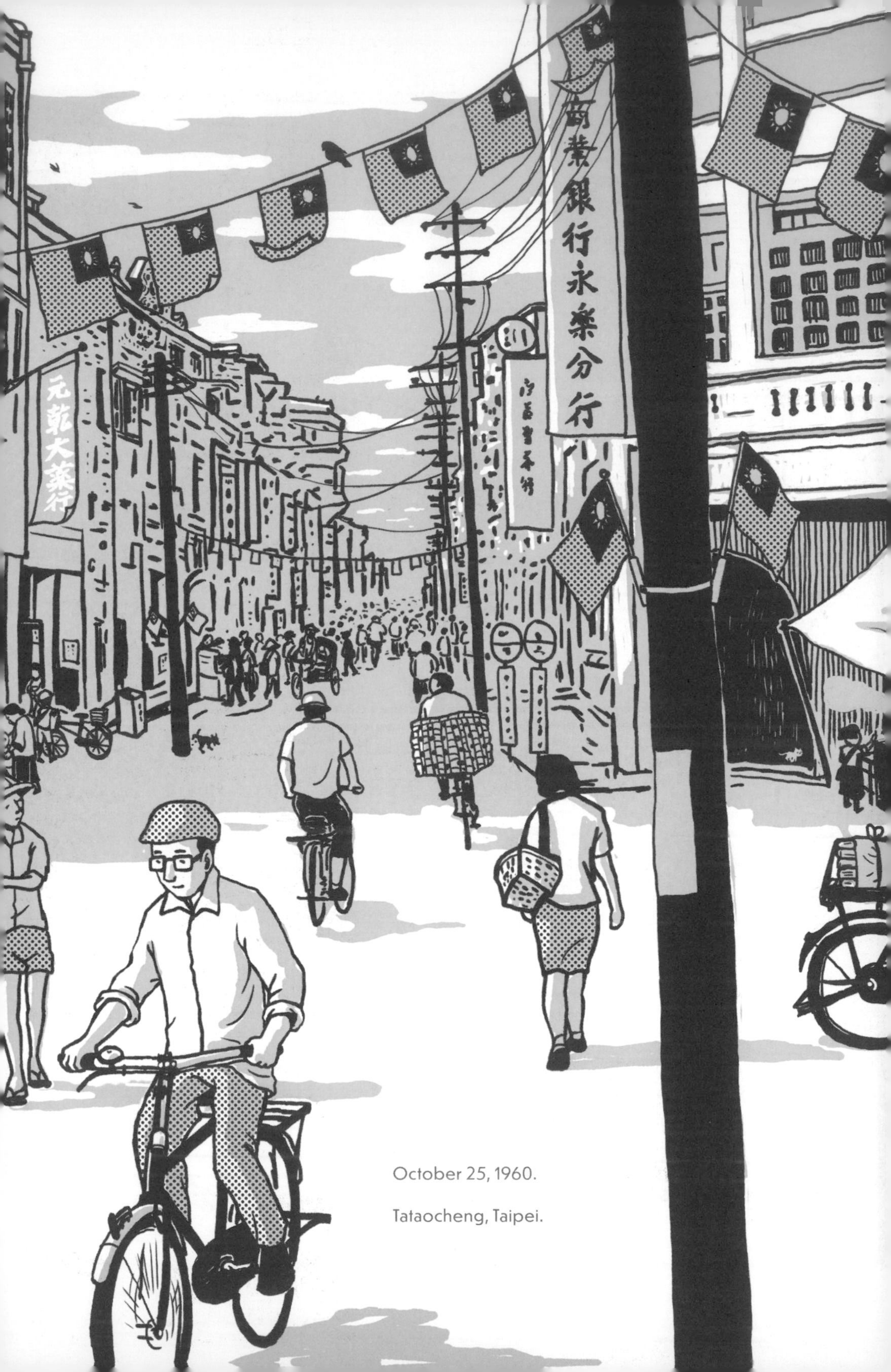

商業銀行永樂分行
元乾大藥行
October 25, 1960.
Tataocheng, Taipei.

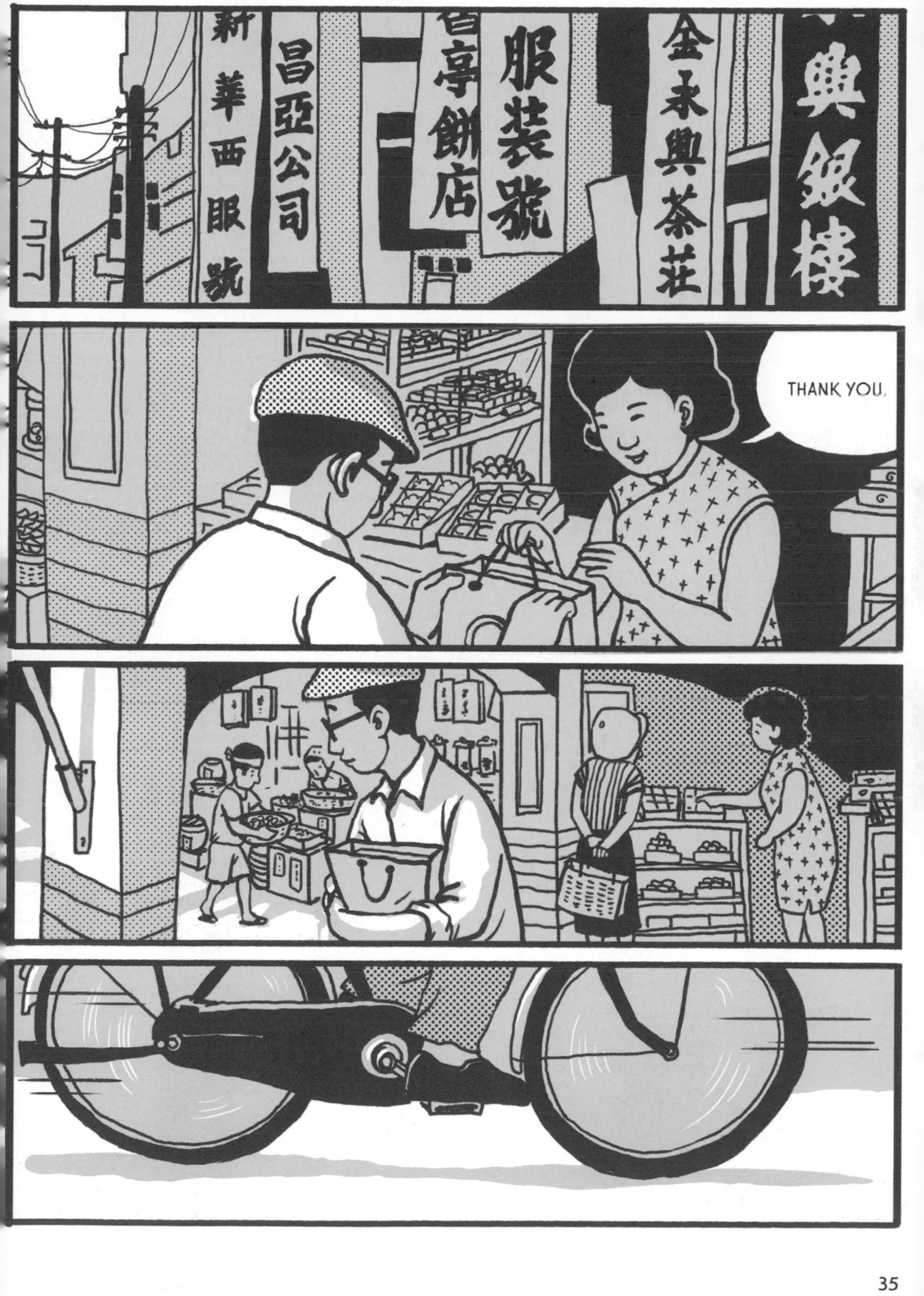
新華西服號
昌亞公司
亭餅店
服裝號
金永興茶莊
興銀樓
THANK YOU.

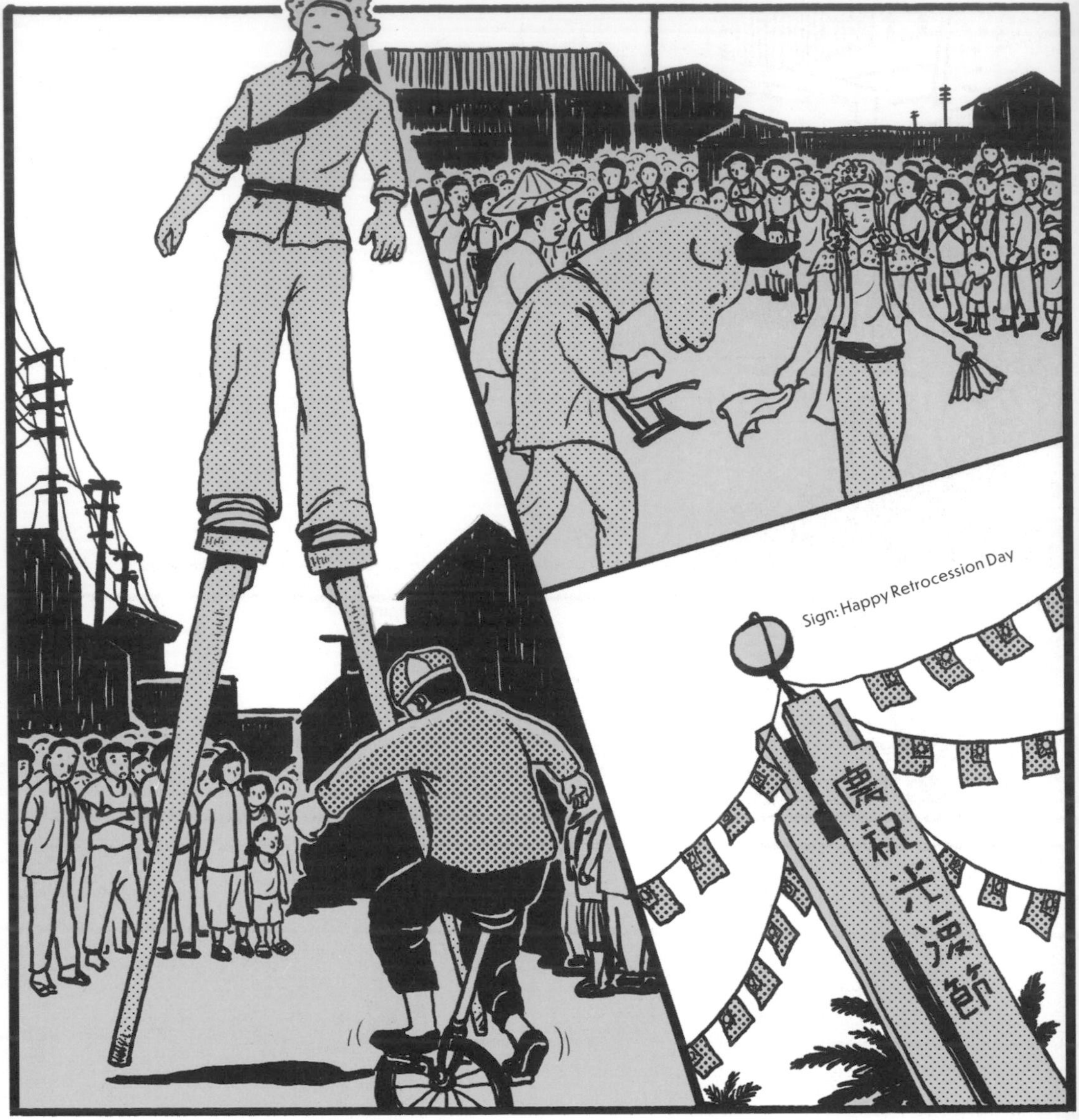
Sign: Happy Retrocession Day
慶祝光復節

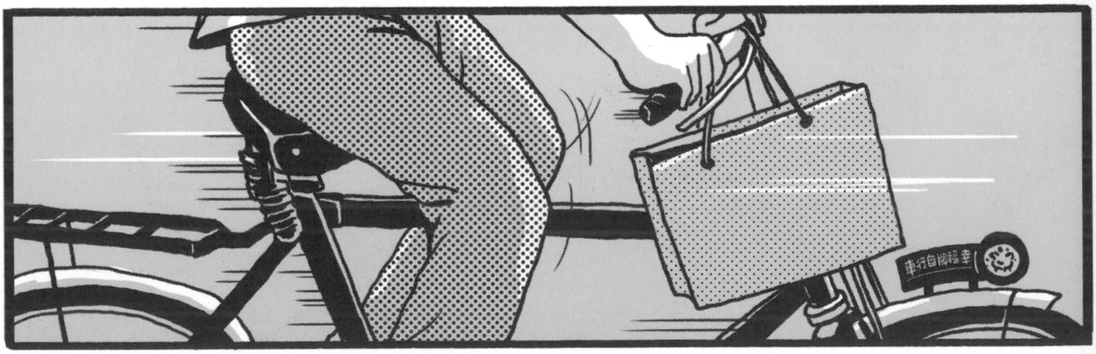

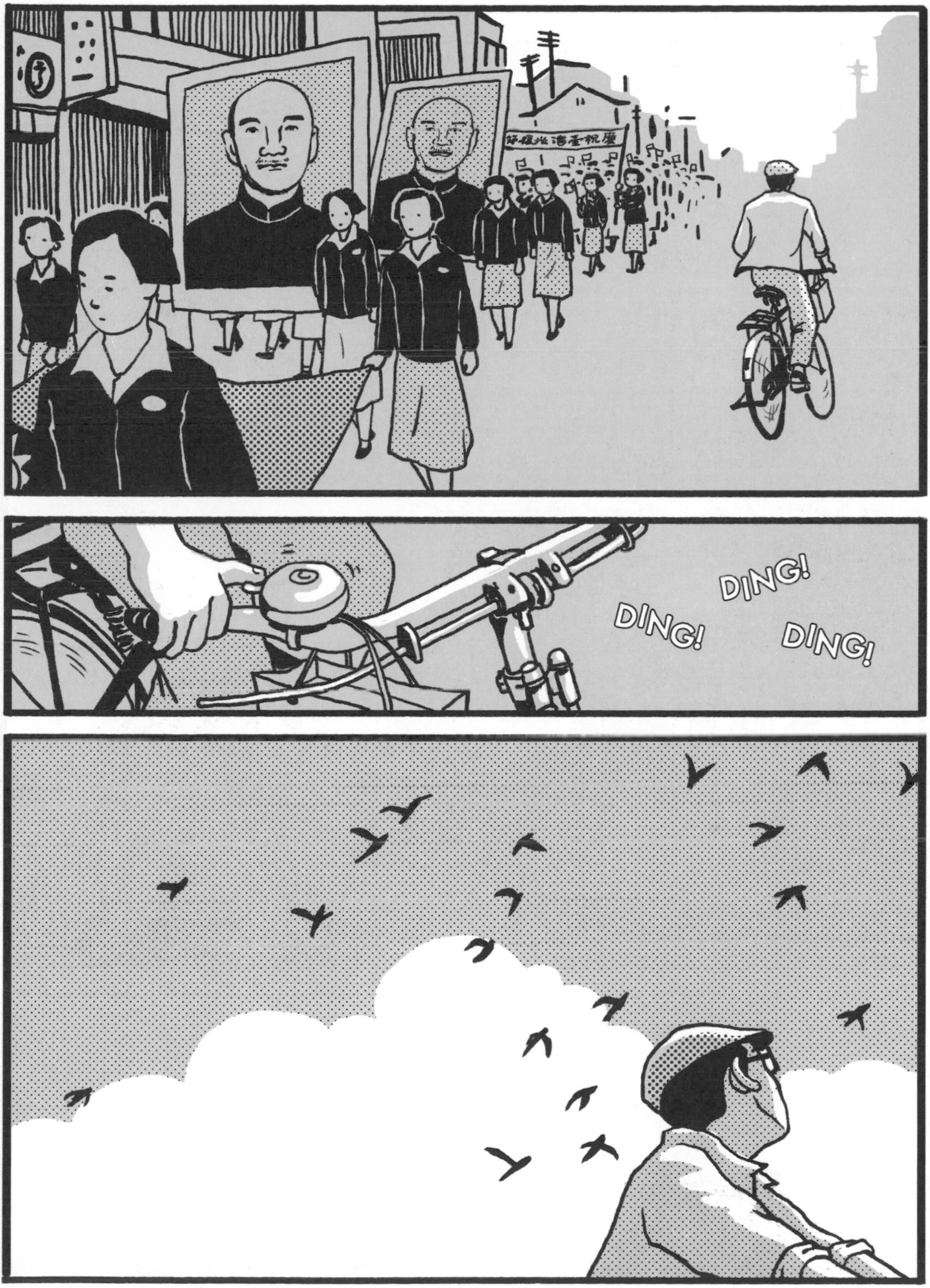
慶祝臺灣光復節
DING!
DING!
DING!

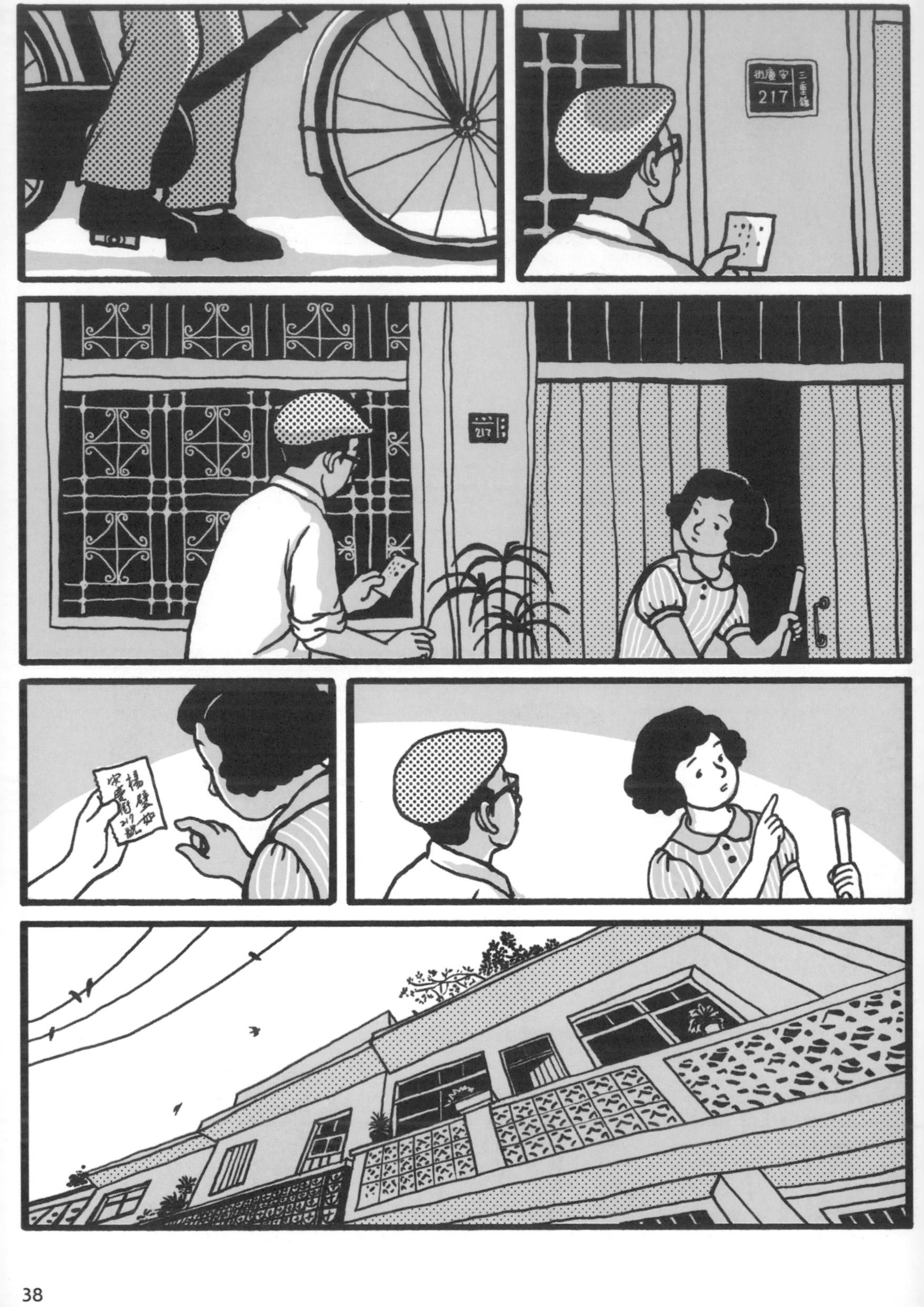

街慶安
217
三重鎮
楊璧如
安慶街217號

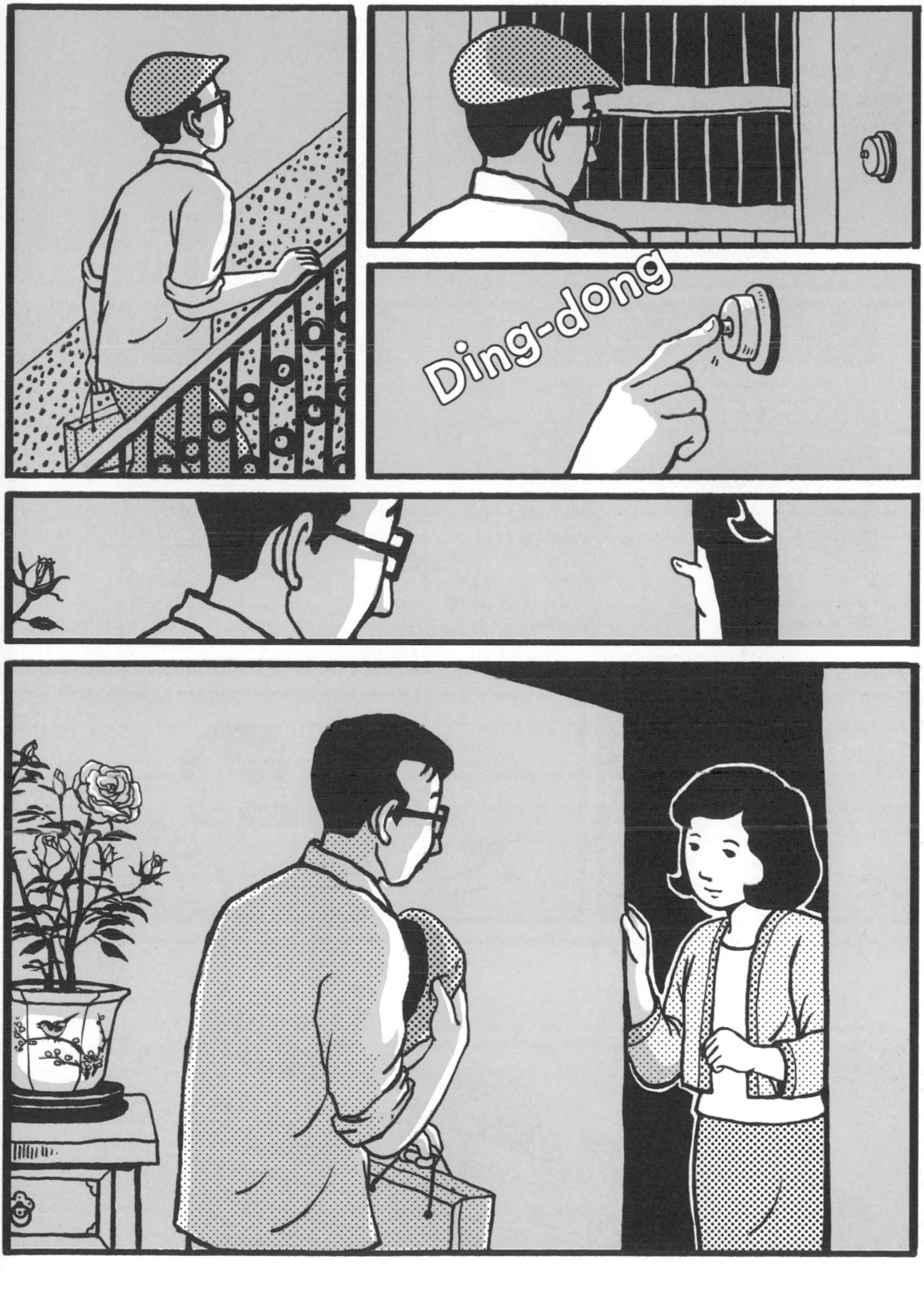
Ding-dong

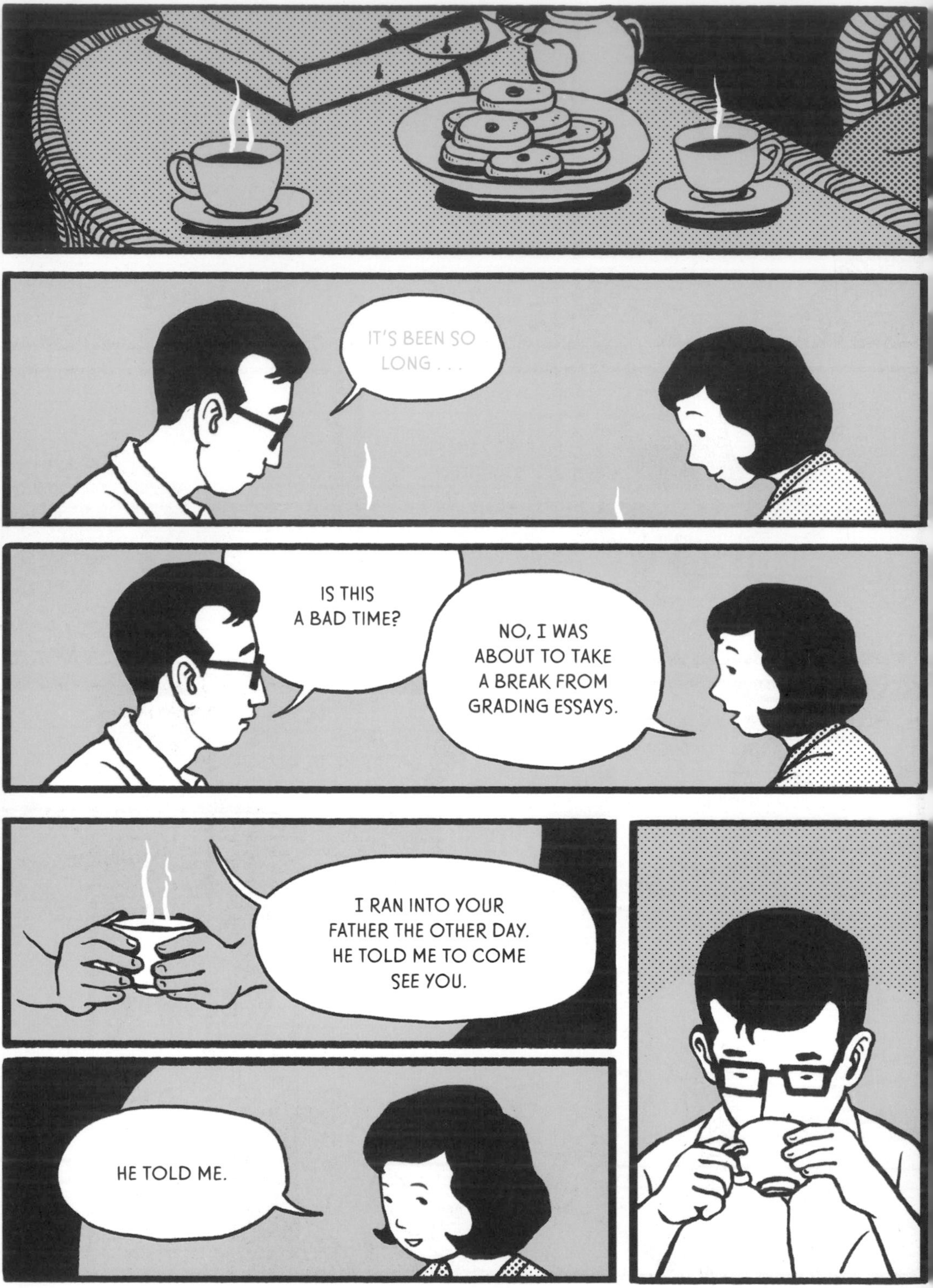
IT'S BEEN SO LONG . . .
IS THIS A BAD TIME?
NO, I WAS ABOUT TO TAKE A BREAK FROM GRADING ESSAYS.
I RAN INTO YOUR FATHER THE OTHER DAY. HE TOLD ME TO COME SEE YOU.
HE TOLD ME.

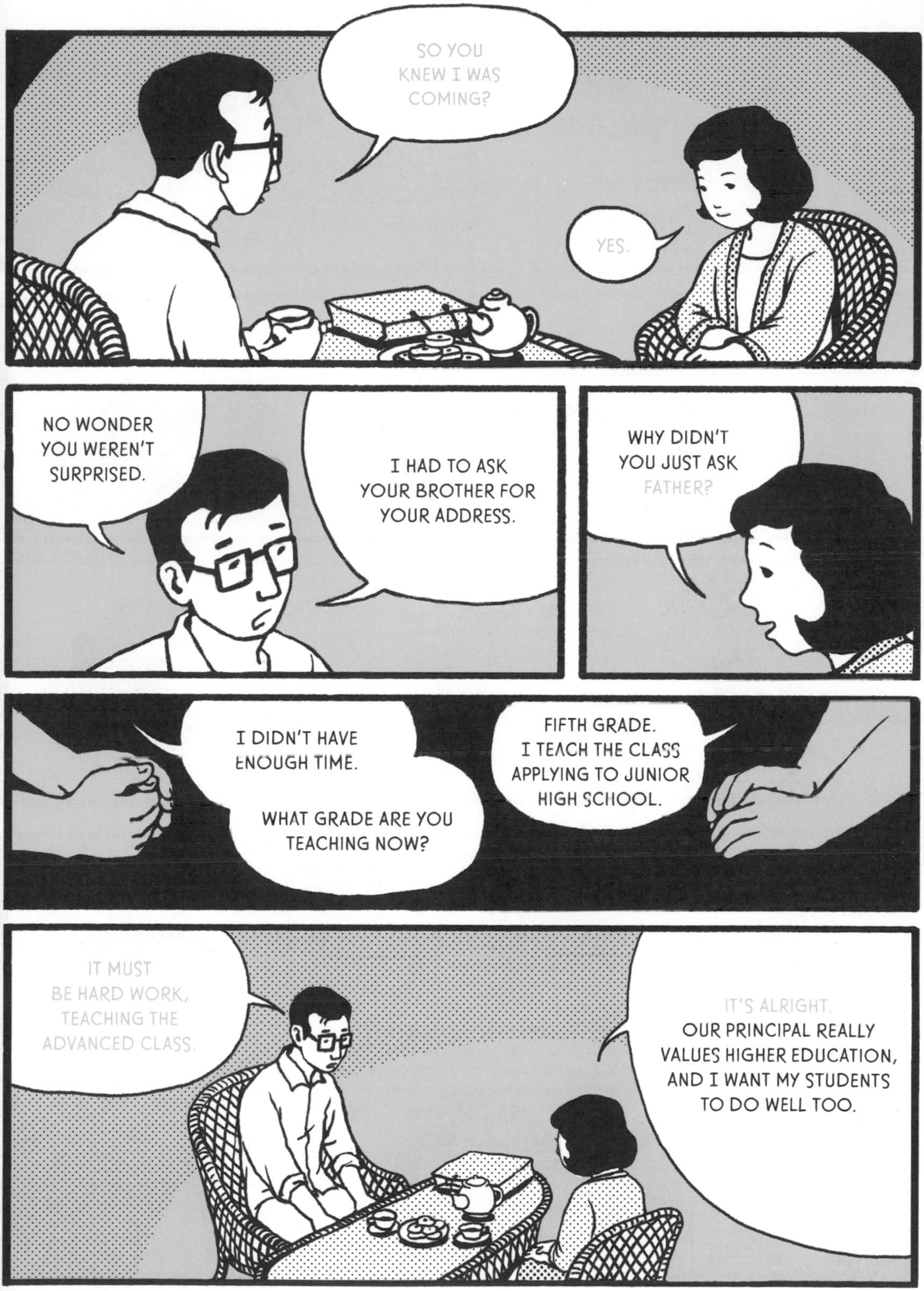
SO YOU KNEW I WAS COMING?
YES.
NO WONDER YOU WEREN'T SURPRISED.
I HAD TO ASK YOUR BROTHER FOR YOUR ADDRESS.
WHY DIDN'T YOU JUST ASK FATHER?
I DIDN'T HAVE ENOUGH TIME.
WHAT GRADE ARE YOU TEACHING NOW?
FIFTH GRADE. I TEACH THE CLASS APPLYING TO JUNIOR HIGH SCHOOL.
IT MUST BE HARD WORK, TEACHING THE ADVANCED CLASS.
IT'S ALRIGHT. OUR PRINCIPAL REALLY VALUES HIGHER EDUCATION, AND I WANT MY STUDENTS TO DO WELL TOO.

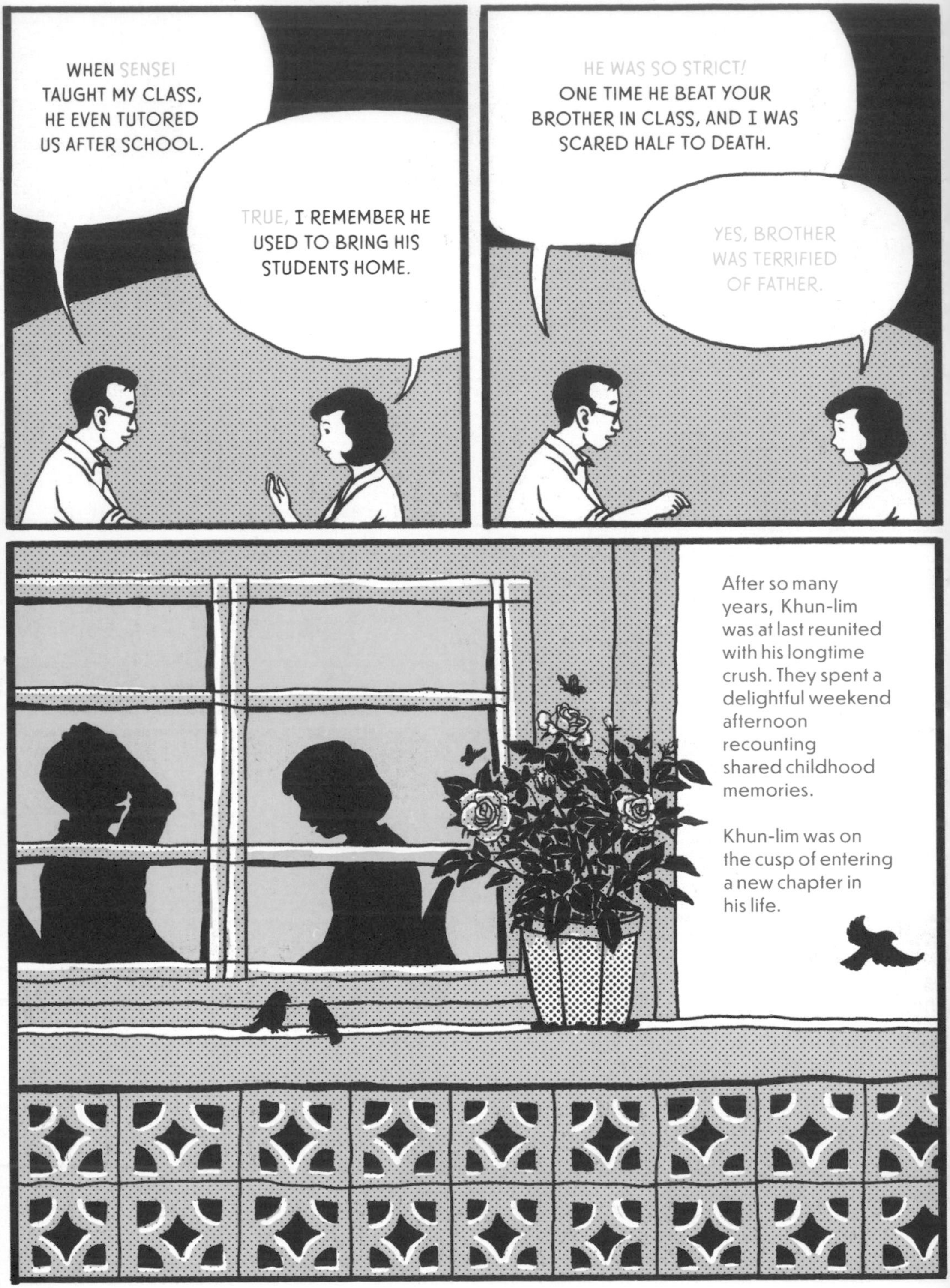
WHEN SENSEI TAUGHT MY CLASS, HE EVEN TUTORED US AFTER SCHOOL.
TRUE, I REMEMBER HE USED TO BRING HIS STUDENTS HOME.
HE WAS SO STRICT! ONE TIME HE BEAT YOUR BROTHER IN CLASS, AND I WAS SCARED HALF TO DEATH.
YES, BROTHER WAS TERRIFIED OF FATHER.
After so many years, Khun-lim was at last reunited with his longtime crush. They spent a delightful weekend afternoon recounting shared childhood memories.
Khun-lim was on the cusp of entering a new chapter in his life.

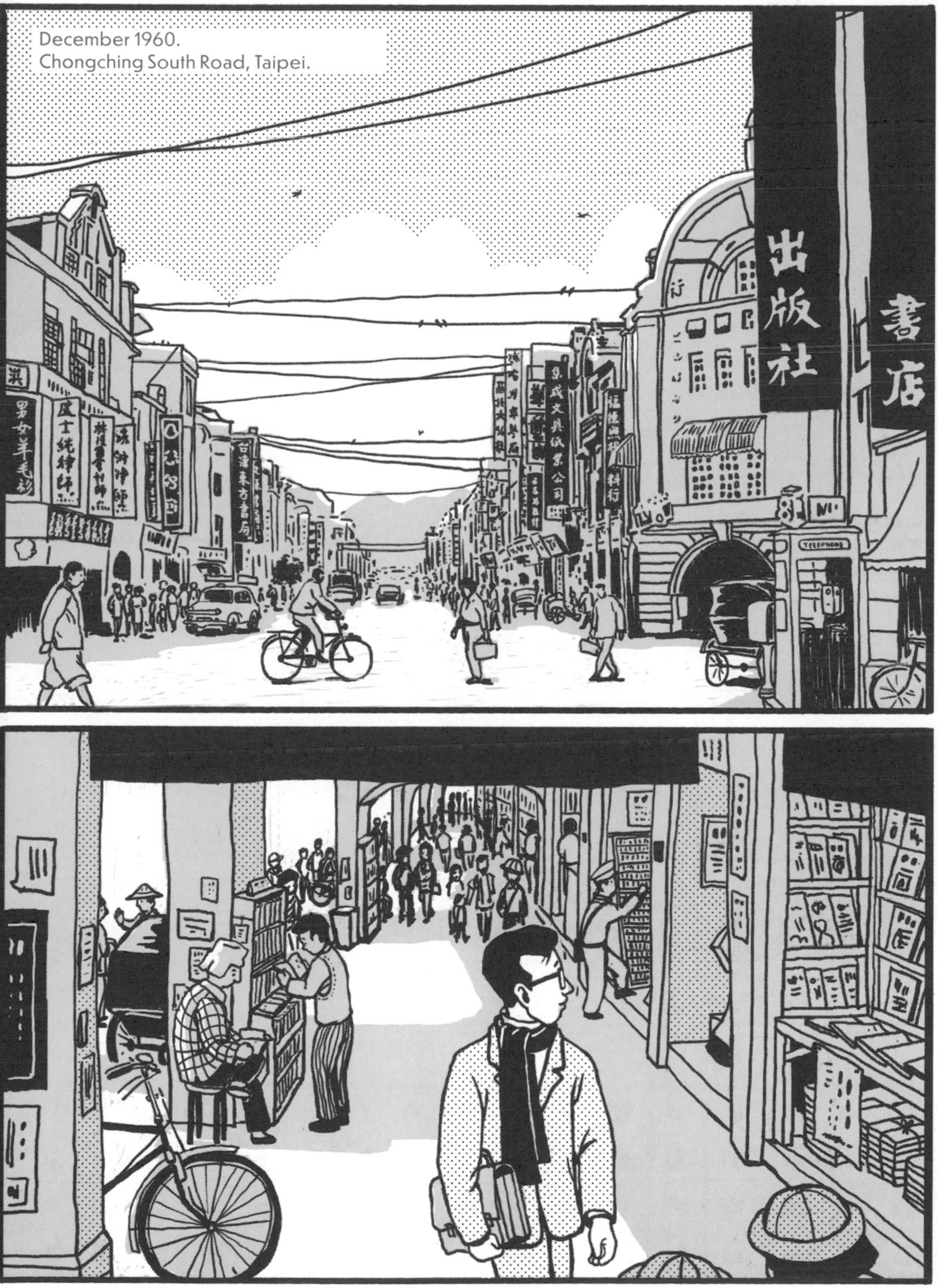
December 1960.
Chongching South Road, Taipei.
出版社
書店

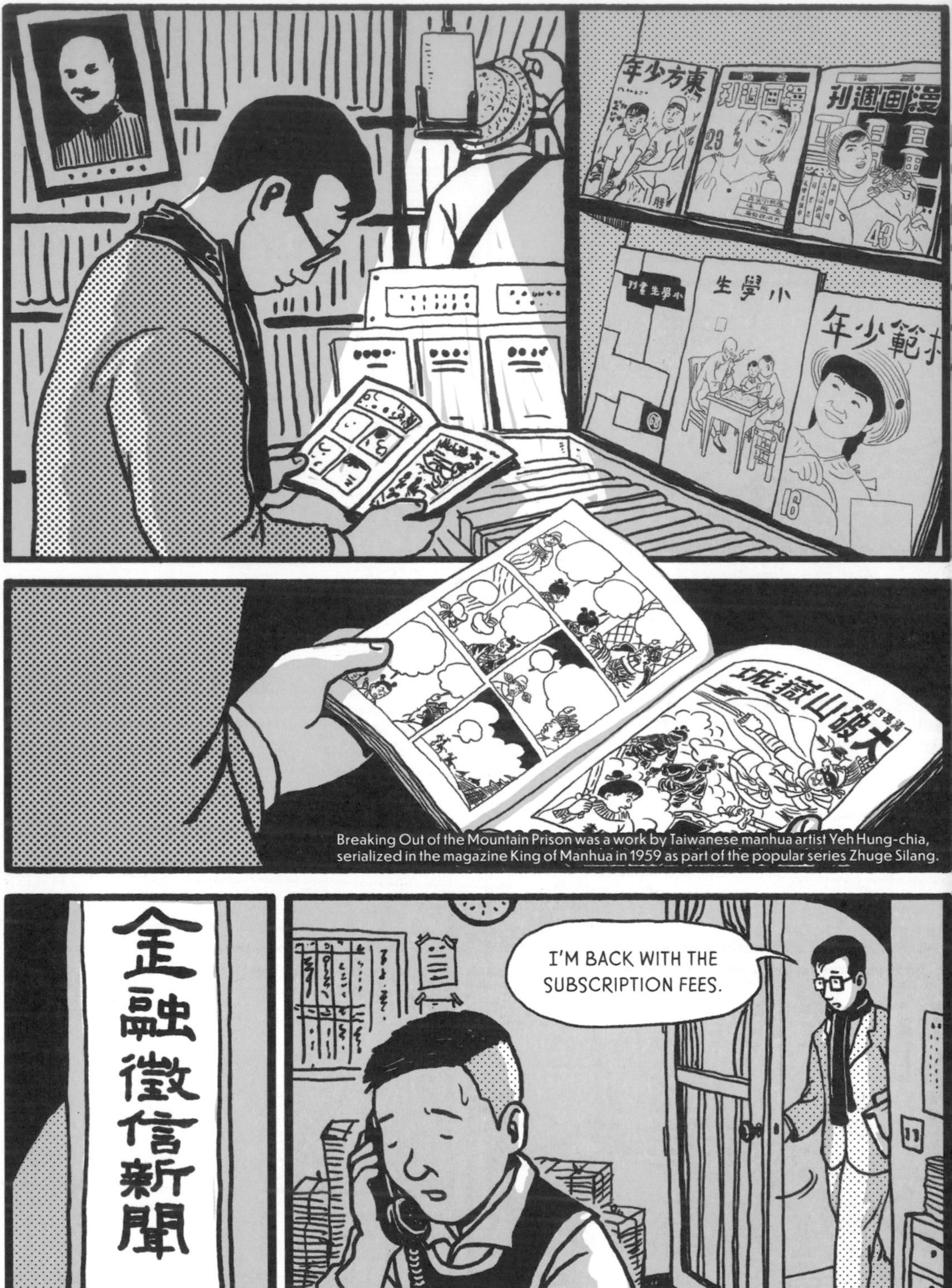
Breaking Out of the Mountain Prison was a work by Taiwanese manhua artist Yeh Hung-chia, serialized in the magazine King of Manhua in 1959 as part of the popular series Zhuge Silang.
金融徵信新聞
I'M BACK WITH THE SUBSCRIPTION FEES.

Sign: Financial Credit News

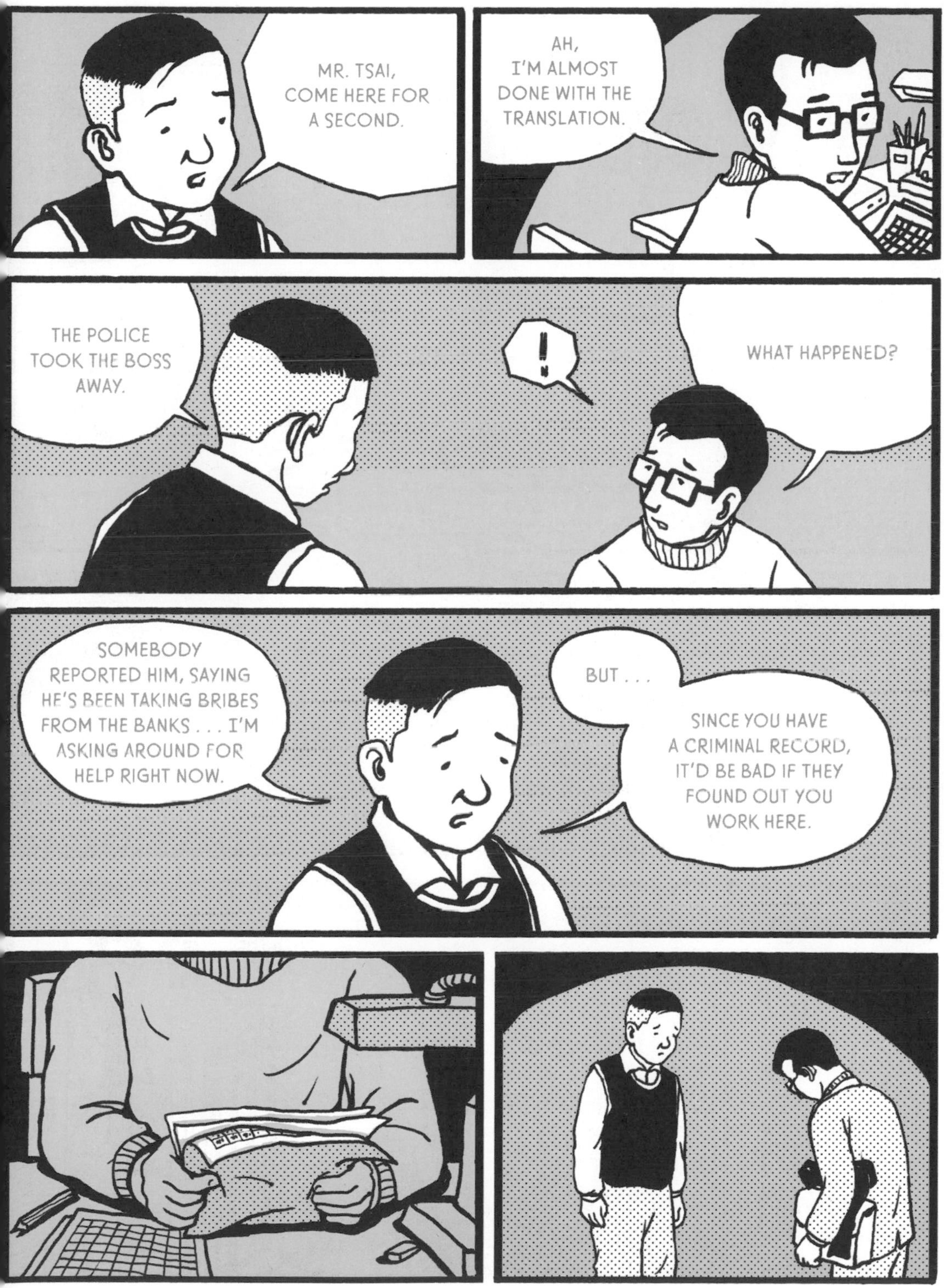
MR. TSAI, COME HERE FOR A SECOND.
AH, I'M ALMOST DONE WITH THE TRANSLATION.
THE POLICE TOOK THE BOSS AWAY.
!
WHAT HAPPENED?
SOMEBODY REPORTED HIM, SAYING HE'S BEEN TAKING BRIBES FROM THE BANKS . . . I'M ASKING AROUND FOR HELP RIGHT NOW.
BUT . . .
SINCE YOU HAVE A CRIMINAL RECORD, IT'D BE BAD IF THEY FOUND OUT YOU WORK HERE.

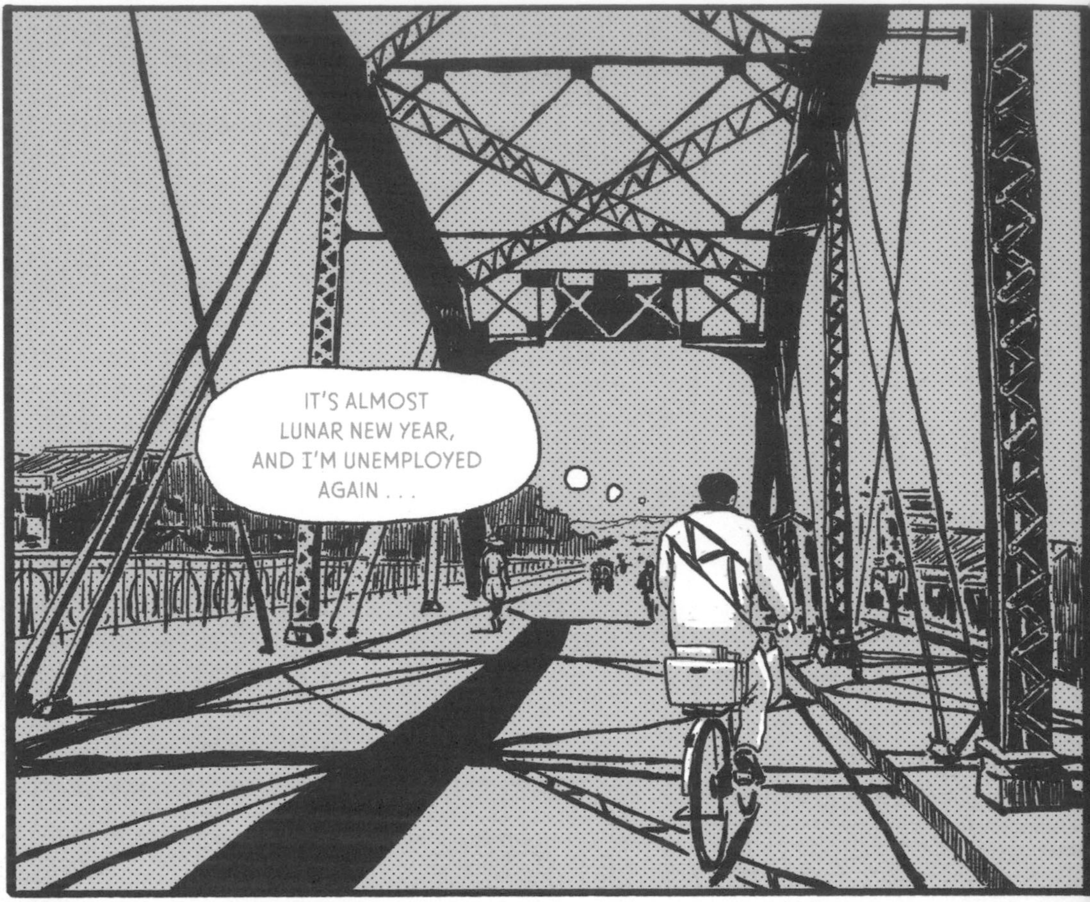
IT'S ALMOST LUNAR NEW YEAR, AND I'M UNEMPLOYED AGAIN . . .

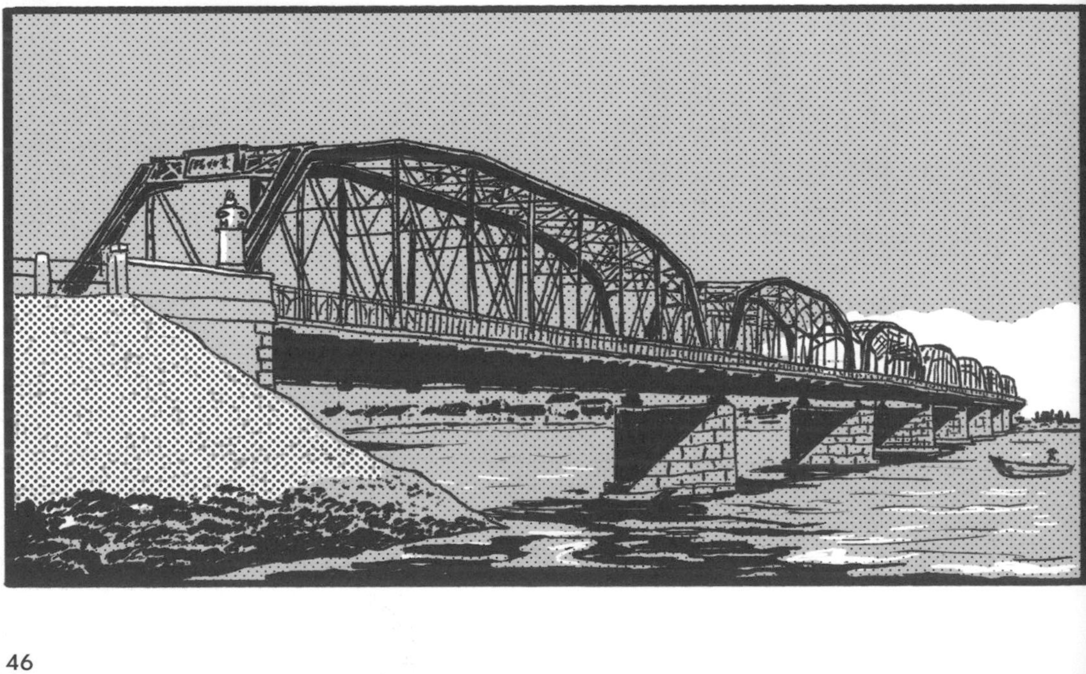

Banner: Jewel Press

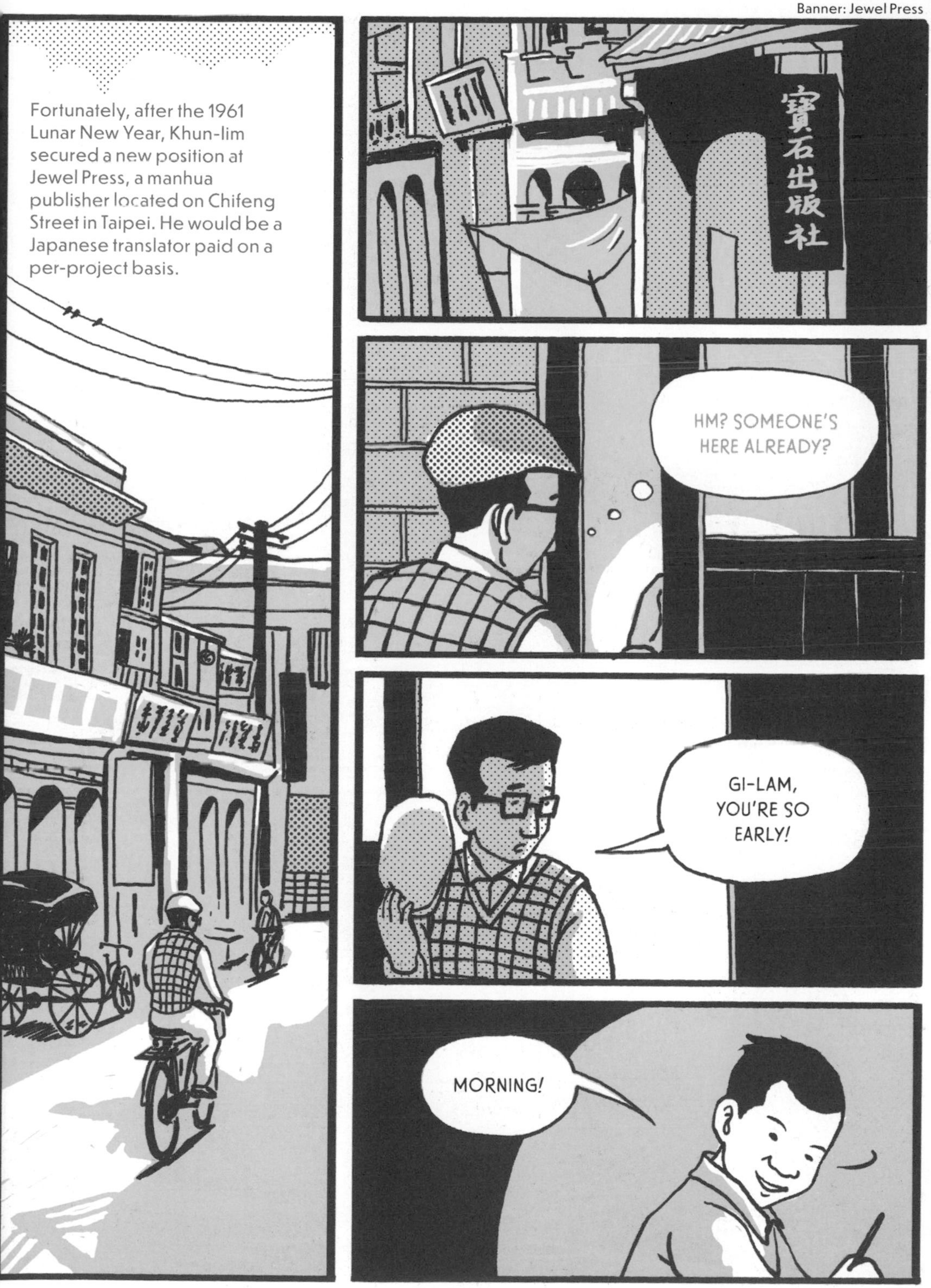

Fortunately, after the 1961 Lunar New Year, Khun-lim secured a new position at Jewel Press, a manhua publisher located on Chifeng Street in Taipei. He would be a Japanese translator paid on a per-project basis.
寶石出版社
HM? SOMEONE'S HERE ALREADY?
GI-LAM, YOU'RE SO EARLY!
MORNING!

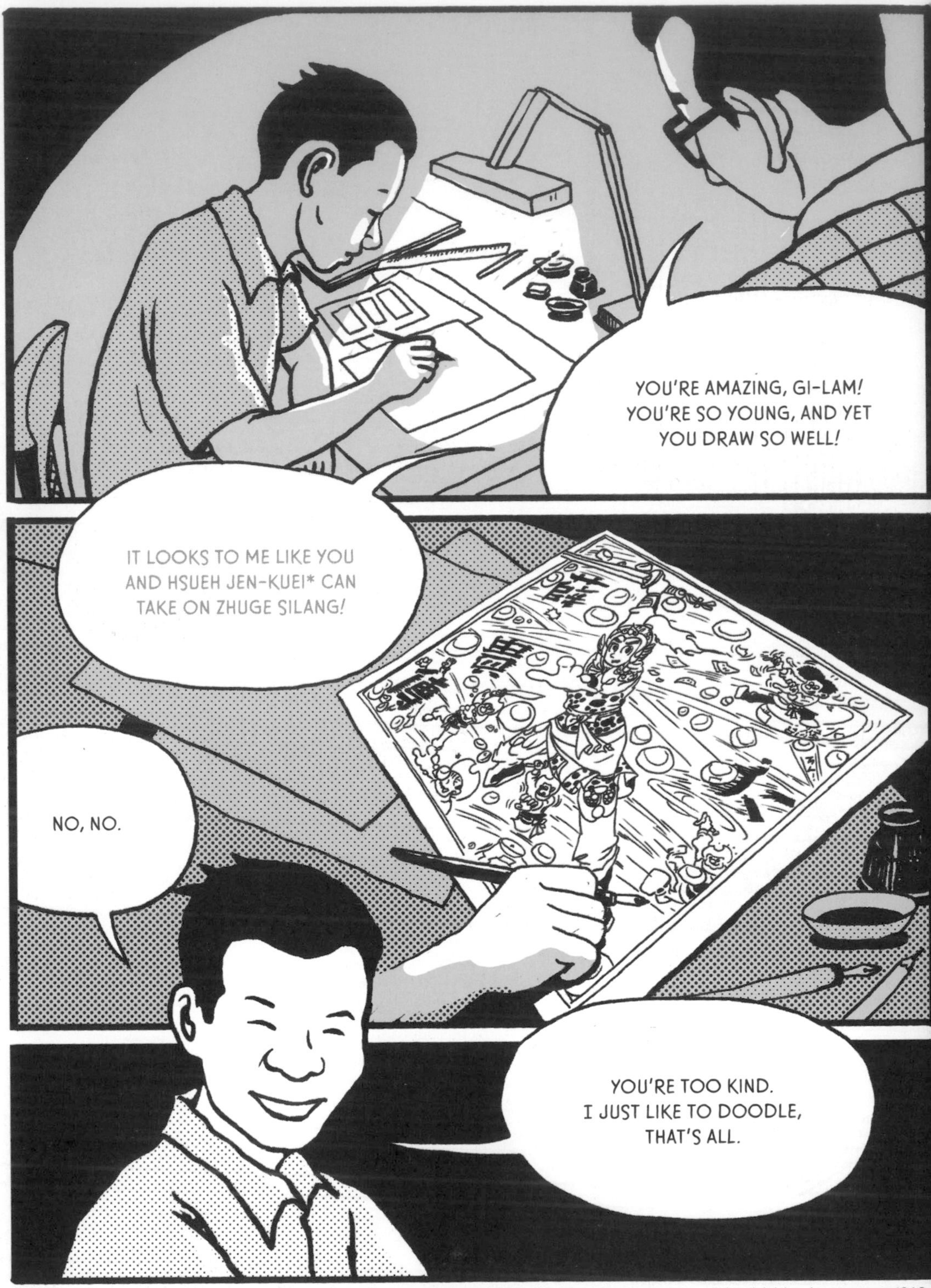
YOU'RE AMAZING, GI-LAM! YOU'RE SO YOUNG, AND YET YOU DRAW SO WELL!
IT LOOKS TO ME LIKE YOU AND HSUEH JEN-KUEI* CAN TAKE ON ZHUGE SILANG!
NO, NO.
YOU'RE TOO KIND. I JUST LIKE TO DOODLE, THAT'S ALL.

**The Conquests of Hsueh Jen-kuei* was a manhua serialized in Jewel Press's magazine *Schoolchildren* beginning in 1960. Its author, Ang Gi-lam (Mandarin Chinese: Hong I-lan), published under the pen name Stone Monkey.

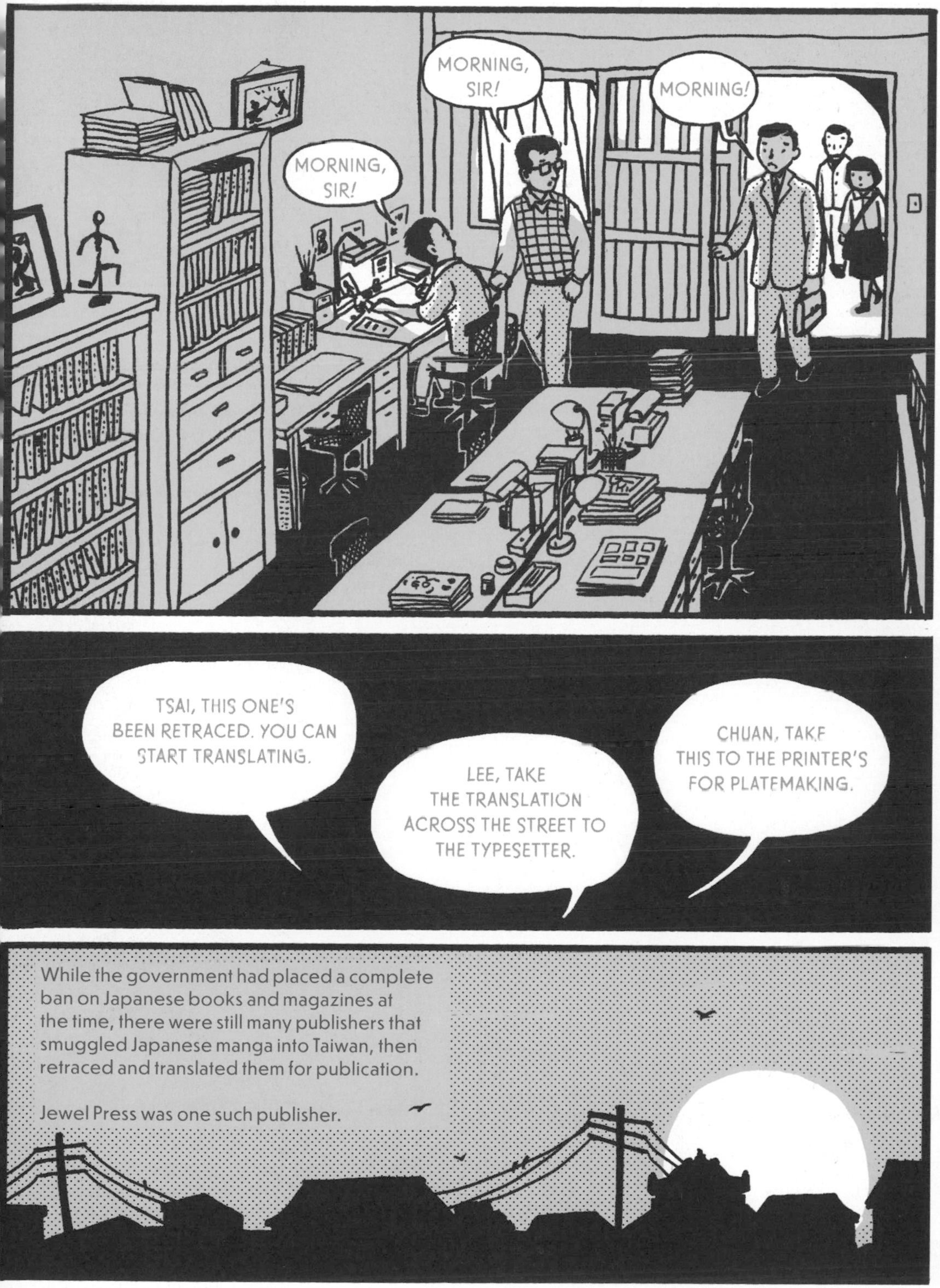
MORNING, SIR!
MORNING, SIR!
MORNING!
TSAI, THIS ONE'S BEEN RETRACED. YOU CAN START TRANSLATING.
LEE, TAKE THE TRANSLATION ACROSS THE STREET TO THE TYPESETTER.
CHUAN, TAKE THIS TO THE PRINTER'S FOR PLATEMAKING.
While the government had placed a complete ban on Japanese books and magazines at the time, there were still many publishers that smuggled Japanese manga into Taiwan, then retraced and translated them for publication.
Jewel Press was one such publisher.

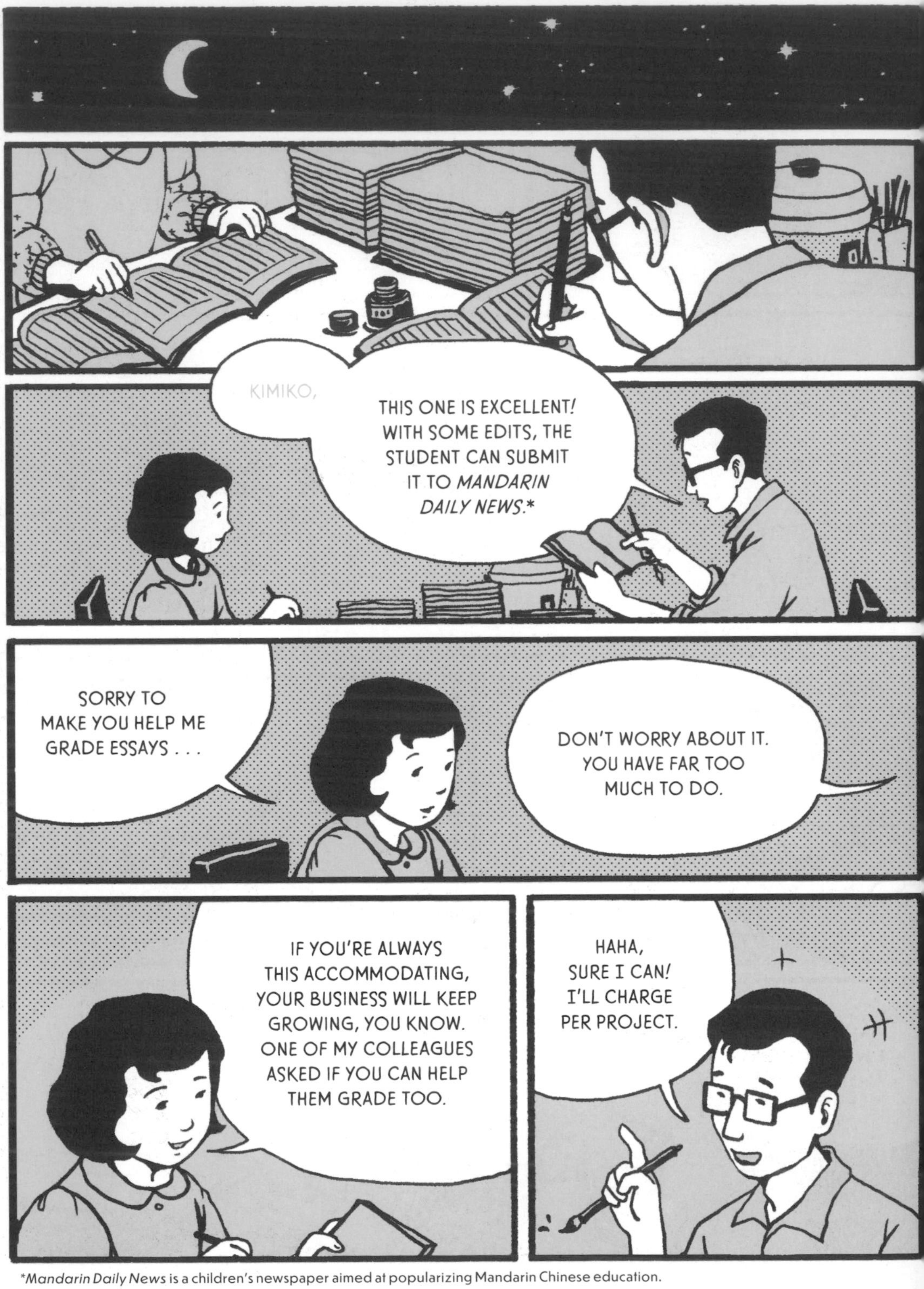
KIMIKO,
THIS ONE IS EXCELLENT! WITH SOME EDITS, THE STUDENT CAN SUBMIT IT TO *MANDARIN DAILY NEWS*.*
SORRY TO MAKE YOU HELP ME GRADE ESSAYS . . .
DON'T WORRY ABOUT IT. YOU HAVE FAR TOO MUCH TO DO.
IF YOU'RE ALWAYS THIS ACCOMMODATING, YOUR BUSINESS WILL KEEP GROWING, YOU KNOW. ONE OF MY COLLEAGUES ASKED IF YOU CAN HELP THEM GRADE TOO.
HAHA, SURE I CAN! I'LL CHARGE PER PROJECT.

**Mandarin Daily News* is a children's newspaper aimed at popularizing Mandarin Chinese education.

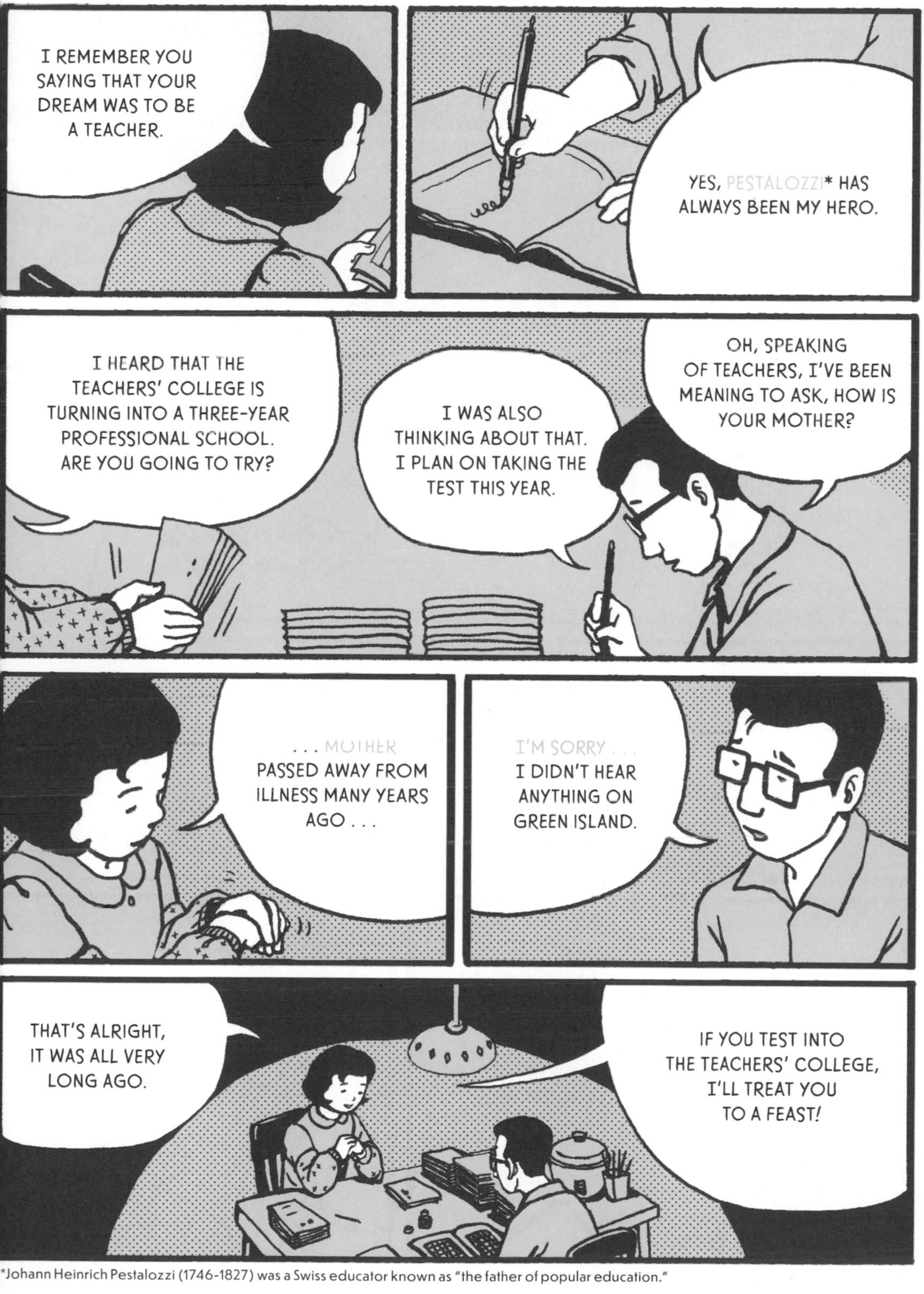
I REMEMBER YOU SAYING THAT YOUR DREAM WAS TO BE A TEACHER.
YES, PESTALOZZI* HAS ALWAYS BEEN MY HERO.
I HEARD THAT THE TEACHERS' COLLEGE IS TURNING INTO A THREE-YEAR PROFESSIONAL SCHOOL. ARE YOU GOING TO TRY?
I WAS ALSO THINKING ABOUT THAT. I PLAN ON TAKING THE TEST THIS YEAR.
OH, SPEAKING OF TEACHERS, I'VE BEEN MEANING TO ASK, HOW IS YOUR MOTHER?
. . . MOTHER PASSED AWAY FROM ILLNESS MANY YEARS AGO . . .
I'M SORRY . . . I DIDN'T HEAR ANYTHING ON GREEN ISLAND.
THAT'S ALRIGHT, IT WAS ALL VERY LONG AGO.
IF YOU TEST INTO THE TEACHERS' COLLEGE, I'LL TREAT YOU TO A FEAST!

*Johann Heinrich Pestalozzi (1746-1827) was a Swiss educator known as "the father of popular education."

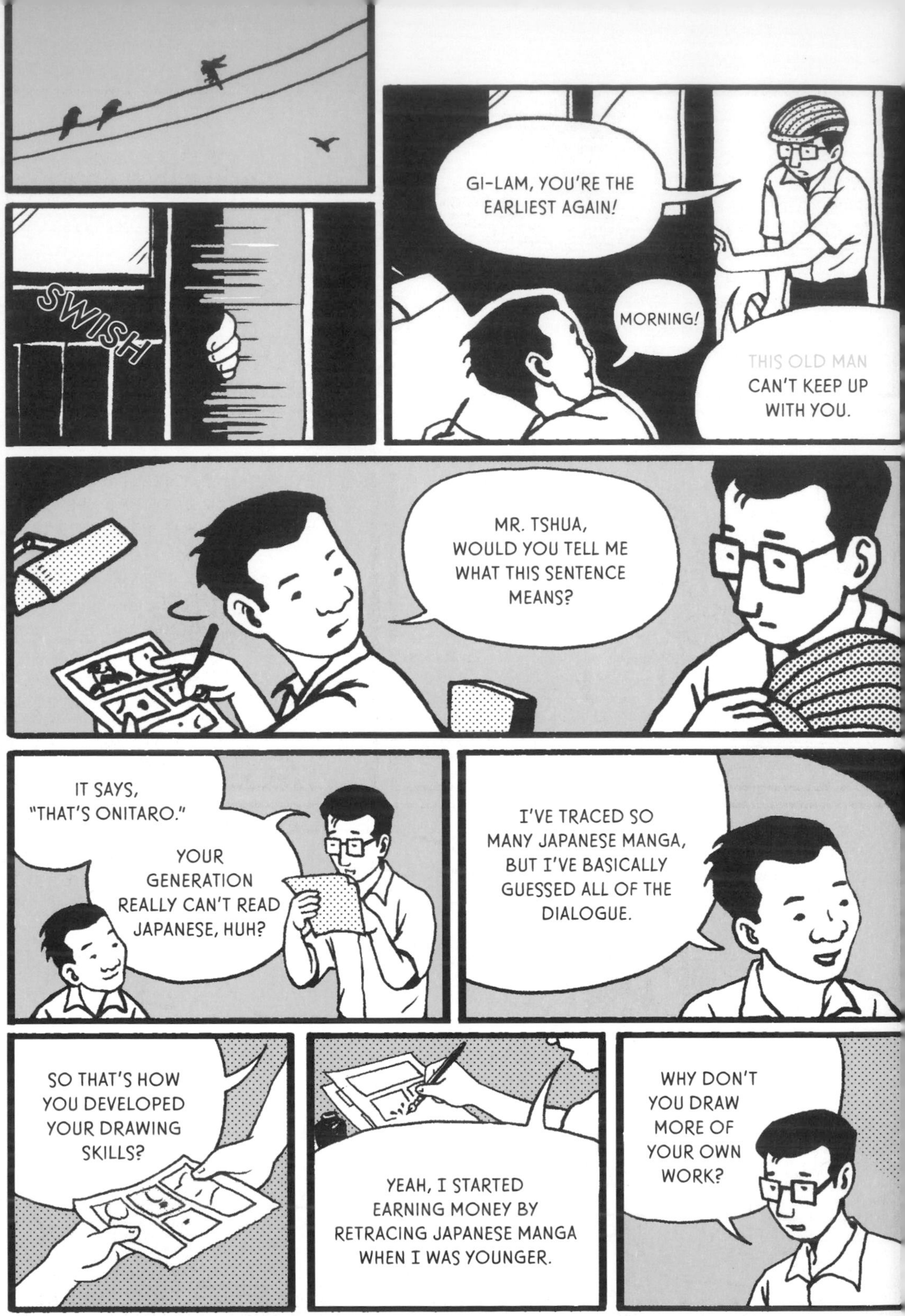
SWISH
GI-LAM, YOU'RE THE EARLIEST AGAIN!
MORNING!
THIS OLD MAN CAN'T KEEP UP WITH YOU.
MR. TSHUA, WOULD YOU TELL ME WHAT THIS SENTENCE MEANS?
IT SAYS, "THAT'S ONITARO."
YOUR GENERATION REALLY CAN'T READ JAPANESE, HUH?
I'VE TRACED SO MANY JAPANESE MANGA, BUT I'VE BASICALLY GUESSED ALL OF THE DIALOGUE.
SO THAT'S HOW YOU DEVELOPED YOUR DRAWING SKILLS?
YEAH, I STARTED EARNING MONEY BY RETRACING JAPANESE MANGA WHEN I WAS YOUNGER.
WHY DON'T YOU DRAW MORE OF YOUR OWN WORK?

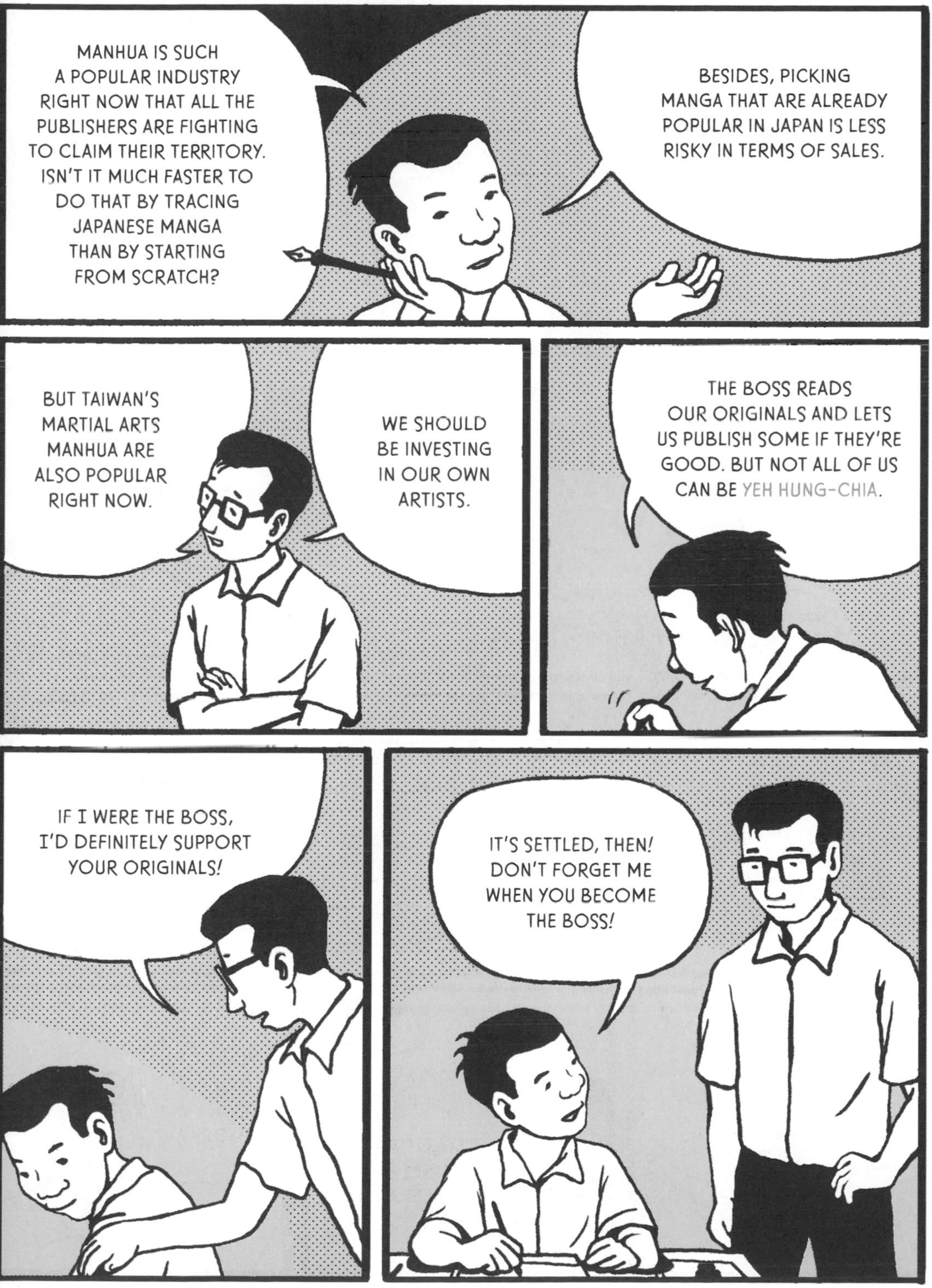
MANHUA IS SUCH A POPULAR INDUSTRY RIGHT NOW THAT ALL THE PUBLISHERS ARE FIGHTING TO CLAIM THEIR TERRITORY. ISN'T IT MUCH FASTER TO DO THAT BY TRACING JAPANESE MANGA THAN BY STARTING FROM SCRATCH?
BESIDES, PICKING MANGA THAT ARE ALREADY POPULAR IN JAPAN IS LESS RISKY IN TERMS OF SALES.
BUT TAIWAN'S MARTIAL ARTS MANHUA ARE ALSO POPULAR RIGHT NOW.
WE SHOULD BE INVESTING IN OUR OWN ARTISTS.
THE BOSS READS OUR ORIGINALS AND LETS US PUBLISH SOME IF THEY'RE GOOD. BUT NOT ALL OF US CAN BE YEH HUNG-CHIA.
IF I WERE THE BOSS, I'D DEFINITELY SUPPORT YOUR ORIGINALS!
IT'S SETTLED, THEN! DON'T FORGET ME WHEN YOU BECOME THE BOSS!

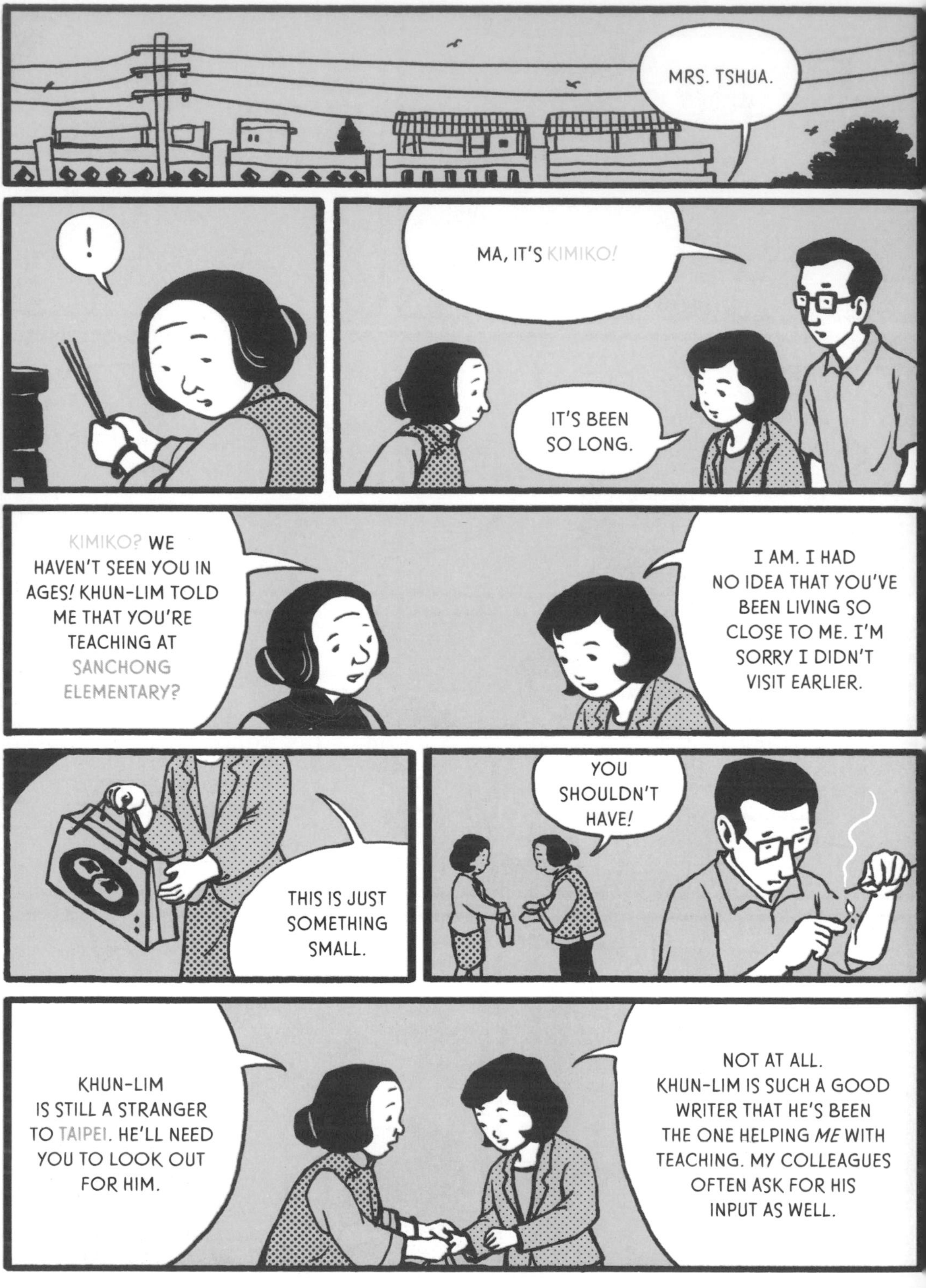
MRS. TSHUA.
!
MA, IT'S KIMIKO!
IT'S BEEN SO LONG.
KIMIKO? WE HAVEN'T SEEN YOU IN AGES! KHUN-LIM TOLD ME THAT YOU'RE TEACHING AT SANCHONG ELEMENTARY?
I AM. I HAD NO IDEA THAT YOU'VE BEEN LIVING SO CLOSE TO ME. I'M SORRY I DIDN'T VISIT EARLIER.
THIS IS JUST SOMETHING SMALL.
YOU SHOULDN'T HAVE!
KHUN-LIM IS STILL A STRANGER TO TAIPEI. HE'LL NEED YOU TO LOOK OUT FOR HIM.
NOT AT ALL. KHUN-LIM IS SUCH A GOOD WRITER THAT HE'S BEEN THE ONE HELPING *ME* WITH TEACHING. MY COLLEAGUES OFTEN ASK FOR HIS INPUT AS WELL.

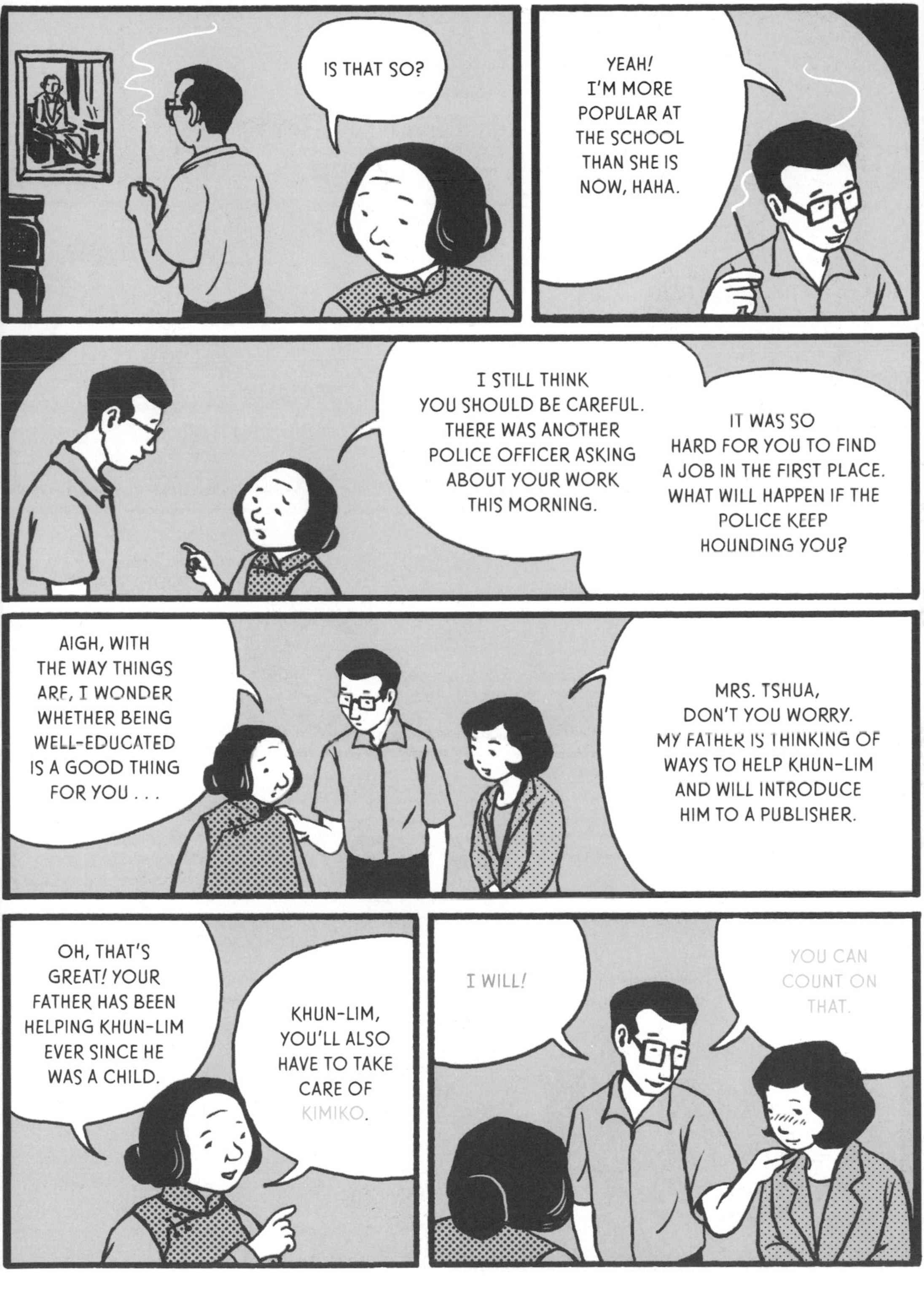
IS THAT SO?
YEAH! I'M MORE POPULAR AT THE SCHOOL THAN SHE IS NOW, HAHA.
I STILL THINK YOU SHOULD BE CAREFUL. THERE WAS ANOTHER POLICE OFFICER ASKING ABOUT YOUR WORK THIS MORNING.
IT WAS SO HARD FOR YOU TO FIND A JOB IN THE FIRST PLACE. WHAT WILL HAPPEN IF THE POLICE KEEP HOUNDING YOU?
AIGH, WITH THE WAY THINGS ARE, I WONDER WHETHER BEING WELL-EDUCATED IS A GOOD THING FOR YOU . . .
MRS. TSHUA, DON'T YOU WORRY. MY FATHER IS THINKING OF WAYS TO HELP KHUN-LIM AND WILL INTRODUCE HIM TO A PUBLISHER.
OH, THAT'S GREAT! YOUR FATHER HAS BEEN HELPING KHUN-LIM EVER SINCE HE WAS A CHILD.
KHUN-LIM, YOU'LL ALSO HAVE TO TAKE CARE OF KIMIKO.
I WILL!
YOU CAN COUNT ON THAT.

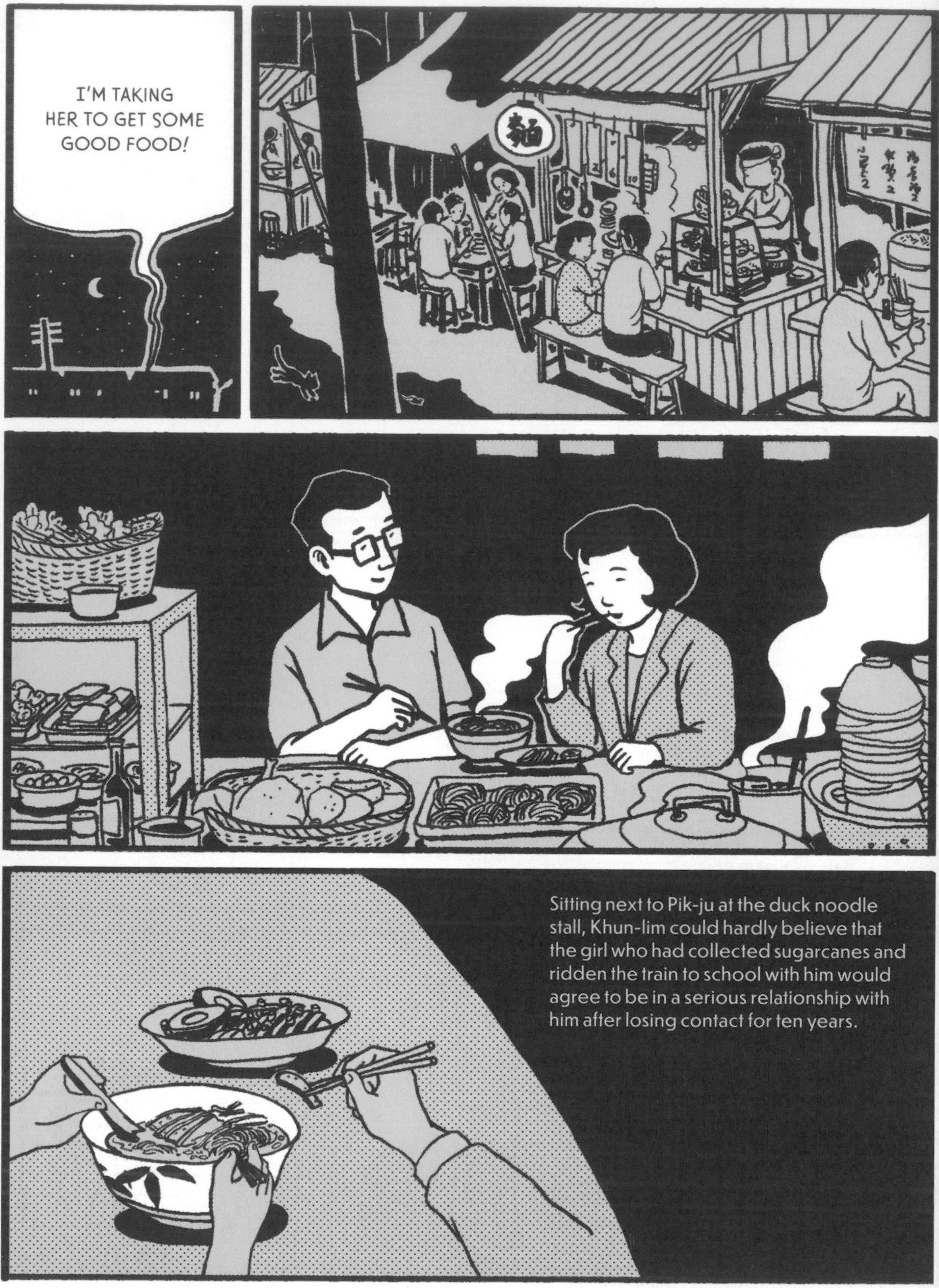
I'M TAKING HER TO GET SOME GOOD FOOD!
Sitting next to Pik-ju at the duck noodle stall, Khun-lim could hardly believe that the girl who had collected sugarcanes and ridden the train to school with him would agree to be in a serious relationship with him after losing contact for ten years.

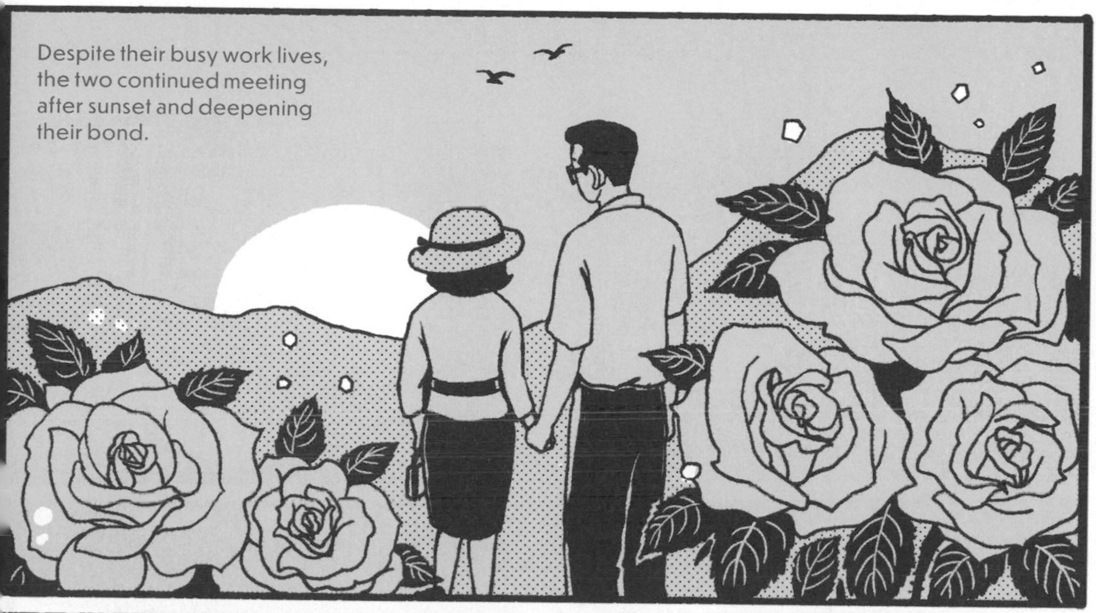
Despite their busy work lives, the two continued meeting after sunset and deepening their bond.

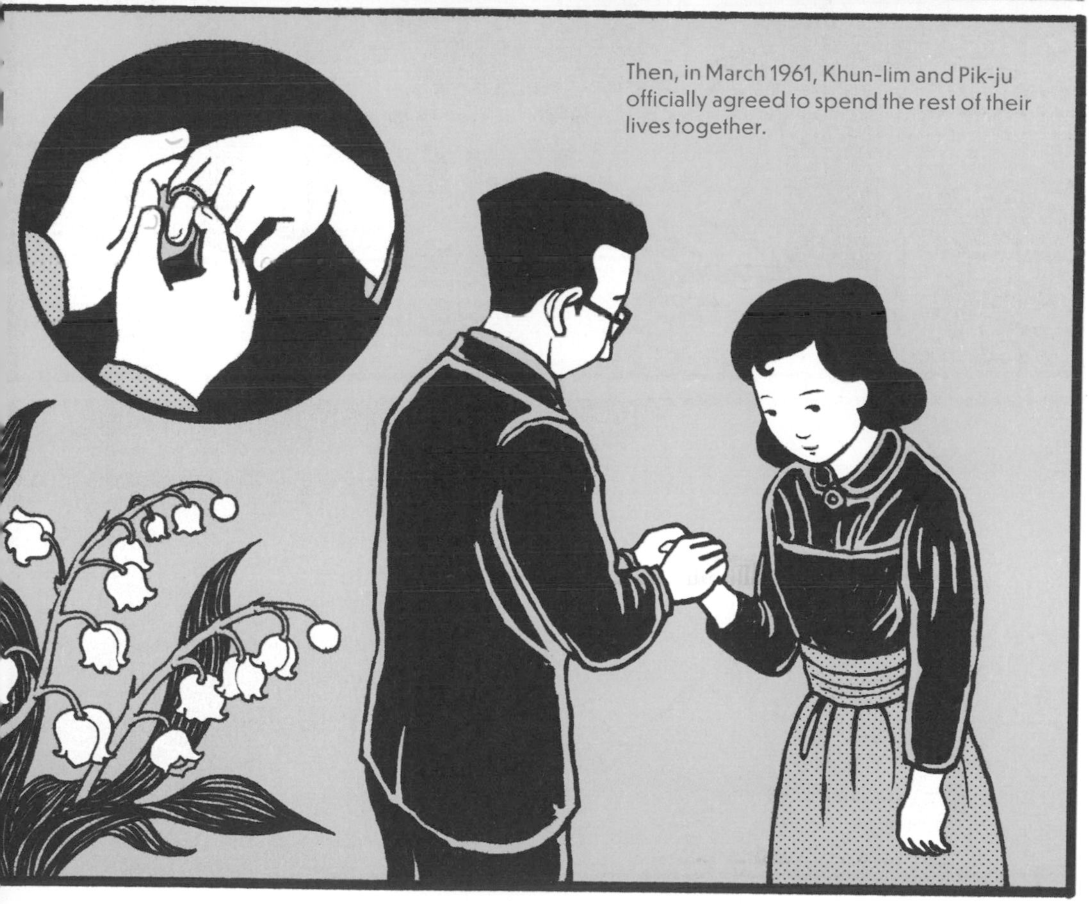
Then, in March 1961, Khun-lim and Pik-ju officially agreed to spend the rest of their lives together.

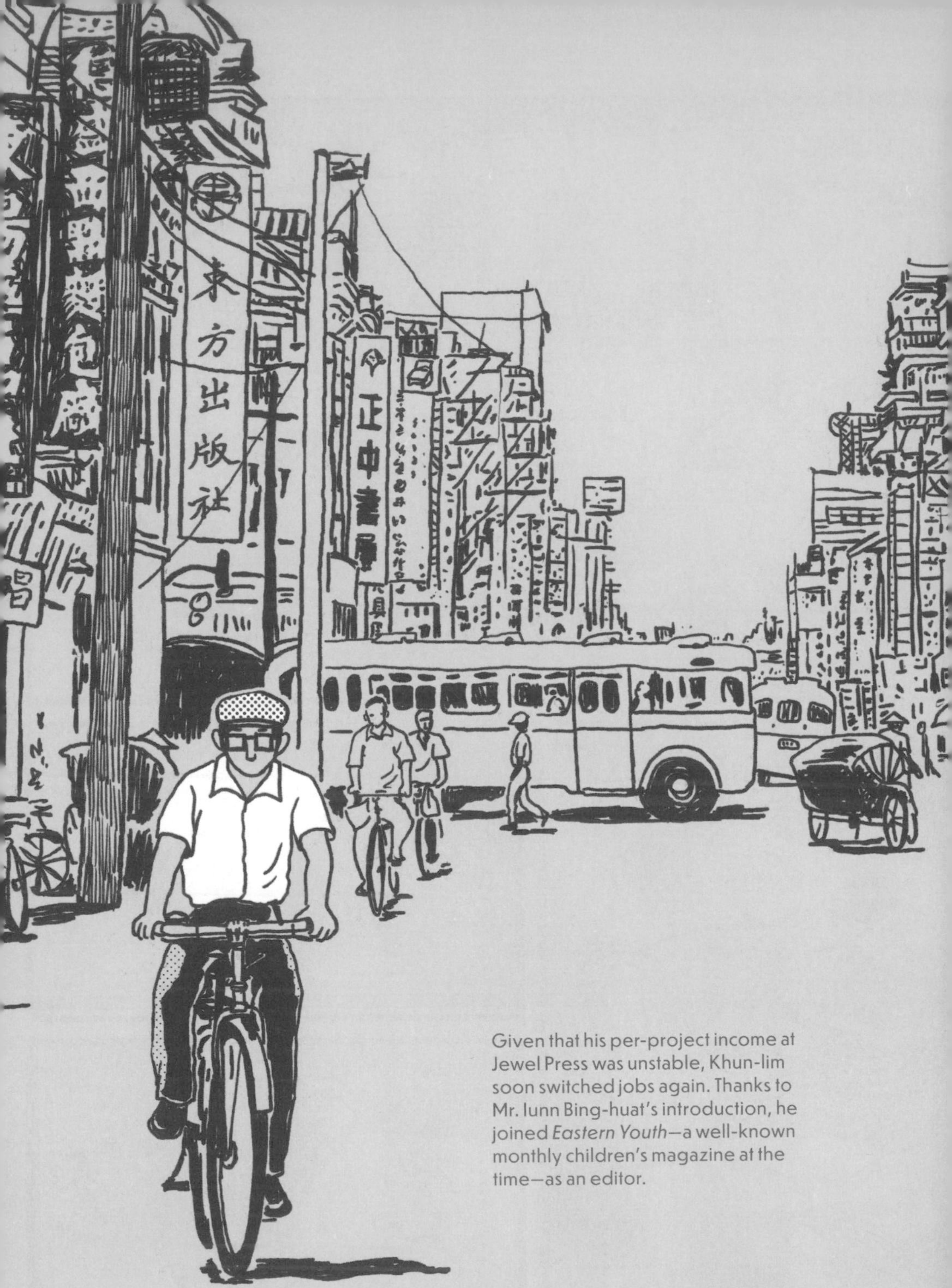
東方出版社
正中書局

Given that his per-project income at Jewel Press was unstable, Khun-lim soon switched jobs again. Thanks to Mr. Iunn Bing-huat's introduction, he joined *Eastern Youth*—a well-known monthly children's magazine at the time—as an editor.

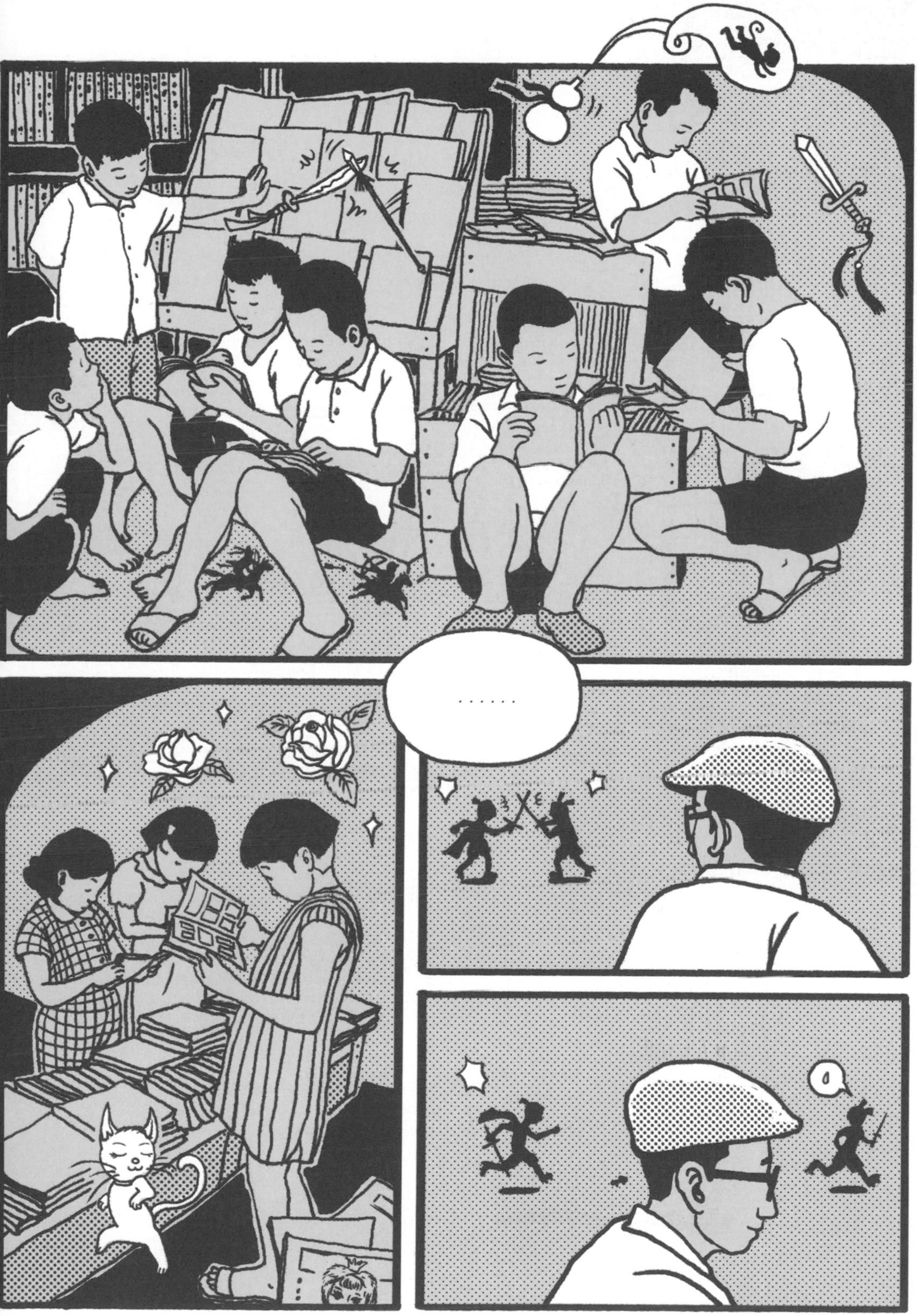
......

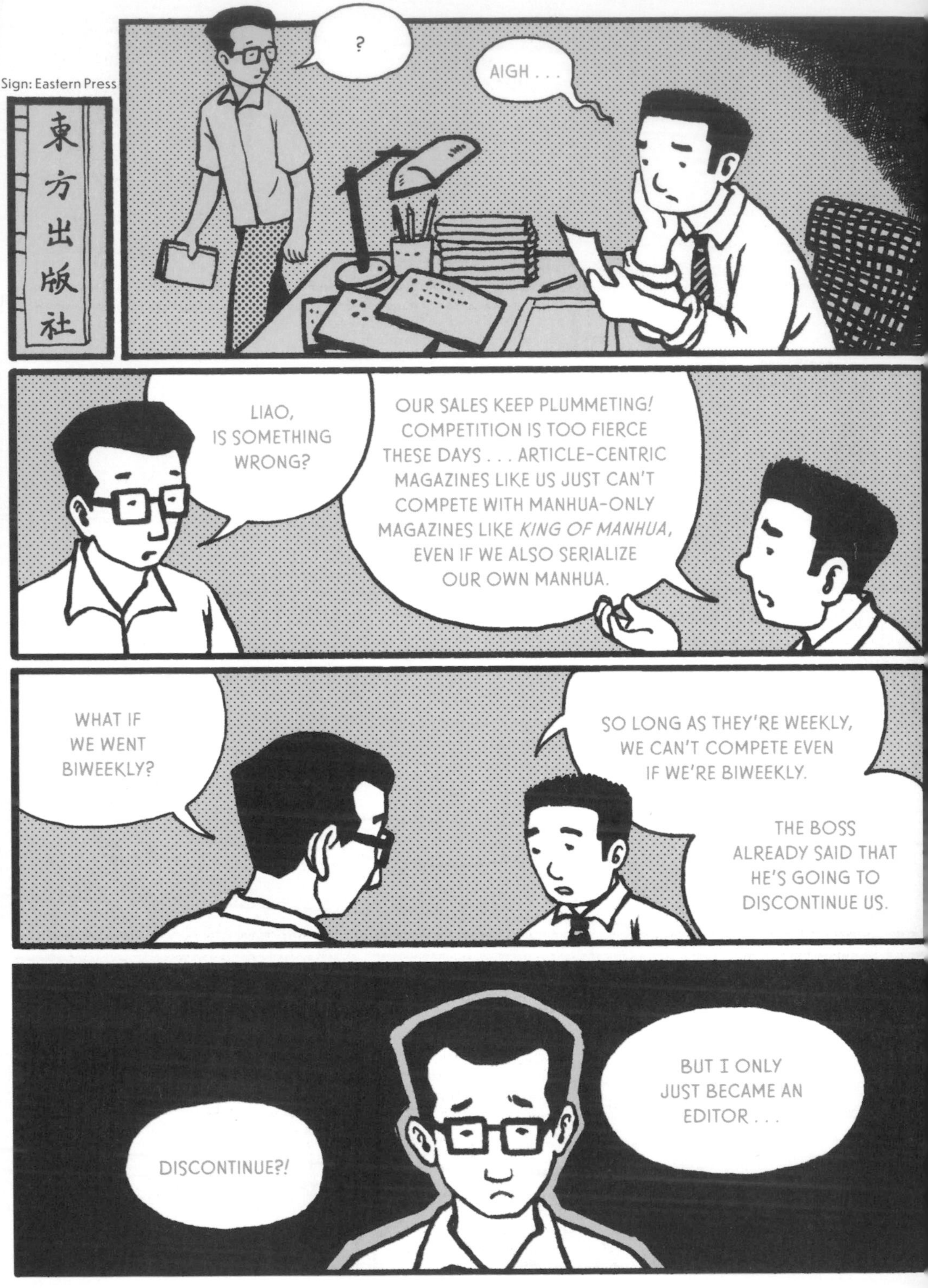
Sign: Eastern Press
東方出版社
?
AIGH . . .
LIAO, IS SOMETHING WRONG?
OUR SALES KEEP PLUMMETING! COMPETITION IS TOO FIERCE THESE DAYS . . . ARTICLE-CENTRIC MAGAZINES LIKE US JUST CAN'T COMPETE WITH MANHUA-ONLY MAGAZINES LIKE *KING OF MANHUA*, EVEN IF WE ALSO SERIALIZE OUR OWN MANHUA.
WHAT IF WE WENT BIWEEKLY?
SO LONG AS THEY'RE WEEKLY, WE CAN'T COMPETE EVEN IF WE'RE BIWEEKLY.
THE BOSS ALREADY SAID THAT HE'S GOING TO DISCONTINUE US.
DISCONTINUE?!
BUT I ONLY JUST BECAME AN EDITOR . . .

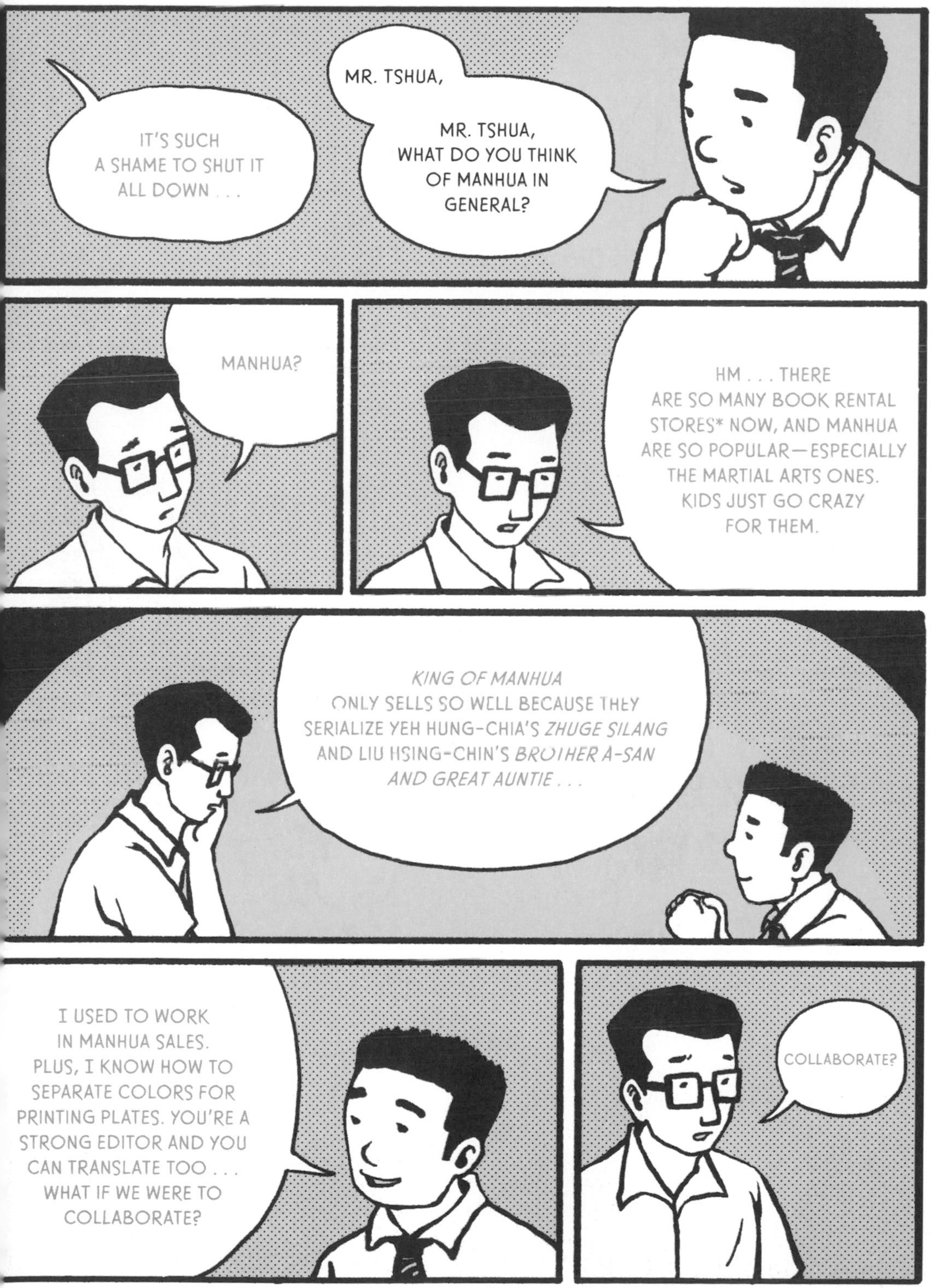
IT'S SUCH A SHAME TO SHUT IT ALL DOWN . . .
MR. TSHUA,
MR. TSHUA, WHAT DO YOU THINK OF MANHUA IN GENERAL?
MANHUA?
HM . . . THERE ARE SO MANY BOOK RENTAL STORES* NOW, AND MANHUA ARE SO POPULAR—ESPECIALLY THE MARTIAL ARTS ONES. KIDS JUST GO CRAZY FOR THEM.
KING OF MANHUA ONLY SELLS SO WELL BECAUSE THEY SERIALIZE YEH HUNG-CHIA'S *ZHUGE SILANG* AND LIU HSING-CHIN'S *BROTHER A-SAN AND GREAT AUNTIE . . .*
I USED TO WORK IN MANHUA SALES. PLUS, I KNOW HOW TO SEPARATE COLORS FOR PRINTING PLATES. YOU'RE A STRONG EDITOR AND YOU CAN TRANSLATE TOO . . . WHAT IF WE WERE TO COLLABORATE?
COLLABORATE?

t the time, magazines and single-volume manhua were sold through separate channels. Magazines were sold in regular bookstores, ıereas manhua volumes were sold to book rental stores instead of directly to readers.

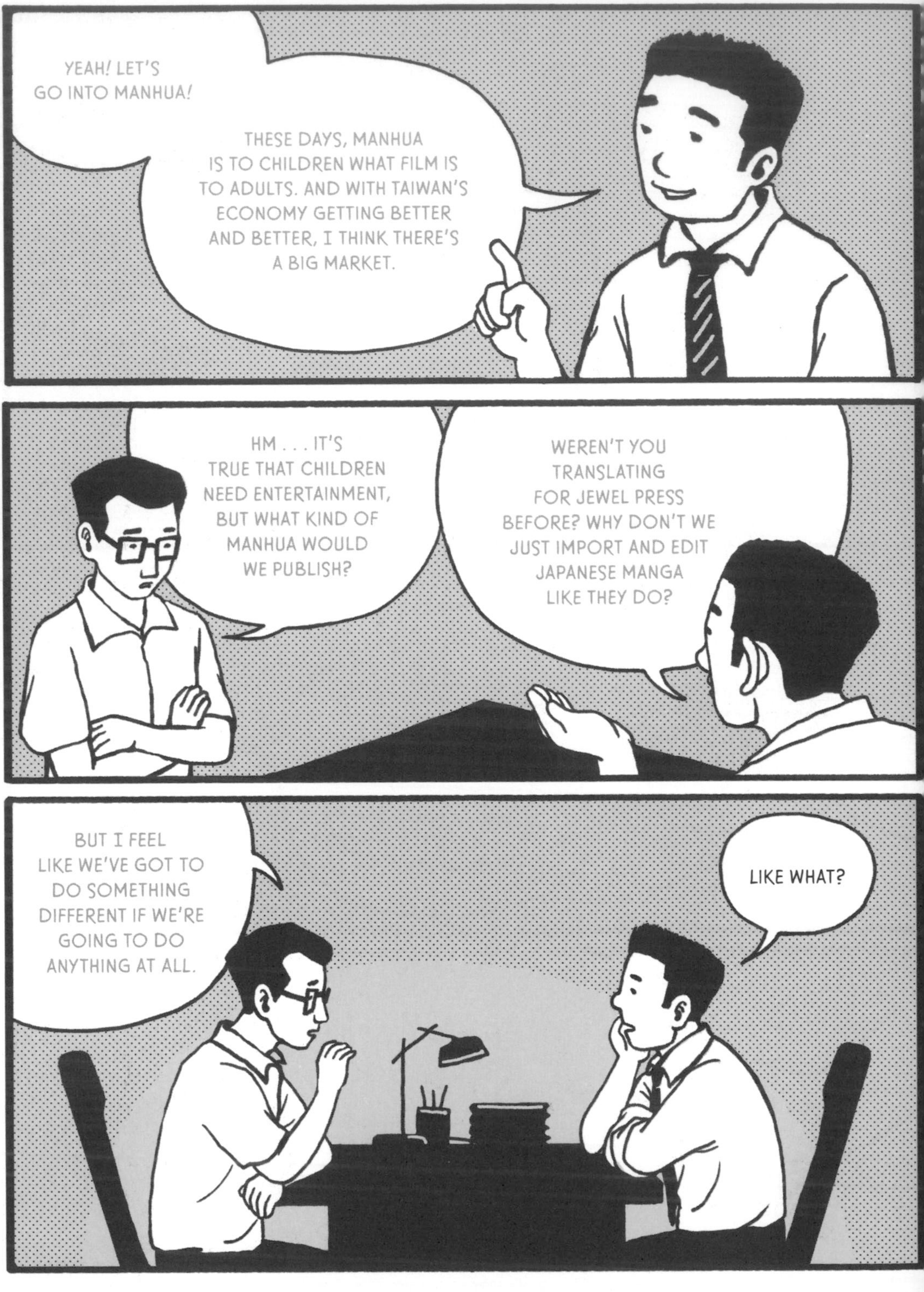
YEAH! LET'S GO INTO MANHUA!
THESE DAYS, MANHUA IS TO CHILDREN WHAT FILM IS TO ADULTS. AND WITH TAIWAN'S ECONOMY GETTING BETTER AND BETTER, I THINK THERE'S A BIG MARKET.
HM . . . IT'S TRUE THAT CHILDREN NEED ENTERTAINMENT, BUT WHAT KIND OF MANHUA WOULD WE PUBLISH?
WEREN'T YOU TRANSLATING FOR JEWEL PRESS BEFORE? WHY DON'T WE JUST IMPORT AND EDIT JAPANESE MANGA LIKE THEY DO?
BUT I FEEL LIKE WE'VE GOT TO DO SOMETHING DIFFERENT IF WE'RE GOING TO DO ANYTHING AT ALL.
LIKE WHAT?

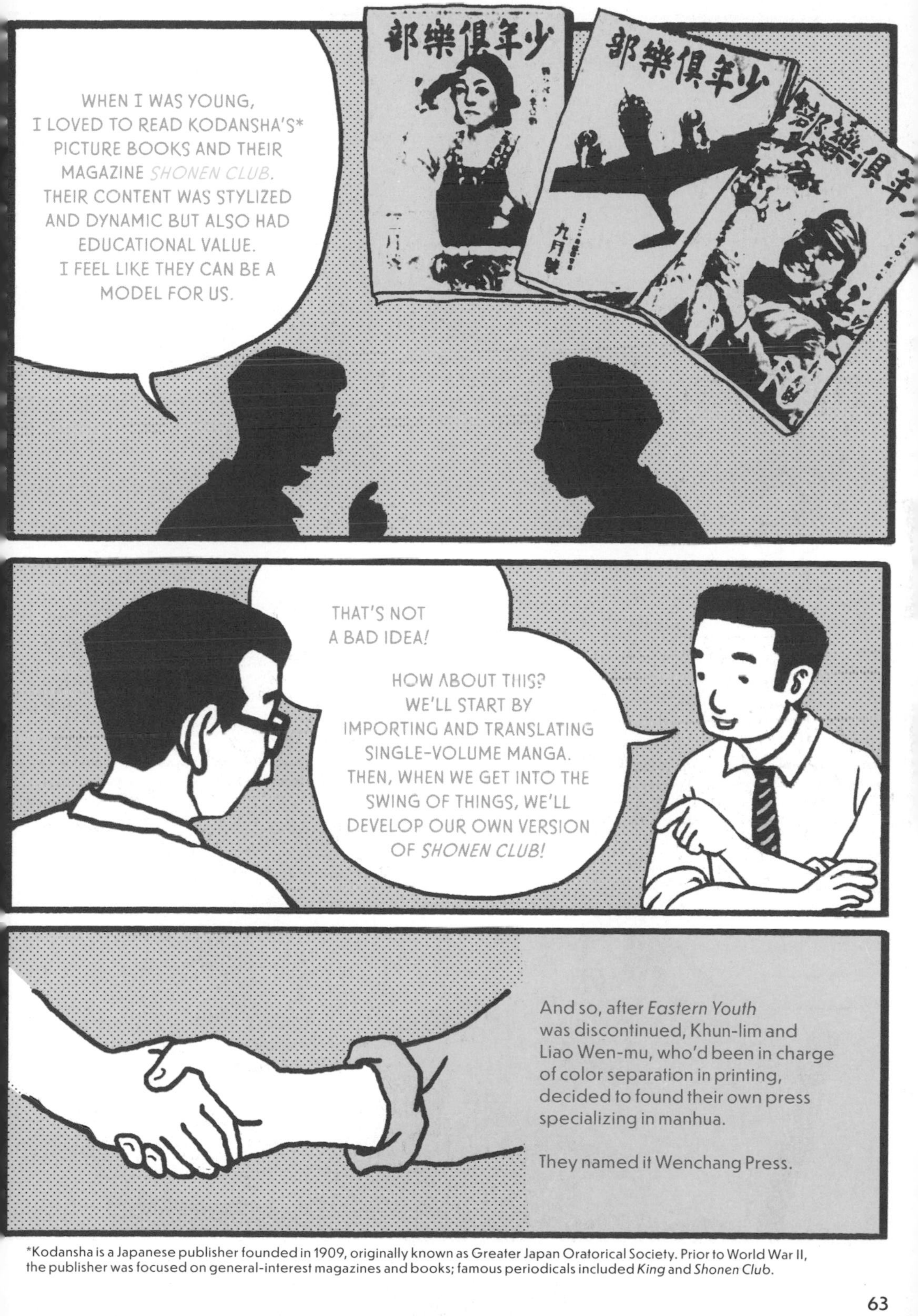

少年倶樂部
少年倶樂部
九月號
WHEN I WAS YOUNG, I LOVED TO READ KODANSHA'S* PICTURE BOOKS AND THEIR MAGAZINE *SHONEN CLUB*. THEIR CONTENT WAS STYLIZED AND DYNAMIC BUT ALSO HAD EDUCATIONAL VALUE. I FEEL LIKE THEY CAN BE A MODEL FOR US.
THAT'S NOT A BAD IDEA!
HOW ABOUT THIS? WE'LL START BY IMPORTING AND TRANSLATING SINGLE-VOLUME MANGA. THEN, WHEN WE GET INTO THE SWING OF THINGS, WE'LL DEVELOP OUR OWN VERSION OF *SHONEN CLUB*!
And so, after *Eastern Youth* was discontinued, Khun-lim and Liao Wen-mu, who'd been in charge of color separation in printing, decided to found their own press specializing in manhua.
They named it Wenchang Press.

*Kodansha is a Japanese publisher founded in 1909, originally known as Greater Japan Oratorical Society. Prior to World War II, the publisher was focused on general-interest magazines and books; famous periodicals included *King* and *Shonen Club*.

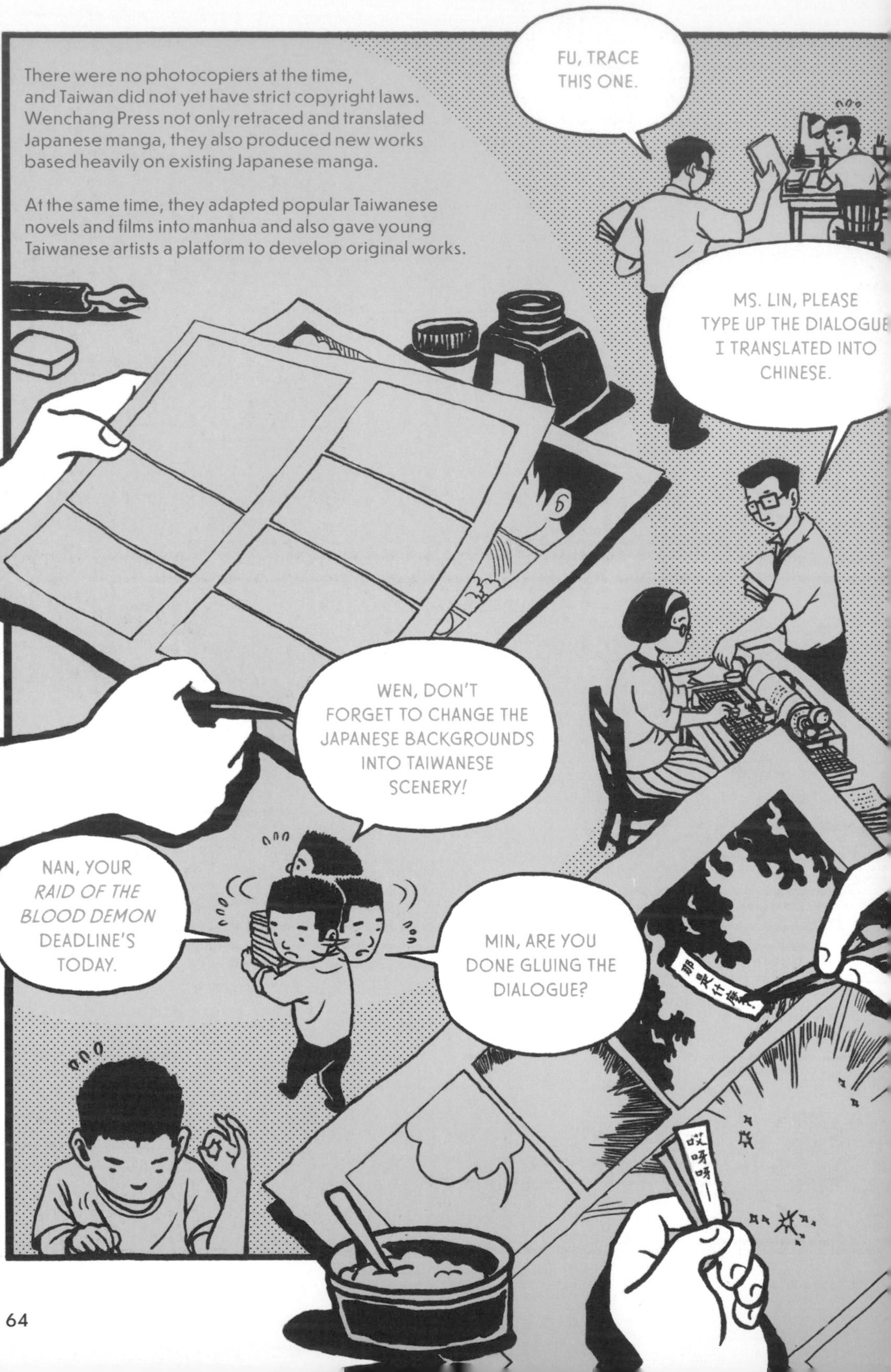
There were no photocopiers at the time, and Taiwan did not yet have strict copyright laws. Wenchang Press not only retraced and translated Japanese manga, they also produced new works based heavily on existing Japanese manga.
At the same time, they adapted popular Taiwanese novels and films into manhua and also gave young Taiwanese artists a platform to develop original works.
FU, TRACE THIS ONE.
MS. LIN, PLEASE TYPE UP THE DIALOGUE I TRANSLATED INTO CHINESE.
WEN, DON'T FORGET TO CHANGE THE JAPANESE BACKGROUNDS INTO TAIWANESE SCENERY!
NAN, YOUR *RAID OF THE BLOOD DEMON* DEADLINE'S TODAY.
MIN, ARE YOU DONE GLUING THE DIALOGUE?
那是什麼?
哎呀呀—

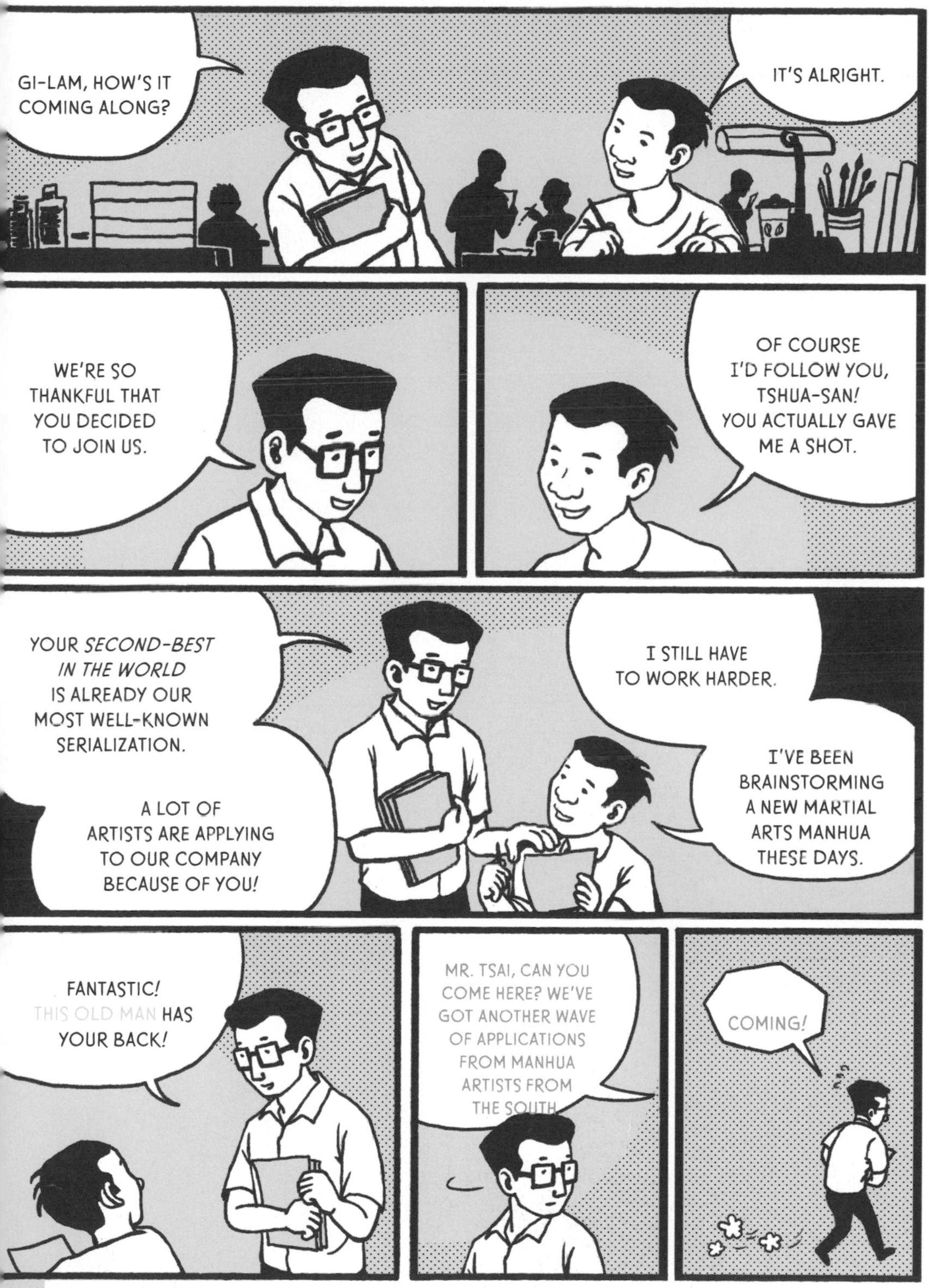
GI-LAM, HOW'S IT COMING ALONG?
IT'S ALRIGHT.
WE'RE SO THANKFUL THAT YOU DECIDED TO JOIN US.
OF COURSE I'D FOLLOW YOU, TSHUA-SAN! YOU ACTUALLY GAVE ME A SHOT.
YOUR *SECOND-BEST IN THE WORLD* IS ALREADY OUR MOST WELL-KNOWN SERIALIZATION.
A LOT OF ARTISTS ARE APPLYING TO OUR COMPANY BECAUSE OF YOU!
I STILL HAVE TO WORK HARDER.
I'VE BEEN BRAINSTORMING A NEW MARTIAL ARTS MANHUA THESE DAYS.
FANTASTIC! THIS OLD MAN HAS YOUR BACK!
MR. TSAI, CAN YOU COME HERE? WE'VE GOT ANOTHER WAVE OF APPLICATIONS FROM MANHUA ARTISTS FROM THE SOUTH.
COMING!

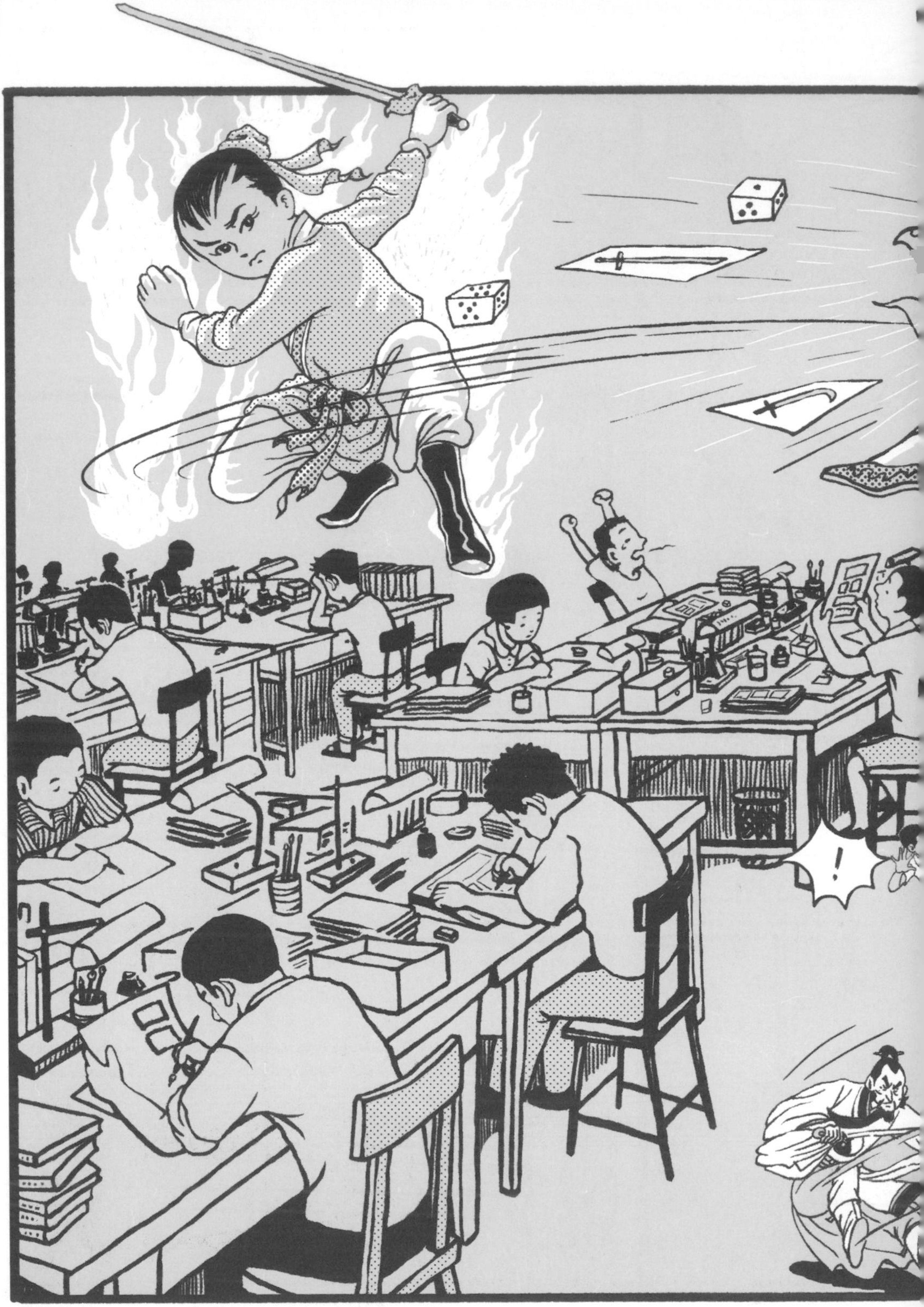
!

Top left: Fang Wan-nan, *The Dashing Swordsman* (1964). Top right: Ang Gi-lam (Mandarin Chinese: Hong I-nan) *The Plaque of Heaven and Earth* (1965). Center: Ang Gi-lam and Hong Cheng-hsiung, *The Vampire* (1963).

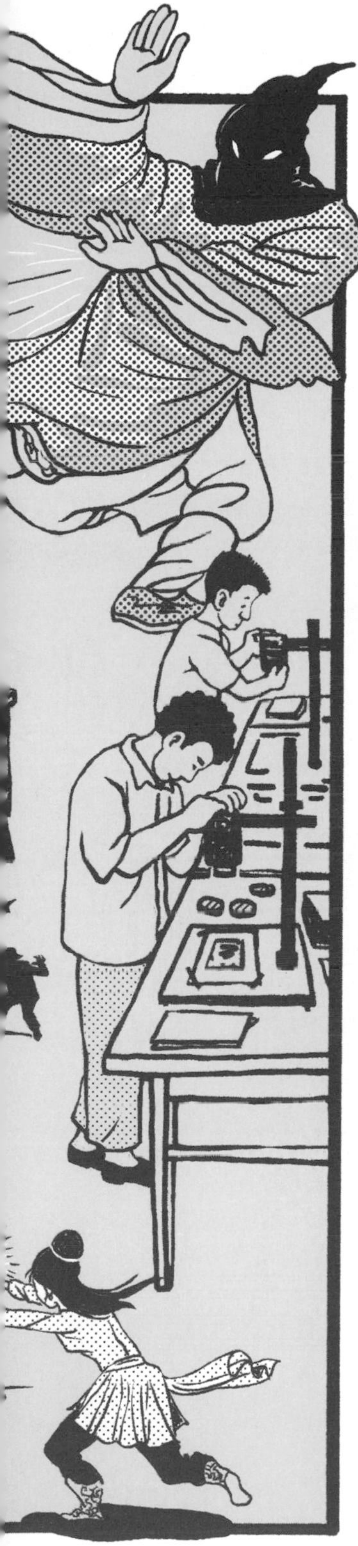

Wenchang Press soon made a name for itself in the manhua industry, attracting to their door many young people aspiring to become manhua artists. These included Fang Wan-nan (pen name Fang I-nan), Tsai Chi-chong, and Chen I-nan.

Slowly, this postwar generation of young Taiwanese creators began to develop their own style of manhua.

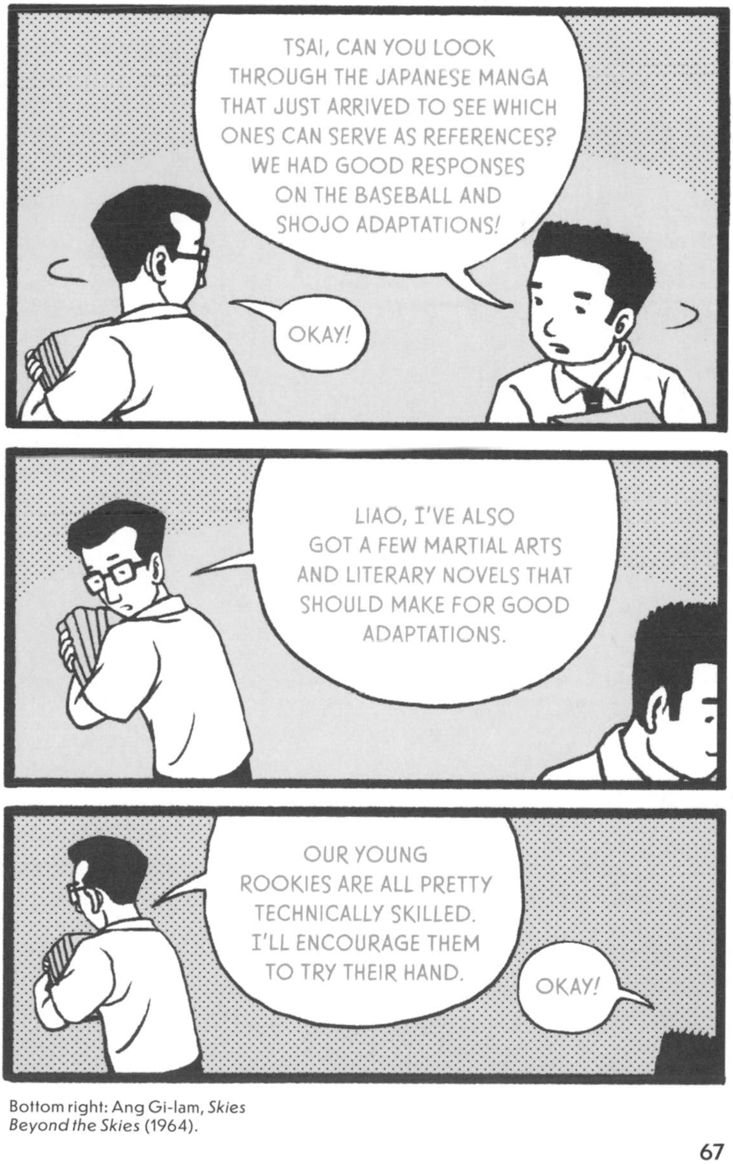
TSAI, CAN YOU LOOK THROUGH THE JAPANESE MANGA THAT JUST ARRIVED TO SEE WHICH ONES CAN SERVE AS REFERENCES? WE HAD GOOD RESPONSES ON THE BASEBALL AND SHOJO ADAPTATIONS!
OKAY!
LIAO, I'VE ALSO GOT A FEW MARTIAL ARTS AND LITERARY NOVELS THAT SHOULD MAKE FOR GOOD ADAPTATIONS.
OUR YOUNG ROOKIES ARE ALL PRETTY TECHNICALLY SKILLED. I'LL ENCOURAGE THEM TO TRY THEIR HAND.
OKAY!

Bottom right: Ang Gi-lam, *Skies Beyond the Skies* (1964).

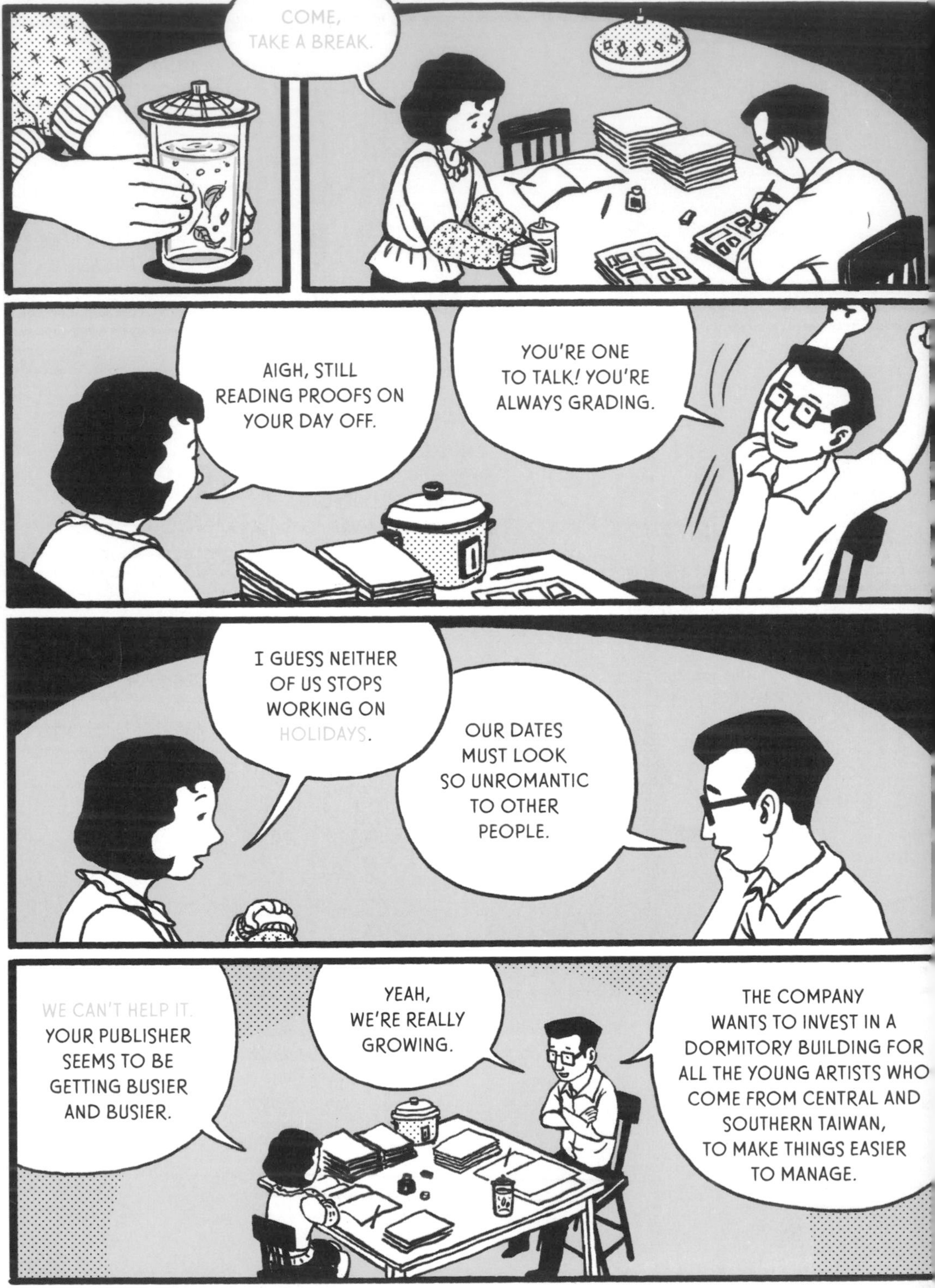
COME, TAKE A BREAK.
AIGH, STILL READING PROOFS ON YOUR DAY OFF.
YOU'RE ONE TO TALK! YOU'RE ALWAYS GRADING.
I GUESS NEITHER OF US STOPS WORKING ON HOLIDAYS.
OUR DATES MUST LOOK SO UNROMANTIC TO OTHER PEOPLE.
WE CAN'T HELP IT. YOUR PUBLISHER SEEMS TO BE GETTING BUSIER AND BUSIER.
YEAH, WE'RE REALLY GROWING.
THE COMPANY WANTS TO INVEST IN A DORMITORY BUILDING FOR ALL THE YOUNG ARTISTS WHO COME FROM CENTRAL AND SOUTHERN TAIWAN, TO MAKE THINGS EASIER TO MANAGE.

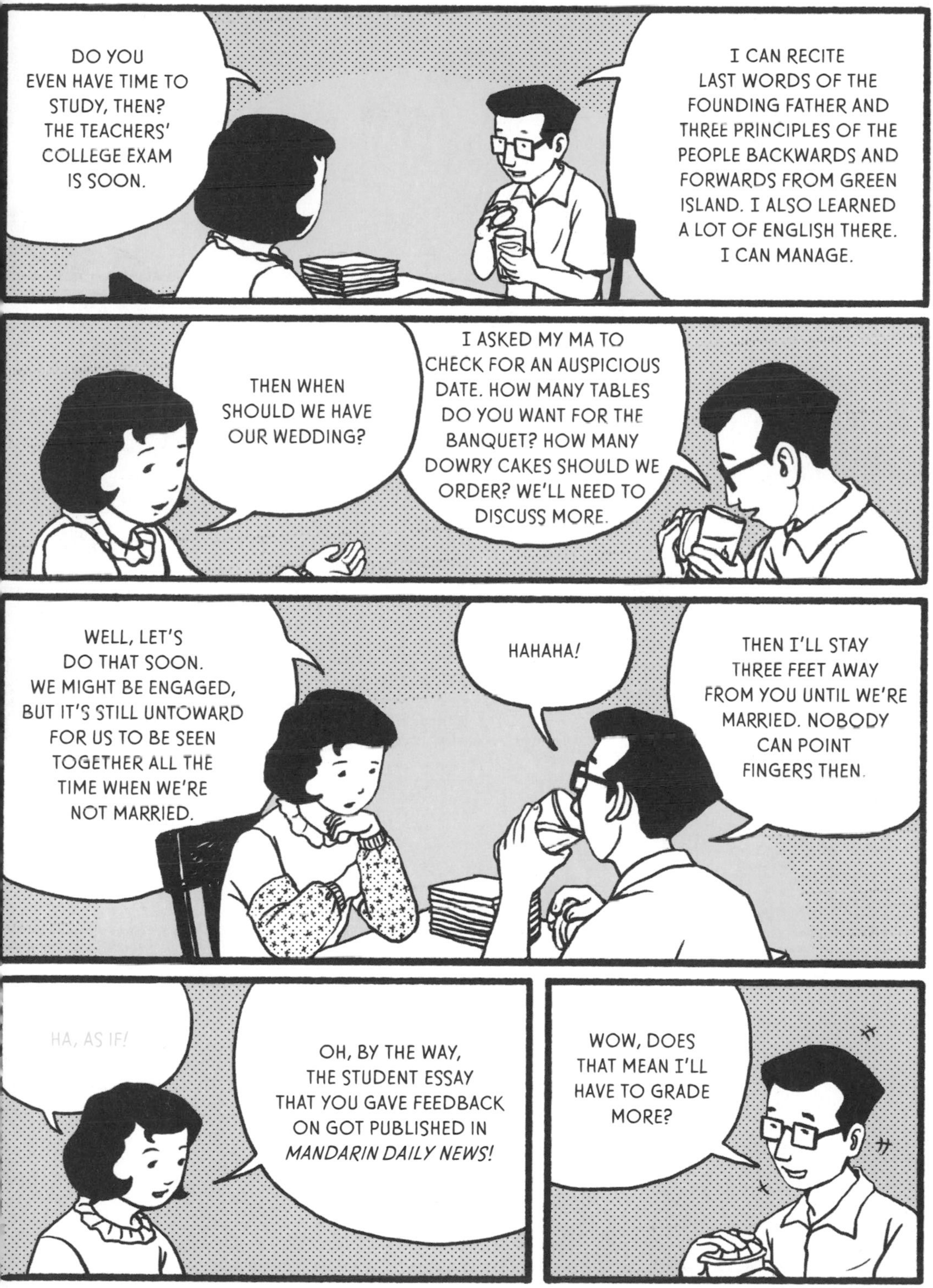
DO YOU EVEN HAVE TIME TO STUDY, THEN? THE TEACHERS' COLLEGE EXAM IS SOON.
I CAN RECITE LAST WORDS OF THE FOUNDING FATHER AND THREE PRINCIPLES OF THE PEOPLE BACKWARDS AND FORWARDS FROM GREEN ISLAND. I ALSO LEARNED A LOT OF ENGLISH THERE. I CAN MANAGE.
THEN WHEN SHOULD WE HAVE OUR WEDDING?
I ASKED MY MA TO CHECK FOR AN AUSPICIOUS DATE. HOW MANY TABLES DO YOU WANT FOR THE BANQUET? HOW MANY DOWRY CAKES SHOULD WE ORDER? WE'LL NEED TO DISCUSS MORE.
WELL, LET'S DO THAT SOON. WE MIGHT BE ENGAGED, BUT IT'S STILL UNTOWARD FOR US TO BE SEEN TOGETHER ALL THE TIME WHEN WE'RE NOT MARRIED.
HAHAHA!
THEN I'LL STAY THREE FEET AWAY FROM YOU UNTIL WE'RE MARRIED. NOBODY CAN POINT FINGERS THEN.
HA, AS IF!
OH, BY THE WAY, THE STUDENT ESSAY THAT YOU GAVE FEEDBACK ON GOT PUBLISHED IN *MANDARIN DAILY NEWS!*
WOW, DOES THAT MEAN I'LL HAVE TO GRADE MORE?

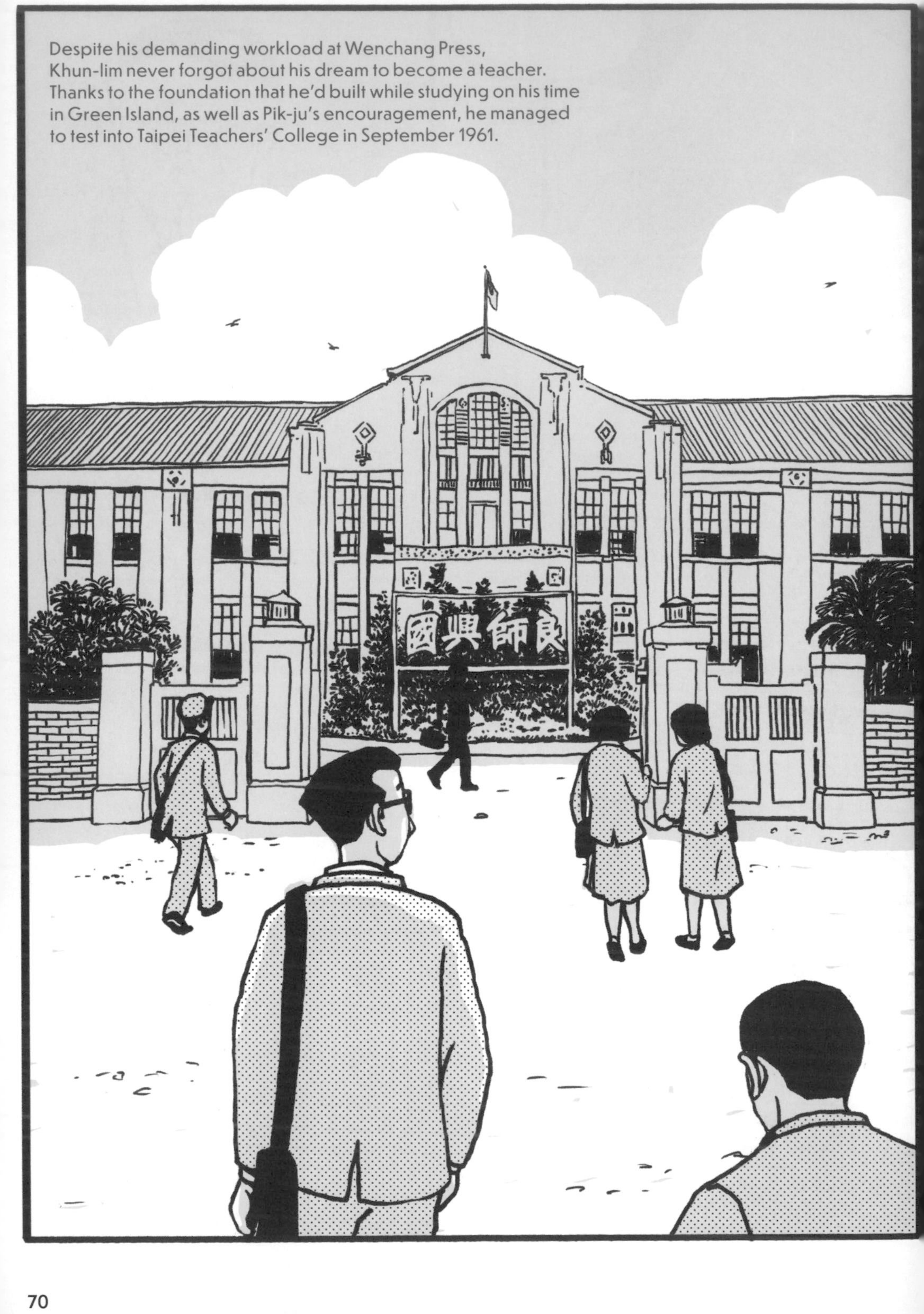
Despite his demanding workload at Wenchang Press, Khun-lim never forgot about his dream to become a teacher. Thanks to the foundation that he'd built while studying on his time in Green Island, as well as Pik-ju's encouragement, he managed to test into Taipei Teachers' College in September 1961.
良師興國

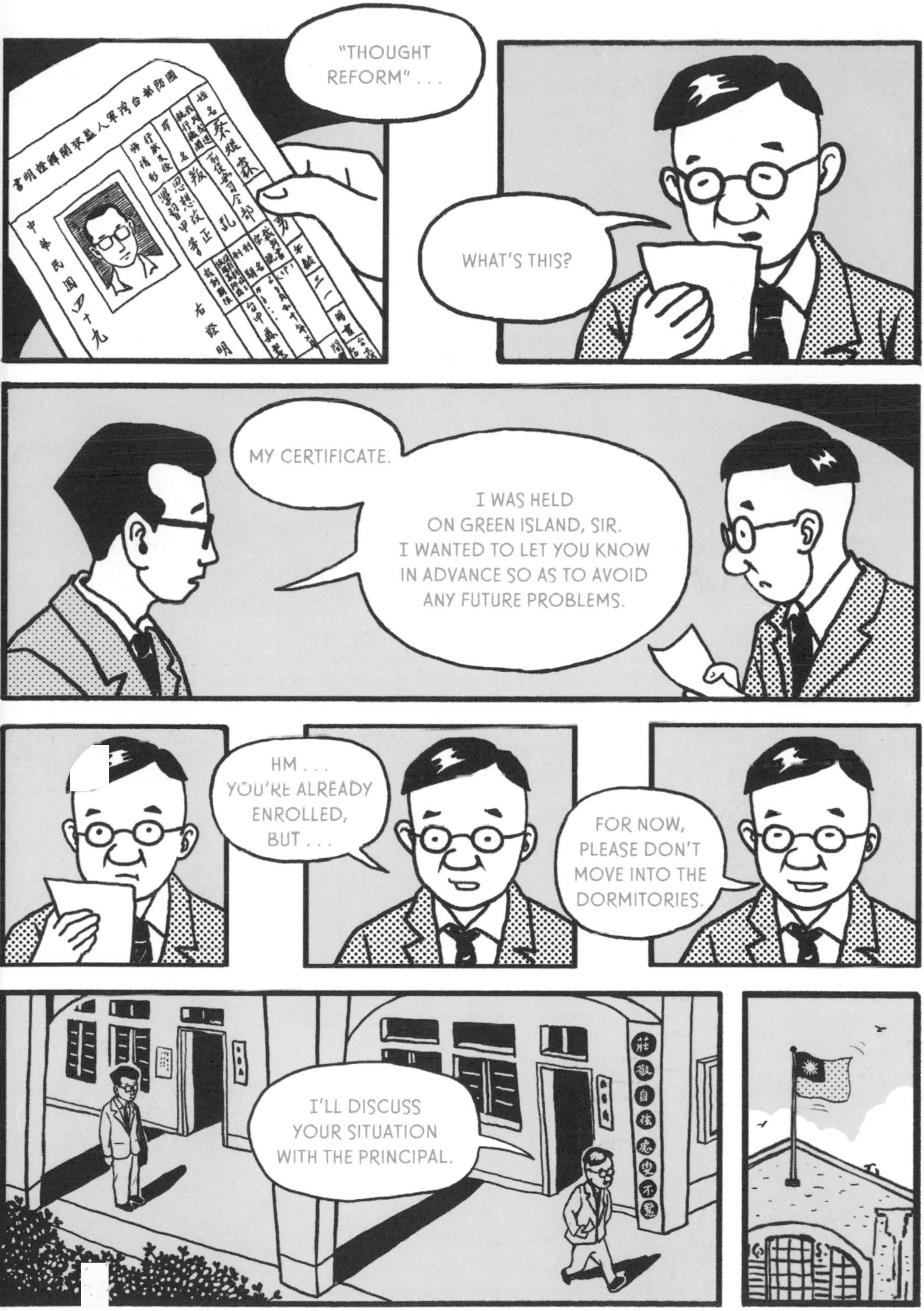
"THOUGHT REFORM" . . .
WHAT'S THIS?
MY CERTIFICATE.
I WAS HELD ON GREEN ISLAND, SIR. I WANTED TO LET YOU KNOW IN ADVANCE SO AS TO AVOID ANY FUTURE PROBLEMS.
HM . . . YOU'RE ALREADY ENROLLED, BUT . . .
FOR NOW, PLEASE DON'T MOVE INTO THE DORMITORIES.
I'LL DISCUSS YOUR SITUATION WITH THE PRINCIPAL.

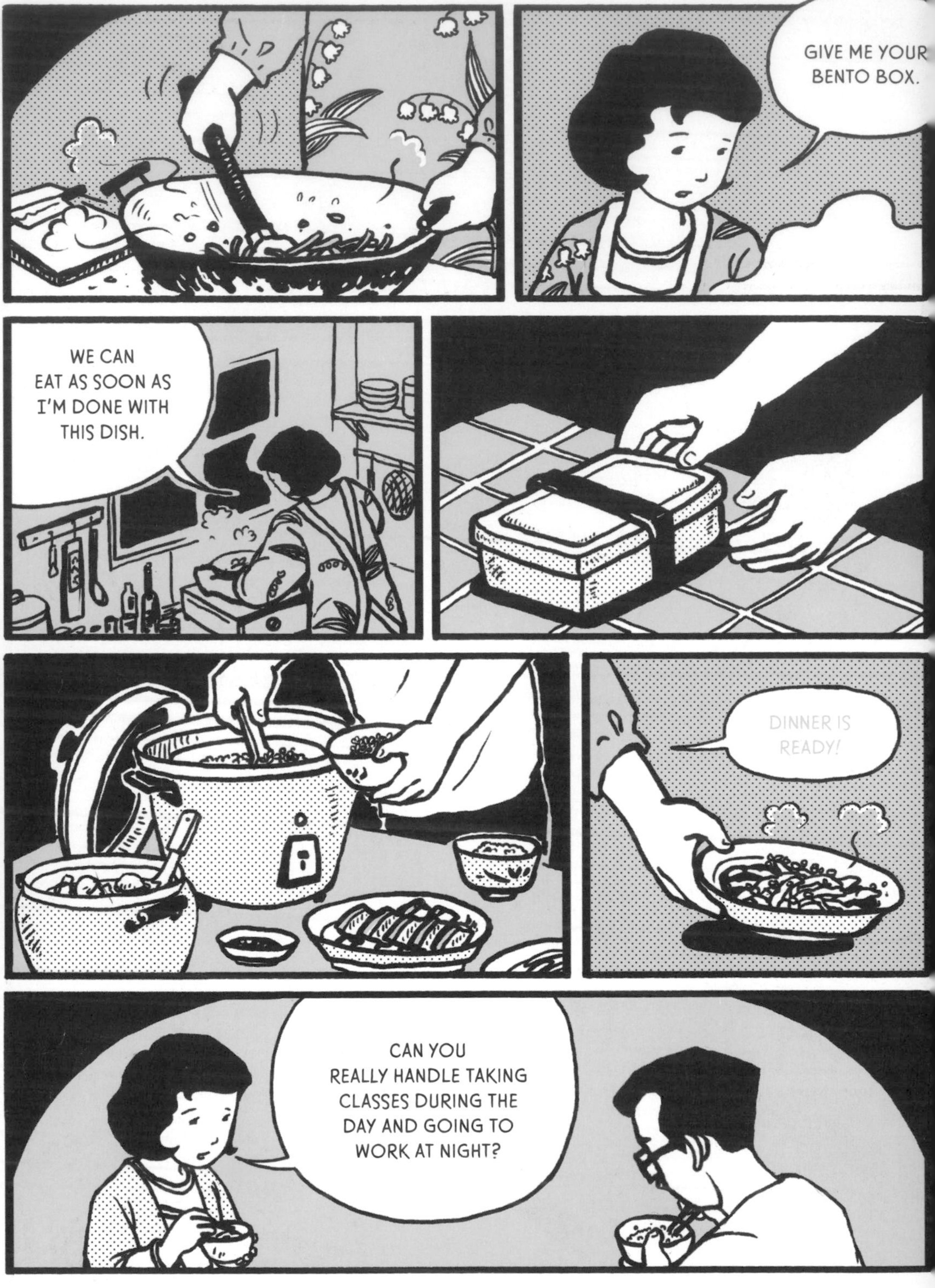
GIVE ME YOUR BENTO BOX.
WE CAN EAT AS SOON AS I'M DONE WITH THIS DISH.
DINNER IS READY!
CAN YOU REALLY HANDLE TAKING CLASSES DURING THE DAY AND GOING TO WORK AT NIGHT?

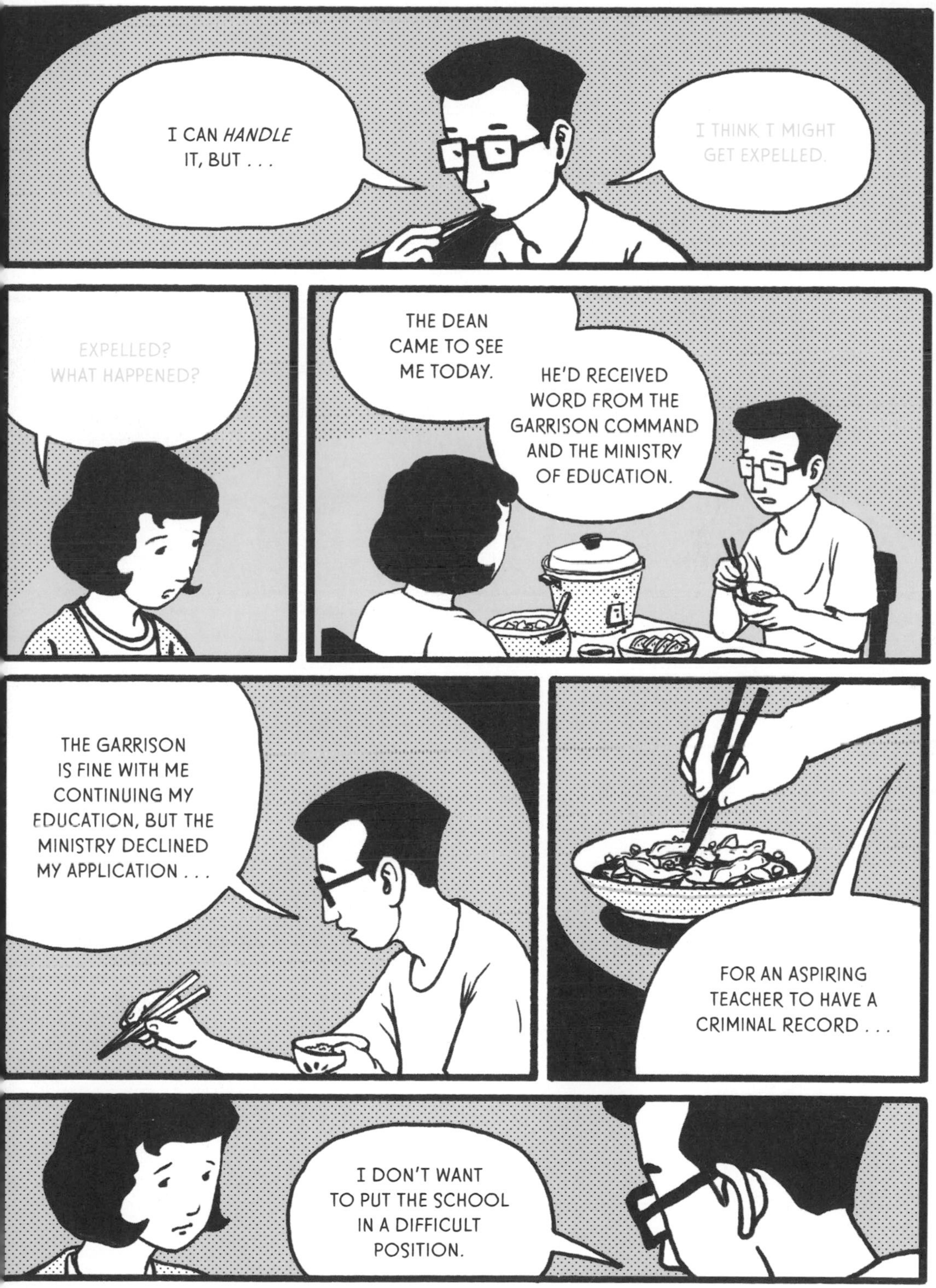

I CAN *HANDLE* IT, BUT . . .
I THINK I MIGHT GET EXPELLED.
EXPELLED? WHAT HAPPENED?
THE DEAN CAME TO SEE ME TODAY.
HE'D RECEIVED WORD FROM THE GARRISON COMMAND AND THE MINISTRY OF EDUCATION.
THE GARRISON IS FINE WITH ME CONTINUING MY EDUCATION, BUT THE MINISTRY DECLINED MY APPLICATION . . .
FOR AN ASPIRING TEACHER TO HAVE A CRIMINAL RECORD . . .
I DON'T WANT TO PUT THE SCHOOL IN A DIFFICULT POSITION.

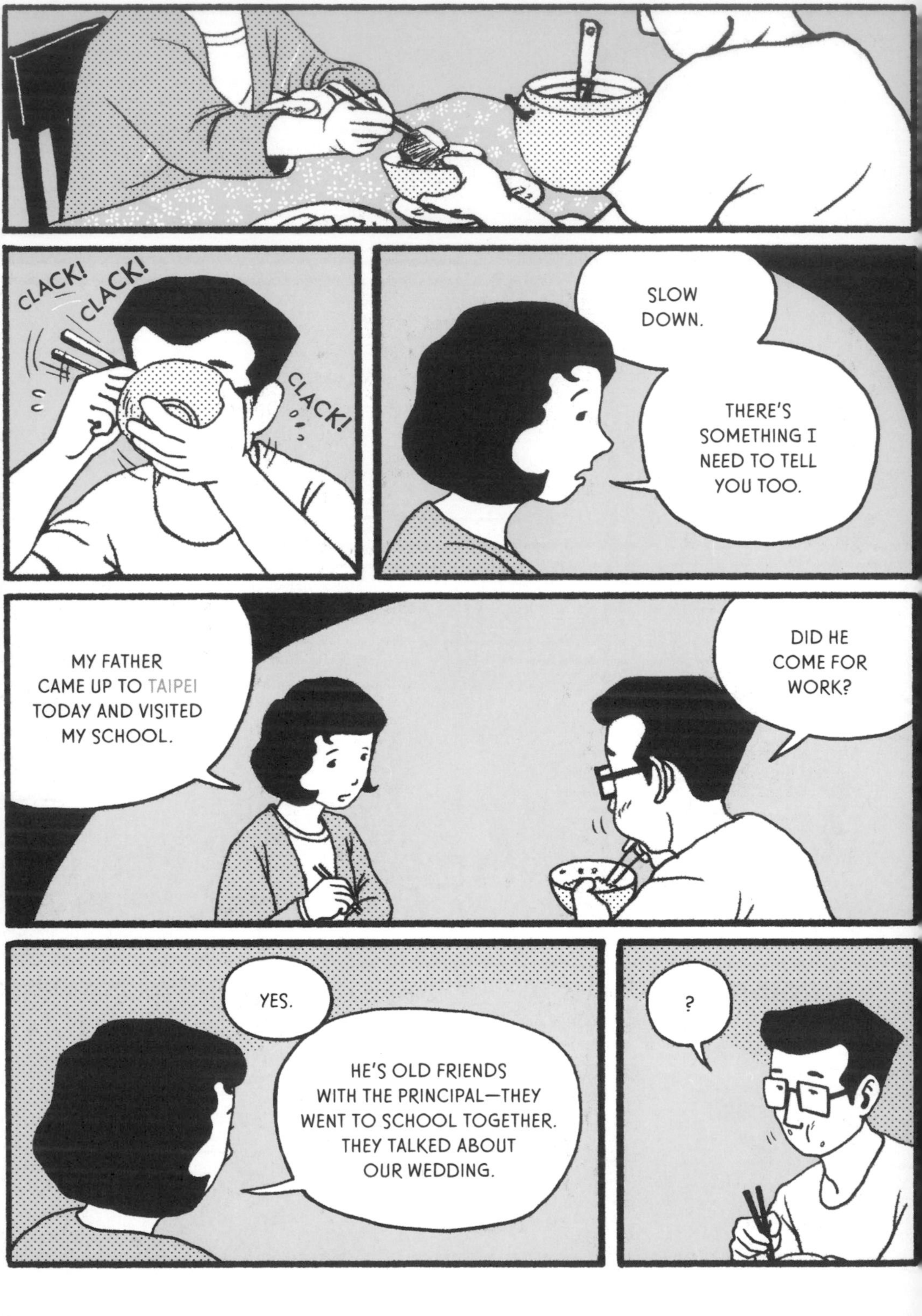
CLACK! CLACK!
CLACK!
SLOW DOWN.
THERE'S SOMETHING I NEED TO TELL YOU TOO.
MY FATHER CAME UP TO TAIPEI TODAY AND VISITED MY SCHOOL.
DID HE COME FOR WORK?
YES.
HE'S OLD FRIENDS WITH THE PRINCIPAL—THEY WENT TO SCHOOL TOGETHER. THEY TALKED ABOUT OUR WEDDING.
?

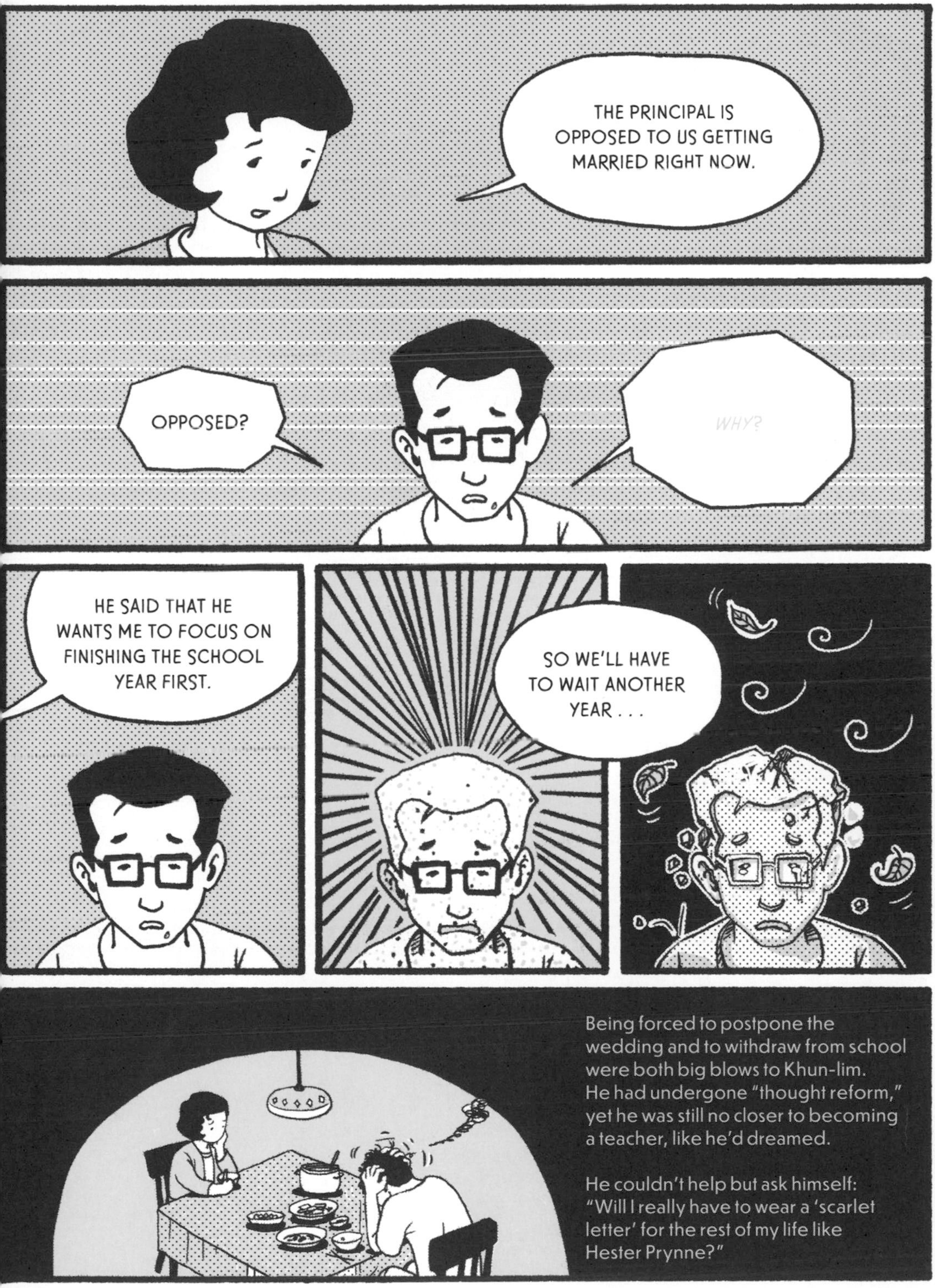
THE PRINCIPAL IS OPPOSED TO US GETTING MARRIED RIGHT NOW.
OPPOSED?
WHY?
HE SAID THAT HE WANTS ME TO FOCUS ON FINISHING THE SCHOOL YEAR FIRST.
SO WE'LL HAVE TO WAIT ANOTHER YEAR . . .
Being forced to postpone the wedding and to withdraw from school were both big blows to Khun-lim. He had undergone "thought reform," yet he was still no closer to becoming a teacher, like he'd dreamed.
He couldn't help but ask himself: "Will I really have to wear a 'scarlet letter' for the rest of my life like Hester Prynne?"

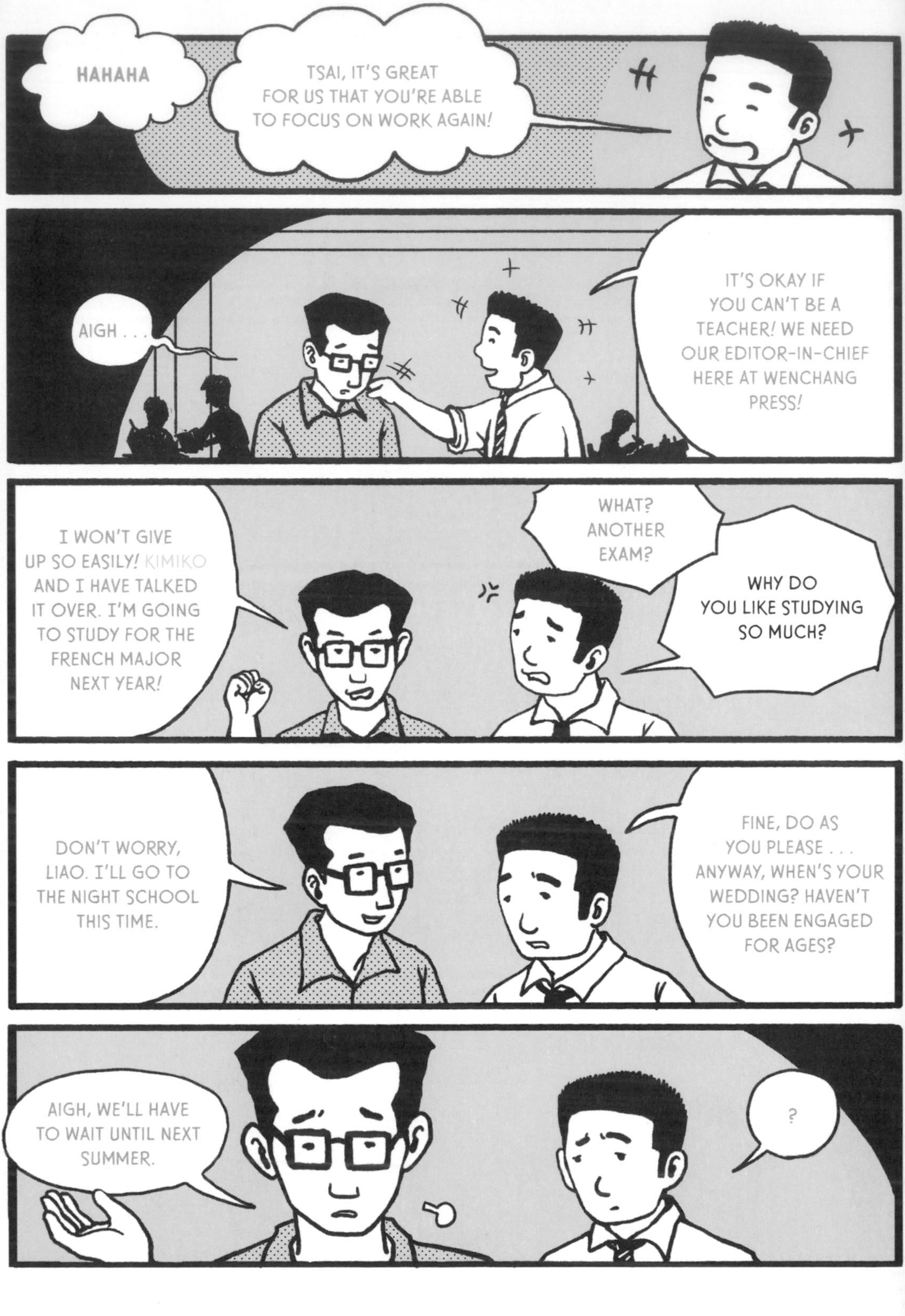
HAHAHA
TSAI, IT'S GREAT FOR US THAT YOU'RE ABLE TO FOCUS ON WORK AGAIN!
AIGH . . .
IT'S OKAY IF YOU CAN'T BE A TEACHER! WE NEED OUR EDITOR-IN-CHIEF HERE AT WENCHANG PRESS!
I WON'T GIVE UP SO EASILY! KIMIKO AND I HAVE TALKED IT OVER. I'M GOING TO STUDY FOR THE FRENCH MAJOR NEXT YEAR!
WHAT? ANOTHER EXAM?
WHY DO YOU LIKE STUDYING SO MUCH?
DON'T WORRY, LIAO. I'LL GO TO THE NIGHT SCHOOL THIS TIME.
FINE, DO AS YOU PLEASE . . . ANYWAY, WHEN'S YOUR WEDDING? HAVEN'T YOU BEEN ENGAGED FOR AGES?
AIGH, WE'LL HAVE TO WAIT UNTIL NEXT SUMMER.
?

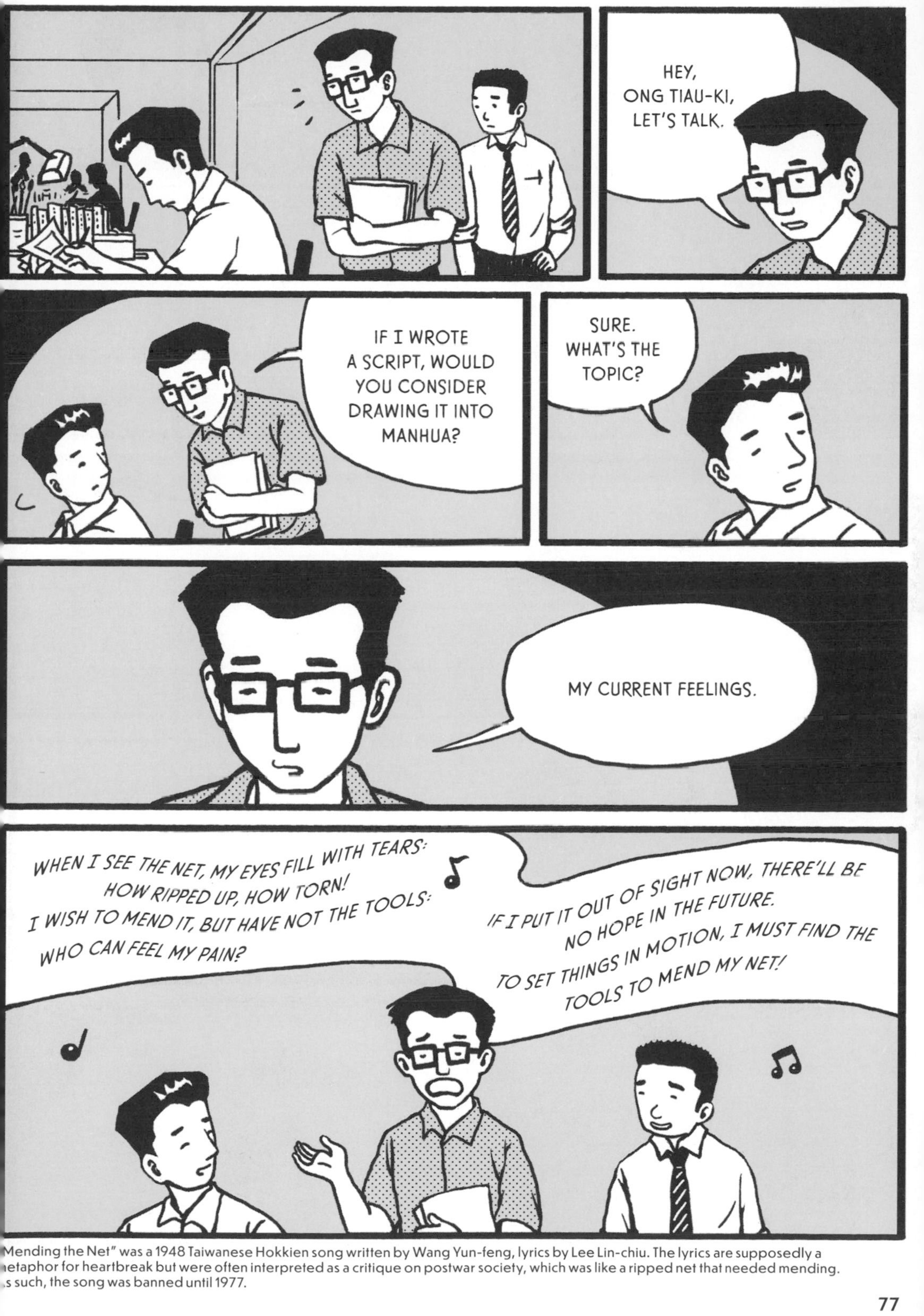
HEY, ONG TIAU-KI, LET'S TALK.
IF I WROTE A SCRIPT, WOULD YOU CONSIDER DRAWING IT INTO MANHUA?
SURE. WHAT'S THE TOPIC?
MY CURRENT FEELINGS.
WHEN I SEE THE NET, MY EYES FILL WITH TEARS: HOW RIPPED UP, HOW TORN! I WISH TO MEND IT, BUT HAVE NOT THE TOOLS: WHO CAN FEEL MY PAIN?
IF I PUT IT OUT OF SIGHT NOW, THERE'LL BE NO HOPE IN THE FUTURE. TO SET THINGS IN MOTION, I MUST FIND THE TOOLS TO MEND MY NET!

"Mending the Net" was a 1948 Taiwanese Hokkien song written by Wang Yun-feng, lyrics by Lee Lin-chiu. The lyrics are supposedly a metaphor for heartbreak but were often interpreted as a critique on postwar society, which was like a ripped net that needed mending. As such, the song was banned until 1977.

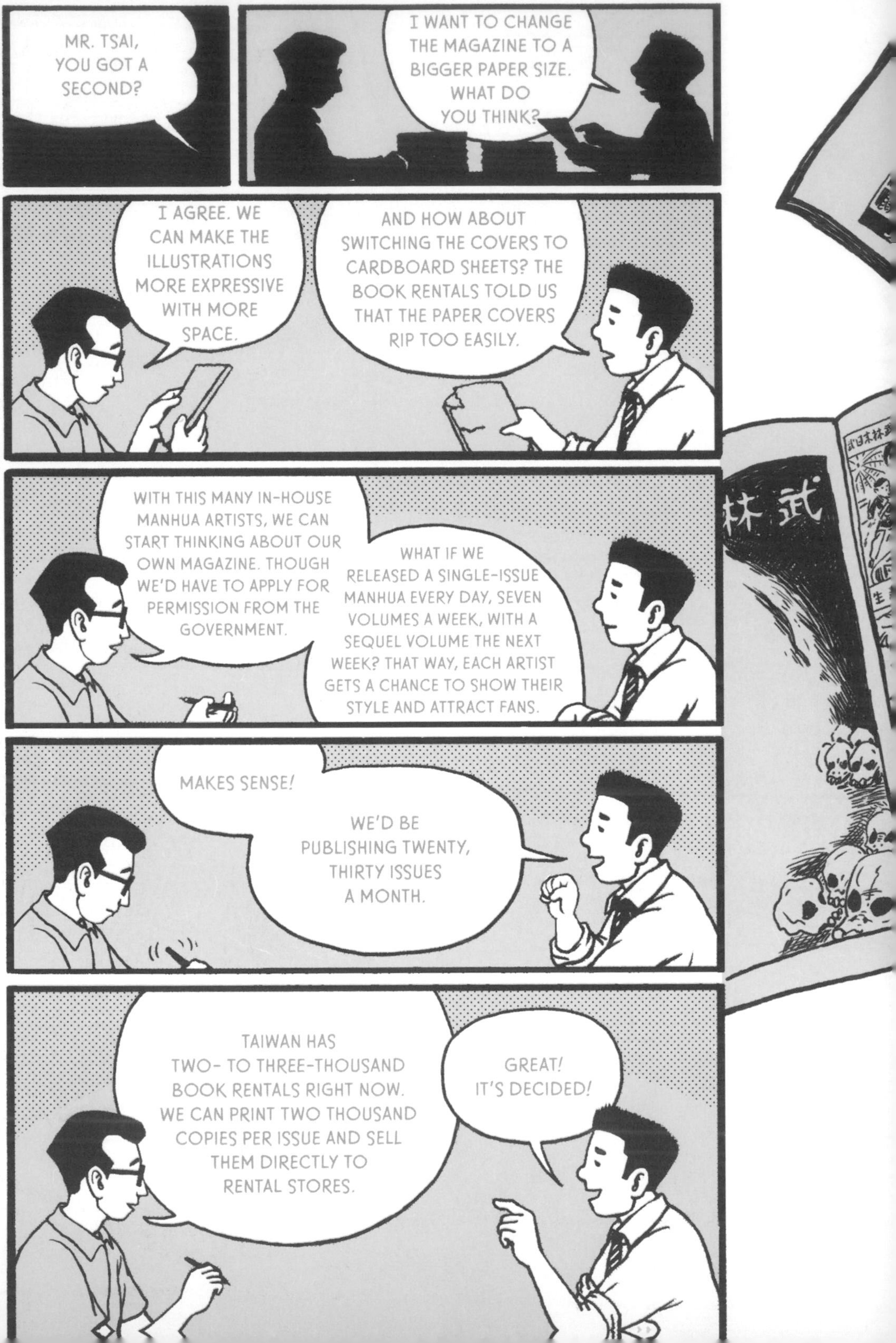
MR. TSAI, YOU GOT A SECOND?
I WANT TO CHANGE THE MAGAZINE TO A BIGGER PAPER SIZE. WHAT DO YOU THINK?
I AGREE. WE CAN MAKE THE ILLUSTRATIONS MORE EXPRESSIVE WITH MORE SPACE.
AND HOW ABOUT SWITCHING THE COVERS TO CARDBOARD SHEETS? THE BOOK RENTALS TOLD US THAT THE PAPER COVERS RIP TOO EASILY.
WITH THIS MANY IN-HOUSE MANHUA ARTISTS, WE CAN START THINKING ABOUT OUR OWN MAGAZINE. THOUGH WE'D HAVE TO APPLY FOR PERMISSION FROM THE GOVERNMENT.
WHAT IF WE RELEASED A SINGLE-ISSUE MANHUA EVERY DAY, SEVEN VOLUMES A WEEK, WITH A SEQUEL VOLUME THE NEXT WEEK? THAT WAY, EACH ARTIST GETS A CHANCE TO SHOW THEIR STYLE AND ATTRACT FANS.
MAKES SENSE!
WE'D BE PUBLISHING TWENTY, THIRTY ISSUES A MONTH.
TAIWAN HAS TWO- TO THREE-THOUSAND BOOK RENTALS RIGHT NOW. WE CAN PRINT TWO THOUSAND COPIES PER ISSUE AND SELL THEM DIRECTLY TO RENTAL STORES.
GREAT! IT'S DECIDED!
林武

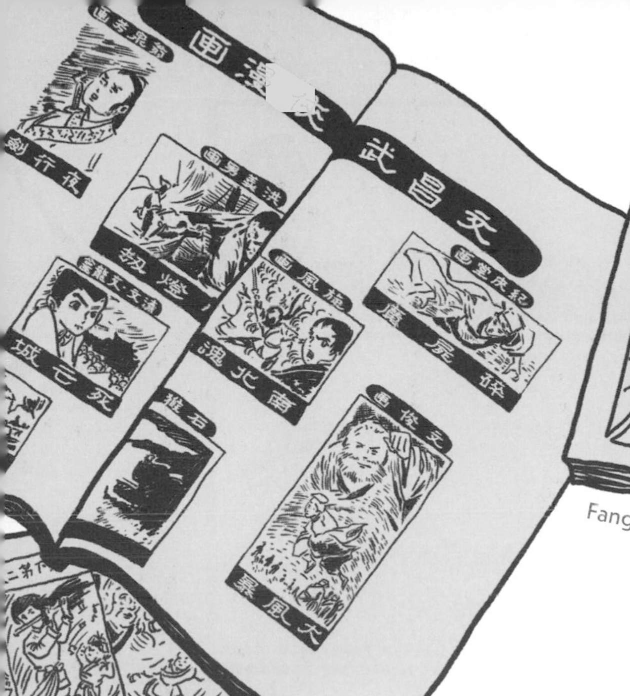

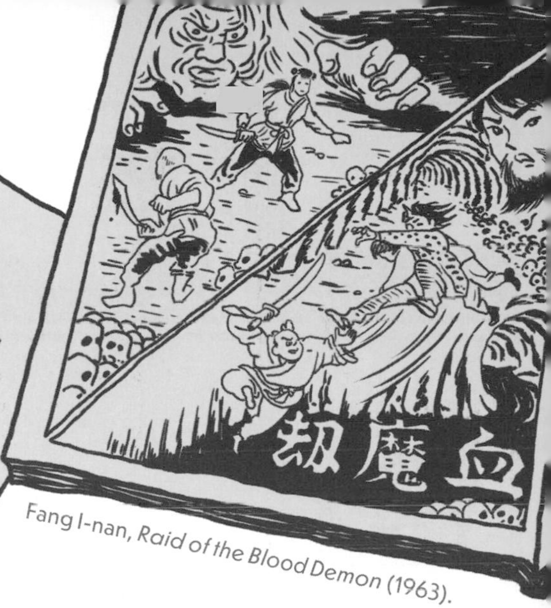
血魔劫

Fang I-nan, *Raid of the Blood Demon* (1963).

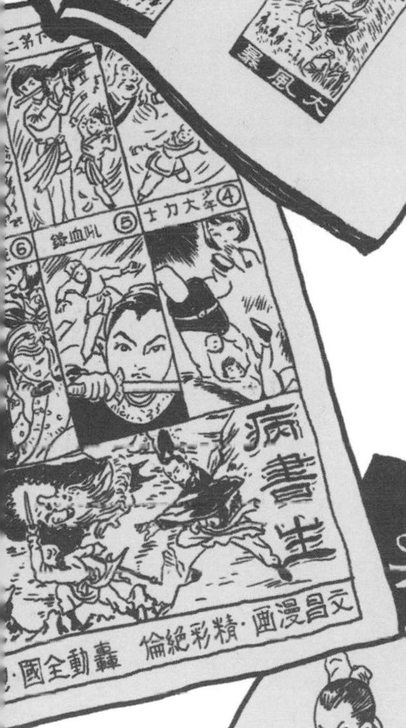
病書生
文昌漫画·精彩絕倫
轟動全國

The many hurdles that Khun-lim faced in other aspects of his life made him devote himself all the more to Wenchang Press.

Wenchang not only pioneered a new form of publishing, it also supported a large cohort of young manhua artists who grew to be wildly popular. They continuously put out one riveting original manhua after another, pushing Taiwan's domestic manhua to new heights.

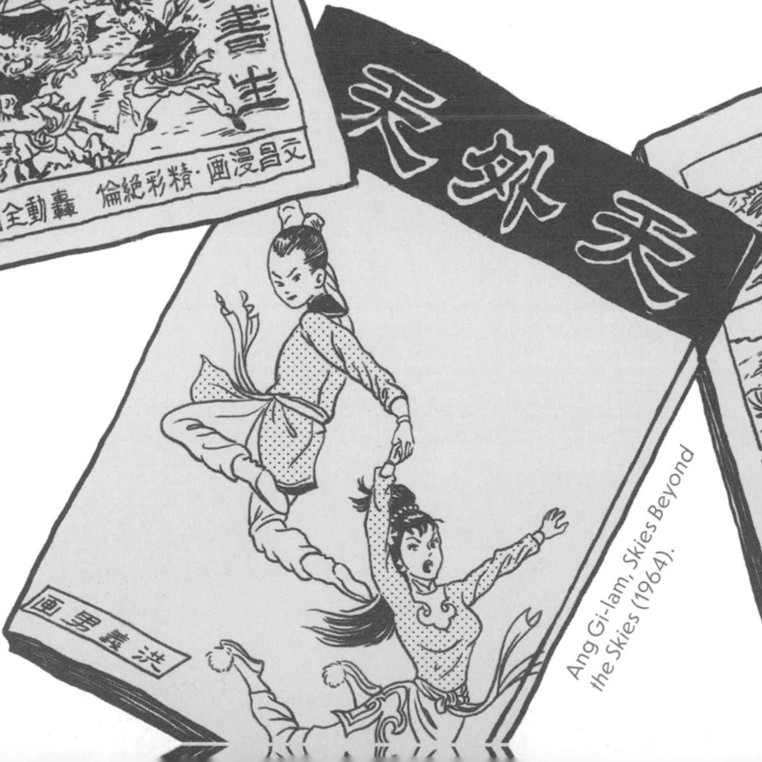
天外天
洪義男画

Ang Gi-lam, *Skies Beyond the Skies* (1964).

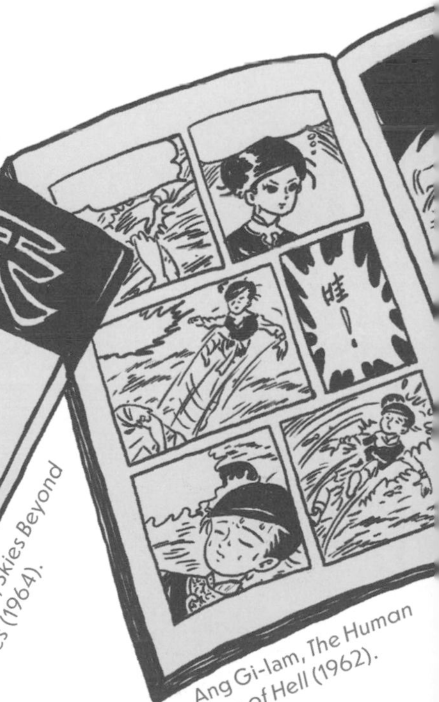
哇!

Ang Gi-lam, *The Human King of Hell* (1962).

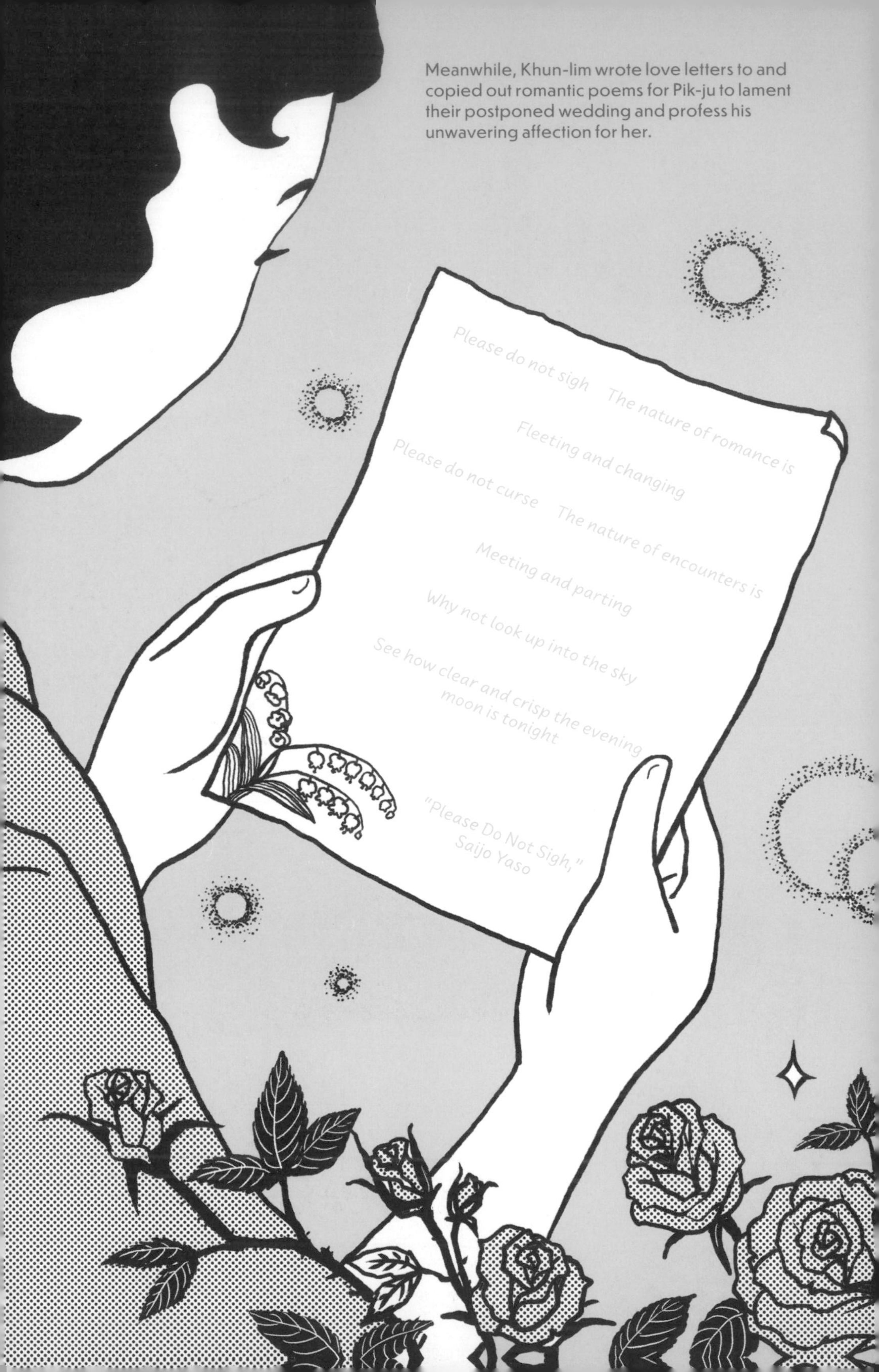
Meanwhile, Khun-lim wrote love letters to and copied out romantic poems for Pik-ju to lament their postponed wedding and profess his unwavering affection for her.
Please do not sigh The nature of romance is
Fleeting and changing
Please do not curse The nature of encounters is
Meeting and parting
Why not look up into the sky
See how clear and crisp the evening moon is tonight
"Please Do Not Sigh," Saijo Yaso

On July 29, 1962, Khun-lim and Pik-ju
were married at last.

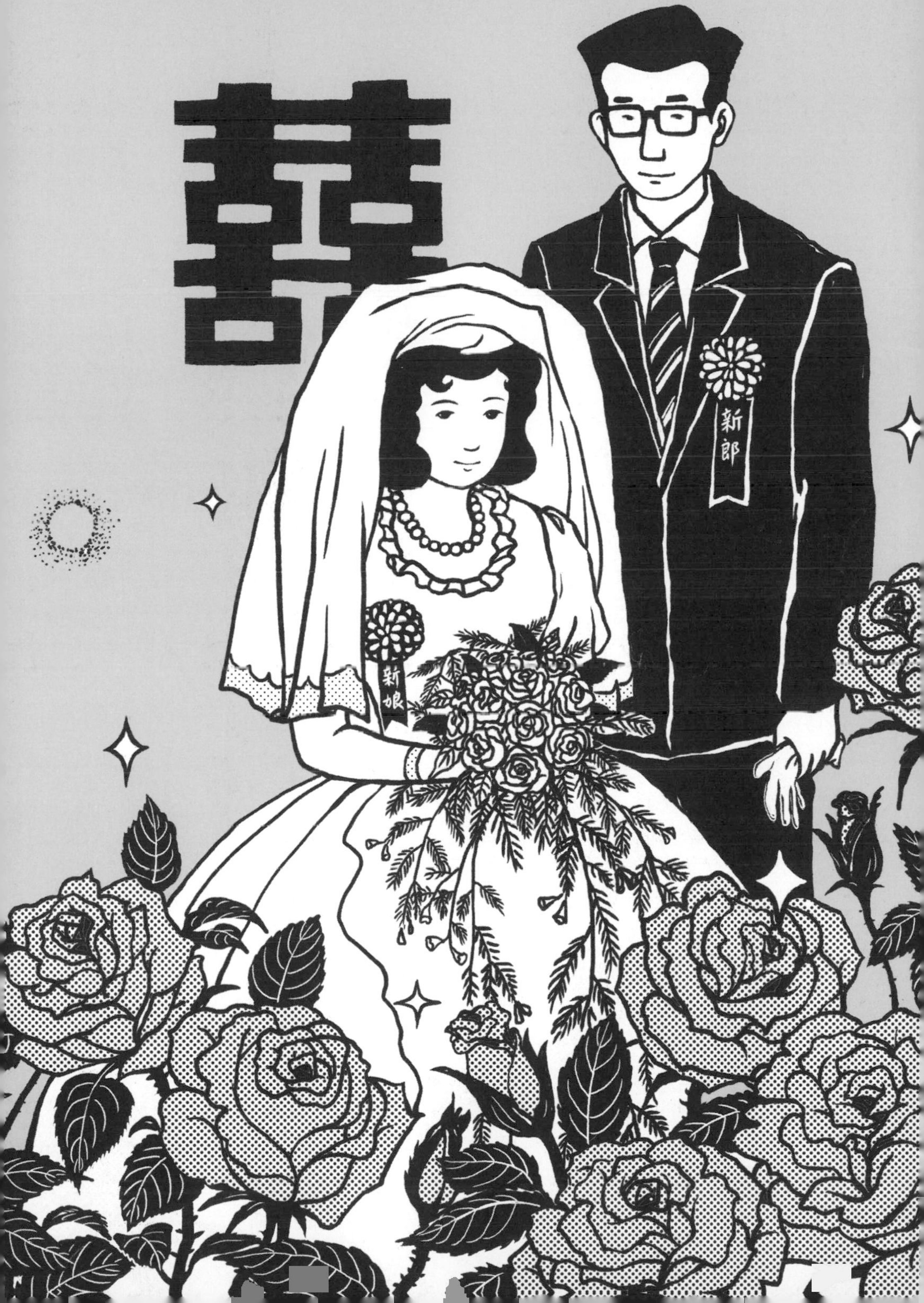
囍
新娘
新郎

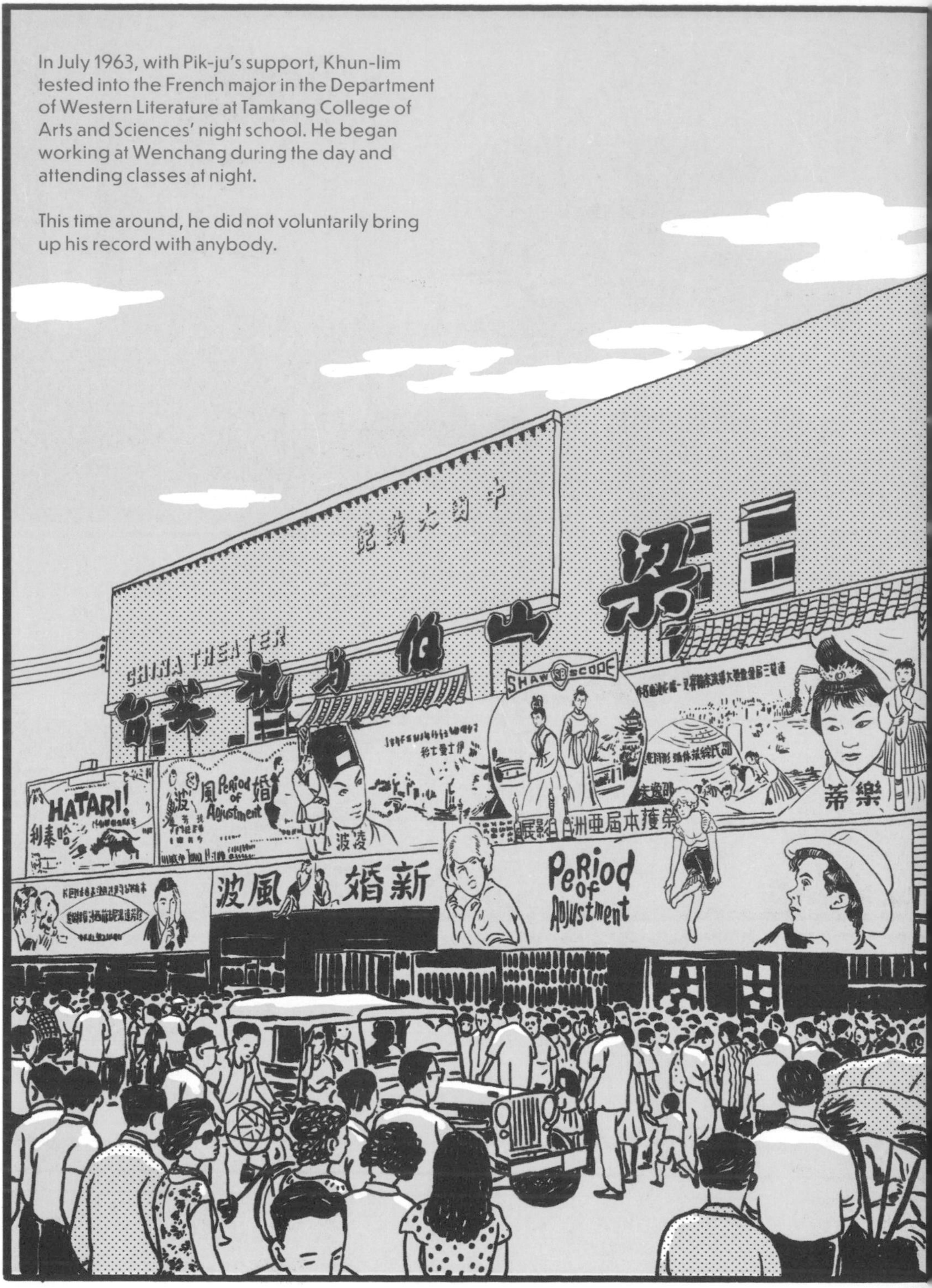
In July 1963, with Pik-ju's support, Khun-lim tested into the French major in the Department of Western Literature at Tamkang College of Arts and Sciences' night school. He began working at Wenchang during the day and attending classes at night.
This time around, he did not voluntarily bring up his record with anybody.
CHINA THEATER
梁山伯与祝英台
SHAW SCOPE
HATARI!
Period of Adjustment
凌波
樂蒂
新婚風波
Period of Adjustment

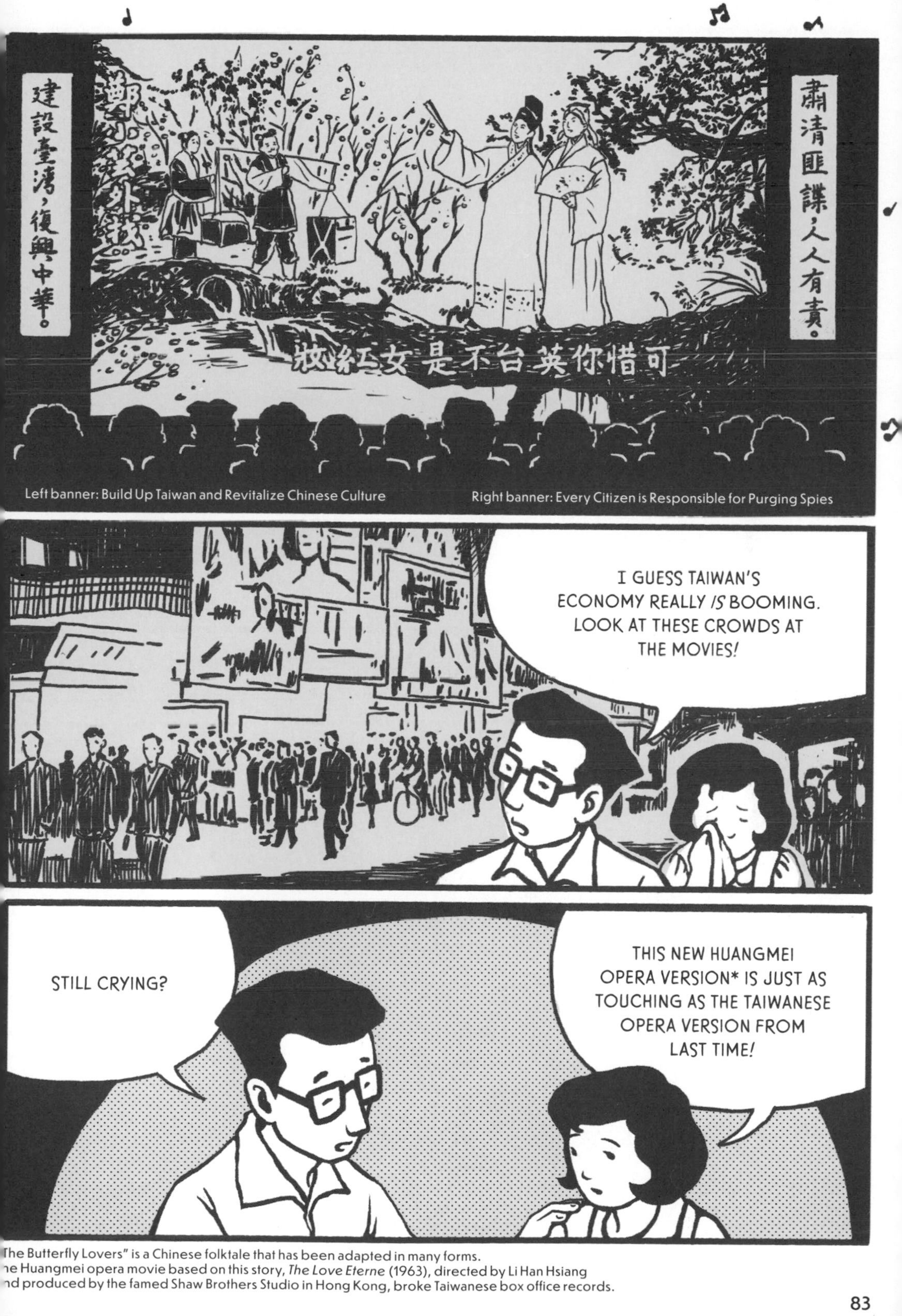
建設臺灣，復興中華。
肅清匪諜，人人有責。
可惜你英台不是女紅妝
Left banner: Build Up Taiwan and Revitalize Chinese Culture
Right banner: Every Citizen is Responsible for Purging Spies
I GUESS TAIWAN'S ECONOMY REALLY *IS* BOOMING. LOOK AT THESE CROWDS AT THE MOVIES!
STILL CRYING?
THIS NEW HUANGMEI OPERA VERSION* IS JUST AS TOUCHING AS THE TAIWANESE OPERA VERSION FROM LAST TIME!

The Butterfly Lovers" is a Chinese folktale that has been adapted in many forms.
he Huangmei opera movie based on this story, *The Love Eterne* (1963), directed by Li Han Hsiang
nd produced by the famed Shaw Brothers Studio in Hong Kong, broke Taiwanese box office records.

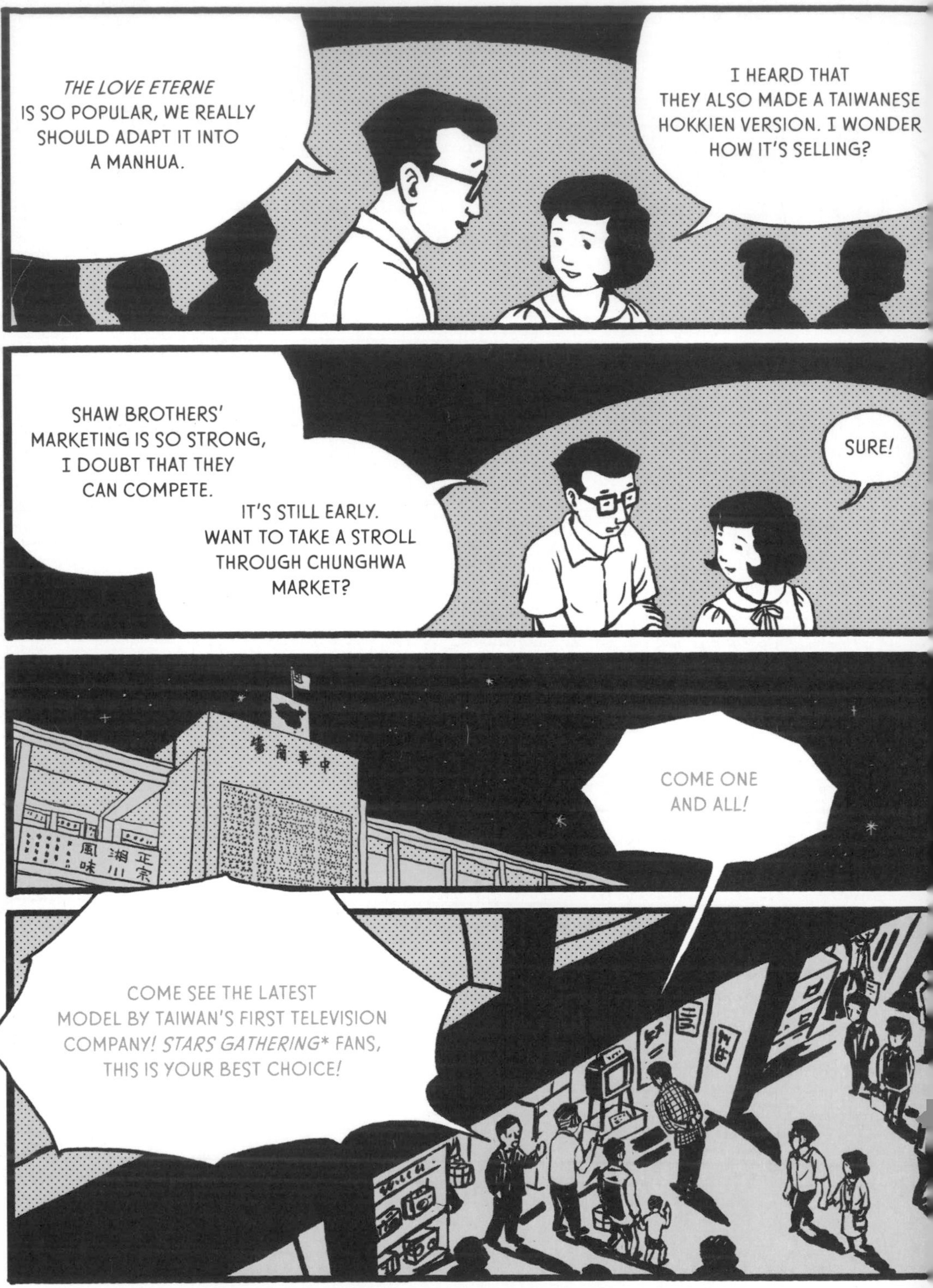
THE LOVE ETERNE IS SO POPULAR, WE REALLY SHOULD ADAPT IT INTO A MANHUA.
I HEARD THAT THEY ALSO MADE A TAIWANESE HOKKIEN VERSION. I WONDER HOW IT'S SELLING?
SHAW BROTHERS' MARKETING IS SO STRONG, I DOUBT THAT THEY CAN COMPETE.
IT'S STILL EARLY. WANT TO TAKE A STROLL THROUGH CHUNGHWA MARKET?
SURE!
中華商場
正宗湘川風味
COME ONE AND ALL!
COME SEE THE LATEST MODEL BY TAIWAN'S FIRST TELEVISION COMPANY! *STARS GATHERING** FANS, THIS IS YOUR BEST CHOICE!

**Stars Gathering* was a Mandarin Chinese singing variety show—the first of its kind in Taiwan. The first episode aired on October 10, 1962, on the station Taiwan Television.

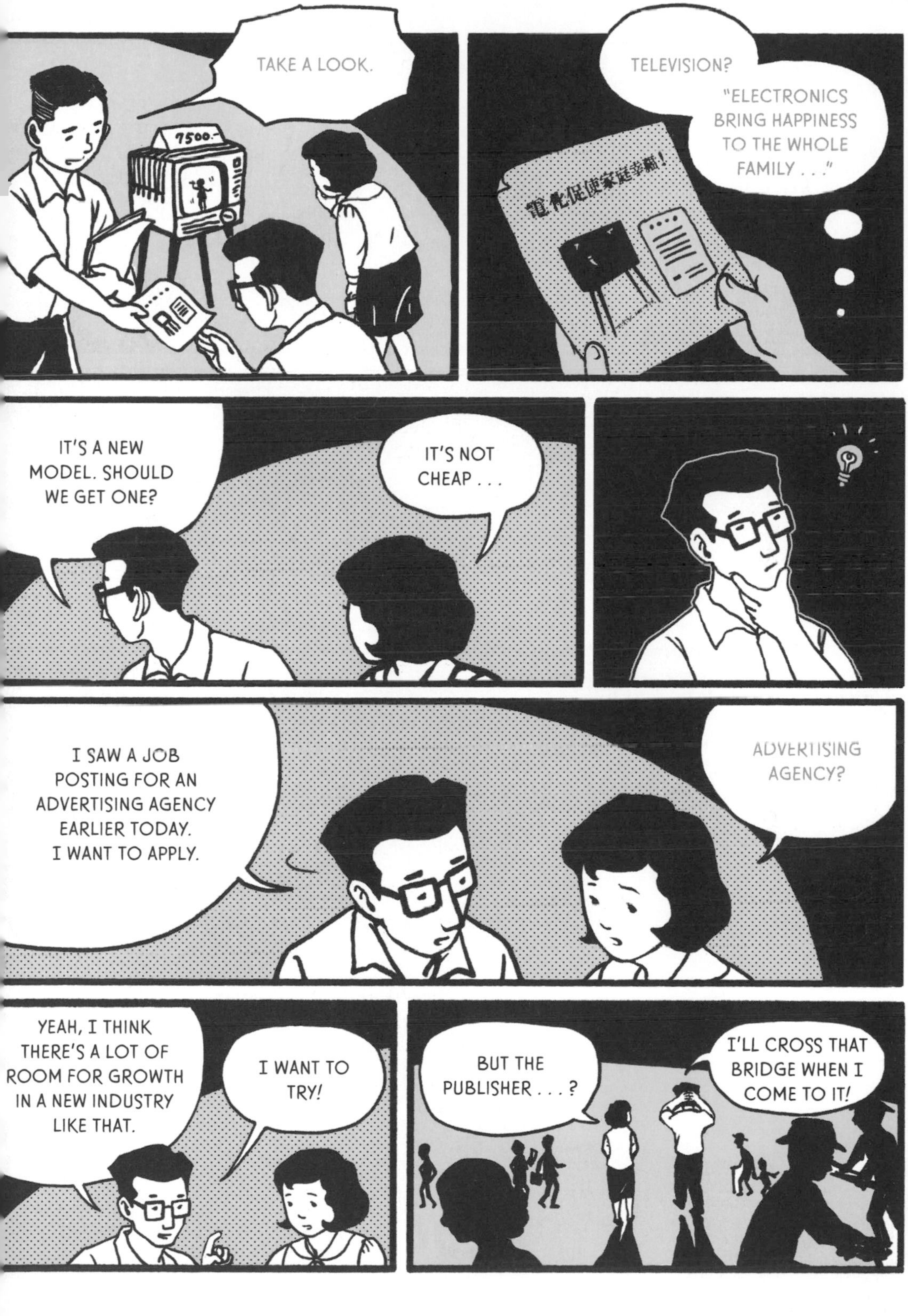

TAKE A LOOK.
7500.-
TELEVISION?
"ELECTRONICS BRING HAPPINESS TO THE WHOLE FAMILY . . ."
電化促使家庭幸福!
IT'S A NEW MODEL. SHOULD WE GET ONE?
IT'S NOT CHEAP . . .
I SAW A JOB POSTING FOR AN ADVERTISING AGENCY EARLIER TODAY. I WANT TO APPLY.
ADVERTISING AGENCY?
YEAH, I THINK THERE'S A LOT OF ROOM FOR GROWTH IN A NEW INDUSTRY LIKE THAT.
I WANT TO TRY!
BUT THE PUBLISHER . . . ?
I'LL CROSS THAT BRIDGE WHEN I COME TO IT!

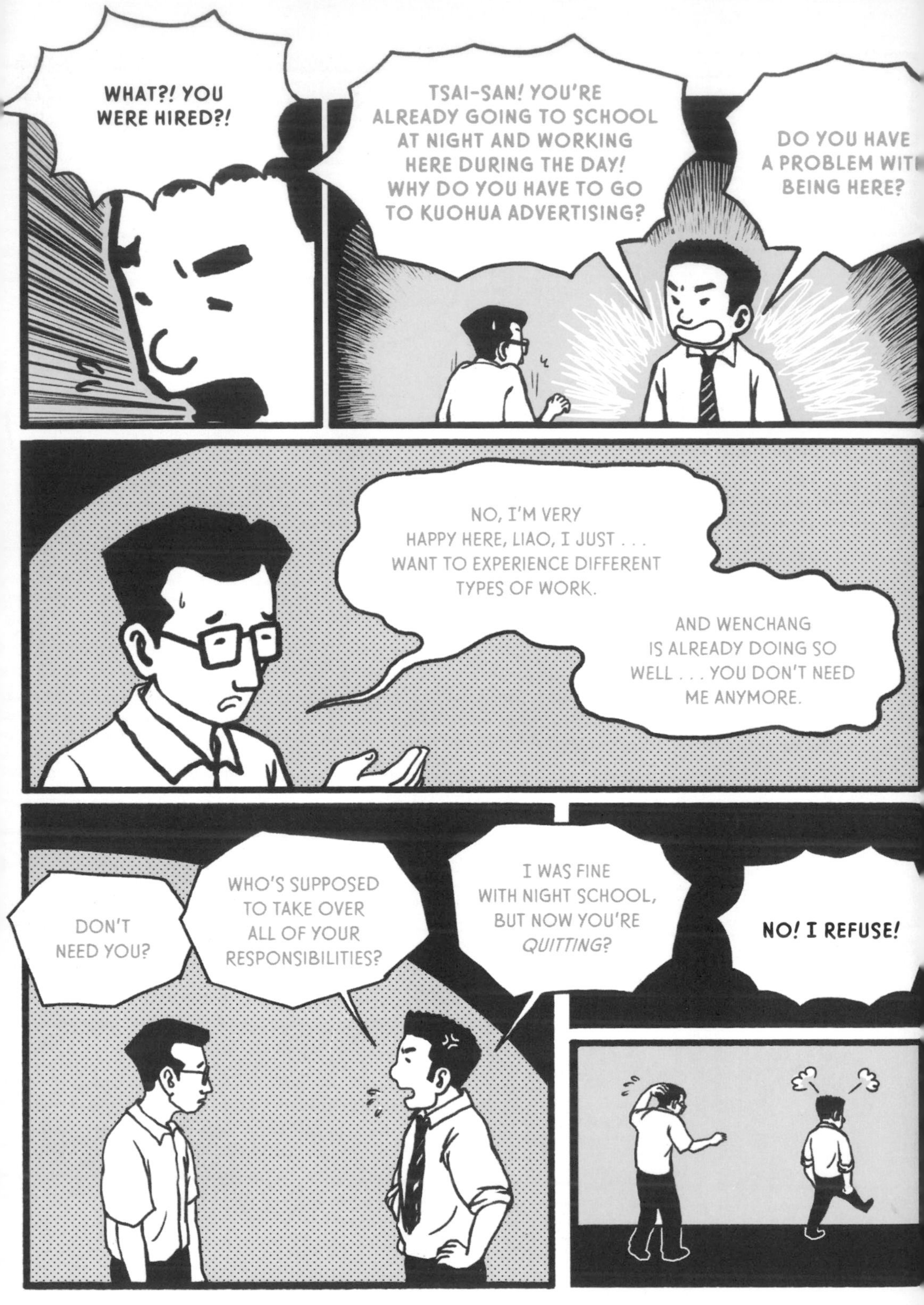
WHAT?! YOU WERE HIRED?!
TSAI-SAN! YOU'RE ALREADY GOING TO SCHOOL AT NIGHT AND WORKING HERE DURING THE DAY! WHY DO YOU HAVE TO GO TO KUOHUA ADVERTISING?
DO YOU HAVE A PROBLEM WIT BEING HERE?
NO, I'M VERY HAPPY HERE, LIAO, I JUST . . . WANT TO EXPERIENCE DIFFERENT TYPES OF WORK.
AND WENCHANG IS ALREADY DOING SO WELL . . . YOU DON'T NEED ME ANYMORE.
DON'T NEED YOU?
WHO'S SUPPOSED TO TAKE OVER ALL OF YOUR RESPONSIBILITIES?
I WAS FINE WITH NIGHT SCHOOL, BUT NOW YOU'RE *QUITTING*?
NO! I REFUSE!

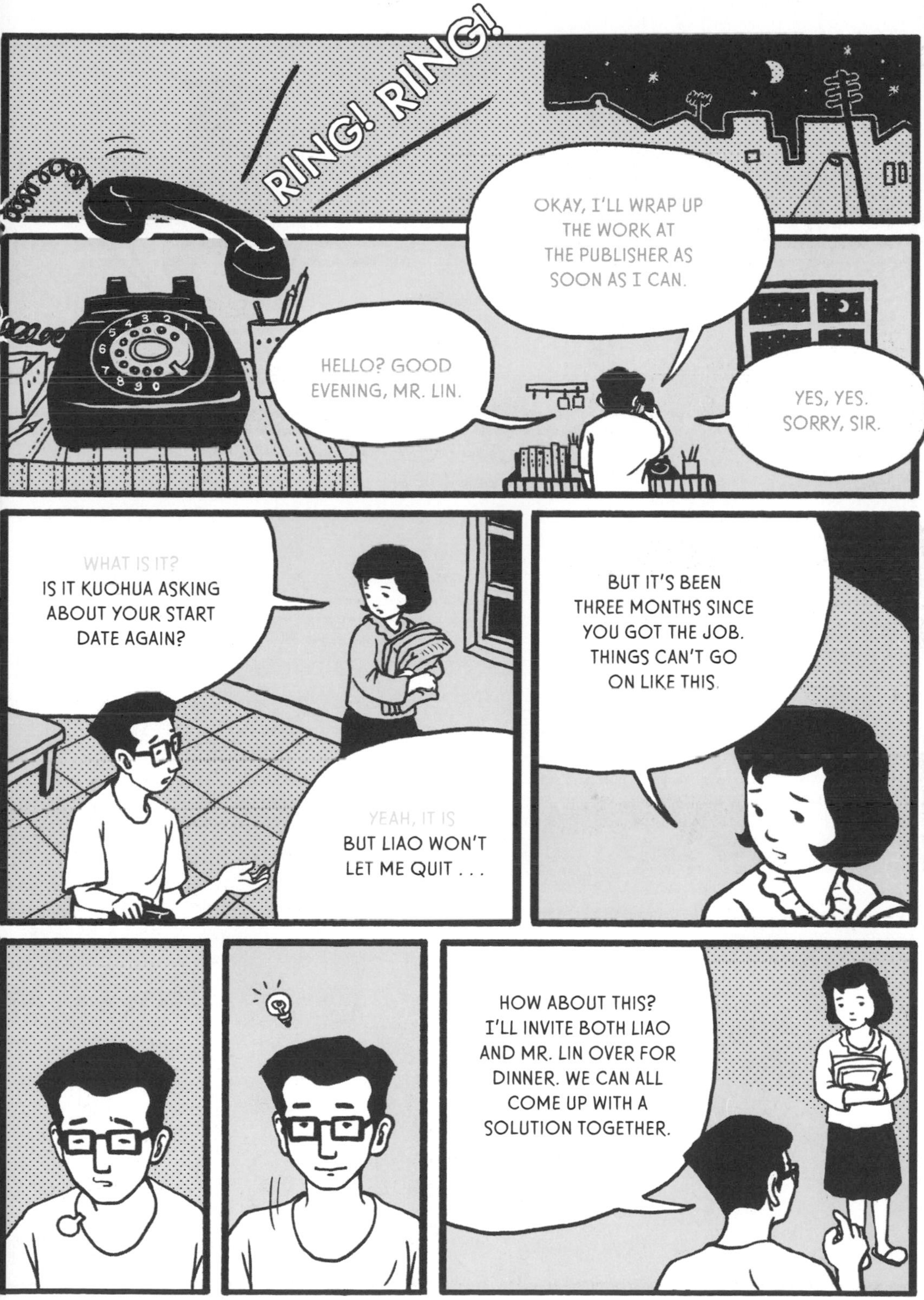
RING! RING!
HELLO? GOOD EVENING, MR. LIN.
OKAY, I'LL WRAP UP THE WORK AT THE PUBLISHER AS SOON AS I CAN.
YES, YES. SORRY, SIR.
WHAT IS IT? IS IT KUOHUA ASKING ABOUT YOUR START DATE AGAIN?
YEAH, IT IS. BUT LIAO WON'T LET ME QUIT . . .
BUT IT'S BEEN THREE MONTHS SINCE YOU GOT THE JOB. THINGS CAN'T GO ON LIKE THIS.
HOW ABOUT THIS? I'LL INVITE BOTH LIAO AND MR. LIN OVER FOR DINNER. WE CAN ALL COME UP WITH A SOLUTION TOGETHER.

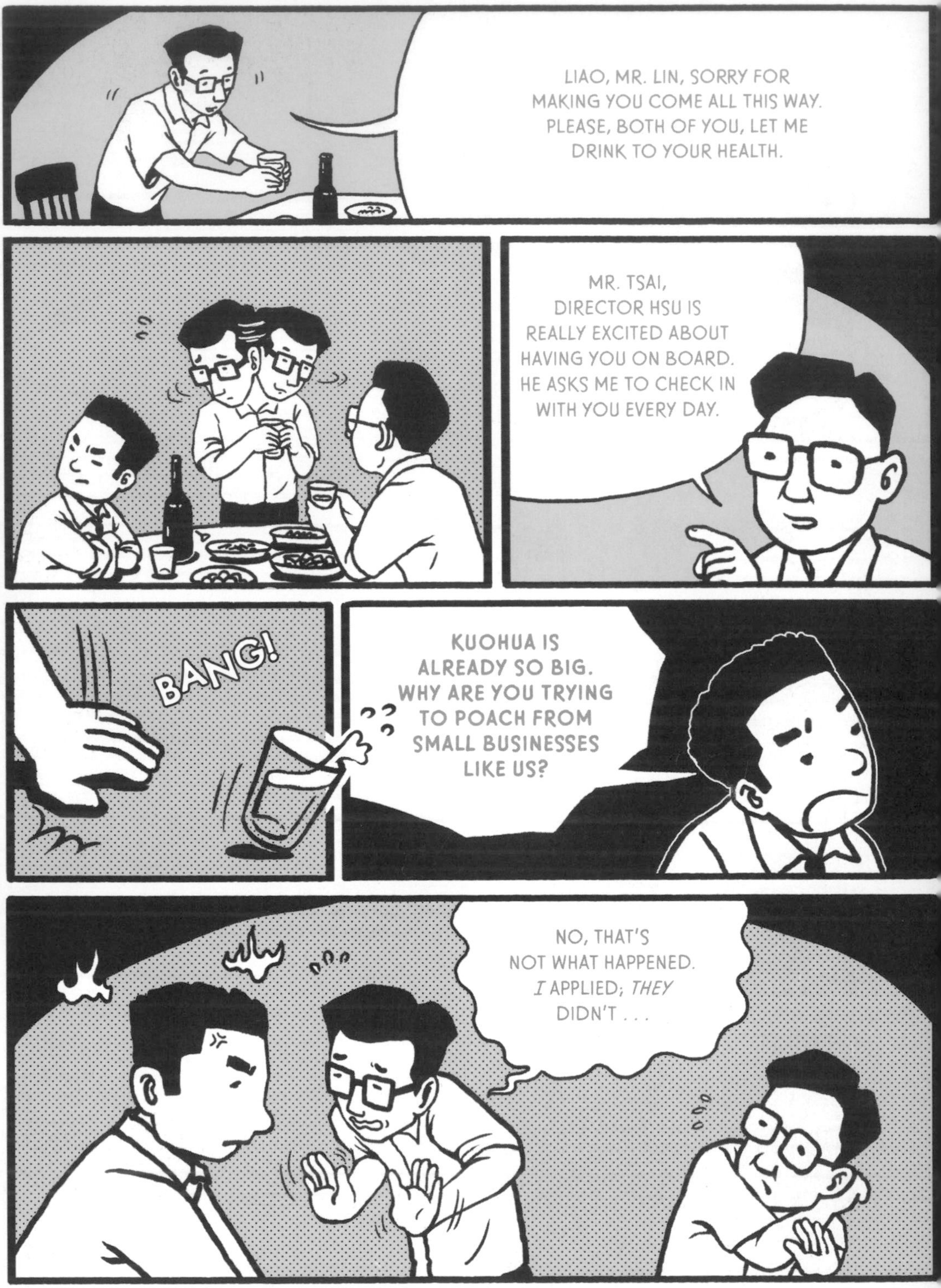
LIAO, MR. LIN, SORRY FOR MAKING YOU COME ALL THIS WAY. PLEASE, BOTH OF YOU, LET ME DRINK TO YOUR HEALTH.
MR. TSAI, DIRECTOR HSU IS REALLY EXCITED ABOUT HAVING YOU ON BOARD. HE ASKS ME TO CHECK IN WITH YOU EVERY DAY.
BANG!
KUOHUA IS ALREADY SO BIG. WHY ARE YOU TRYING TO POACH FROM SMALL BUSINESSES LIKE US?
NO, THAT'S NOT WHAT HAPPENED. *I* APPLIED; *THEY* DIDN'T . . .

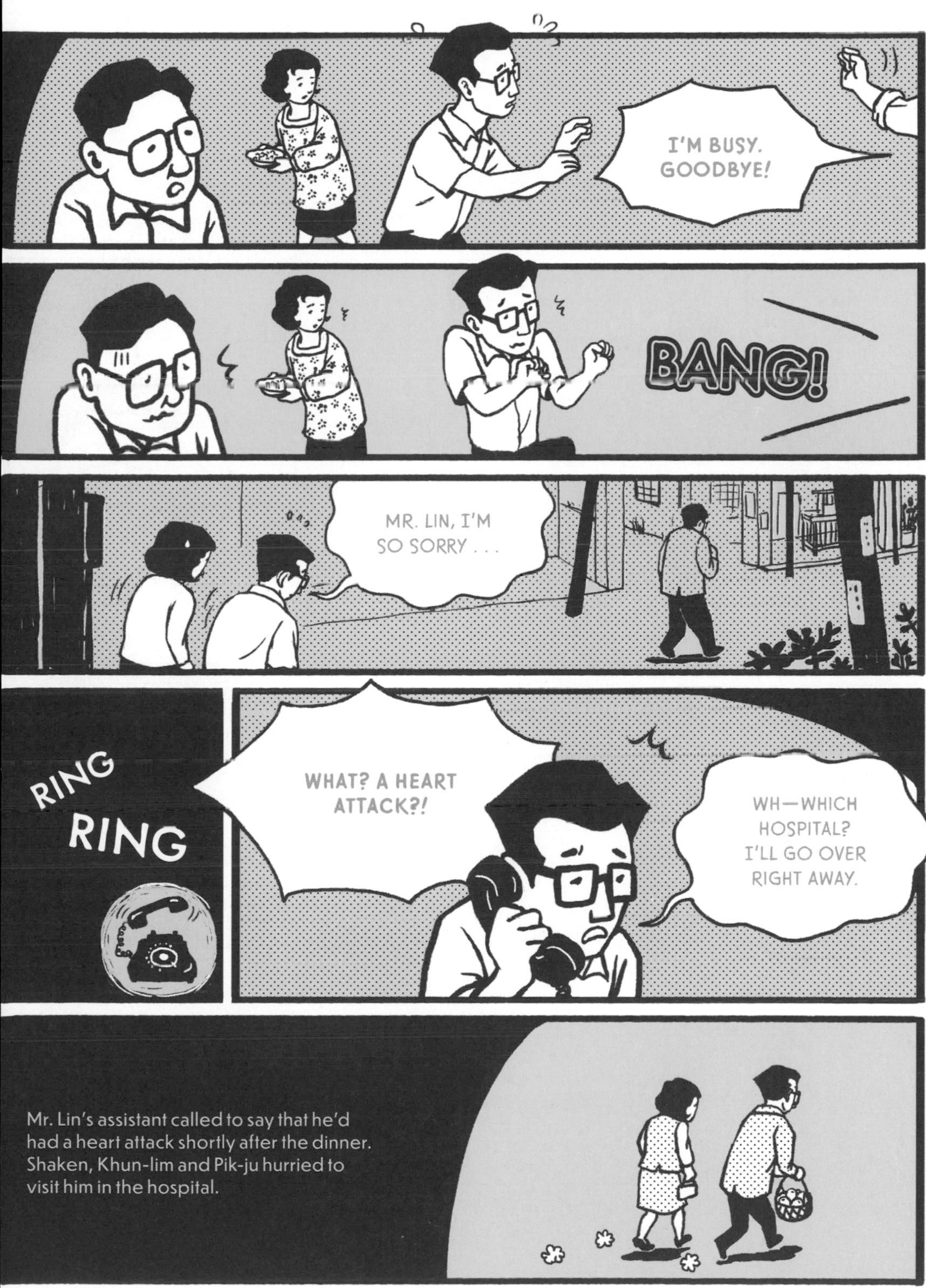
I'M BUSY. GOODBYE!
BANG!
MR. LIN, I'M SO SORRY . . .
RING
RING
WHAT? A HEART ATTACK?!
WH—WHICH HOSPITAL? I'LL GO OVER RIGHT AWAY.
Mr. Lin's assistant called to say that he'd had a heart attack shortly after the dinner. Shaken, Khun-lim and Pik-ju hurried to visit him in the hospital.

Following this whirlwind, and only after Khun-lim made more earnest appeals while promising that he would continue helping out at Wenchang Press in his free time, Liao Wen-mu grudgingly agreed to let him go to Kuohua Advertising.

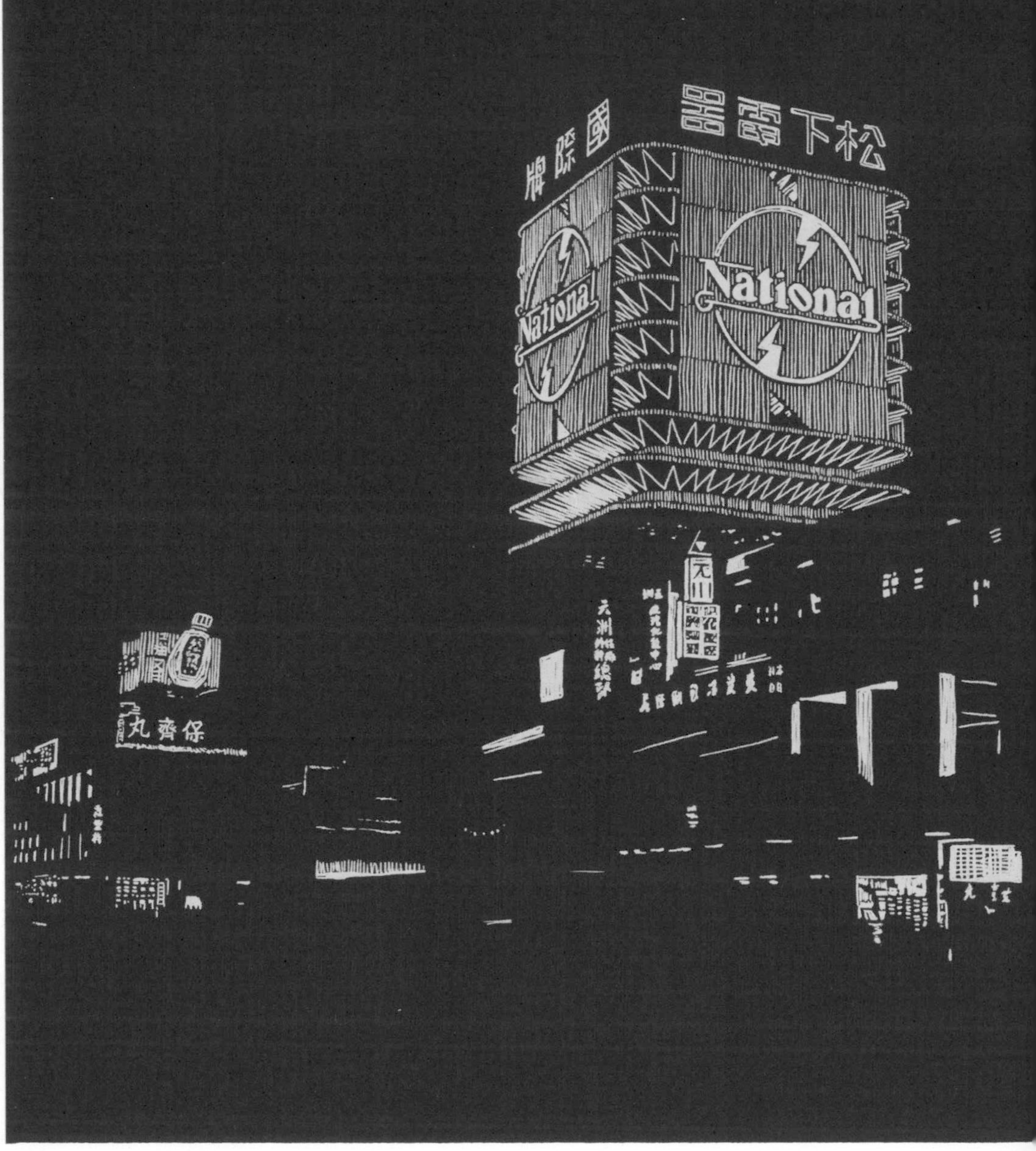

國際牌
松下電器
National
National
保齊丸

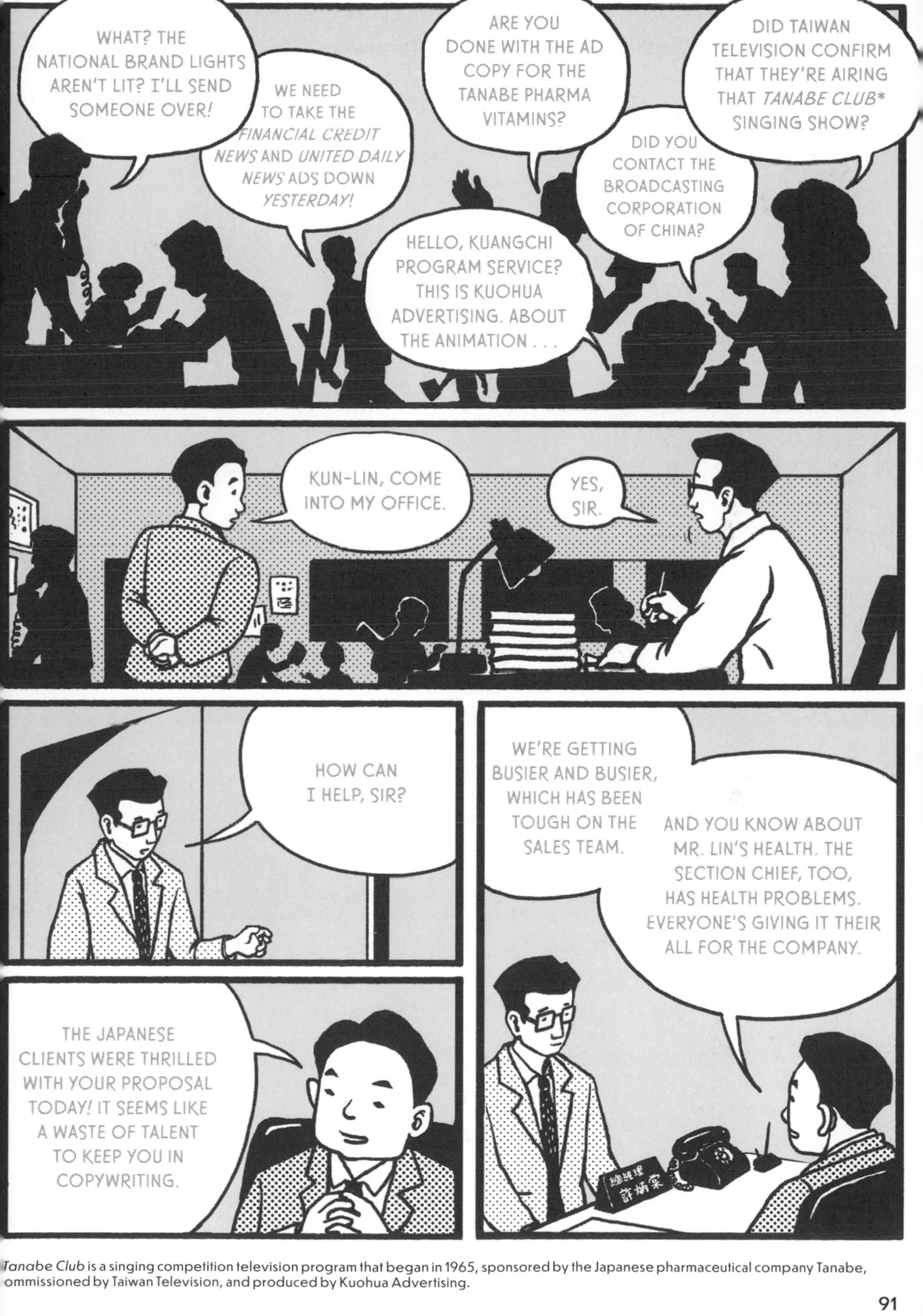
WHAT? THE NATIONAL BRAND LIGHTS AREN'T LIT? I'LL SEND SOMEONE OVER!
WE NEED TO TAKE THE *FINANCIAL CREDIT NEWS* AND *UNITED DAILY NEWS* ADS DOWN *YESTERDAY!*
ARE YOU DONE WITH THE AD COPY FOR THE TANABE PHARMA VITAMINS?
HELLO, KUANGCHI PROGRAM SERVICE? THIS IS KUOHUA ADVERTISING. ABOUT THE ANIMATION . . .
DID YOU CONTACT THE BROADCASTING CORPORATION OF CHINA?
DID TAIWAN TELEVISION CONFIRM THAT THEY'RE AIRING THAT *TANABE CLUB** SINGING SHOW?
KUN-LIN, COME INTO MY OFFICE.
YES, SIR.
HOW CAN I HELP, SIR?
THE JAPANESE CLIENTS WERE THRILLED WITH YOUR PROPOSAL TODAY! IT SEEMS LIKE A WASTE OF TALENT TO KEEP YOU IN COPYWRITING.
WE'RE GETTING BUSIER AND BUSIER, WHICH HAS BEEN TOUGH ON THE SALES TEAM.
AND YOU KNOW ABOUT MR. LIN'S HEALTH. THE SECTION CHIEF, TOO, HAS HEALTH PROBLEMS. EVERYONE'S GIVING IT THEIR ALL FOR THE COMPANY.

Tanabe Club is a singing competition television program that began in 1965, sponsored by the Japanese pharmaceutical company Tanabe, ommissioned by Taiwan Television, and produced by Kuohua Advertising.

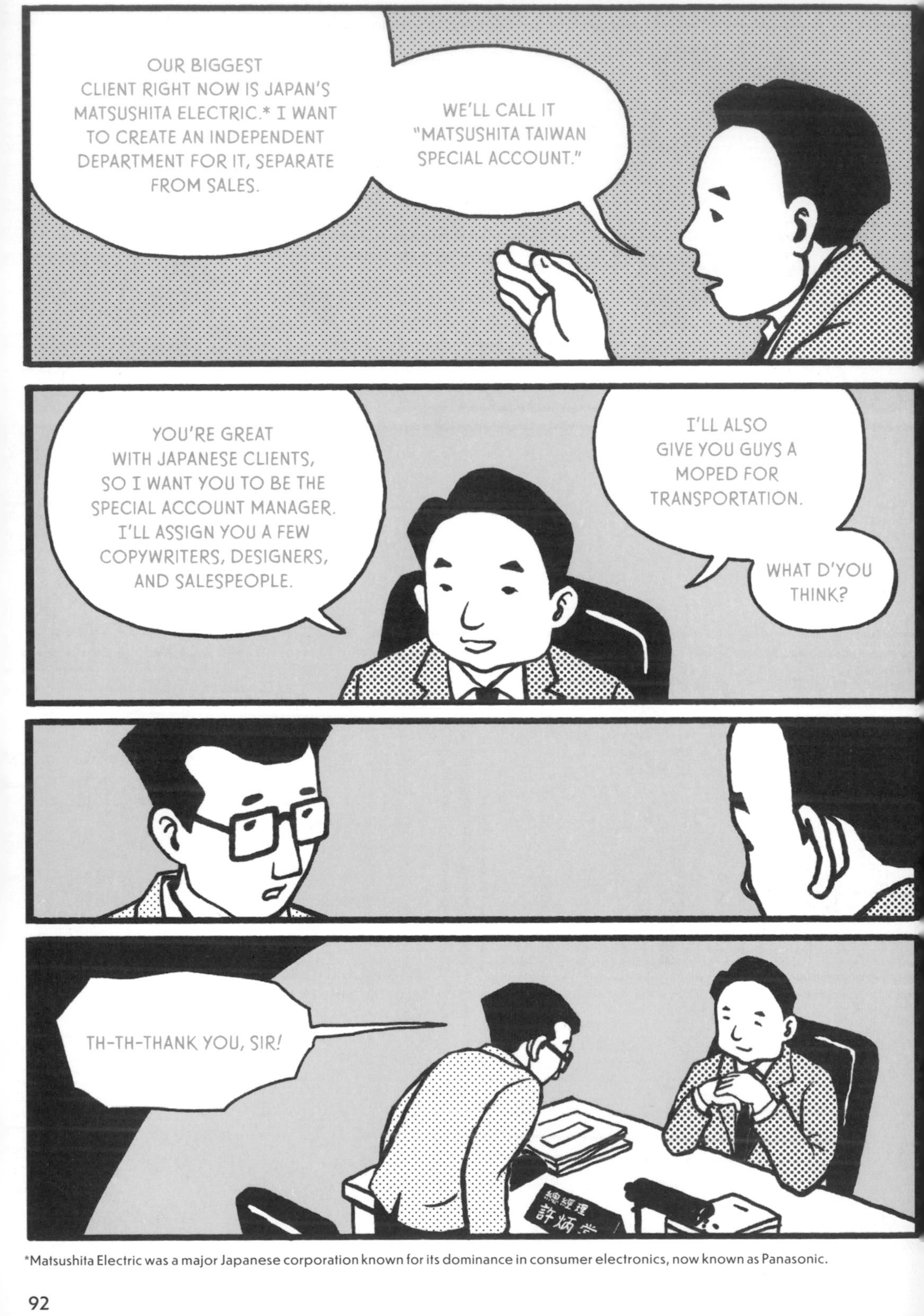
OUR BIGGEST CLIENT RIGHT NOW IS JAPAN'S MATSUSHITA ELECTRIC.* I WANT TO CREATE AN INDEPENDENT DEPARTMENT FOR IT, SEPARATE FROM SALES.
WE'LL CALL IT "MATSUSHITA TAIWAN SPECIAL ACCOUNT."
YOU'RE GREAT WITH JAPANESE CLIENTS, SO I WANT YOU TO BE THE SPECIAL ACCOUNT MANAGER. I'LL ASSIGN YOU A FEW COPYWRITERS, DESIGNERS, AND SALESPEOPLE.
I'LL ALSO GIVE YOU GUYS A MOPED FOR TRANSPORTATION.
WHAT D'YOU THINK?
TH-TH-THANK YOU, SIR!
總經理

*Matsushita Electric was a major Japanese corporation known for its dominance in consumer electronics, now known as Panasonic.

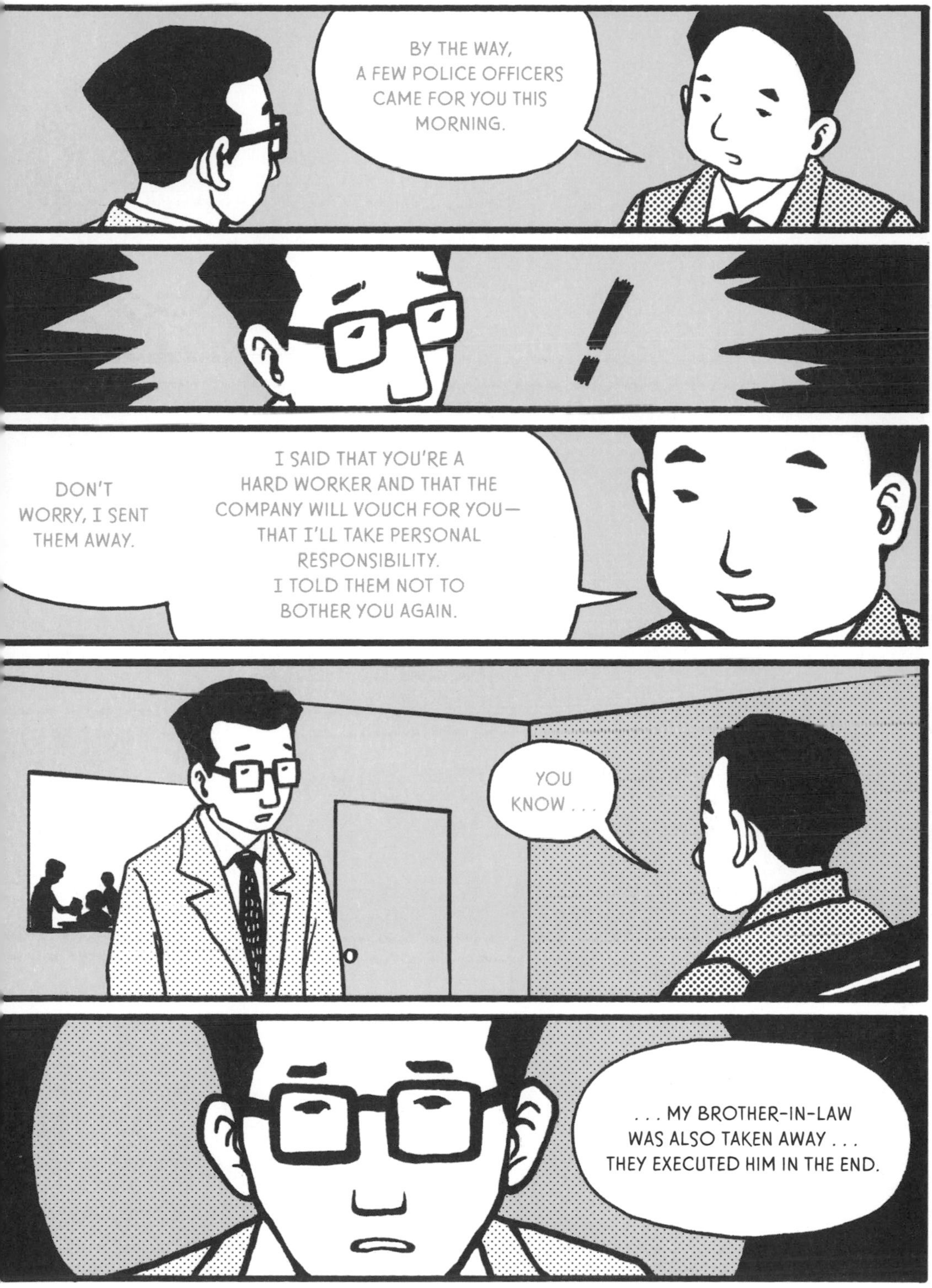
BY THE WAY, A FEW POLICE OFFICERS CAME FOR YOU THIS MORNING.
!
DON'T WORRY, I SENT THEM AWAY.
I SAID THAT YOU'RE A HARD WORKER AND THAT THE COMPANY WILL VOUCH FOR YOU— THAT I'LL TAKE PERSONAL RESPONSIBILITY. I TOLD THEM NOT TO BOTHER YOU AGAIN.
YOU KNOW . . .
. . . MY BROTHER-IN-LAW WAS ALSO TAKEN AWAY . . . THEY EXECUTED HIM IN THE END.

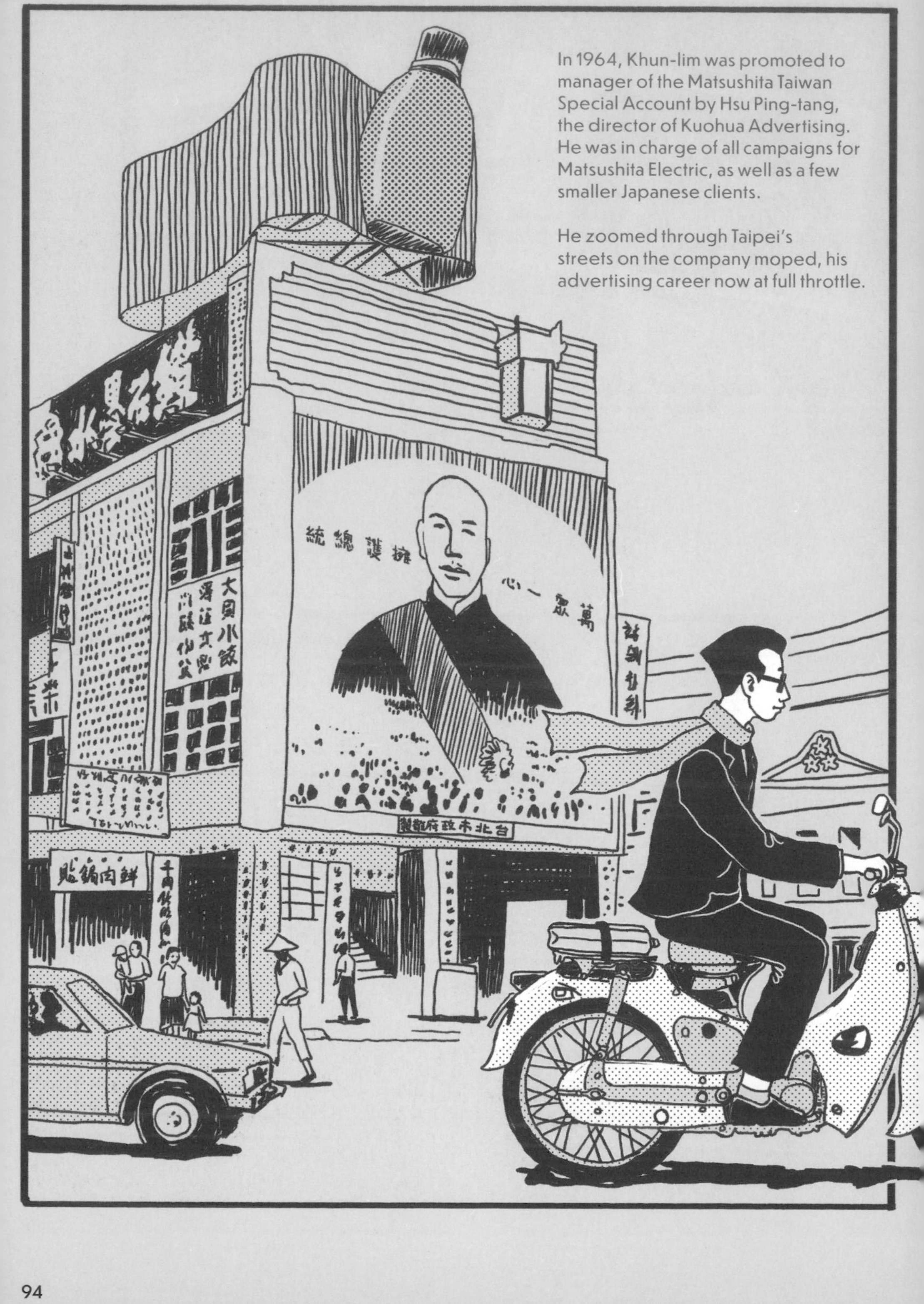
In 1964, Khun-lim was promoted to manager of the Matsushita Taiwan Special Account by Hsu Ping-tang, the director of Kuohua Advertising. He was in charge of all campaigns for Matsushita Electric, as well as a few smaller Japanese clients.
He zoomed through Taipei's streets on the company moped, his advertising career now at full throttle.
擁護總統
萬衆一心
台北市政府敬製
鮮肉鍋貼

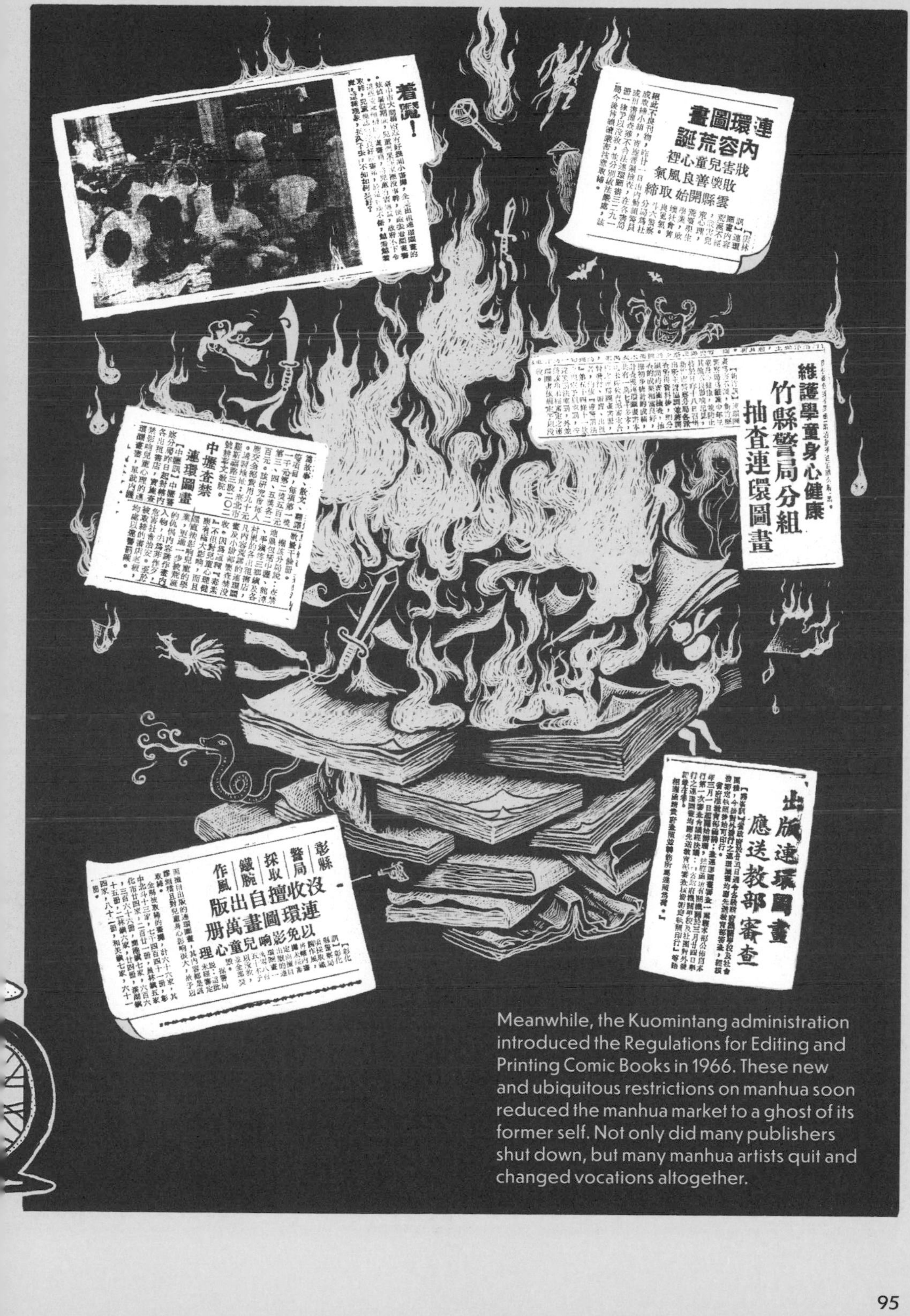
着魔！
連環圖畫
內容荒誕
戕害兒童心裡
敗壞善良風氣
雲縣開始取締
維護學童身心健康
竹縣警局分組
抽查連環圖畫
中壢查禁
連環圖畫
出版連環圖畫
應送教部審查
彰縣警局
採取鐵腕作風
沒收擅自出版
連環圖畫萬冊
以免影響兒童心理

Meanwhile, the Kuomintang administration introduced the Regulations for Editing and Printing Comic Books in 1966. These new and ubiquitous restrictions on manhua soon reduced the manhua market to a ghost of its former self. Not only did many publishers shut down, but many manhua artists quit and changed vocations altogether.

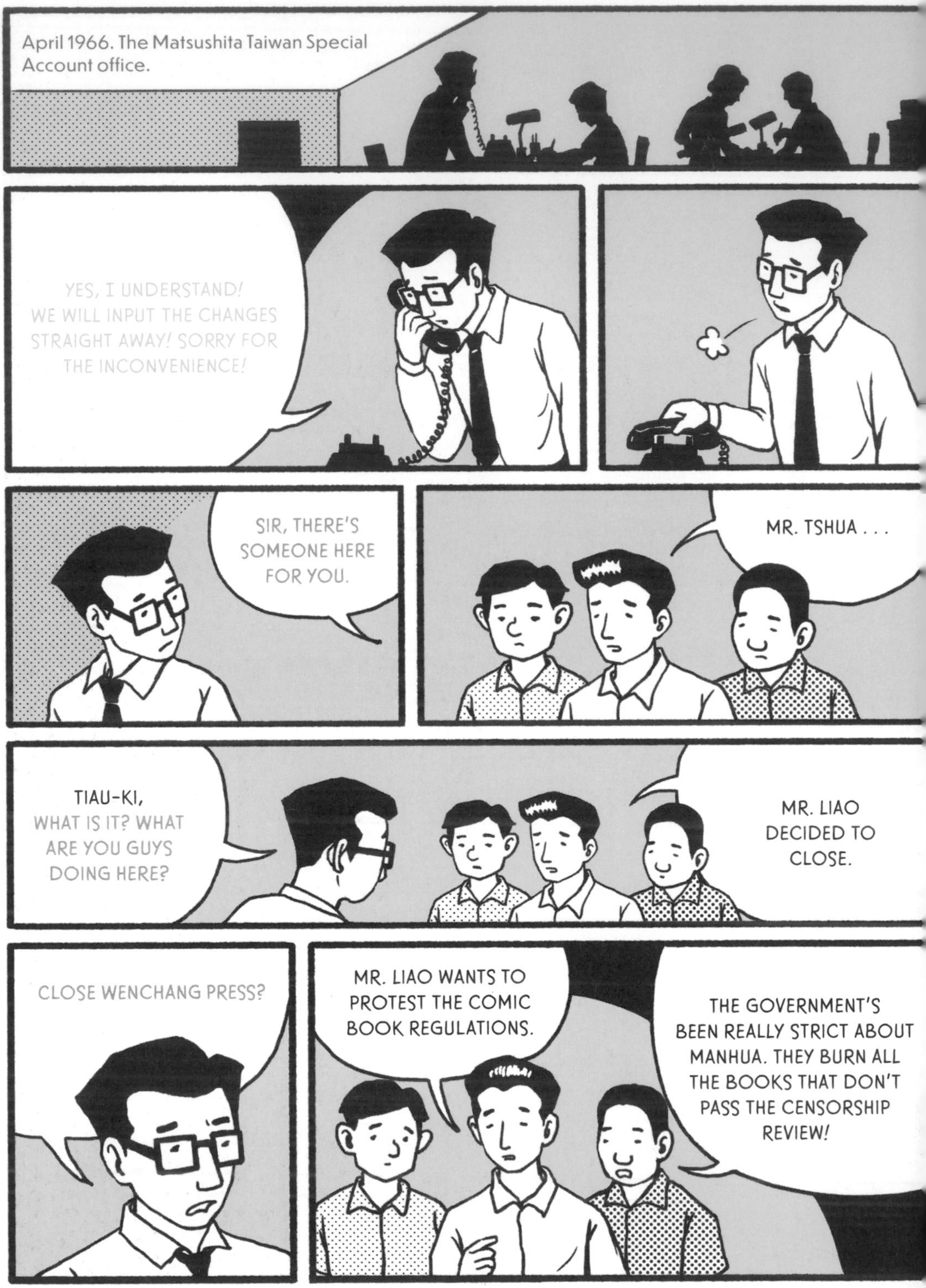
April 1966. The Matsushita Taiwan Special Account office.
YES, I UNDERSTAND! WE WILL INPUT THE CHANGES STRAIGHT AWAY! SORRY FOR THE INCONVENIENCE!
SIR, THERE'S SOMEONE HERE FOR YOU.
MR. TSHUA . . .
TIAU-KI, WHAT IS IT? WHAT ARE YOU GUYS DOING HERE?
MR. LIAO DECIDED TO CLOSE.
CLOSE WENCHANG PRESS?
MR. LIAO WANTS TO PROTEST THE COMIC BOOK REGULATIONS.
THE GOVERNMENT'S BEEN REALLY STRICT ABOUT MANHUA. THEY BURN ALL THE BOOKS THAT DON'T PASS THE CENSORSHIP REVIEW!

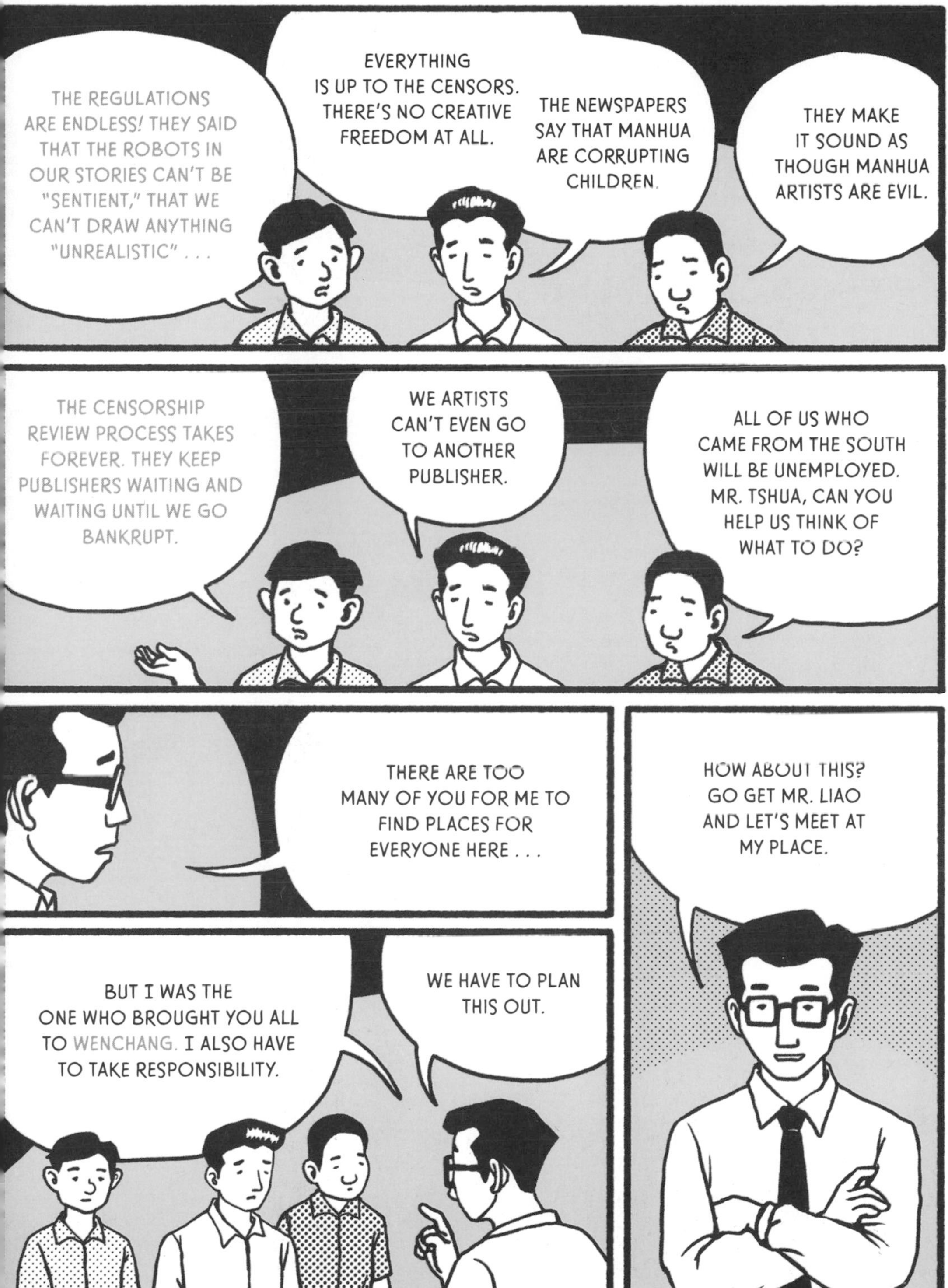
THE REGULATIONS ARE ENDLESS! THEY SAID THAT THE ROBOTS IN OUR STORIES CAN'T BE "SENTIENT," THAT WE CAN'T DRAW ANYTHING "UNREALISTIC" . . .
EVERYTHING IS UP TO THE CENSORS. THERE'S NO CREATIVE FREEDOM AT ALL.
THE NEWSPAPERS SAY THAT MANHUA ARE CORRUPTING CHILDREN.
THEY MAKE IT SOUND AS THOUGH MANHUA ARTISTS ARE EVIL.
THE CENSORSHIP REVIEW PROCESS TAKES FOREVER. THEY KEEP PUBLISHERS WAITING AND WAITING UNTIL WE GO BANKRUPT.
WE ARTISTS CAN'T EVEN GO TO ANOTHER PUBLISHER.
ALL OF US WHO CAME FROM THE SOUTH WILL BE UNEMPLOYED. MR. TSHUA, CAN YOU HELP US THINK OF WHAT TO DO?
THERE ARE TOO MANY OF YOU FOR ME TO FIND PLACES FOR EVERYONE HERE . . .
BUT I WAS THE ONE WHO BROUGHT YOU ALL TO WENCHANG. I ALSO HAVE TO TAKE RESPONSIBILITY.
WE HAVE TO PLAN THIS OUT.
HOW ABOUT THIS? GO GET MR. LIAO AND LET'S MEET AT MY PLACE.

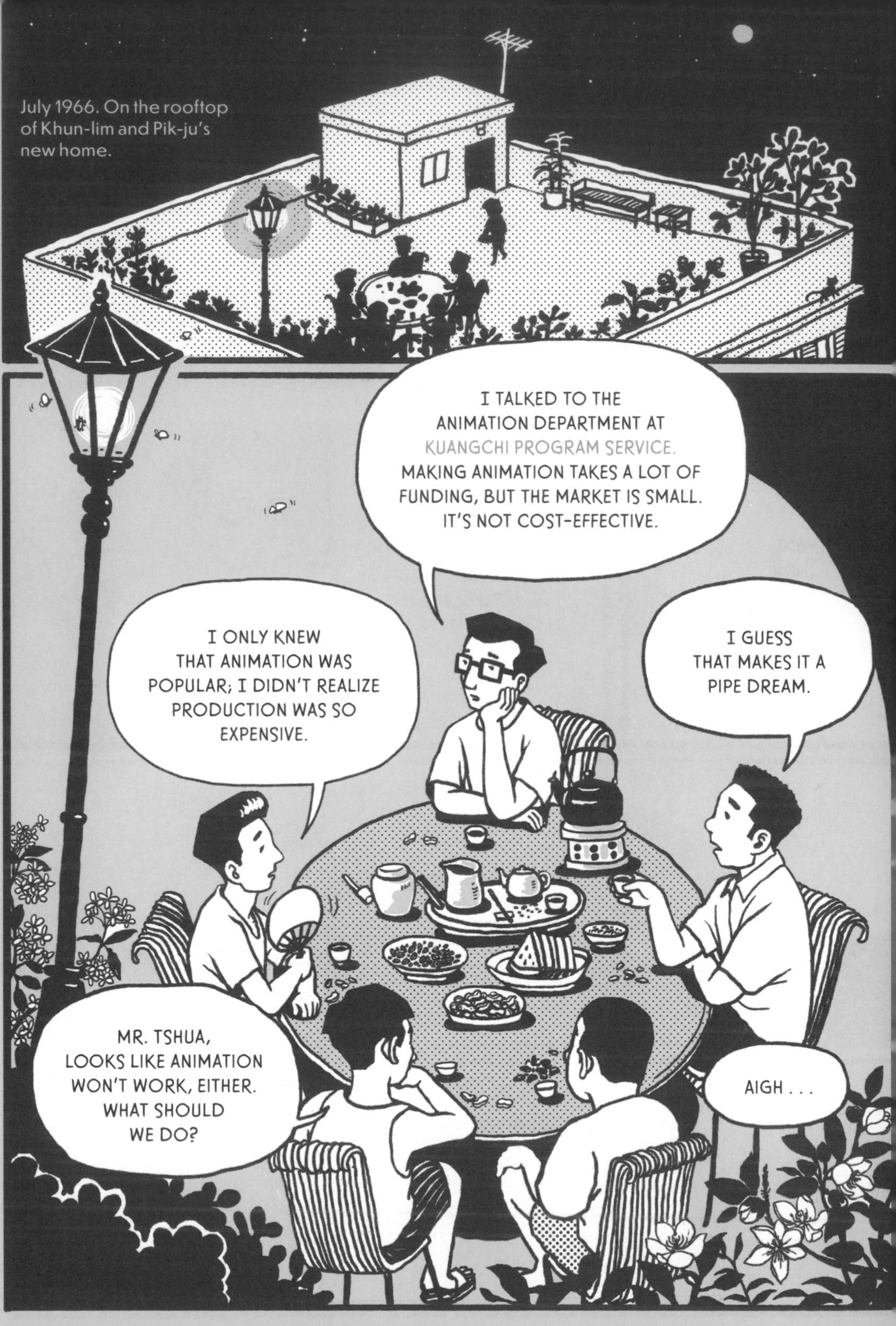
July 1966. On the rooftop of Khun-lim and Pik-ju's new home.
I TALKED TO THE ANIMATION DEPARTMENT AT KUANGCHI PROGRAM SERVICE. MAKING ANIMATION TAKES A LOT OF FUNDING, BUT THE MARKET IS SMALL. IT'S NOT COST-EFFECTIVE.
I ONLY KNEW THAT ANIMATION WAS POPULAR; I DIDN'T REALIZE PRODUCTION WAS SO EXPENSIVE.
I GUESS THAT MAKES IT A PIPE DREAM.
MR. TSHUA, LOOKS LIKE ANIMATION WON'T WORK, EITHER. WHAT SHOULD WE DO?
AIGH . . .

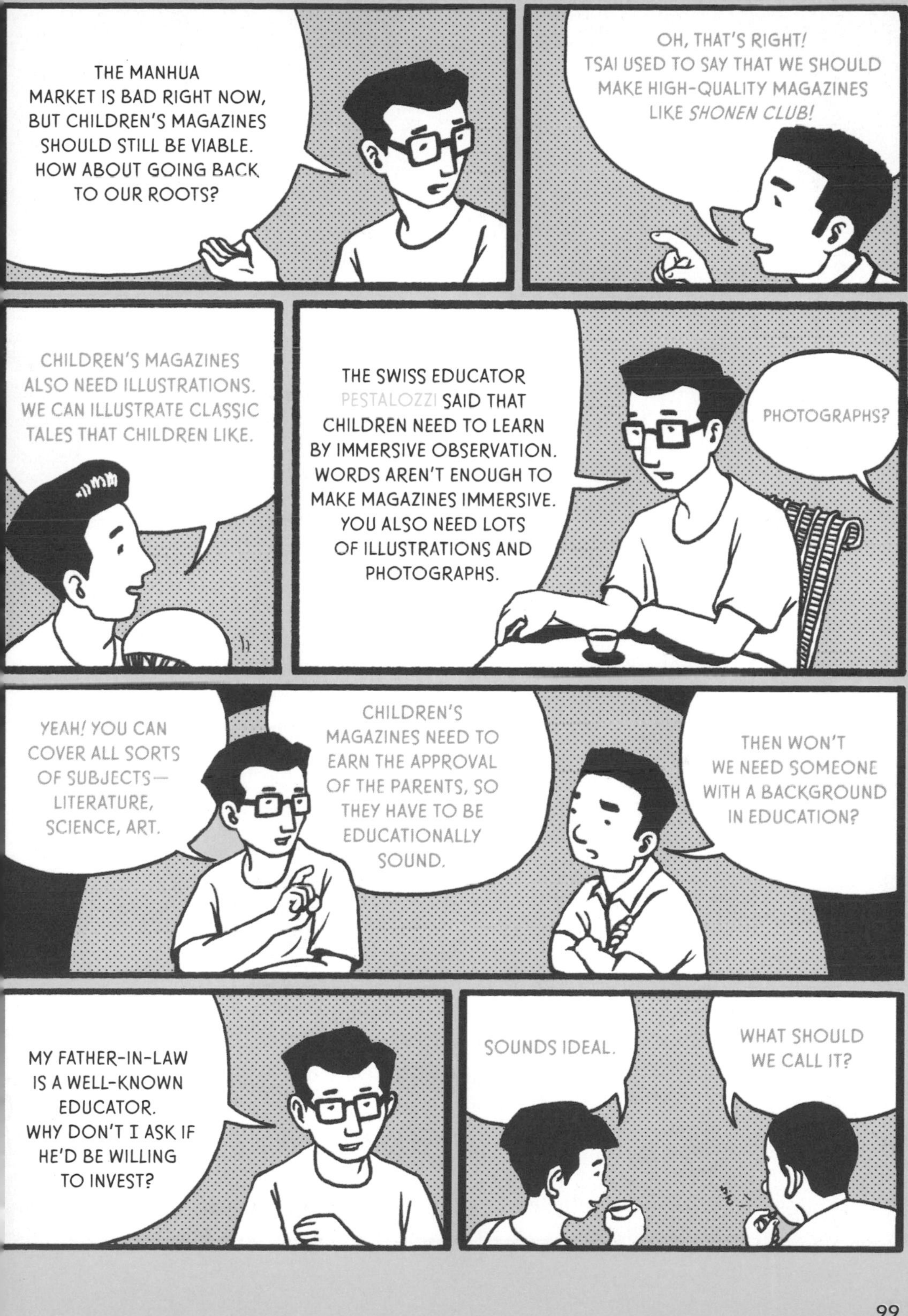
THE MANHUA MARKET IS BAD RIGHT NOW, BUT CHILDREN'S MAGAZINES SHOULD STILL BE VIABLE. HOW ABOUT GOING BACK TO OUR ROOTS?
OH, THAT'S RIGHT! TSAI USED TO SAY THAT WE SHOULD MAKE HIGH-QUALITY MAGAZINES LIKE *SHONEN CLUB!*
CHILDREN'S MAGAZINES ALSO NEED ILLUSTRATIONS. WE CAN ILLUSTRATE CLASSIC TALES THAT CHILDREN LIKE.
THE SWISS EDUCATOR PESTALOZZI SAID THAT CHILDREN NEED TO LEARN BY IMMERSIVE OBSERVATION. WORDS AREN'T ENOUGH TO MAKE MAGAZINES IMMERSIVE. YOU ALSO NEED LOTS OF ILLUSTRATIONS AND PHOTOGRAPHS.
PHOTOGRAPHS?
YEAH! YOU CAN COVER ALL SORTS OF SUBJECTS—LITERATURE, SCIENCE, ART.
CHILDREN'S MAGAZINES NEED TO EARN THE APPROVAL OF THE PARENTS, SO THEY HAVE TO BE EDUCATIONALLY SOUND.
THEN WON'T WE NEED SOMEONE WITH A BACKGROUND IN EDUCATION?
MY FATHER-IN-LAW IS A WELL-KNOWN EDUCATOR. WHY DON'T I ASK IF HE'D BE WILLING TO INVEST?
SOUNDS IDEAL.
WHAT SHOULD WE CALL IT?

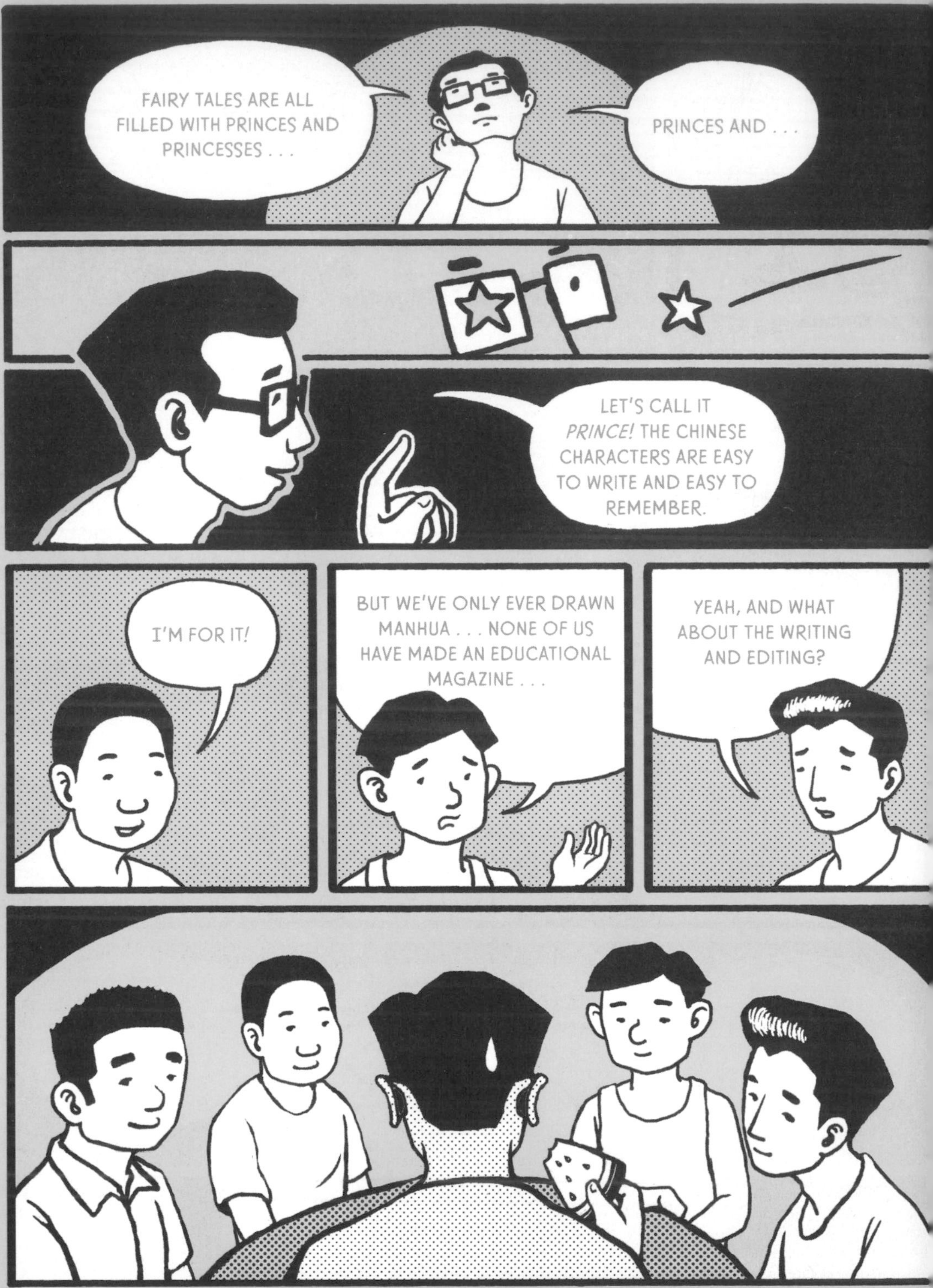
FAIRY TALES ARE ALL FILLED WITH PRINCES AND PRINCESSES . . .
PRINCES AND . . .
LET'S CALL IT *PRINCE!* THE CHINESE CHARACTERS ARE EASY TO WRITE AND EASY TO REMEMBER.
I'M FOR IT!
BUT WE'VE ONLY EVER DRAWN MANHUA . . . NONE OF US HAVE MADE AN EDUCATIONAL MAGAZINE . . .
YEAH, AND WHAT ABOUT THE WRITING AND EDITING?

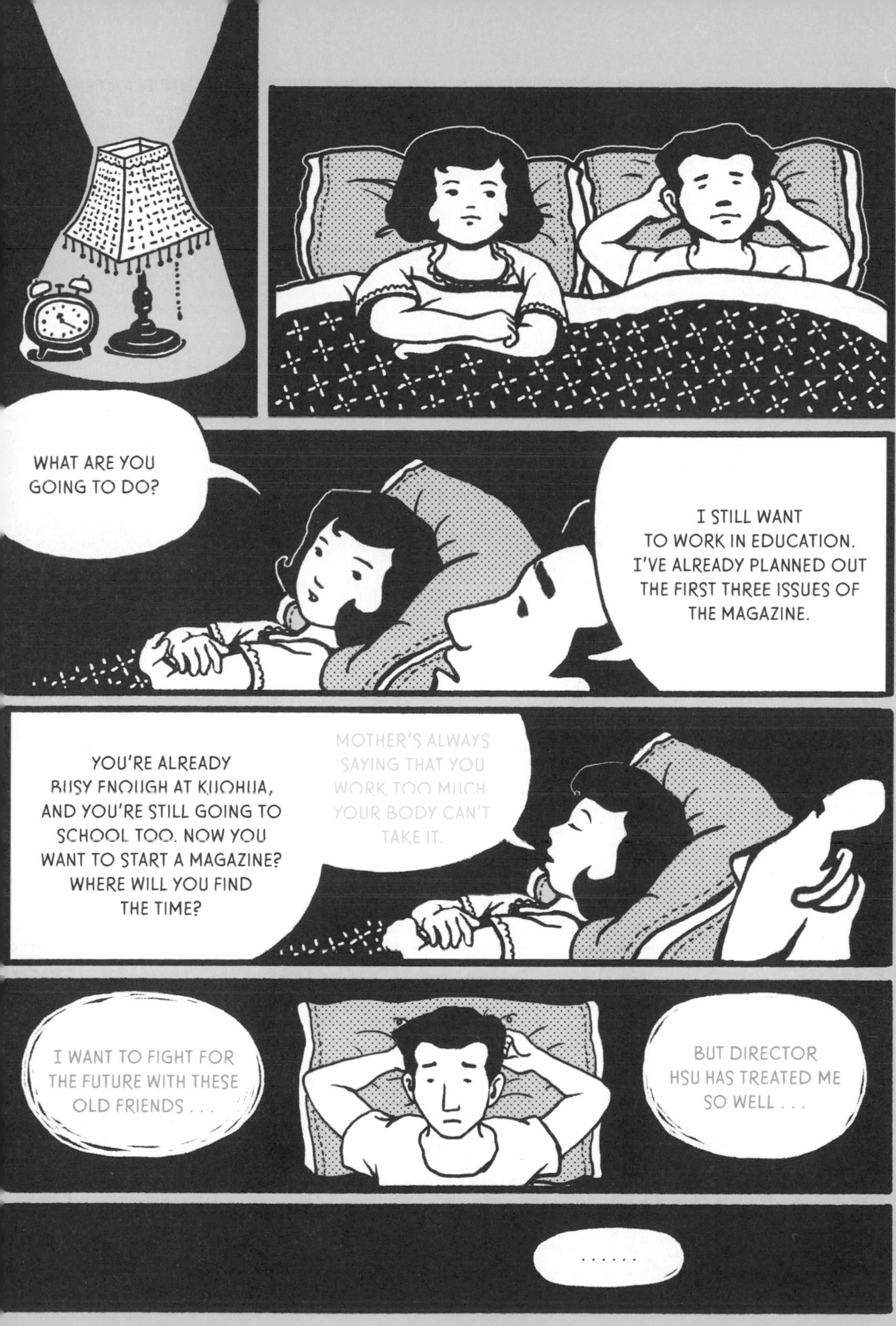
WHAT ARE YOU GOING TO DO?
I STILL WANT TO WORK IN EDUCATION. I'VE ALREADY PLANNED OUT THE FIRST THREE ISSUES OF THE MAGAZINE.
YOU'RE ALREADY BUSY ENOUGH AT KUOHUA, AND YOU'RE STILL GOING TO SCHOOL TOO. NOW YOU WANT TO START A MAGAZINE? WHERE WILL YOU FIND THE TIME?
MOTHER'S ALWAYS SAYING THAT YOU WORK TOO MUCH YOUR BODY CAN'T TAKE IT.
I WANT TO FIGHT FOR THE FUTURE WITH THESE OLD FRIENDS . . .
BUT DIRECTOR HSU HAS TREATED ME SO WELL . . .
. . . . . .

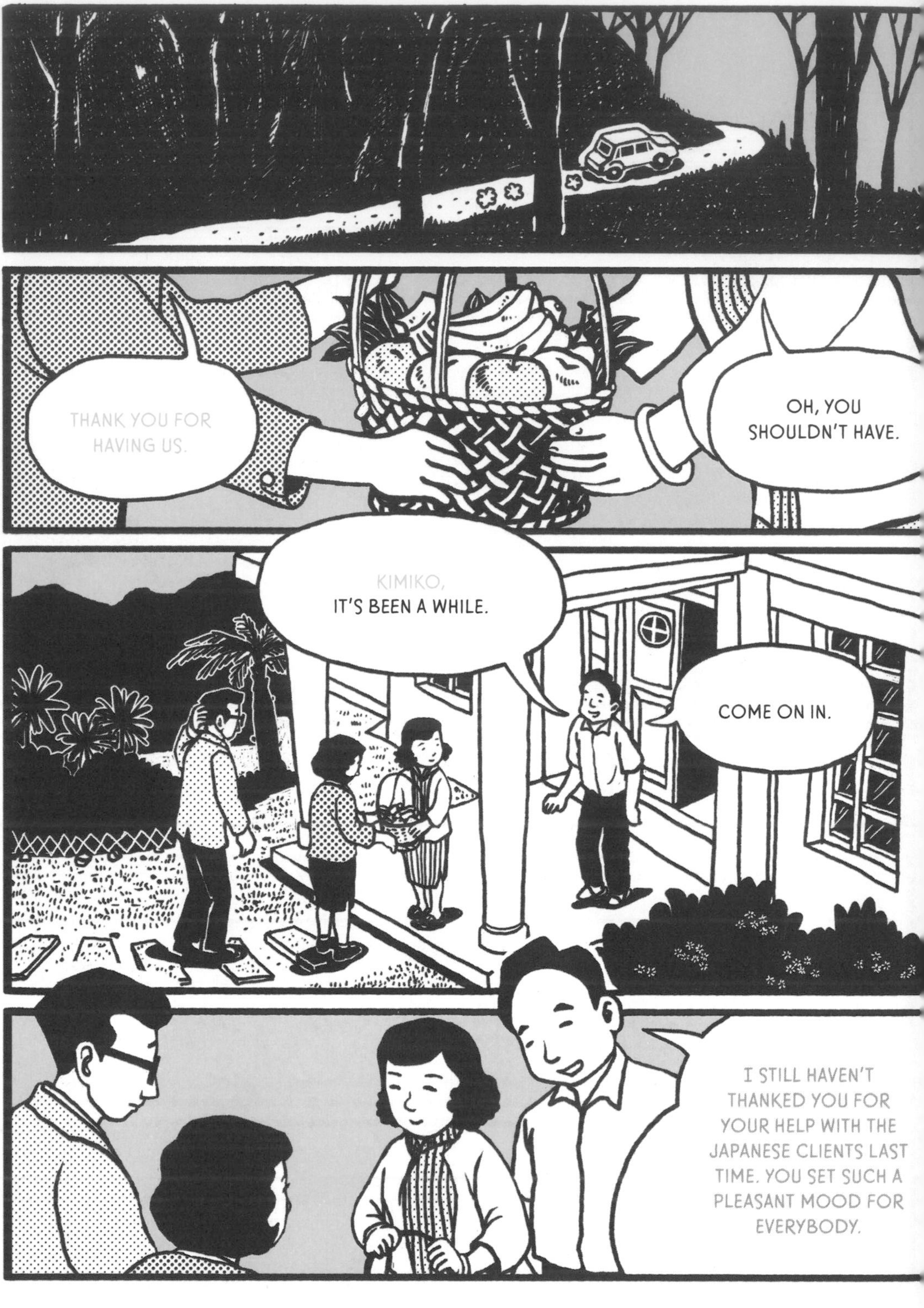
THANK YOU FOR HAVING US.
OH, YOU SHOULDN'T HAVE.
KIMIKO,
IT'S BEEN A WHILE.
COME ON IN.
I STILL HAVEN'T THANKED YOU FOR YOUR HELP WITH THE JAPANESE CLIENTS LAST TIME. YOU SET SUCH A PLEASANT MOOD FOR EVERYBODY.

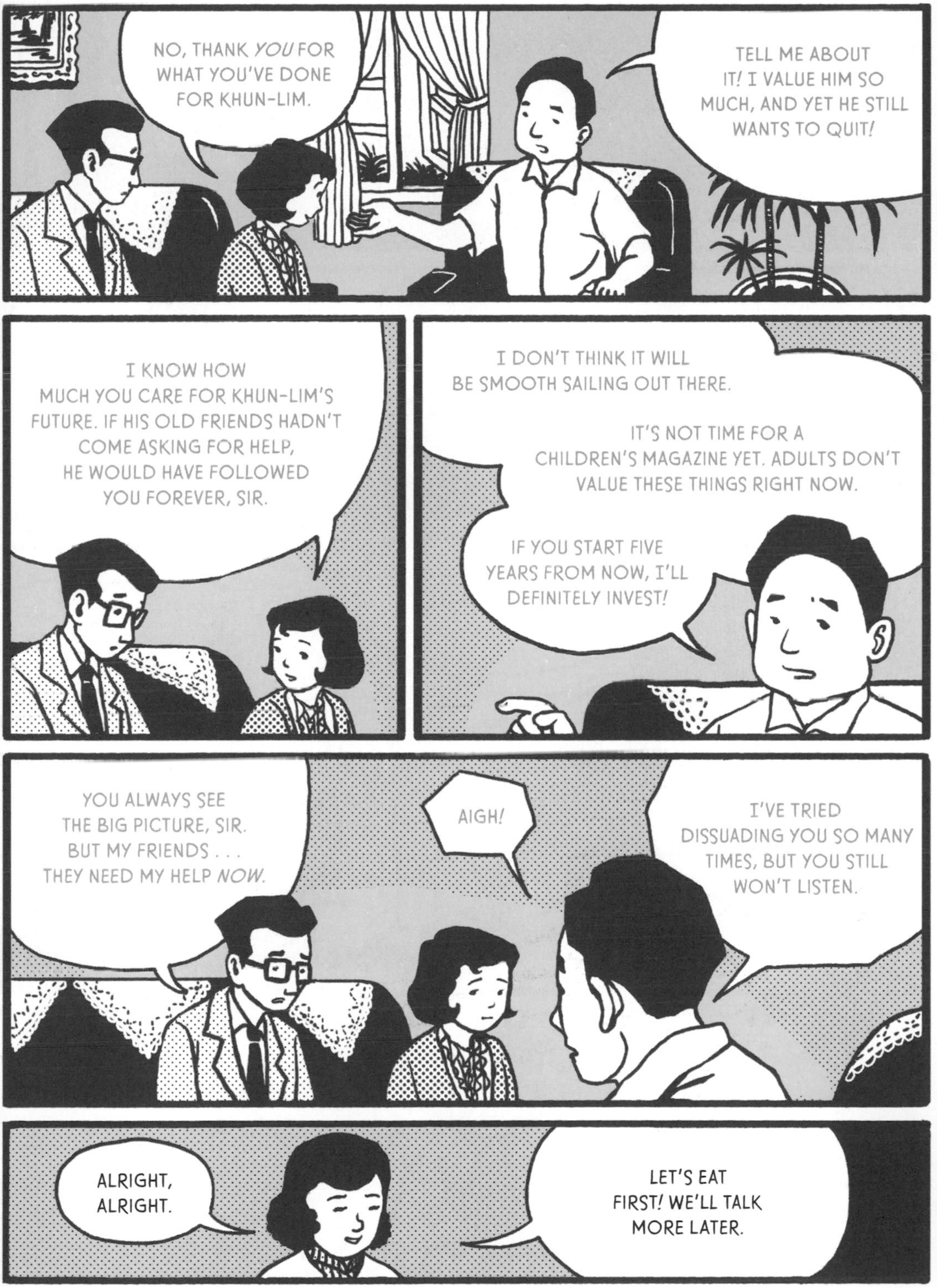
NO, THANK *YOU* FOR WHAT YOU'VE DONE FOR KHUN-LIM.
TELL ME ABOUT IT! I VALUE HIM SO MUCH, AND YET HE STILL WANTS TO QUIT!
I KNOW HOW MUCH YOU CARE FOR KHUN-LIM'S FUTURE. IF HIS OLD FRIENDS HADN'T COME ASKING FOR HELP, HE WOULD HAVE FOLLOWED YOU FOREVER, SIR.
I DON'T THINK IT WILL BE SMOOTH SAILING OUT THERE.
IT'S NOT TIME FOR A CHILDREN'S MAGAZINE YET. ADULTS DON'T VALUE THESE THINGS RIGHT NOW.
IF YOU START FIVE YEARS FROM NOW, I'LL DEFINITELY INVEST!
YOU ALWAYS SEE THE BIG PICTURE, SIR. BUT MY FRIENDS . . . THEY NEED MY HELP *NOW*.
AIGH!
I'VE TRIED DISSUADING YOU SO MANY TIMES, BUT YOU STILL WON'T LISTEN.
ALRIGHT, ALRIGHT.
LET'S EAT FIRST! WE'LL TALK MORE LATER.

Khun-lim's plans could never keep up with reality. The government's enforcement of manhua censorship transformed him from an advertising executive to a children's magazine founder.

His decision to pursue this new path was due in part to his loyalty to his former colleagues, but also in part to his longstanding wish to work in education and serve children.

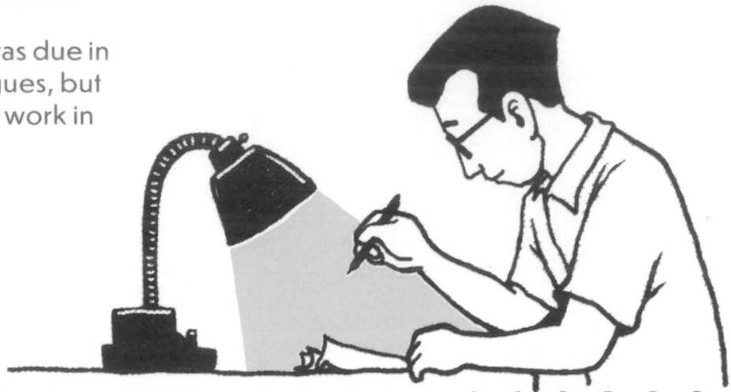

王子創刊詞

Editor's Note for *Prince* Magazine's Inaugural Issue

Have you ever witnessed a plant shoot breaking ground? Perhaps you were surprised: where does a soft bud like that find the strength to break through the hard earth? This—the power of growth—is Nature's great secret! "Growing up" is a young person's right and the most meaningful part of life, yet it also comes at an extremely high cost. How could the shoot have pushed through the soil if the seed hadn't been storing up nutrients for months or maybe years? If it hadn't struggled underground, how could it have ever seen the sun or the sky?

My dear young friends: you are currently in the most dazzling period of your life. Whether you spend your days in school or a factory, farm, or shopfront; whether you are burying yourself in books or sweating down your back in labor; all of this is part of your growth—part of the journey you must endure in order to climb upward.

Prince, our bimonthly magazine, hopes to work and fight alongside you as you grow up. We hope our magazine will act as your walking stick, stepping stone, and spiritual sustenance while you navigate this journey. If you feel as though the path before you is pitch black, then hopefully this magazine can shed light on human reason, sound values, and scientific knowledge. The road ahead may be treacherous, but here we will share stories of people who have achieved great feats and in whose footsteps you might follow. Perhaps you will find yourself tired—then come to us for funny manhua and other absorbing tales to ease your exhaustion. Perhaps you will find yourself lonely—then we hope you can find companionship in your countless fellow readers. From now on, neither of us will be alone. *Prince* will be your friend, growing up with you and improving as you do.

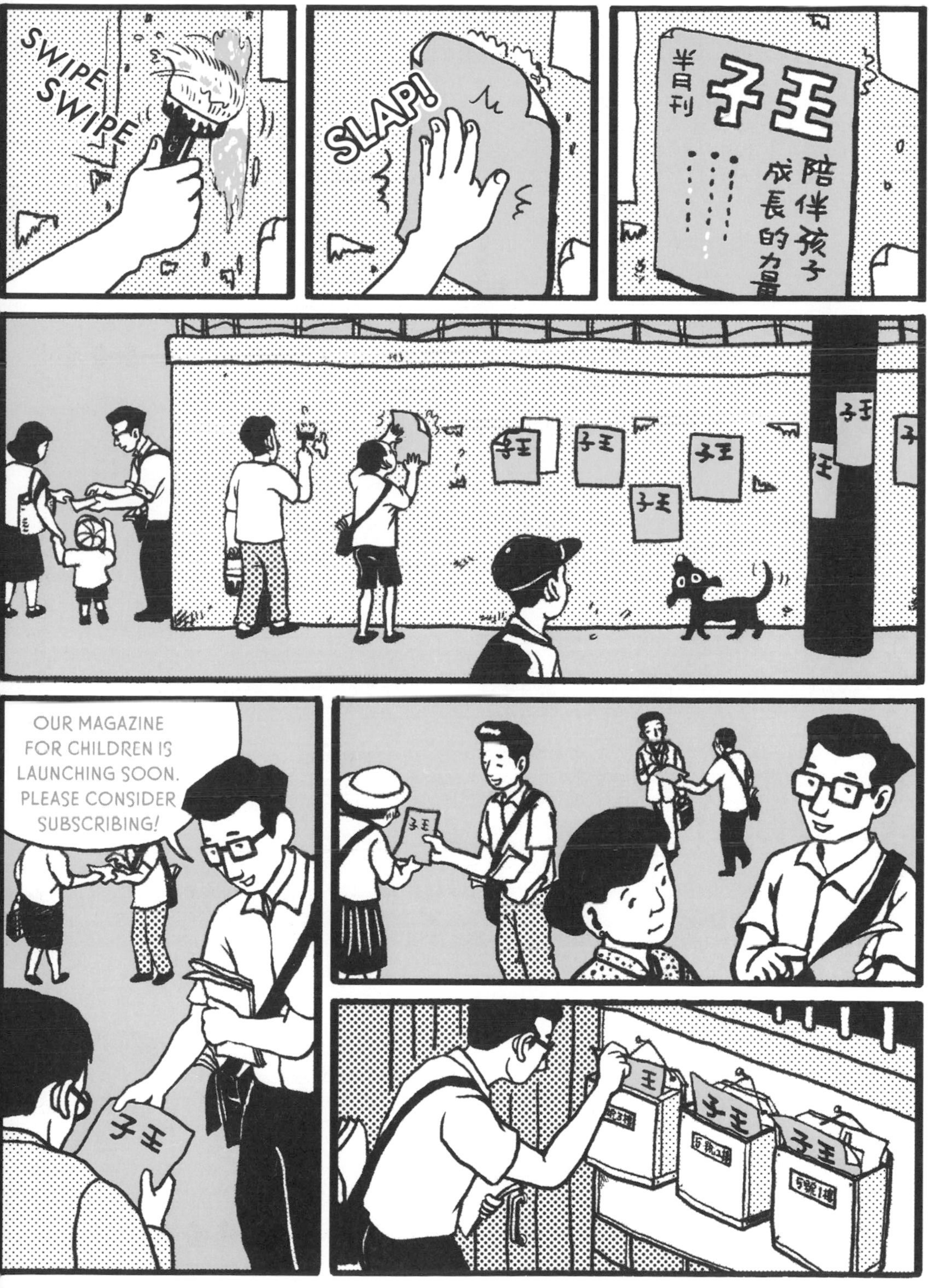
SWIPE SWIPE
SLAP!
半月刊
子王
陪伴孩子
成長的力量
子王
OUR MAGAZINE FOR CHILDREN IS LAUNCHING SOON. PLEASE CONSIDER SUBSCRIBING!
子王

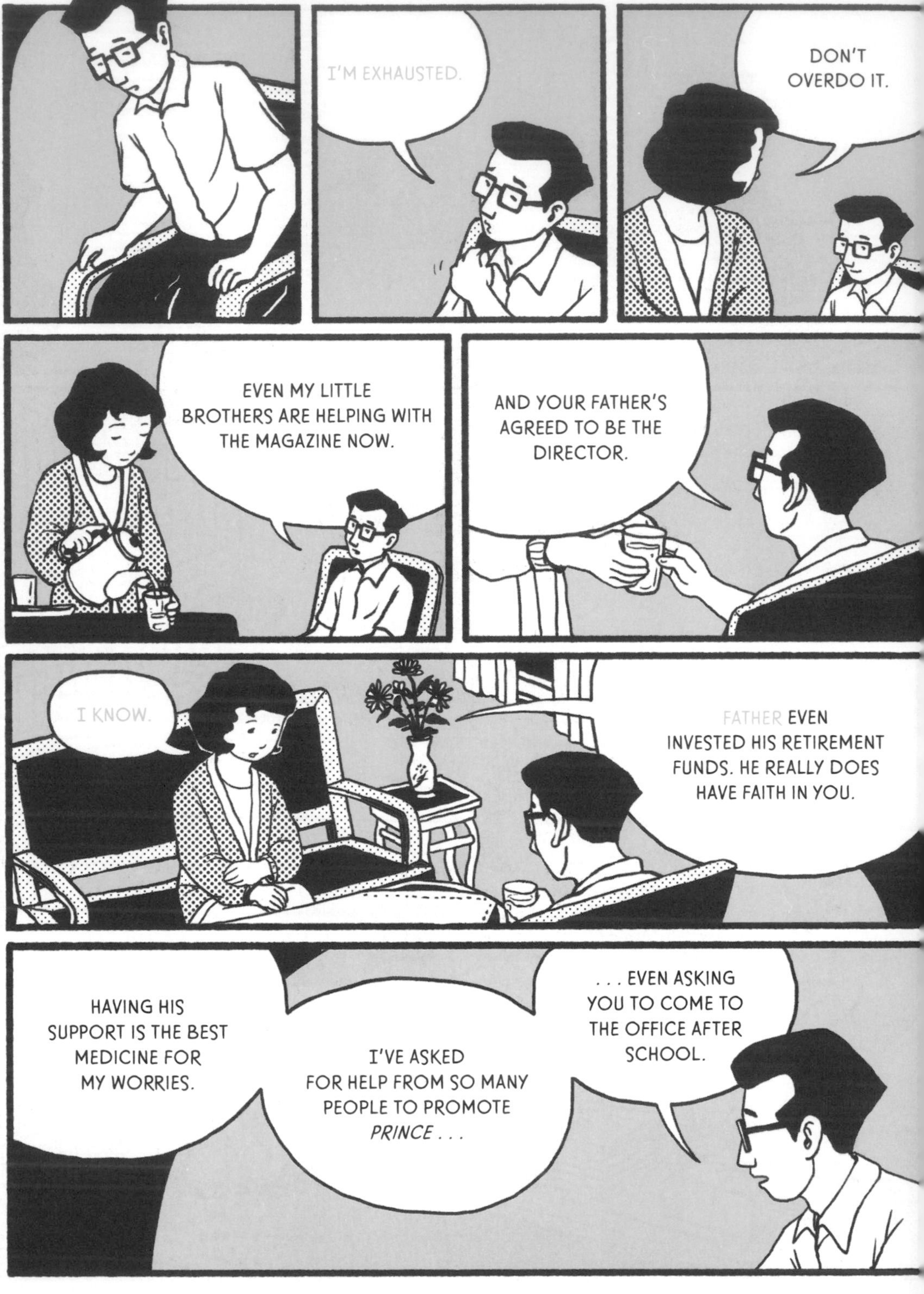
I'M EXHAUSTED.
DON'T OVERDO IT.
EVEN MY LITTLE BROTHERS ARE HELPING WITH THE MAGAZINE NOW.
AND YOUR FATHER'S AGREED TO BE THE DIRECTOR.
I KNOW.
FATHER EVEN INVESTED HIS RETIREMENT FUNDS. HE REALLY DOES HAVE FAITH IN YOU.
HAVING HIS SUPPORT IS THE BEST MEDICINE FOR MY WORRIES.
I'VE ASKED FOR HELP FROM SO MANY PEOPLE TO PROMOTE *PRINCE* . . .
. . . EVEN ASKING YOU TO COME TO THE OFFICE AFTER SCHOOL.

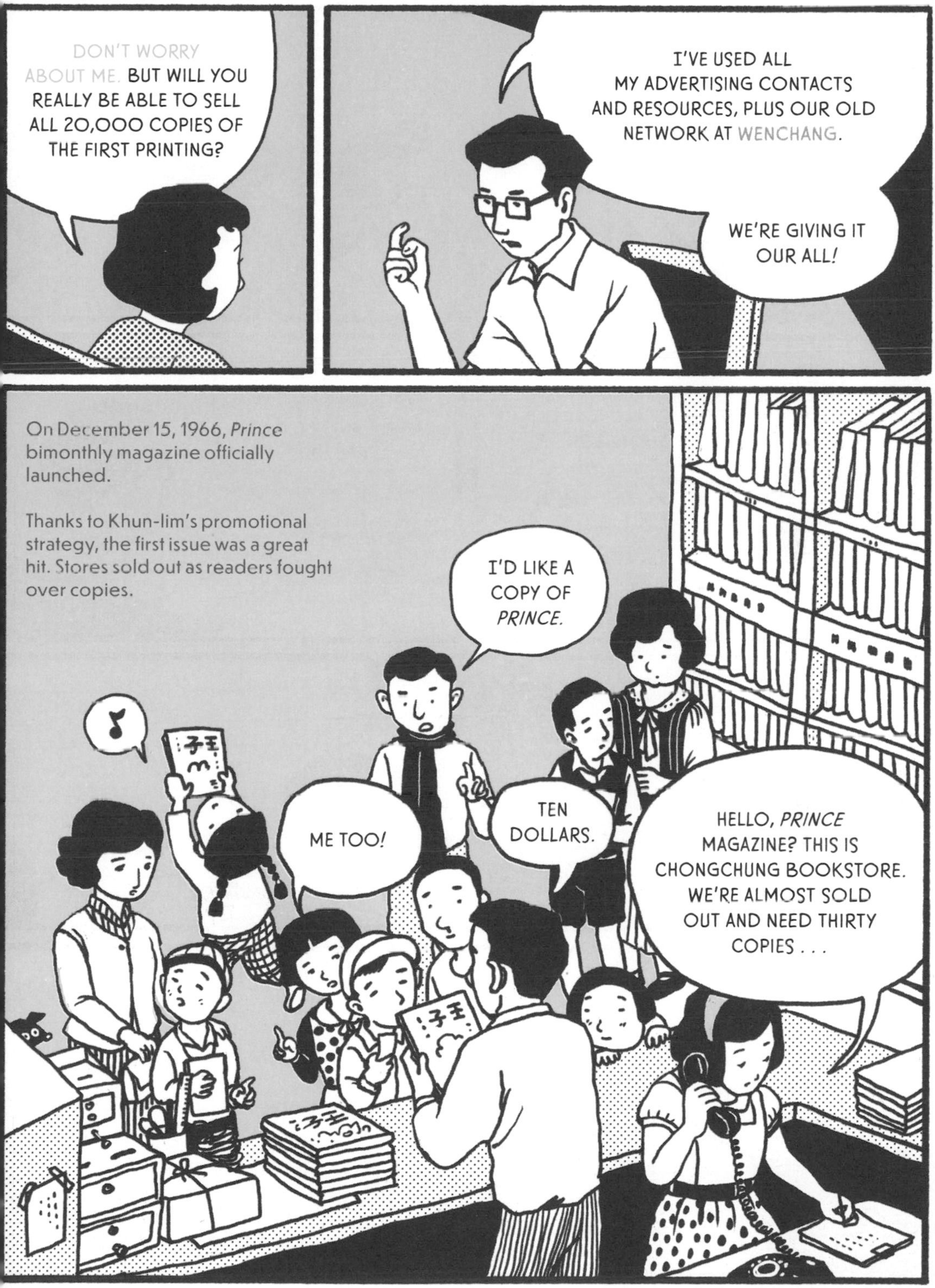
DON'T WORRY ABOUT ME. BUT WILL YOU REALLY BE ABLE TO SELL ALL 20,000 COPIES OF THE FIRST PRINTING?
I'VE USED ALL MY ADVERTISING CONTACTS AND RESOURCES, PLUS OUR OLD NETWORK AT WENCHANG.
WE'RE GIVING IT OUR ALL!
On December 15, 1966, *Prince* bimonthly magazine officially launched.
Thanks to Khun-lim's promotional strategy, the first issue was a great hit. Stores sold out as readers fought over copies.
I'D LIKE A COPY OF *PRINCE.*
ME TOO!
TEN DOLLARS.
HELLO, *PRINCE* MAGAZINE? THIS IS CHONGCHUNG BOOKSTORE. WE'RE ALMOST SOLD OUT AND NEED THIRTY COPIES . . .

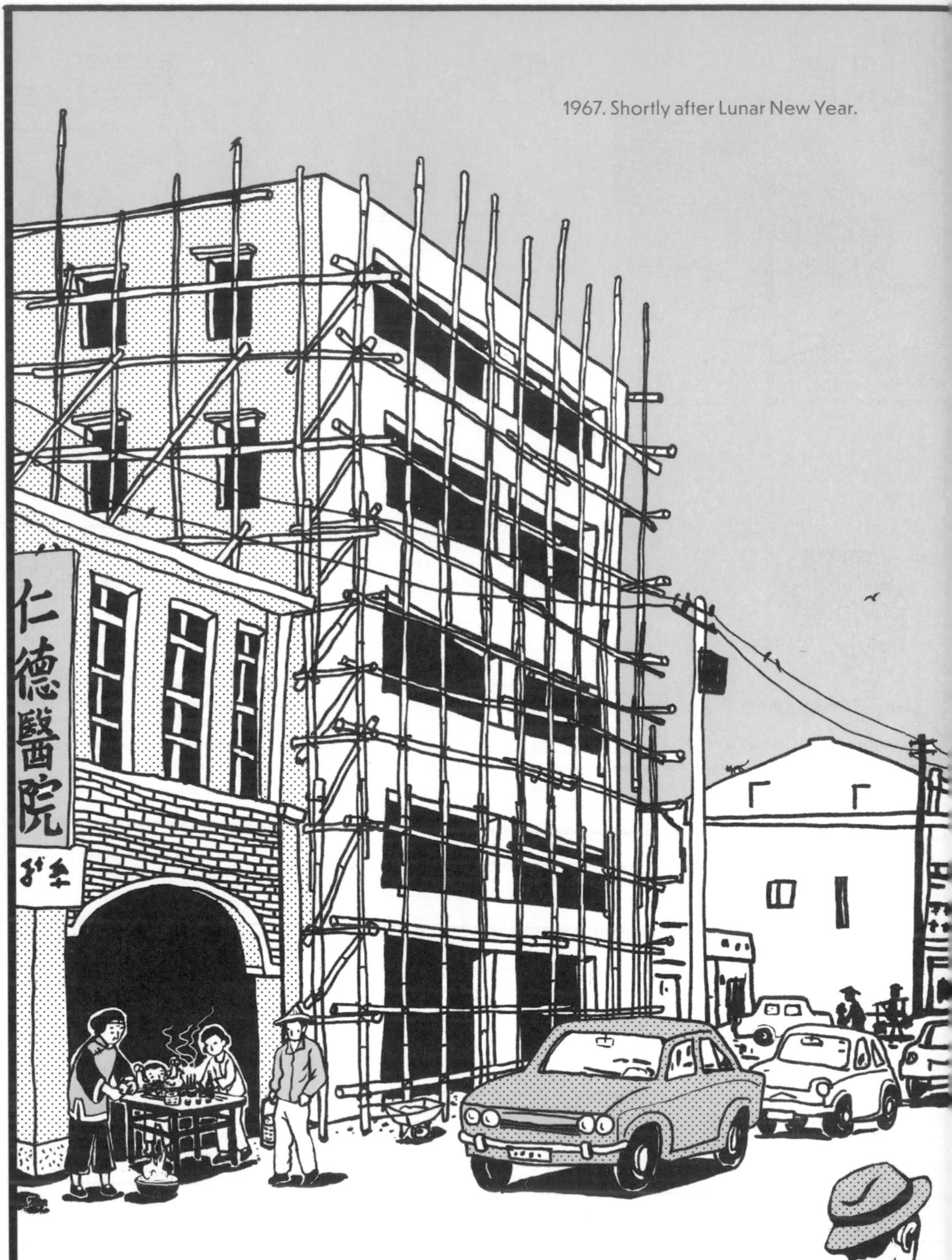
1967. Shortly after Lunar New Year.
仁德醫院

Prince Press Conference Room

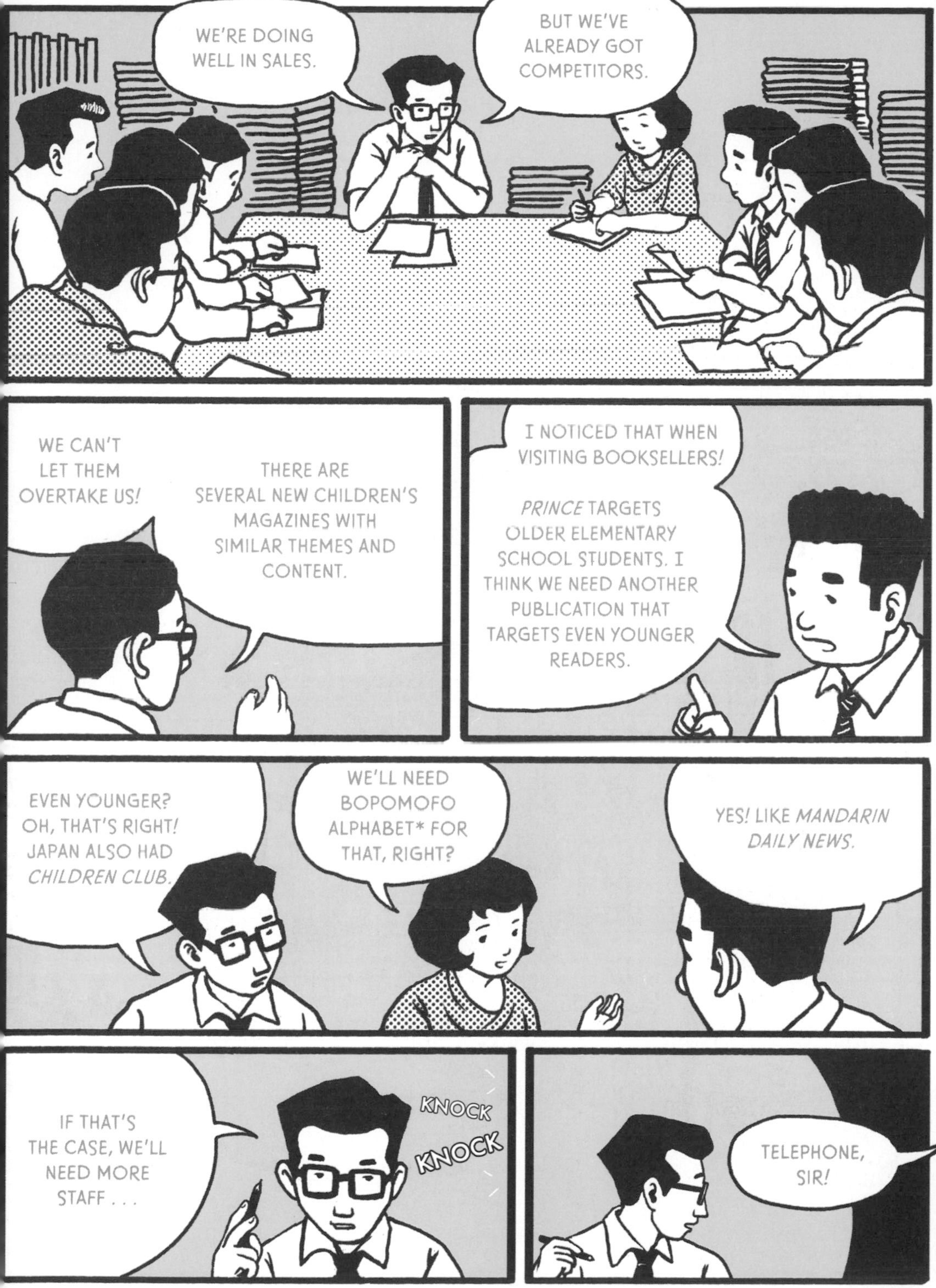
WE'RE DOING WELL IN SALES.
BUT WE'VE ALREADY GOT COMPETITORS.
WE CAN'T LET THEM OVERTAKE US!
THERE ARE SEVERAL NEW CHILDREN'S MAGAZINES WITH SIMILAR THEMES AND CONTENT.
I NOTICED THAT WHEN VISITING BOOKSELLERS!
PRINCE TARGETS OLDER ELEMENTARY SCHOOL STUDENTS. I THINK WE NEED ANOTHER PUBLICATION THAT TARGETS EVEN YOUNGER READERS.
EVEN YOUNGER? OH, THAT'S RIGHT! JAPAN ALSO HAD *CHILDREN CLUB*.
WE'LL NEED BOPOMOFO ALPHABET* FOR THAT, RIGHT?
YES! LIKE *MANDARIN DAILY NEWS*.
IF THAT'S THE CASE, WE'LL NEED MORE STAFF . . .
KNOCK
KNOCK
TELEPHONE, SIR!

*Bopomofo is the alphabet system used to teach children the pronunciation of Mandarin characters in Taiwan, which does not use the romanized Pinyin system for early education.

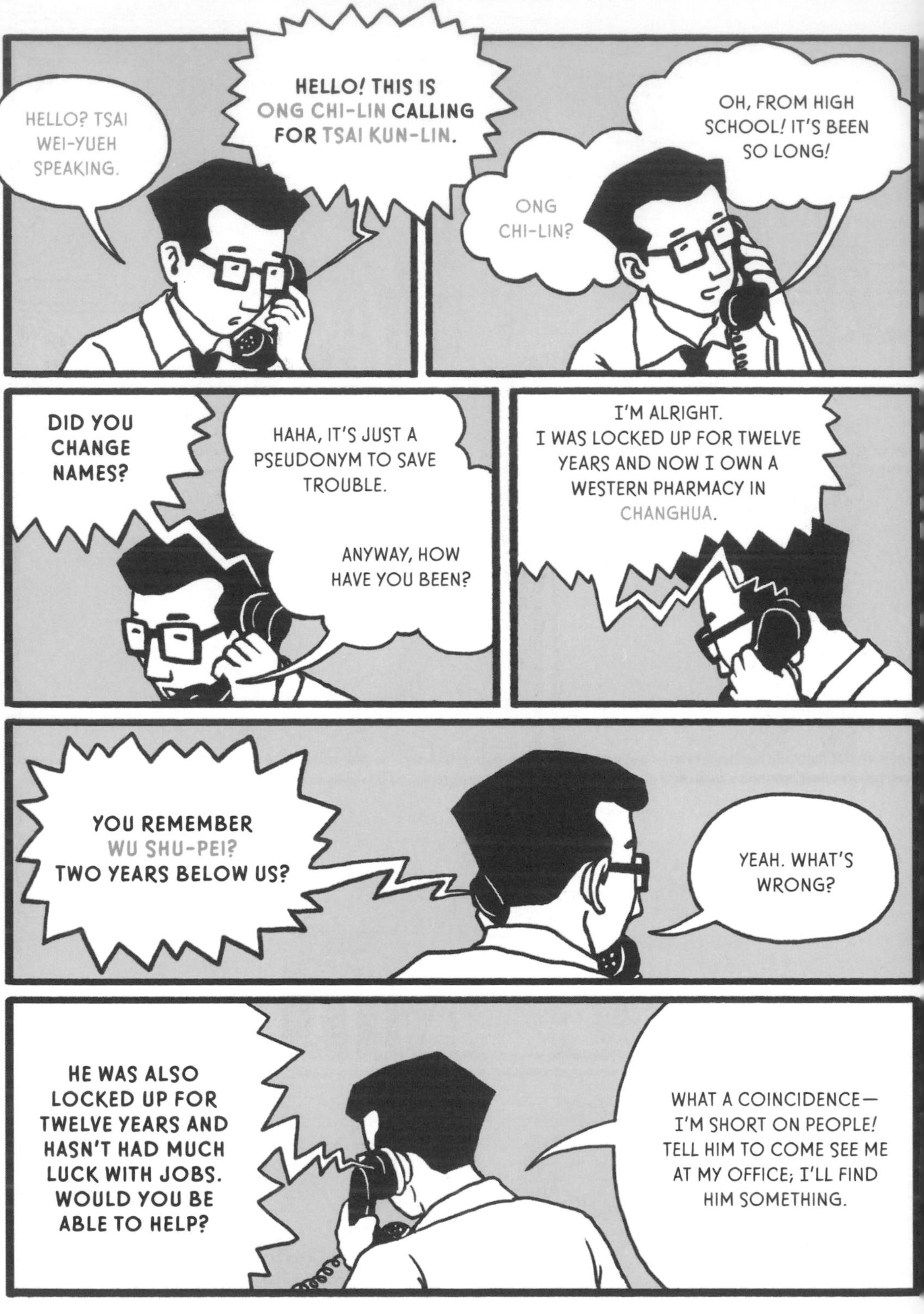
HELLO? TSAI WEI-YUEH SPEAKING.
HELLO! THIS IS ONG CHI-LIN CALLING FOR TSAI KUN-LIN.
ONG CHI-LIN?
OH, FROM HIGH SCHOOL! IT'S BEEN SO LONG!
DID YOU CHANGE NAMES?
HAHA, IT'S JUST A PSEUDONYM TO SAVE TROUBLE.
ANYWAY, HOW HAVE YOU BEEN?
I'M ALRIGHT. I WAS LOCKED UP FOR TWELVE YEARS AND NOW I OWN A WESTERN PHARMACY IN CHANGHUA.
YOU REMEMBER WU SHU-PEI? TWO YEARS BELOW US?
YEAH. WHAT'S WRONG?
HE WAS ALSO LOCKED UP FOR TWELVE YEARS AND HASN'T HAD MUCH LUCK WITH JOBS. WOULD YOU BE ABLE TO HELP?
WHAT A COINCIDENCE— I'M SHORT ON PEOPLE! TELL HIM TO COME SEE ME AT MY OFFICE; I'LL FIND HIM SOMETHING.

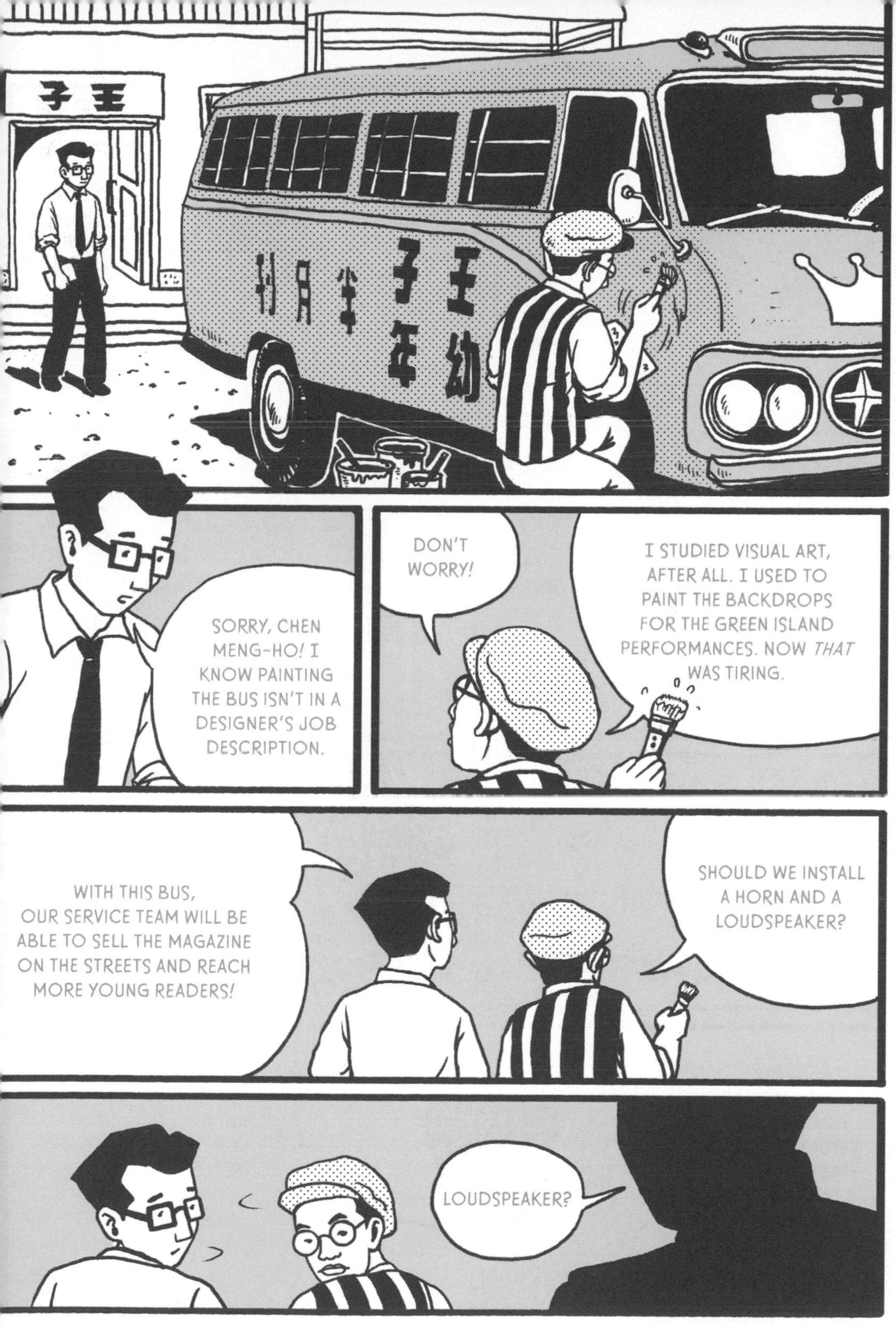
SORRY, CHEN MENG-HO! I KNOW PAINTING THE BUS ISN'T IN A DESIGNER'S JOB DESCRIPTION.
DON'T WORRY!
I STUDIED VISUAL ART, AFTER ALL. I USED TO PAINT THE BACKDROPS FOR THE GREEN ISLAND PERFORMANCES. NOW *THAT* WAS TIRING.
WITH THIS BUS, OUR SERVICE TEAM WILL BE ABLE TO SELL THE MAGAZINE ON THE STREETS AND REACH MORE YOUNG READERS!
SHOULD WE INSTALL A HORN AND A LOUDSPEAKER?
LOUDSPEAKER?

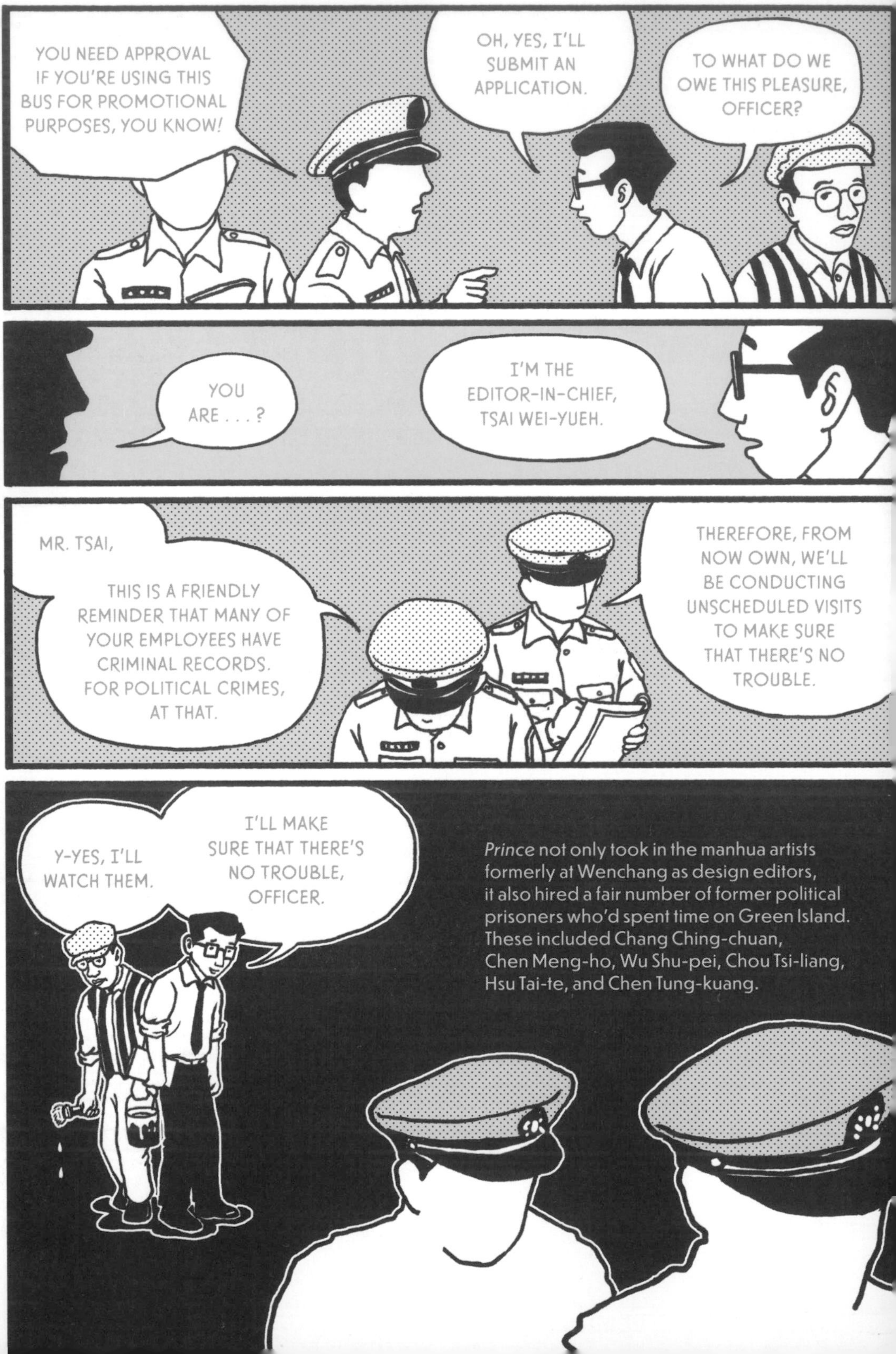
YOU NEED APPROVAL IF YOU'RE USING THIS BUS FOR PROMOTIONAL PURPOSES, YOU KNOW!
OH, YES, I'LL SUBMIT AN APPLICATION.
TO WHAT DO WE OWE THIS PLEASURE, OFFICER?
YOU ARE . . . ?
I'M THE EDITOR-IN-CHIEF, TSAI WEI-YUEH.
MR. TSAI,
THIS IS A FRIENDLY REMINDER THAT MANY OF YOUR EMPLOYEES HAVE CRIMINAL RECORDS. FOR POLITICAL CRIMES, AT THAT.
THEREFORE, FROM NOW OWN, WE'LL BE CONDUCTING UNSCHEDULED VISITS TO MAKE SURE THAT THERE'S NO TROUBLE.
Y-YES, I'LL WATCH THEM.
I'LL MAKE SURE THAT THERE'S NO TROUBLE, OFFICER.
Prince not only took in the manhua artists formerly at Wenchang as design editors, it also hired a fair number of former political prisoners who'd spent time on Green Island. These included Chang Ching-chuan, Chen Meng-ho, Wu Shu-pei, Chou Tsi-liang, Hsu Tai-te, and Chen Tung-kuang.

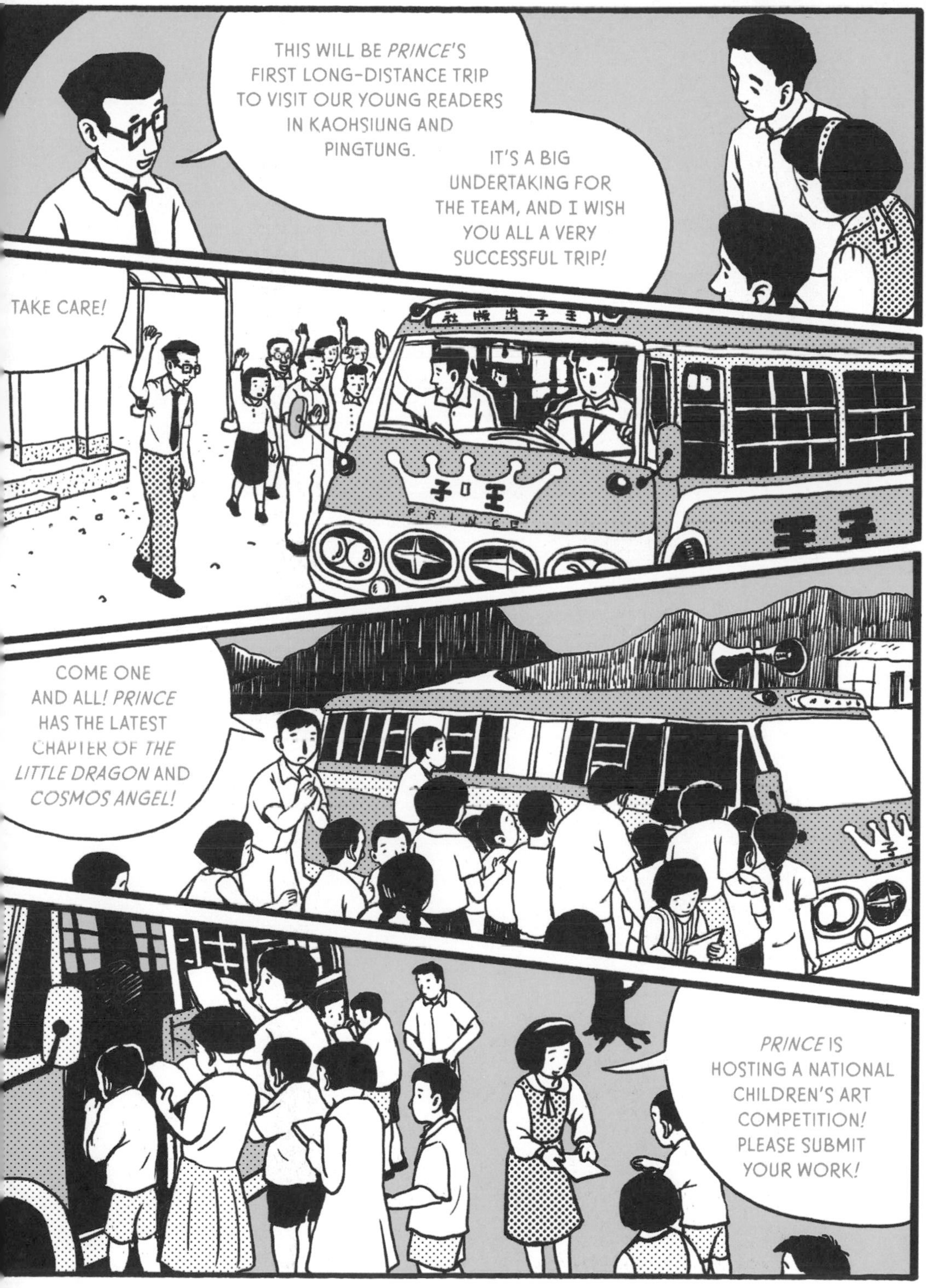
THIS WILL BE *PRINCE*'S FIRST LONG-DISTANCE TRIP TO VISIT OUR YOUNG READERS IN KAOHSIUNG AND PINGTUNG.
IT'S A BIG UNDERTAKING FOR THE TEAM, AND I WISH YOU ALL A VERY SUCCESSFUL TRIP!
TAKE CARE!
COME ONE AND ALL! *PRINCE* HAS THE LATEST CHAPTER OF *THE LITTLE DRAGON* AND *COSMOS ANGEL*!
PRINCE IS HOSTING A NATIONAL CHILDREN'S ART COMPETITION! PLEASE SUBMIT YOUR WORK!

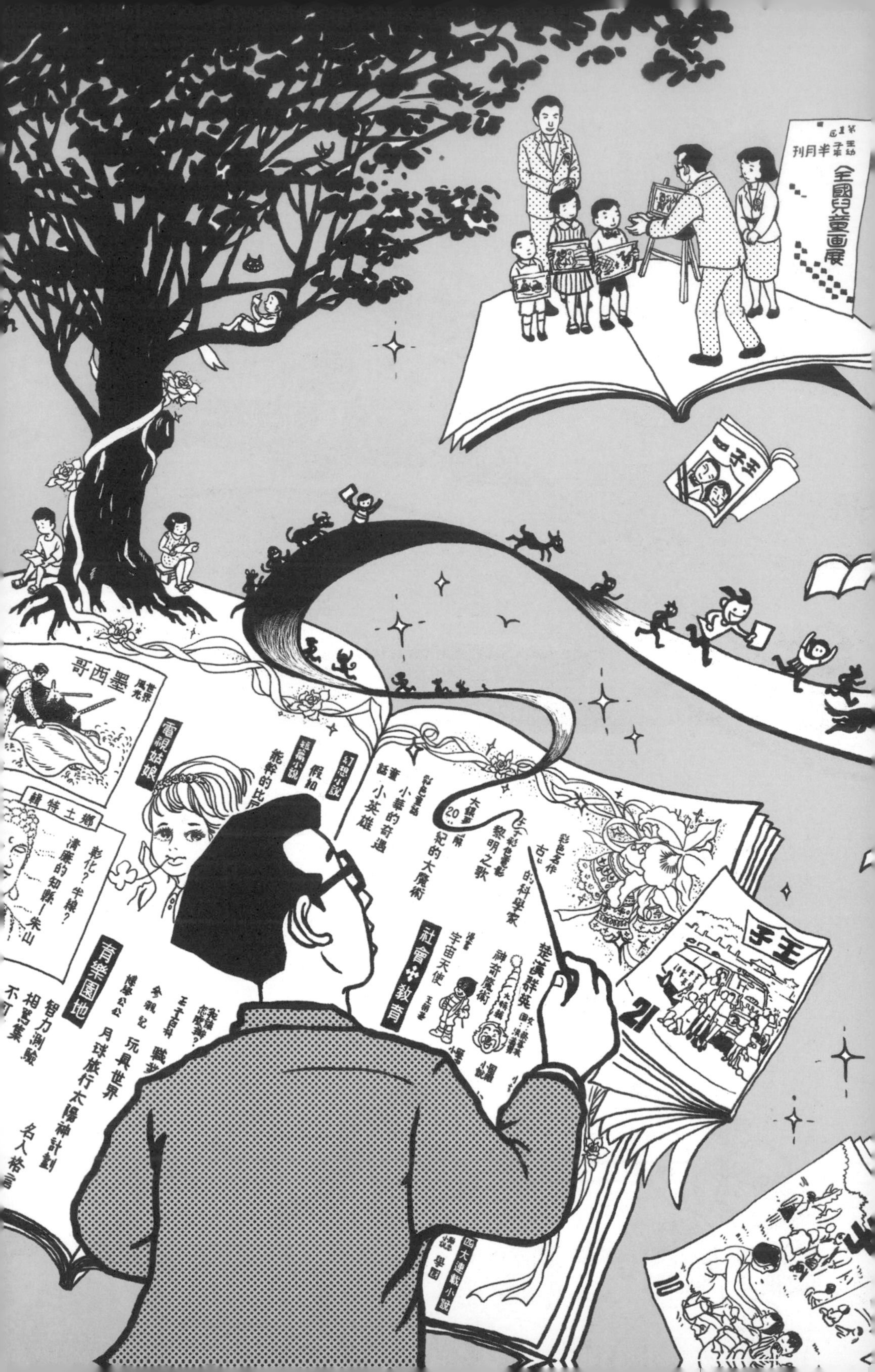

王子半月刊
全國兒童畫展
王子
墨西哥
世界風光
電視姑娘
鄉土特輯
彰化？半線？
清廉的知縣－朱山
音樂園地
智力測驗
玩具世界
月球旅行太陽神計劃
名人格言
幻想小說
長篇小說
假如
彩色童話
小華的奇遇
童話
小英雄
大銀幕
20世紀的大魔術
彩色名作
黎明之歌
的科學家
社會教育
宇宙天使
神奇魔術
楚漢群英
大連載小說
王子

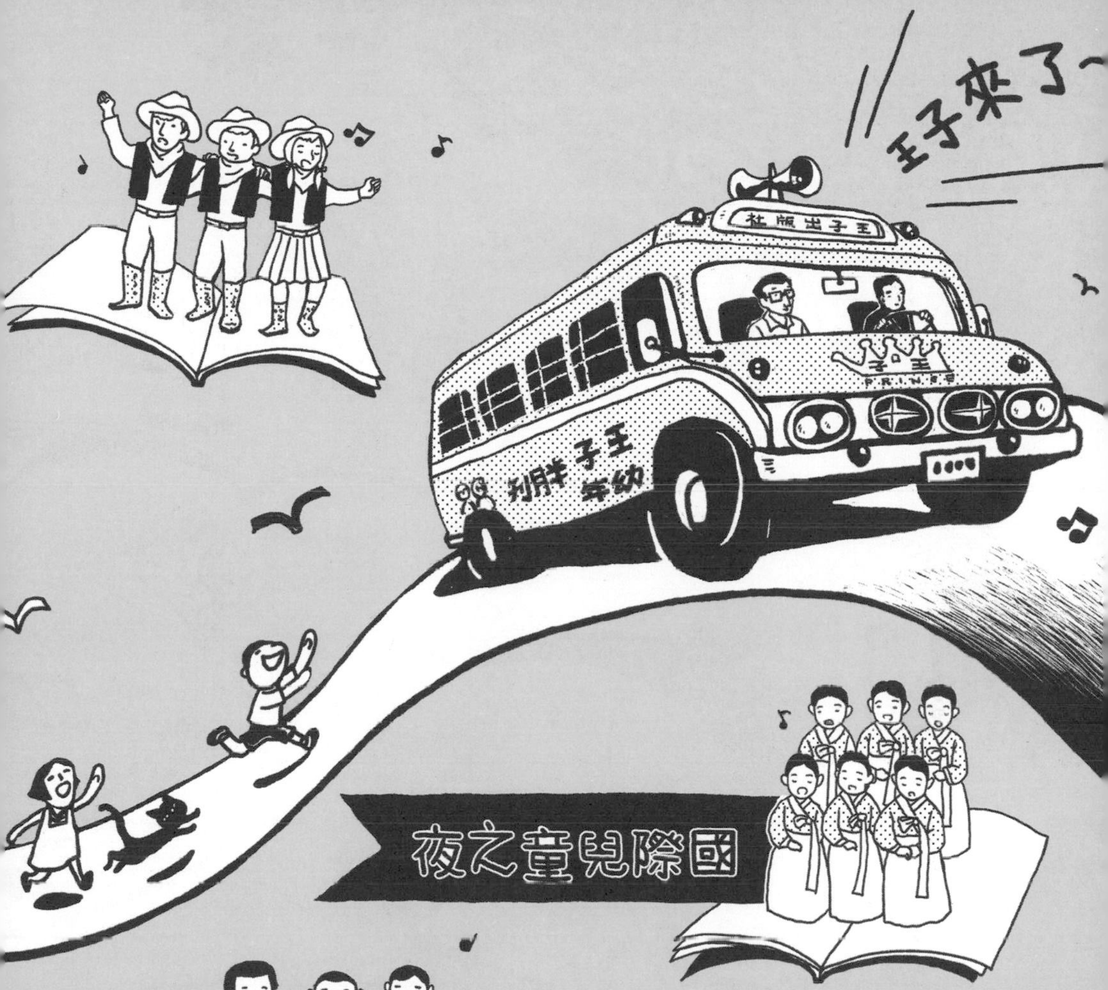
王子來了～
王子出版社
王子
PRINCE
幼年王子
半月刊
國際兒童之夜

International Children's Night

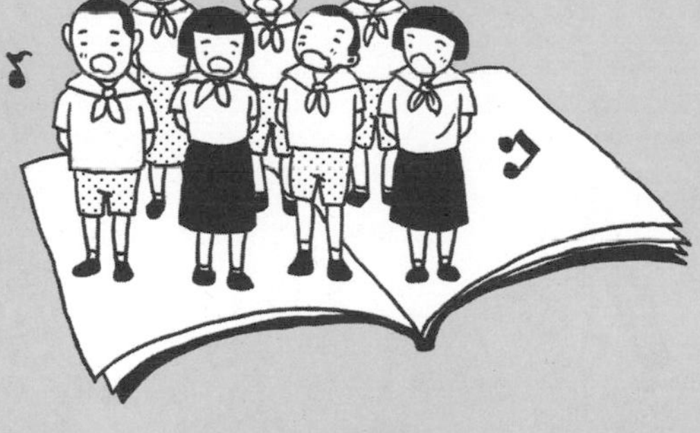

In the year after founding *Prince*, Khun-lim not only worked on curating high-quality content for the magazine but also hosted numerous events and contests for children. His staff grew to fifty-eight in number.

His hard work paid off. *Prince* was soon the undisputed leader in children's periodicals.

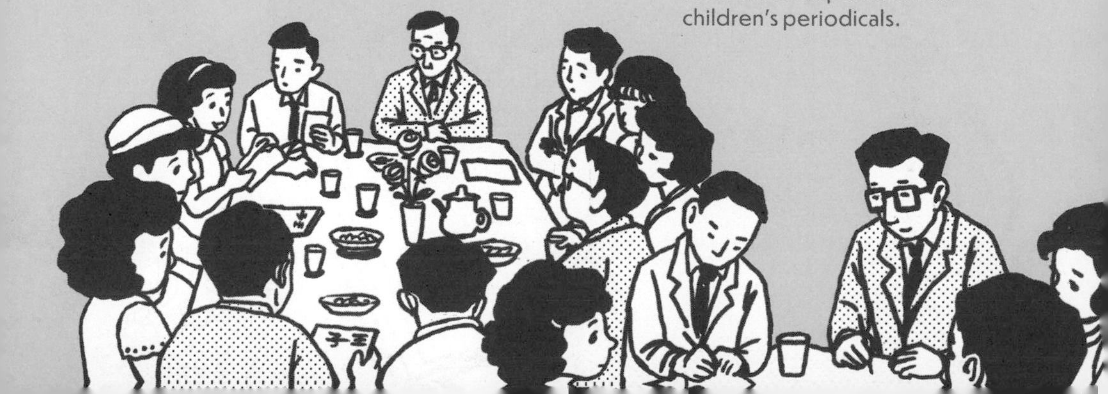
王子

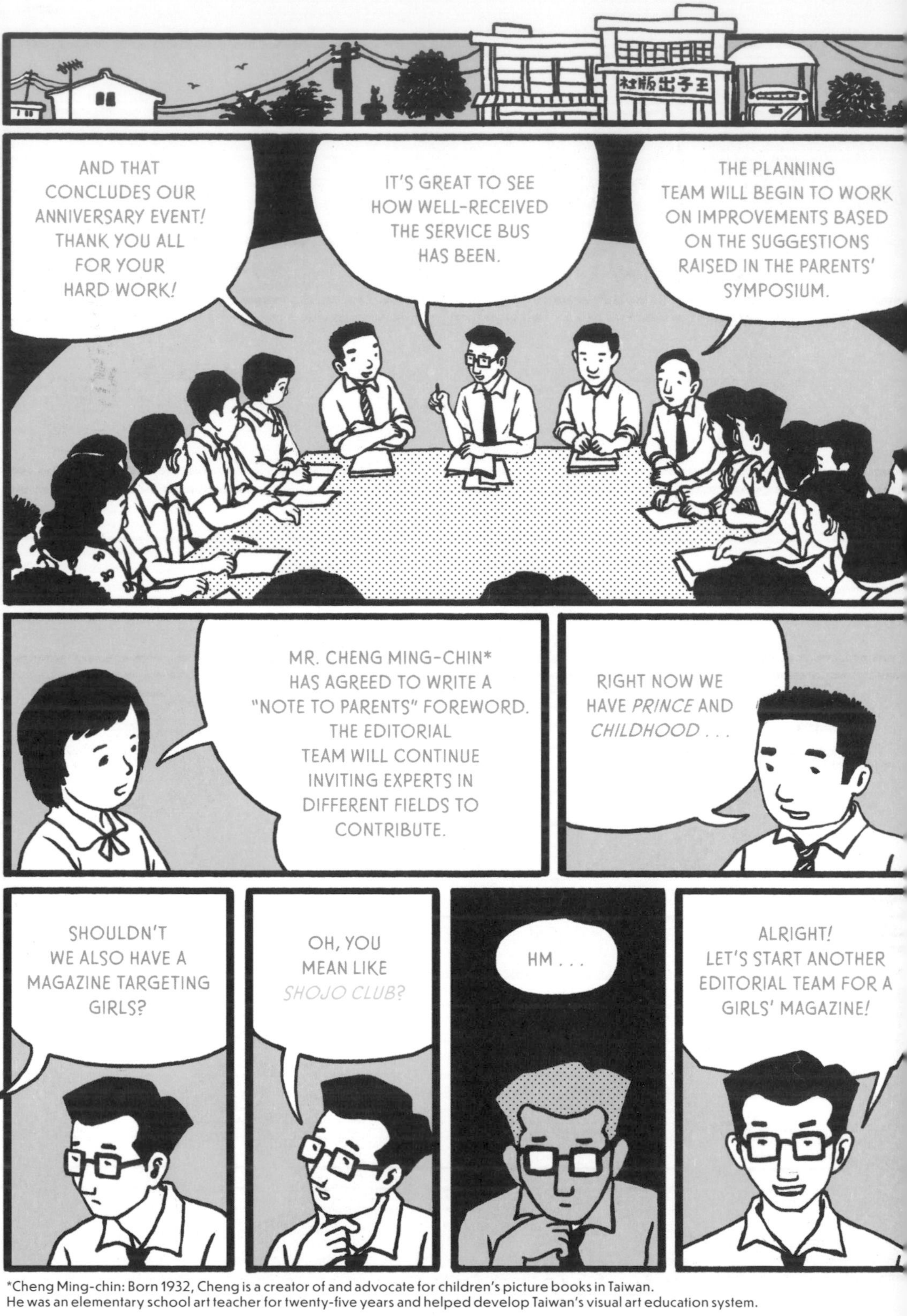
AND THAT CONCLUDES OUR ANNIVERSARY EVENT! THANK YOU ALL FOR YOUR HARD WORK!
IT'S GREAT TO SEE HOW WELL-RECEIVED THE SERVICE BUS HAS BEEN.
THE PLANNING TEAM WILL BEGIN TO WORK ON IMPROVEMENTS BASED ON THE SUGGESTIONS RAISED IN THE PARENTS' SYMPOSIUM.
MR. CHENG MING-CHIN* HAS AGREED TO WRITE A "NOTE TO PARENTS" FOREWORD. THE EDITORIAL TEAM WILL CONTINUE INVITING EXPERTS IN DIFFERENT FIELDS TO CONTRIBUTE.
RIGHT NOW WE HAVE *PRINCE* AND *CHILDHOOD* . . .
SHOULDN'T WE ALSO HAVE A MAGAZINE TARGETING GIRLS?
OH, YOU MEAN LIKE *SHOJO CLUB*?
HM . . .
ALRIGHT! LET'S START ANOTHER EDITORIAL TEAM FOR A GIRLS' MAGAZINE!

*Cheng Ming-chin: Born 1932, Cheng is a creator of and advocate for children's picture books in Taiwan. He was an elementary school art teacher for twenty-five years and helped develop Taiwan's visual art education system.

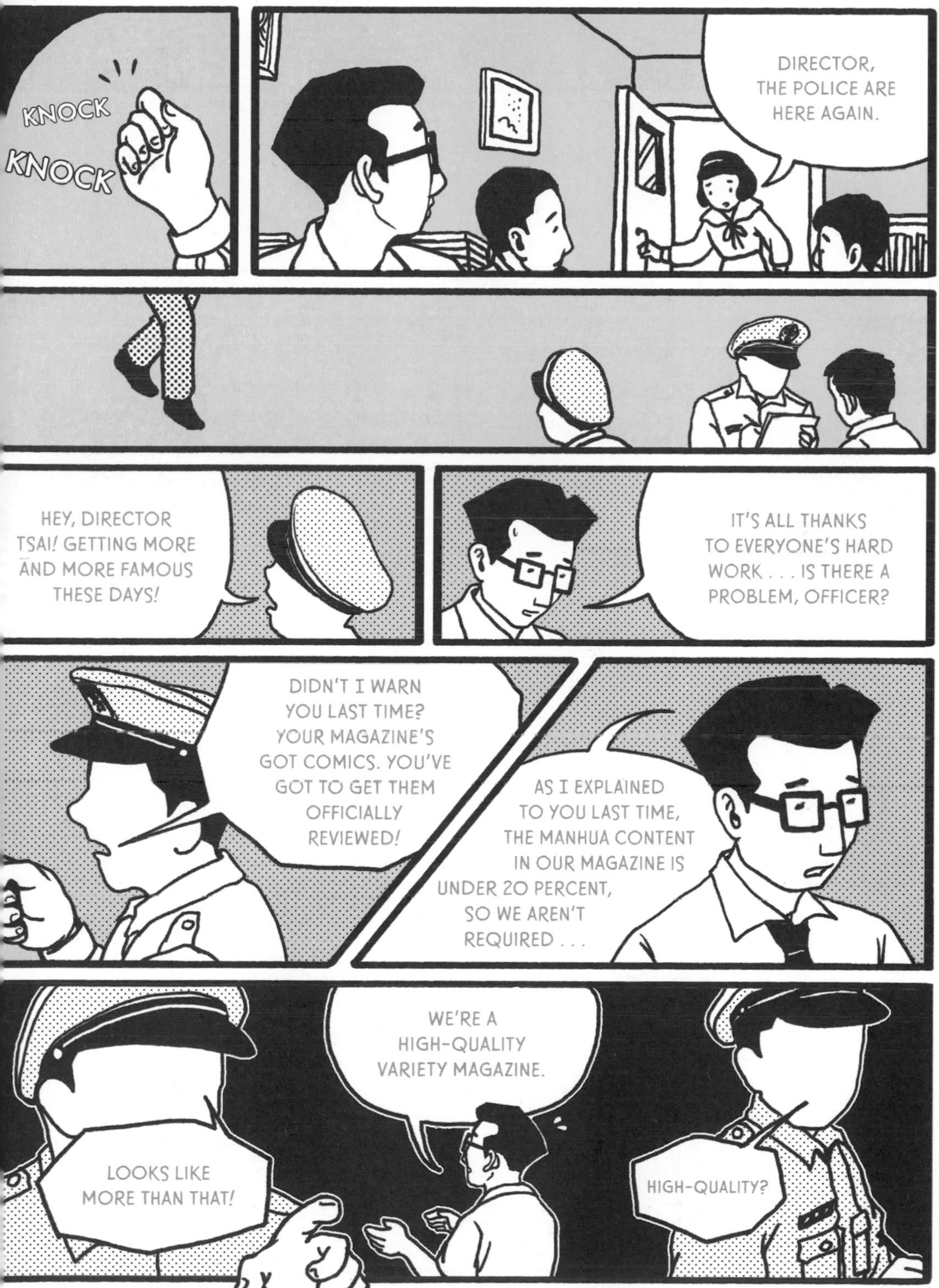
KNOCK
KNOCK
DIRECTOR, THE POLICE ARE HERE AGAIN.
HEY, DIRECTOR TSAI! GETTING MORE AND MORE FAMOUS THESE DAYS!
IT'S ALL THANKS TO EVERYONE'S HARD WORK . . . IS THERE A PROBLEM, OFFICER?
DIDN'T I WARN YOU LAST TIME? YOUR MAGAZINE'S GOT COMICS. YOU'VE GOT TO GET THEM OFFICIALLY REVIEWED!
AS I EXPLAINED TO YOU LAST TIME, THE MANHUA CONTENT IN OUR MAGAZINE IS UNDER 20 PERCENT, SO WE AREN'T REQUIRED . . .
WE'RE A HIGH-QUALITY VARIETY MAGAZINE.
LOOKS LIKE MORE THAN THAT!
HIGH-QUALITY?

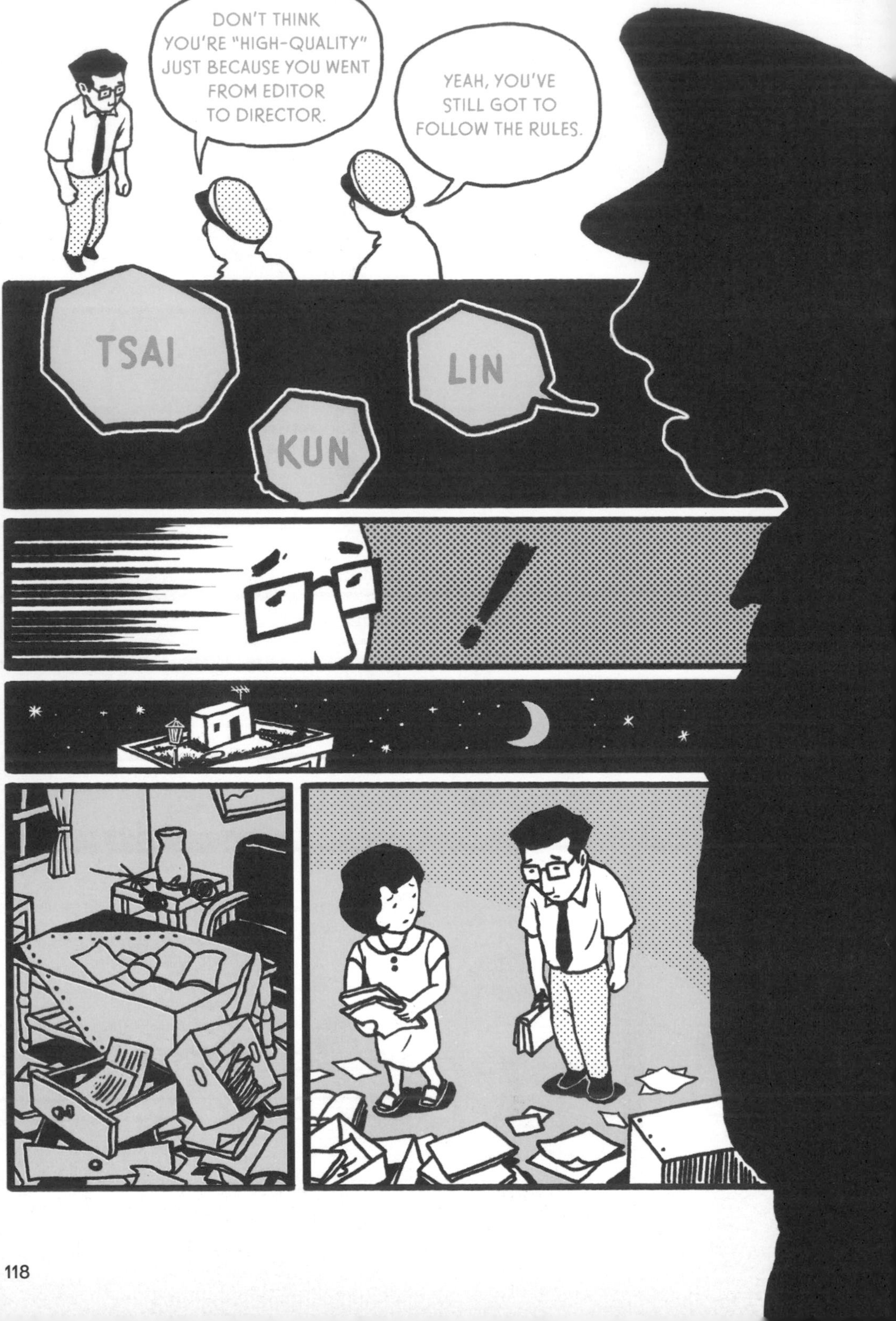

DON'T THINK YOU'RE "HIGH-QUALITY" JUST BECAUSE YOU WENT FROM EDITOR TO DIRECTOR.
YEAH, YOU'VE STILL GOT TO FOLLOW THE RULES.
TSAI
KUN
LIN
!

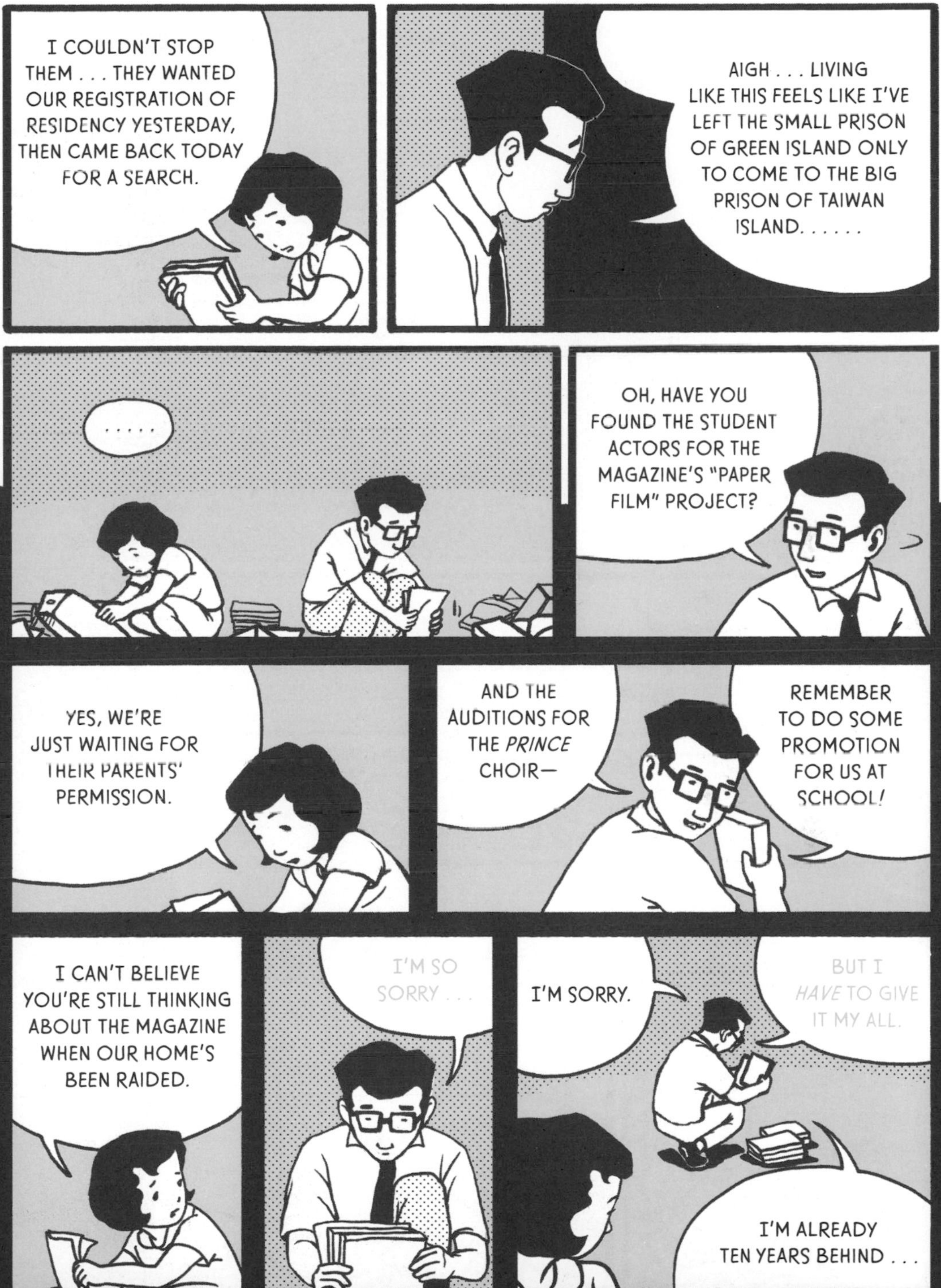
I COULDN'T STOP THEM . . . THEY WANTED OUR REGISTRATION OF RESIDENCY YESTERDAY, THEN CAME BACK TODAY FOR A SEARCH.
AIGH . . . LIVING LIKE THIS FEELS LIKE I'VE LEFT THE SMALL PRISON OF GREEN ISLAND ONLY TO COME TO THE BIG PRISON OF TAIWAN ISLAND. . . . . .
. . . . . .
OH, HAVE YOU FOUND THE STUDENT ACTORS FOR THE MAGAZINE'S "PAPER FILM" PROJECT?
YES, WE'RE JUST WAITING FOR THEIR PARENTS' PERMISSION.
AND THE AUDITIONS FOR THE *PRINCE* CHOIR—
REMEMBER TO DO SOME PROMOTION FOR US AT SCHOOL!
I CAN'T BELIEVE YOU'RE STILL THINKING ABOUT THE MAGAZINE WHEN OUR HOME'S BEEN RAIDED.
I'M SO SORRY . . .
I'M SORRY.
BUT I *HAVE* TO GIVE IT MY ALL.
I'M ALREADY TEN YEARS BEHIND . . .

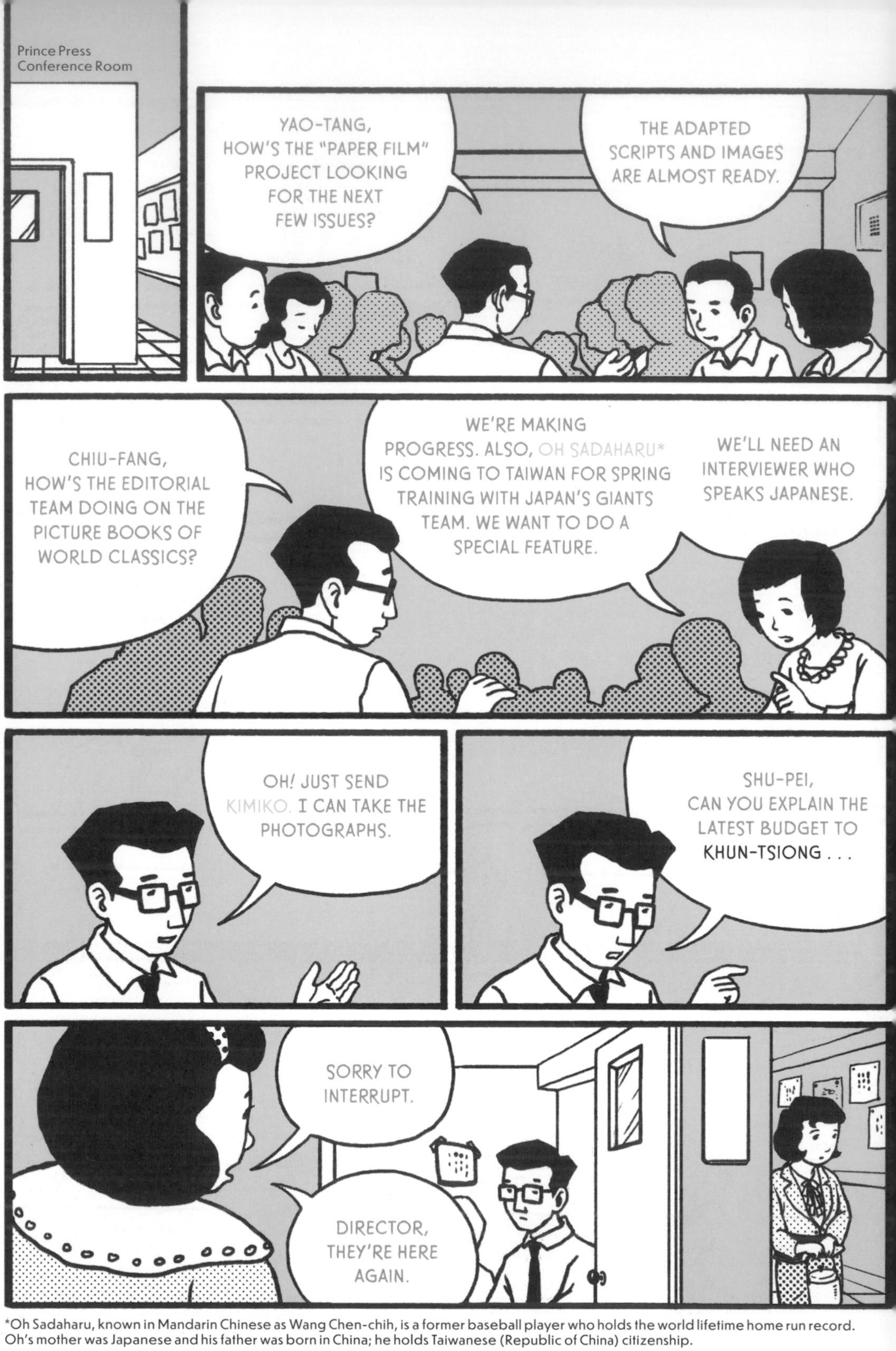
Prince Press
Conference Room
YAO-TANG, HOW'S THE "PAPER FILM" PROJECT LOOKING FOR THE NEXT FEW ISSUES?
THE ADAPTED SCRIPTS AND IMAGES ARE ALMOST READY.
CHIU-FANG, HOW'S THE EDITORIAL TEAM DOING ON THE PICTURE BOOKS OF WORLD CLASSICS?
WE'RE MAKING PROGRESS. ALSO, OH SADAHARU* IS COMING TO TAIWAN FOR SPRING TRAINING WITH JAPAN'S GIANTS TEAM. WE WANT TO DO A SPECIAL FEATURE.
WE'LL NEED AN INTERVIEWER WHO SPEAKS JAPANESE.
OH! JUST SEND KIMIKO. I CAN TAKE THE PHOTOGRAPHS.
SHU-PEI, CAN YOU EXPLAIN THE LATEST BUDGET TO KHUN-TSIONG . . .
SORRY TO INTERRUPT.
DIRECTOR, THEY'RE HERE AGAIN.

*Oh Sadaharu, known in Mandarin Chinese as Wang Chen-chih, is a former baseball player who holds the world lifetime home run record. Oh's mother was Japanese and his father was born in China; he holds Taiwanese (Republic of China) citizenship.

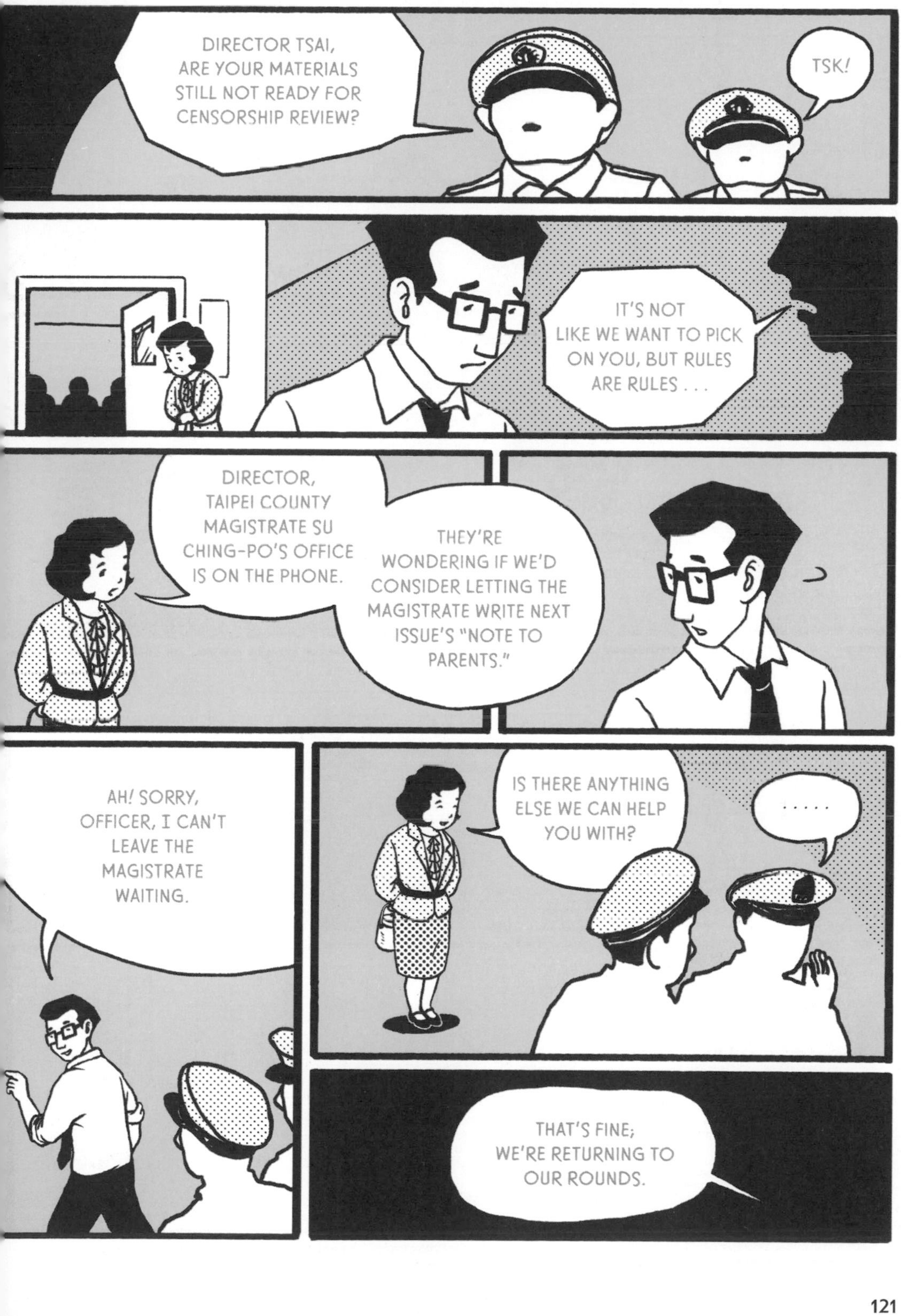
DIRECTOR TSAI, ARE YOUR MATERIALS STILL NOT READY FOR CENSORSHIP REVIEW?
TSK!
IT'S NOT LIKE WE WANT TO PICK ON YOU, BUT RULES ARE RULES . . .
DIRECTOR, TAIPEI COUNTY MAGISTRATE SU CHING-PO'S OFFICE IS ON THE PHONE.
THEY'RE WONDERING IF WE'D CONSIDER LETTING THE MAGISTRATE WRITE NEXT ISSUE'S "NOTE TO PARENTS."
AH! SORRY, OFFICER, I CAN'T LEAVE THE MAGISTRATE WAITING.
IS THERE ANYTHING ELSE WE CAN HELP YOU WITH?
. . . . .
THAT'S FINE; WE'RE RETURNING TO OUR ROUNDS.

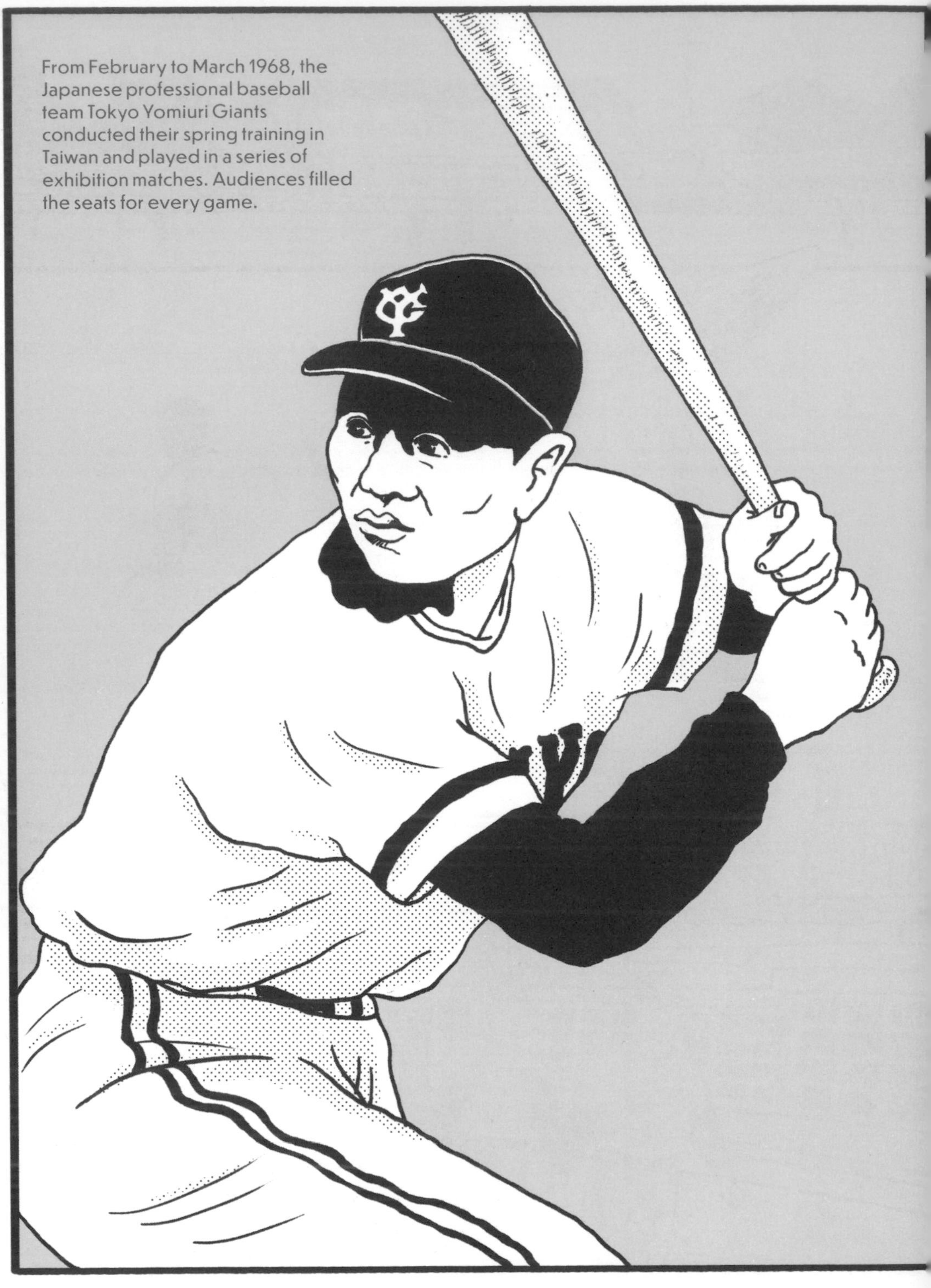
From February to March 1968, the Japanese professional baseball team Tokyo Yomiuri Giants conducted their spring training in Taiwan and played in a series of exhibition matches. Audiences filled the seats for every game.

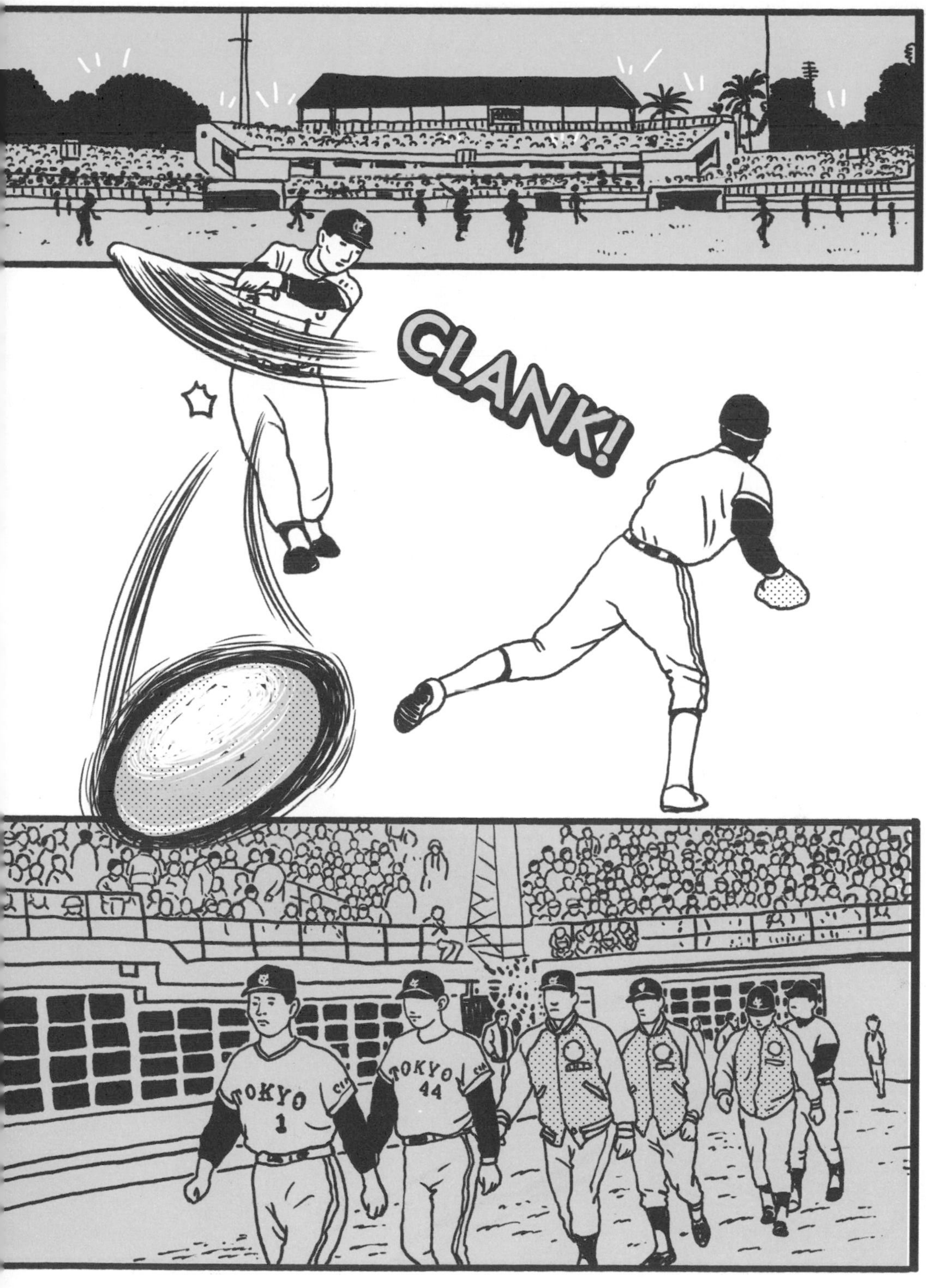
CLANK!
TOKYO
1
TOKYO
44

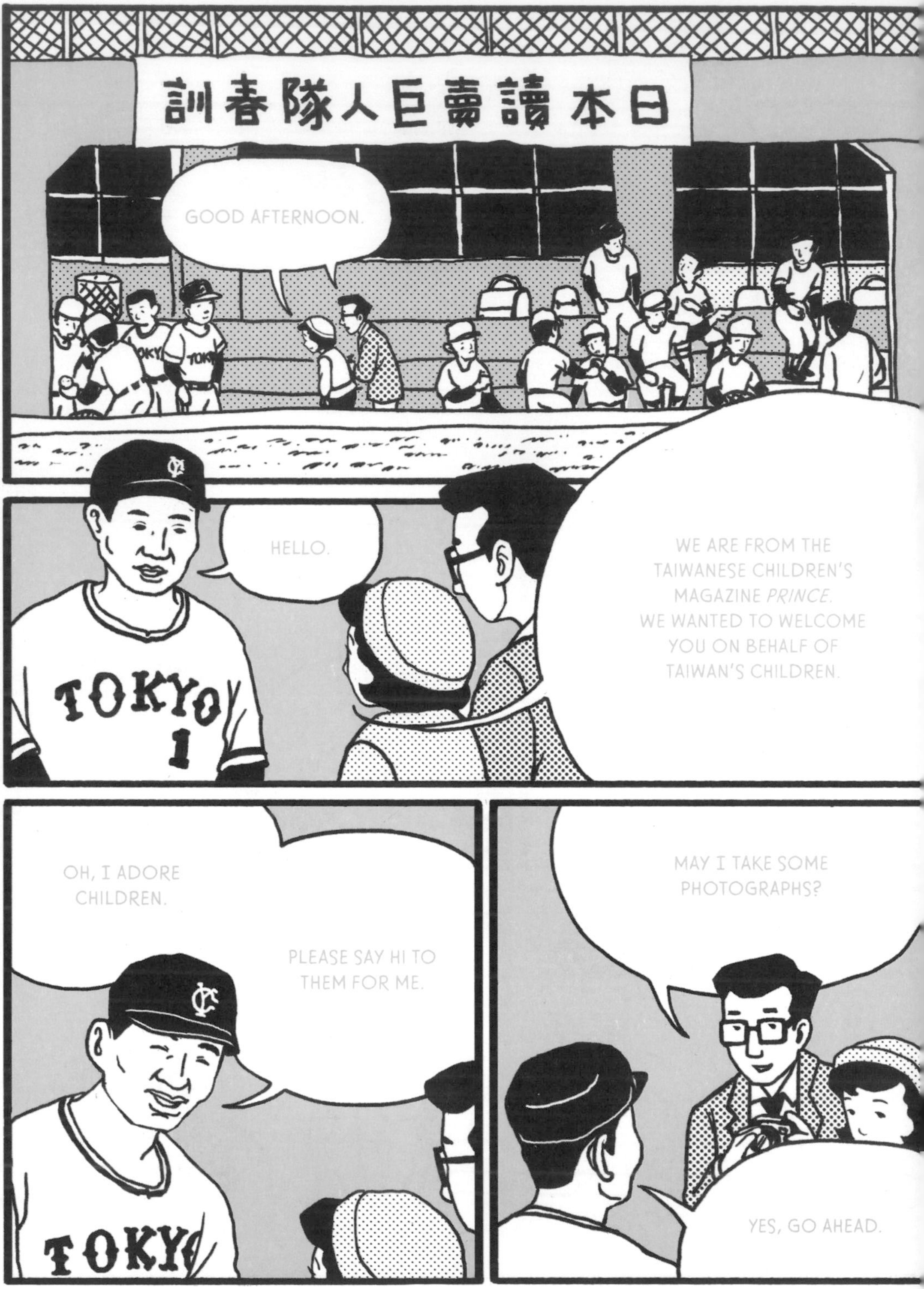
訓春隊人巨賣讀本日
GOOD AFTERNOON.
HELLO.
WE ARE FROM THE TAIWANESE CHILDREN'S MAGAZINE *PRINCE*. WE WANTED TO WELCOME YOU ON BEHALF OF TAIWAN'S CHILDREN.
OH, I ADORE CHILDREN.
PLEASE SAY HI TO THEM FOR ME.
MAY I TAKE SOME PHOTOGRAPHS?
YES, GO AHEAD.

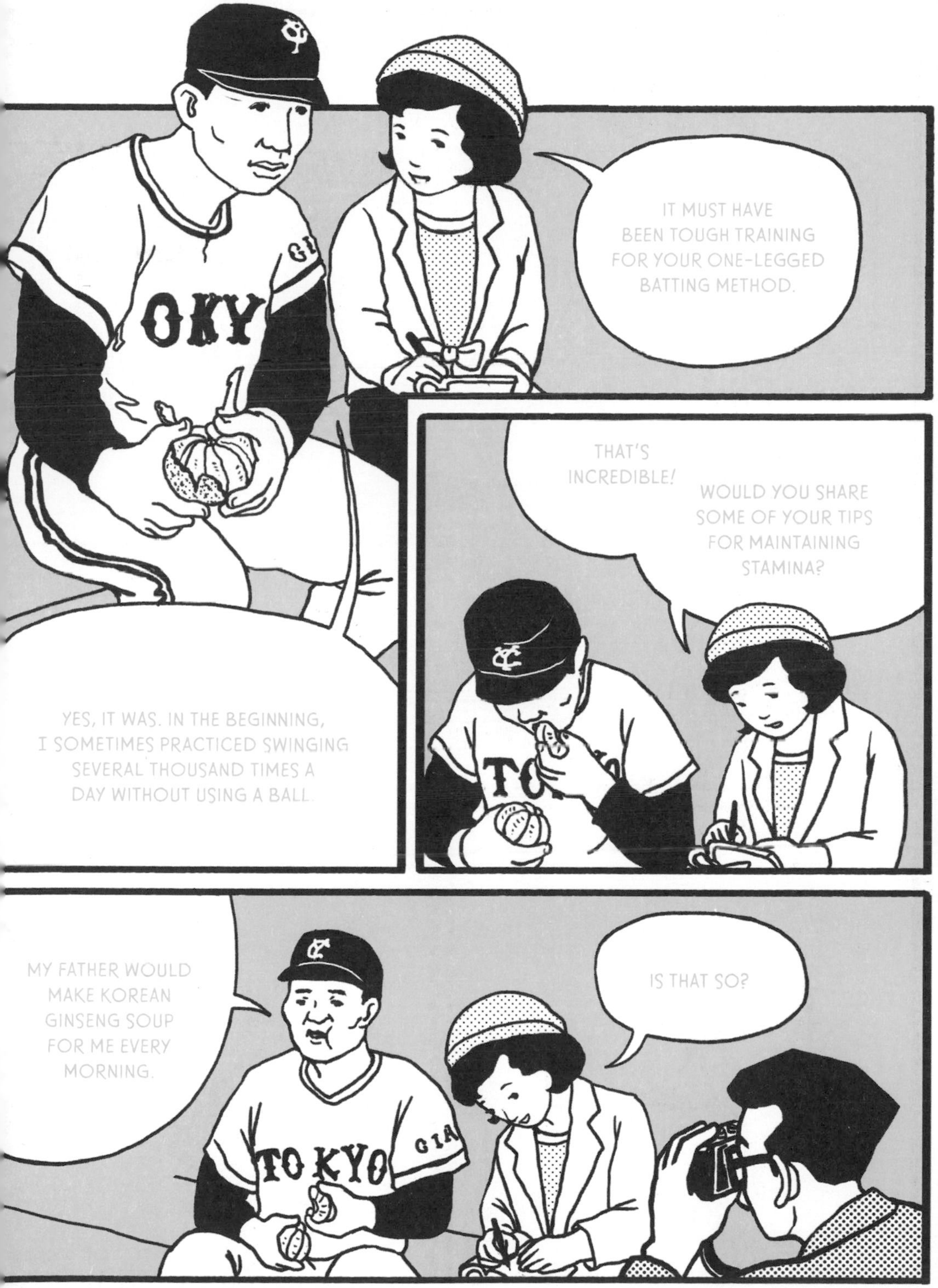
IT MUST HAVE BEEN TOUGH TRAINING FOR YOUR ONE-LEGGED BATTING METHOD.
YES, IT WAS. IN THE BEGINNING, I SOMETIMES PRACTICED SWINGING SEVERAL THOUSAND TIMES A DAY WITHOUT USING A BALL.
THAT'S INCREDIBLE!
WOULD YOU SHARE SOME OF YOUR TIPS FOR MAINTAINING STAMINA?
MY FATHER WOULD MAKE KOREAN GINSENG SOUP FOR ME EVERY MORNING.
IS THAT SO?

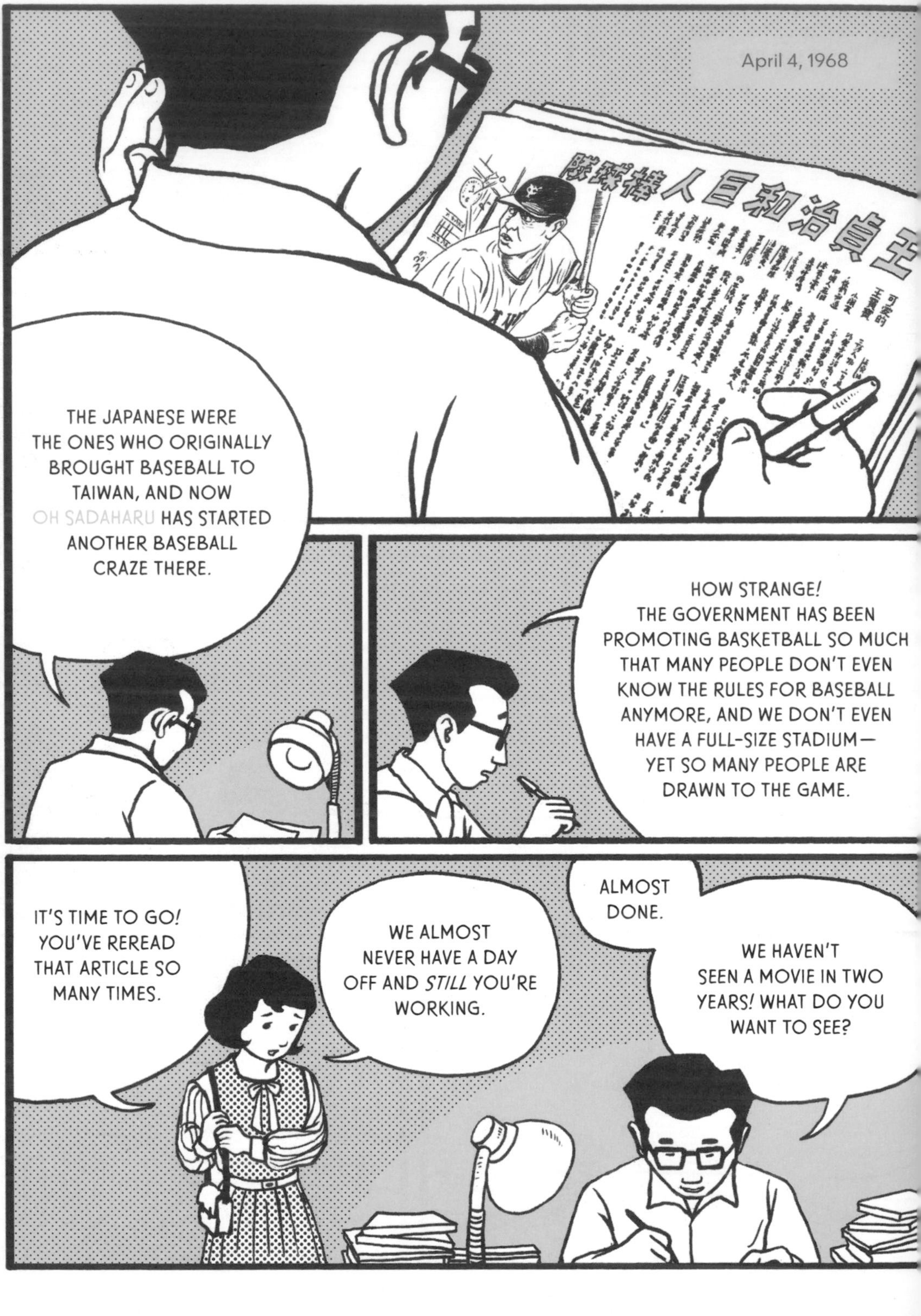
April 4, 1968
王貞治和巨人棒球隊
THE JAPANESE WERE THE ONES WHO ORIGINALLY BROUGHT BASEBALL TO TAIWAN, AND NOW OH SADAHARU HAS STARTED ANOTHER BASEBALL CRAZE THERE.
HOW STRANGE! THE GOVERNMENT HAS BEEN PROMOTING BASKETBALL SO MUCH THAT MANY PEOPLE DON'T EVEN KNOW THE RULES FOR BASEBALL ANYMORE, AND WE DON'T EVEN HAVE A FULL-SIZE STADIUM— YET SO MANY PEOPLE ARE DRAWN TO THE GAME.
IT'S TIME TO GO! YOU'VE REREAD THAT ARTICLE SO MANY TIMES.
WE ALMOST NEVER HAVE A DAY OFF AND *STILL* YOU'RE WORKING.
ALMOST DONE.
WE HAVEN'T SEEN A MOVIE IN TWO YEARS! WHAT DO YOU WANT TO SEE?

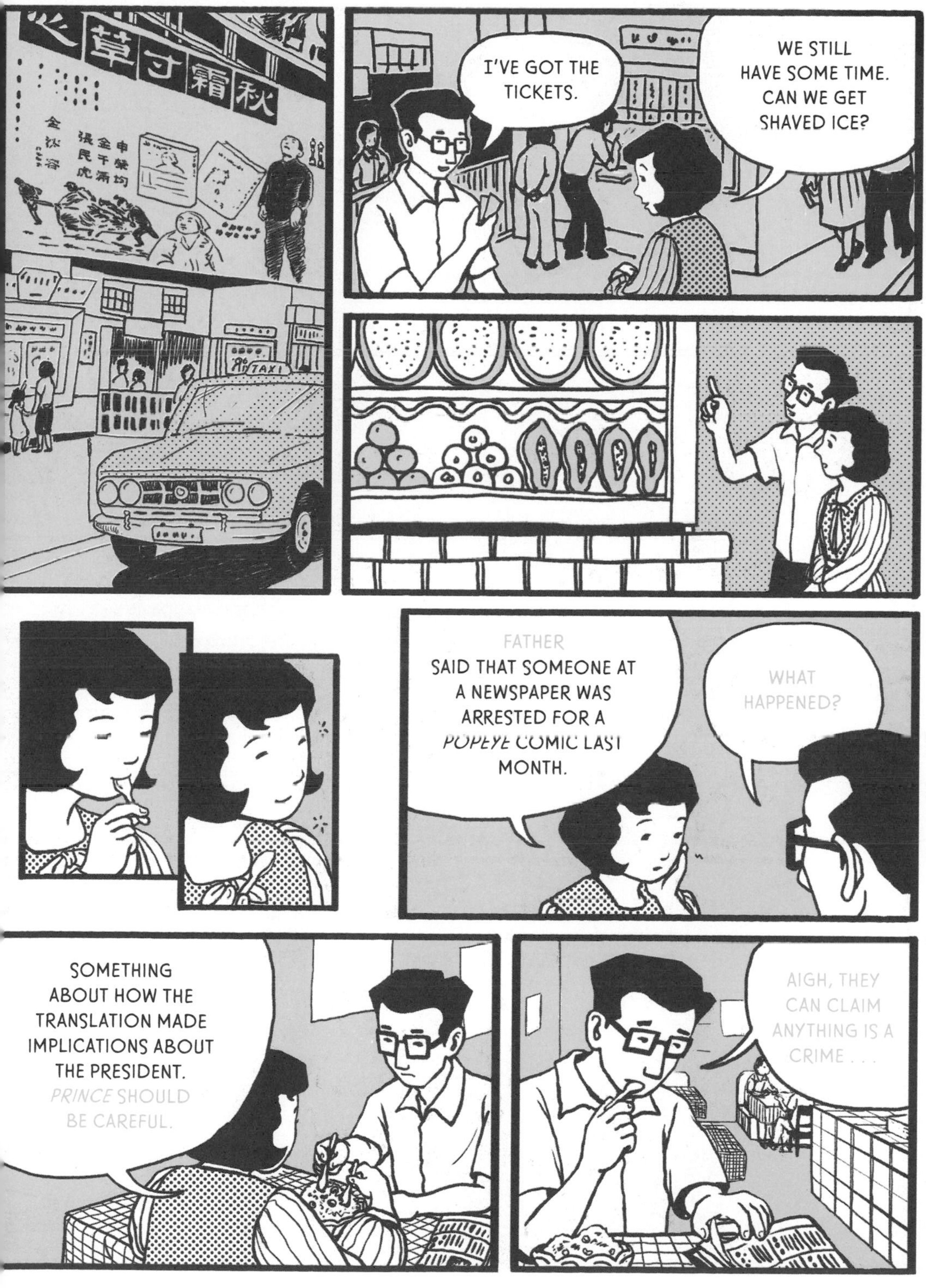
TAXI
I'VE GOT THE TICKETS.
WE STILL HAVE SOME TIME. CAN WE GET SHAVED ICE?
FATHER SAID THAT SOMEONE AT A NEWSPAPER WAS ARRESTED FOR A *POPEYE* COMIC LAST MONTH.
WHAT HAPPENED?
SOMETHING ABOUT HOW THE TRANSLATION MADE IMPLICATIONS ABOUT THE PRESIDENT. *PRINCE* SHOULD BE CAREFUL.
AIGH, THEY CAN CLAIM ANYTHING IS A CRIME . . .

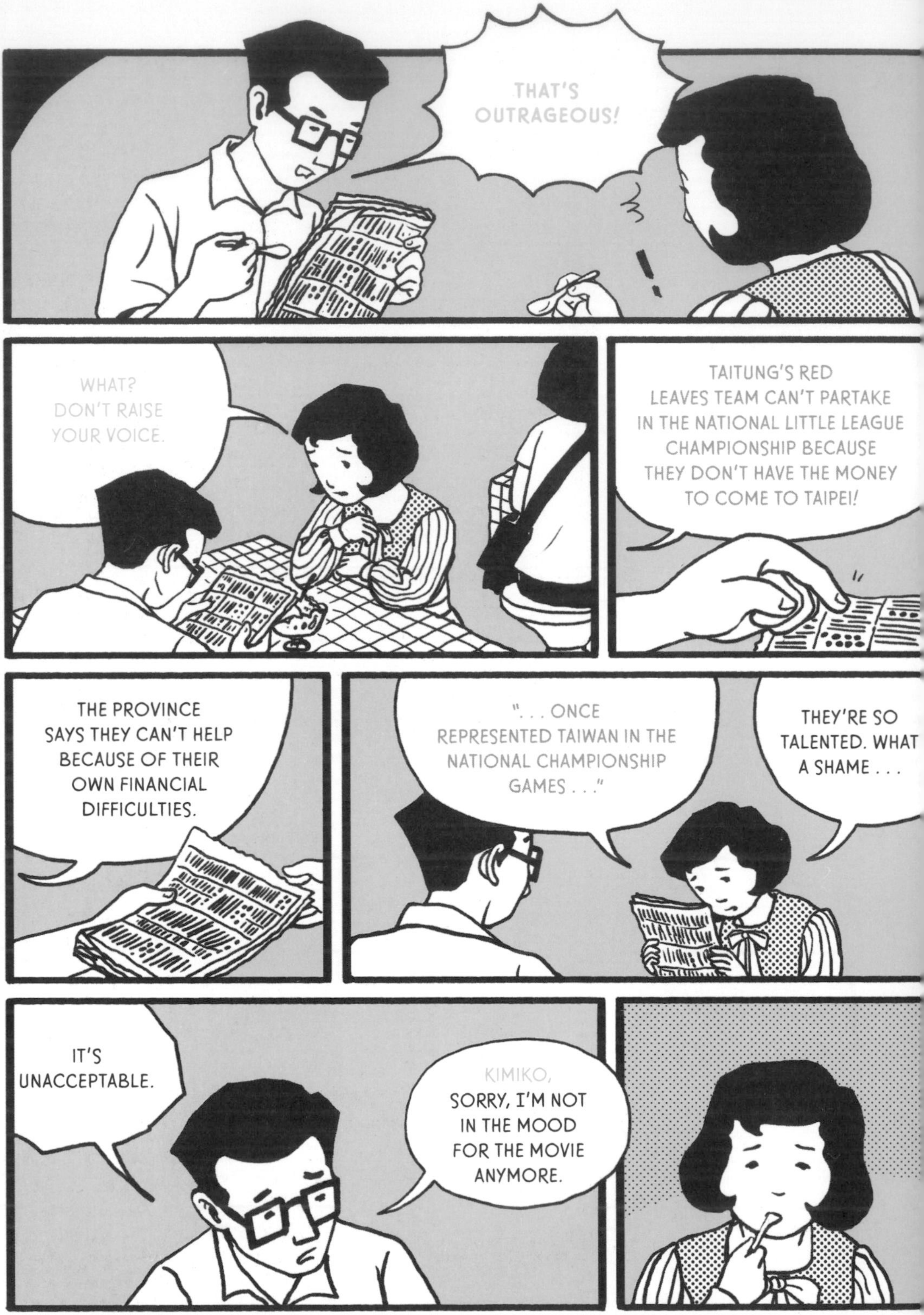
THAT'S OUTRAGEOUS!
WHAT? DON'T RAISE YOUR VOICE.
TAITUNG'S RED LEAVES TEAM CAN'T PARTAKE IN THE NATIONAL LITTLE LEAGUE CHAMPIONSHIP BECAUSE THEY DON'T HAVE THE MONEY TO COME TO TAIPEI!
THE PROVINCE SAYS THEY CAN'T HELP BECAUSE OF THEIR OWN FINANCIAL DIFFICULTIES.
". . . ONCE REPRESENTED TAIWAN IN THE NATIONAL CHAMPIONSHIP GAMES . . ."
THEY'RE SO TALENTED. WHAT A SHAME . . .
IT'S UNACCEPTABLE.
KIMIKO, SORRY, I'M NOT IN THE MOOD FOR THE MOVIE ANYMORE.

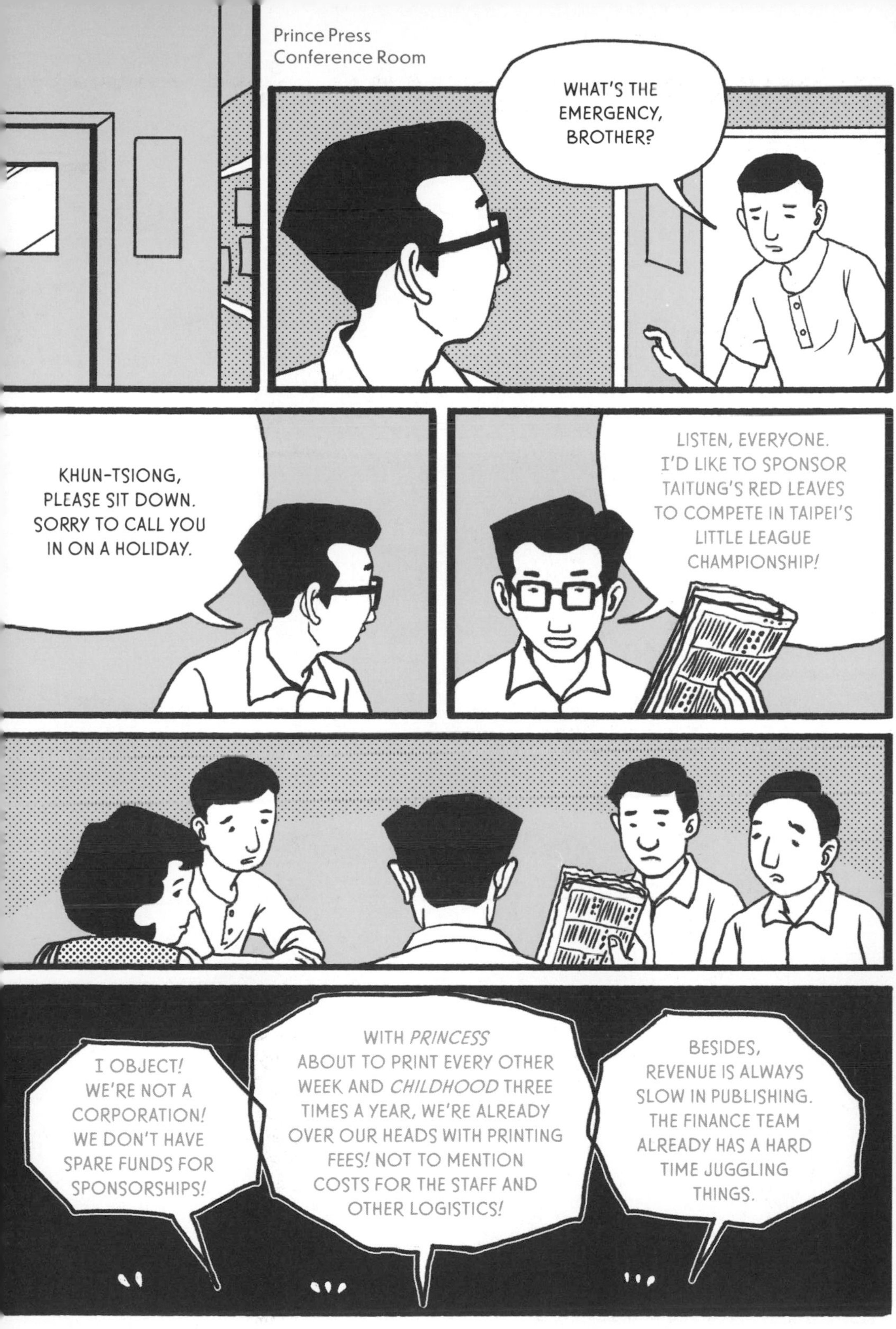
Prince Press
Conference Room
WHAT'S THE EMERGENCY, BROTHER?
KHUN-TSIONG, PLEASE SIT DOWN. SORRY TO CALL YOU IN ON A HOLIDAY.
LISTEN, EVERYONE. I'D LIKE TO SPONSOR TAITUNG'S RED LEAVES TO COMPETE IN TAIPEI'S LITTLE LEAGUE CHAMPIONSHIP!
I OBJECT! WE'RE NOT A CORPORATION! WE DON'T HAVE SPARE FUNDS FOR SPONSORSHIPS!
WITH *PRINCESS* ABOUT TO PRINT EVERY OTHER WEEK AND *CHILDHOOD* THREE TIMES A YEAR, WE'RE ALREADY OVER OUR HEADS WITH PRINTING FEES! NOT TO MENTION COSTS FOR THE STAFF AND OTHER LOGISTICS!
BESIDES, REVENUE IS ALWAYS SLOW IN PUBLISHING. THE FINANCE TEAM ALREADY HAS A HARD TIME JUGGLING THINGS.

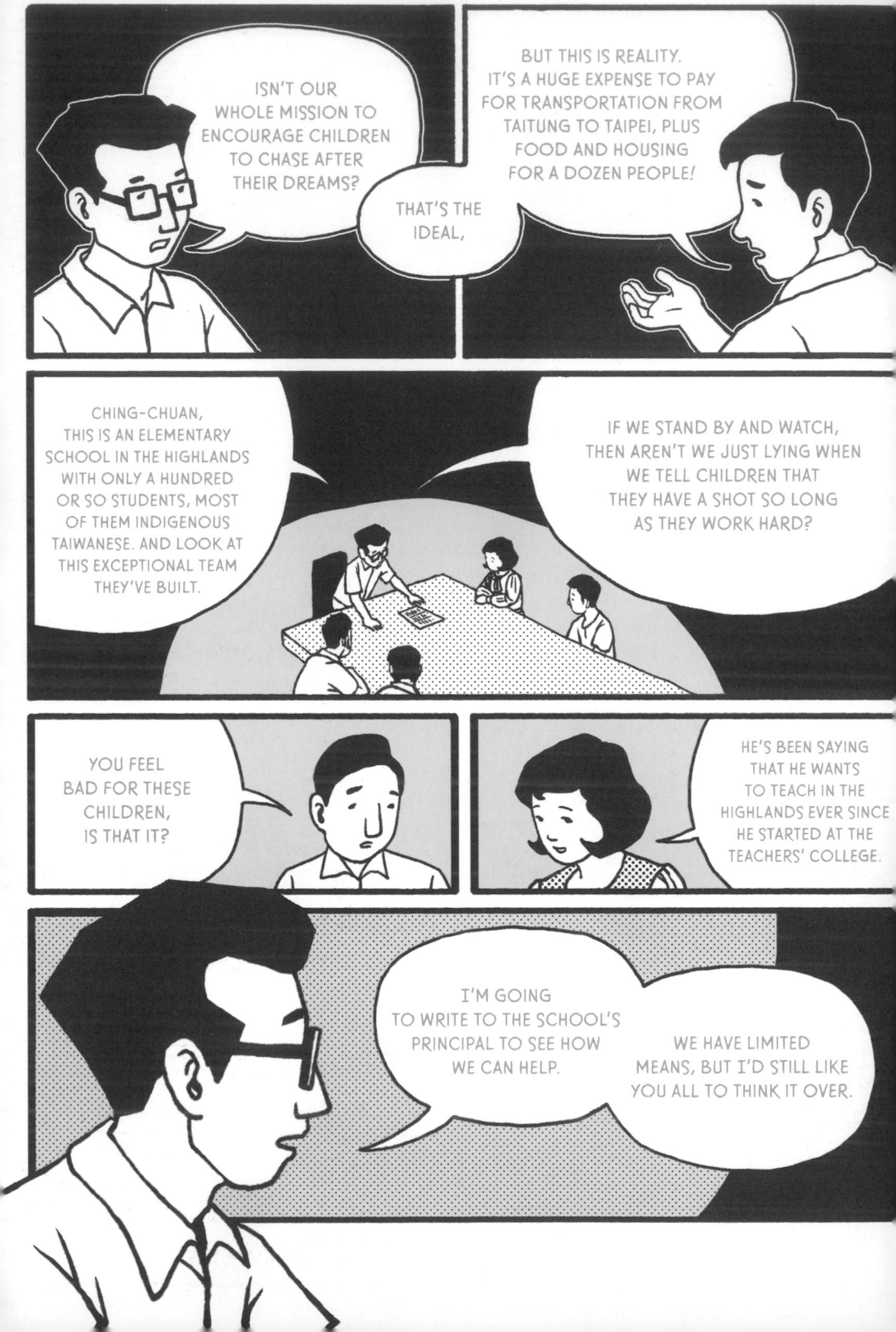
ISN'T OUR WHOLE MISSION TO ENCOURAGE CHILDREN TO CHASE AFTER THEIR DREAMS?
THAT'S THE IDEAL,
BUT THIS IS REALITY. IT'S A HUGE EXPENSE TO PAY FOR TRANSPORTATION FROM TAITUNG TO TAIPEI, PLUS FOOD AND HOUSING FOR A DOZEN PEOPLE!
CHING-CHUAN, THIS IS AN ELEMENTARY SCHOOL IN THE HIGHLANDS WITH ONLY A HUNDRED OR SO STUDENTS, MOST OF THEM INDIGENOUS TAIWANESE. AND LOOK AT THIS EXCEPTIONAL TEAM THEY'VE BUILT.
IF WE STAND BY AND WATCH, THEN AREN'T WE JUST LYING WHEN WE TELL CHILDREN THAT THEY HAVE A SHOT SO LONG AS THEY WORK HARD?
YOU FEEL BAD FOR THESE CHILDREN, IS THAT IT?
HE'S BEEN SAYING THAT HE WANTS TO TEACH IN THE HIGHLANDS EVER SINCE HE STARTED AT THE TEACHERS' COLLEGE.
I'M GOING TO WRITE TO THE SCHOOL'S PRINCIPAL TO SEE HOW WE CAN HELP.
WE HAVE LIMITED MEANS, BUT I'D STILL LIKE YOU ALL TO THINK IT OVER.

One week later.

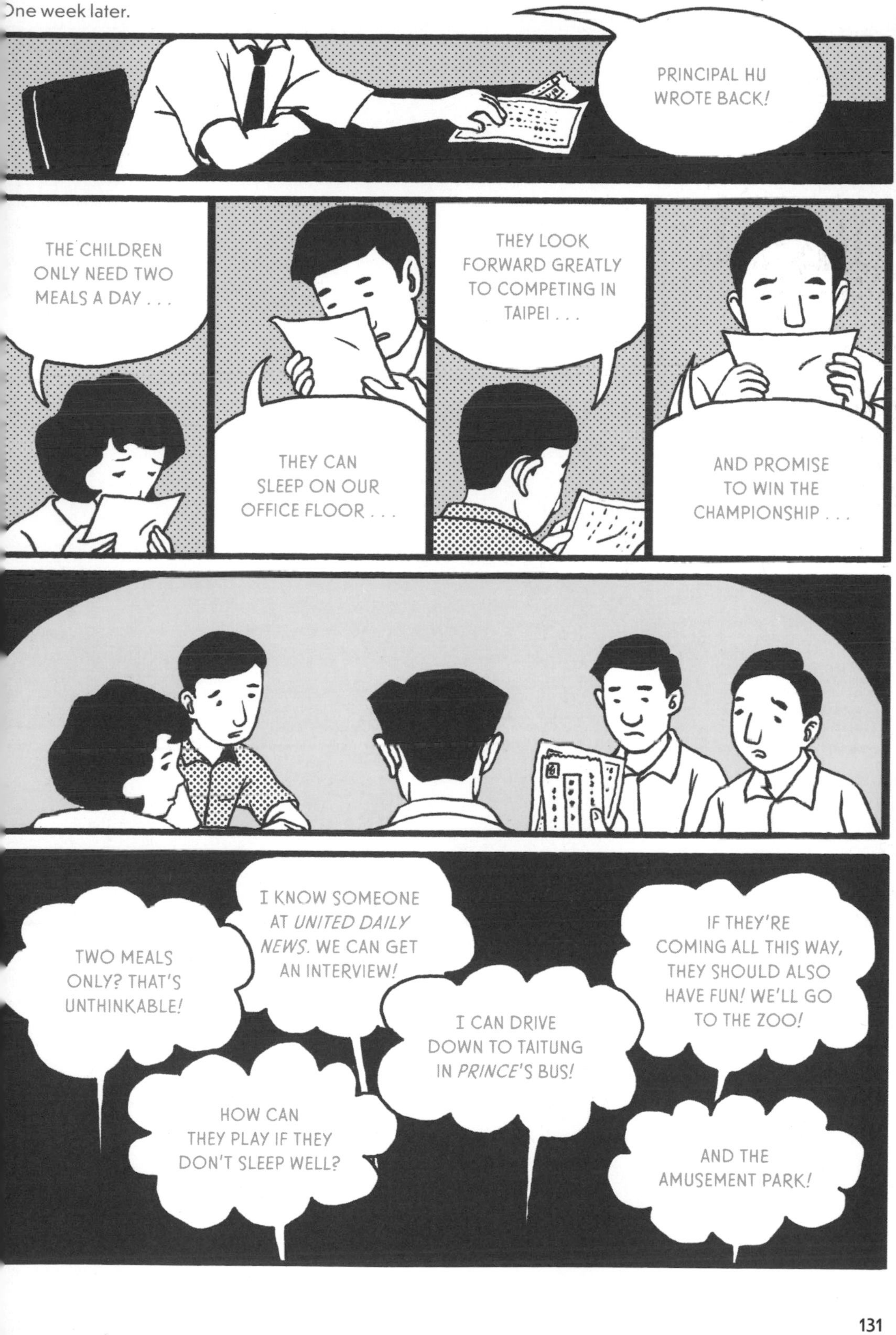
PRINCIPAL HU WROTE BACK!
THE CHILDREN ONLY NEED TWO MEALS A DAY . . .
THEY CAN SLEEP ON OUR OFFICE FLOOR . . .
THEY LOOK FORWARD GREATLY TO COMPETING IN TAIPEI . . .
AND PROMISE TO WIN THE CHAMPIONSHIP . . .
TWO MEALS ONLY? THAT'S UNTHINKABLE!
I KNOW SOMEONE AT *UNITED DAILY NEWS*. WE CAN GET AN INTERVIEW!
HOW CAN THEY PLAY IF THEY DON'T SLEEP WELL?
I CAN DRIVE DOWN TO TAITUNG IN *PRINCE*'S BUS!
IF THEY'RE COMING ALL THIS WAY, THEY SHOULD ALSO HAVE FUN! WE'LL GO TO THE ZOO!
AND THE AMUSEMENT PARK!

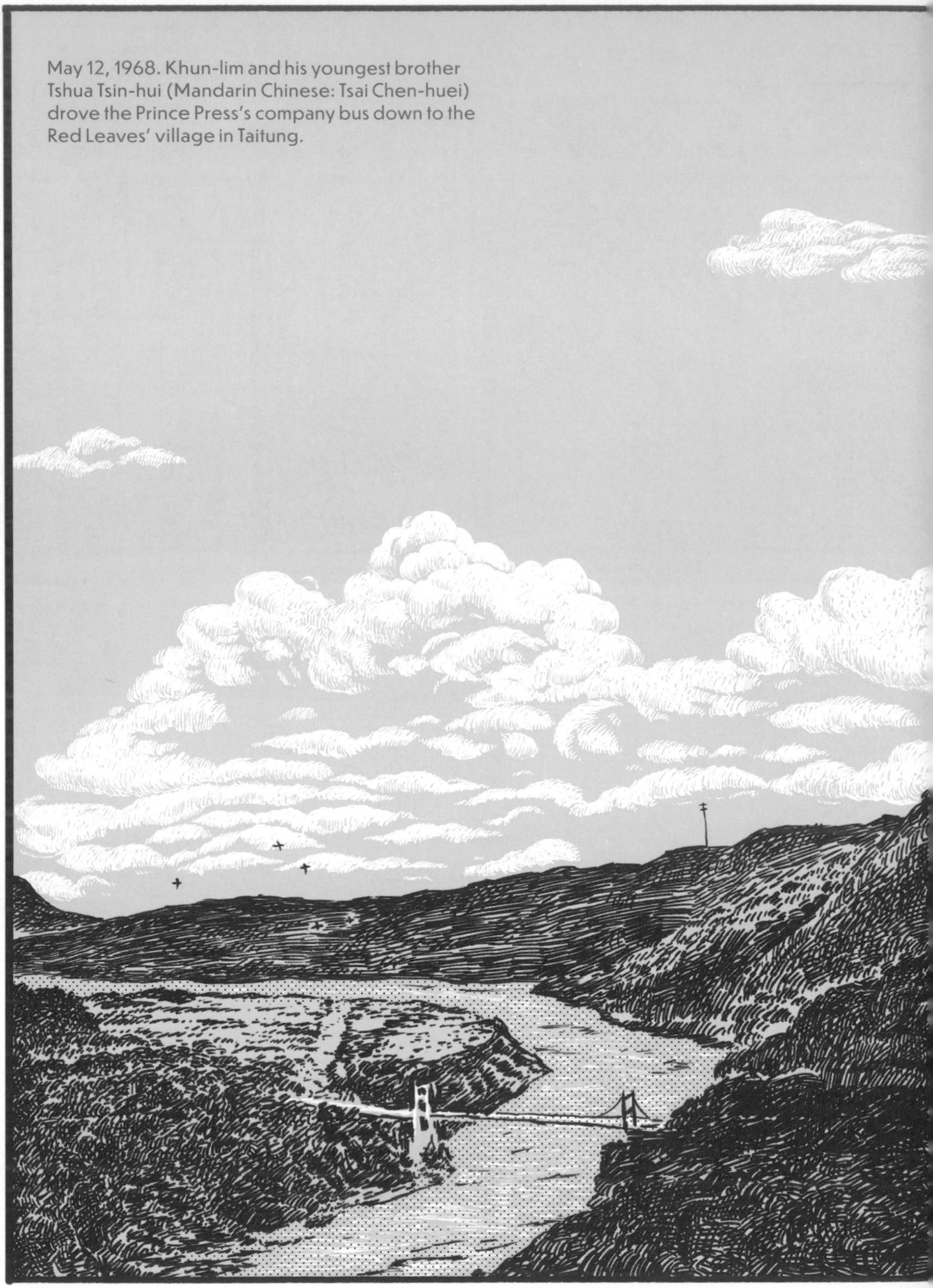
May 12, 1968. Khun-lim and his youngest brother Tshua Tsin-hui (Mandarin Chinese: Tsai Chen-huei) drove the Prince Press's company bus down to the Red Leaves' village in Taitung.

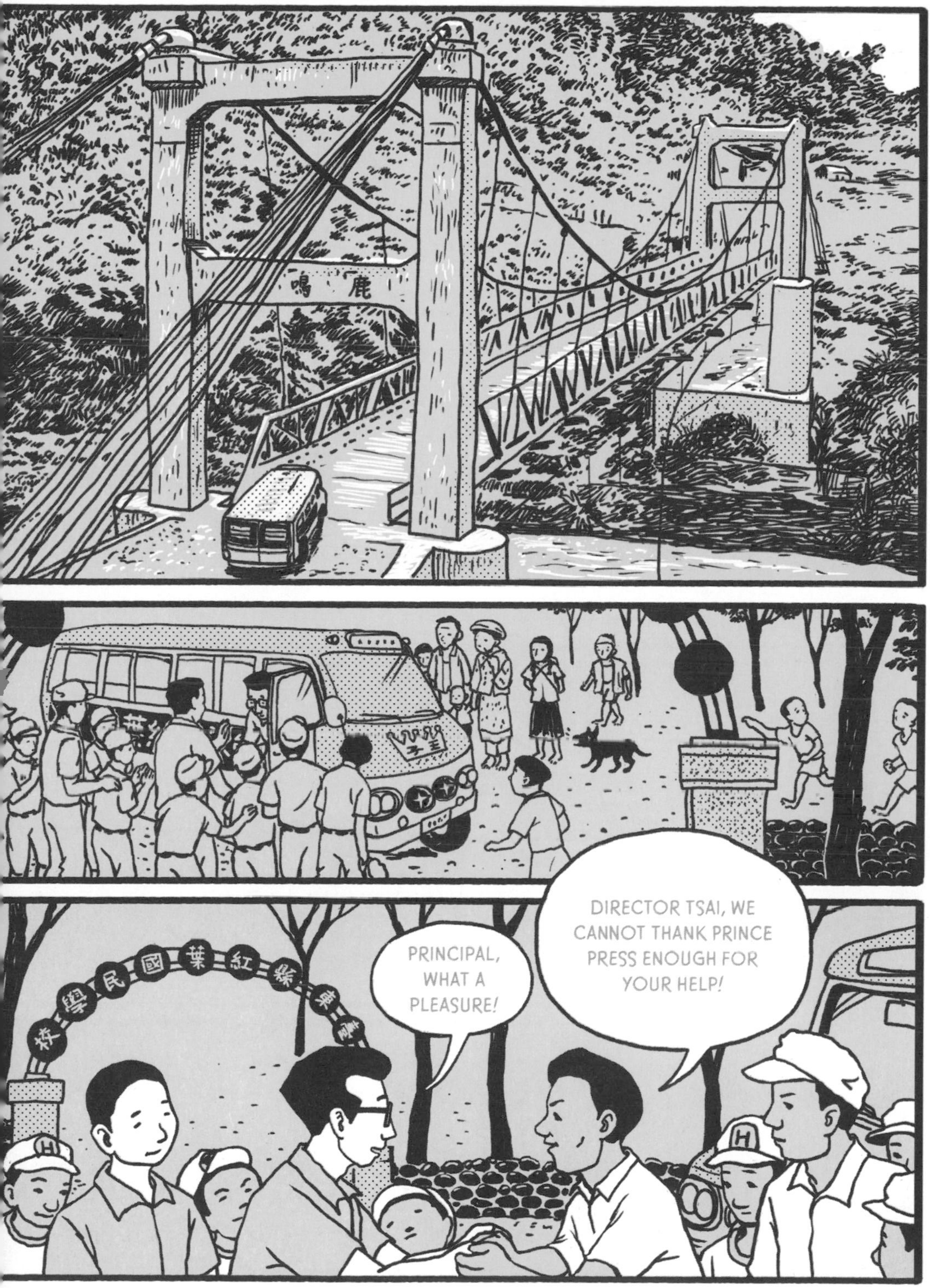
鹿鳴
PRINCIPAL, WHAT A PLEASURE!
DIRECTOR TSAI, WE CANNOT THANK PRINCE PRESS ENOUGH FOR YOUR HELP!

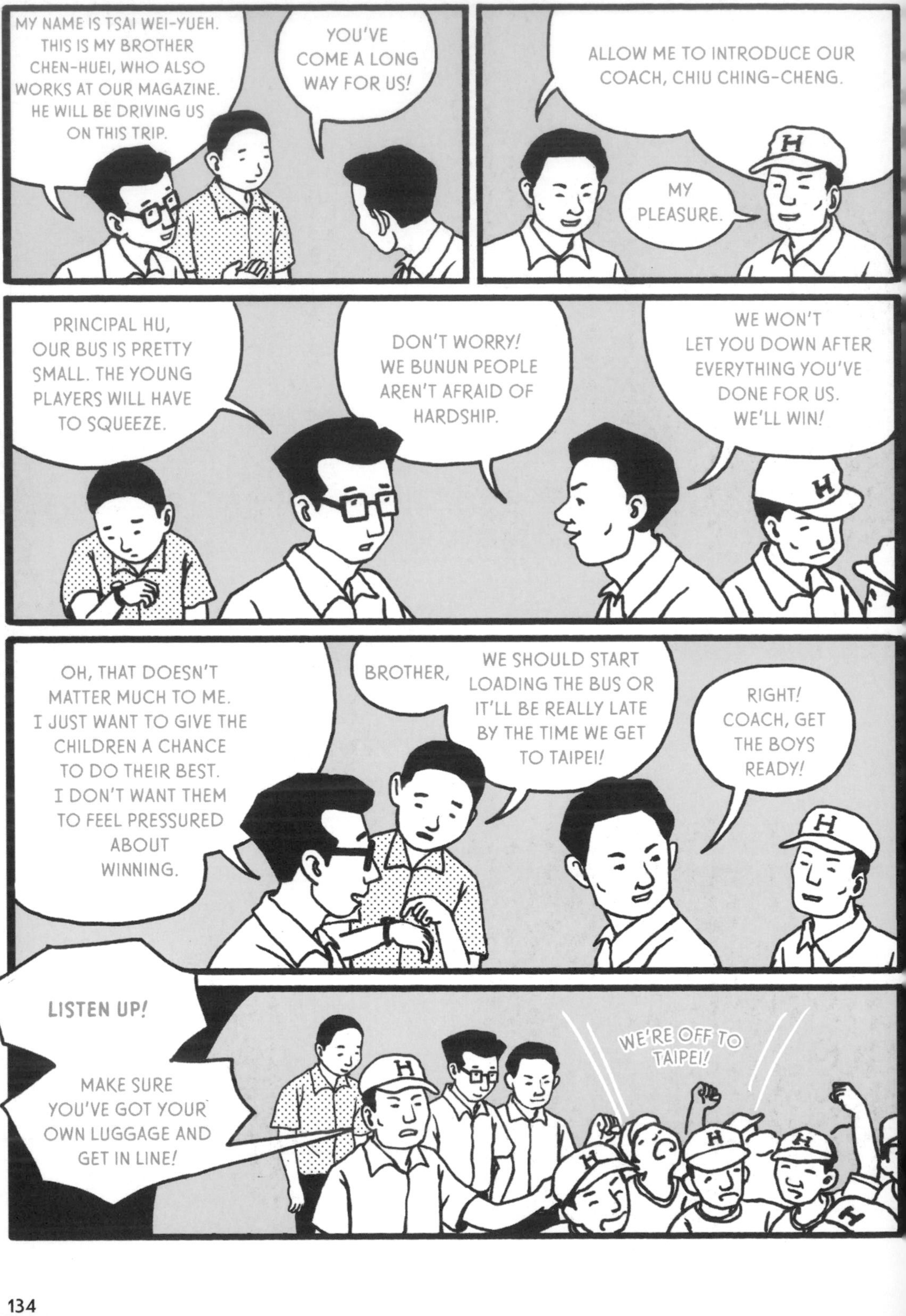
MY NAME IS TSAI WEI-YUEH. THIS IS MY BROTHER CHEN-HUEI, WHO ALSO WORKS AT OUR MAGAZINE. HE WILL BE DRIVING US ON THIS TRIP.
YOU'VE COME A LONG WAY FOR US!
ALLOW ME TO INTRODUCE OUR COACH, CHIU CHING-CHENG.
MY PLEASURE.
PRINCIPAL HU, OUR BUS IS PRETTY SMALL. THE YOUNG PLAYERS WILL HAVE TO SQUEEZE.
DON'T WORRY! WE BUNUN PEOPLE AREN'T AFRAID OF HARDSHIP.
WE WON'T LET YOU DOWN AFTER EVERYTHING YOU'VE DONE FOR US. WE'LL WIN!
OH, THAT DOESN'T MATTER MUCH TO ME. I JUST WANT TO GIVE THE CHILDREN A CHANCE TO DO THEIR BEST. I DON'T WANT THEM TO FEEL PRESSURED ABOUT WINNING.
BROTHER,
WE SHOULD START LOADING THE BUS OR IT'LL BE REALLY LATE BY THE TIME WE GET TO TAIPEI!
RIGHT! COACH, GET THE BOYS READY!
LISTEN UP!
MAKE SURE YOU'VE GOT YOUR OWN LUGGAGE AND GET IN LINE!
WE'RE OFF TO TAIPEI!

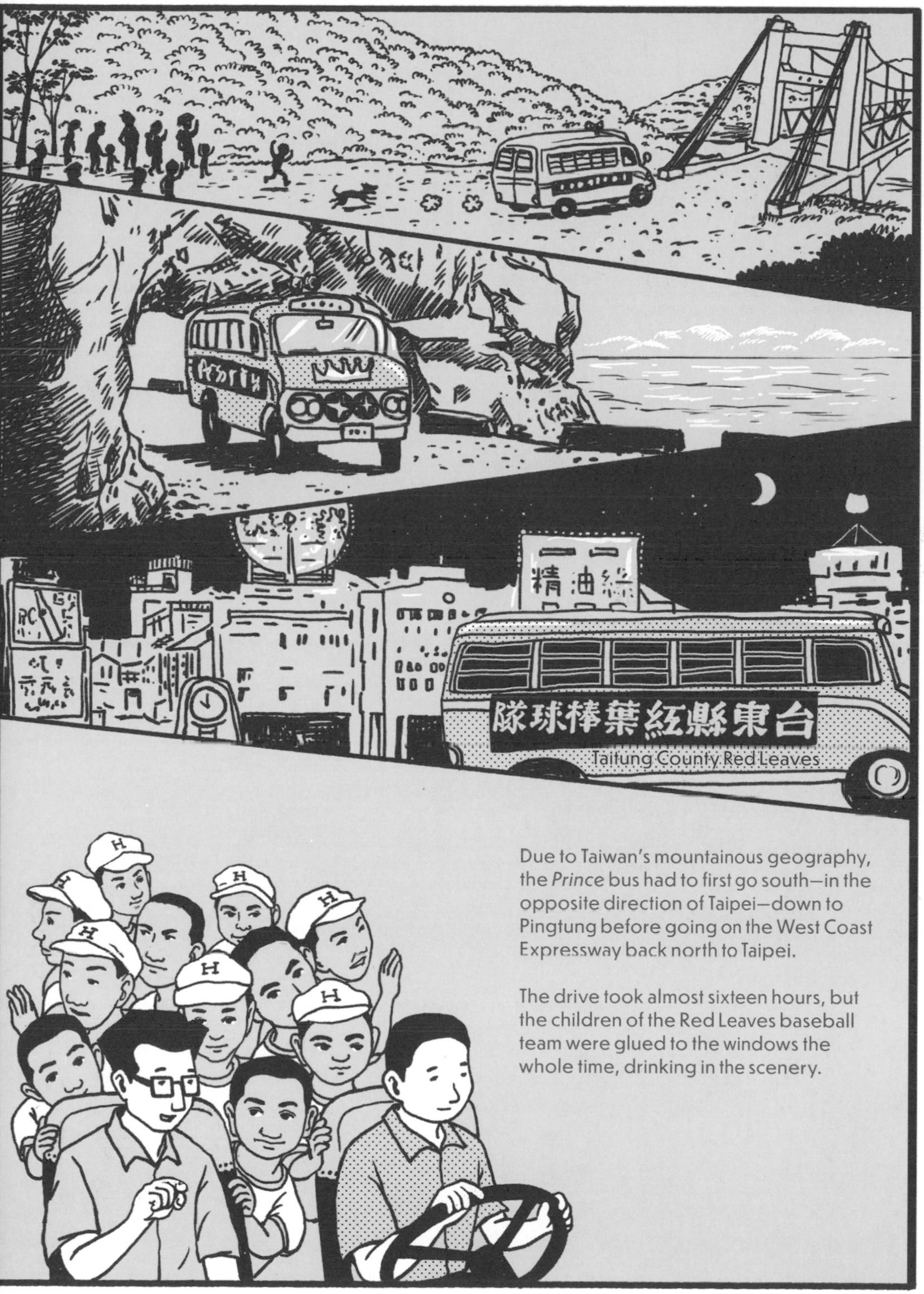
台東縣紅葉棒球隊
Taitung County Red Leaves
Due to Taiwan's mountainous geography, the *Prince* bus had to first go south—in the opposite direction of Taipei—down to Pingtung before going on the West Coast Expressway back north to Taipei.
The drive took almost sixteen hours, but the children of the Red Leaves baseball team were glued to the windows the whole time, drinking in the scenery.

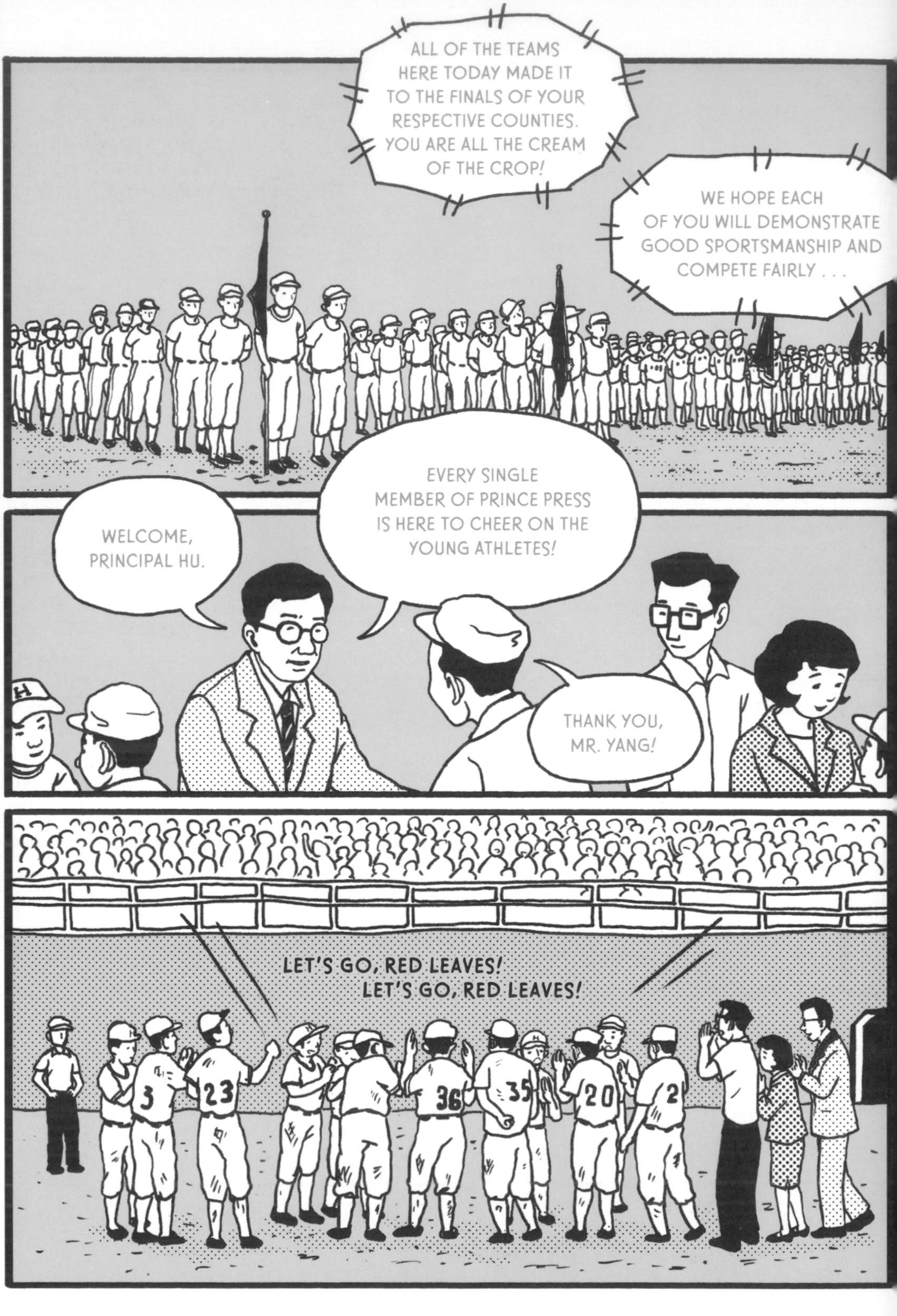
ALL OF THE TEAMS HERE TODAY MADE IT TO THE FINALS OF YOUR RESPECTIVE COUNTIES. YOU ARE ALL THE CREAM OF THE CROP!
WE HOPE EACH OF YOU WILL DEMONSTRATE GOOD SPORTSMANSHIP AND COMPETE FAIRLY . . .
WELCOME, PRINCIPAL HU.
EVERY SINGLE MEMBER OF PRINCE PRESS IS HERE TO CHEER ON THE YOUNG ATHLETES!
THANK YOU, MR. YANG!
LET'S GO, RED LEAVES!
LET'S GO, RED LEAVES!

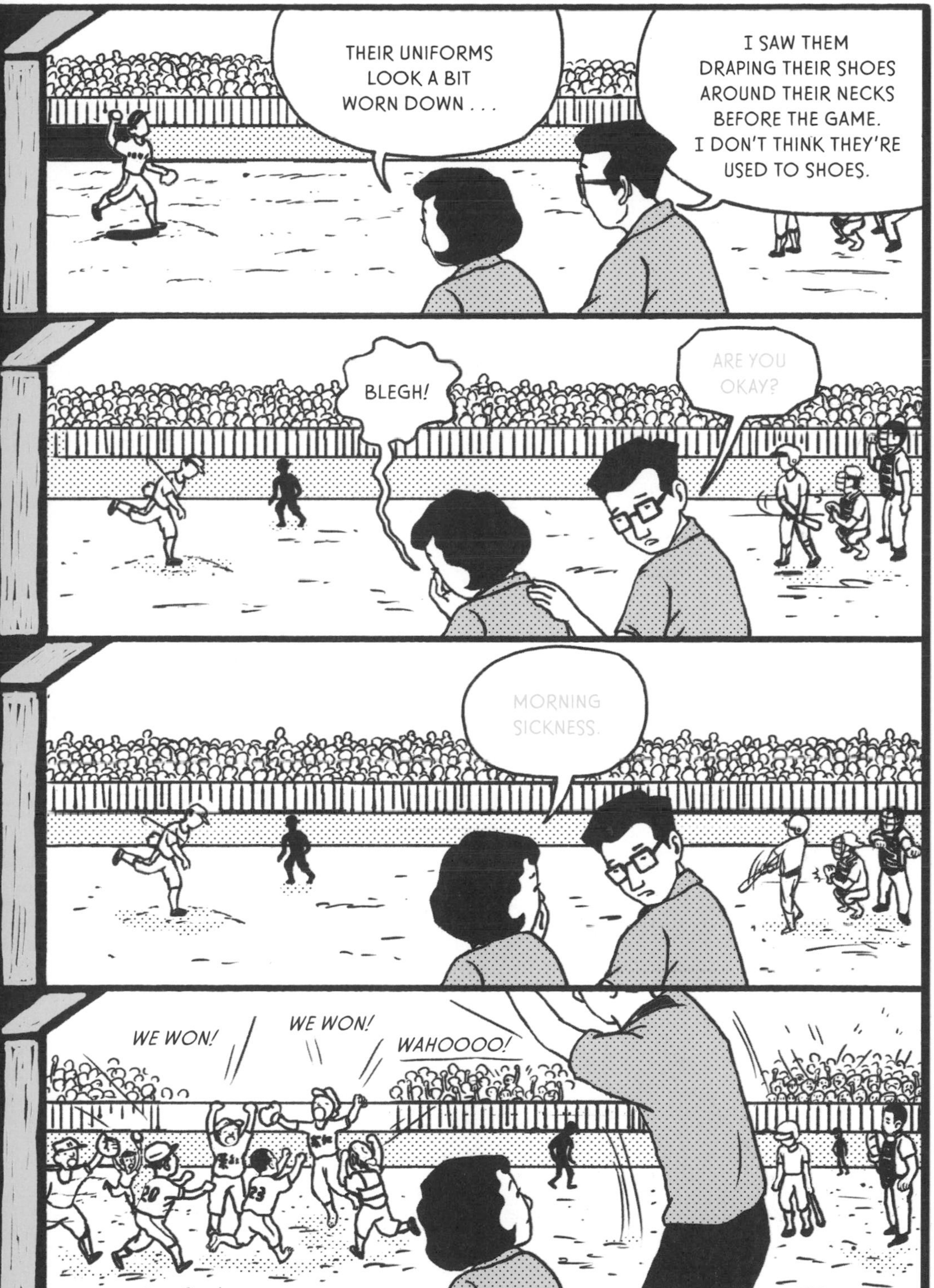
THEIR UNIFORMS LOOK A BIT WORN DOWN . . .
I SAW THEM DRAPING THEIR SHOES AROUND THEIR NECKS BEFORE THE GAME. I DON'T THINK THEY'RE USED TO SHOES.
BLEGH!
ARE YOU OKAY?
MORNING SICKNESS.
WE WON!
WE WON!
WAHOOOO!

May 21, 1968. Dawn.

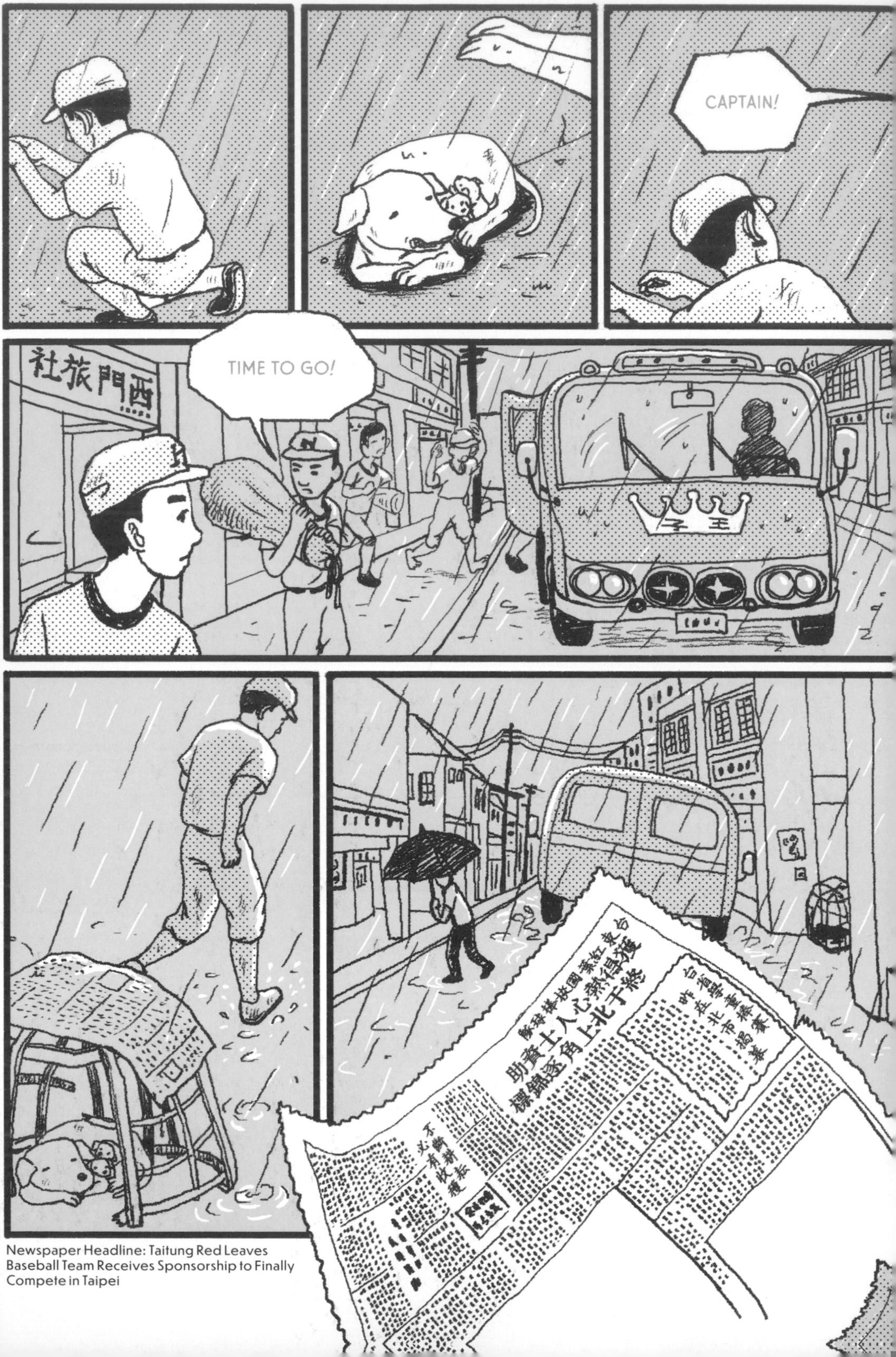
CAPTAIN!
西門旅社
TIME TO GO!
王子
台東紅葉棒球隊
獲得熱心人士資助
終於北上逐角錦標
台省學童棒賽
昨在北市揭幕

Newspaper Headline: Taitung Red Leaves Baseball Team Receives Sponsorship to Finally Compete in Taipei

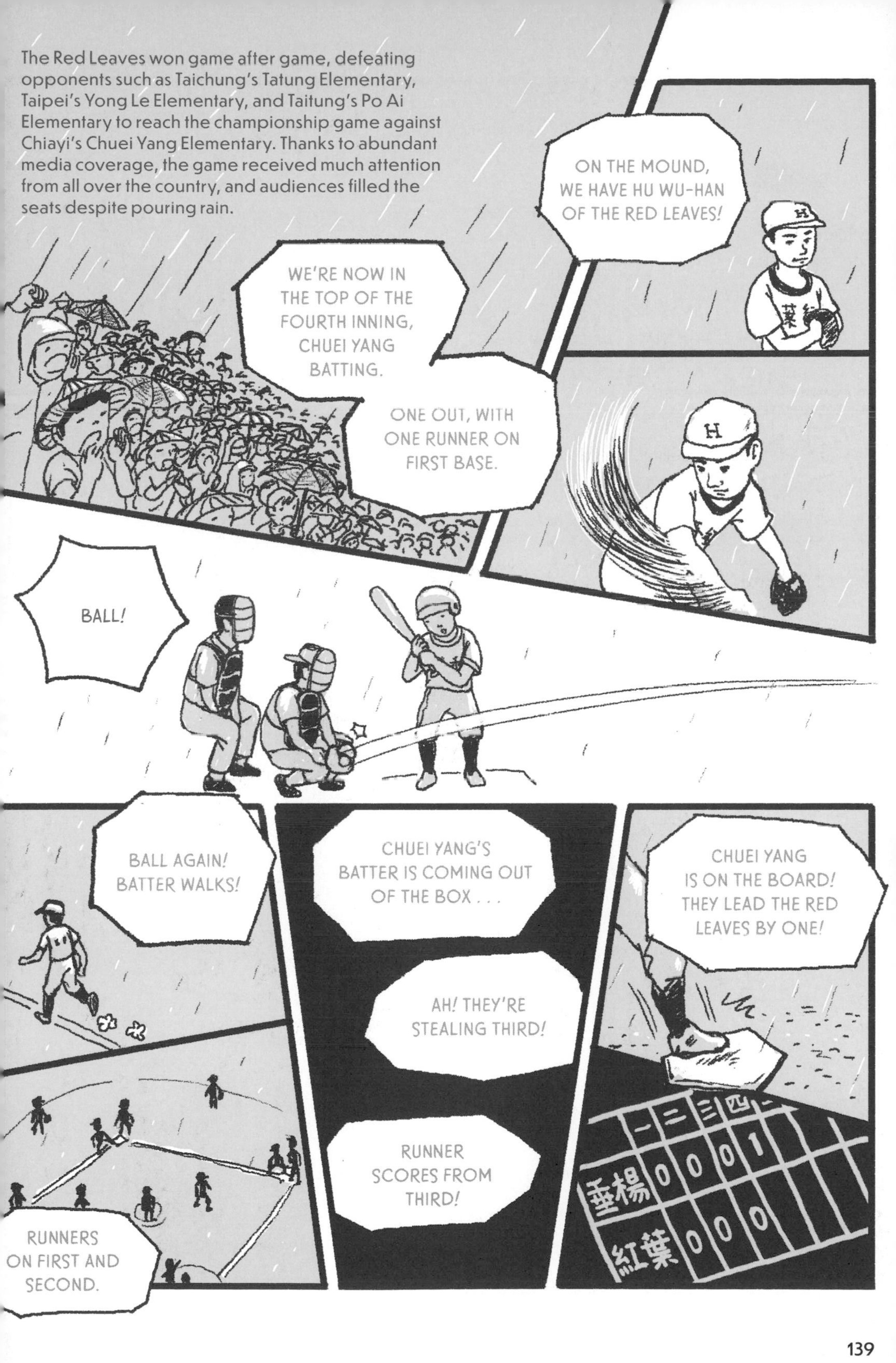
The Red Leaves won game after game, defeating opponents such as Taichung's Tatung Elementary, Taipei's Yong Le Elementary, and Taitung's Po Ai Elementary to reach the championship game against Chiayi's Chuei Yang Elementary. Thanks to abundant media coverage, the game received much attention from all over the country, and audiences filled the seats despite pouring rain.
ON THE MOUND, WE HAVE HU WU-HAN OF THE RED LEAVES!
WE'RE NOW IN THE TOP OF THE FOURTH INNING, CHUEI YANG BATTING.
ONE OUT, WITH ONE RUNNER ON FIRST BASE.
BALL!
BALL AGAIN! BATTER WALKS!
RUNNERS ON FIRST AND SECOND.
CHUEI YANG'S BATTER IS COMING OUT OF THE BOX . . .
AH! THEY'RE STEALING THIRD!
RUNNER SCORES FROM THIRD!
CHUEI YANG IS ON THE BOARD! THEY LEAD THE RED LEAVES BY ONE!
一 二 三 四
垂楊 0 0 0 1
紅葉 0 0 0

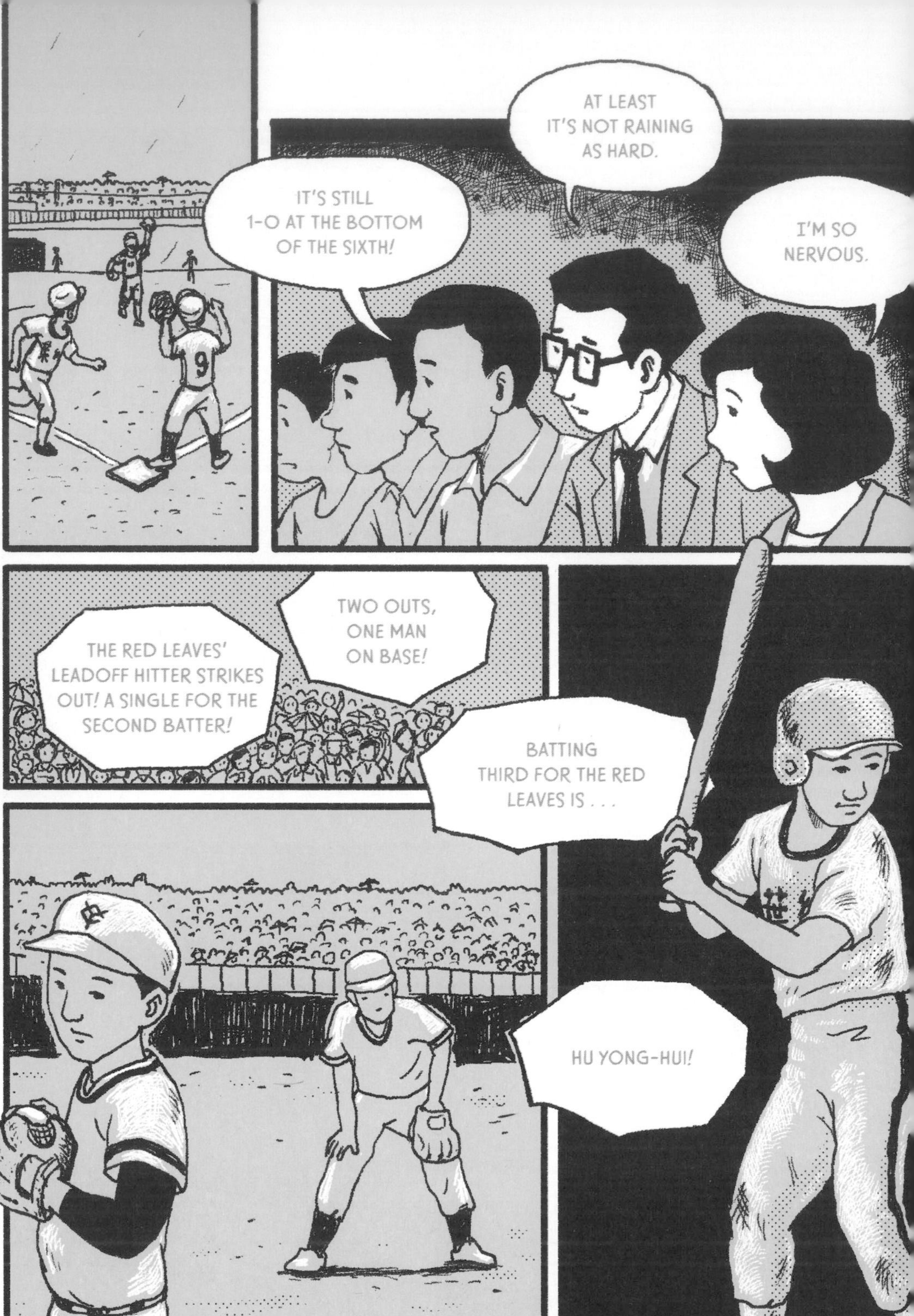
IT'S STILL 1-0 AT THE BOTTOM OF THE SIXTH!
AT LEAST IT'S NOT RAINING AS HARD.
I'M SO NERVOUS.
THE RED LEAVES' LEADOFF HITTER STRIKES OUT! A SINGLE FOR THE SECOND BATTER!
TWO OUTS, ONE MAN ON BASE!
BATTING THIRD FOR THE RED LEAVES IS . . .
HU YONG-HUI!

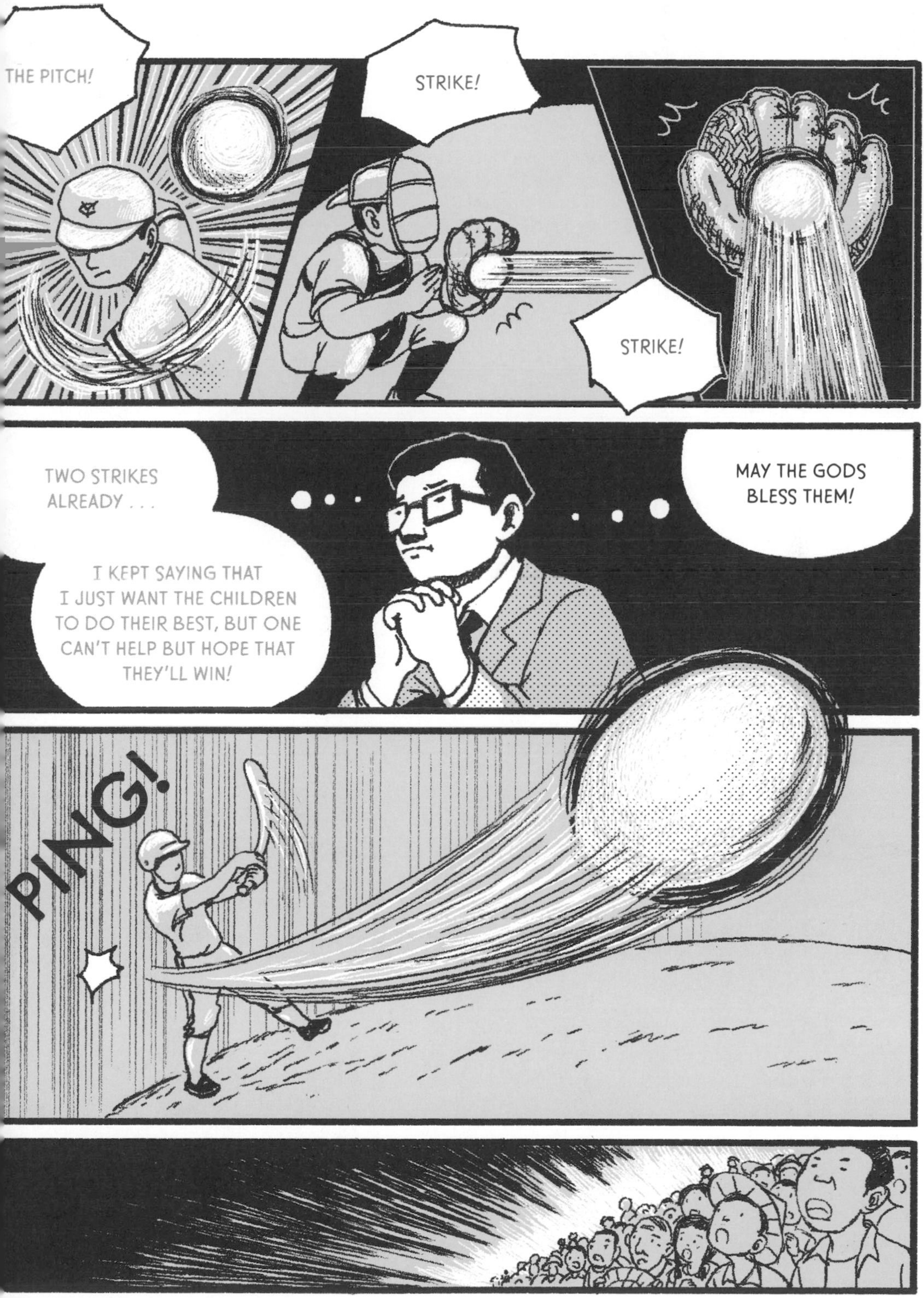
THE PITCH!
STRIKE!
STRIKE!
TWO STRIKES ALREADY . . .
MAY THE GODS BLESS THEM!
I KEPT SAYING THAT I JUST WANT THE CHILDREN TO DO THEIR BEST, BUT ONE CAN'T HELP BUT HOPE THAT THEY'LL WIN!
PING!

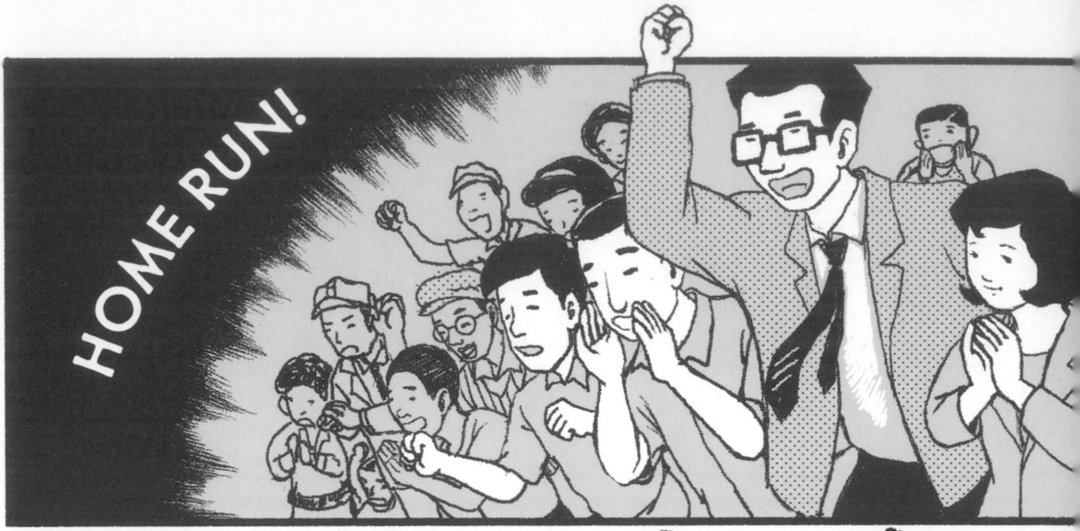
HOME RUN!

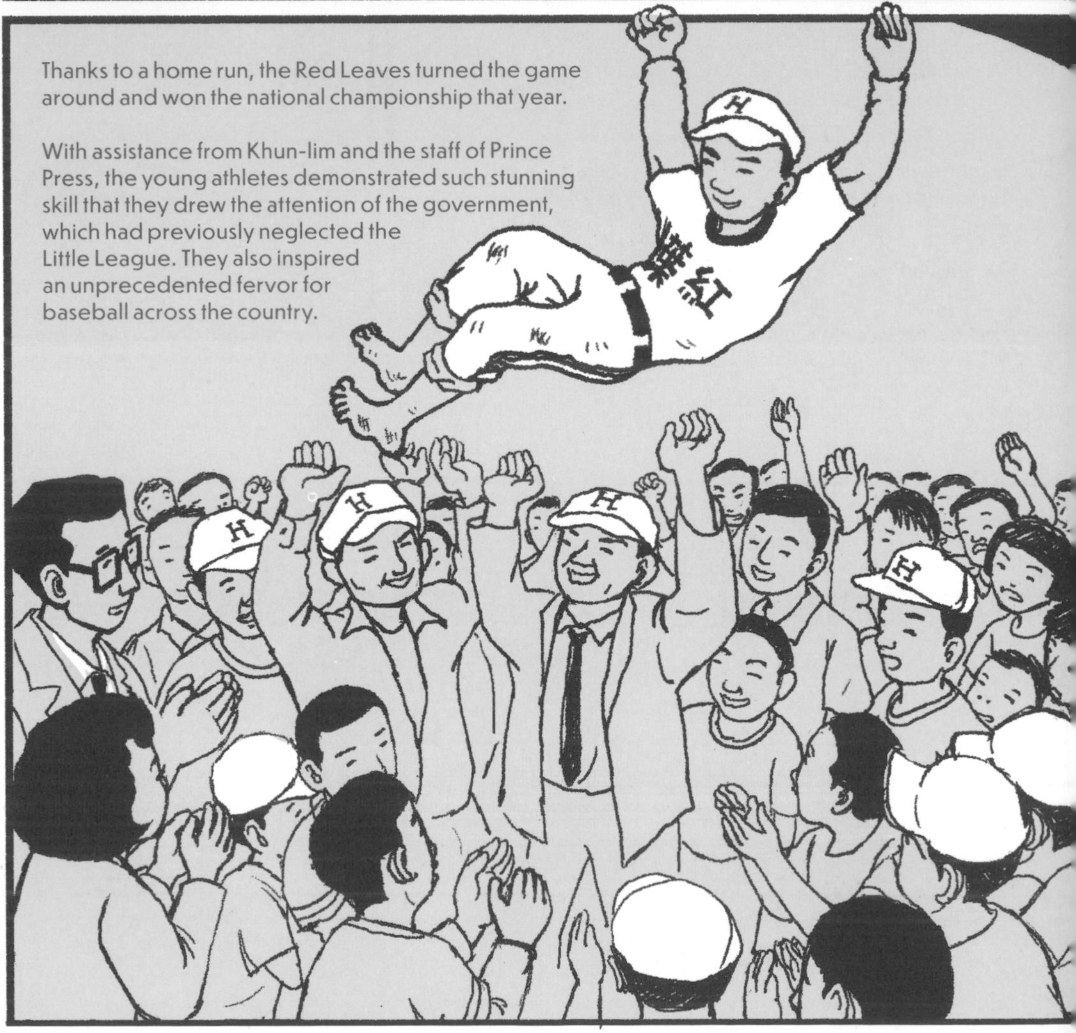
Thanks to a home run, the Red Leaves turned the game around and won the national championship that year.
With assistance from Khun-lim and the staff of Prince Press, the young athletes demonstrated such stunning skill that they drew the attention of the government, which had previously neglected the Little League. They also inspired an unprecedented fervor for baseball across the country.

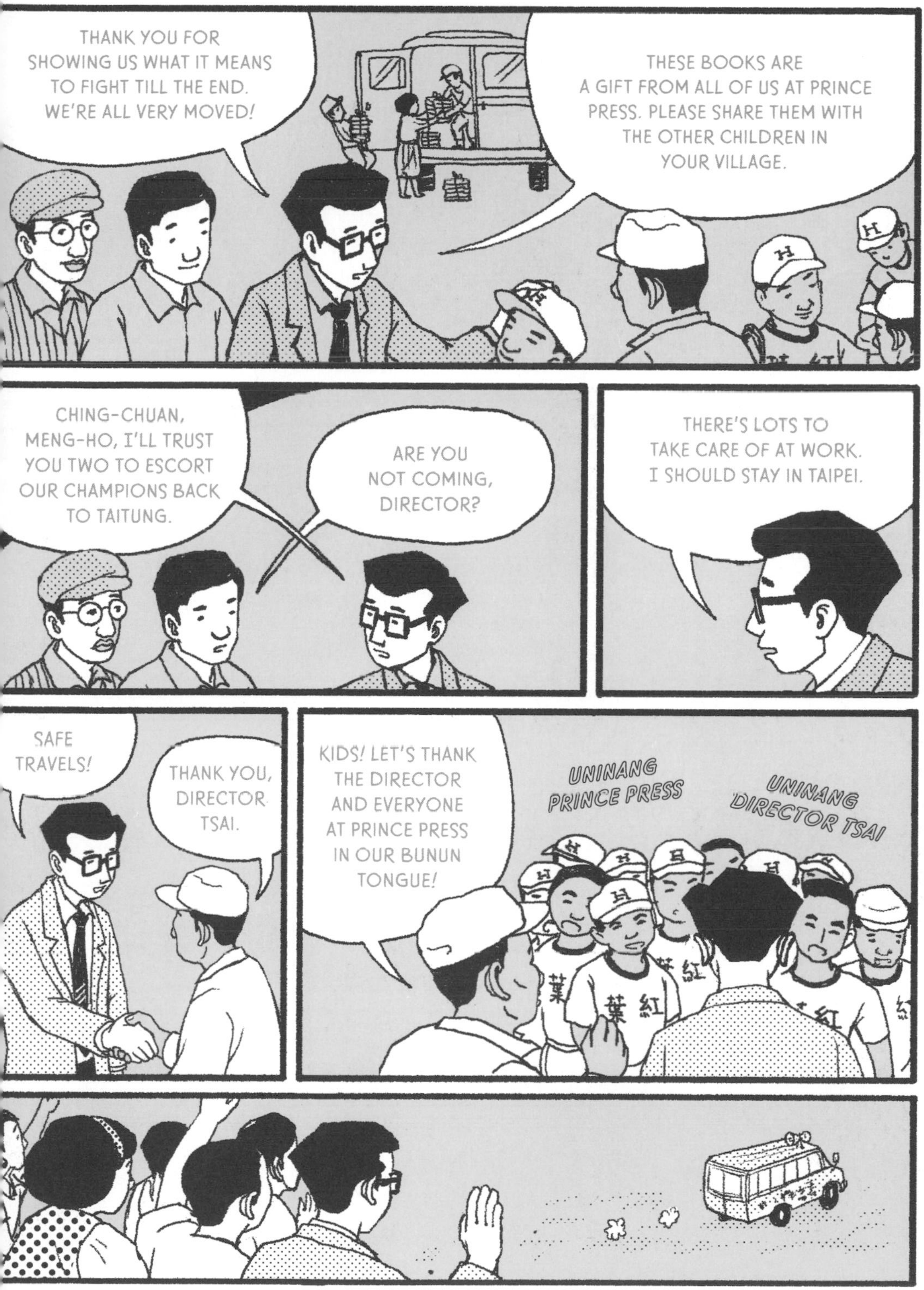
THANK YOU FOR SHOWING US WHAT IT MEANS TO FIGHT TILL THE END. WE'RE ALL VERY MOVED!
THESE BOOKS ARE A GIFT FROM ALL OF US AT PRINCE PRESS. PLEASE SHARE THEM WITH THE OTHER CHILDREN IN YOUR VILLAGE.
CHING-CHUAN, MENG-HO, I'LL TRUST YOU TWO TO ESCORT OUR CHAMPIONS BACK TO TAITUNG.
ARE YOU NOT COMING, DIRECTOR?
THERE'S LOTS TO TAKE CARE OF AT WORK. I SHOULD STAY IN TAIPEI.
SAFE TRAVELS!
THANK YOU, DIRECTOR TSAI.
KIDS! LET'S THANK THE DIRECTOR AND EVERYONE AT PRINCE PRESS IN OUR BUNUN TONGUE!
UNINANG PRINCE PRESS
UNINANG DIRECTOR TSAI

One week later.

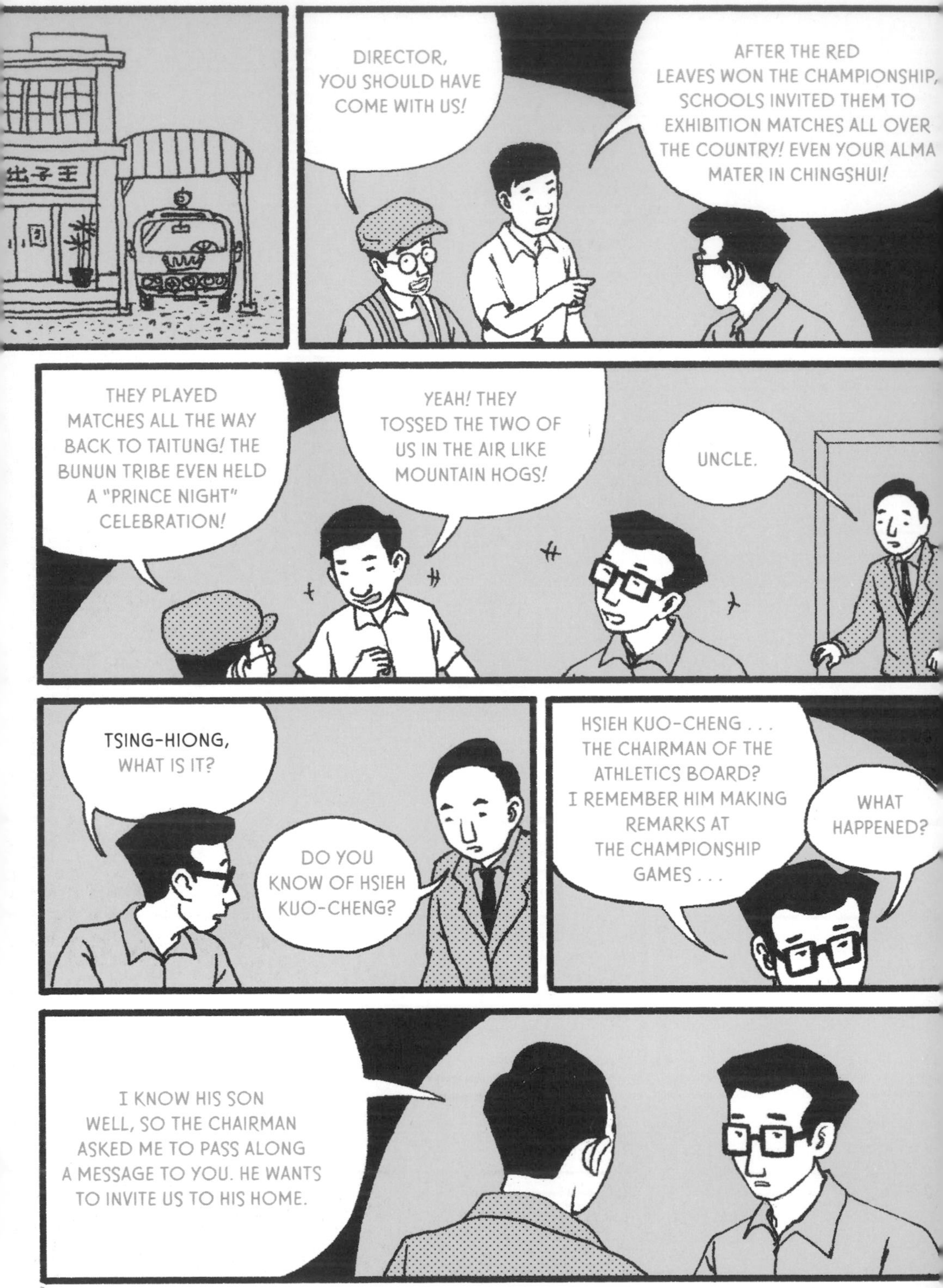

DIRECTOR, YOU SHOULD HAVE COME WITH US!
AFTER THE RED LEAVES WON THE CHAMPIONSHIP, SCHOOLS INVITED THEM TO EXHIBITION MATCHES ALL OVER THE COUNTRY! EVEN YOUR ALMA MATER IN CHINGSHUI!
THEY PLAYED MATCHES ALL THE WAY BACK TO TAITUNG! THE BUNUN TRIBE EVEN HELD A "PRINCE NIGHT" CELEBRATION!
YEAH! THEY TOSSED THE TWO OF US IN THE AIR LIKE MOUNTAIN HOGS!
UNCLE.
TSING-HIONG, WHAT IS IT?
DO YOU KNOW OF HSIEH KUO-CHENG?
HSIEH KUO-CHENG . . . THE CHAIRMAN OF THE ATHLETICS BOARD? I REMEMBER HIM MAKING REMARKS AT THE CHAMPIONSHIP GAMES . . .
WHAT HAPPENED?
I KNOW HIS SON WELL, SO THE CHAIRMAN ASKED ME TO PASS ALONG A MESSAGE TO YOU. HE WANTS TO INVITE US TO HIS HOME.

ne Hsieh residence.

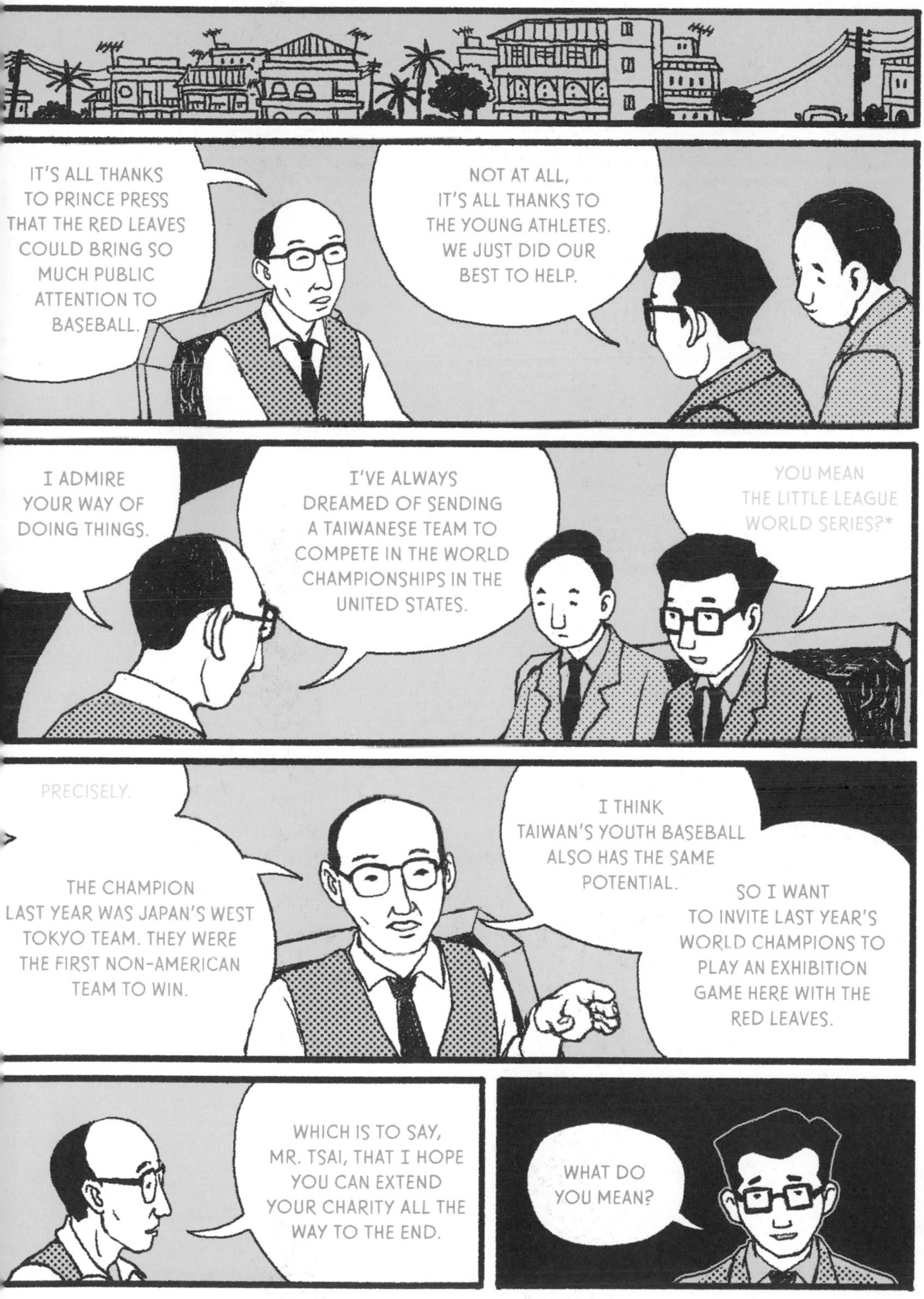

IT'S ALL THANKS TO PRINCE PRESS THAT THE RED LEAVES COULD BRING SO MUCH PUBLIC ATTENTION TO BASEBALL.
NOT AT ALL, IT'S ALL THANKS TO THE YOUNG ATHLETES. WE JUST DID OUR BEST TO HELP.
I ADMIRE YOUR WAY OF DOING THINGS.
I'VE ALWAYS DREAMED OF SENDING A TAIWANESE TEAM TO COMPETE IN THE WORLD CHAMPIONSHIPS IN THE UNITED STATES.
YOU MEAN THE LITTLE LEAGUE WORLD SERIES?*
PRECISELY.
THE CHAMPION LAST YEAR WAS JAPAN'S WEST TOKYO TEAM. THEY WERE THE FIRST NON-AMERICAN TEAM TO WIN.
I THINK TAIWAN'S YOUTH BASEBALL ALSO HAS THE SAME POTENTIAL.
SO I WANT TO INVITE LAST YEAR'S WORLD CHAMPIONS TO PLAY AN EXHIBITION GAME HERE WITH THE RED LEAVES.
WHICH IS TO SAY, MR. TSAI, THAT I HOPE YOU CAN EXTEND YOUR CHARITY ALL THE WAY TO THE END.
WHAT DO YOU MEAN?

tle League Baseball was founded in 1939 by Carl Stotz, based in Williamsport, Pennsylvania.
League is responsible for holding the Little League Baseball World Series, among other tournaments.

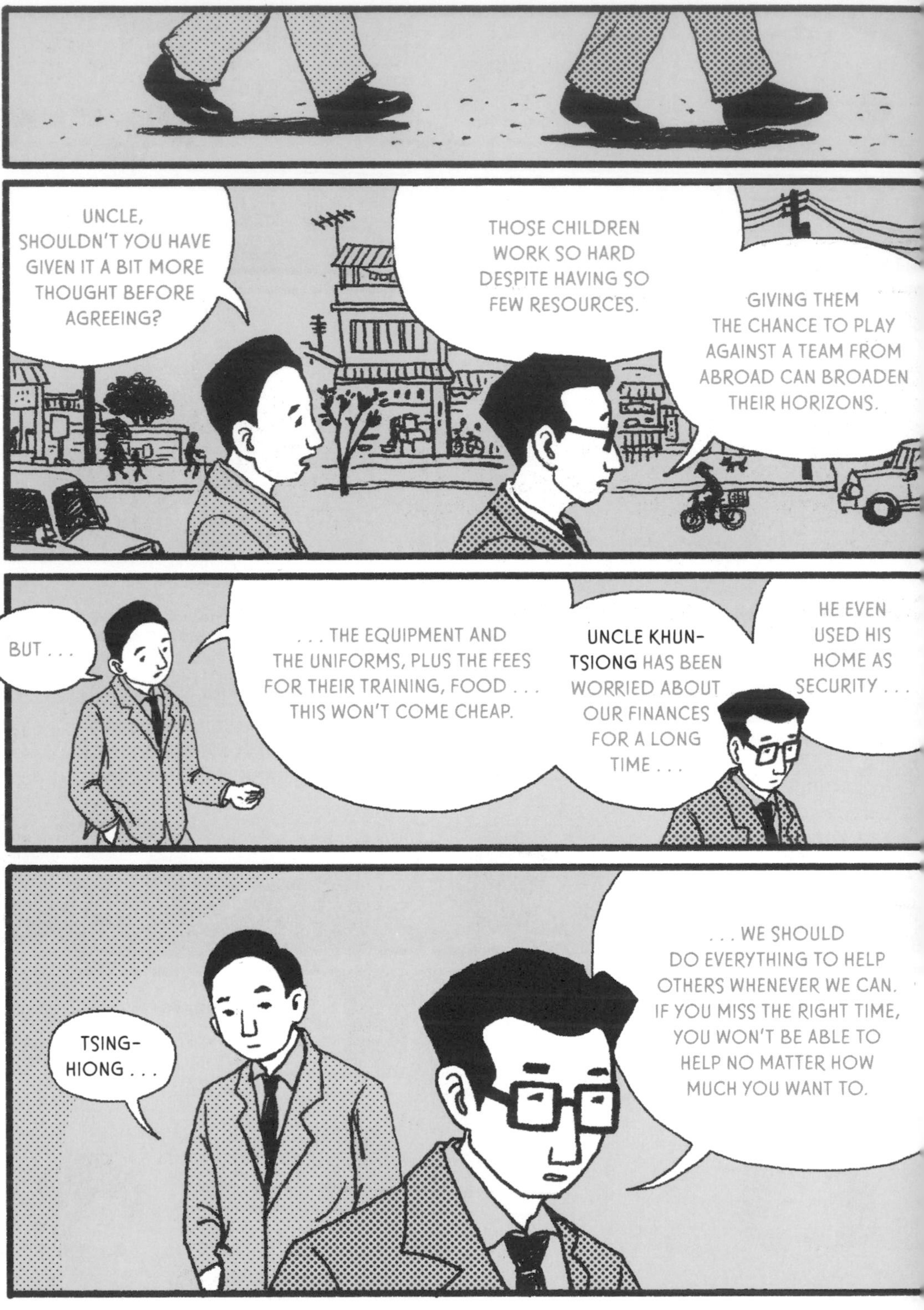
UNCLE, SHOULDN'T YOU HAVE GIVEN IT A BIT MORE THOUGHT BEFORE AGREEING?
THOSE CHILDREN WORK SO HARD DESPITE HAVING SO FEW RESOURCES.
GIVING THEM THE CHANCE TO PLAY AGAINST A TEAM FROM ABROAD CAN BROADEN THEIR HORIZONS.
BUT . . .
. . . THE EQUIPMENT AND THE UNIFORMS, PLUS THE FEES FOR THEIR TRAINING, FOOD . . . THIS WON'T COME CHEAP.
UNCLE KHUN-TSIONG HAS BEEN WORRIED ABOUT OUR FINANCES FOR A LONG TIME . . .
HE EVEN USED HIS HOME AS SECURITY . . .
TSING-HIONG . . .
. . . WE SHOULD DO EVERYTHING TO HELP OTHERS WHENEVER WE CAN. IF YOU MISS THE RIGHT TIME, YOU WON'T BE ABLE TO HELP NO MATTER HOW MUCH YOU WANT TO.

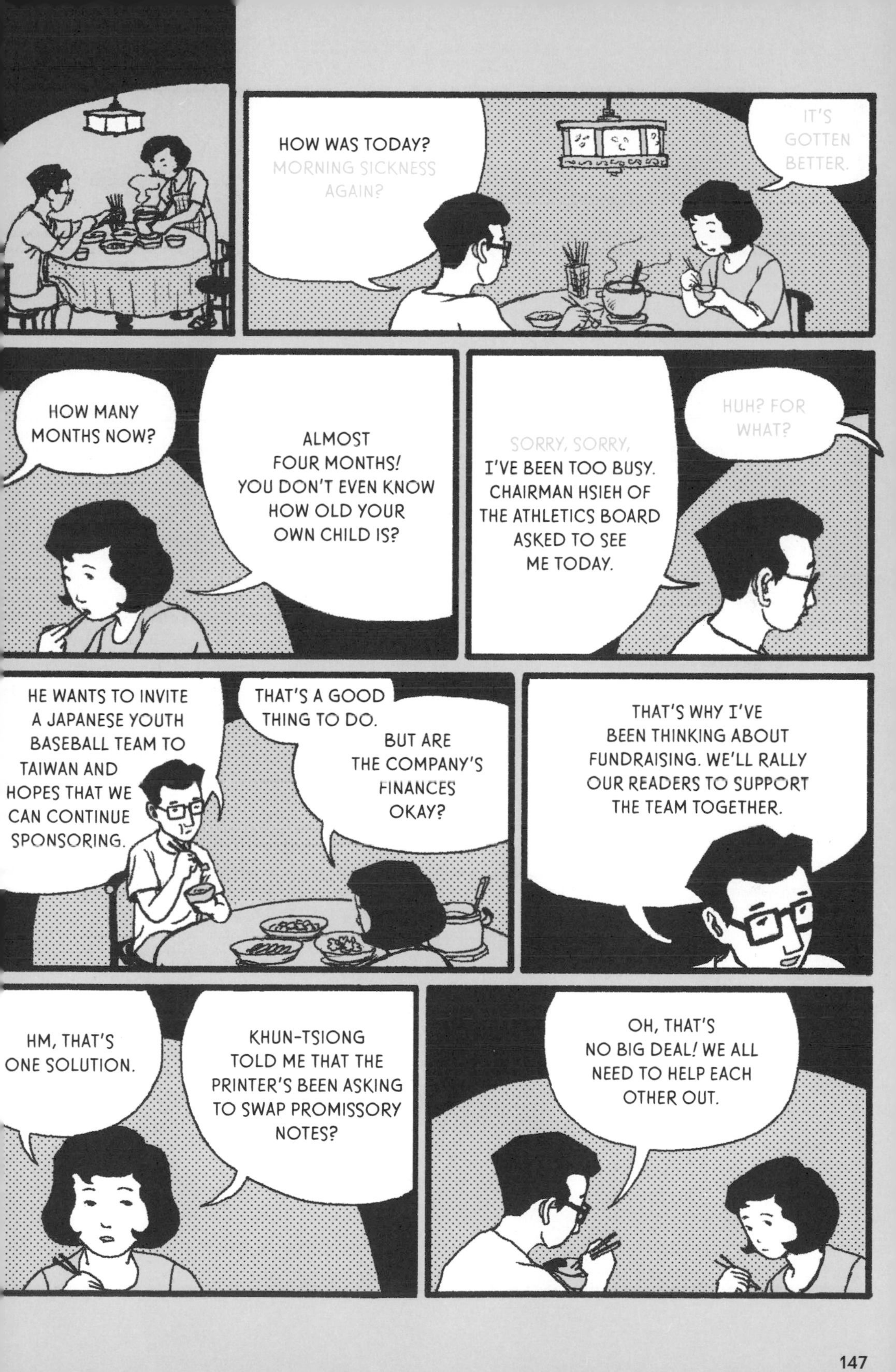
HOW WAS TODAY? MORNING SICKNESS AGAIN?
IT'S GOTTEN BETTER.
HOW MANY MONTHS NOW?
ALMOST FOUR MONTHS! YOU DON'T EVEN KNOW HOW OLD YOUR OWN CHILD IS?
SORRY, SORRY, I'VE BEEN TOO BUSY. CHAIRMAN HSIEH OF THE ATHLETICS BOARD ASKED TO SEE ME TODAY.
HUH? FOR WHAT?
HE WANTS TO INVITE A JAPANESE YOUTH BASEBALL TEAM TO TAIWAN AND HOPES THAT WE CAN CONTINUE SPONSORING.
THAT'S A GOOD THING TO DO.
BUT ARE THE COMPANY'S FINANCES OKAY?
THAT'S WHY I'VE BEEN THINKING ABOUT FUNDRAISING. WE'LL RALLY OUR READERS TO SUPPORT THE TEAM TOGETHER.
HM, THAT'S ONE SOLUTION.
KHUN-TSIONG TOLD ME THAT THE PRINTER'S BEEN ASKING TO SWAP PROMISSORY NOTES?
OH, THAT'S NO BIG DEAL! WE ALL NEED TO HELP EACH OTHER OUT.

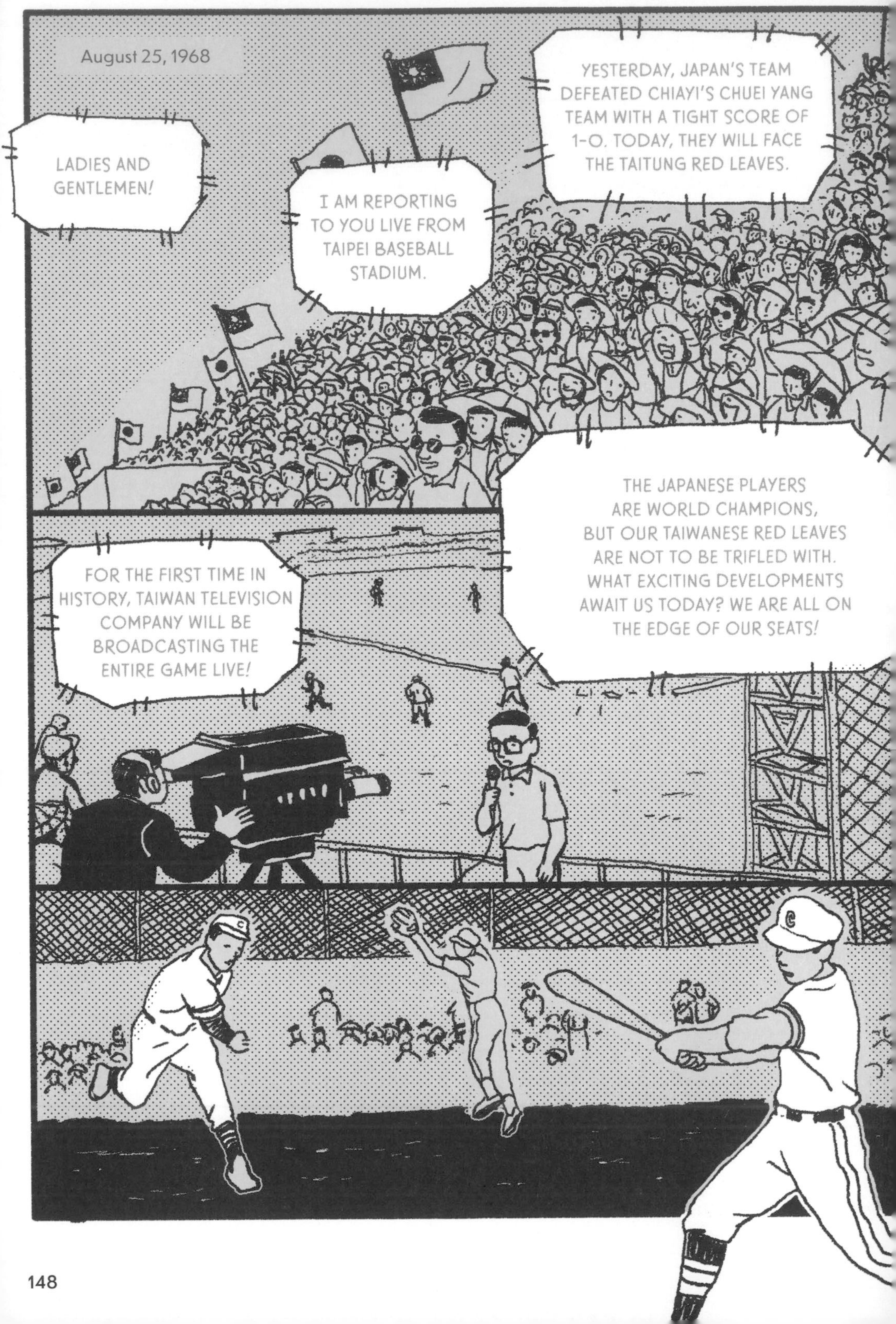

August 25, 1968
LADIES AND GENTLEMEN!
I AM REPORTING TO YOU LIVE FROM TAIPEI BASEBALL STADIUM.
YESTERDAY, JAPAN'S TEAM DEFEATED CHIAYI'S CHUEI YANG TEAM WITH A TIGHT SCORE OF 1-0. TODAY, THEY WILL FACE THE TAITUNG RED LEAVES.
FOR THE FIRST TIME IN HISTORY, TAIWAN TELEVISION COMPANY WILL BE BROADCASTING THE ENTIRE GAME LIVE!
THE JAPANESE PLAYERS ARE WORLD CHAMPIONS, BUT OUR TAIWANESE RED LEAVES ARE NOT TO BE TRIFLED WITH. WHAT EXCITING DEVELOPMENTS AWAIT US TODAY? WE ARE ALL ON THE EDGE OF OUR SEATS!

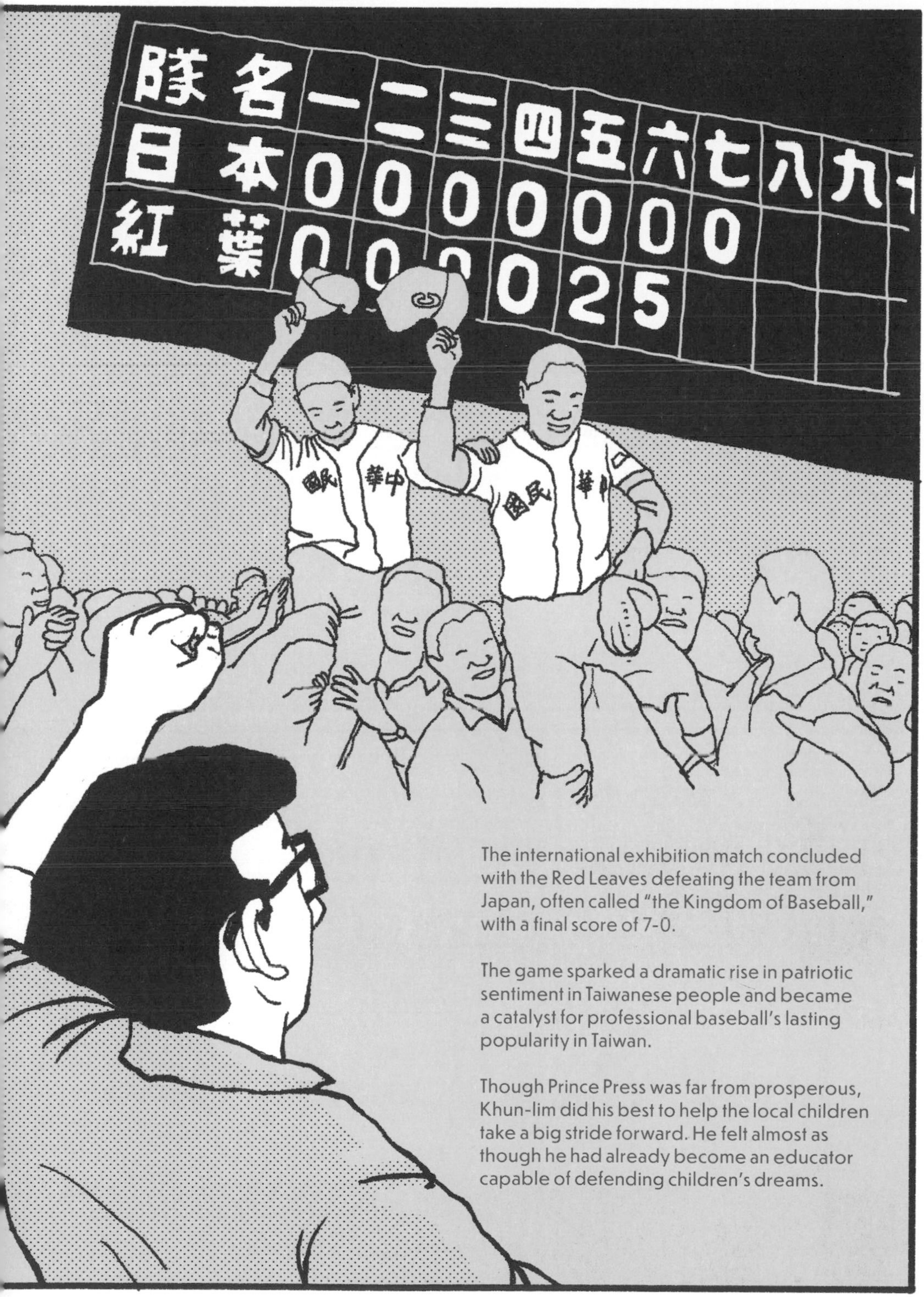
隊 名 一 二 三 四 五 六 七 八 九
日 本 0 0 0 0 0 0 0
紅 葉 0 0 2 5
The international exhibition match concluded with the Red Leaves defeating the team from Japan, often called "the Kingdom of Baseball," with a final score of 7-0.
The game sparked a dramatic rise in patriotic sentiment in Taiwanese people and became a catalyst for professional baseball's lasting popularity in Taiwan.
Though Prince Press was far from prosperous, Khun-lim did his best to help the local children take a big stride forward. He felt almost as though he had already become an educator capable of defending children's dreams.

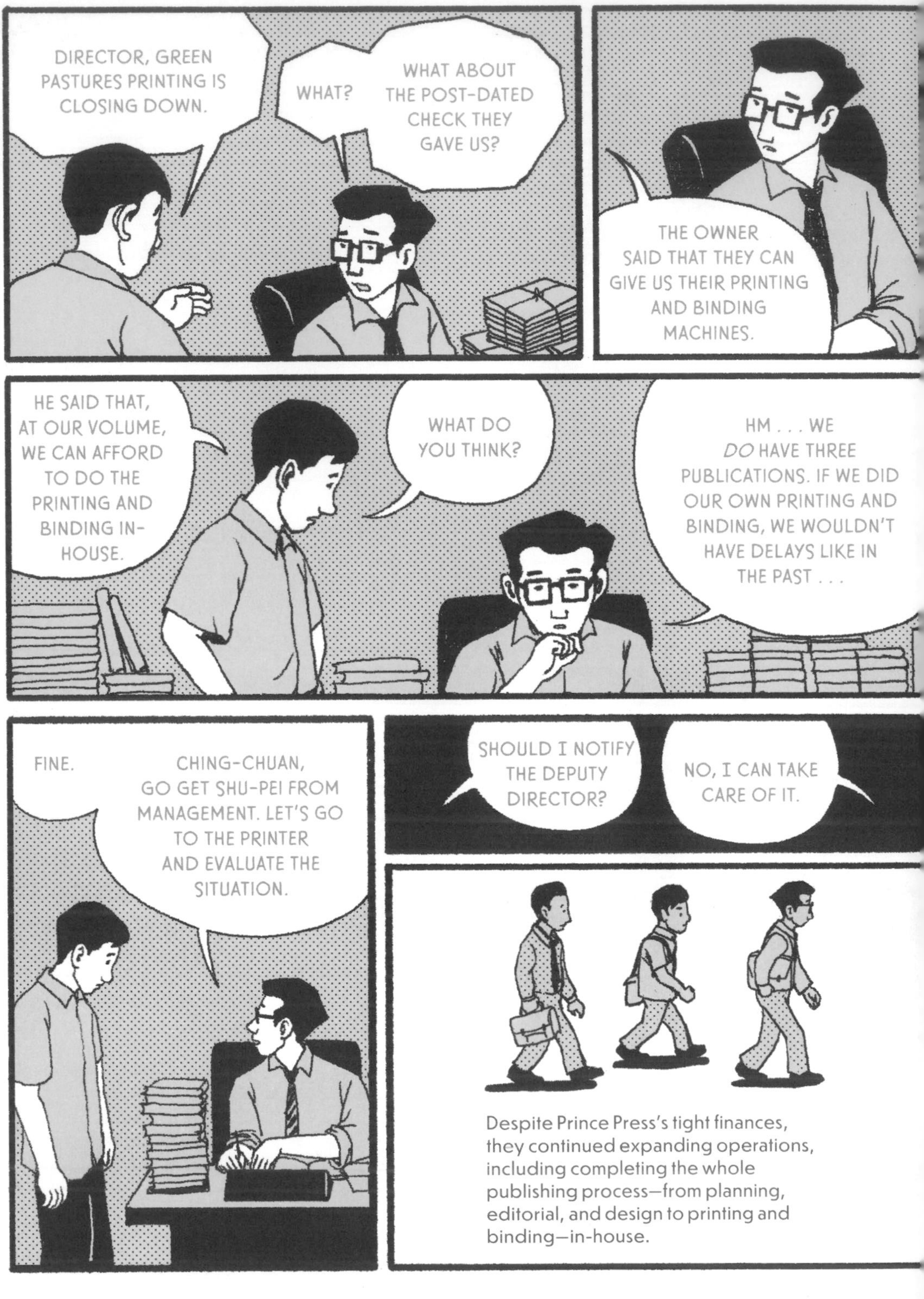
DIRECTOR, GREEN PASTURES PRINTING IS CLOSING DOWN.
WHAT?
WHAT ABOUT THE POST-DATED CHECK THEY GAVE US?
THE OWNER SAID THAT THEY CAN GIVE US THEIR PRINTING AND BINDING MACHINES.
HE SAID THAT, AT OUR VOLUME, WE CAN AFFORD TO DO THE PRINTING AND BINDING IN-HOUSE.
WHAT DO YOU THINK?
HM . . . WE *DO* HAVE THREE PUBLICATIONS. IF WE DID OUR OWN PRINTING AND BINDING, WE WOULDN'T HAVE DELAYS LIKE IN THE PAST . . .
FINE.
CHING-CHUAN, GO GET SHU-PEI FROM MANAGEMENT. LET'S GO TO THE PRINTER AND EVALUATE THE SITUATION.
SHOULD I NOTIFY THE DEPUTY DIRECTOR?
NO, I CAN TAKE CARE OF IT.

Despite Prince Press's tight finances, they continued expanding operations, including completing the whole publishing process—from planning, editorial, and design to printing and binding—in-house.

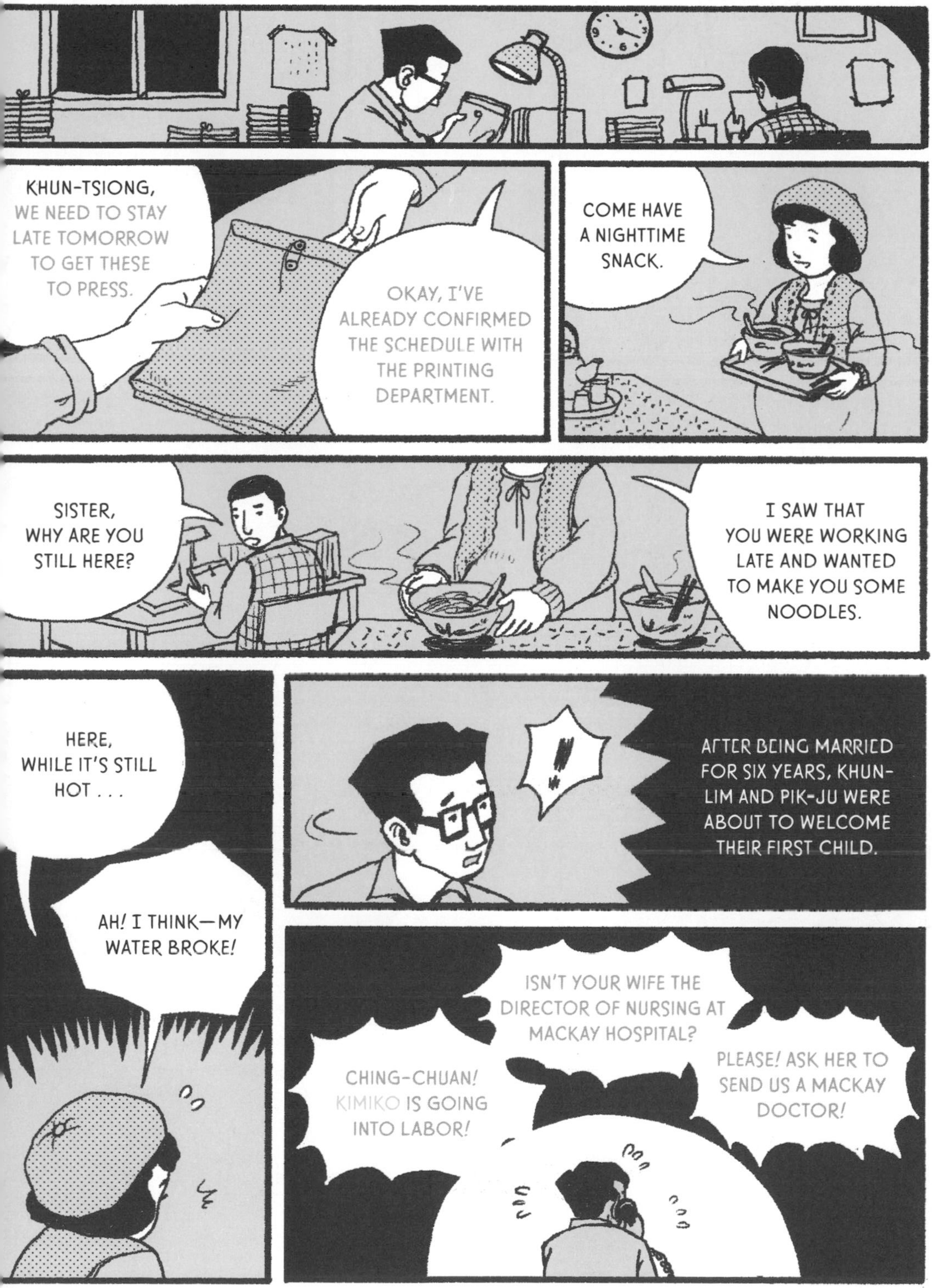
KHUN-TSIONG, WE NEED TO STAY LATE TOMORROW TO GET THESE TO PRESS.
OKAY, I'VE ALREADY CONFIRMED THE SCHEDULE WITH THE PRINTING DEPARTMENT.
COME HAVE A NIGHTTIME SNACK.
SISTER, WHY ARE YOU STILL HERE?
I SAW THAT YOU WERE WORKING LATE AND WANTED TO MAKE YOU SOME NOODLES.
HERE, WHILE IT'S STILL HOT . . .
AH! I THINK—MY WATER BROKE!
!!
AFTER BEING MARRIED FOR SIX YEARS, KHUN-LIM AND PIK-JU WERE ABOUT TO WELCOME THEIR FIRST CHILD.
ISN'T YOUR WIFE THE DIRECTOR OF NURSING AT MACKAY HOSPITAL?
CHING-CHUAN! KIMIKO IS GOING INTO LABOR!
PLEASE! ASK HER TO SEND US A MACKAY DOCTOR!

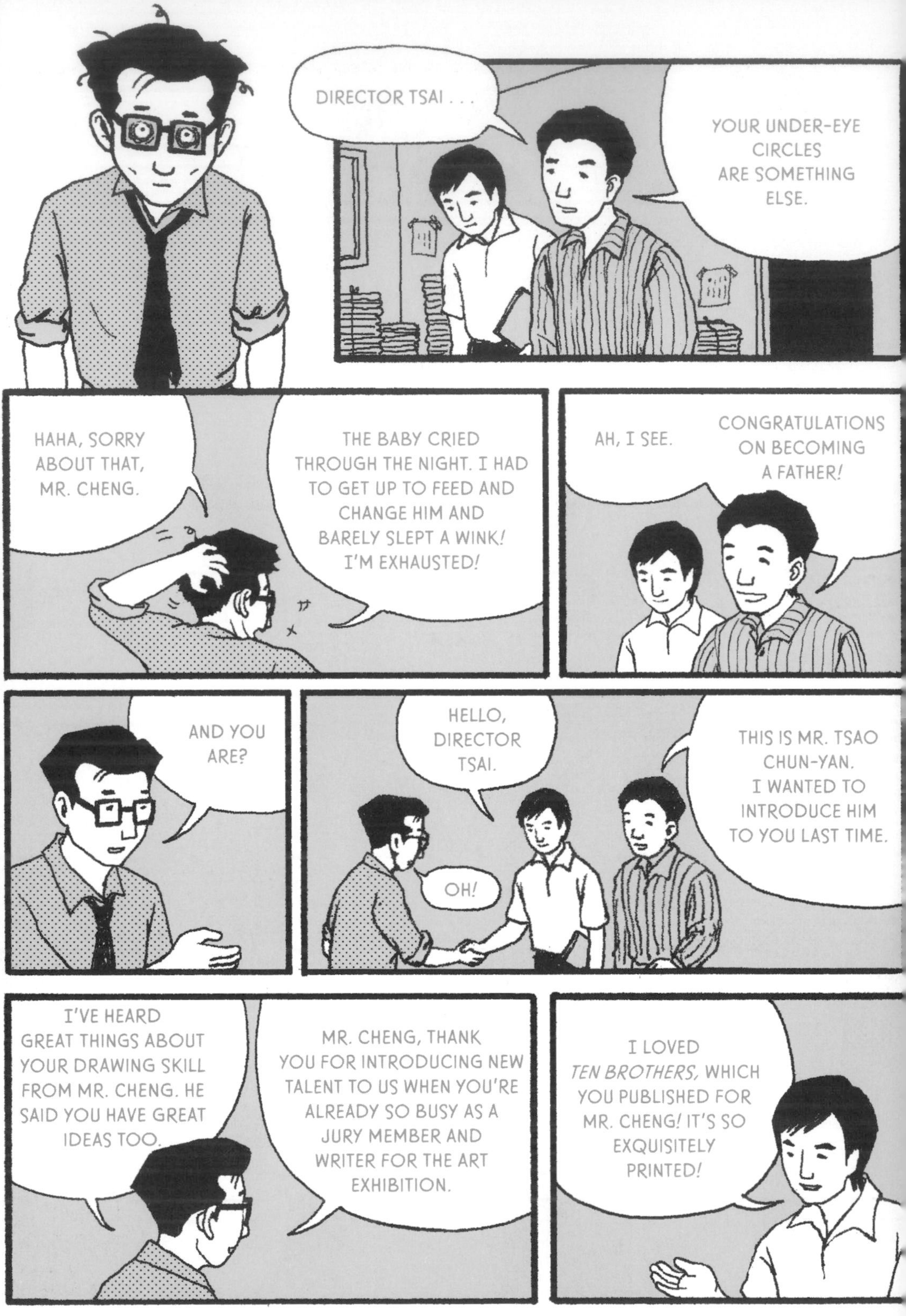
DIRECTOR TSAI . . .
YOUR UNDER-EYE CIRCLES ARE SOMETHING ELSE.
HAHA, SORRY ABOUT THAT, MR. CHENG.
THE BABY CRIED THROUGH THE NIGHT. I HAD TO GET UP TO FEED AND CHANGE HIM AND BARELY SLEPT A WINK! I'M EXHAUSTED!
AH, I SEE.
CONGRATULATIONS ON BECOMING A FATHER!
AND YOU ARE?
HELLO, DIRECTOR TSAI.
OH!
THIS IS MR. TSAO CHUN-YAN. I WANTED TO INTRODUCE HIM TO YOU LAST TIME.
I'VE HEARD GREAT THINGS ABOUT YOUR DRAWING SKILL FROM MR. CHENG. HE SAID YOU HAVE GREAT IDEAS TOO.
MR. CHENG, THANK YOU FOR INTRODUCING NEW TALENT TO US WHEN YOU'RE ALREADY SO BUSY AS A JURY MEMBER AND WRITER FOR THE ART EXHIBITION.
I LOVED *TEN BROTHERS,* WHICH YOU PUBLISHED FOR MR. CHENG! IT'S SO EXQUISITELY PRINTED!

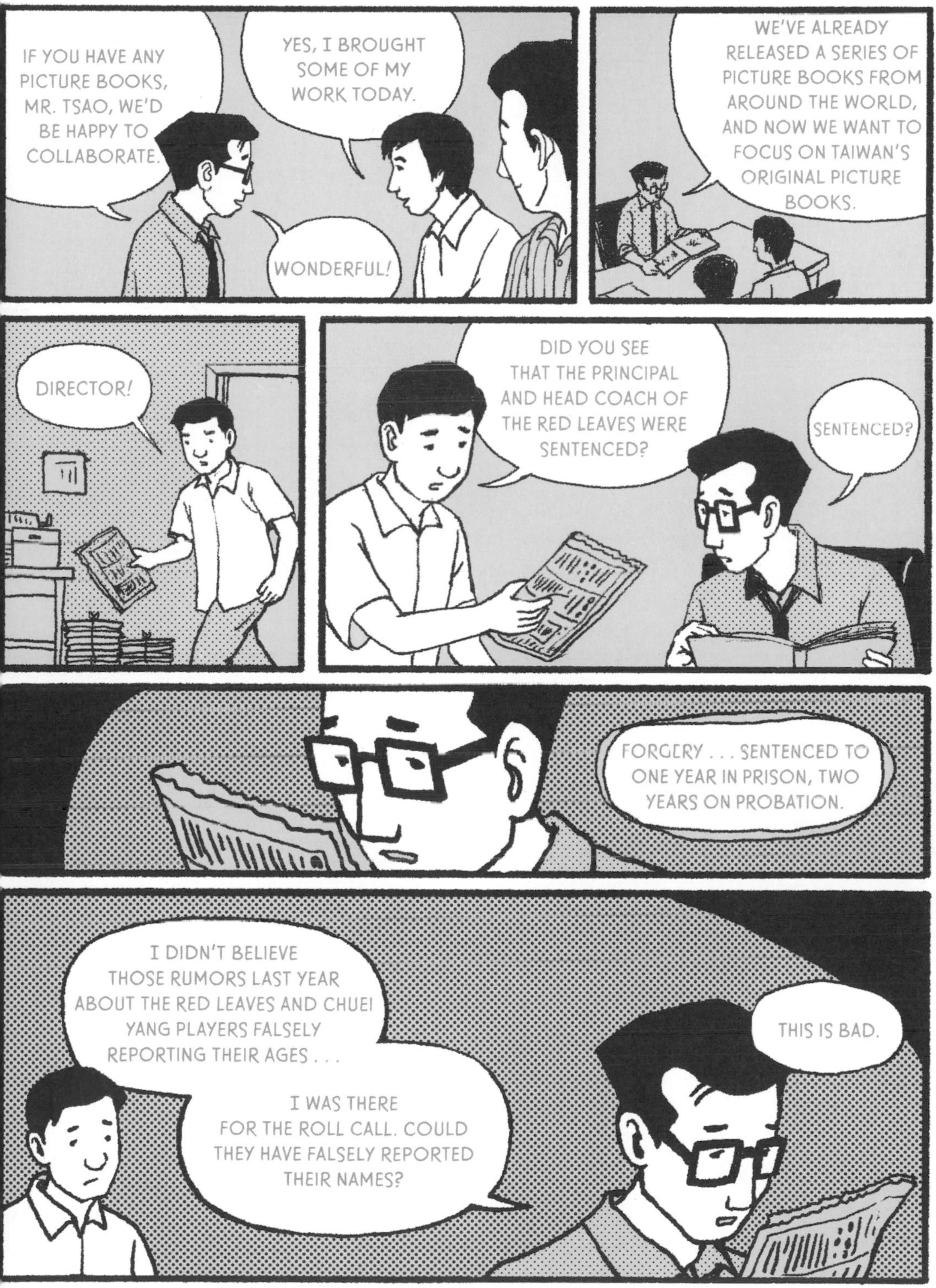
IF YOU HAVE ANY PICTURE BOOKS, MR. TSAO, WE'D BE HAPPY TO COLLABORATE.
YES, I BROUGHT SOME OF MY WORK TODAY.
WONDERFUL!
WE'VE ALREADY RELEASED A SERIES OF PICTURE BOOKS FROM AROUND THE WORLD, AND NOW WE WANT TO FOCUS ON TAIWAN'S ORIGINAL PICTURE BOOKS.
DIRECTOR!
DID YOU SEE THAT THE PRINCIPAL AND HEAD COACH OF THE RED LEAVES WERE SENTENCED?
SENTENCED?
FORGERY . . . SENTENCED TO ONE YEAR IN PRISON, TWO YEARS ON PROBATION.
I DIDN'T BELIEVE THOSE RUMORS LAST YEAR ABOUT THE RED LEAVES AND CHUEI YANG PLAYERS FALSELY REPORTING THEIR AGES . . .
I WAS THERE FOR THE ROLL CALL. COULD THEY HAVE FALSELY REPORTED THEIR NAMES?
THIS IS BAD.

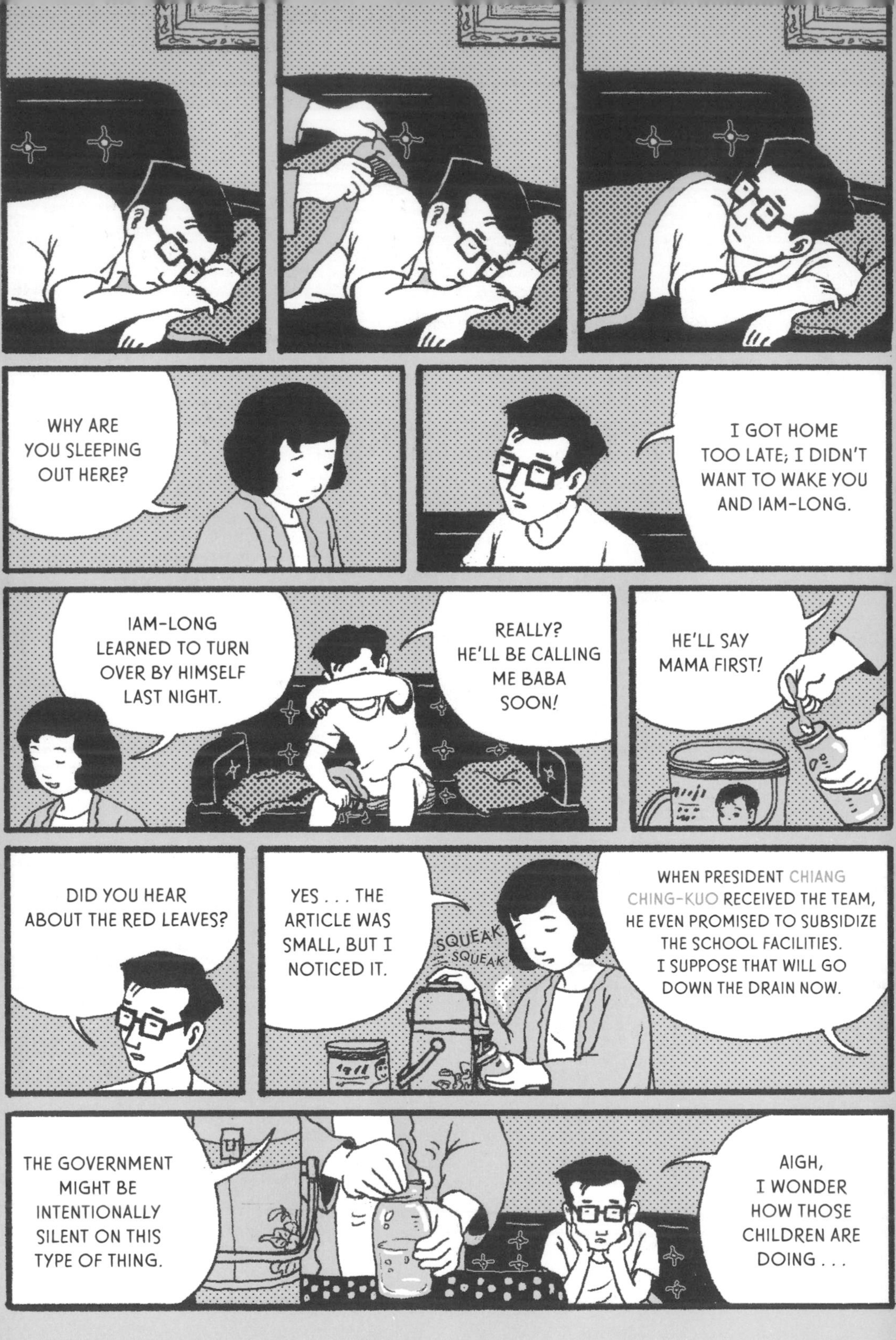
WHY ARE YOU SLEEPING OUT HERE?
I GOT HOME TOO LATE; I DIDN'T WANT TO WAKE YOU AND IAM-LONG.
IAM-LONG LEARNED TO TURN OVER BY HIMSELF LAST NIGHT.
REALLY? HE'LL BE CALLING ME BABA SOON!
HE'LL SAY MAMA FIRST!
DID YOU HEAR ABOUT THE RED LEAVES?
YES . . . THE ARTICLE WAS SMALL, BUT I NOTICED IT.
SQUEAK
SQUEAK
WHEN PRESIDENT CHIANG CHING-KUO RECEIVED THE TEAM, HE EVEN PROMISED TO SUBSIDIZE THE SCHOOL FACILITIES. I SUPPOSE THAT WILL GO DOWN THE DRAIN NOW.
THE GOVERNMENT MIGHT BE INTENTIONALLY SILENT ON THIS TYPE OF THING.
AIGH, I WONDER HOW THOSE CHILDREN ARE DOING . . .

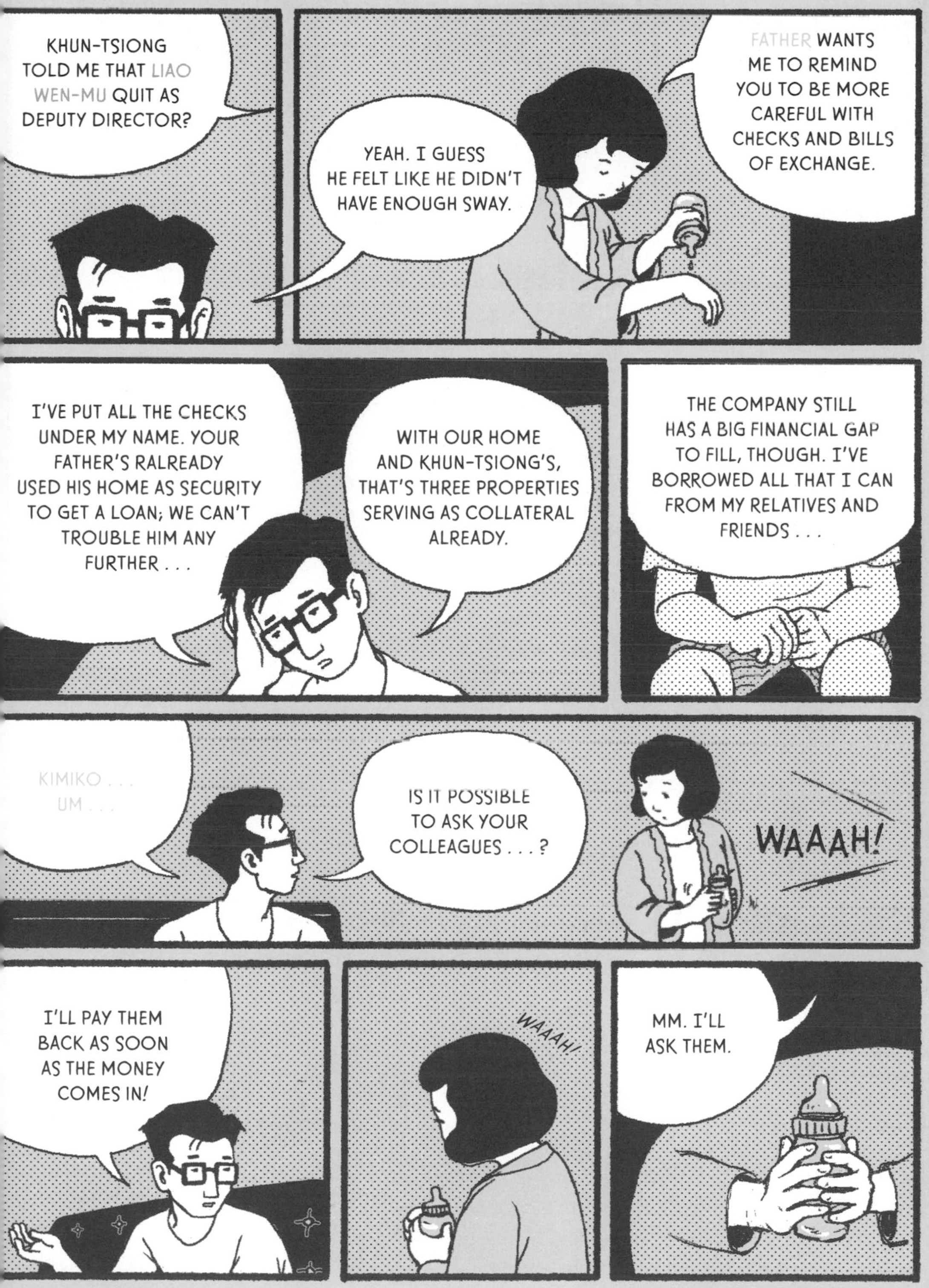
KHUN-TSIONG TOLD ME THAT LIAO WEN-MU QUIT AS DEPUTY DIRECTOR?
YEAH. I GUESS HE FELT LIKE HE DIDN'T HAVE ENOUGH SWAY.
FATHER WANTS ME TO REMIND YOU TO BE MORE CAREFUL WITH CHECKS AND BILLS OF EXCHANGE.
I'VE PUT ALL THE CHECKS UNDER MY NAME. YOUR FATHER'S RALREADY USED HIS HOME AS SECURITY TO GET A LOAN; WE CAN'T TROUBLE HIM ANY FURTHER . . .
WITH OUR HOME AND KHUN-TSIONG'S, THAT'S THREE PROPERTIES SERVING AS COLLATERAL ALREADY.
THE COMPANY STILL HAS A BIG FINANCIAL GAP TO FILL, THOUGH. I'VE BORROWED ALL THAT I CAN FROM MY RELATIVES AND FRIENDS . . .
KIMIKO . . . UM . . .
IS IT POSSIBLE TO ASK YOUR COLLEAGUES . . . ?
WAAAH!
I'LL PAY THEM BACK AS SOON AS THE MONEY COMES IN!
WAAAH!
MM. I'LL ASK THEM.

September 8, 1969

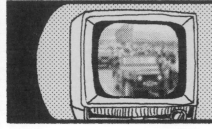
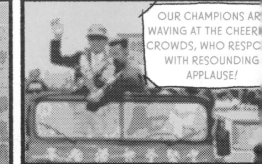
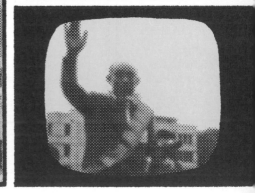

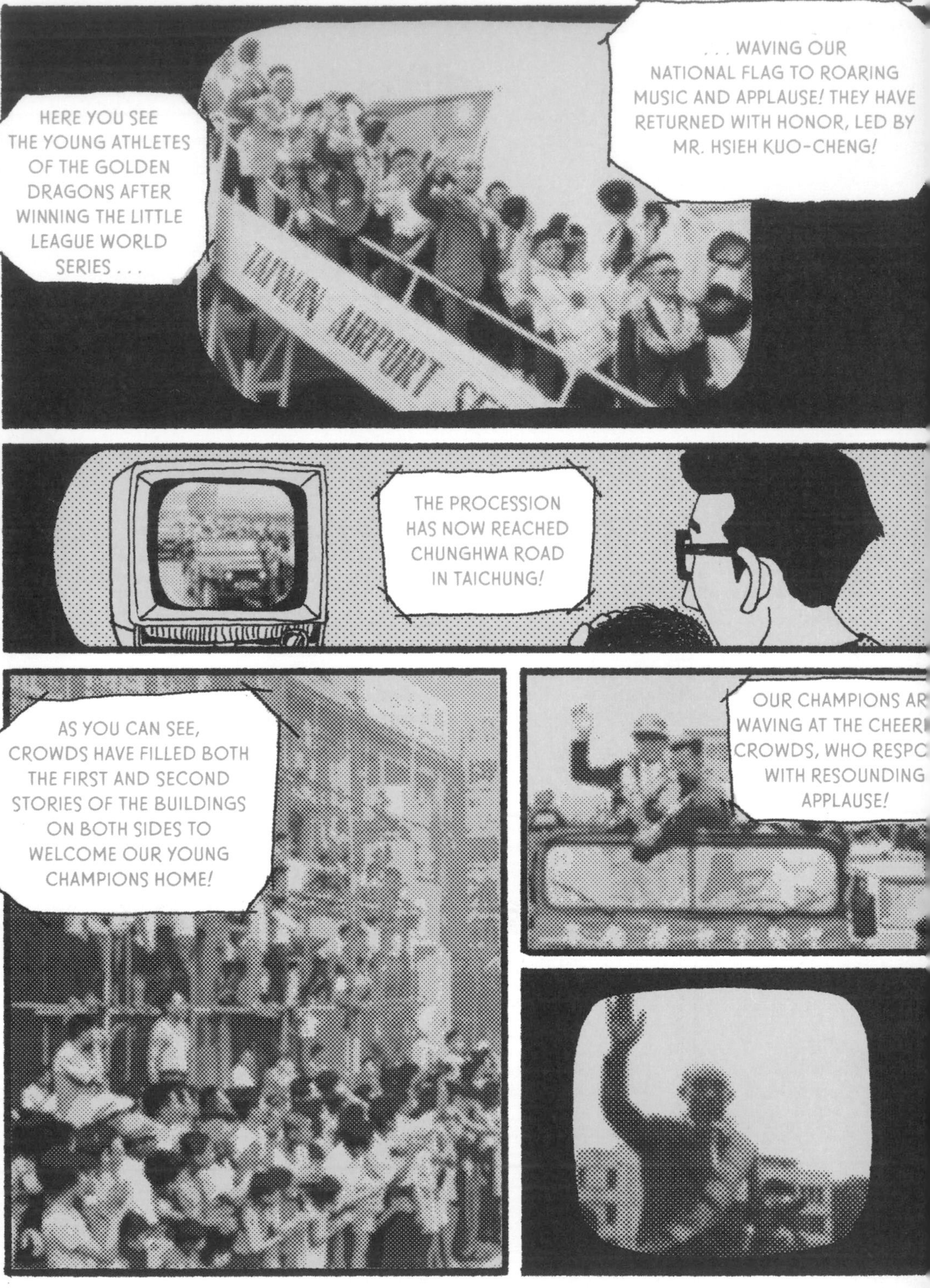

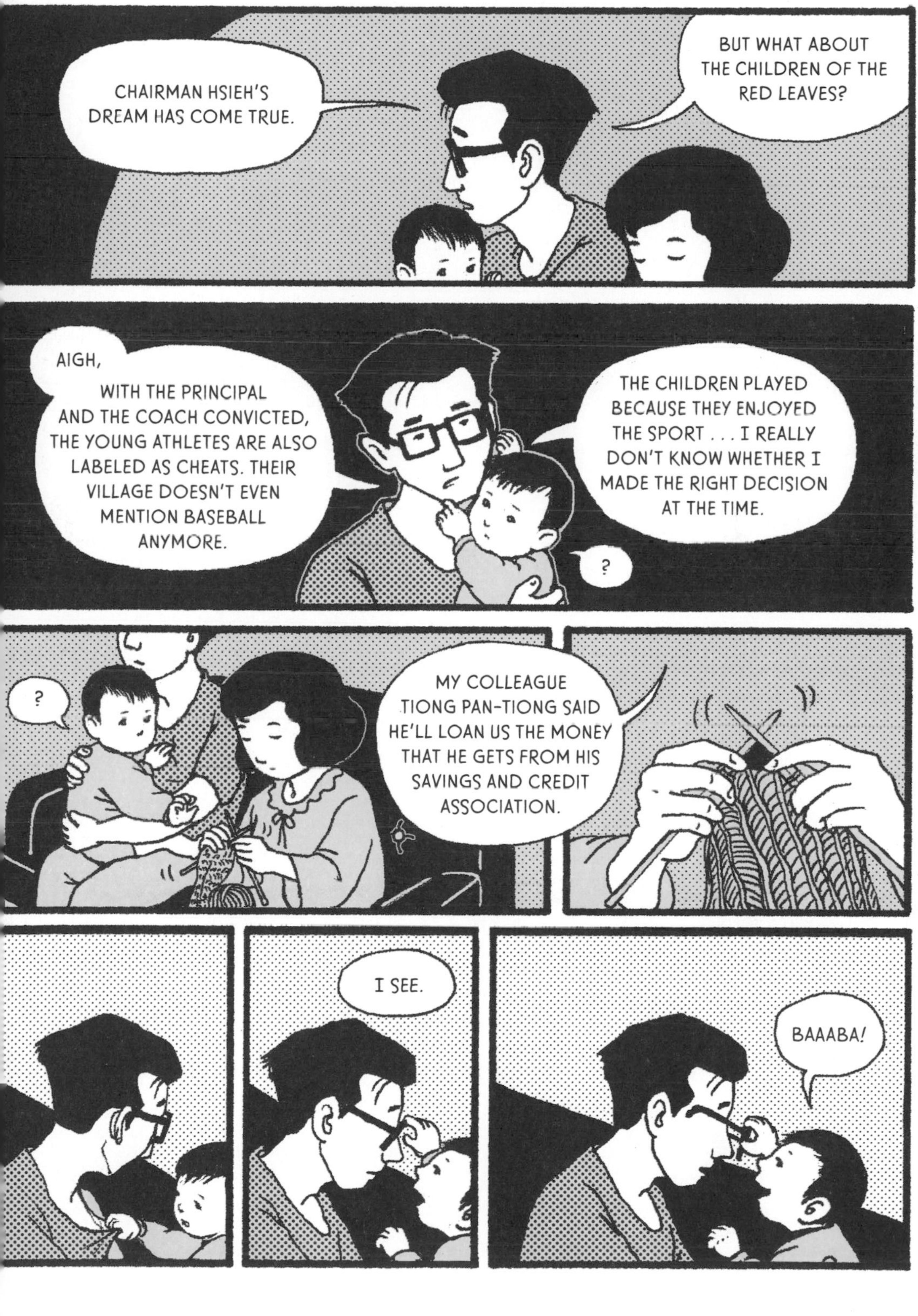
CHAIRMAN HSIEH'S DREAM HAS COME TRUE.
BUT WHAT ABOUT THE CHILDREN OF THE RED LEAVES?
AIGH,
WITH THE PRINCIPAL AND THE COACH CONVICTED, THE YOUNG ATHLETES ARE ALSO LABELED AS CHEATS. THEIR VILLAGE DOESN'T EVEN MENTION BASEBALL ANYMORE.
THE CHILDREN PLAYED BECAUSE THEY ENJOYED THE SPORT . . . I REALLY DON'T KNOW WHETHER I MADE THE RIGHT DECISION AT THE TIME.
?
?
MY COLLEAGUE TIONG PAN-TIONG SAID HE'LL LOAN US THE MONEY THAT HE GETS FROM HIS SAVINGS AND CREDIT ASSOCIATION.
I SEE.
BAAABA!

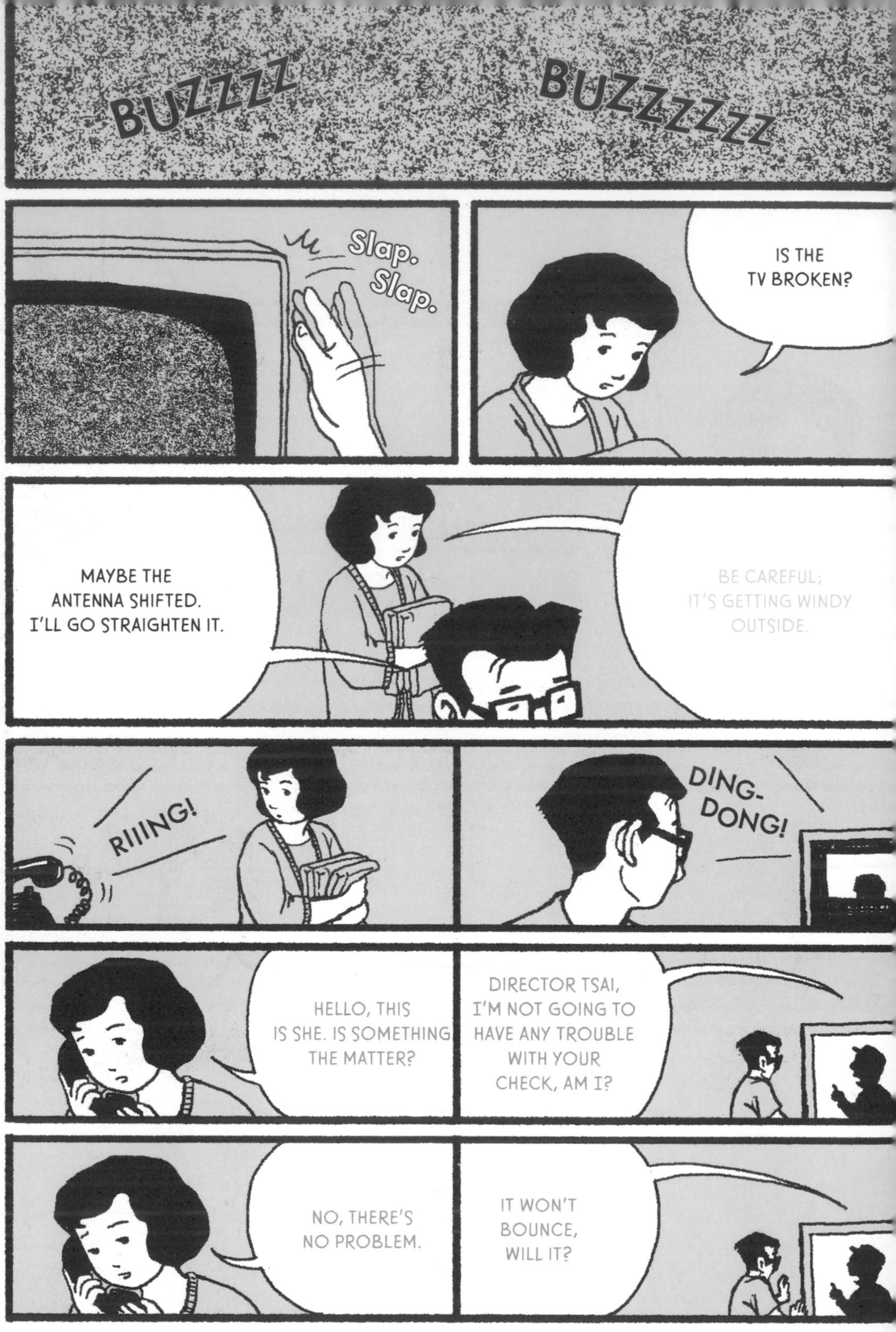
BUZZZZ
BUZZZZZZZ
Slap.
Slap.
IS THE TV BROKEN?
MAYBE THE ANTENNA SHIFTED. I'LL GO STRAIGHTEN IT.
BE CAREFUL; IT'S GETTING WINDY OUTSIDE.
RIIING!
DING-DONG!
HELLO, THIS IS SHE. IS SOMETHING THE MATTER?
DIRECTOR TSAI, I'M NOT GOING TO HAVE ANY TROUBLE WITH YOUR CHECK, AM I?
NO, THERE'S NO PROBLEM.
IT WON'T BOUNCE, WILL IT?

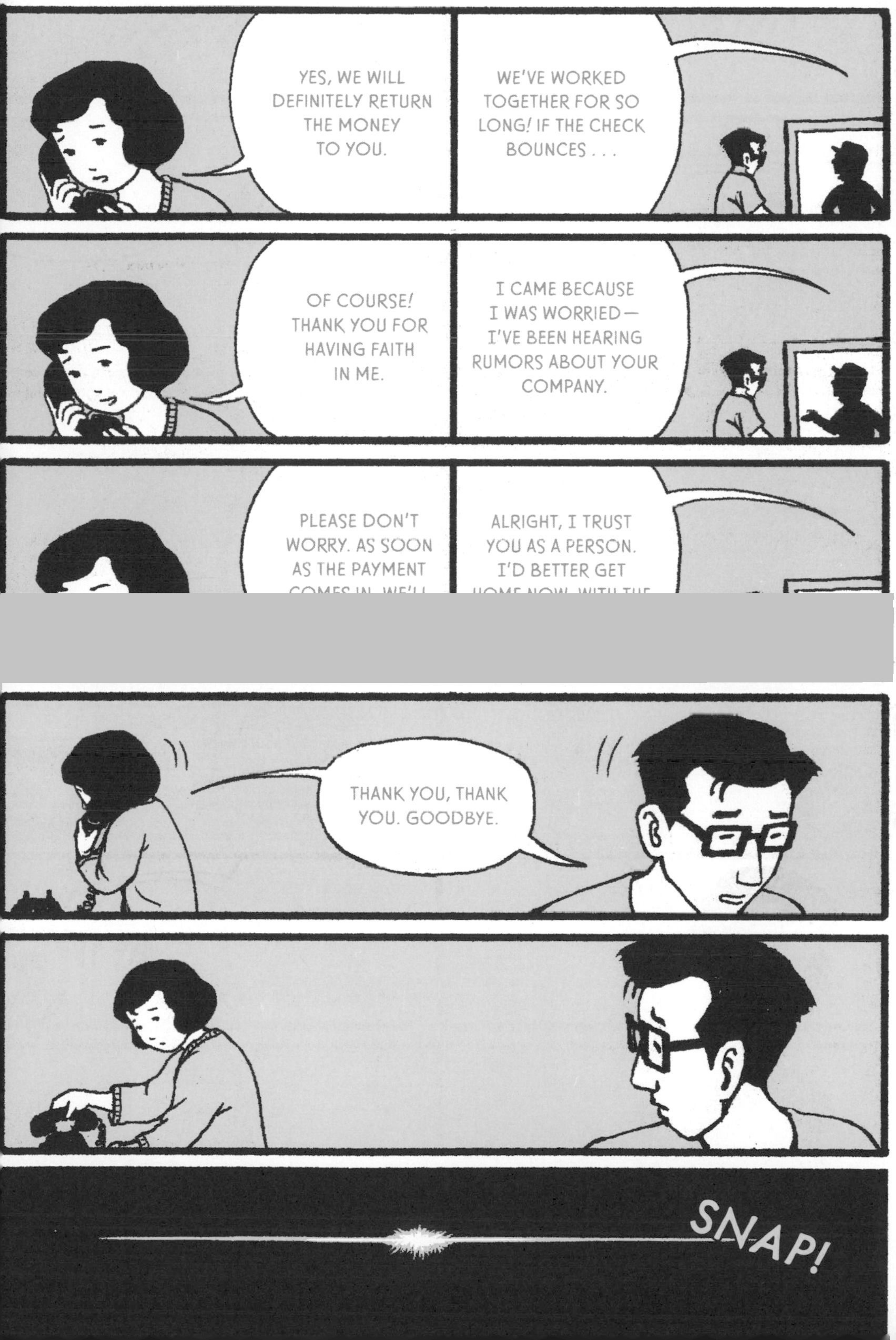
YES, WE WILL DEFINITELY RETURN THE MONEY TO YOU.
WE'VE WORKED TOGETHER FOR SO LONG! IF THE CHECK BOUNCES . . .
OF COURSE! THANK YOU FOR HAVING FAITH IN ME.
I CAME BECAUSE I WAS WORRIED— I'VE BEEN HEARING RUMORS ABOUT YOUR COMPANY.
PLEASE DON'T WORRY. AS SOON AS THE PAYMENT
ALRIGHT, I TRUST YOU AS A PERSON. I'D BETTER GET
THANK YOU, THANK YOU. GOODBYE.
SNAP!

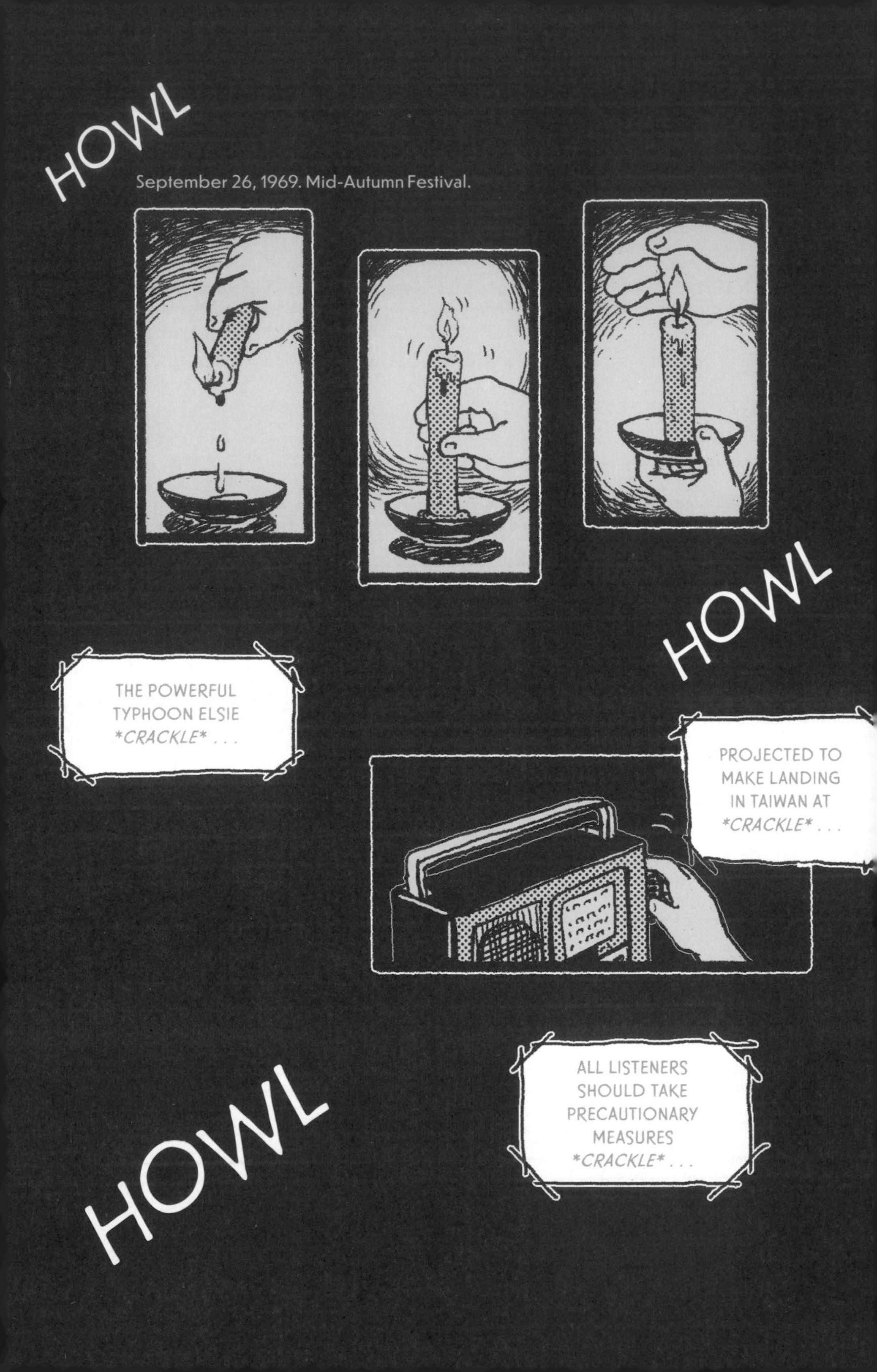
HOWL
September 26, 1969. Mid-Autumn Festival.
HOWL
THE POWERFUL TYPHOON ELSIE *CRACKLE* . . .
PROJECTED TO MAKE LANDING IN TAIWAN AT *CRACKLE* . . .
HOWL
ALL LISTENERS SHOULD TAKE PRECAUTIONARY MEASURES *CRACKLE* . . .

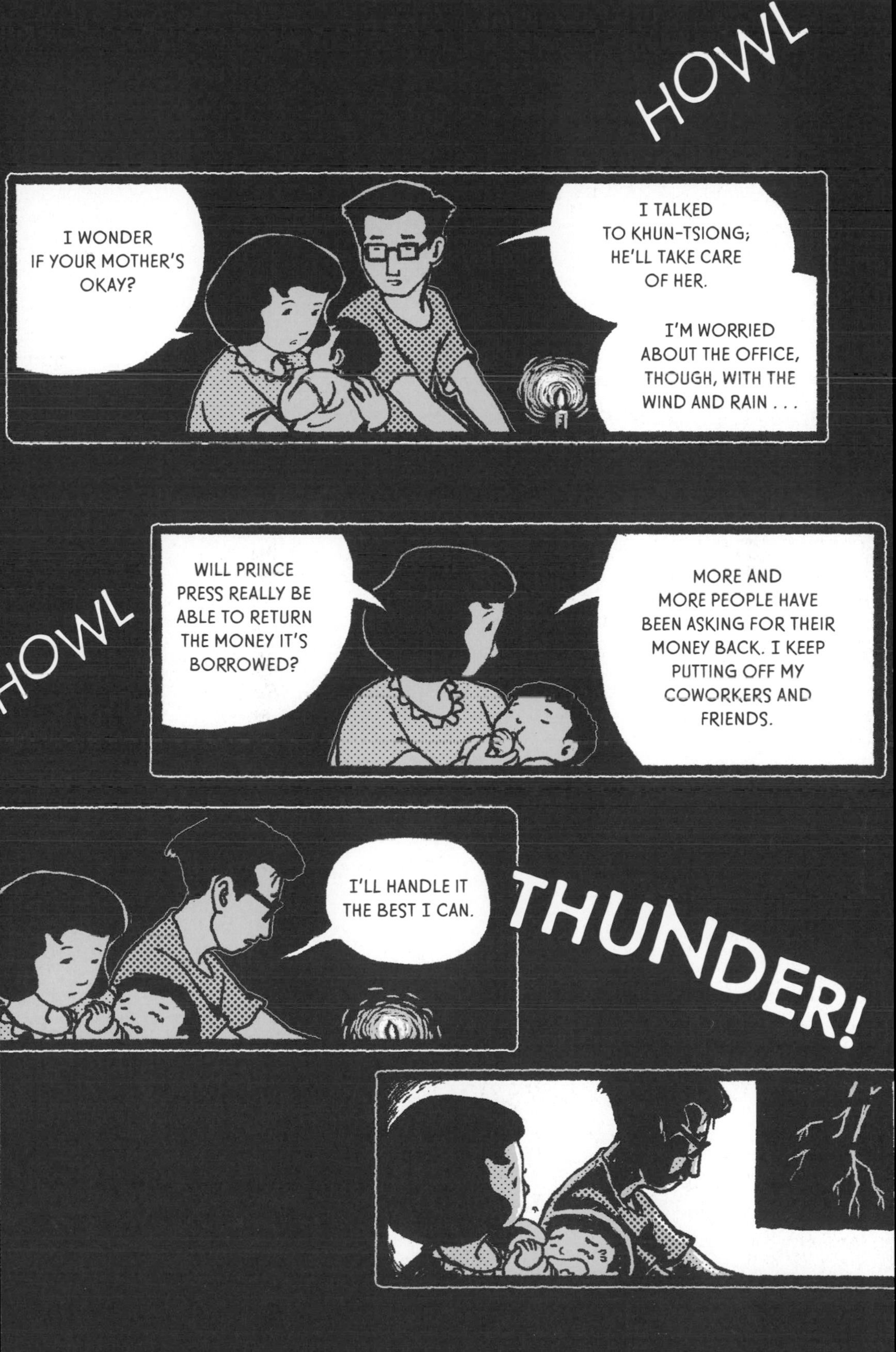
HOWL
I WONDER IF YOUR MOTHER'S OKAY?
I TALKED TO KHUN-TSIONG; HE'LL TAKE CARE OF HER.
I'M WORRIED ABOUT THE OFFICE, THOUGH, WITH THE WIND AND RAIN . . .
HOWL
WILL PRINCE PRESS REALLY BE ABLE TO RETURN THE MONEY IT'S BORROWED?
MORE AND MORE PEOPLE HAVE BEEN ASKING FOR THEIR MONEY BACK. I KEEP PUTTING OFF MY COWORKERS AND FRIENDS.
I'LL HANDLE IT THE BEST I CAN.
THUNDER!

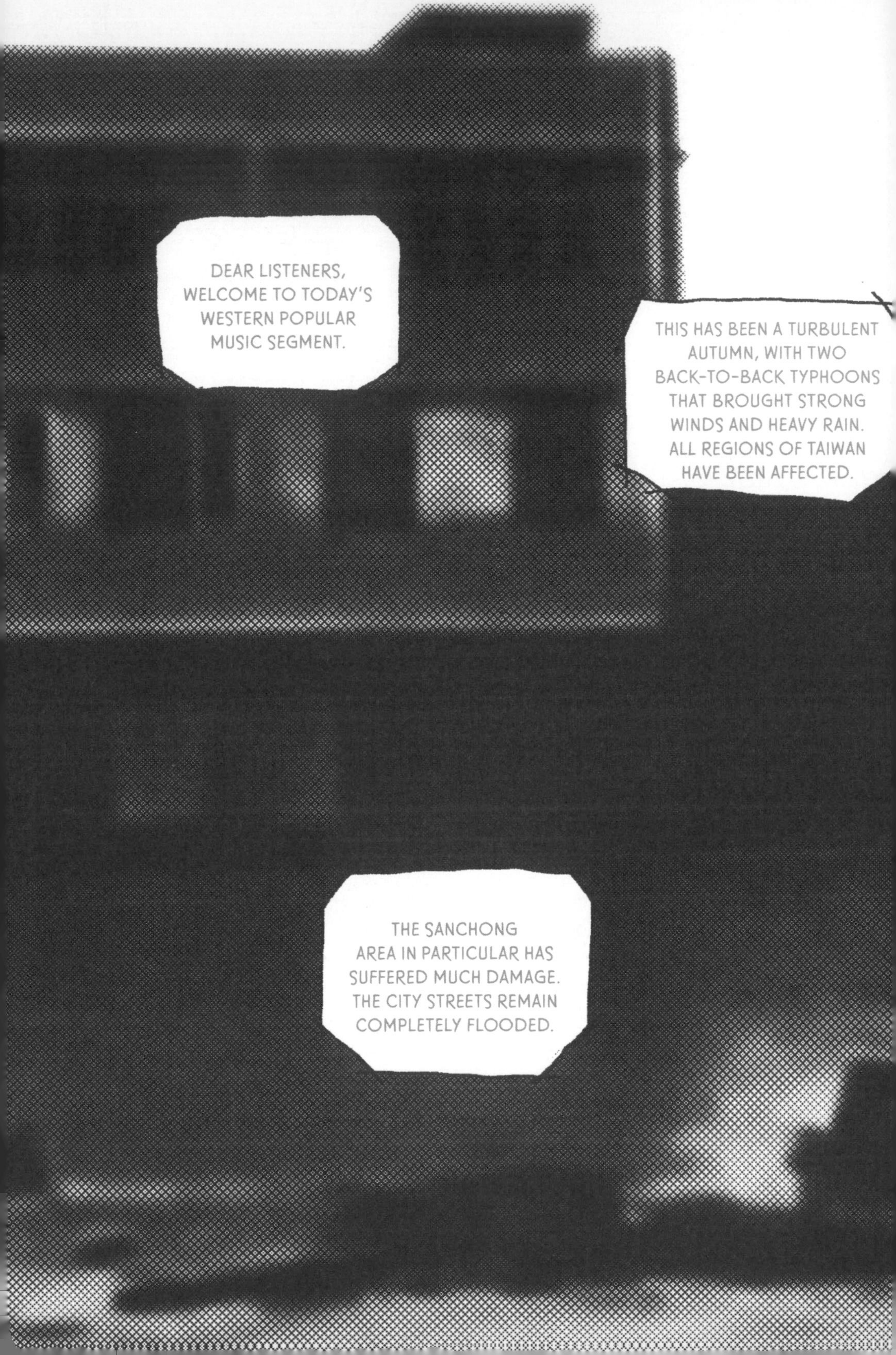
DEAR LISTENERS, WELCOME TO TODAY'S WESTERN POPULAR MUSIC SEGMENT.
THIS HAS BEEN A TURBULENT AUTUMN, WITH TWO BACK-TO-BACK TYPHOONS THAT BROUGHT STRONG WINDS AND HEAVY RAIN. ALL REGIONS OF TAIWAN HAVE BEEN AFFECTED.
THE SANCHONG AREA IN PARTICULAR HAS SUFFERED MUCH DAMAGE. THE CITY STREETS REMAIN COMPLETELY FLOODED.

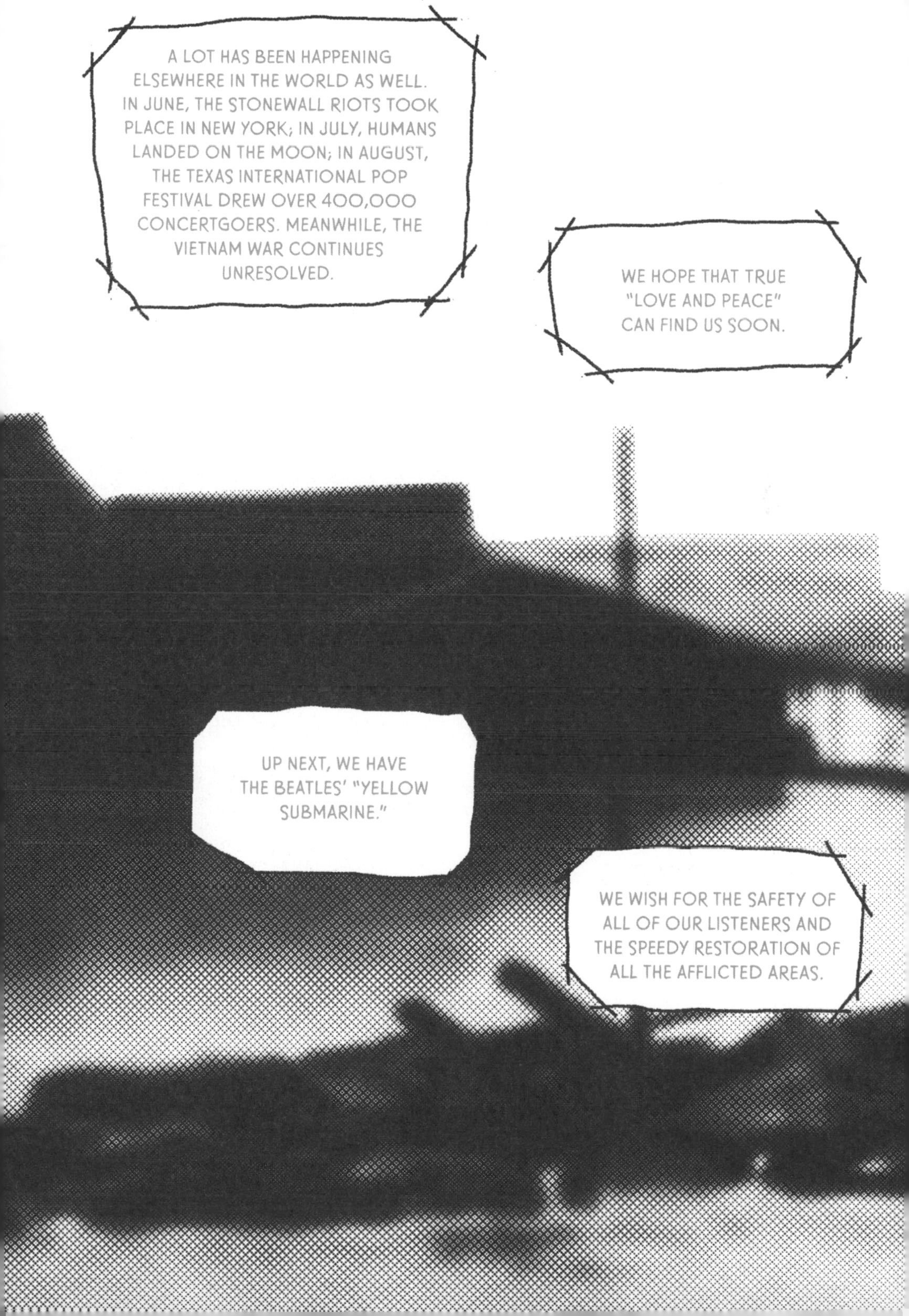
A LOT HAS BEEN HAPPENING ELSEWHERE IN THE WORLD AS WELL. IN JUNE, THE STONEWALL RIOTS TOOK PLACE IN NEW YORK; IN JULY, HUMANS LANDED ON THE MOON; IN AUGUST, THE TEXAS INTERNATIONAL POP FESTIVAL DREW OVER 400,000 CONCERTGOERS. MEANWHILE, THE VIETNAM WAR CONTINUES UNRESOLVED.
WE HOPE THAT TRUE "LOVE AND PEACE" CAN FIND US SOON.
UP NEXT, WE HAVE THE BEATLES' "YELLOW SUBMARINE."
WE WISH FOR THE SAFETY OF ALL OF OUR LISTENERS AND THE SPEEDY RESTORATION OF ALL THE AFFLICTED AREAS.

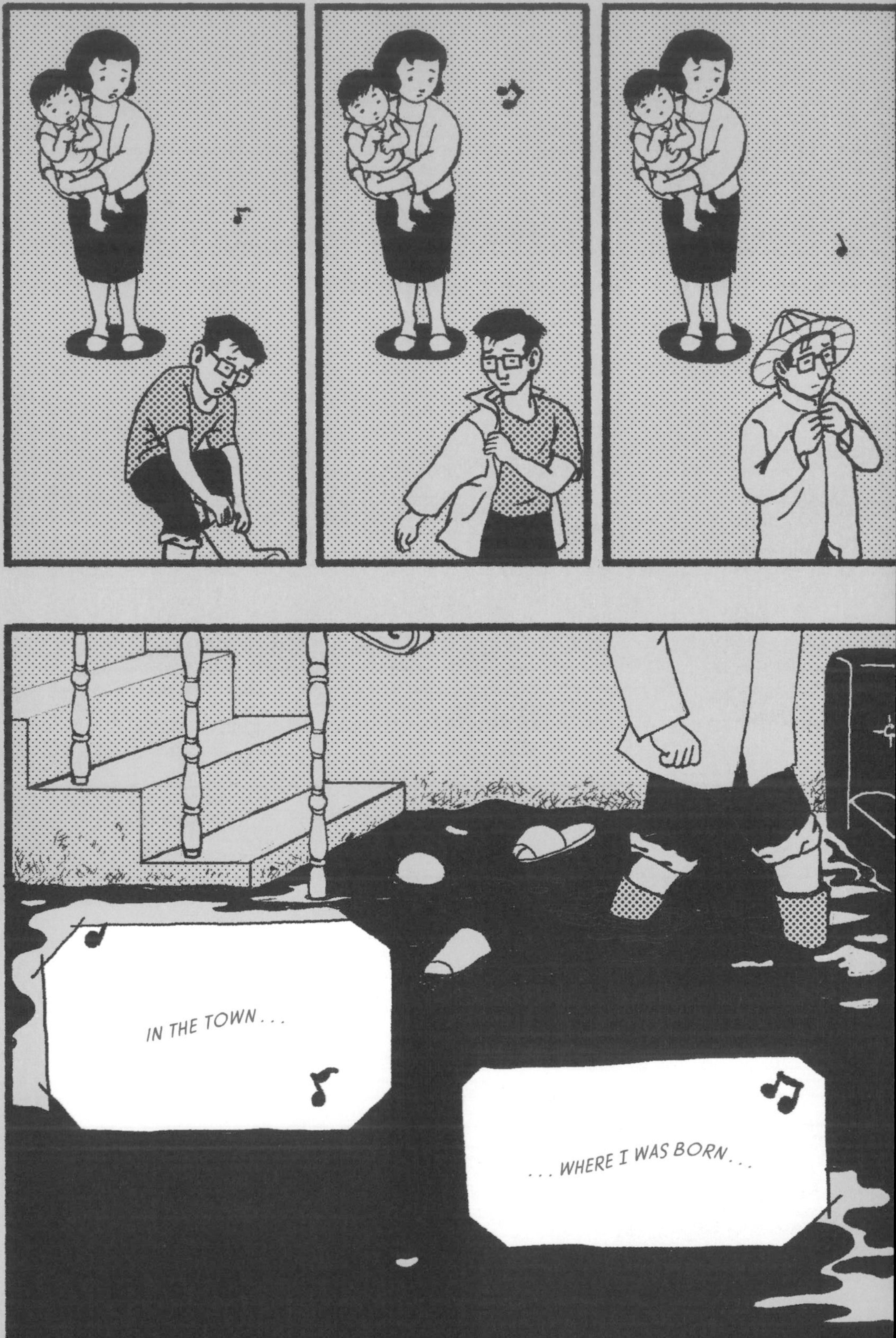
IN THE TOWN . . .
. . . WHERE I WAS BORN . . .

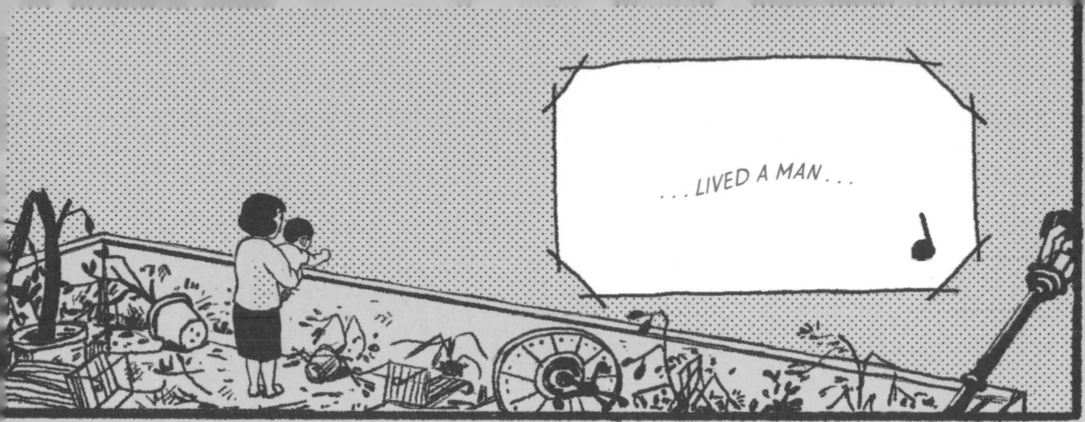

. . . LIVED A MAN . . .

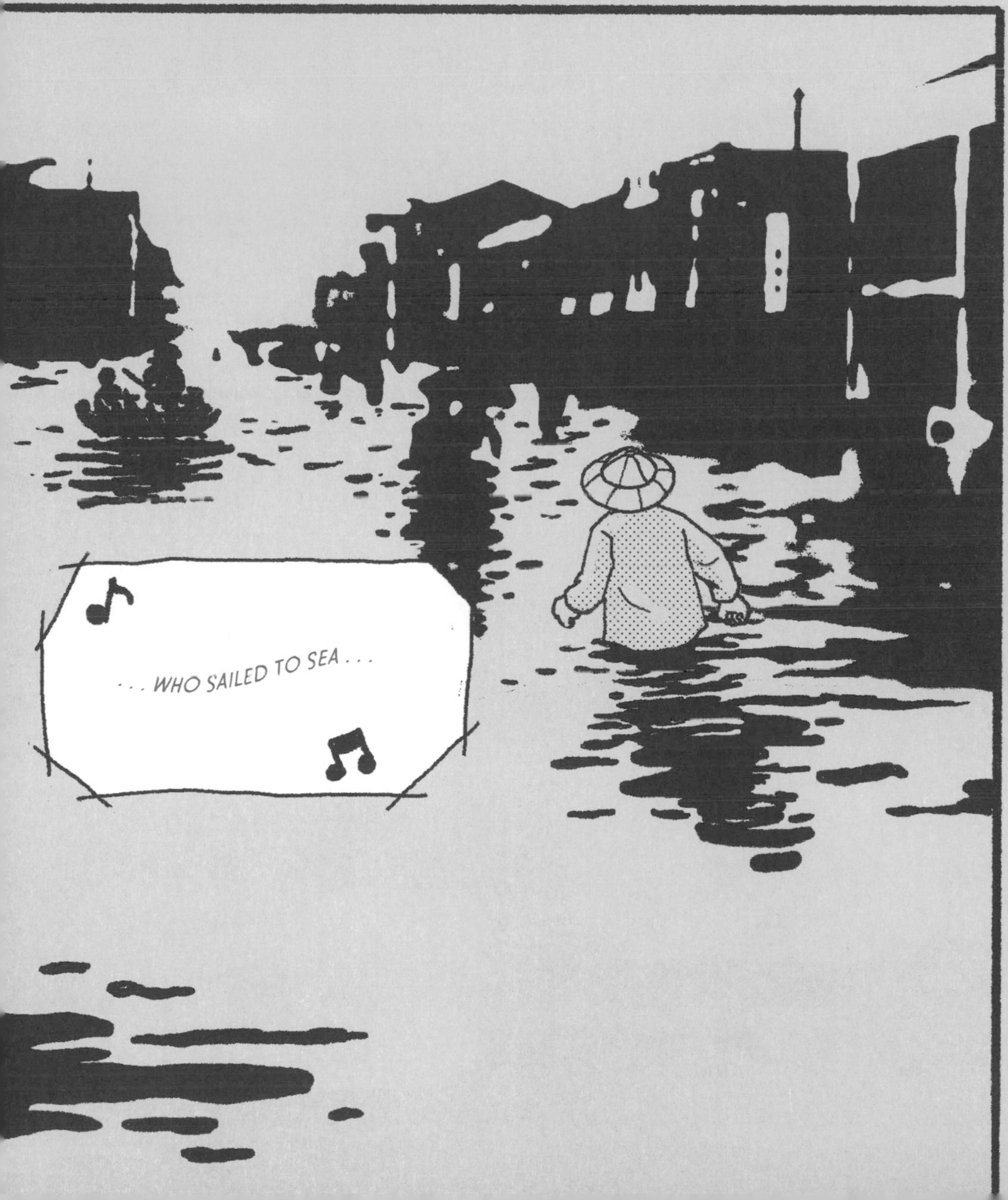

. . . WHO SAILED TO SEA . . .

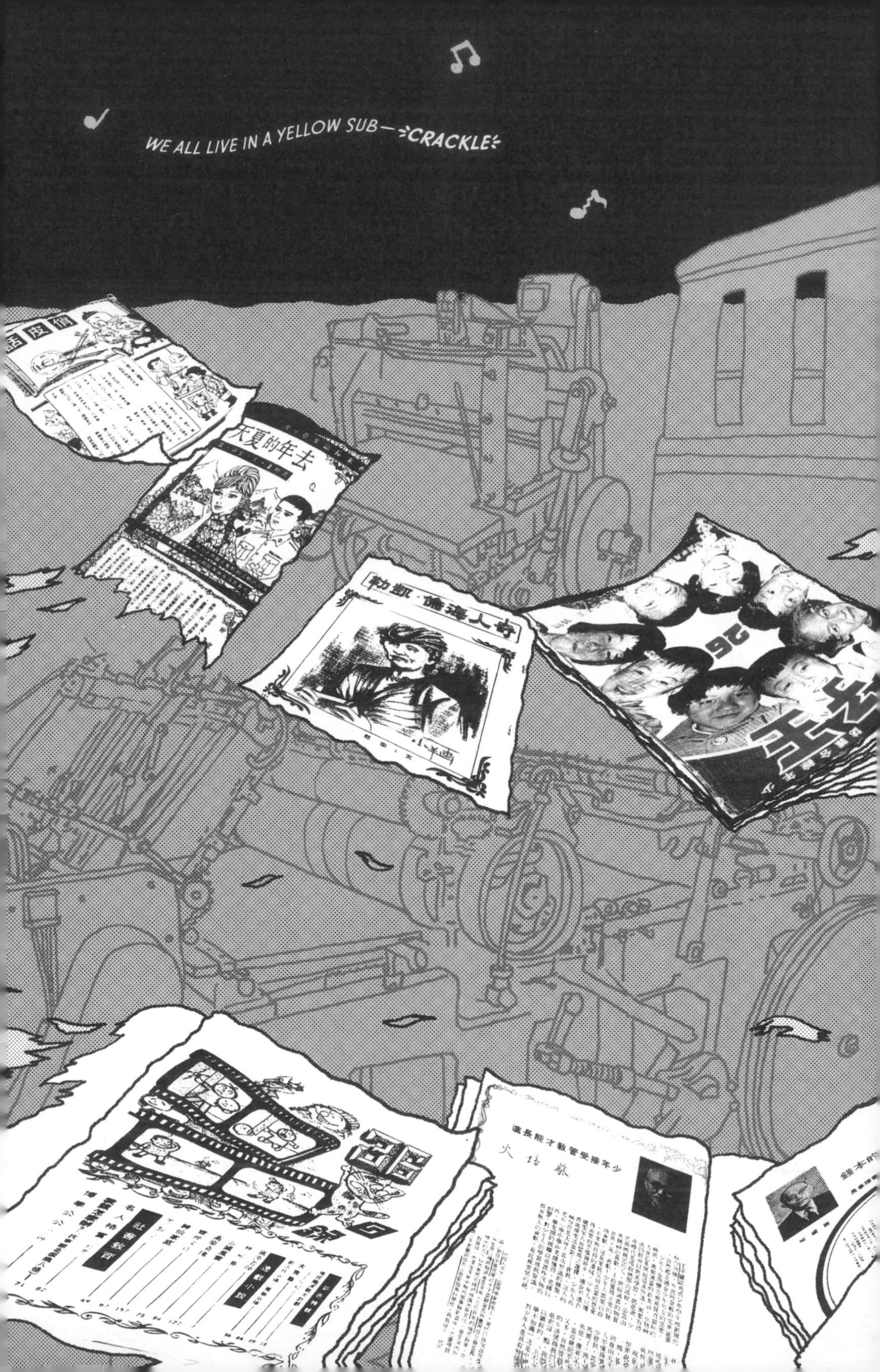
WE ALL LIVE IN A YELLOW SUB—
CRACKLE

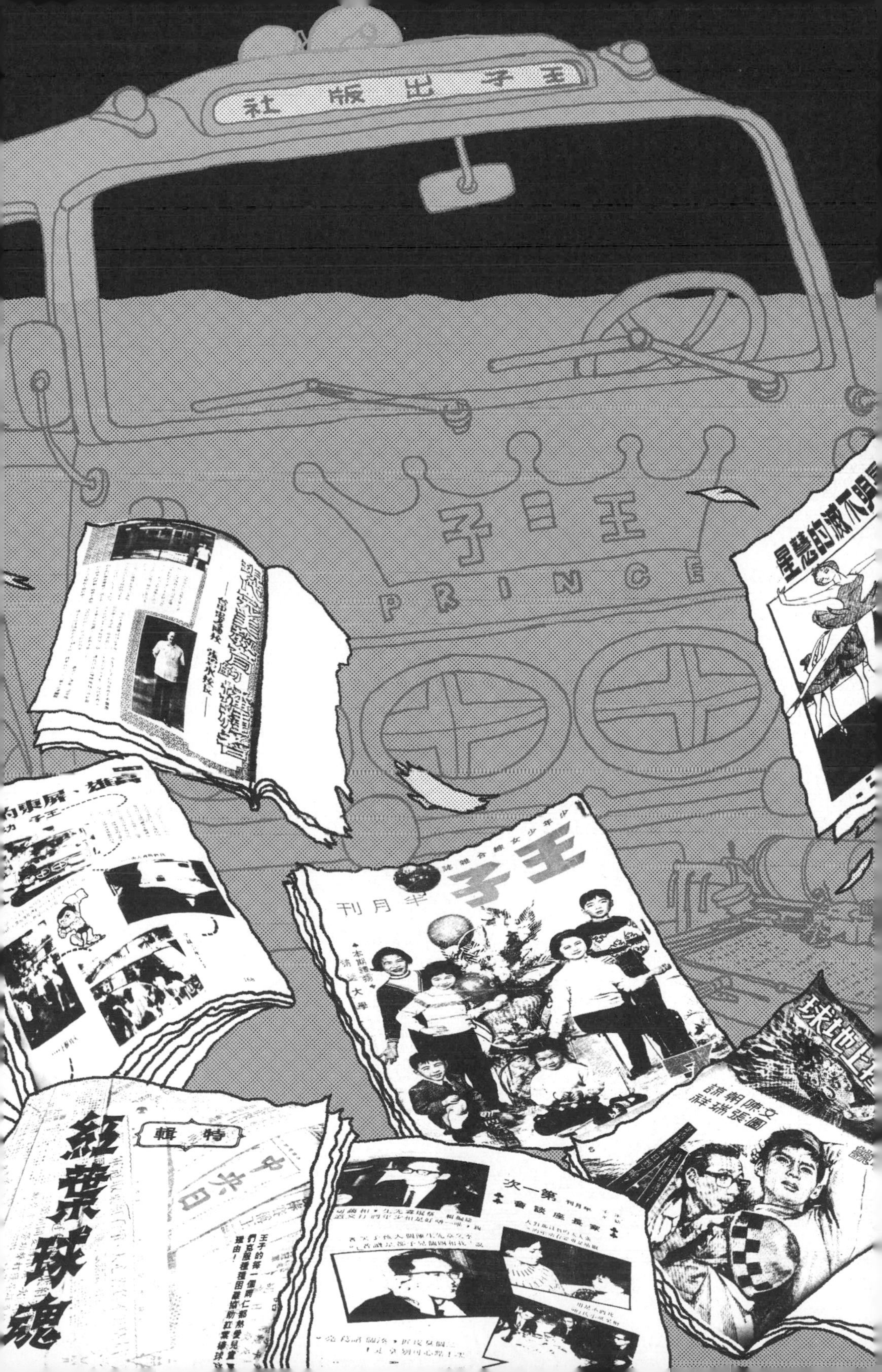

王子出版社
PRINCE
少年少女綜合雜誌
王子
半月刊
特輯
紅葉球魂
第一次
座談會

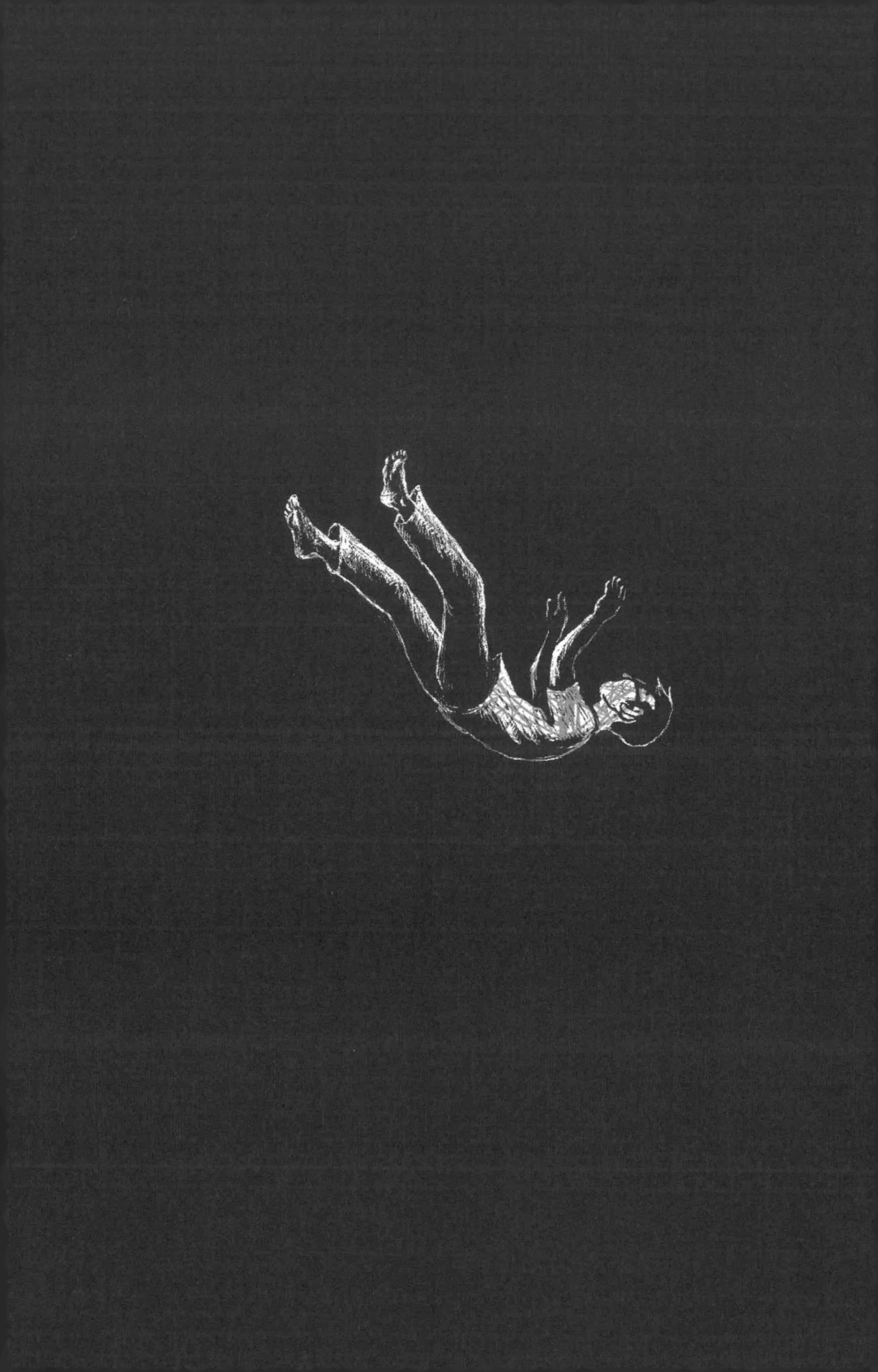

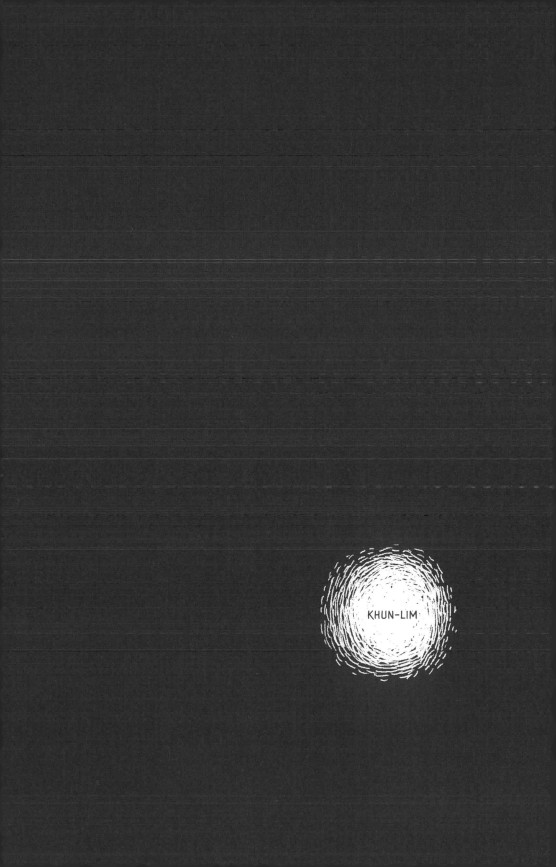

KHUN-LIM

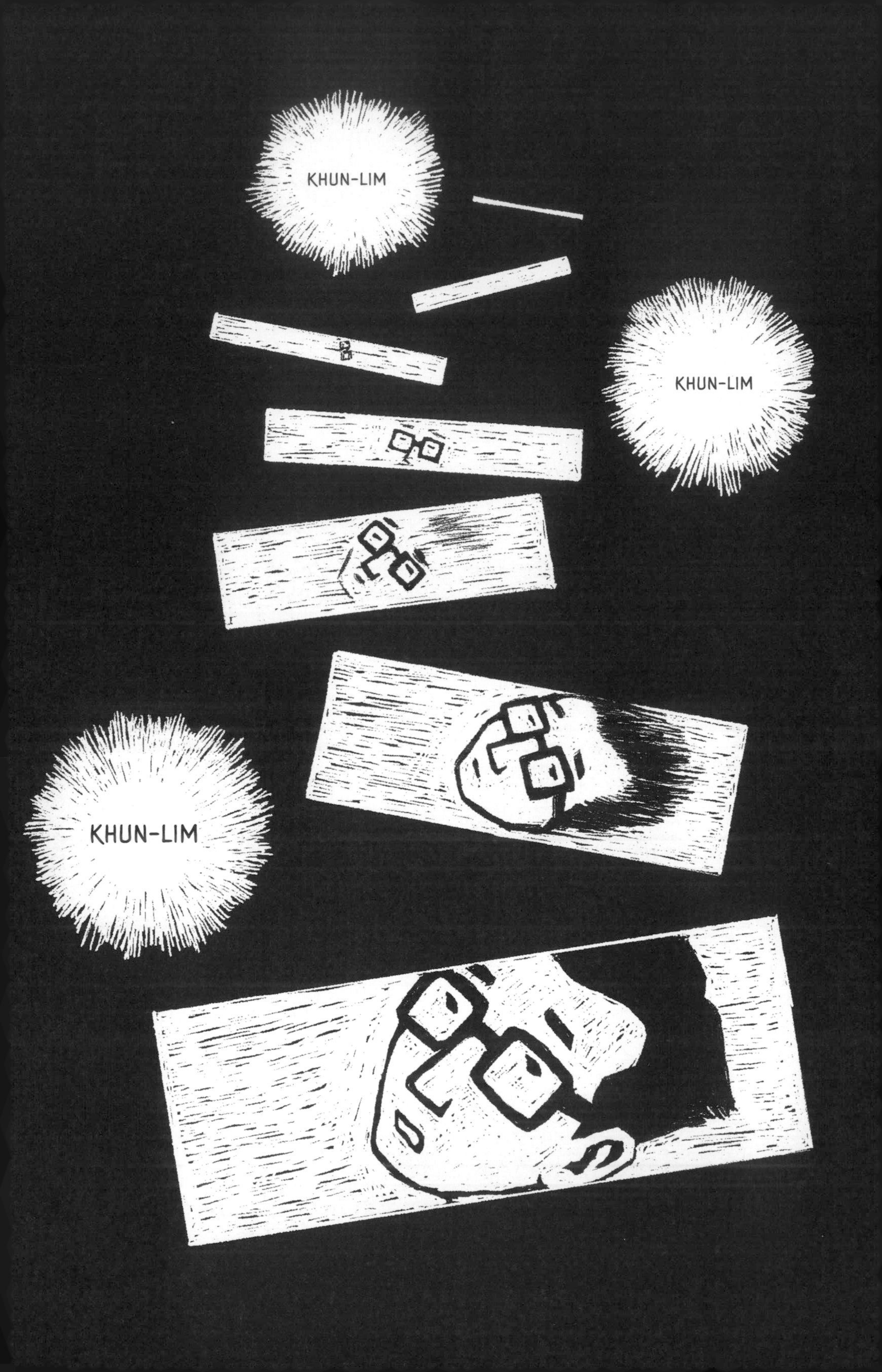
KHUN-LIM
KHUN-LIM
KHUN-LIM

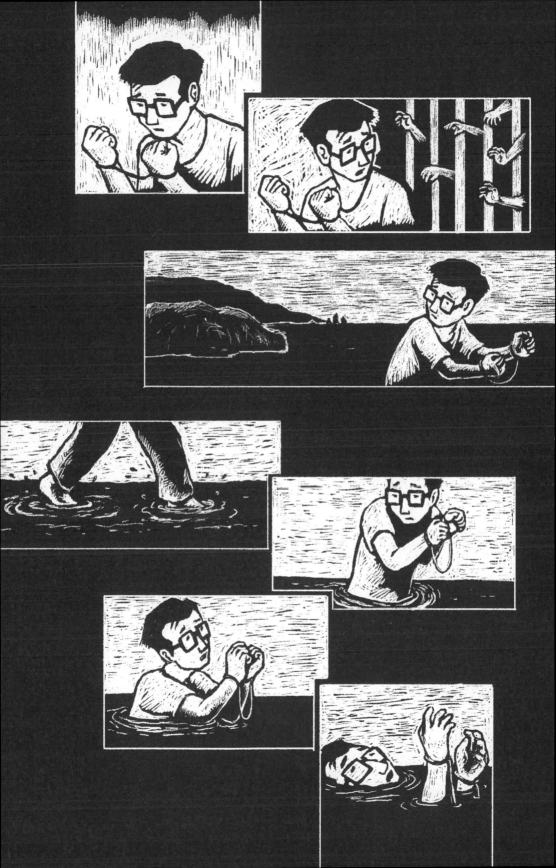

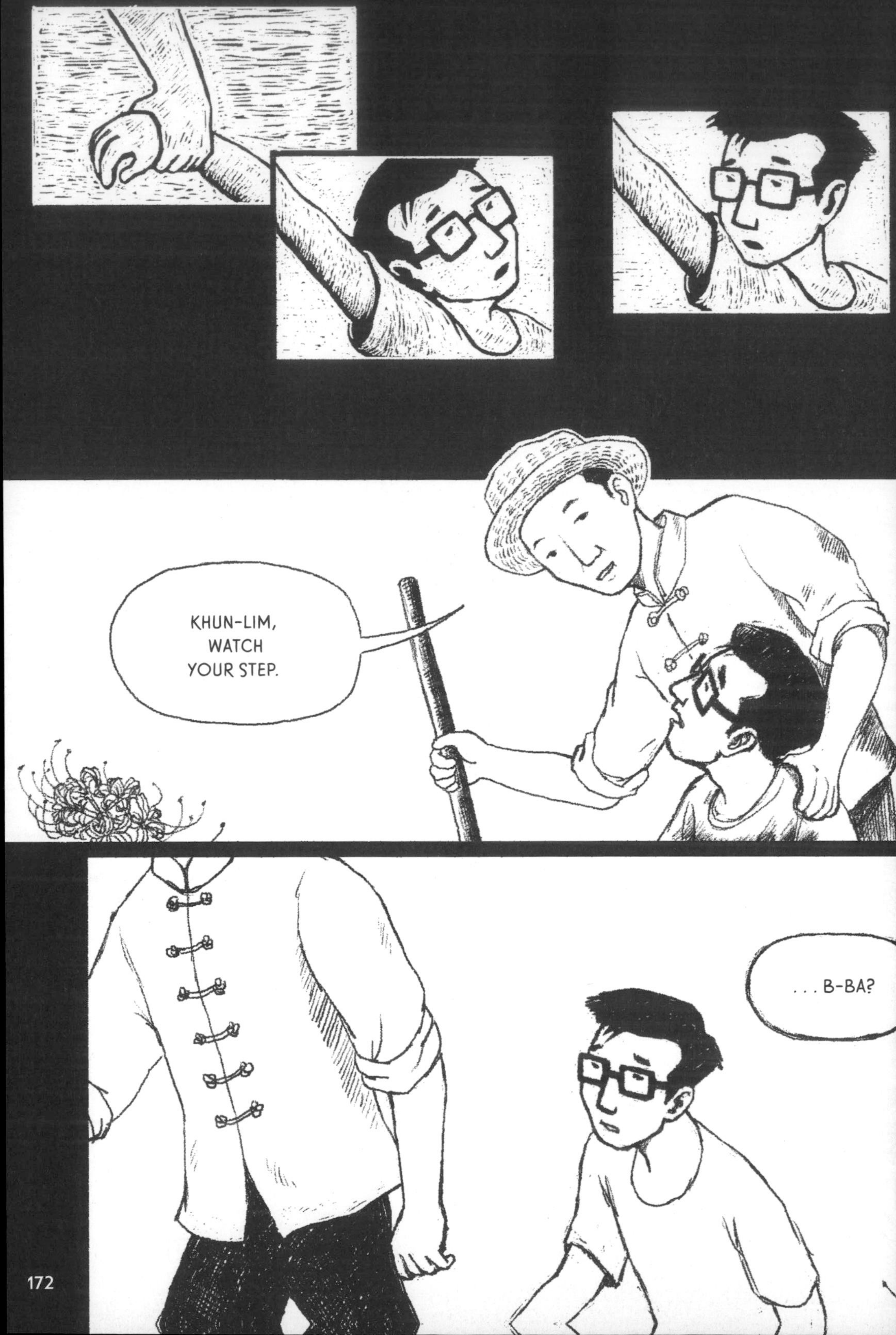
KHUN-LIM, WATCH YOUR STEP.
. . . B-BA?

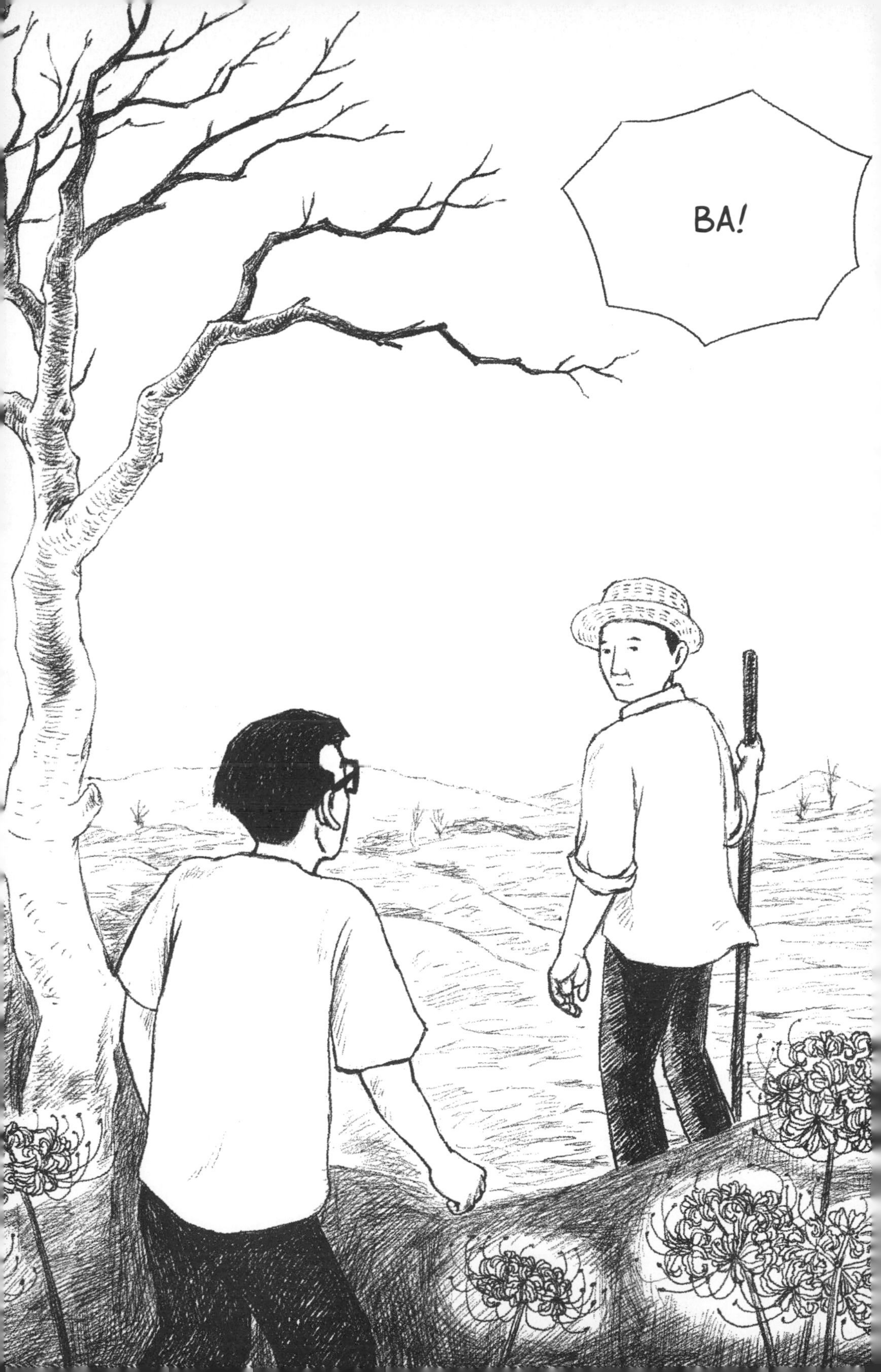
BA!

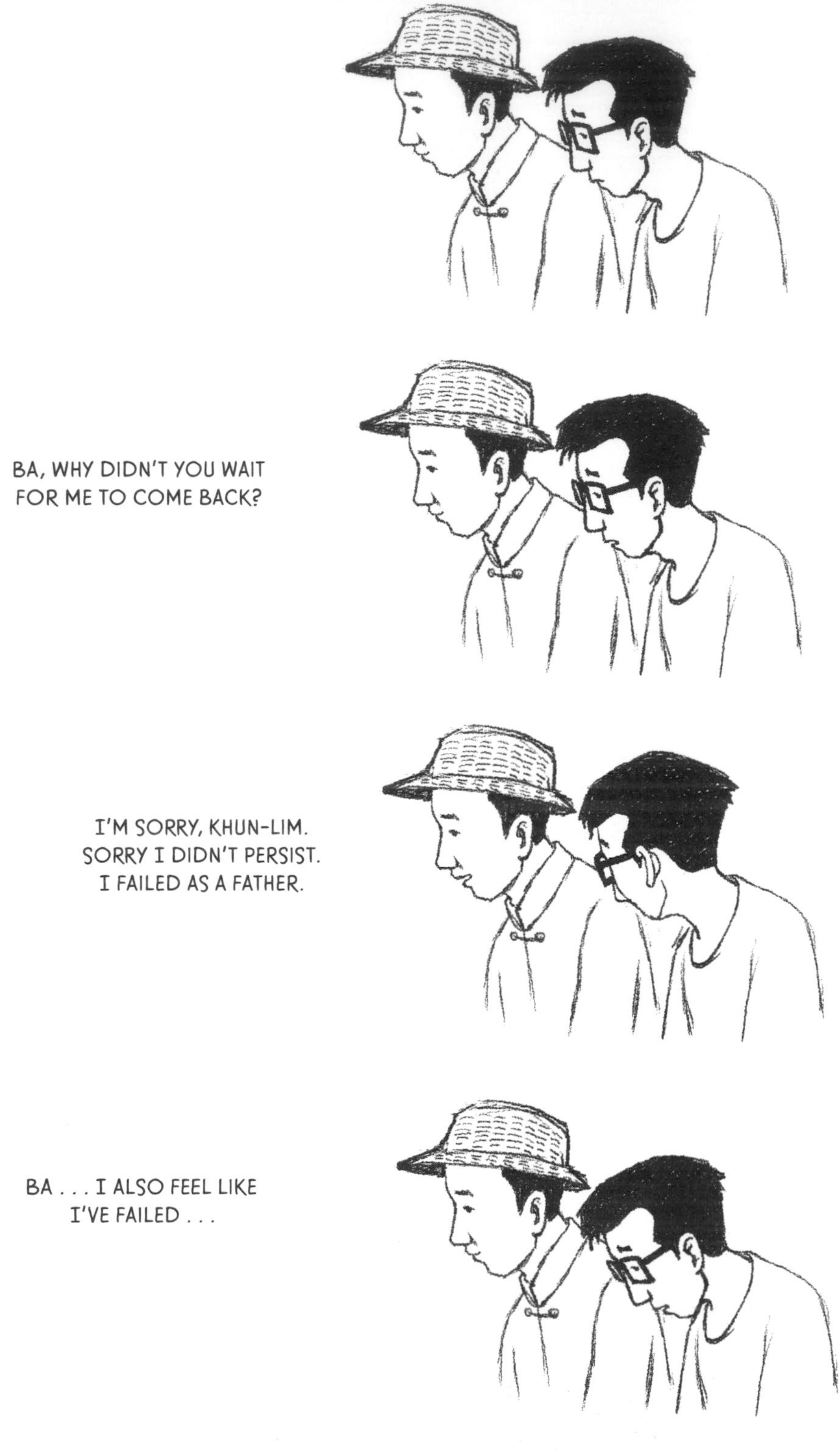
BA, WHY DIDN'T YOU WAIT FOR ME TO COME BACK?
I'M SORRY, KHUN-LIM. SORRY I DIDN'T PERSIST. I FAILED AS A FATHER.
BA . . . I ALSO FEEL LIKE I'VE FAILED . . .

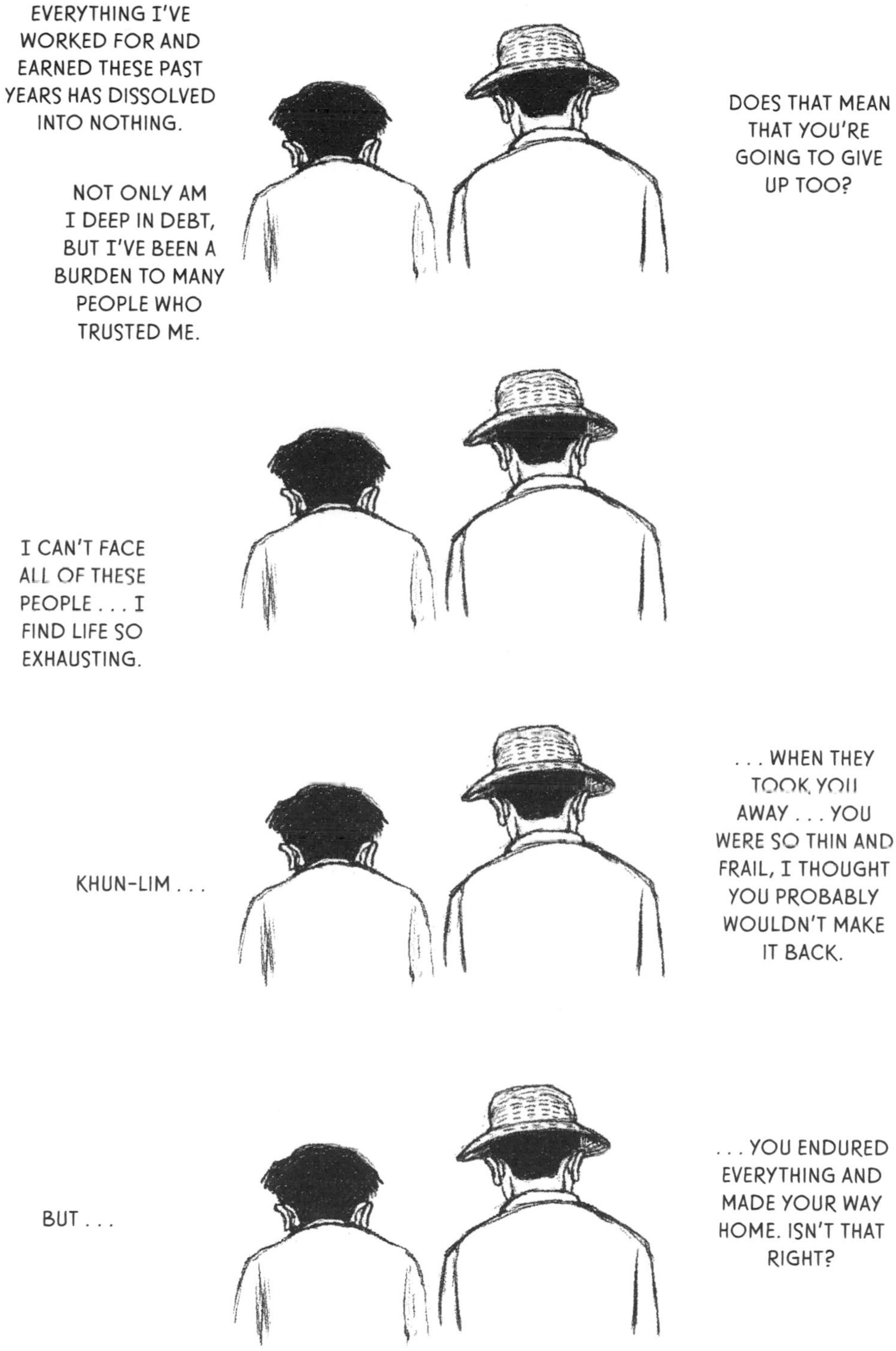
EVERYTHING I'VE WORKED FOR AND EARNED THESE PAST YEARS HAS DISSOLVED INTO NOTHING.
NOT ONLY AM I DEEP IN DEBT, BUT I'VE BEEN A BURDEN TO MANY PEOPLE WHO TRUSTED ME.
DOES THAT MEAN THAT YOU'RE GOING TO GIVE UP TOO?
I CAN'T FACE ALL OF THESE PEOPLE . . . I FIND LIFE SO EXHAUSTING.
KHUN-LIM . . .
. . . WHEN THEY TOOK YOU AWAY . . . YOU WERE SO THIN AND FRAIL, I THOUGHT YOU PROBABLY WOULDN'T MAKE IT BACK.
BUT . . .
. . . YOU ENDURED EVERYTHING AND MADE YOUR WAY HOME. ISN'T THAT RIGHT?

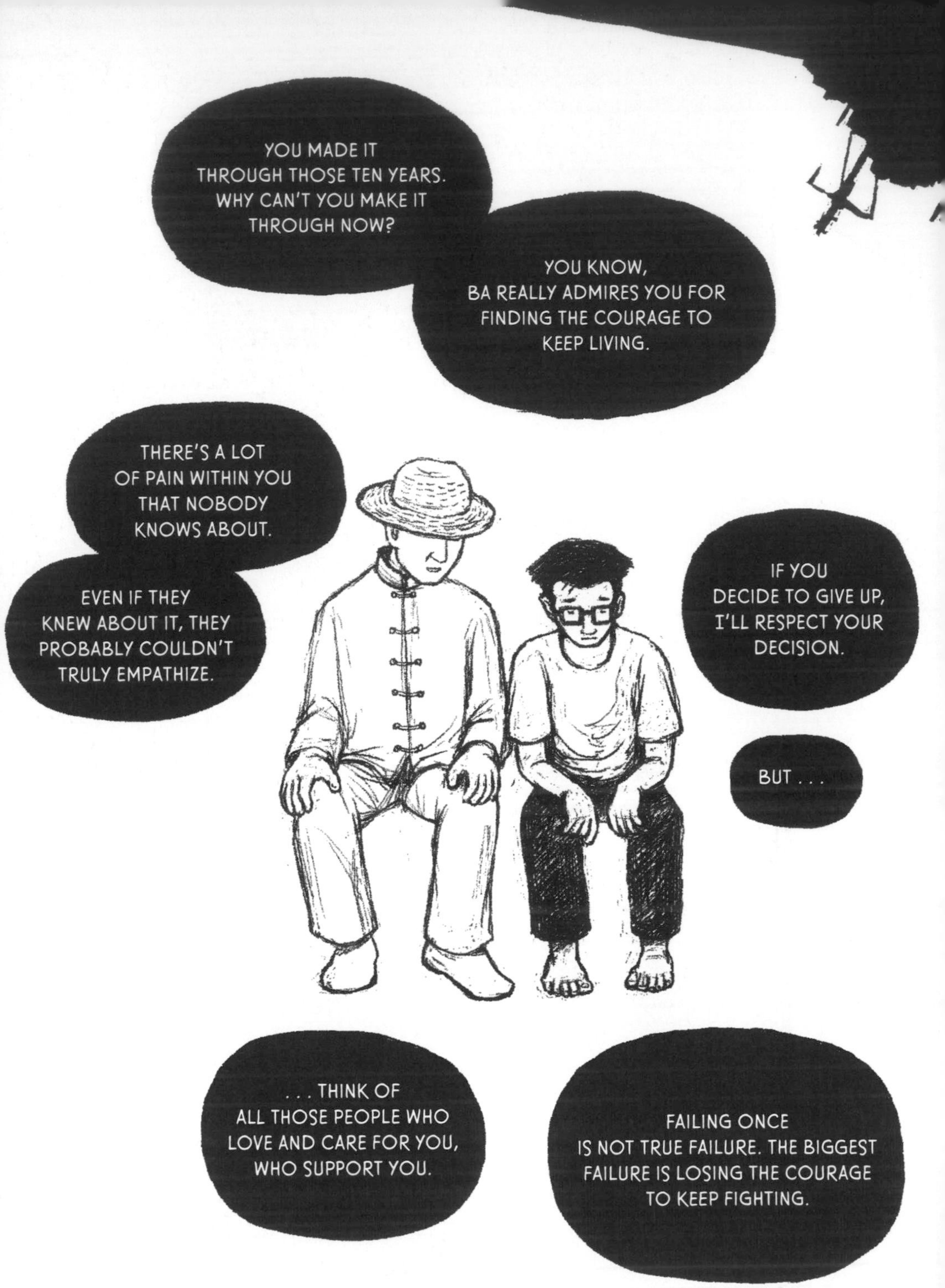
YOU MADE IT THROUGH THOSE TEN YEARS. WHY CAN'T YOU MAKE IT THROUGH NOW?
YOU KNOW, BA REALLY ADMIRES YOU FOR FINDING THE COURAGE TO KEEP LIVING.
THERE'S A LOT OF PAIN WITHIN YOU THAT NOBODY KNOWS ABOUT.
EVEN IF THEY KNEW ABOUT IT, THEY PROBABLY COULDN'T TRULY EMPATHIZE.
IF YOU DECIDE TO GIVE UP, I'LL RESPECT YOUR DECISION.
BUT . . .
. . . THINK OF ALL THOSE PEOPLE WHO LOVE AND CARE FOR YOU, WHO SUPPORT YOU.
FAILING ONCE IS NOT TRUE FAILURE. THE BIGGEST FAILURE IS LOSING THE COURAGE TO KEEP FIGHTING.

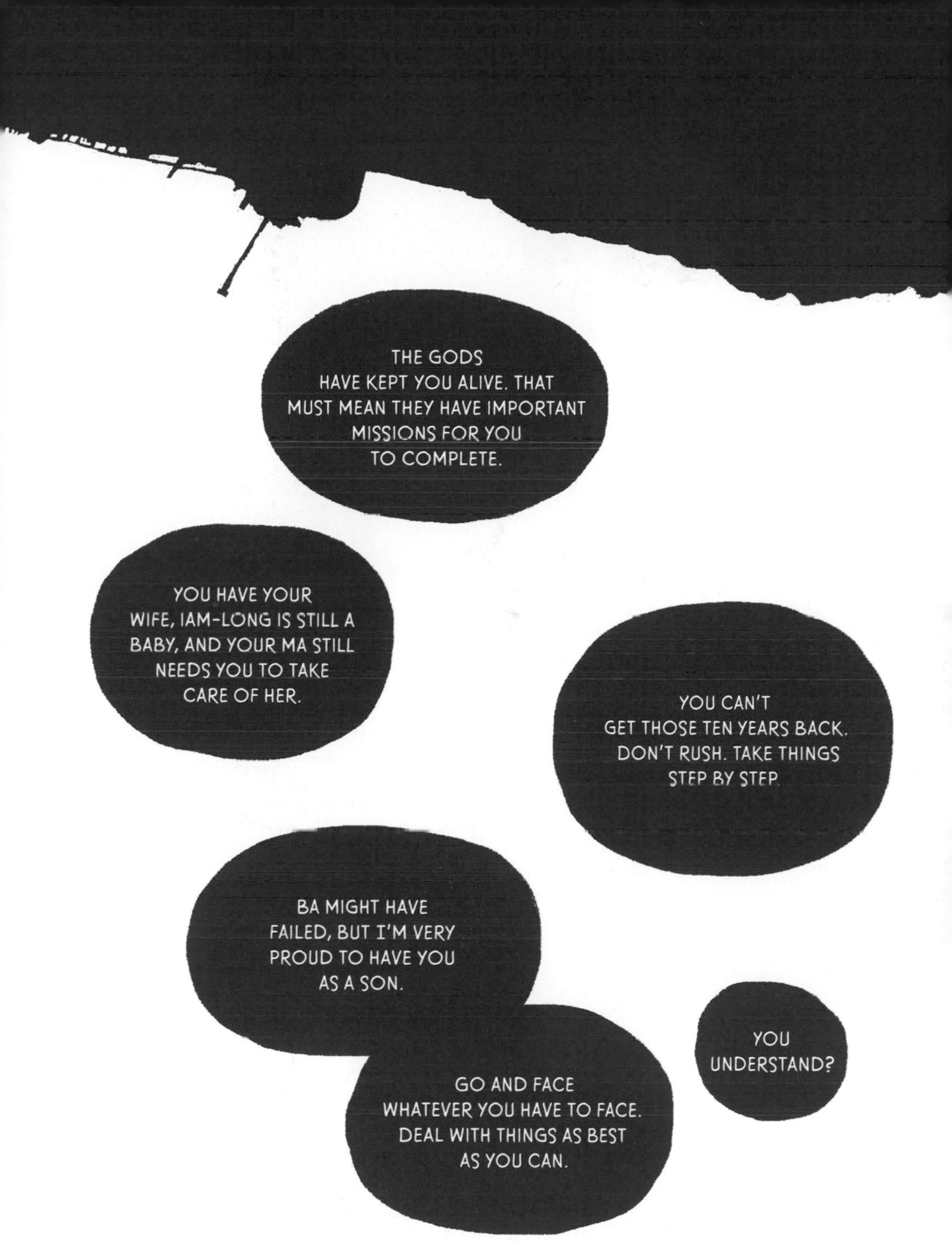
THE GODS HAVE KEPT YOU ALIVE. THAT MUST MEAN THEY HAVE IMPORTANT MISSIONS FOR YOU TO COMPLETE.
YOU HAVE YOUR WIFE, IAM-LONG IS STILL A BABY, AND YOUR MA STILL NEEDS YOU TO TAKE CARE OF HER.
YOU CAN'T GET THOSE TEN YEARS BACK. DON'T RUSH. TAKE THINGS STEP BY STEP.
BA MIGHT HAVE FAILED, BUT I'M VERY PROUD TO HAVE YOU AS A SON.
GO AND FACE WHATEVER YOU HAVE TO FACE. DEAL WITH THINGS AS BEST AS YOU CAN.
YOU UNDERSTAND?

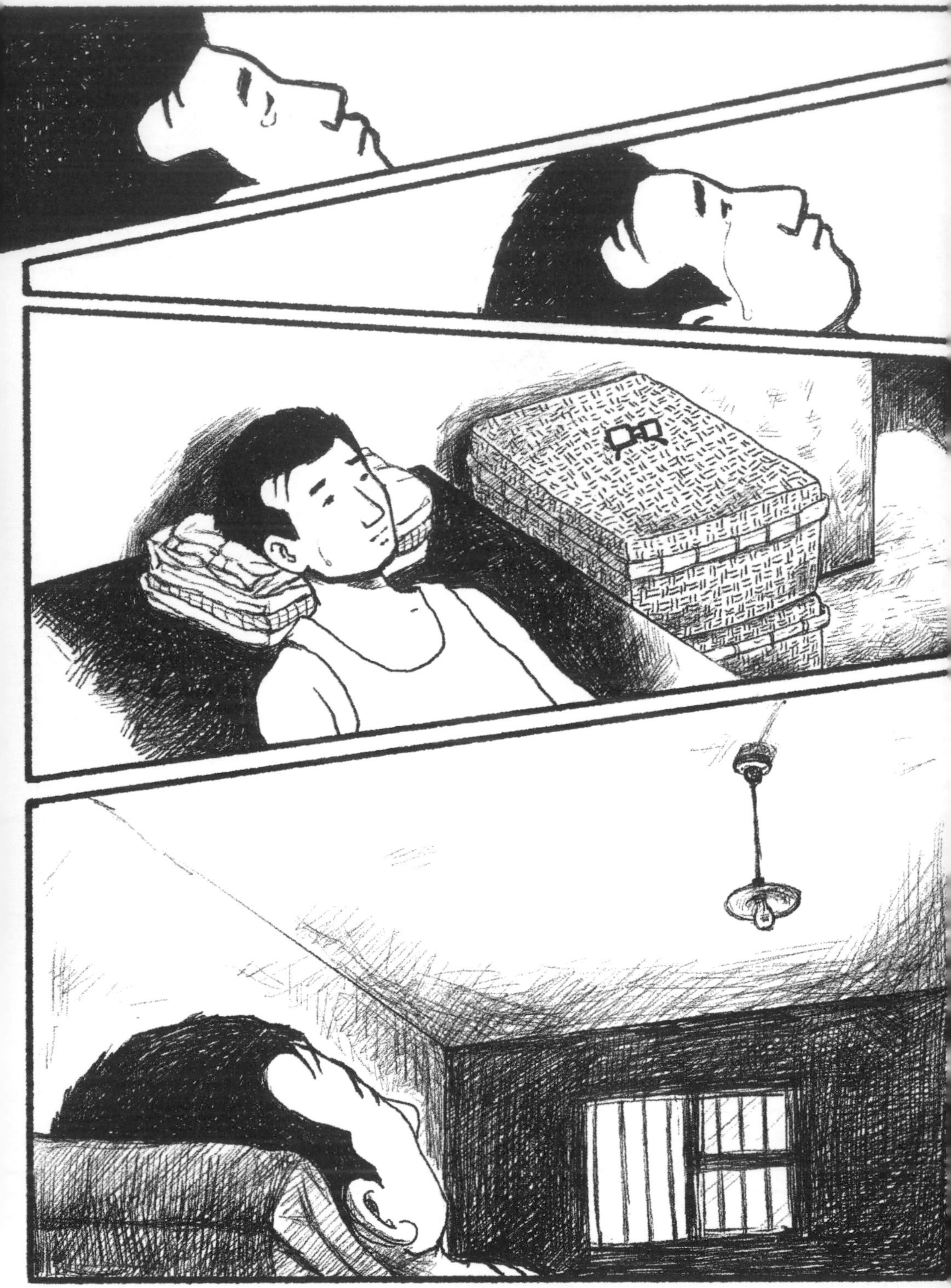

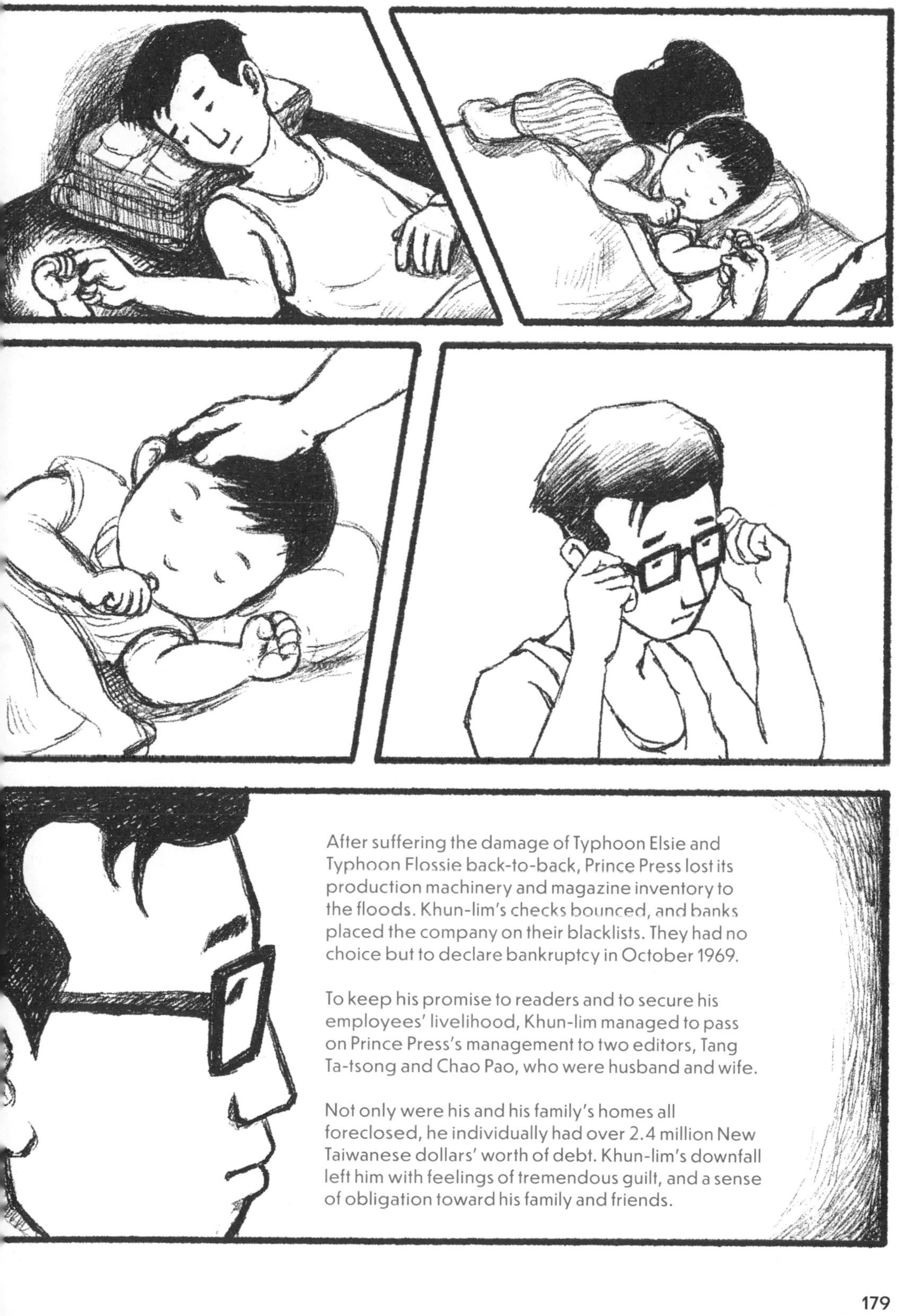
After suffering the damage of Typhoon Elsie and Typhoon Flossie back-to-back, Prince Press lost its production machinery and magazine inventory to the floods. Khun-lim's checks bounced, and banks placed the company on their blacklists. They had no choice but to declare bankruptcy in October 1969.
To keep his promise to readers and to secure his employees' livelihood, Khun-lim managed to pass on Prince Press's management to two editors, Tang Ta-tsong and Chao Pao, who were husband and wife.
Not only were his and his family's homes all foreclosed, he individually had over 2.4 million New Taiwanese dollars' worth of debt. Khun-lim's downfall left him with feelings of tremendous guilt, and a sense of obligation toward his family and friends.

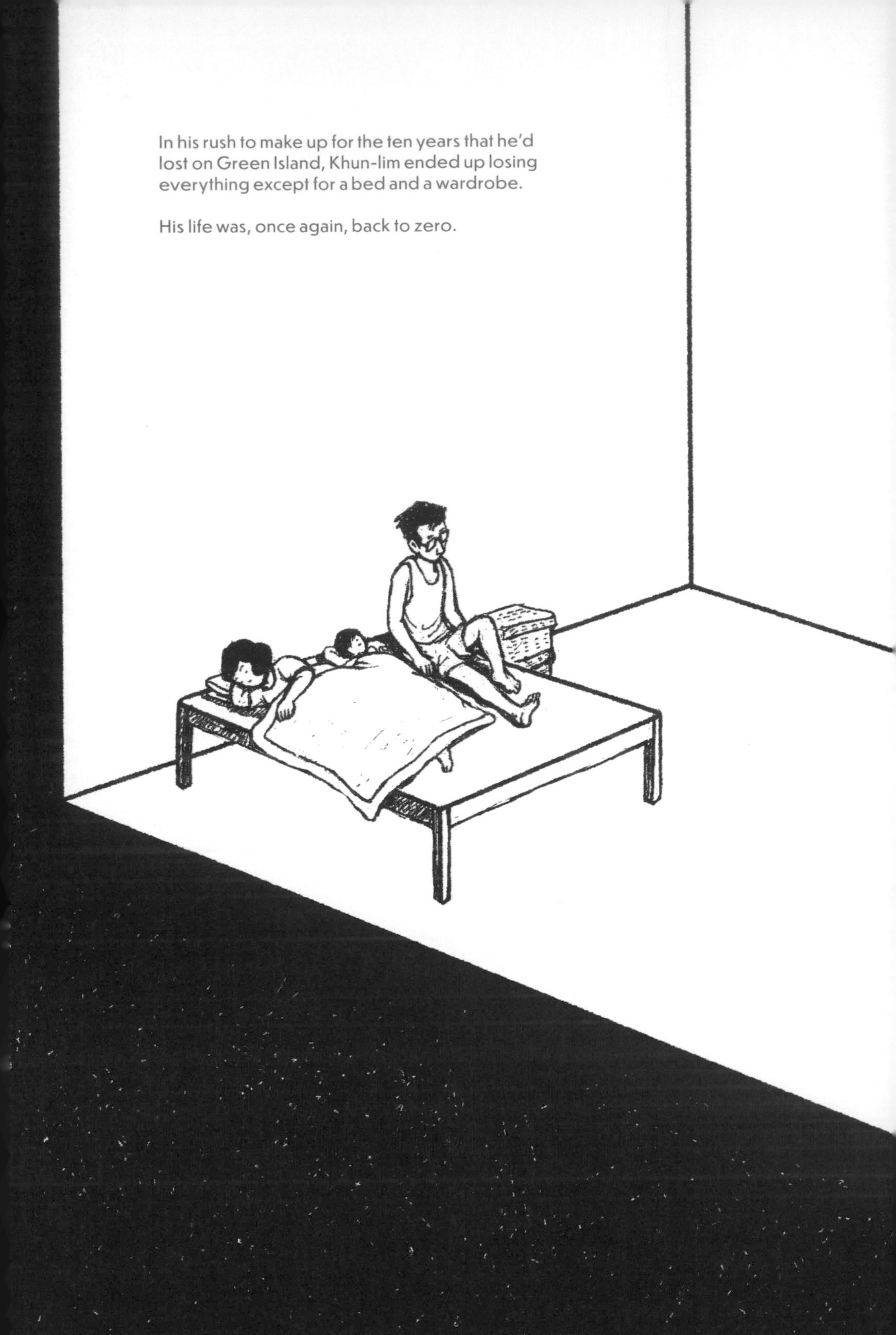
In his rush to make up for the ten years that he'd lost on Green Island, Khun-lim ended up losing everything except for a bed and a wardrobe.
His life was, once again, back to zero.

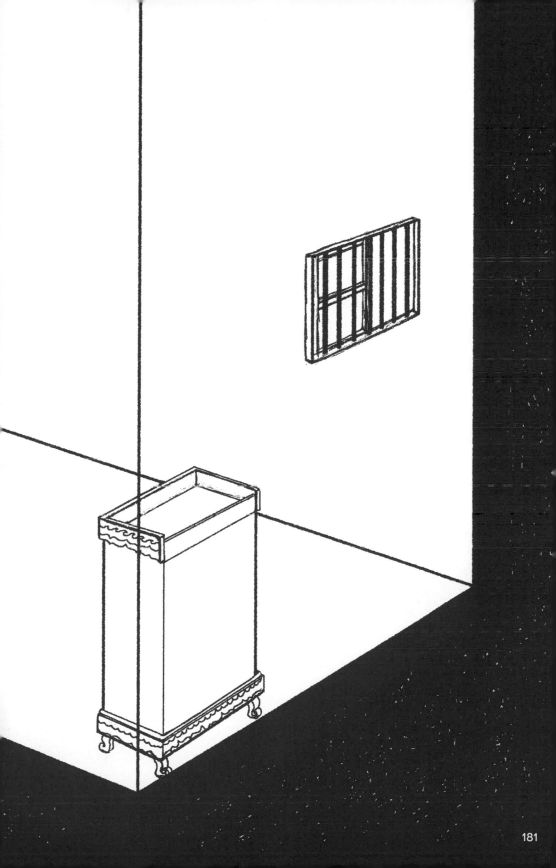

PART 4
A THOUSAND WINDS

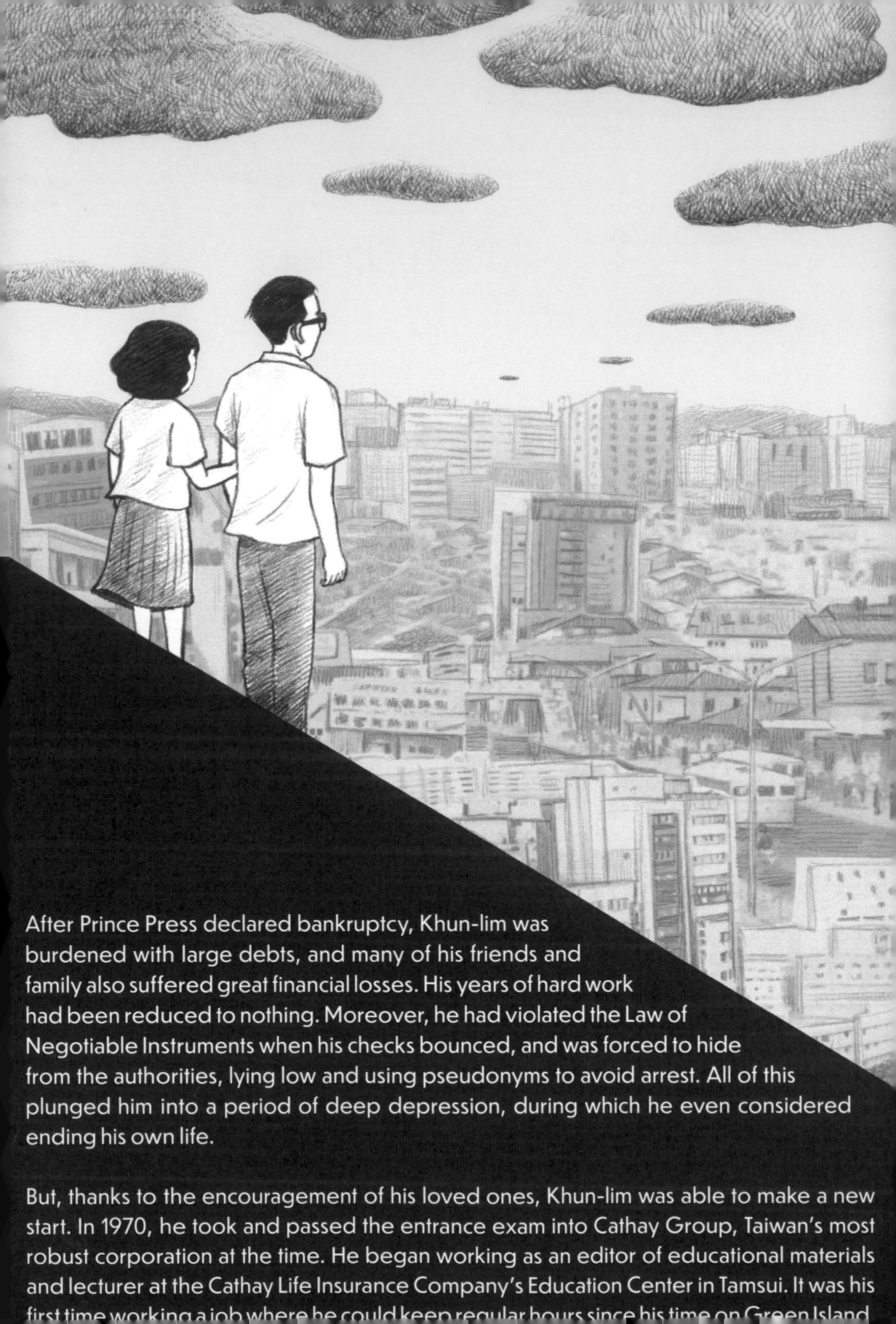

After Prince Press declared bankruptcy, Khun-lim was burdened with large debts, and many of his friends and family also suffered great financial losses. His years of hard work had been reduced to nothing. Moreover, he had violated the Law of Negotiable Instruments when his checks bounced, and was forced to hide from the authorities, lying low and using pseudonyms to avoid arrest. All of this plunged him into a period of deep depression, during which he even considered ending his own life.

But, thanks to the encouragement of his loved ones, Khun-lim was able to make a new start. In 1970, he took and passed the entrance exam into Cathay Group, Taiwan's most robust corporation at the time. He began working as an editor of educational materials and lecturer at the Cathay Life Insurance Company's Education Center in Tamsui. It was his first time working a job where he could keep regular hours since his time on Green Island

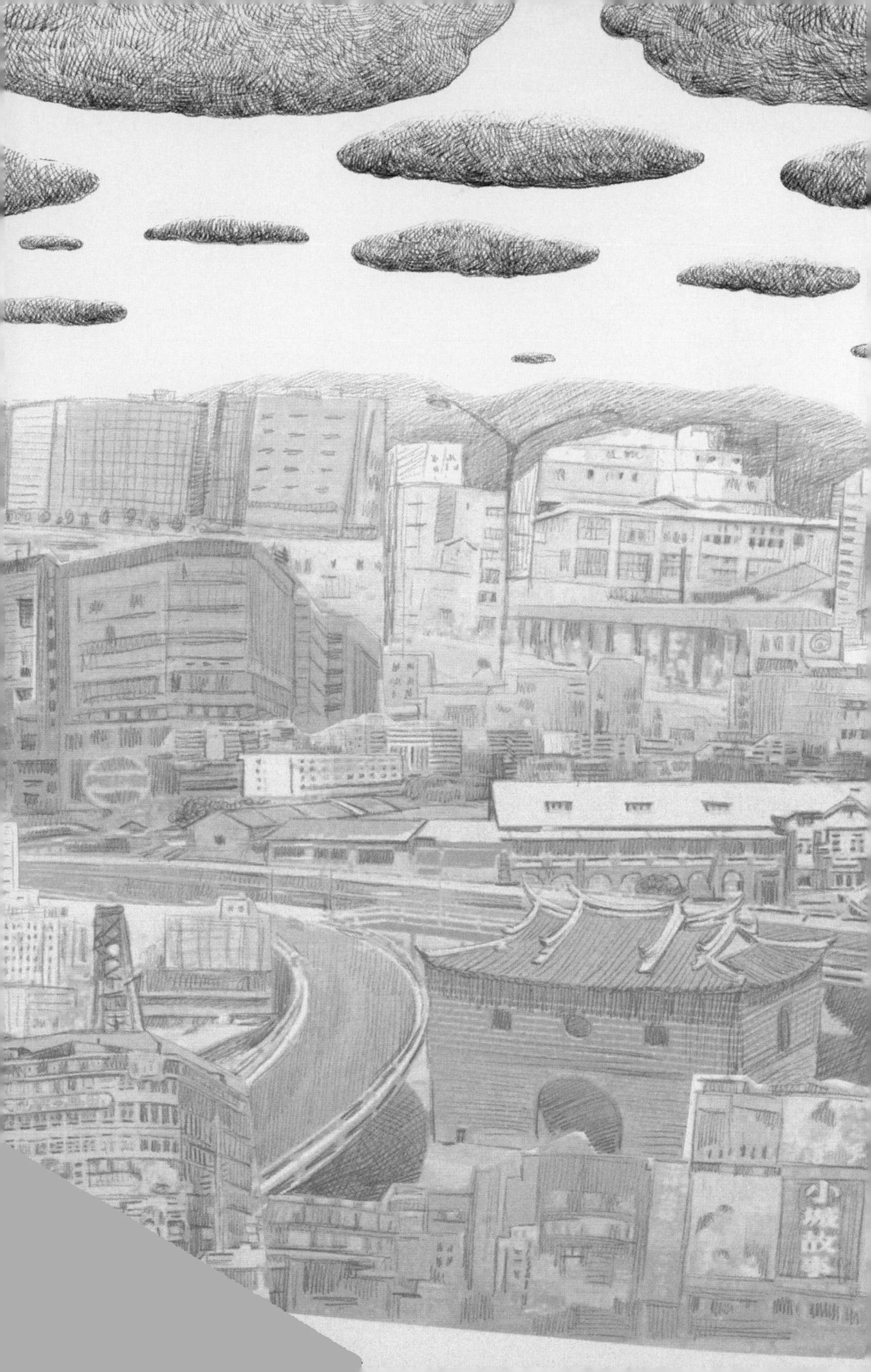

On October 1, 1949, Chairman Mao Zedong of the Chinese Communist Party (CCP) declared a "new China" in Beijing, establishing the People's Republic of China (PRC). Meanwhile, President Chiang Kai-shek of the Kuomintang (KMT), leader of the Republic of China (ROC), retreated across the Taiwan Strait and began preparing to "defeat the Communists and restore the Chinese nation" from his new base in Taiwan. Both the PRC and the ROC insisted that they and they alone represented China; the international community proceeded to "choose sides" according to each country's own interests.

Beginning in the late 1960s, more and more countries began breaking the ice and establishing diplomatic relations with the PRC. In 1971, the United Nations General Assembly passed Resolution 2758, officially replacing Chiang Kai-shek's ROC with Mao Zedong's PRC as "the only legitimate representative of China to the United Nations."

Mao Zedong

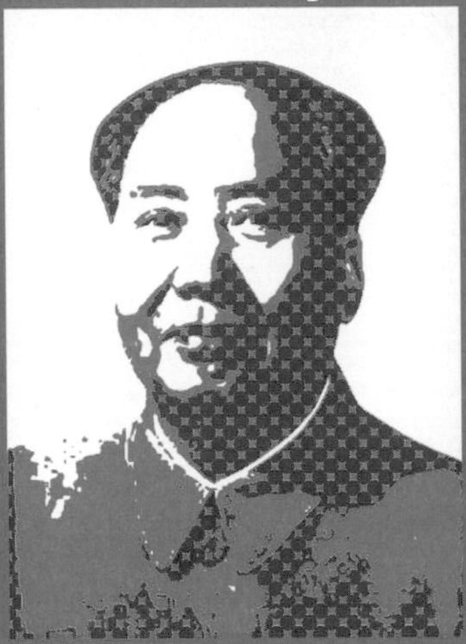

毛澤東 1949–1976

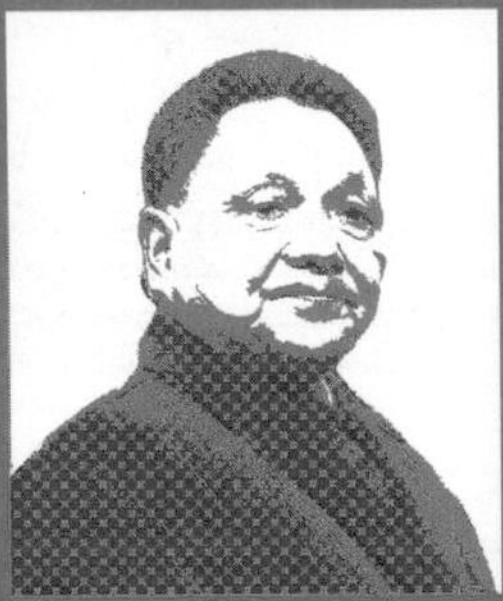

鄧小平 1978–1989

Deng Xiaoping

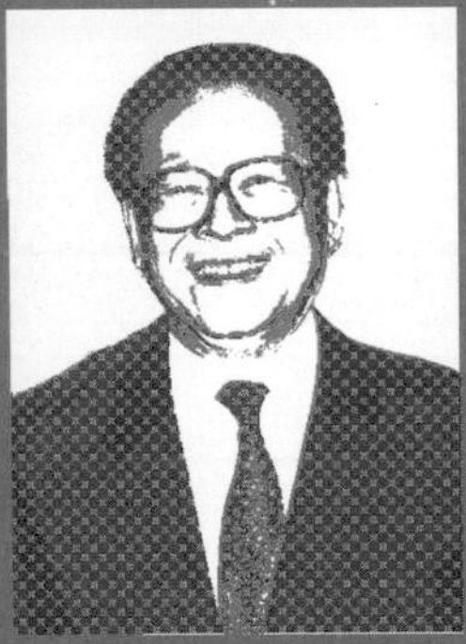

江澤民 1989–2004

Jiang Zemin

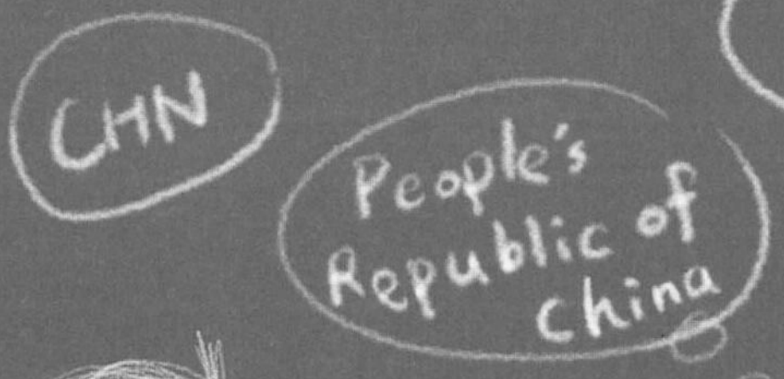
CHN
People's Republic of China

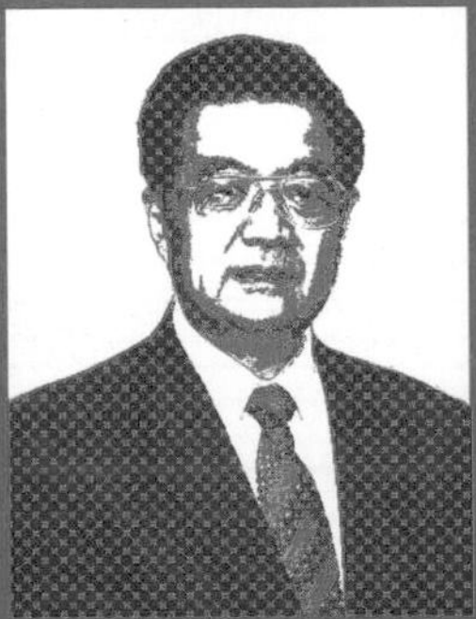

胡錦濤 2004–2012

Hu Jintao

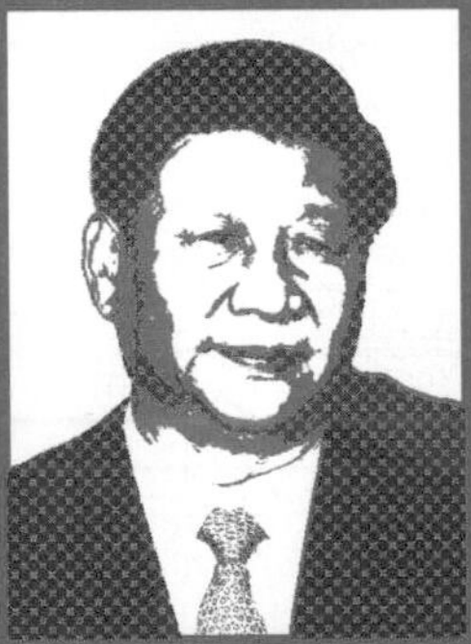

習近平 2012–

Xi Jinping

ations

In the years that followed, many countries revoked diplomatic relations with the ROC, which was increasingly excluded from international alliances due to pressure from the PRC. The PRC refused to recognize the region governed by the ROC as a self-governing nation, and instead demanded that its diplomatic allies officially proclaim Taiwan's islands as "part of China," and that there was only "one China"—meaning the PRC.

This rift has lasted over seventy years. The two administrations across the strait have each evolved over time into completely different political landscapes relative to what they were in 1971, and the ROC is now more commonly known simply as "Taiwan," instead of as "the Republic of China." Although Taiwan has now held democratic presidential elections for more than twenty years and undergone multiple peaceful transitions of power between different political parties, and though it manages its own military and diplomatic relations, it is still subject to the "one China" stance held by many countries around the world. To this day, Taiwan, the Republic of China, cannot gain universal recognition as an official country.

Chiang Kai-shek

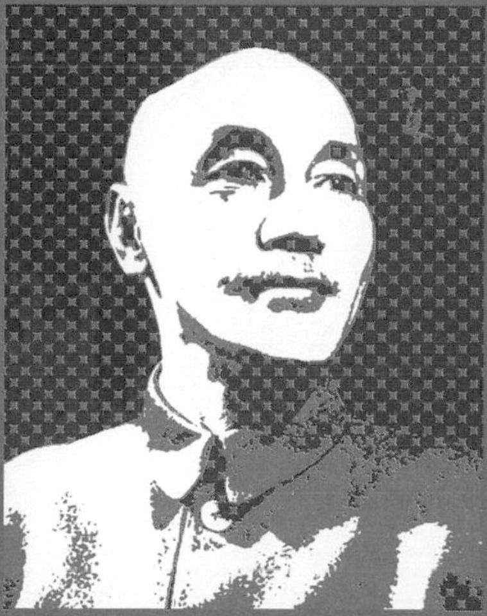

蔣介石 1948–1975

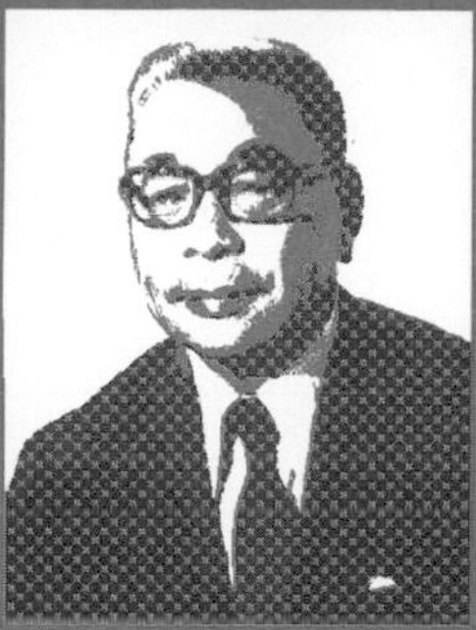

蔣經國 1978–1988
Chiang Ching-kuo

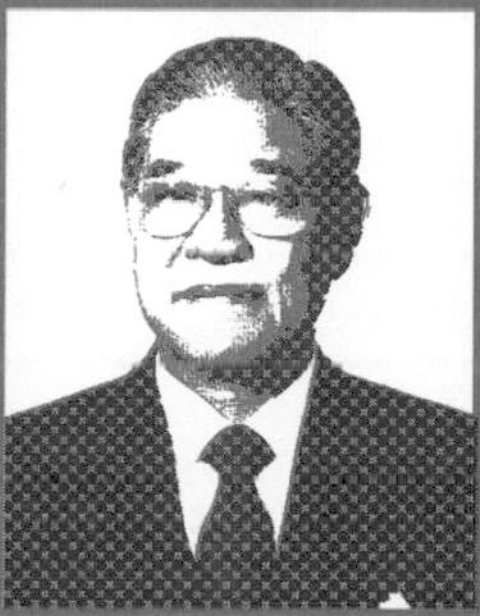

李登輝 1988–2000
Lee Teng-hui

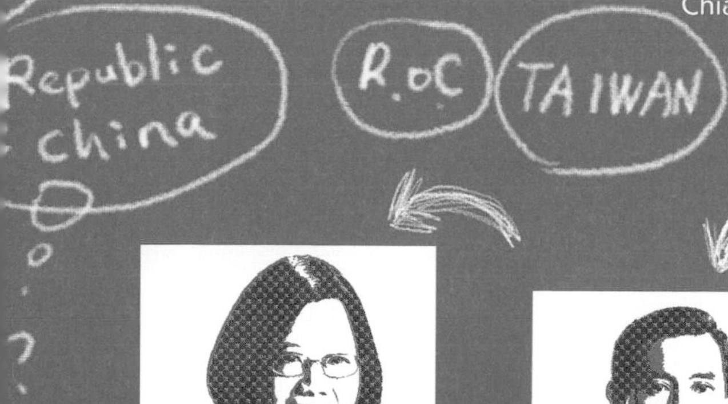

Republic china
R.OC
TAIWAN

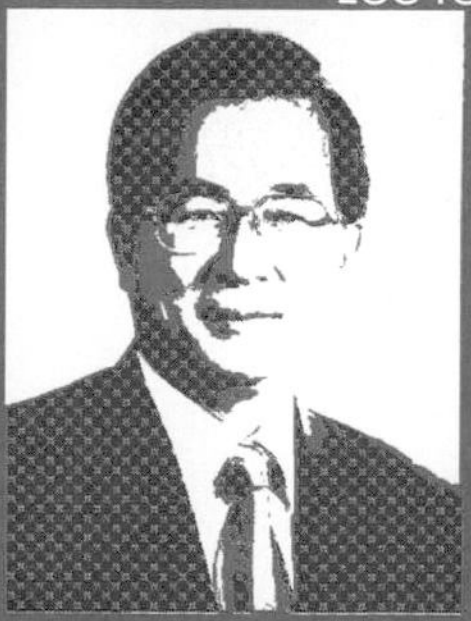

陳水扁 2000–2008
Chen Shui-bian

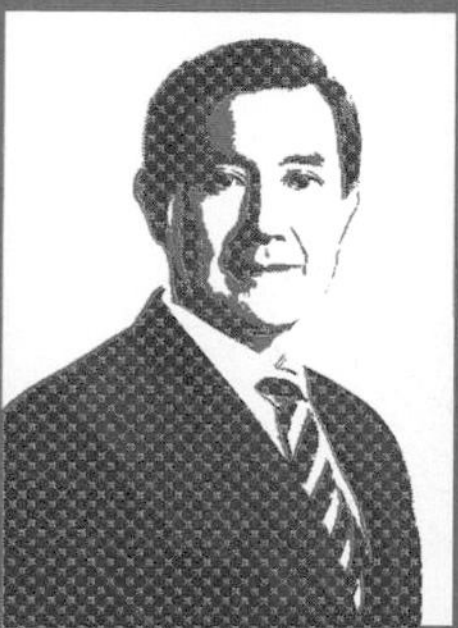

馬英九 2008–2016
Ma Ying-jeou

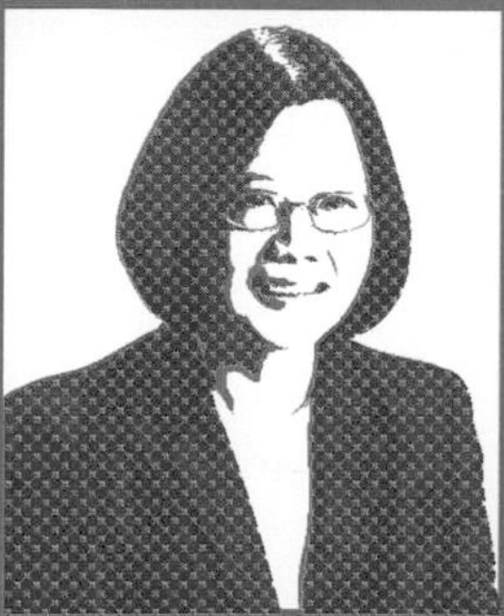

蔡英文 2016–
Tsai Ing-wen

January 2018. National Human Rights
Museum Development Office.

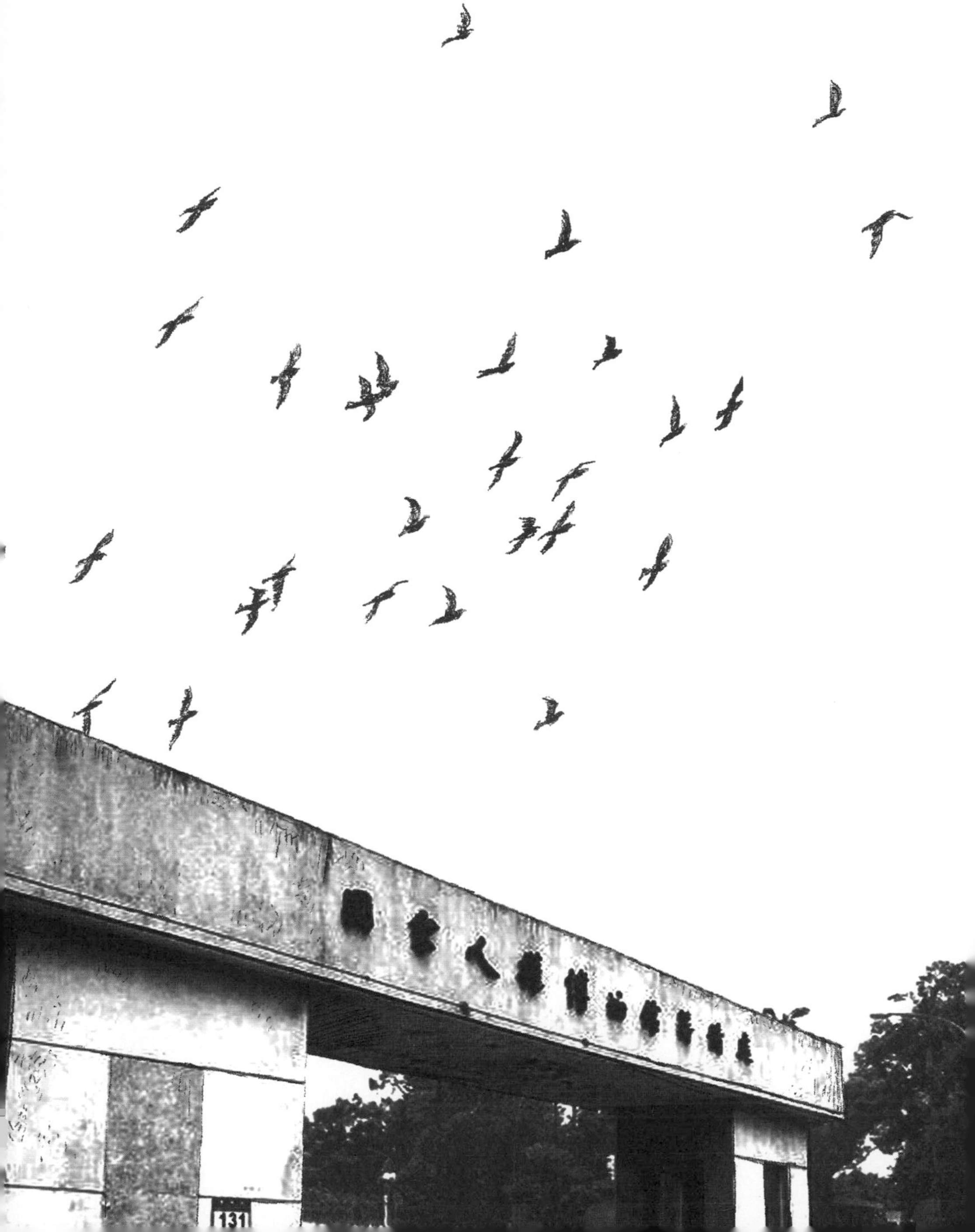
131

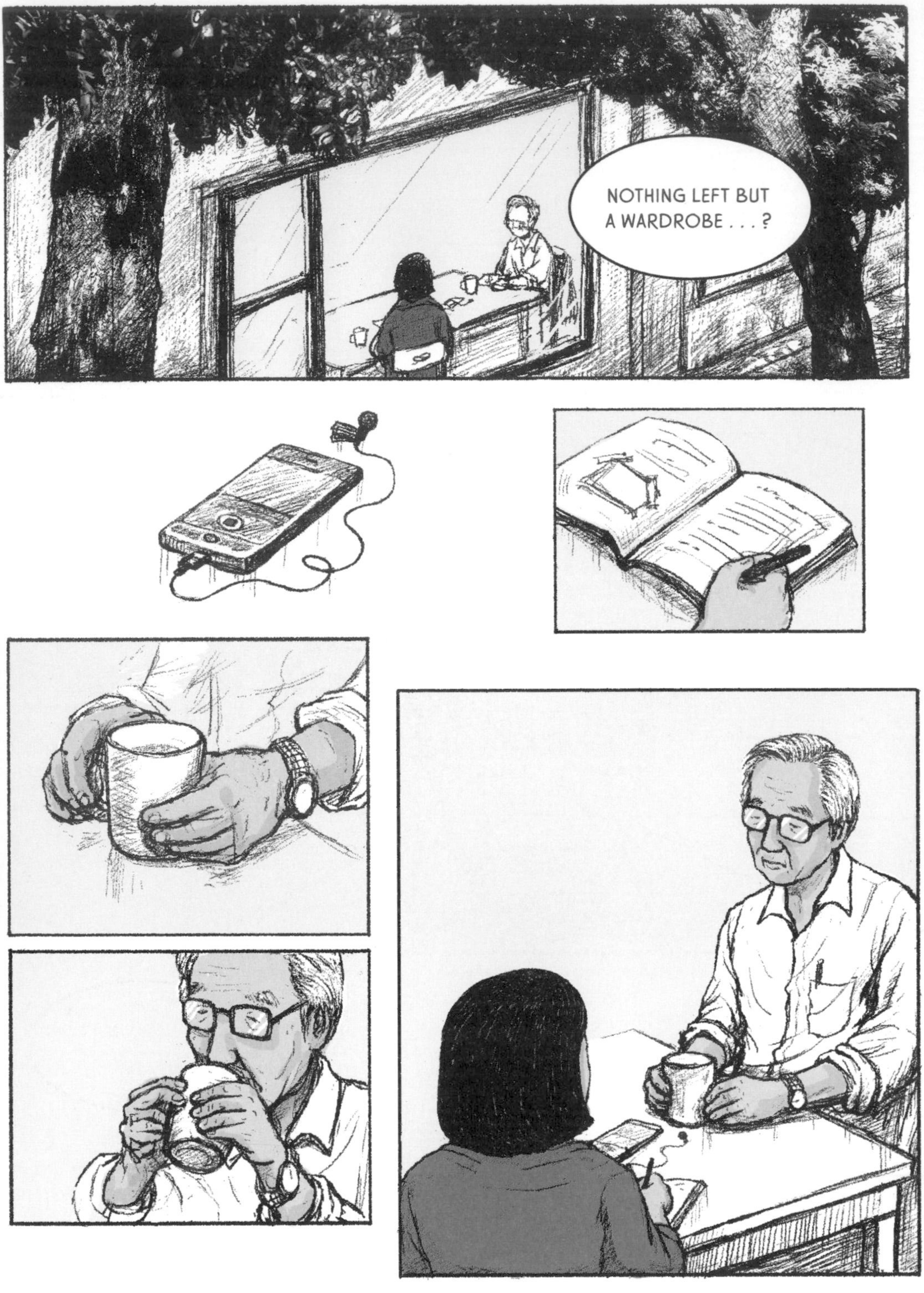
NOTHING LEFT BUT
A WARDROBE . . . ?

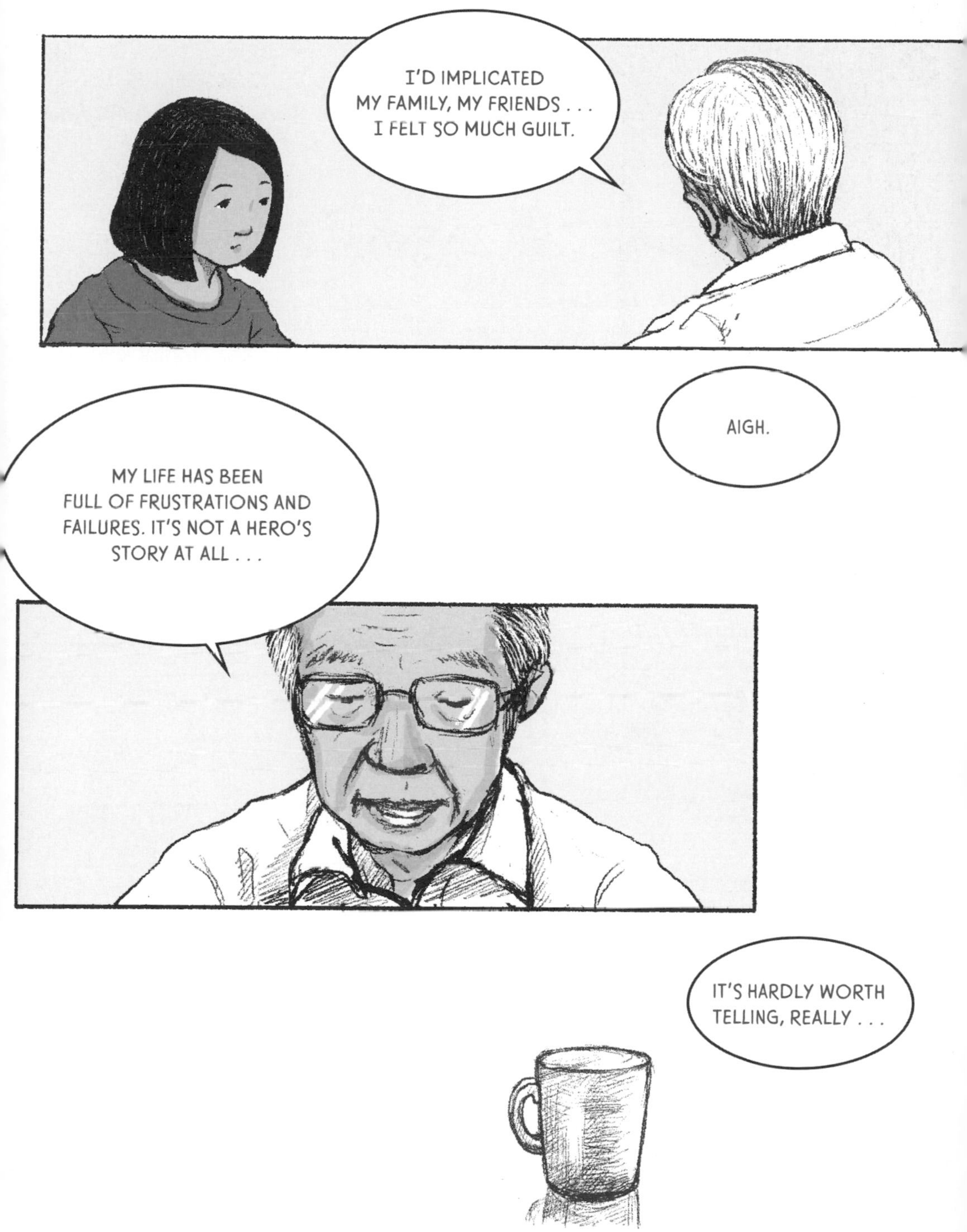
I'D IMPLICATED MY FAMILY, MY FRIENDS . . . I FELT SO MUCH GUILT.
AIGH.
MY LIFE HAS BEEN FULL OF FRUSTRATIONS AND FAILURES. IT'S NOT A HERO'S STORY AT ALL . . .
IT'S HARDLY WORTH TELLING, REALLY . . .

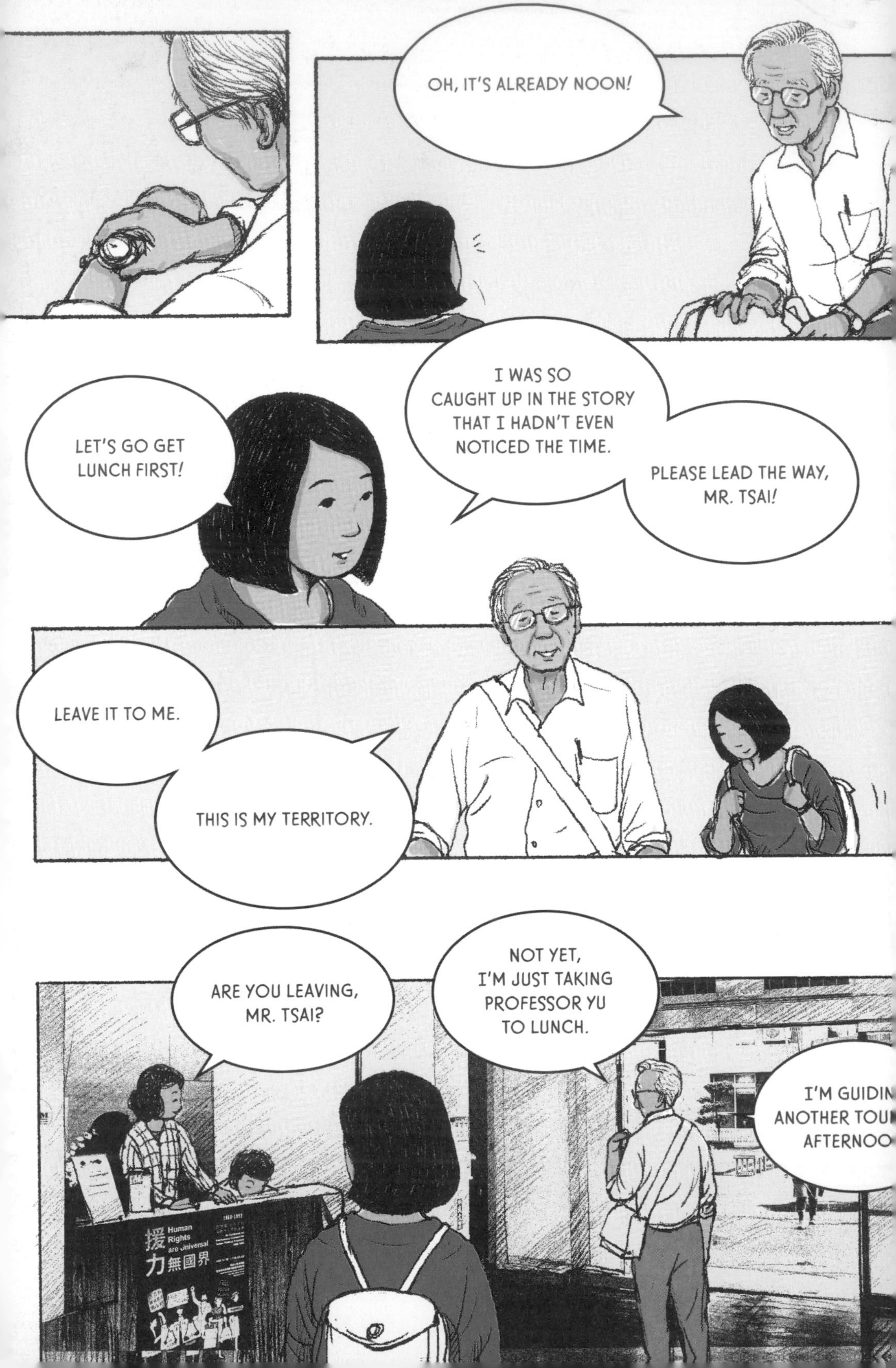
OH, IT'S ALREADY NOON!
I WAS SO CAUGHT UP IN THE STORY THAT I HADN'T EVEN NOTICED THE TIME.
LET'S GO GET LUNCH FIRST!
PLEASE LEAD THE WAY, MR. TSAI!
LEAVE IT TO ME.
THIS IS MY TERRITORY.
ARE YOU LEAVING, MR. TSAI?
NOT YET, I'M JUST TAKING PROFESSOR YU TO LUNCH.
I'M GUIDIN
ANOTHER TOU
AFTERNOO
援力無國界
Human Rights are Universal

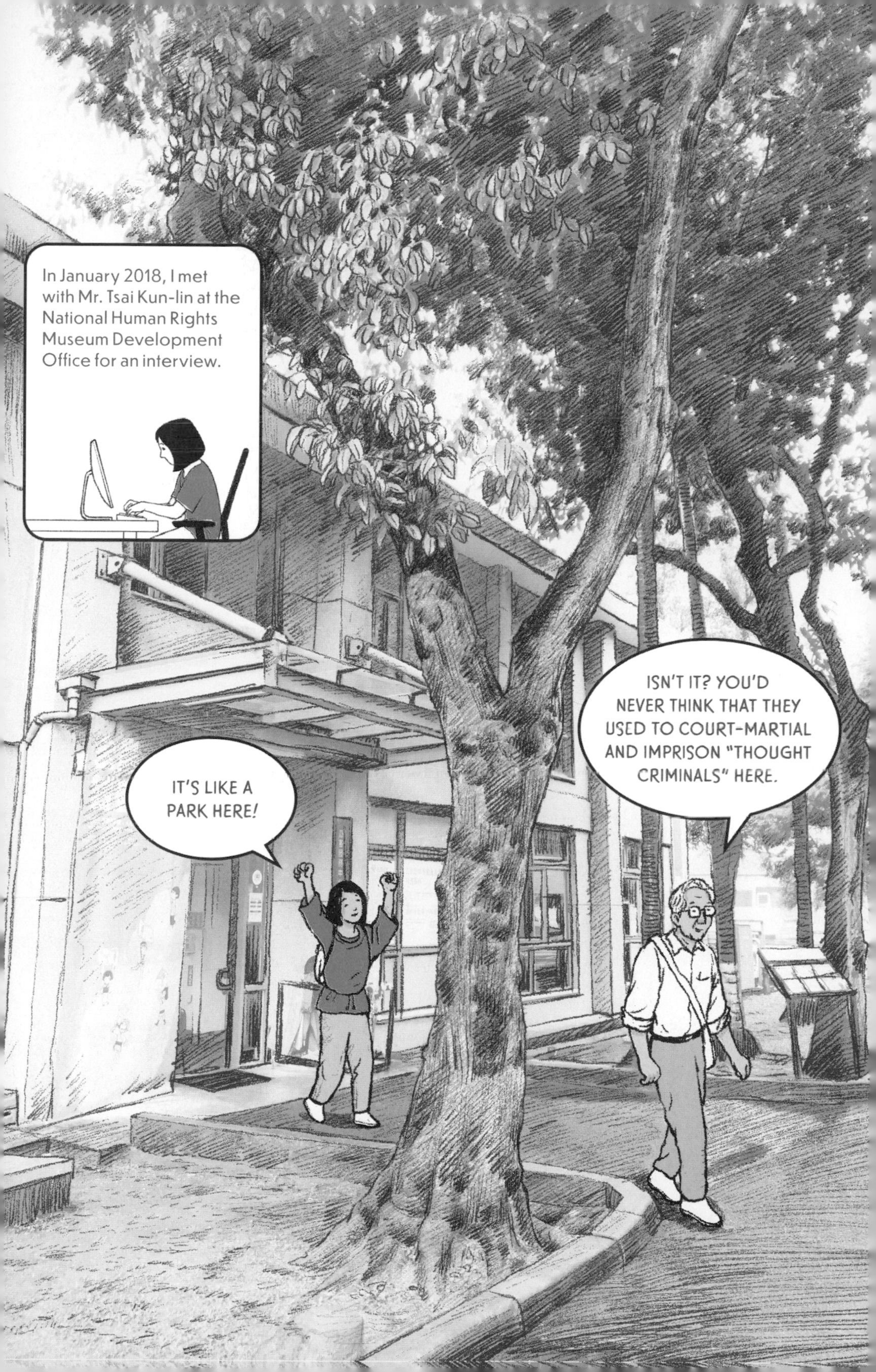
In January 2018, I met with Mr. Tsai Kun-lin at the National Human Rights Museum Development Office for an interview.
IT'S LIKE A PARK HERE!
ISN'T IT? YOU'D NEVER THINK THAT THEY USED TO COURT-MARTIAL AND IMPRISON "THOUGHT CRIMINALS" HERE.

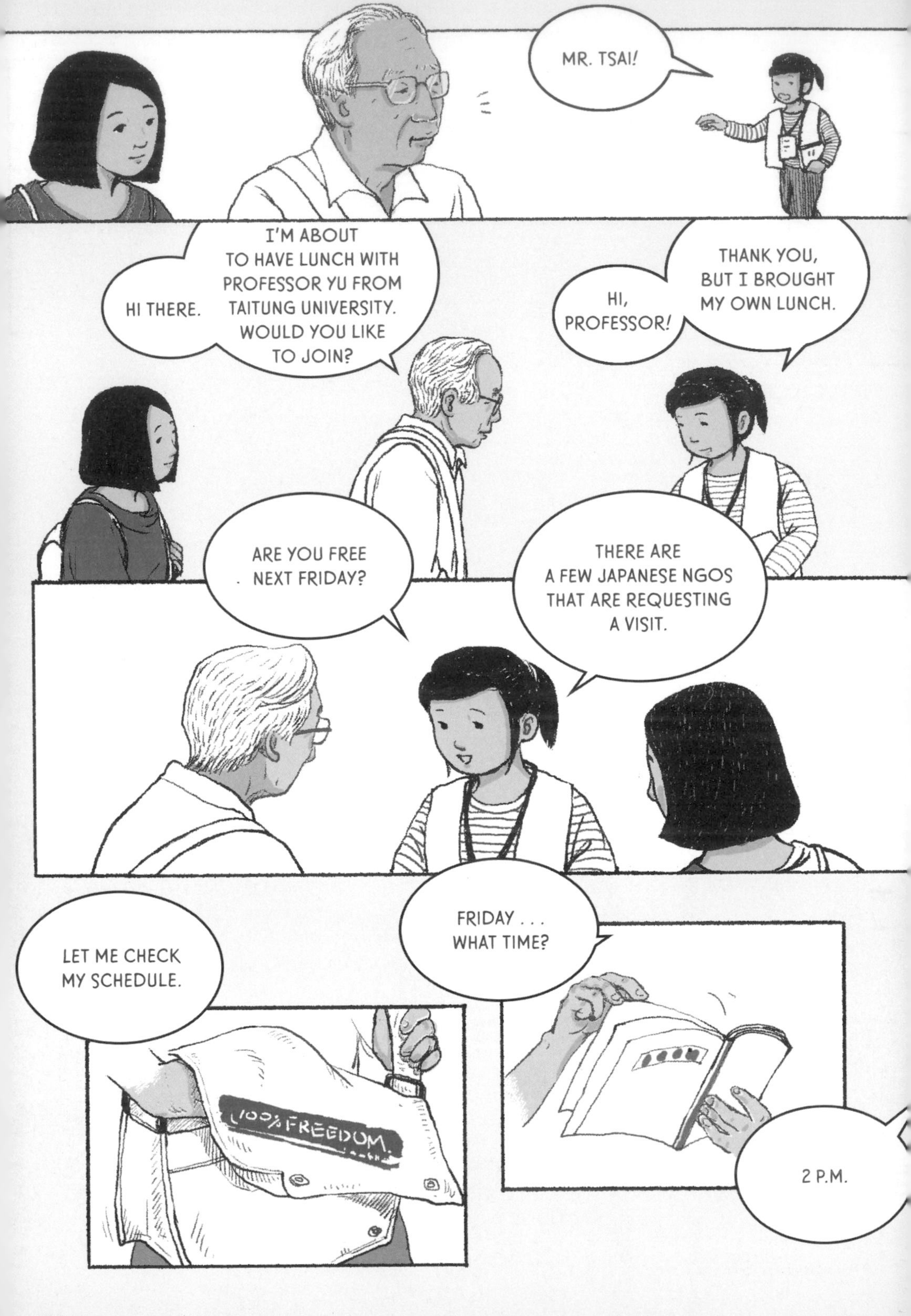
MR. TSAI!
HI THERE.
I'M ABOUT TO HAVE LUNCH WITH PROFESSOR YU FROM TAITUNG UNIVERSITY. WOULD YOU LIKE TO JOIN?
HI, PROFESSOR!
THANK YOU, BUT I BROUGHT MY OWN LUNCH.
ARE YOU FREE NEXT FRIDAY?
THERE ARE A FEW JAPANESE NGOS THAT ARE REQUESTING A VISIT.
LET ME CHECK MY SCHEDULE.
FRIDAY . . . WHAT TIME?
100% FREEDOM
2 P.M.

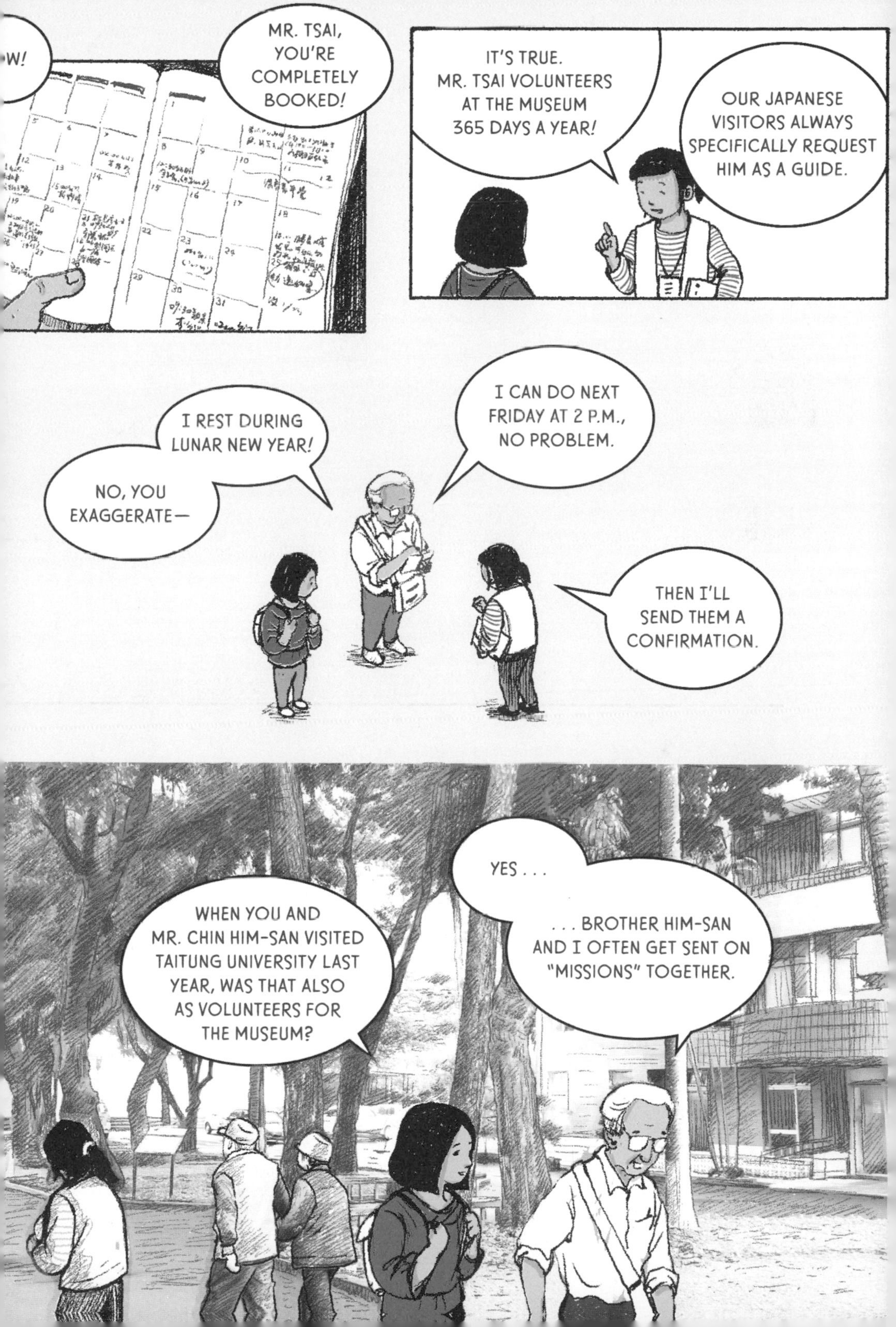
W!
MR. TSAI, YOU'RE COMPLETELY BOOKED!
IT'S TRUE. MR. TSAI VOLUNTEERS AT THE MUSEUM 365 DAYS A YEAR!
OUR JAPANESE VISITORS ALWAYS SPECIFICALLY REQUEST HIM AS A GUIDE.
NO, YOU EXAGGERATE—
I REST DURING LUNAR NEW YEAR!
I CAN DO NEXT FRIDAY AT 2 P.M., NO PROBLEM.
THEN I'LL SEND THEM A CONFIRMATION.
WHEN YOU AND MR. CHIN HIM-SAN VISITED TAITUNG UNIVERSITY LAST YEAR, WAS THAT ALSO AS VOLUNTEERS FOR THE MUSEUM?
YES . . .
. . . BROTHER HIM-SAN AND I OFTEN GET SENT ON "MISSIONS" TOGETHER.

In April 2016, the Children's Literature Research Institute at Taitung University—where I teach—hosted a special exhibition curated by the National Human Rights Museum titled "Delayed, with Love: Last Letters from Victims of White Terror Era Political Persecution."

The exhibition presented letters that victims of the White Terror wrote before being executed for political crimes.

These letters had been sealed in the National Archives for more than sixty years. It was only thanks to the investigation and advocacy of the victims' families that the letters were at last released to the families.

Last letter of political victim Huang Wen-kung:

Huang Wen-kung was the director of the Department of Sanitation of Chunri Township in Pingtung County at the time of his arrest in September 1952. He was executed on May 20, 1953, when he was thirty-three years old. In the four hours prior to his execution, he wrote five letters to his family, including to his youngest daughter, Huang Chun-lan, who was only five months old and whom he had never met.

Dearest Chun-lan…   5/19/1953

I was arrested when you were still in your mother's tummy. Alas! Father and child will never meet! There is nothing more miserable than this in the world. Although I have never seen you, held you, or kissed you, I love you just as deeply as I love Ta-yi and Ling-lan. Chun-lan! Will you recognize me as your father? Will you admire and love me? So many regrets! I cannot fulfill my duty to you, Chun-lan—can you ever forgive your poor father?

Chun-lan! I will have to bid farewell to this world soon. I am doing my utmost to calm…

最疼愛的春蘭…

你還在媽的肚子裡面，我就被捕
再也沒有比這更悽慘的了。這
遇疼，但我是和大一、鈴蘭一
做爸的呢？羨愛我嗎？慚
春蘭！你能不能原諒這
春蘭！我不久就要和也簡
心腸，來和你做一次最初而最後……，把你一同
……愛吧！嗚呼！酷於此時不能見我……一面貌吧！
……至恨不盡！

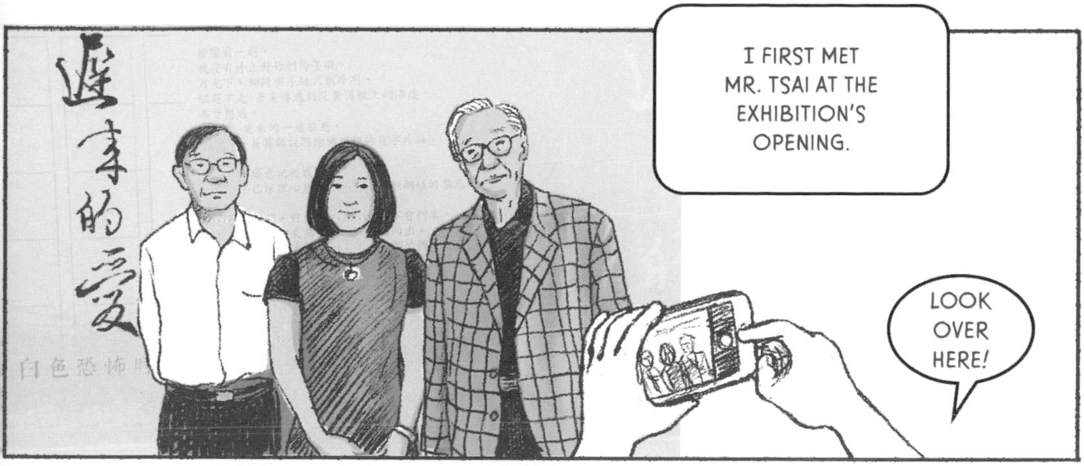
遲來的愛
白色恐怖
I FIRST MET MR. TSAI AT THE EXHIBITION'S OPENING.
LOOK OVER HERE!

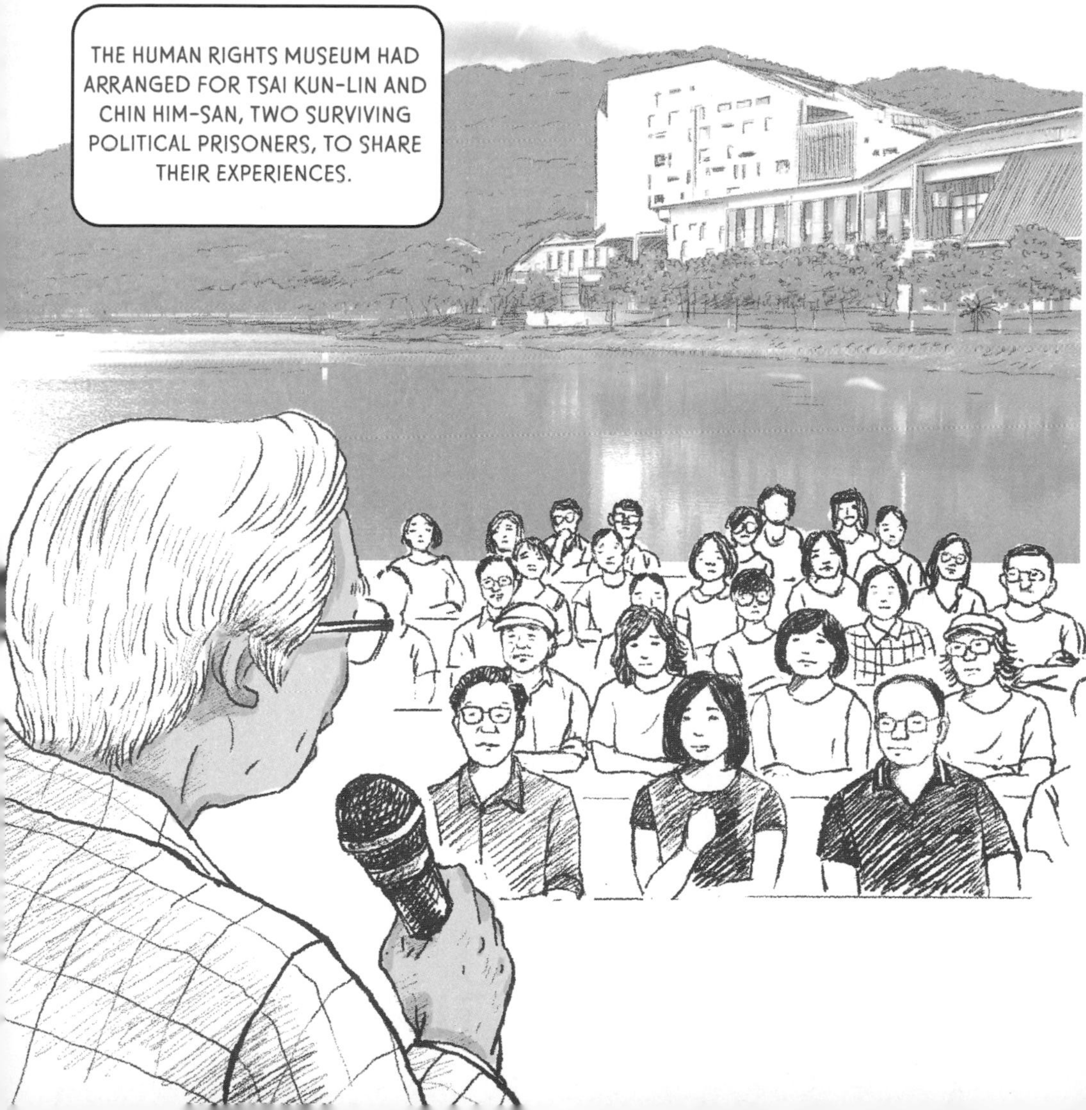
THE HUMAN RIGHTS MUSEUM HAD ARRANGED FOR TSAI KUN-LIN AND CHIN HIM-SAN, TWO SURVIVING POLITICAL PRISONERS, TO SHARE THEIR EXPERIENCES.

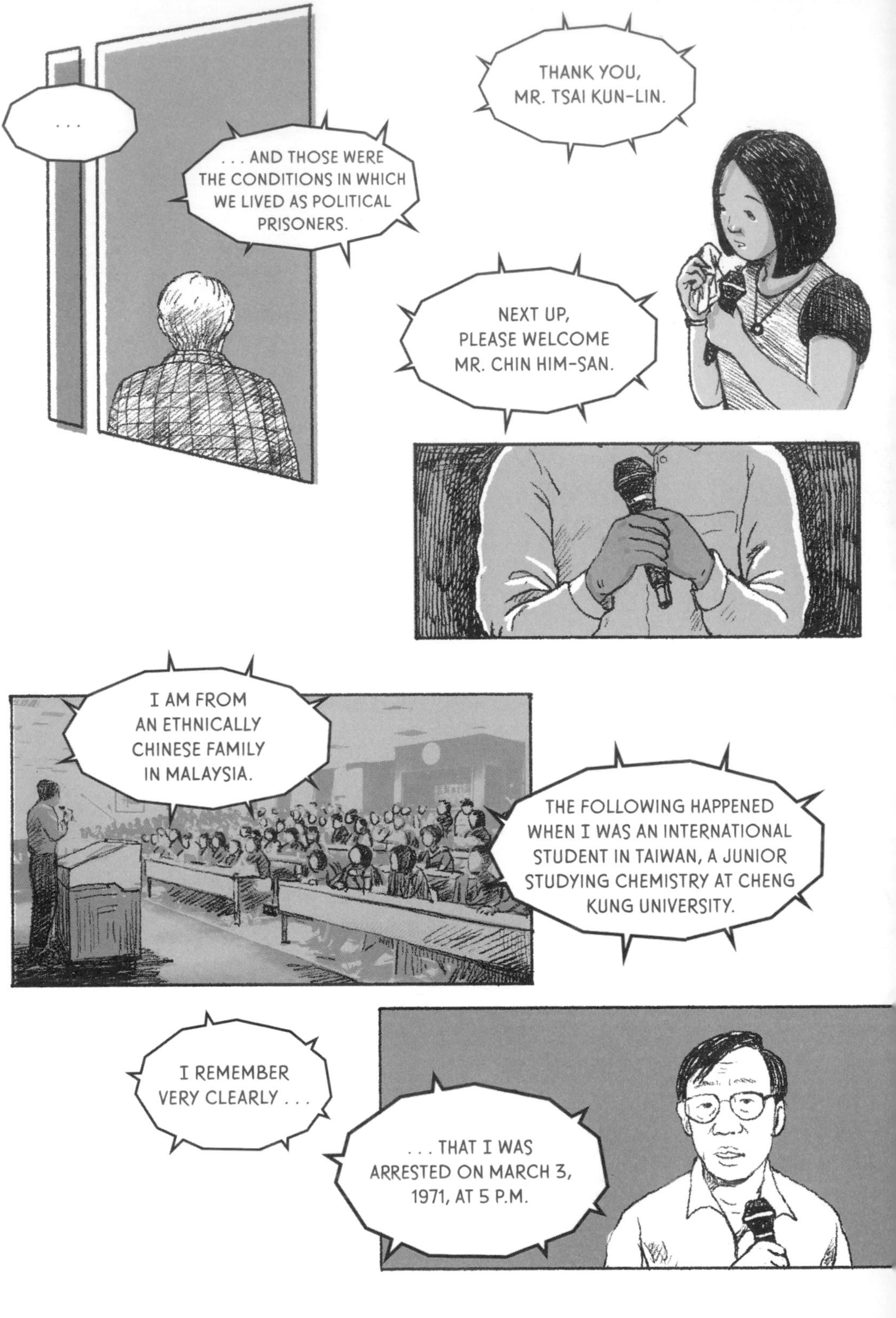
. . .
. . . AND THOSE WERE THE CONDITIONS IN WHICH WE LIVED AS POLITICAL PRISONERS.
THANK YOU, MR. TSAI KUN-LIN.
NEXT UP, PLEASE WELCOME MR. CHIN HIM-SAN.
I AM FROM AN ETHNICALLY CHINESE FAMILY IN MALAYSIA.
THE FOLLOWING HAPPENED WHEN I WAS AN INTERNATIONAL STUDENT IN TAIWAN, A JUNIOR STUDYING CHEMISTRY AT CHENG KUNG UNIVERSITY.
I REMEMBER VERY CLEARLY . . .
. . . THAT I WAS ARRESTED ON MARCH 3, 1971, AT 5 P.M.

THEY SOMEHOW CONNECTED MY NAME TO A BOMBING AT THE US INFORMATION SERVICE OFFICE IN TAINAN. I WAS TORTURED AND FORCED TO WRITE A CONFESSION LETTER.
BECAUSE OF THESE UNFOUNDED CHARGES, I WAS SENTENCED TO TWELVE YEARS IN THE PRISON CAMPS. THIS WAS THE BEGINNING OF DARKNESS IN MY LIFE.
MY MOTHER COULDN'T READ OR WRITE. SHE SPENT AN EXTRAORDINARY AMOUNT OF MONEY SEARCHING FOR ME AND TRAVELED ALL THE WAY FROM MALAYSIA TO VISIT ME ON GREEN ISLAND.
WHEN SHE SUDDENLY APPEARED IN FRONT OF ME AFTER SO MANY YEARS, I FOUND MYSELF UNABLE TO SAY A SINGLE WORD . . .
AFTER I WAS RELEASED, I COULDN'T FIND A JOB BECAUSE I DIDN'T HAVE A TAIWANESE NATIONAL IDENTIFICATION CARD. I WAS ALSO CONTINUALLY HARASSED BY SPECIAL INTELLIGENCE FORCES AND COULD ONLY WANDER TAIPEI'S STREETS, SIFTING THROUGH GARBAGE AS THOUGH I DIDN'T HAVE A HOME . . .
I THOUGHT THAT I WOULD JUST SLOWLY DISAPPEAR INTO NOTHINGNESS HERE IN TAIWAN. BUT THEN I MET A CHEF WHO, AFTER LEARNING ABOUT WHAT HAD HAPPENED TO ME, BEGAN GIVING ME TWO BENTO BOXES FOR FREE EVERY DAY.
I TRULY FELT THE WARMTH OF THE TAIWANESE PEOPLE THEN AND FOUND THE STRENGTH TO KEEP ON LIVING . . .

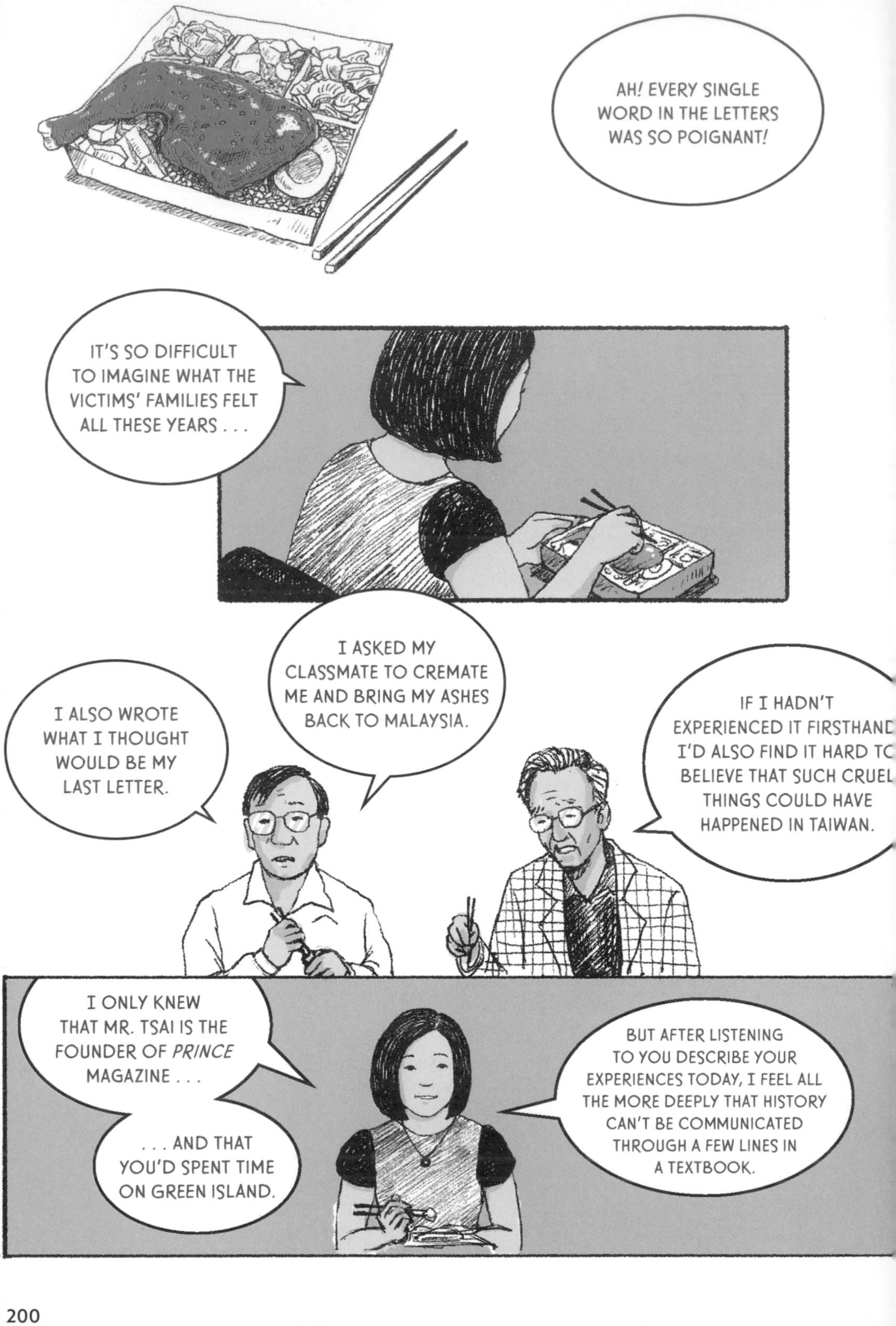
AH! EVERY SINGLE WORD IN THE LETTERS WAS SO POIGNANT!
IT'S SO DIFFICULT TO IMAGINE WHAT THE VICTIMS' FAMILIES FELT ALL THESE YEARS . . .
I ALSO WROTE WHAT I THOUGHT WOULD BE MY LAST LETTER.
I ASKED MY CLASSMATE TO CREMATE ME AND BRING MY ASHES BACK TO MALAYSIA.
IF I HADN'T EXPERIENCED IT FIRSTHAND I'D ALSO FIND IT HARD TO BELIEVE THAT SUCH CRUEL THINGS COULD HAVE HAPPENED IN TAIWAN.
I ONLY KNEW THAT MR. TSAI IS THE FOUNDER OF *PRINCE* MAGAZINE . . .
. . . AND THAT YOU'D SPENT TIME ON GREEN ISLAND.
BUT AFTER LISTENING TO YOU DESCRIBE YOUR EXPERIENCES TODAY, I FEEL ALL THE MORE DEEPLY THAT HISTORY CAN'T BE COMMUNICATED THROUGH A FEW LINES IN A TEXTBOOK.

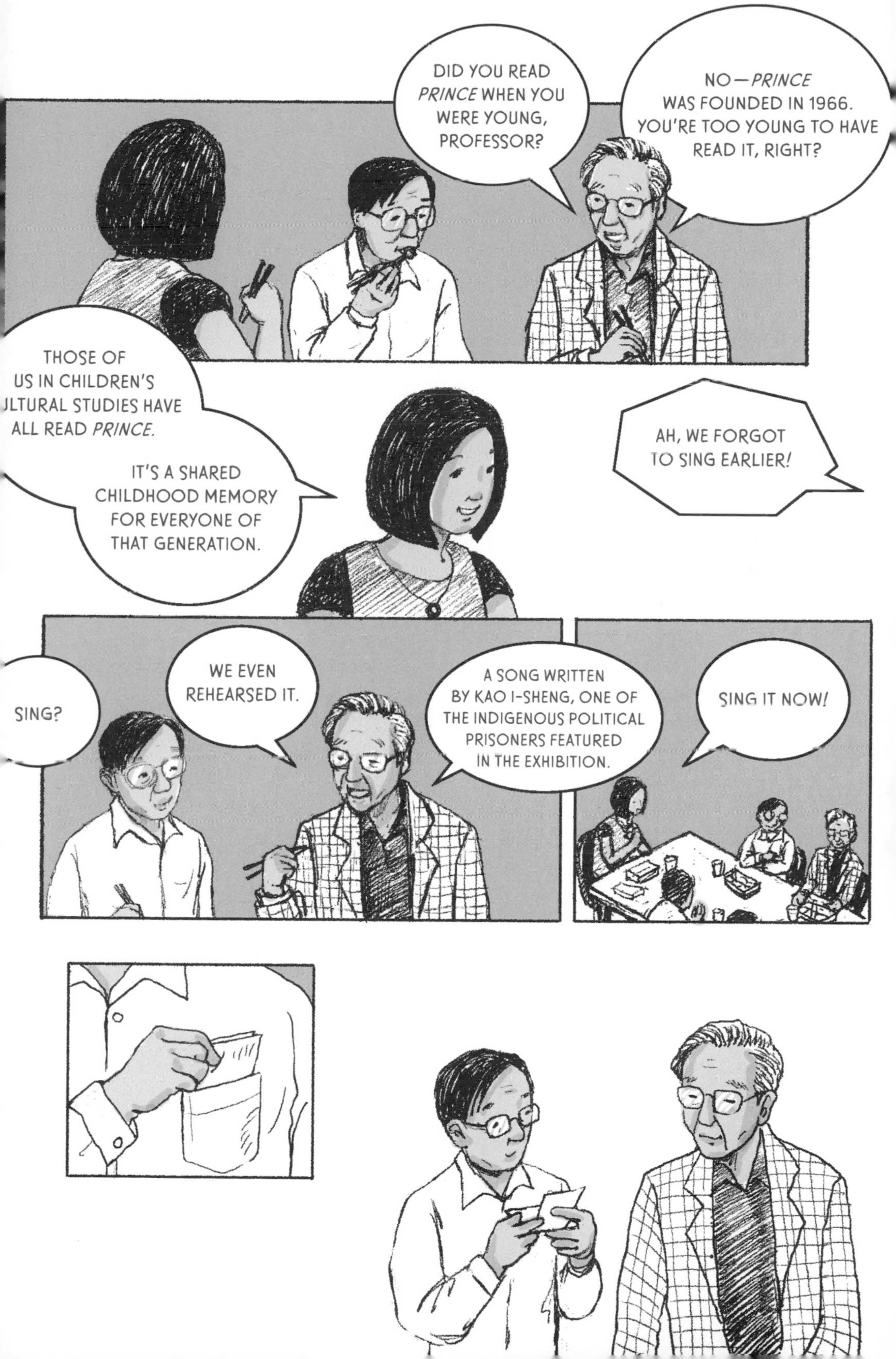
DID YOU READ *PRINCE* WHEN YOU WERE YOUNG, PROFESSOR?
NO—*PRINCE* WAS FOUNDED IN 1966. YOU'RE TOO YOUNG TO HAVE READ IT, RIGHT?
THOSE OF US IN CHILDREN'S ULTURAL STUDIES HAVE ALL READ *PRINCE.*
IT'S A SHARED CHILDHOOD MEMORY FOR EVERYONE OF THAT GENERATION.
AH, WE FORGOT TO SING EARLIER!
SING?
WE EVEN REHEARSED IT.
A SONG WRITTEN BY KAO I-SHENG, ONE OF THE INDIGENOUS POLITICAL PRISONERS FEATURED IN THE EXHIBITION.
SING IT NOW!

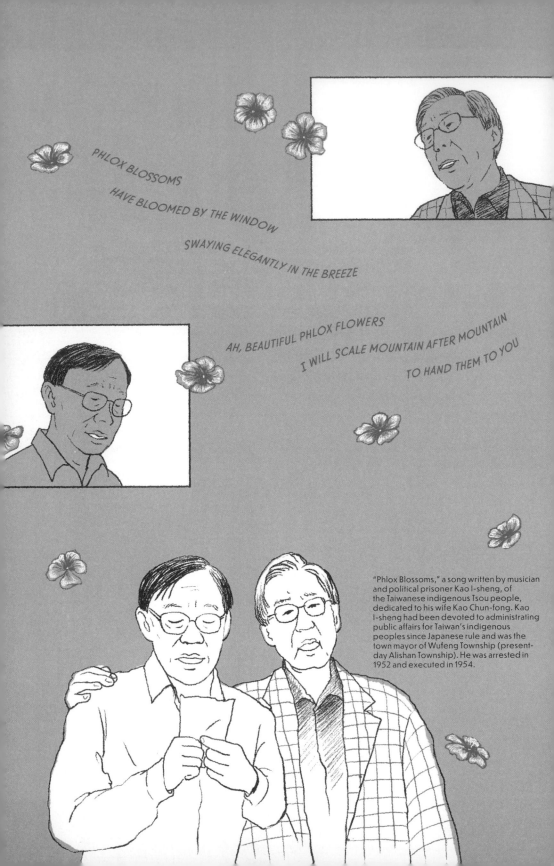

PHLOX BLOSSOMS

HAVE BLOOMED BY THE WINDOW

SWAYING ELEGANTLY IN THE BREEZE

AH, BEAUTIFUL PHLOX FLOWERS

I WILL SCALE MOUNTAIN AFTER MOUNTAIN

TO HAND THEM TO YOU

"Phlox Blossoms," a song written by musician and political prisoner Kao I-sheng, of the Taiwanese indigenous Tsou people, dedicated to his wife Kao Chun-fong. Kao I-sheng had been devoted to administrating public affairs for Taiwan's indigenous peoples since Japanese rule and was the town mayor of Wufeng Township (present-day Alishan Township). He was arrested in 1952 and executed in 1954.

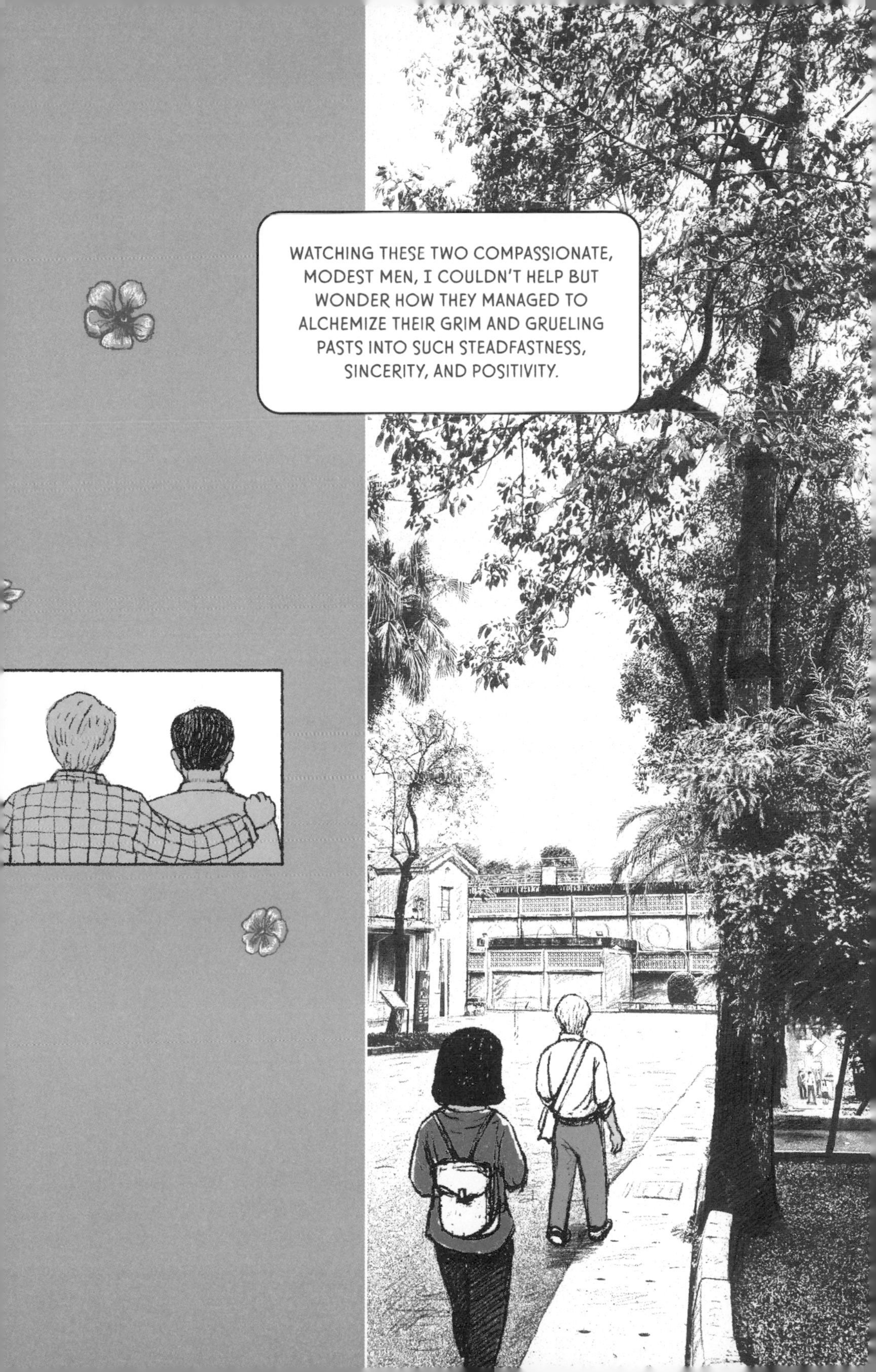
WATCHING THESE TWO COMPASSIONATE, MODEST MEN, I COULDN'T HELP BUT WONDER HOW THEY MANAGED TO ALCHEMIZE THEIR GRIM AND GRUELING PASTS INTO SUCH STEADFASTNESS, SINCERITY, AND POSITIVITY.

1972. Taipei.

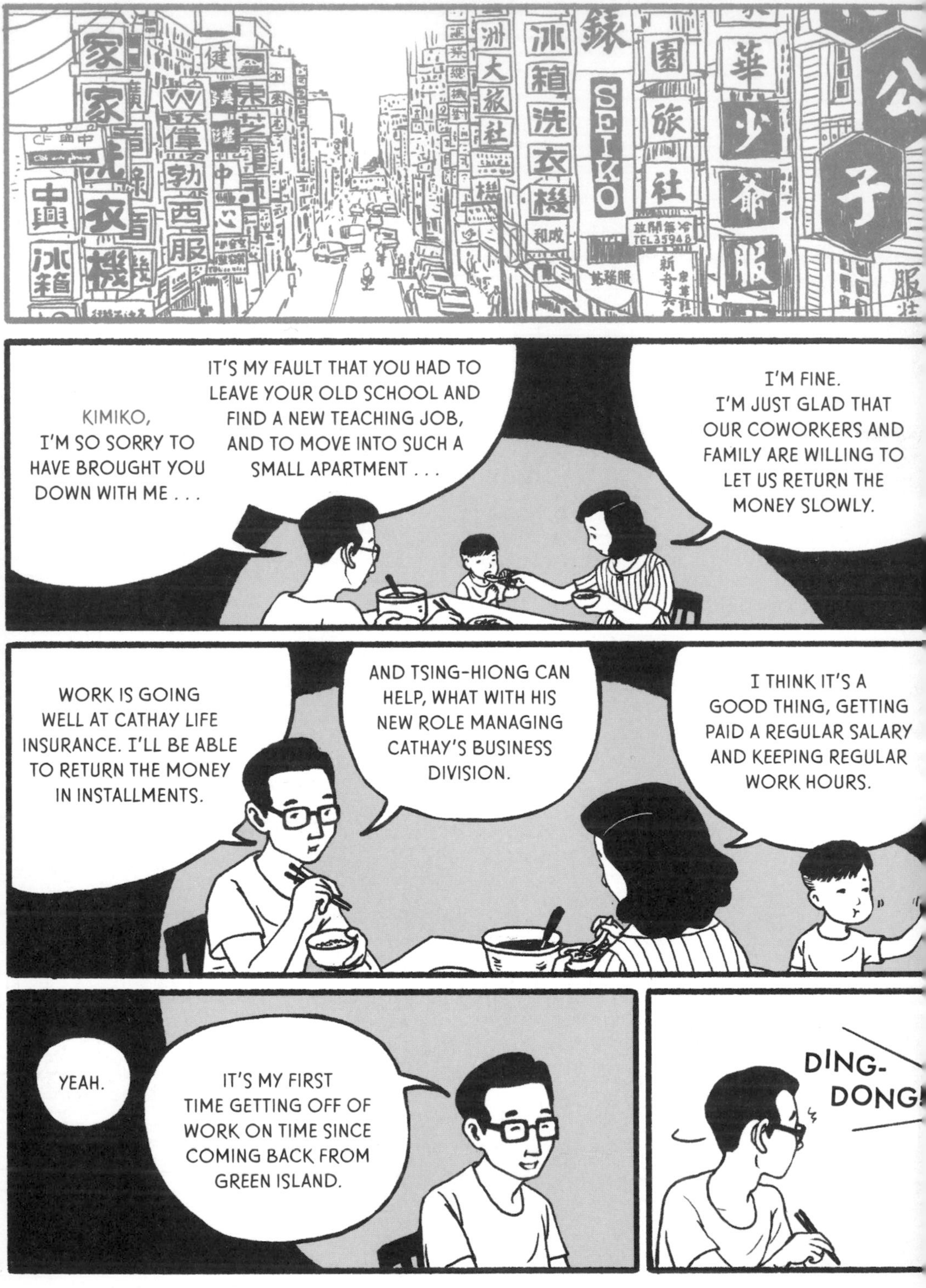
SEIKO
KIMIKO, I'M SO SORRY TO HAVE BROUGHT YOU DOWN WITH ME . . .
IT'S MY FAULT THAT YOU HAD TO LEAVE YOUR OLD SCHOOL AND FIND A NEW TEACHING JOB, AND TO MOVE INTO SUCH A SMALL APARTMENT . . .
I'M FINE. I'M JUST GLAD THAT OUR COWORKERS AND FAMILY ARE WILLING TO LET US RETURN THE MONEY SLOWLY.
WORK IS GOING WELL AT CATHAY LIFE INSURANCE. I'LL BE ABLE TO RETURN THE MONEY IN INSTALLMENTS.
AND TSING-HIONG CAN HELP, WHAT WITH HIS NEW ROLE MANAGING CATHAY'S BUSINESS DIVISION.
I THINK IT'S A GOOD THING, GETTING PAID A REGULAR SALARY AND KEEPING REGULAR WORK HOURS.
YEAH.
IT'S MY FIRST TIME GETTING OFF OF WORK ON TIME SINCE COMING BACK FROM GREEN ISLAND.
DING-DONG!

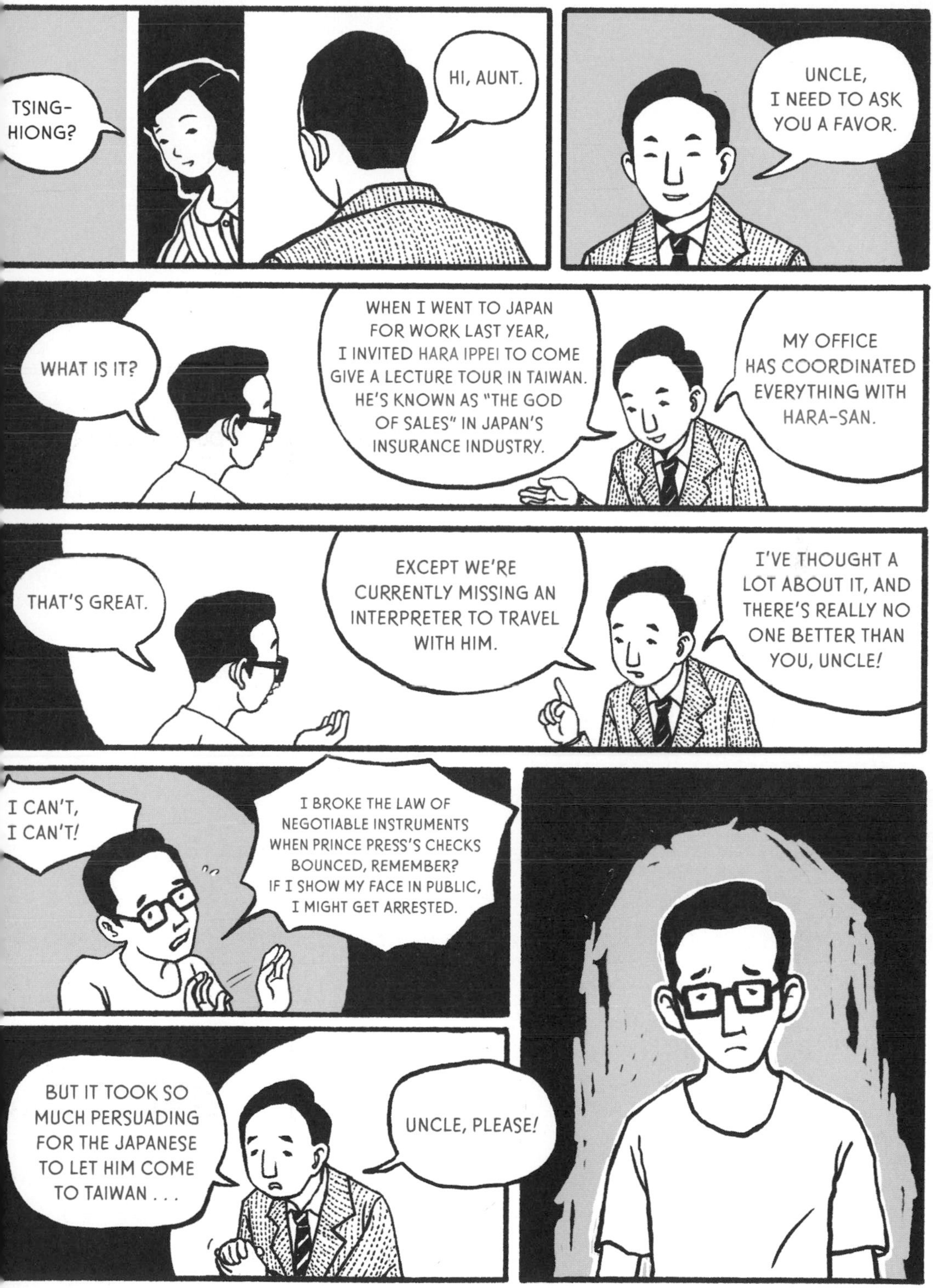
TSING-HIONG?
HI, AUNT.
UNCLE, I NEED TO ASK YOU A FAVOR.
WHAT IS IT?
WHEN I WENT TO JAPAN FOR WORK LAST YEAR, I INVITED HARA IPPEI TO COME GIVE A LECTURE TOUR IN TAIWAN. HE'S KNOWN AS "THE GOD OF SALES" IN JAPAN'S INSURANCE INDUSTRY.
MY OFFICE HAS COORDINATED EVERYTHING WITH HARA-SAN.
THAT'S GREAT.
EXCEPT WE'RE CURRENTLY MISSING AN INTERPRETER TO TRAVEL WITH HIM.
I'VE THOUGHT A LOT ABOUT IT, AND THERE'S REALLY NO ONE BETTER THAN YOU, UNCLE!
I CAN'T, I CAN'T!
I BROKE THE LAW OF NEGOTIABLE INSTRUMENTS WHEN PRINCE PRESS'S CHECKS BOUNCED, REMEMBER? IF I SHOW MY FACE IN PUBLIC, I MIGHT GET ARRESTED.
BUT IT TOOK SO MUCH PERSUADING FOR THE JAPANESE TO LET HIM COME TO TAIWAN . . .
UNCLE, PLEASE!

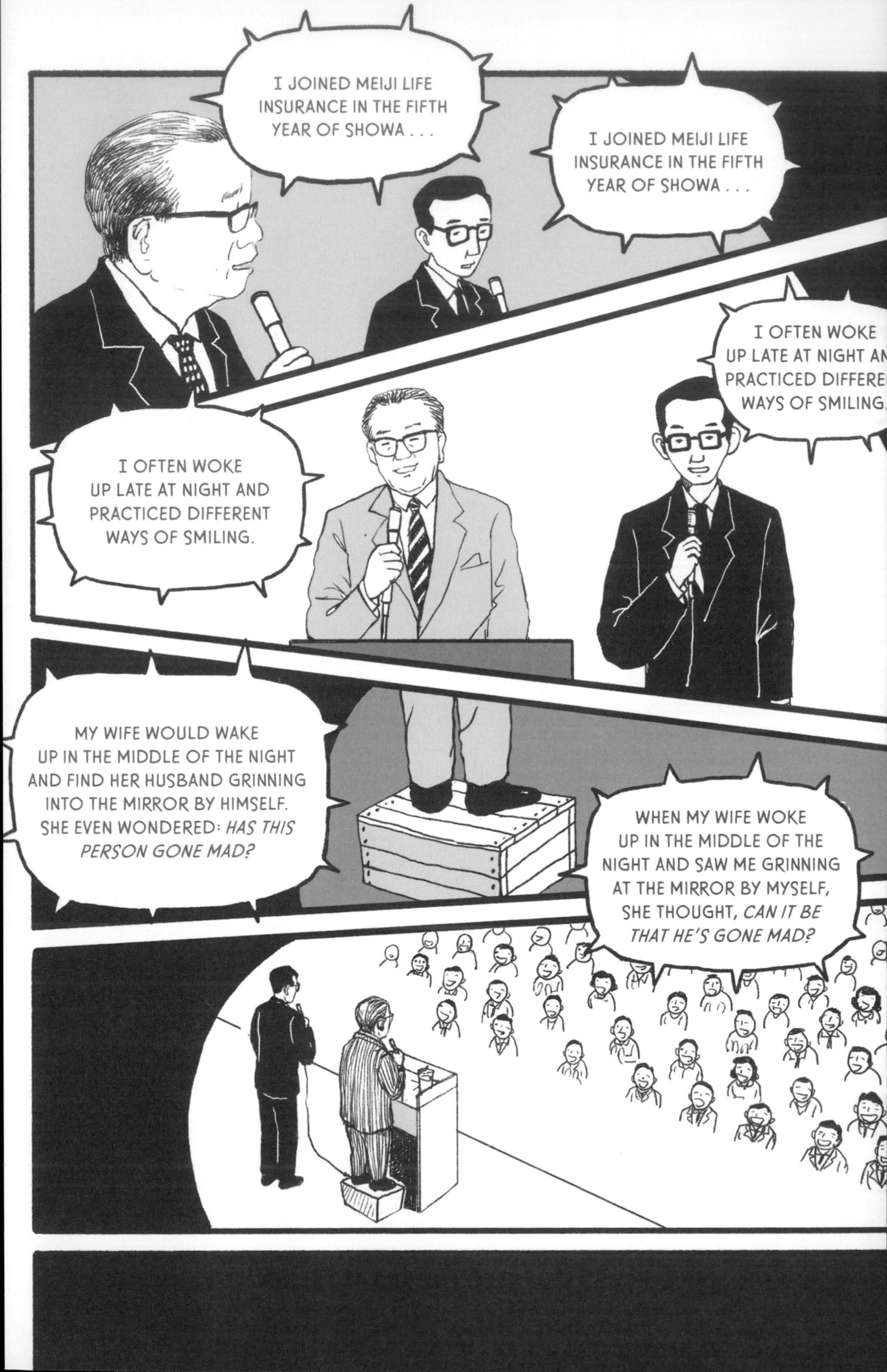
I JOINED MEIJI LIFE INSURANCE IN THE FIFTH YEAR OF SHOWA . . .
I JOINED MEIJI LIFE INSURANCE IN THE FIFTH YEAR OF SHOWA . . .
I OFTEN WOKE UP LATE AT NIGHT AND PRACTICED DIFFERENT WAYS OF SMILING.
I OFTEN WOKE UP LATE AT NIGHT AN PRACTICED DIFFERE WAYS OF SMILING.
MY WIFE WOULD WAKE UP IN THE MIDDLE OF THE NIGHT AND FIND HER HUSBAND GRINNING INTO THE MIRROR BY HIMSELF. SHE EVEN WONDERED: *HAS THIS PERSON GONE MAD?*
WHEN MY WIFE WOKE UP IN THE MIDDLE OF THE NIGHT AND SAW ME GRINNING AT THE MIRROR BY MYSELF, SHE THOUGHT, *CAN IT BE THAT HE'S GONE MAD?*

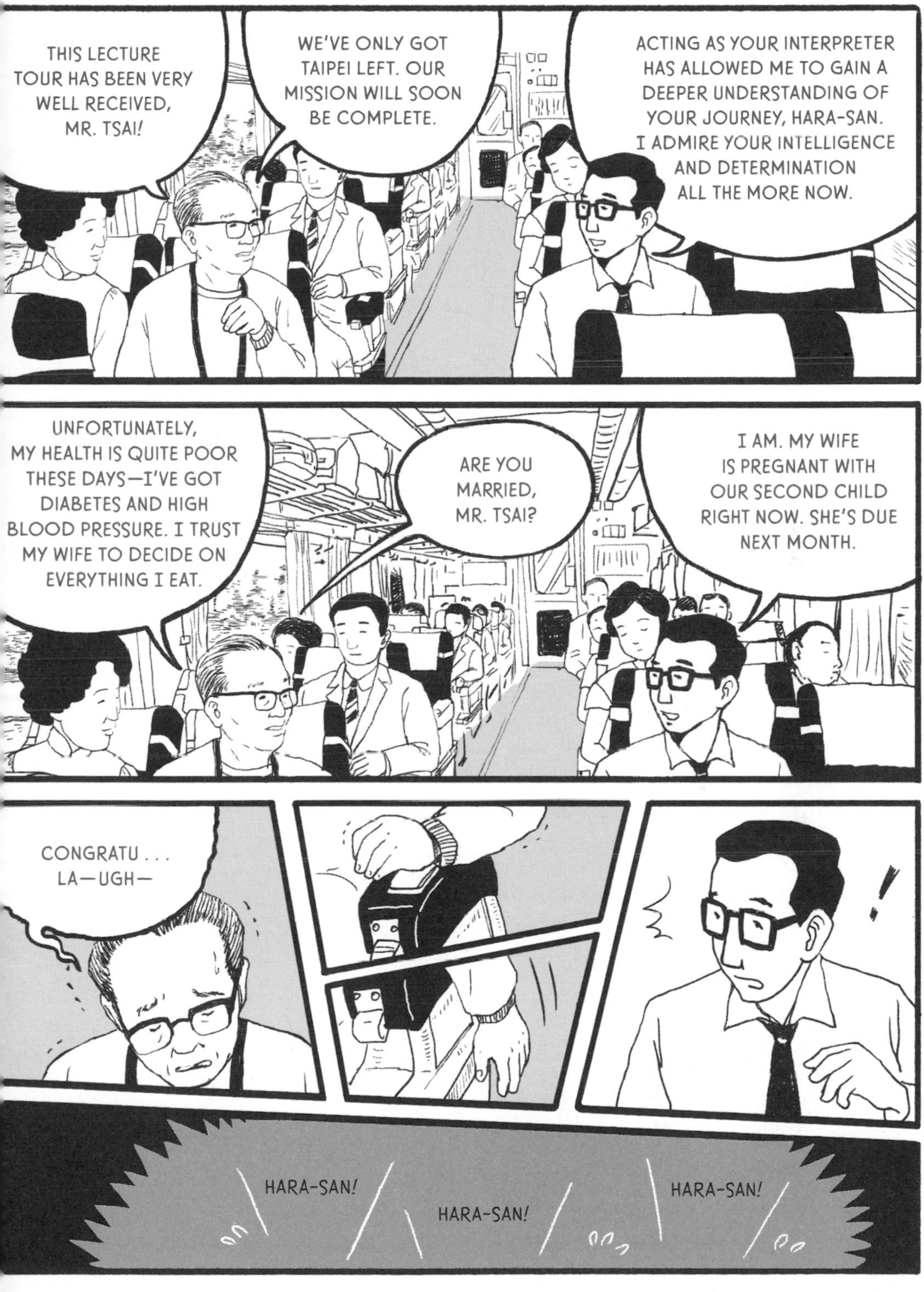
THIS LECTURE TOUR HAS BEEN VERY WELL RECEIVED, MR. TSAI!
WE'VE ONLY GOT TAIPEI LEFT. OUR MISSION WILL SOON BE COMPLETE.
ACTING AS YOUR INTERPRETER HAS ALLOWED ME TO GAIN A DEEPER UNDERSTANDING OF YOUR JOURNEY, HARA-SAN. I ADMIRE YOUR INTELLIGENCE AND DETERMINATION ALL THE MORE NOW.
UNFORTUNATELY, MY HEALTH IS QUITE POOR THESE DAYS—I'VE GOT DIABETES AND HIGH BLOOD PRESSURE. I TRUST MY WIFE TO DECIDE ON EVERYTHING I EAT.
ARE YOU MARRIED, MR. TSAI?
I AM. MY WIFE IS PREGNANT WITH OUR SECOND CHILD RIGHT NOW. SHE'S DUE NEXT MONTH.
CONGRATU . . . LA—UGH—
!
HARA-SAN!
HARA-SAN!
HARA-SAN!

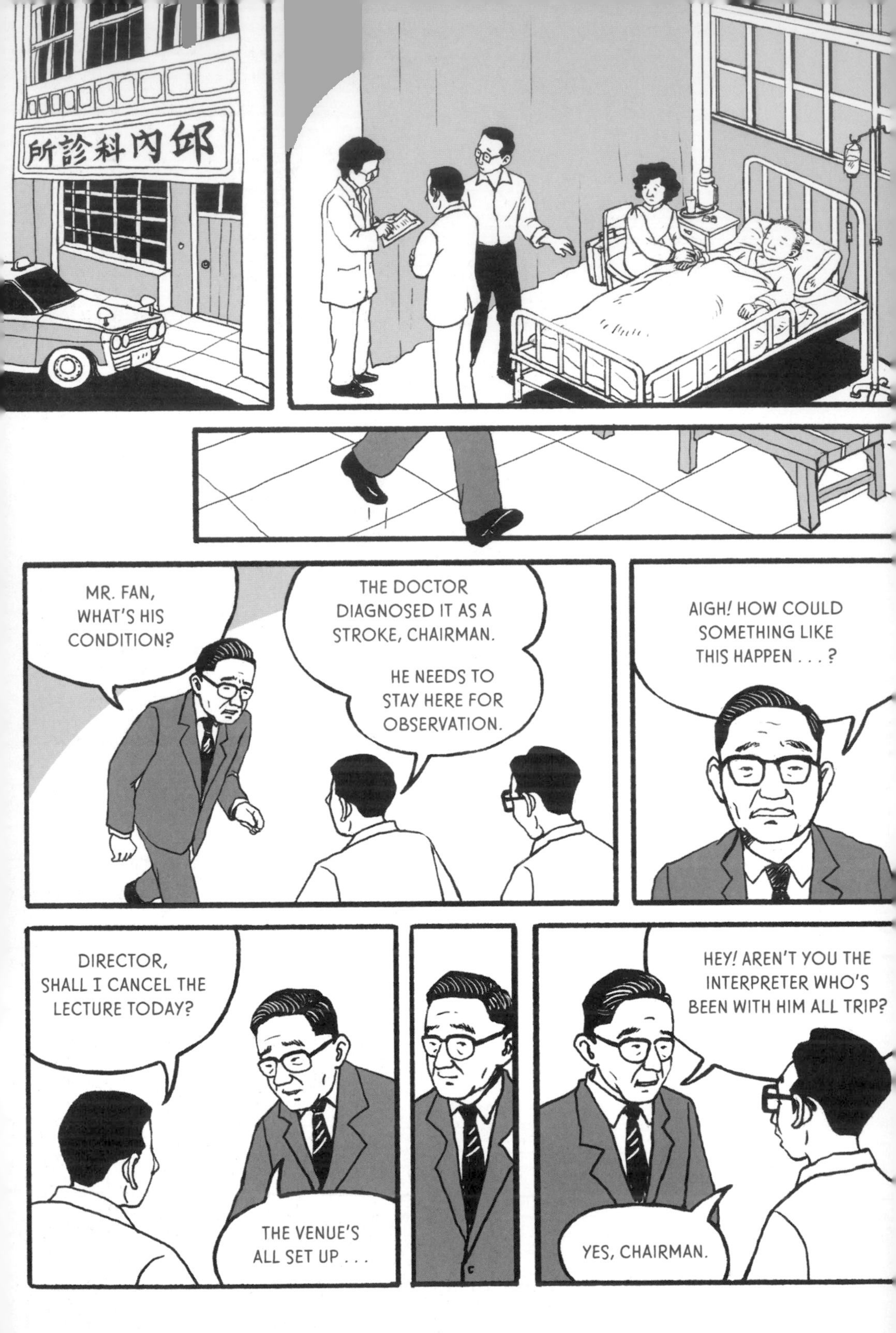

所診科內邱
MR. FAN, WHAT'S HIS CONDITION?
THE DOCTOR DIAGNOSED IT AS A STROKE, CHAIRMAN.
HE NEEDS TO STAY HERE FOR OBSERVATION.
AIGH! HOW COULD SOMETHING LIKE THIS HAPPEN . . . ?
DIRECTOR, SHALL I CANCEL THE LECTURE TODAY?
THE VENUE'S ALL SET UP . . .
HEY! AREN'T YOU THE INTERPRETER WHO'S BEEN WITH HIM ALL TRIP?
YES, CHAIRMAN.

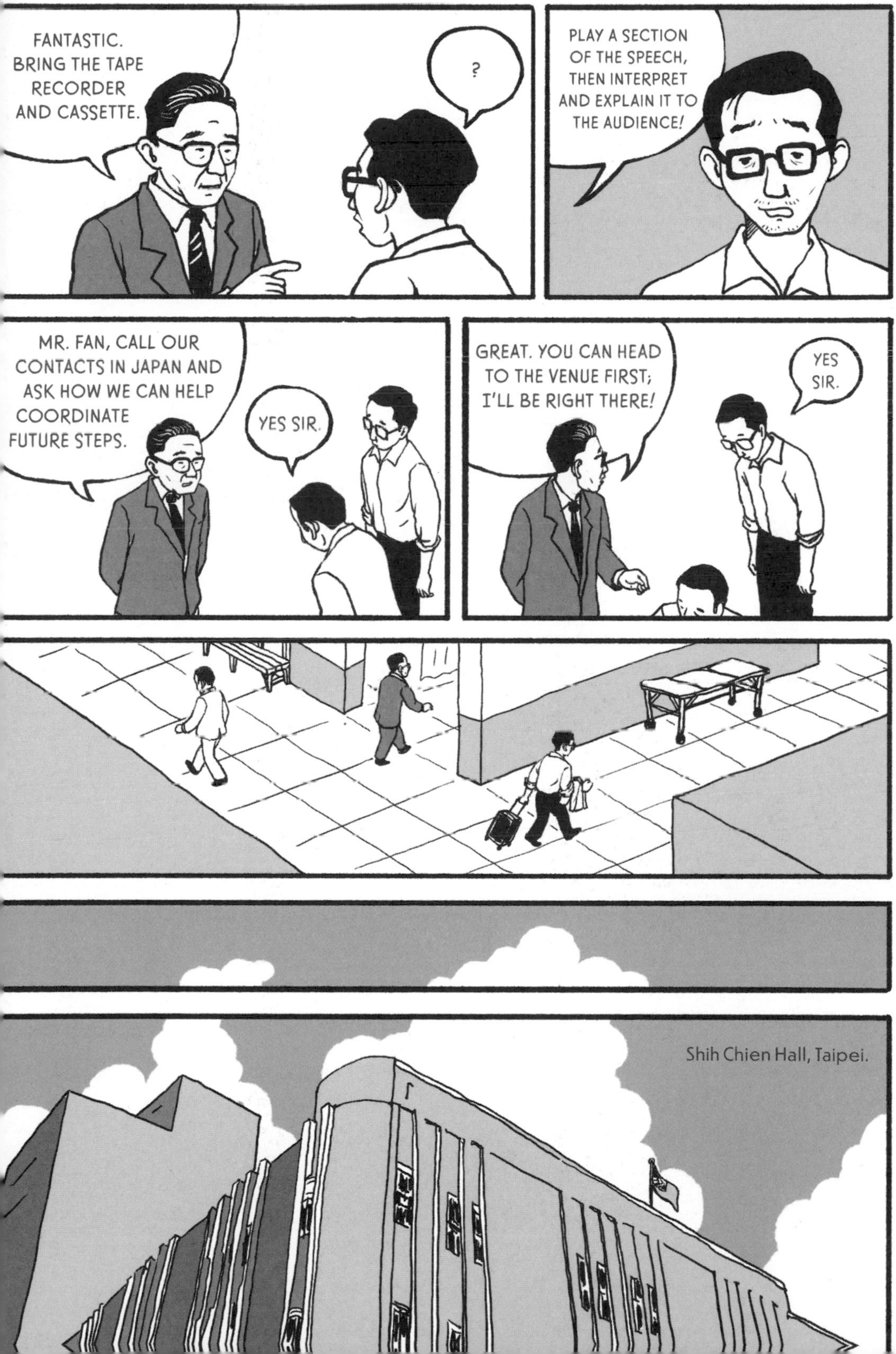
FANTASTIC. BRING THE TAPE RECORDER AND CASSETTE.
?
PLAY A SECTION OF THE SPEECH, THEN INTERPRET AND EXPLAIN IT TO THE AUDIENCE!
MR. FAN, CALL OUR CONTACTS IN JAPAN AND ASK HOW WE CAN HELP COORDINATE FUTURE STEPS.
YES SIR.
GREAT. YOU CAN HEAD TO THE VENUE FIRST; I'LL BE RIGHT THERE!
YES SIR.
Shih Chien Hall, Taipei.

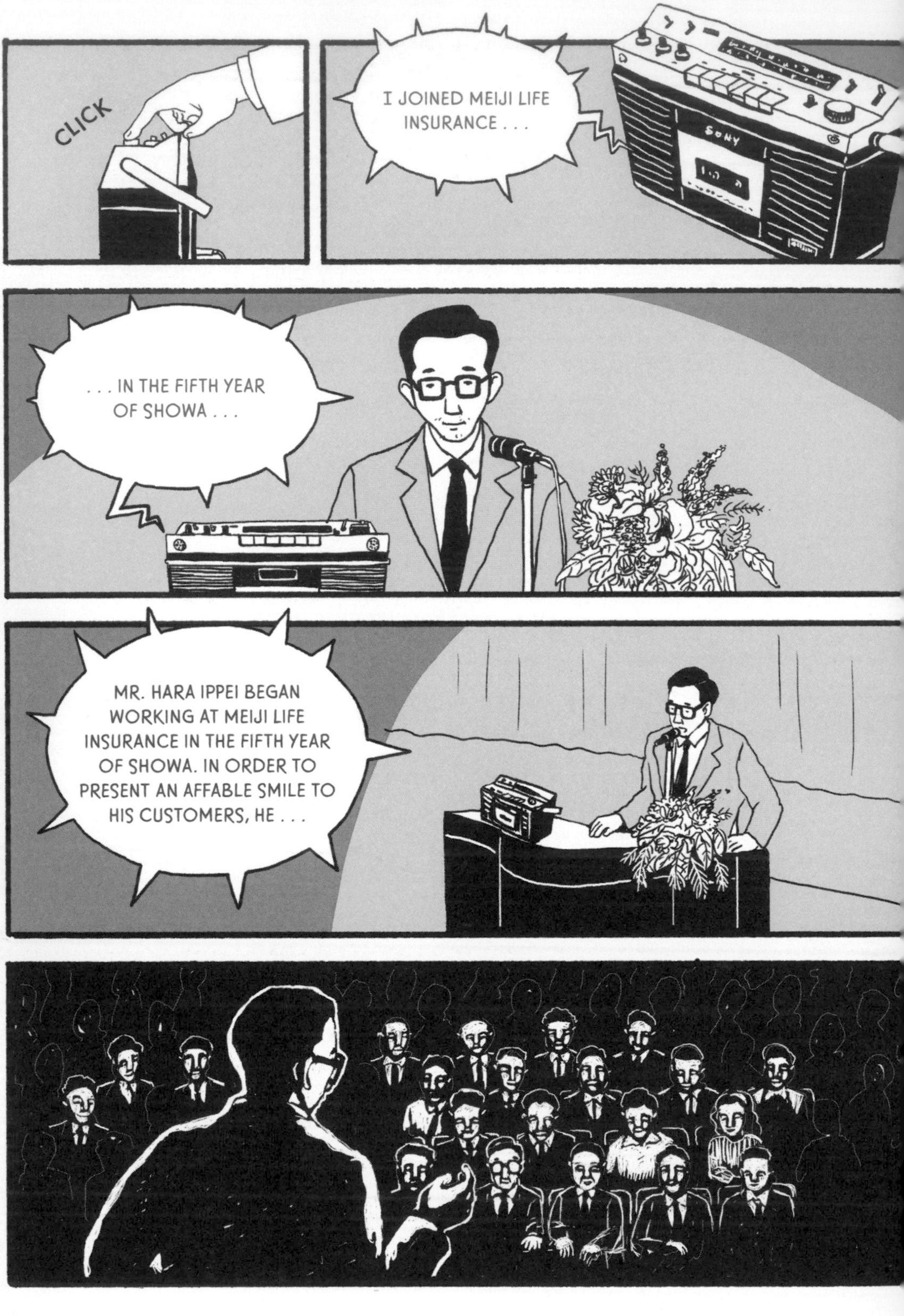
CLICK
I JOINED MEIJI LIFE INSURANCE . . .
SONY
. . . IN THE FIFTH YEAR OF SHOWA . . .
MR. HARA IPPEI BEGAN WORKING AT MEIJI LIFE INSURANCE IN THE FIFTH YEAR OF SHOWA. IN ORDER TO PRESENT AN AFFABLE SMILE TO HIS CUSTOMERS, HE . . .

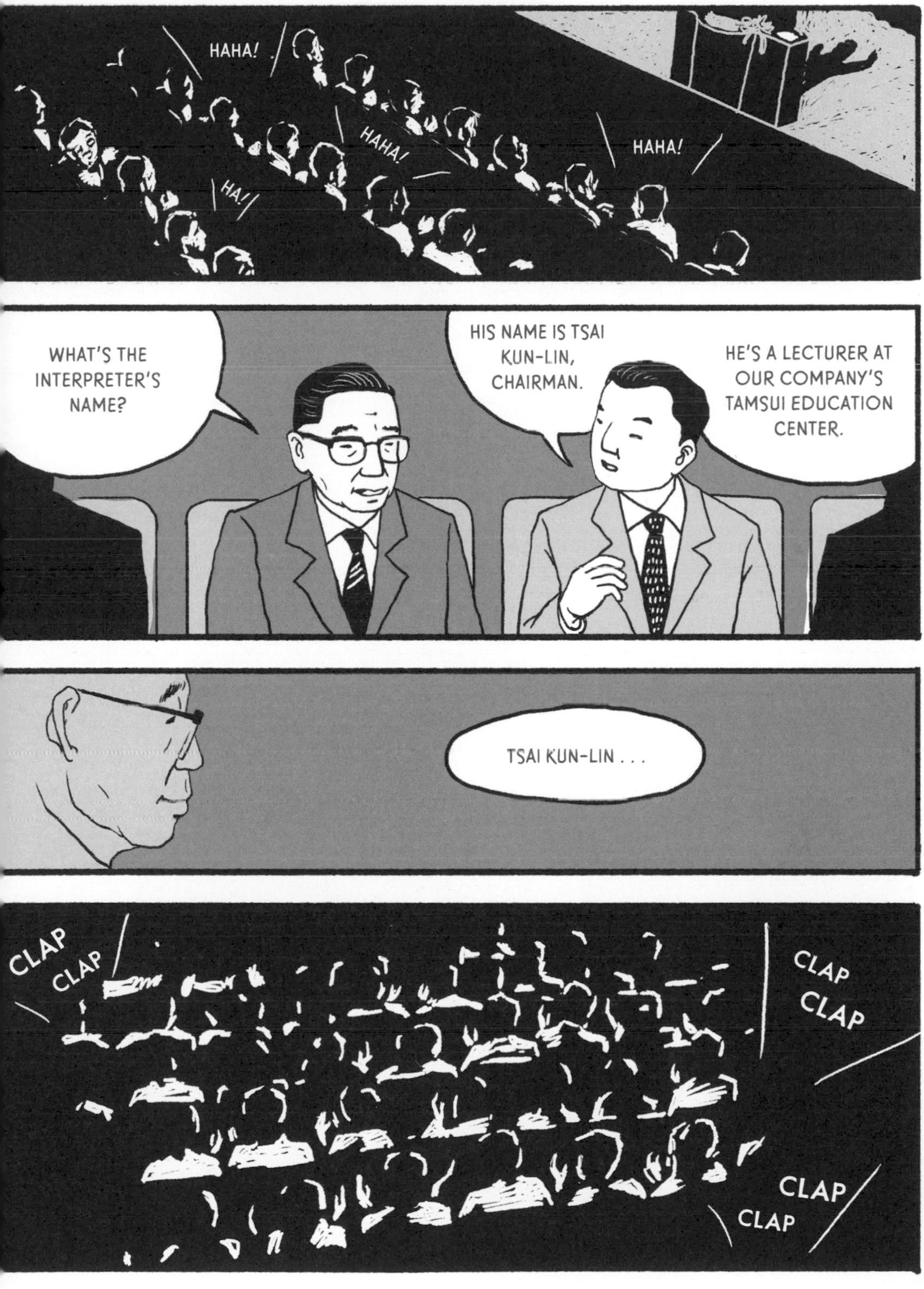
HAHA!
HAHA!
HA!
HAHA!
WHAT'S THE INTERPRETER'S NAME?
HIS NAME IS TSAI KUN-LIN, CHAIRMAN.
HE'S A LECTURER AT OUR COMPANY'S TAMSUI EDUCATION CENTER.
TSAI KUN-LIN . . .
CLAP CLAP
CLAP CLAP
CLAP CLAP

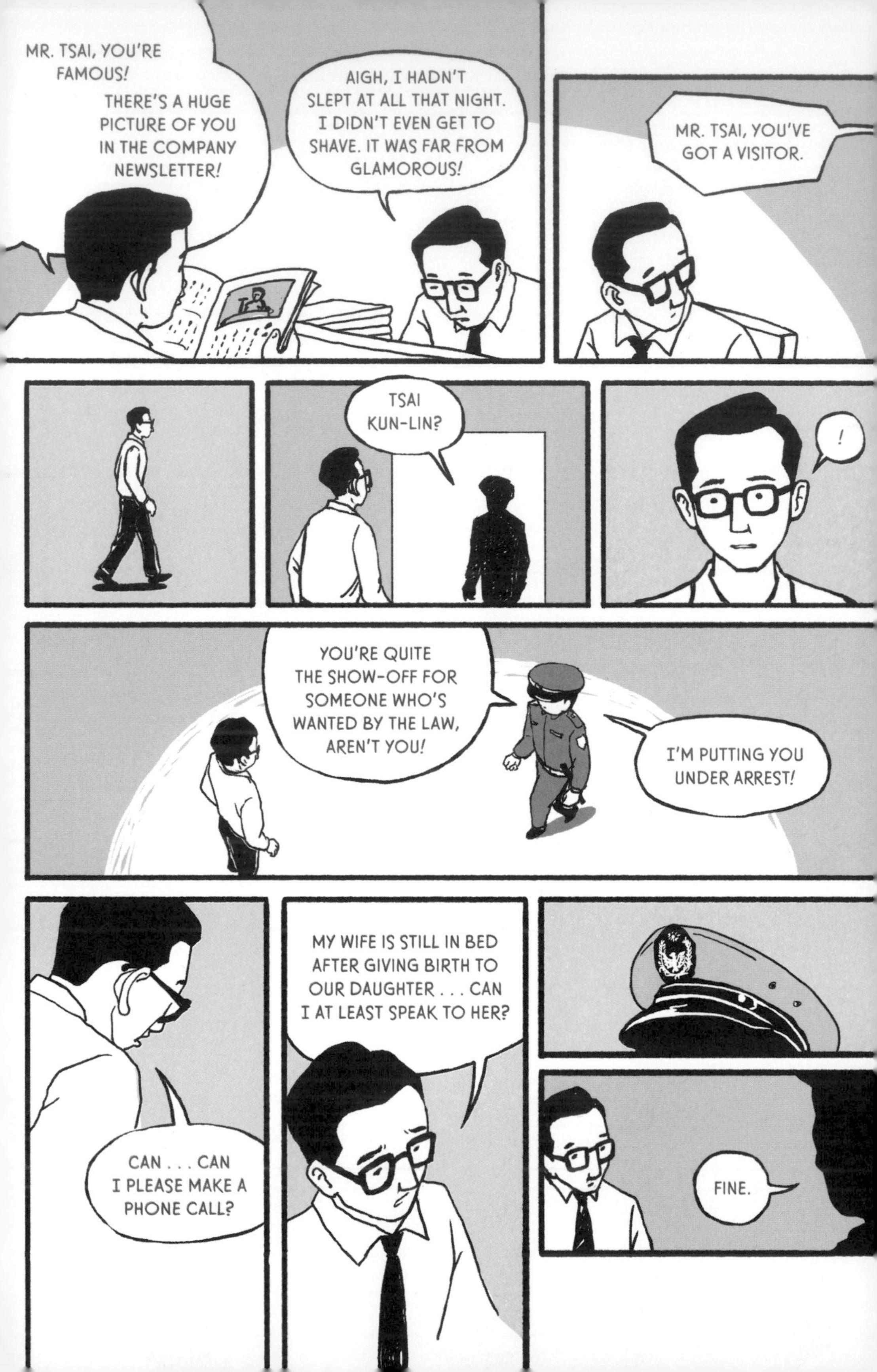
MR. TSAI, YOU'RE FAMOUS!
THERE'S A HUGE PICTURE OF YOU IN THE COMPANY NEWSLETTER!
AIGH, I HADN'T SLEPT AT ALL THAT NIGHT. I DIDN'T EVEN GET TO SHAVE. IT WAS FAR FROM GLAMOROUS!
MR. TSAI, YOU'VE GOT A VISITOR.
TSAI KUN-LIN?
!
YOU'RE QUITE THE SHOW-OFF FOR SOMEONE WHO'S WANTED BY THE LAW, AREN'T YOU!
I'M PUTTING YOU UNDER ARREST!
CAN . . . CAN I PLEASE MAKE A PHONE CALL?
MY WIFE IS STILL IN BED AFTER GIVING BIRTH TO OUR DAUGHTER . . . CAN I AT LEAST SPEAK TO HER?
FINE.

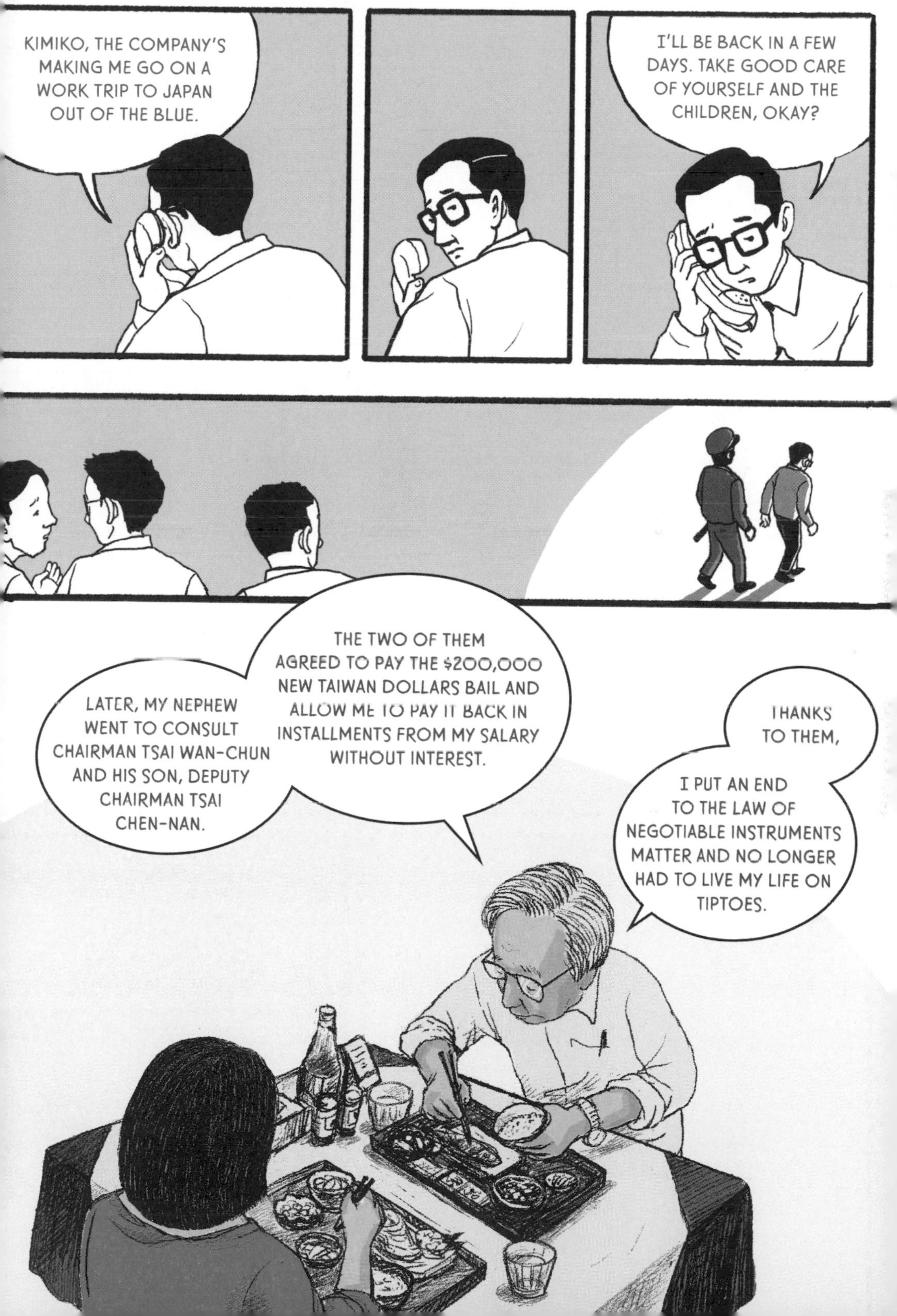
KIMIKO, THE COMPANY'S MAKING ME GO ON A WORK TRIP TO JAPAN OUT OF THE BLUE.
I'LL BE BACK IN A FEW DAYS. TAKE GOOD CARE OF YOURSELF AND THE CHILDREN, OKAY?
LATER, MY NEPHEW WENT TO CONSULT CHAIRMAN TSAI WAN-CHUN AND HIS SON, DEPUTY CHAIRMAN TSAI CHEN-NAN.
THE TWO OF THEM AGREED TO PAY THE $200,000 NEW TAIWAN DOLLARS BAIL AND ALLOW ME TO PAY IT BACK IN INSTALLMENTS FROM MY SALARY WITHOUT INTEREST.
THANKS TO THEM,
I PUT AN END TO THE LAW OF NEGOTIABLE INSTRUMENTS MATTER AND NO LONGER HAD TO LIVE MY LIFE ON TIPTOES.

1972, Cathay Group Headquarters.

MR. TSAI, I HAVE A FAVOR TO ASK.

CHAIRMAN, IT'S NO FAVOR AT ALL. THANK YOU AGAIN FOR HELPING WITH MY BAIL.

WHATEVER YOU NEED, JUST SAY THE WORD.

THE THING IS . . .

AS YOU KNOW, MY THIRD-ELDEST SON STARTED AN ADVERTISING COMPANY RECENTLY.

IT'S ONLY BEEN A MINUTE, BUT NOW HE SAYS HE WANTS TO QUIT.

IT WOULD BE AN INSULT TO CATHAY GROUP'S BRAND!

DURING THE HARA IPPEI LECTURE TOUR, I SAW THAT YOU'RE CLEARLY ABLE TO THINK ON YOUR FEET.

I LOOKED AT YOUR RÉSUMÉ AFTERWARD AND SAW THAT YOU USED TO BE A MANAGER AT KUOHUA ADVERTISING.

SO, IF YOU'RE WILLING, I HOPE YOU CAN LEND YOUR SKILLS TO HIS NEW COMPANY.

HUH? BU YOUR ELD SON ONLY ASKED ME HELP *HIM*

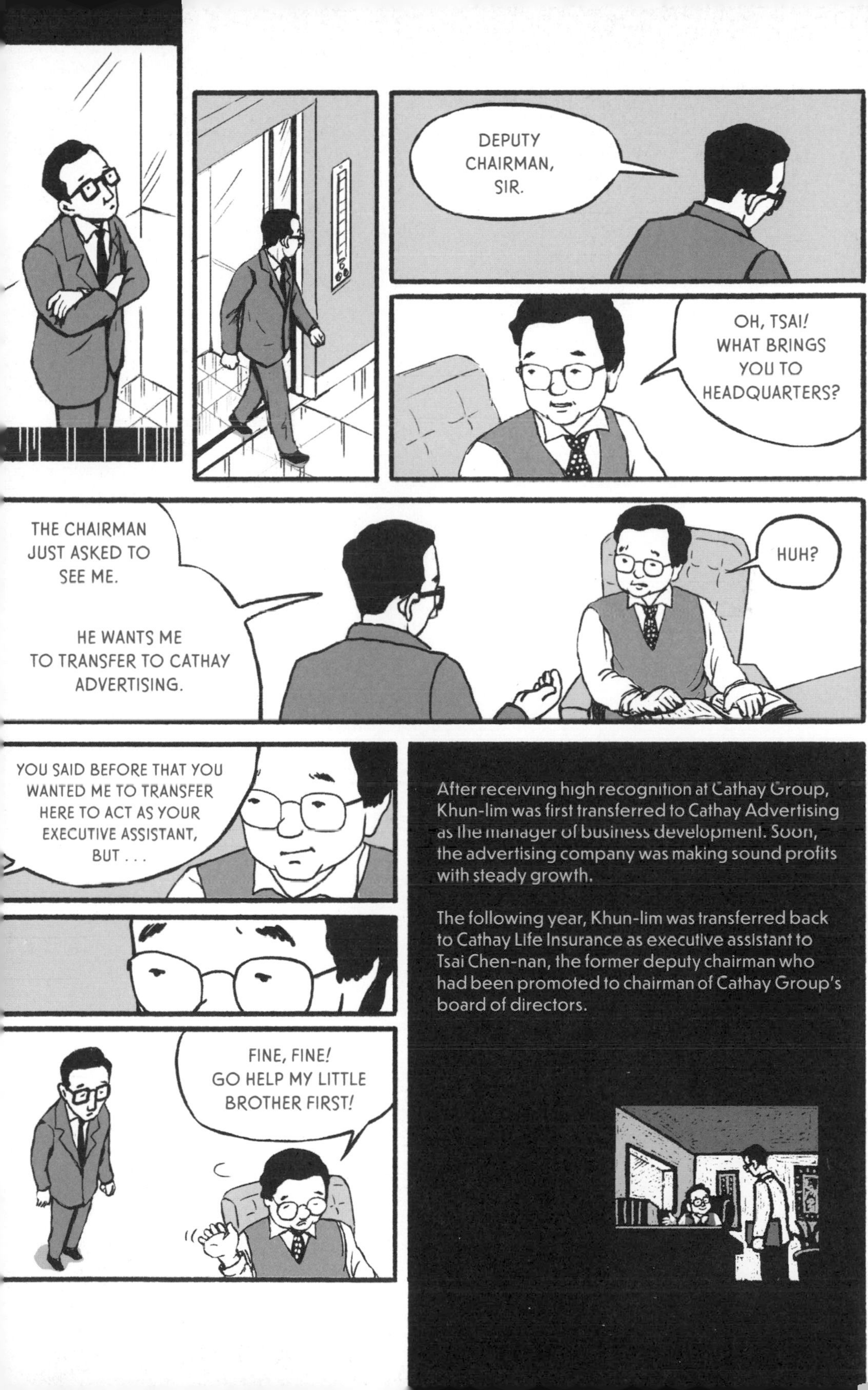
DEPUTY CHAIRMAN, SIR.
OH, TSAI! WHAT BRINGS YOU TO HEADQUARTERS?
THE CHAIRMAN JUST ASKED TO SEE ME.
HE WANTS ME TO TRANSFER TO CATHAY ADVERTISING.
HUH?
YOU SAID BEFORE THAT YOU WANTED ME TO TRANSFER HERE TO ACT AS YOUR EXECUTIVE ASSISTANT, BUT . . .
After receiving high recognition at Cathay Group, Khun-lim was first transferred to Cathay Advertising as the manager of business development. Soon, the advertising company was making sound profits with steady growth.
The following year, Khun-lim was transferred back to Cathay Life Insurance as executive assistant to Tsai Chen-nan, the former deputy chairman who had been promoted to chairman of Cathay Group's board of directors.
FINE, FINE! GO HELP MY LITTLE BROTHER FIRST!

In October 1971, the ROC was forced to withdraw from the United Nations, where representation of China was replaced by the PRC. A little over a year later, US President Richard Nixon visited the PRC for the first time. Japan, too, soon established diplomatic relations with the PRC, drastically shifting the status quo of global affairs.

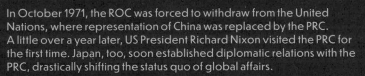

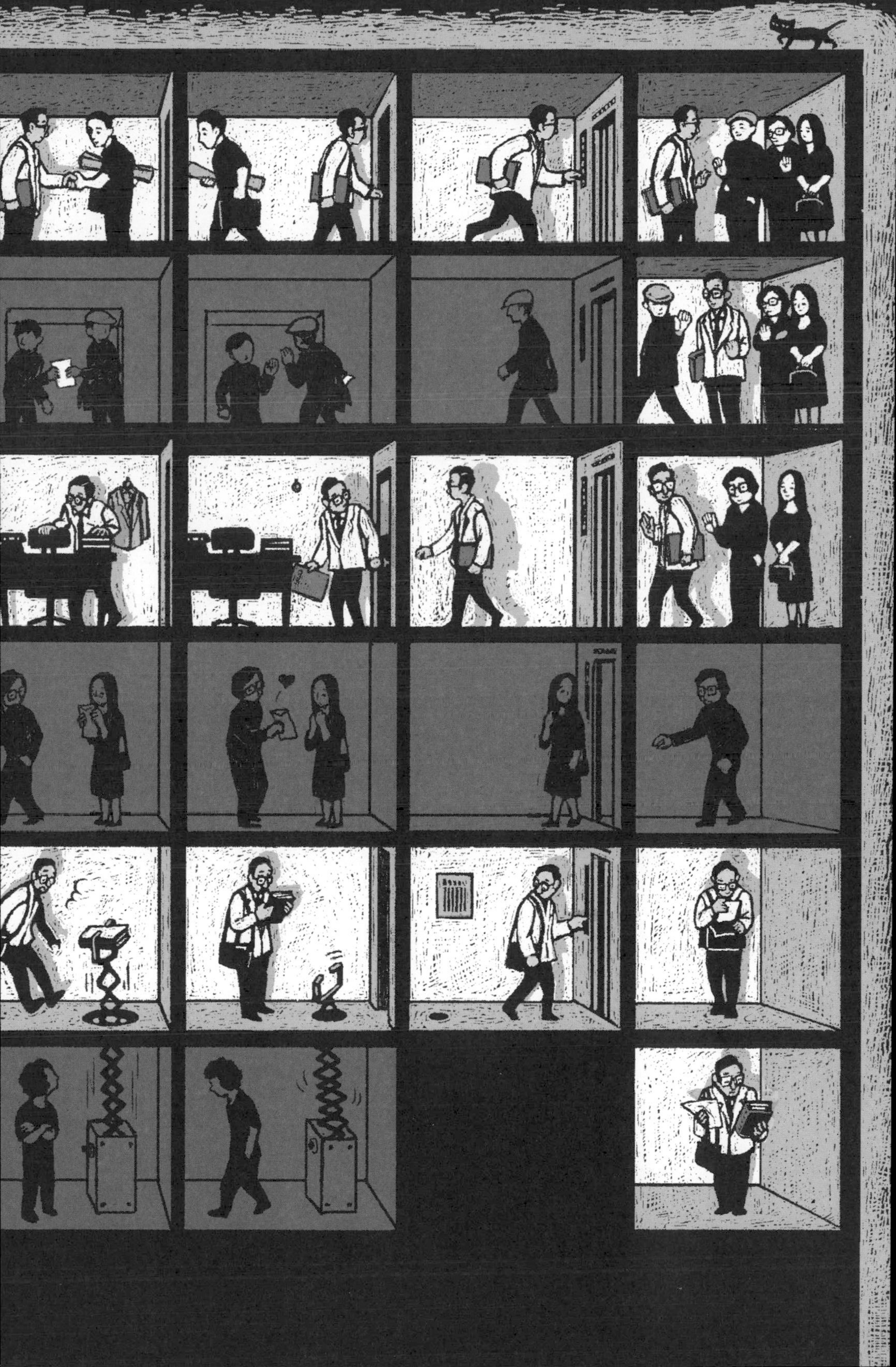

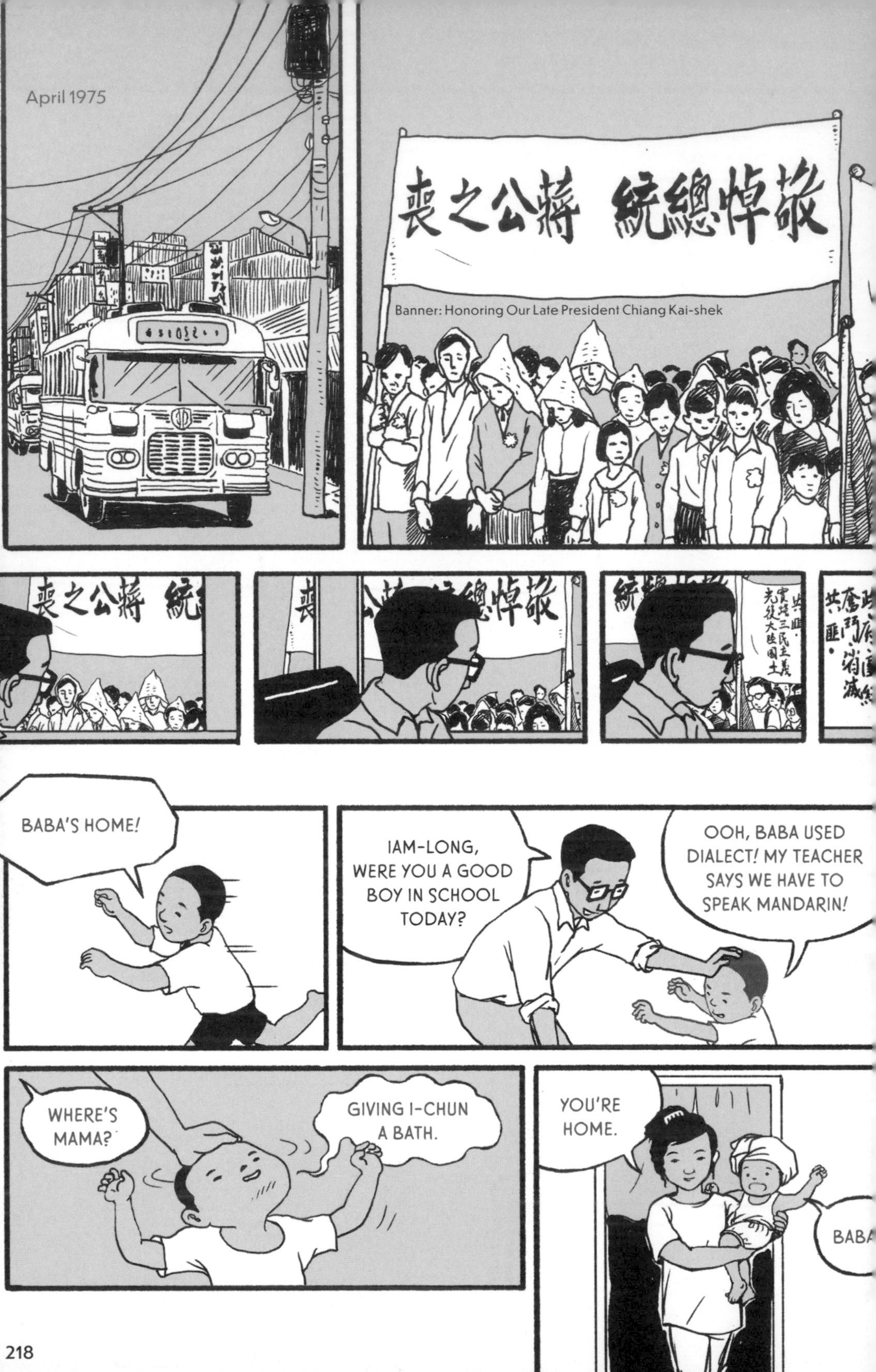
April 1975
敬悼總統 蔣公之喪
Banner: Honoring Our Late President Chiang Kai-shek
BABA'S HOME!
IAM-LONG, WERE YOU A GOOD BOY IN SCHOOL TODAY?
OOH, BABA USED DIALECT! MY TEACHER SAYS WE HAVE TO SPEAK MANDARIN!
WHERE'S MAMA?
GIVING I-CHUN A BATH.
YOU'RE HOME.
BABA

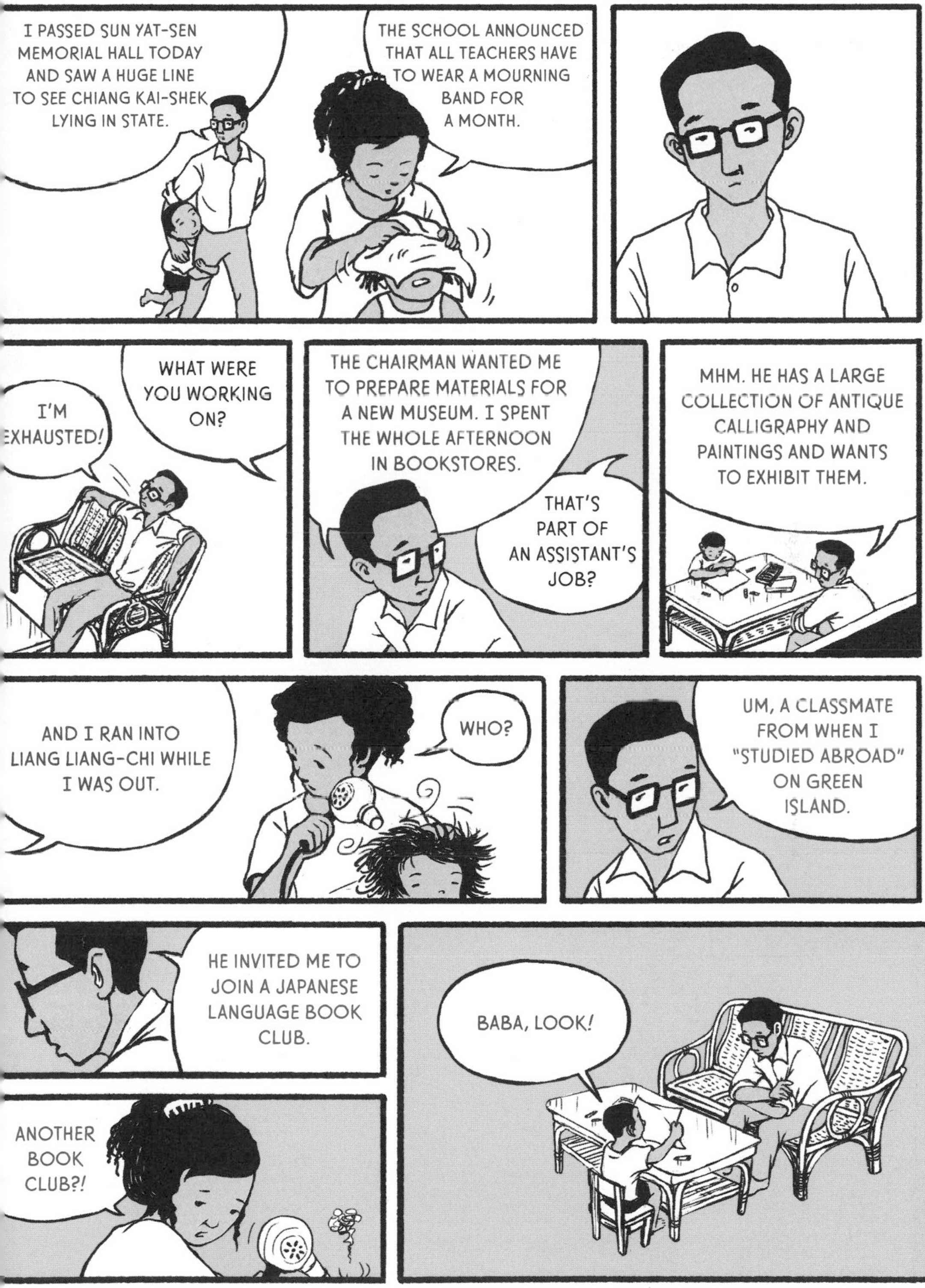
I PASSED SUN YAT-SEN MEMORIAL HALL TODAY AND SAW A HUGE LINE TO SEE CHIANG KAI-SHEK LYING IN STATE.
THE SCHOOL ANNOUNCED THAT ALL TEACHERS HAVE TO WEAR A MOURNING BAND FOR A MONTH.
I'M EXHAUSTED!
WHAT WERE YOU WORKING ON?
THE CHAIRMAN WANTED ME TO PREPARE MATERIALS FOR A NEW MUSEUM. I SPENT THE WHOLE AFTERNOON IN BOOKSTORES.
THAT'S PART OF AN ASSISTANT'S JOB?
MHM. HE HAS A LARGE COLLECTION OF ANTIQUE CALLIGRAPHY AND PAINTINGS AND WANTS TO EXHIBIT THEM.
AND I RAN INTO LIANG LIANG-CHI WHILE I WAS OUT.
WHO?
UM, A CLASSMATE FROM WHEN I "STUDIED ABROAD" ON GREEN ISLAND.
HE INVITED ME TO JOIN A JAPANESE LANGUAGE BOOK CLUB.
ANOTHER BOOK CLUB?!
BABA, LOOK!

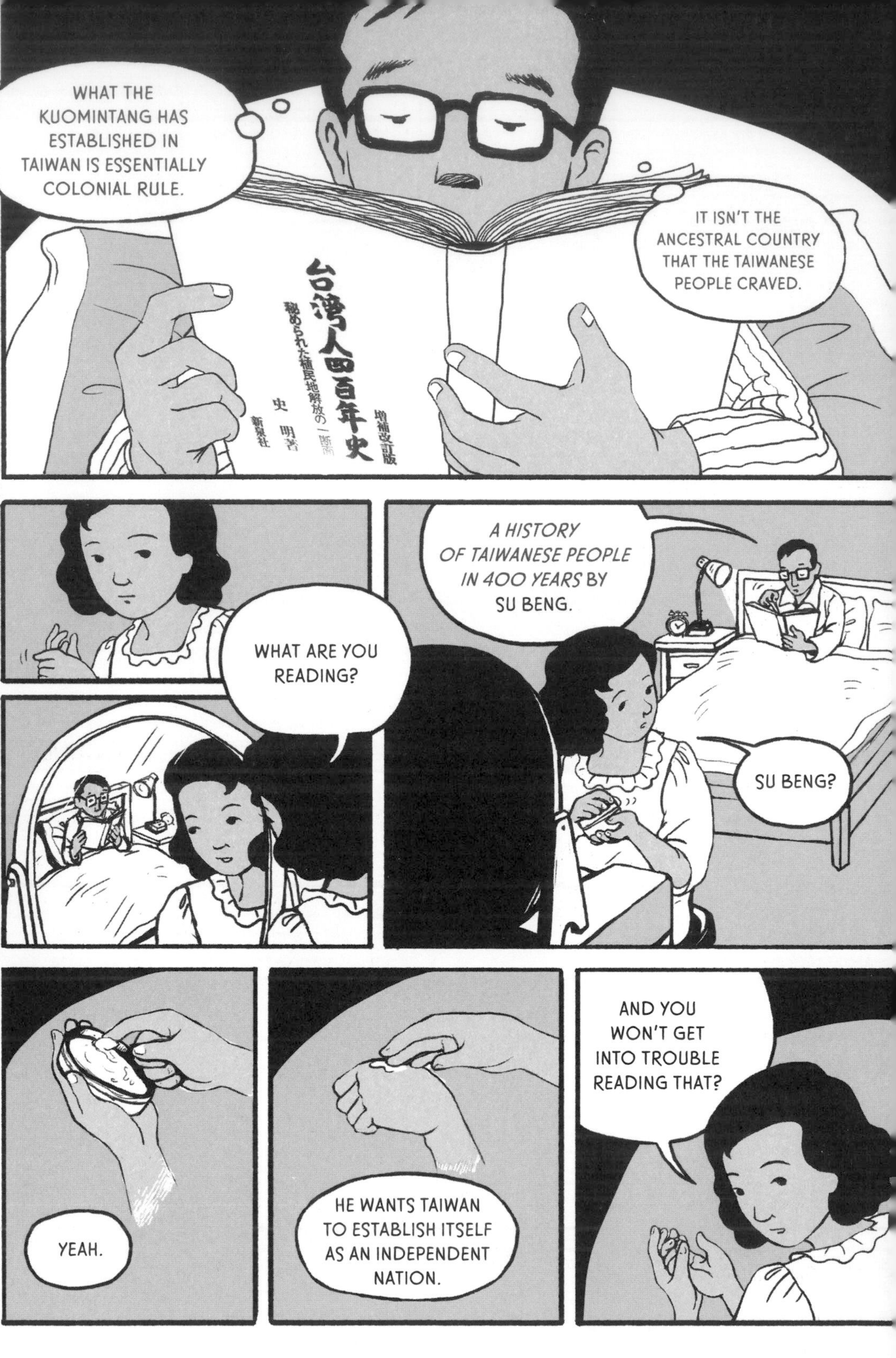
WHAT THE KUOMINTANG HAS ESTABLISHED IN TAIWAN IS ESSENTIALLY COLONIAL RULE.
增補改訂版
台湾人四百年史
秘められた植民地解放の一断面
史 明著
新泉社
IT ISN'T THE ANCESTRAL COUNTRY THAT THE TAIWANESE PEOPLE CRAVED.
WHAT ARE YOU READING?
A HISTORY OF TAIWANESE PEOPLE IN 400 YEARS BY SU BENG.
SU BENG?
YEAH.
HE WANTS TAIWAN TO ESTABLISH ITSELF AS AN INDEPENDENT NATION.
AND YOU WON'T GET INTO TROUBLE READING THAT?

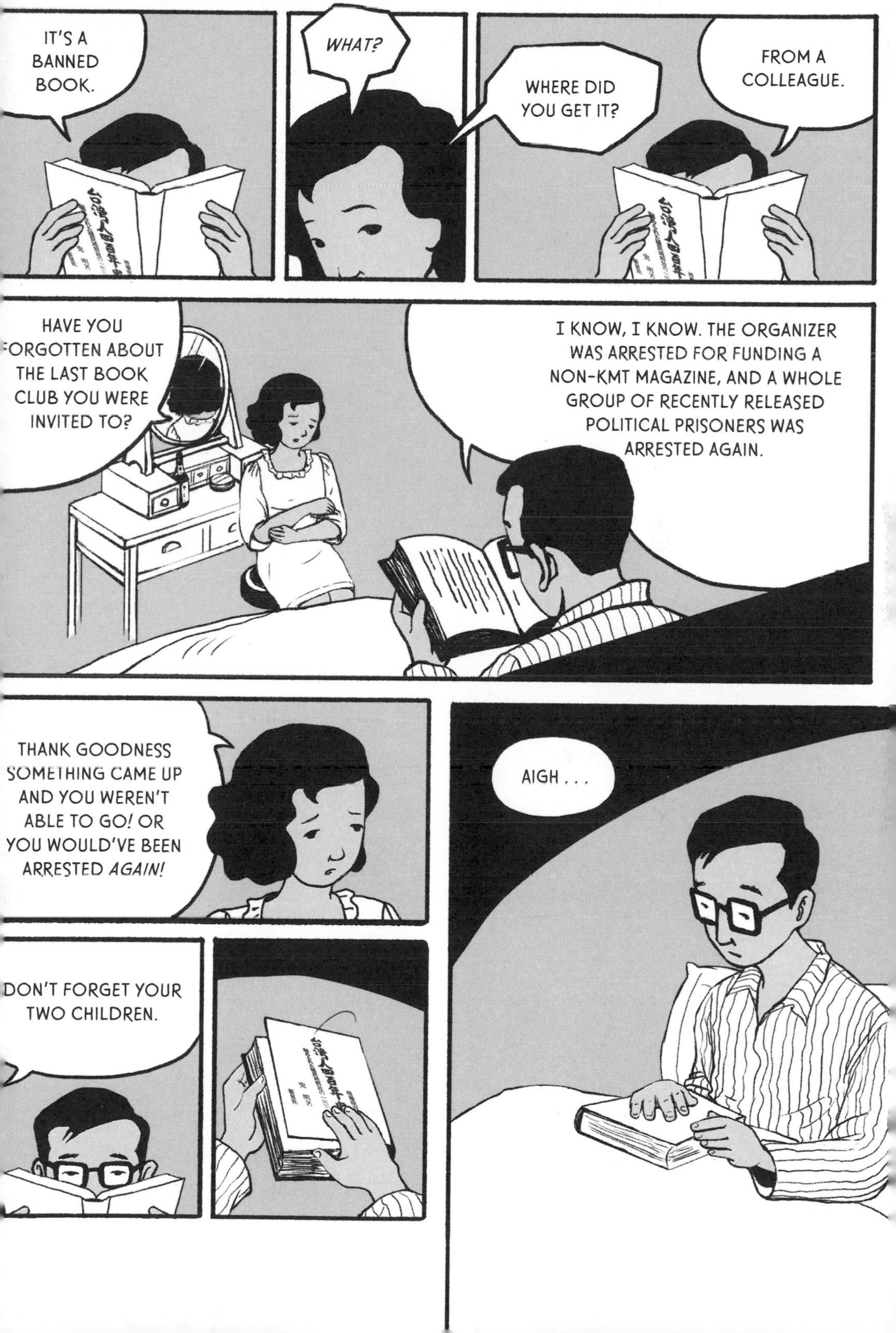
IT'S A BANNED BOOK.
WHAT?
WHERE DID YOU GET IT?
FROM A COLLEAGUE.
HAVE YOU FORGOTTEN ABOUT THE LAST BOOK CLUB YOU WERE INVITED TO?
I KNOW, I KNOW. THE ORGANIZER WAS ARRESTED FOR FUNDING A NON-KMT MAGAZINE, AND A WHOLE GROUP OF RECENTLY RELEASED POLITICAL PRISONERS WAS ARRESTED AGAIN.
THANK GOODNESS SOMETHING CAME UP AND YOU WEREN'T ABLE TO GO! OR YOU WOULD'VE BEEN ARRESTED *AGAIN!*
DON'T FORGET YOUR TWO CHILDREN.
AIGH . . .

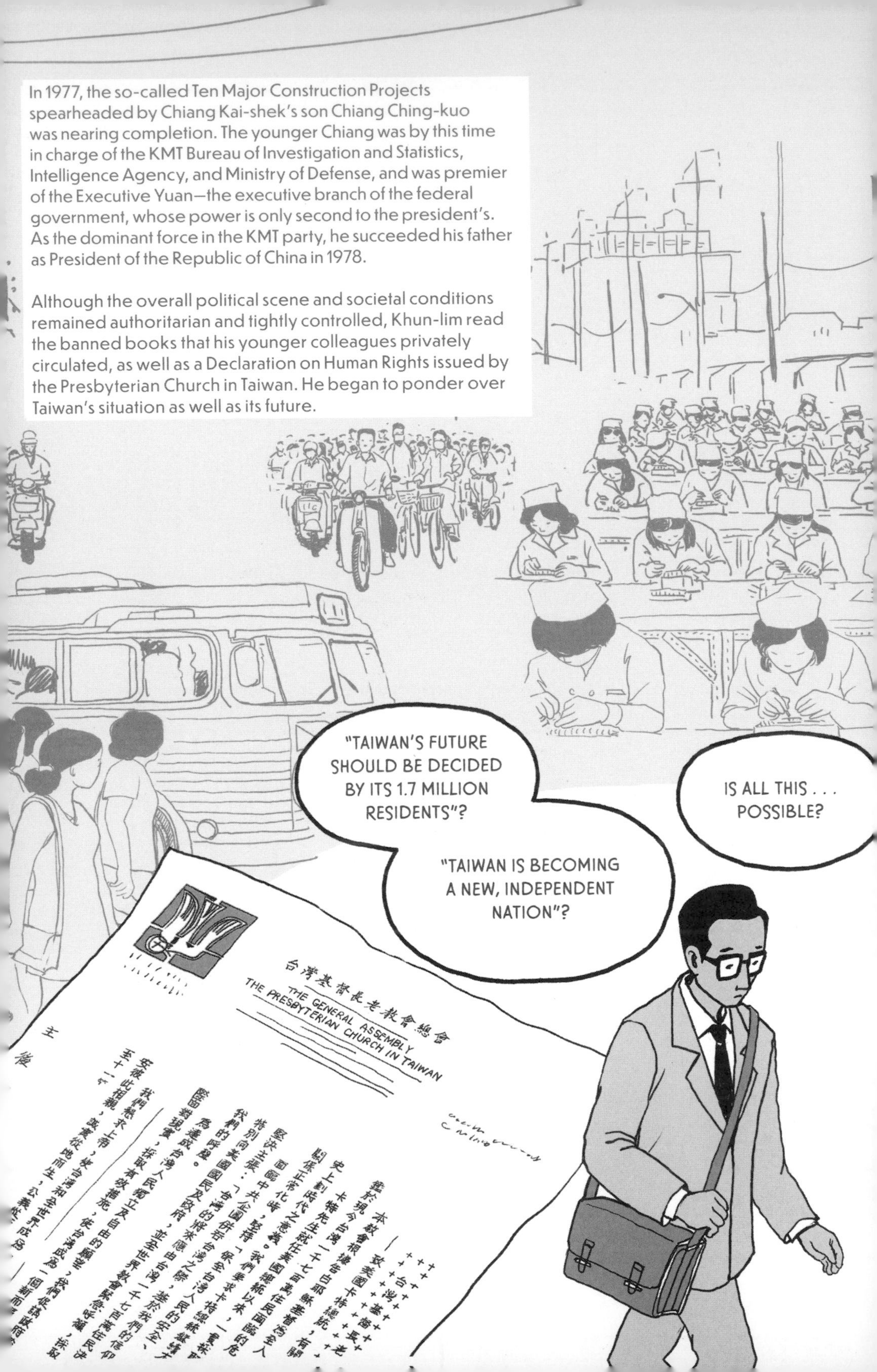
In 1977, the so-called Ten Major Construction Projects spearheaded by Chiang Kai-shek's son Chiang Ching-kuo was nearing completion. The younger Chiang was by this time in charge of the KMT Bureau of Investigation and Statistics, Intelligence Agency, and Ministry of Defense, and was premier of the Executive Yuan—the executive branch of the federal government, whose power is only second to the president's. As the dominant force in the KMT party, he succeeded his father as President of the Republic of China in 1978.
Although the overall political scene and societal conditions remained authoritarian and tightly controlled, Khun-lim read the banned books that his younger colleagues privately circulated, as well as a Declaration on Human Rights issued by the Presbyterian Church in Taiwan. He began to ponder over Taiwan's situation as well as its future.
"TAIWAN'S FUTURE SHOULD BE DECIDED BY ITS 1.7 MILLION RESIDENTS"?
"TAIWAN IS BECOMING A NEW, INDEPENDENT NATION"?
IS ALL THIS . . . POSSIBLE?
台灣基督長老教會總會
THE GENERAL ASSEMBLY
THE PRESBYTERIAN CHURCH IN TAIWAN

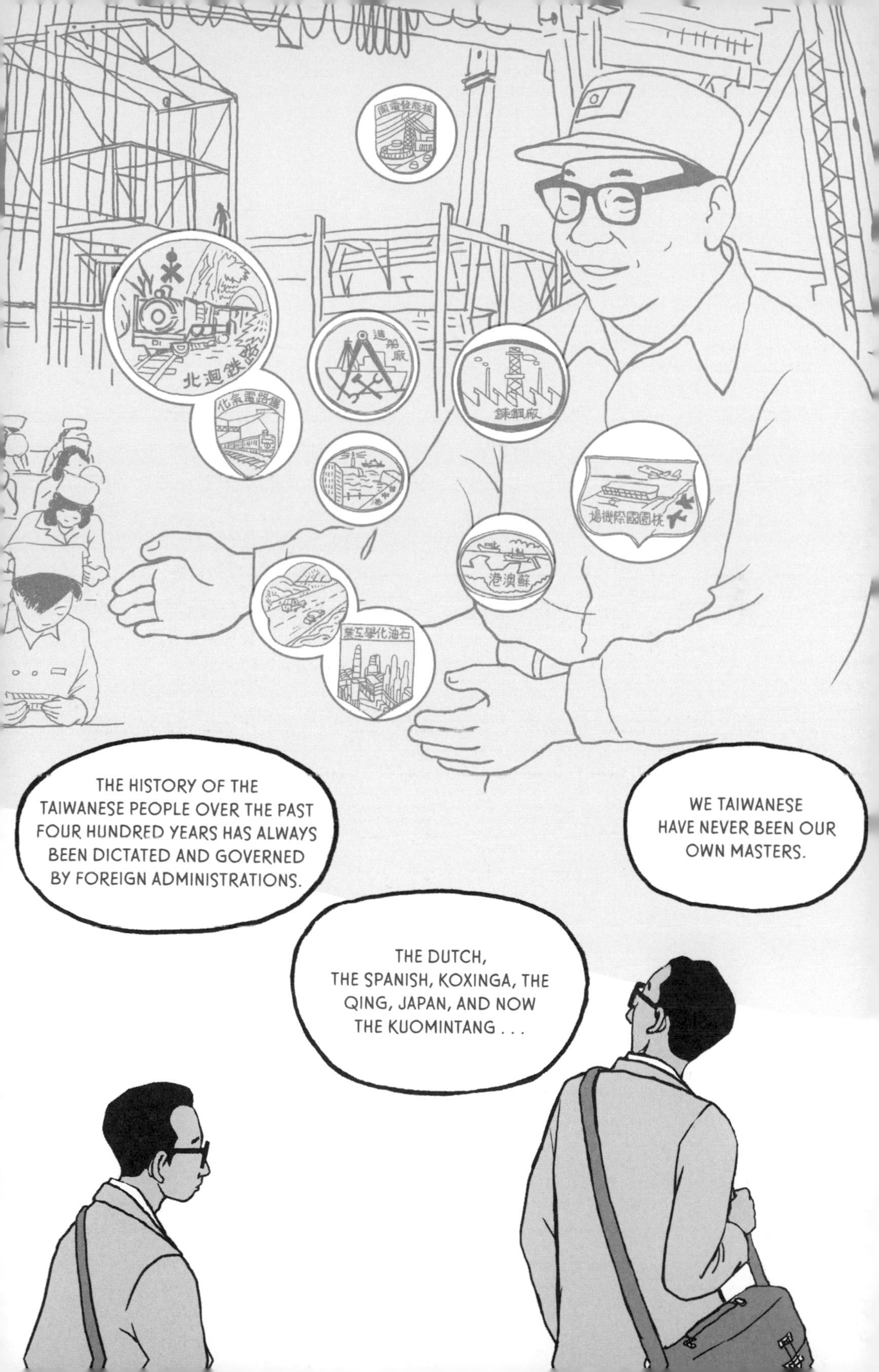

核能發電廠
北迴鐵路
鐵路電氣化
造船廠
煉鋼廠
桃園國際機場
蘇澳港
石油化學工業
THE HISTORY OF THE TAIWANESE PEOPLE OVER THE PAST FOUR HUNDRED YEARS HAS ALWAYS BEEN DICTATED AND GOVERNED BY FOREIGN ADMINISTRATIONS.
WE TAIWANESE HAVE NEVER BEEN OUR OWN MASTERS.
THE DUTCH, THE SPANISH, KOXINGA, THE QING, JAPAN, AND NOW THE KUOMINTANG . . .

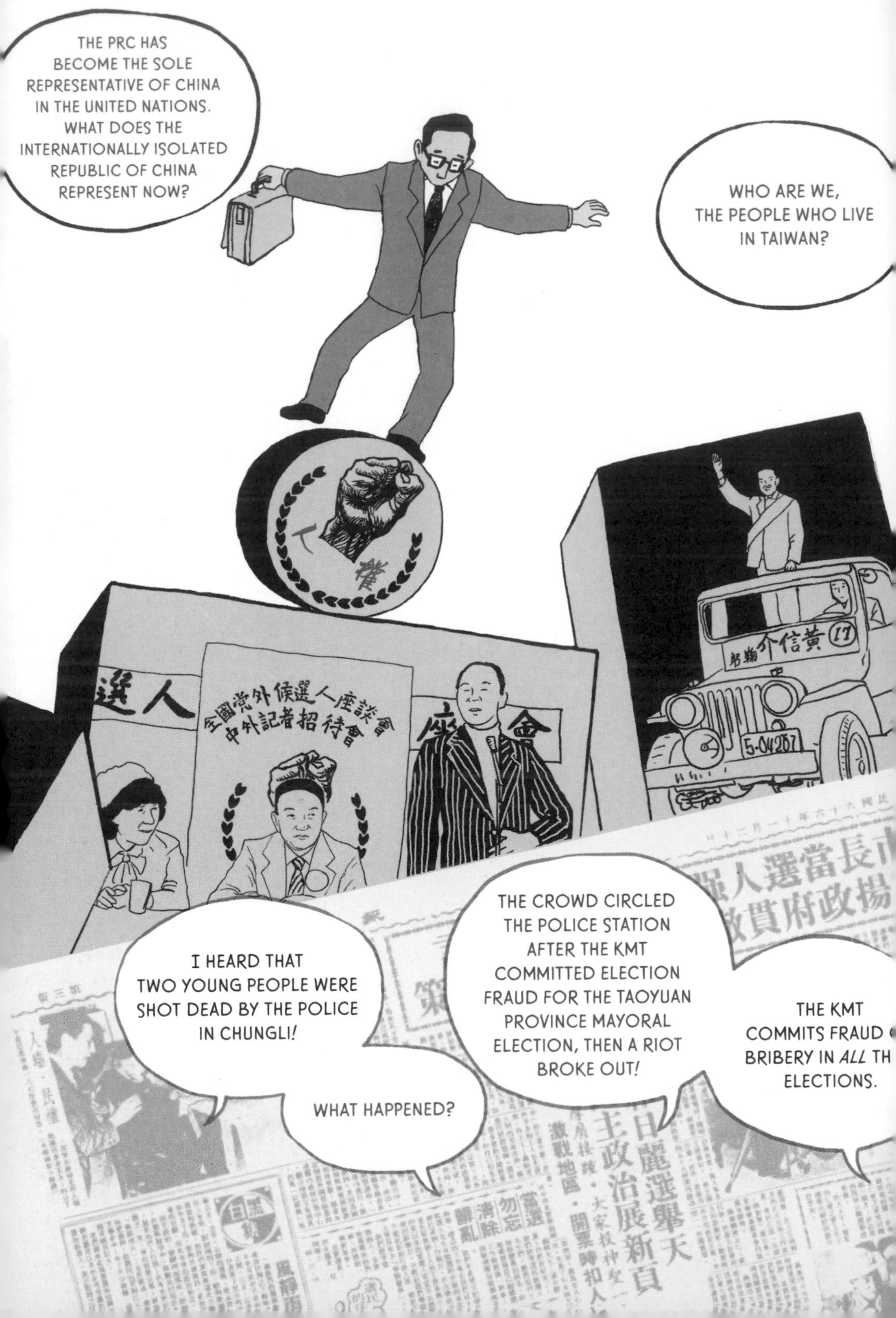

THE PRC HAS BECOME THE SOLE REPRESENTATIVE OF CHINA IN THE UNITED NATIONS. WHAT DOES THE INTERNATIONALLY ISOLATED REPUBLIC OF CHINA REPRESENT NOW?
WHO ARE WE, THE PEOPLE WHO LIVE IN TAIWAN?
選人
全國党外候選人座談會
中外記者招待會
黃信介
5-04207
I HEARD THAT TWO YOUNG PEOPLE WERE SHOT DEAD BY THE POLICE IN CHUNGLI!
WHAT HAPPENED?
THE CROWD CIRCLED THE POLICE STATION AFTER THE KMT COMMITTED ELECTION FRAUD FOR THE TAOYUAN PROVINCE MAYORAL ELECTION, THEN A RIOT BROKE OUT!
THE KMT COMMITS FRAUD
BRIBERY IN *ALL* TH
ELECTIONS.

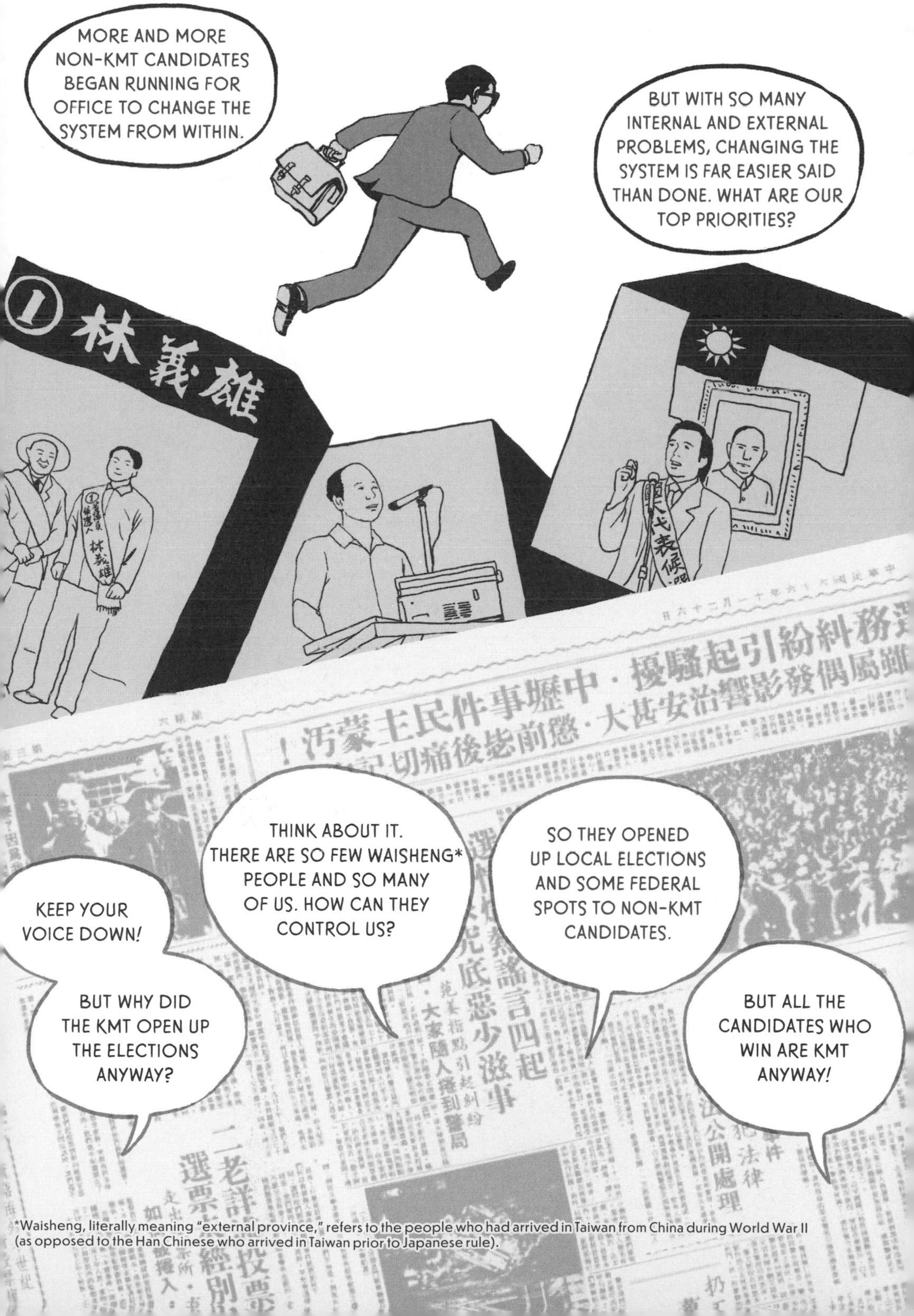

MORE AND MORE NON-KMT CANDIDATES BEGAN RUNNING FOR OFFICE TO CHANGE THE SYSTEM FROM WITHIN.
BUT WITH SO MANY INTERNAL AND EXTERNAL PROBLEMS, CHANGING THE SYSTEM IS FAR EASIER SAID THAN DONE. WHAT ARE OUR TOP PRIORITIES?
林義雄
THINK ABOUT IT. THERE ARE SO FEW WAISHENG* PEOPLE AND SO MANY OF US. HOW CAN THEY CONTROL US?
KEEP YOUR VOICE DOWN!
BUT WHY DID THE KMT OPEN UP THE ELECTIONS ANYWAY?
SO THEY OPENED UP LOCAL ELECTIONS AND SOME FEDERAL SPOTS TO NON-KMT CANDIDATES.
BUT ALL THE CANDIDATES WHO WIN ARE KMT ANYWAY!

*Waisheng, literally meaning "external province," refers to the people who had arrived in Taiwan from China during World War II (as opposed to the Han Chinese who arrived in Taiwan prior to Japanese rule).

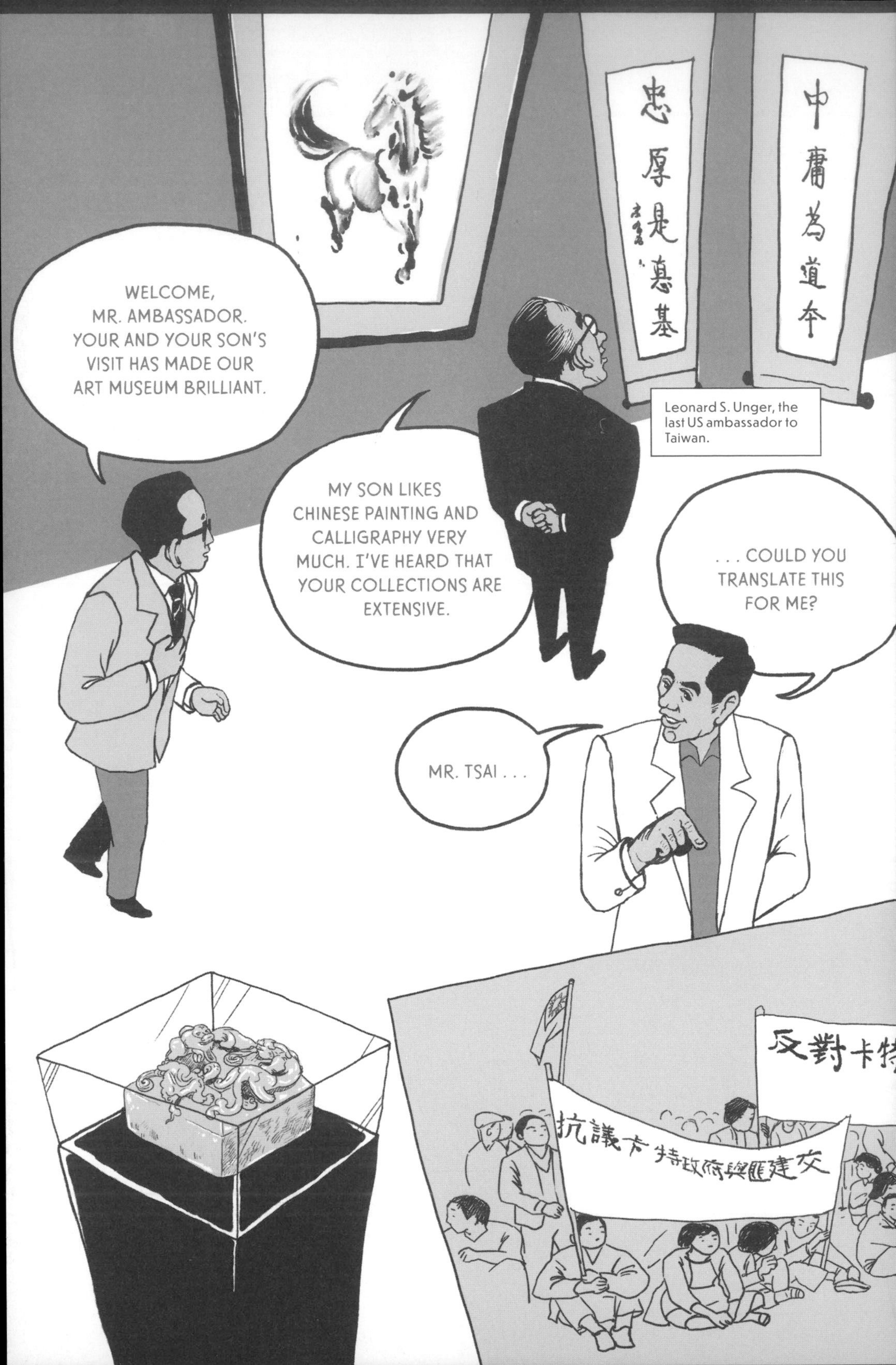

中庸為道本
WELCOME, MR. AMBASSADOR. YOUR AND YOUR SON'S VISIT HAS MADE OUR ART MUSEUM BRILLIANT.
Leonard S. Unger, the last US ambassador to Taiwan.
MY SON LIKES CHINESE PAINTING AND CALLIGRAPHY VERY MUCH. I'VE HEARD THAT YOUR COLLECTIONS ARE EXTENSIVE.
MR. TSAI . . .
. . . COULD YOU TRANSLATE THIS FOR ME?
反對卡特
抗議卡特政府與匪建交

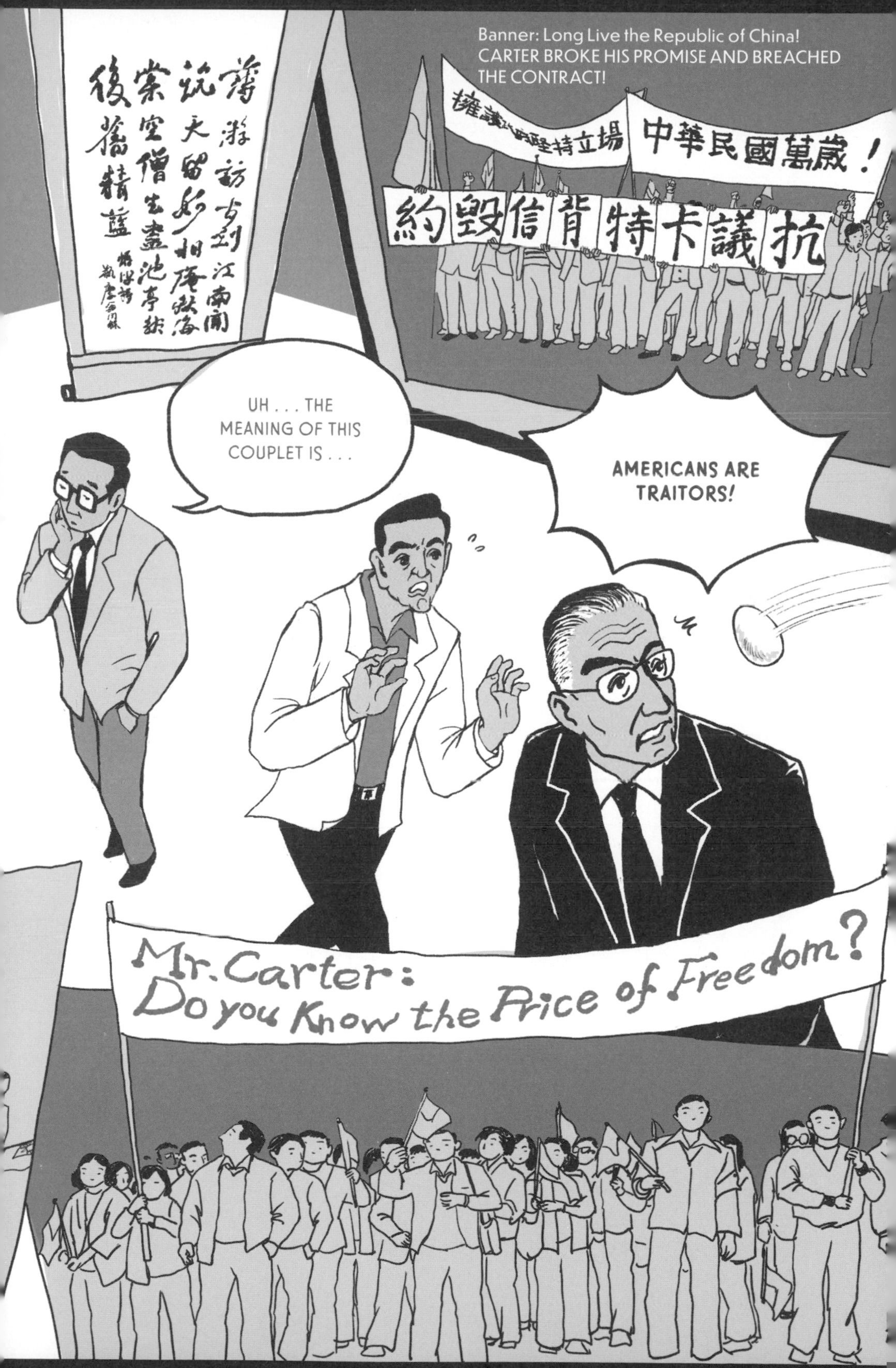
Banner: Long Live the Republic of China! CARTER BROKE HIS PROMISE AND BREACHED THE CONTRACT!
中華民國萬歲！
抗議卡特背信毀約
UH . . . THE MEANING OF THIS COUPLET IS . . .
AMERICANS ARE TRAITORS!
Mr. Carter: Do you Know the Price of Freedom?

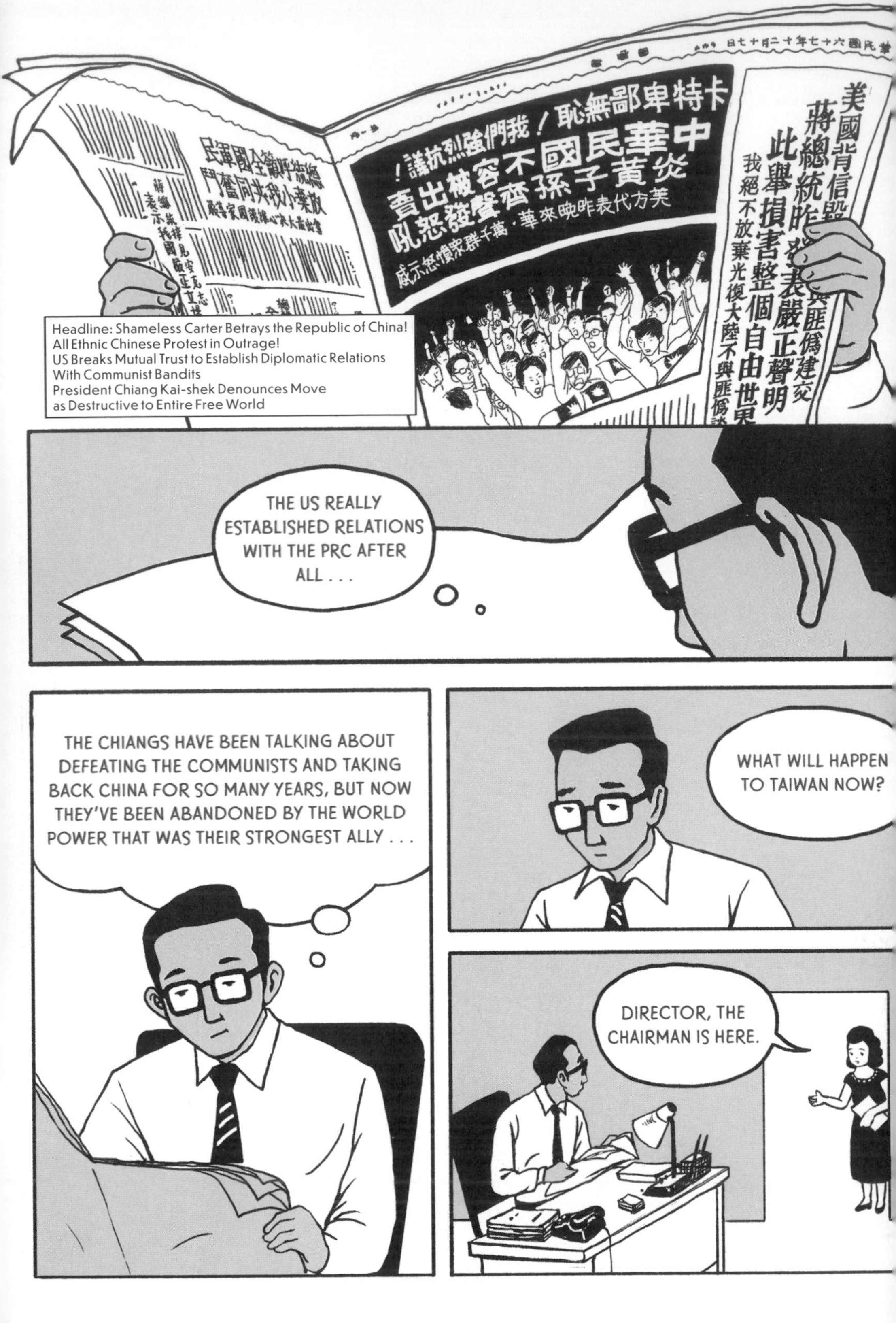
卡特卑鄙無恥！我們強烈抗議！
中華民國不容被出賣
炎黃子孫齊聲發怒吼
美方代表昨晚來華・萬千群眾憤怒示威
Headline: Shameless Carter Betrays the Republic of China!
All Ethnic Chinese Protest in Outrage!
US Breaks Mutual Trust to Establish Diplomatic Relations With Communist Bandits
President Chiang Kai-shek Denounces Move as Destructive to Entire Free World
THE US REALLY ESTABLISHED RELATIONS WITH THE PRC AFTER ALL . . .
THE CHIANGS HAVE BEEN TALKING ABOUT DEFEATING THE COMMUNISTS AND TAKING BACK CHINA FOR SO MANY YEARS, BUT NOW THEY'VE BEEN ABANDONED BY THE WORLD POWER THAT WAS THEIR STRONGEST ALLY . . .
WHAT WILL HAPPEN TO TAIWAN NOW?
DIRECTOR, THE CHAIRMAN IS HERE.

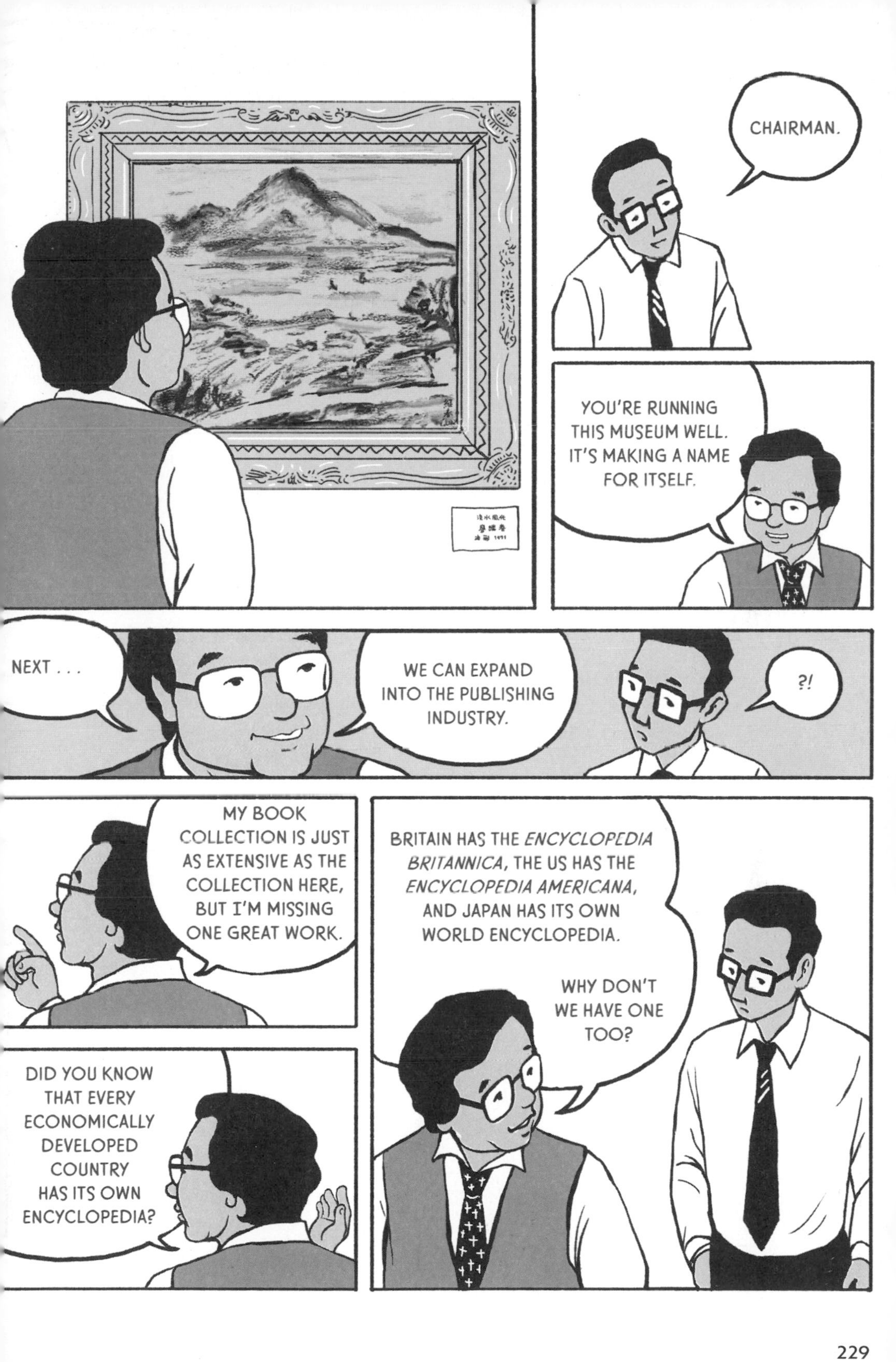
CHAIRMAN.
YOU'RE RUNNING THIS MUSEUM WELL. IT'S MAKING A NAME FOR ITSELF.
NEXT . . .
WE CAN EXPAND INTO THE PUBLISHING INDUSTRY.
?!
MY BOOK COLLECTION IS JUST AS EXTENSIVE AS THE COLLECTION HERE, BUT I'M MISSING ONE GREAT WORK.
DID YOU KNOW THAT EVERY ECONOMICALLY DEVELOPED COUNTRY HAS ITS OWN ENCYCLOPEDIA?
BRITAIN HAS THE *ENCYCLOPEDIA BRITANNICA*, THE US HAS THE *ENCYCLOPEDIA AMERICANA*, AND JAPAN HAS ITS OWN WORLD ENCYCLOPEDIA.
WHY DON'T WE HAVE ONE TOO?

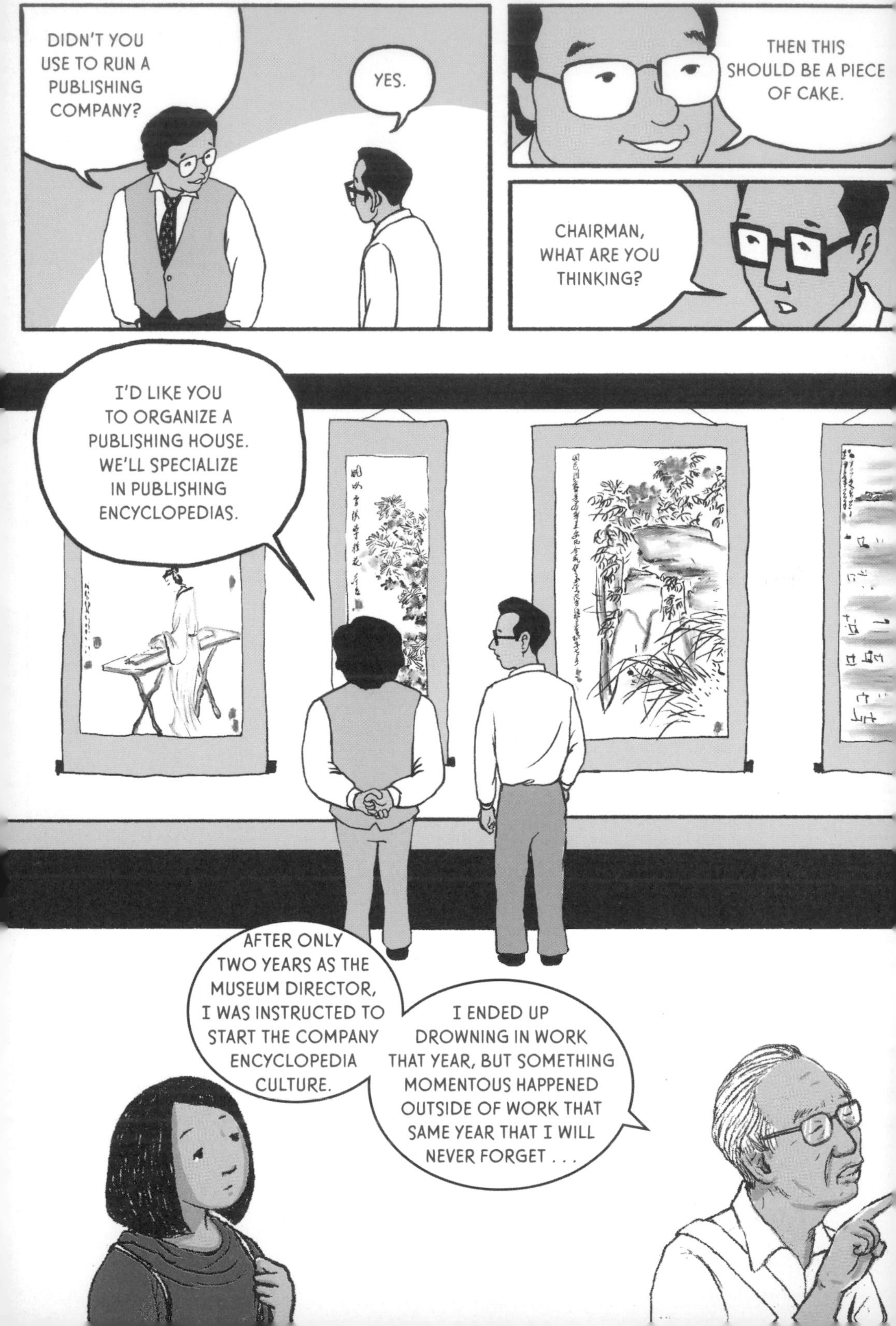
DIDN'T YOU USE TO RUN A PUBLISHING COMPANY?
YES.
THEN THIS SHOULD BE A PIECE OF CAKE.
CHAIRMAN, WHAT ARE YOU THINKING?
I'D LIKE YOU TO ORGANIZE A PUBLISHING HOUSE. WE'LL SPECIALIZE IN PUBLISHING ENCYCLOPEDIAS.
AFTER ONLY TWO YEARS AS THE MUSEUM DIRECTOR, I WAS INSTRUCTED TO START THE COMPANY ENCYCLOPEDIA CULTURE.
I ENDED UP DROWNING IN WORK THAT YEAR, BUT SOMETHING MOMENTOUS HAPPENED OUTSIDE OF WORK THAT SAME YEAR THAT I WILL NEVER FORGET . . .

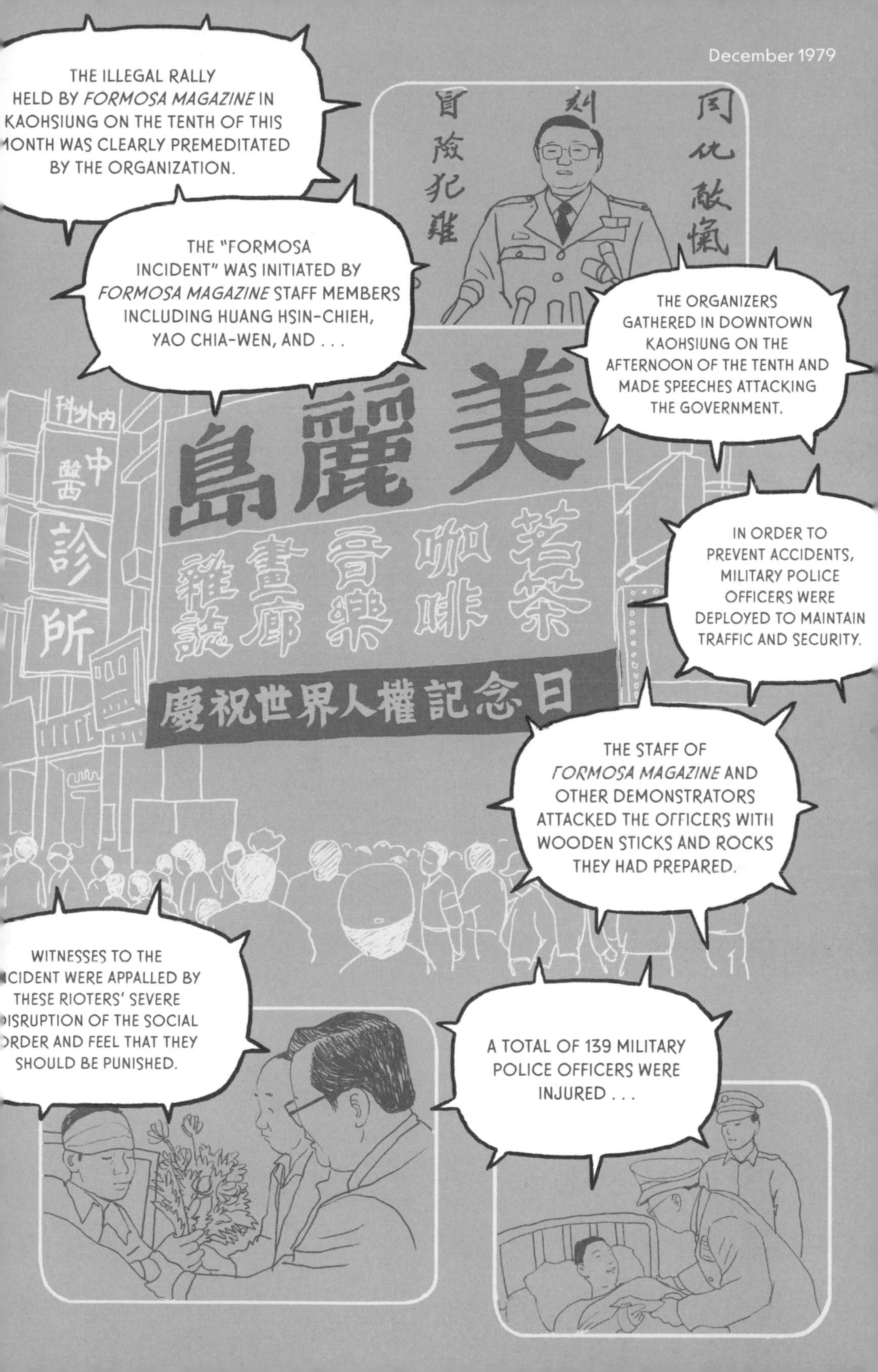
December 1979
THE ILLEGAL RALLY HELD BY *FORMOSA MAGAZINE* IN KAOHSIUNG ON THE TENTH OF THIS MONTH WAS CLEARLY PREMEDITATED BY THE ORGANIZATION.
THE "FORMOSA INCIDENT" WAS INITIATED BY *FORMOSA MAGAZINE* STAFF MEMBERS INCLUDING HUANG HSIN-CHIEH, YAO CHIA-WEN, AND . . .
THE ORGANIZERS GATHERED IN DOWNTOWN KAOHSIUNG ON THE AFTERNOON OF THE TENTH AND MADE SPEECHES ATTACKING THE GOVERNMENT.
美麗島
雜誌 畫廊 音樂 咖啡 茗茶
慶祝世界人權記念日
中醫診所
IN ORDER TO PREVENT ACCIDENTS, MILITARY POLICE OFFICERS WERE DEPLOYED TO MAINTAIN TRAFFIC AND SECURITY.
THE STAFF OF *FORMOSA MAGAZINE* AND OTHER DEMONSTRATORS ATTACKED THE OFFICERS WITH WOODEN STICKS AND ROCKS THEY HAD PREPARED.
WITNESSES TO THE INCIDENT WERE APPALLED BY THESE RIOTERS' SEVERE DISRUPTION OF THE SOCIAL ORDER AND FEEL THAT THEY SHOULD BE PUNISHED.
A TOTAL OF 139 MILITARY POLICE OFFICERS WERE INJURED . . .

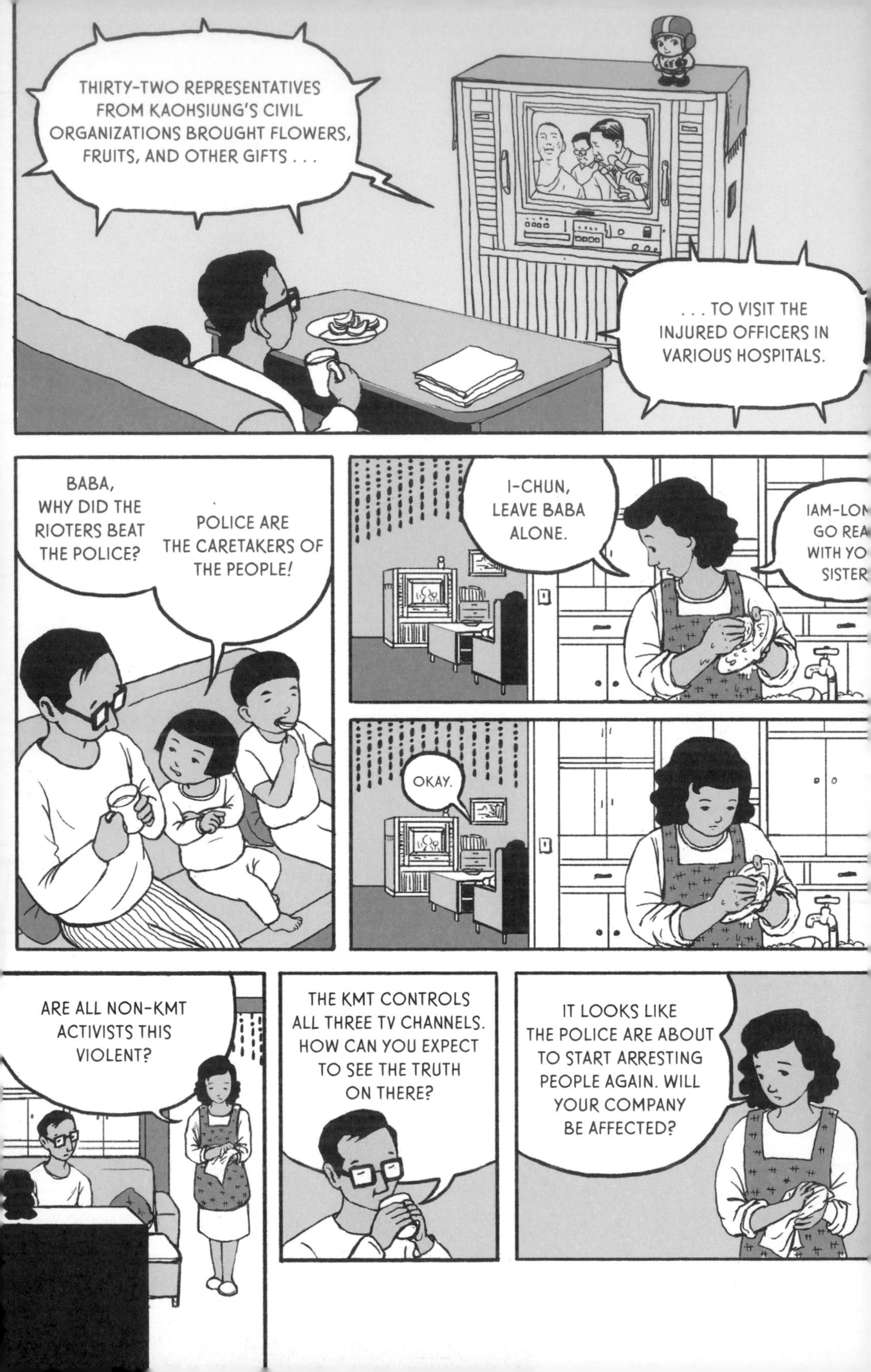
THIRTY-TWO REPRESENTATIVES FROM KAOHSIUNG'S CIVIL ORGANIZATIONS BROUGHT FLOWERS, FRUITS, AND OTHER GIFTS . . .
. . . TO VISIT THE INJURED OFFICERS IN VARIOUS HOSPITALS.
BABA, WHY DID THE RIOTERS BEAT THE POLICE?
POLICE ARE THE CARETAKERS OF THE PEOPLE!
I-CHUN, LEAVE BABA ALONE.
IAM-LON GO REA WITH YO SISTER
OKAY.
ARE ALL NON-KMT ACTIVISTS THIS VIOLENT?
THE KMT CONTROLS ALL THREE TV CHANNELS. HOW CAN YOU EXPECT TO SEE THE TRUTH ON THERE?
IT LOOKS LIKE THE POLICE ARE ABOUT TO START ARRESTING PEOPLE AGAIN. WILL YOUR COMPANY BE AFFECTED?

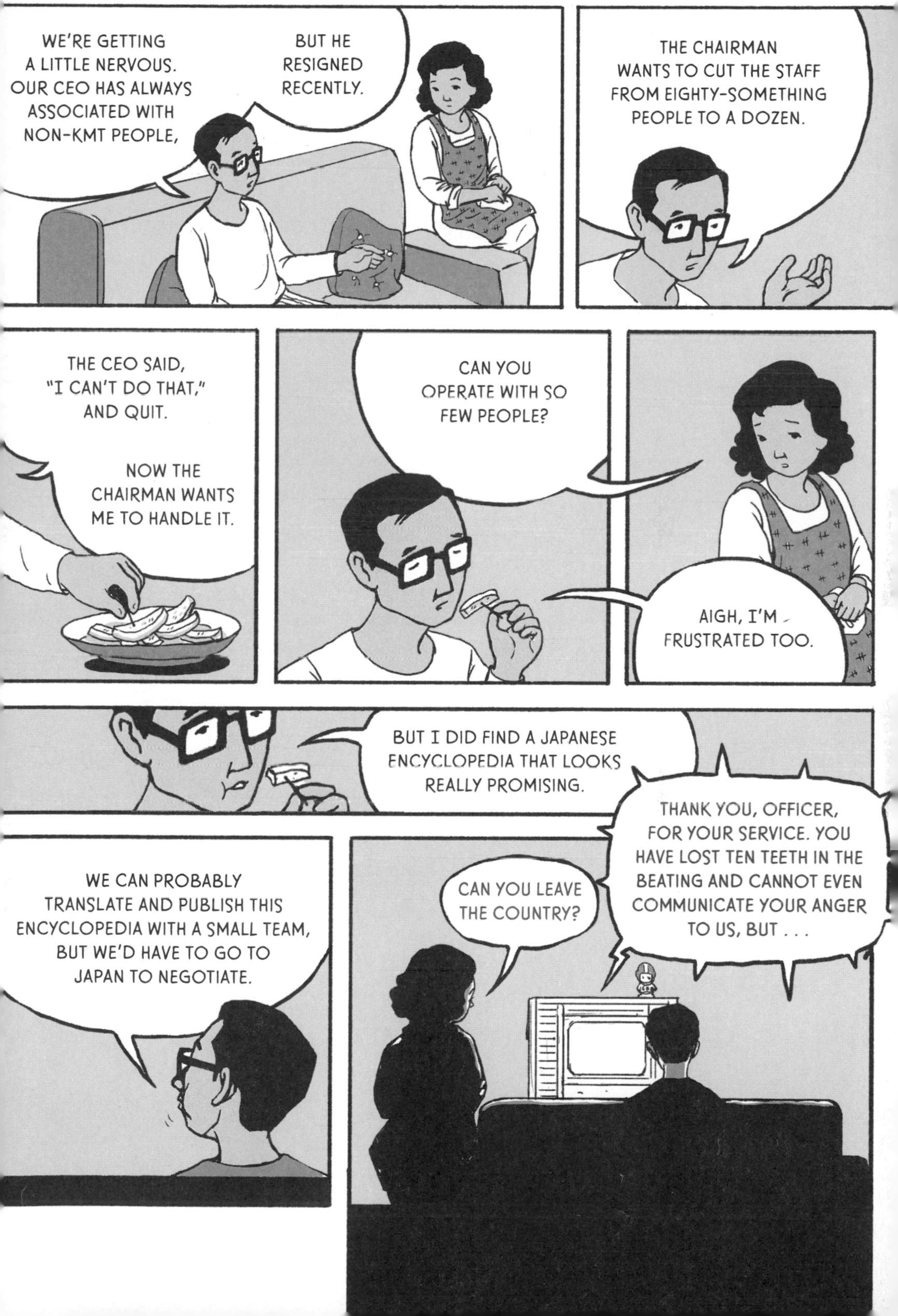
WE'RE GETTING A LITTLE NERVOUS. OUR CEO HAS ALWAYS ASSOCIATED WITH NON-KMT PEOPLE,
BUT HE RESIGNED RECENTLY.
THE CHAIRMAN WANTS TO CUT THE STAFF FROM EIGHTY-SOMETHING PEOPLE TO A DOZEN.
THE CEO SAID, "I CAN'T DO THAT," AND QUIT.
NOW THE CHAIRMAN WANTS ME TO HANDLE IT.
CAN YOU OPERATE WITH SO FEW PEOPLE?
AIGH, I'M FRUSTRATED TOO.
BUT I DID FIND A JAPANESE ENCYCLOPEDIA THAT LOOKS REALLY PROMISING.
WE CAN PROBABLY TRANSLATE AND PUBLISH THIS ENCYCLOPEDIA WITH A SMALL TEAM, BUT WE'D HAVE TO GO TO JAPAN TO NEGOTIATE.
CAN YOU LEAVE THE COUNTRY?
THANK YOU, OFFICER, FOR YOUR SERVICE. YOU HAVE LOST TEN TEETH IN THE BEATING AND CANNOT EVEN COMMUNICATE YOUR ANGER TO US, BUT . . .

February 1980. Taipei.

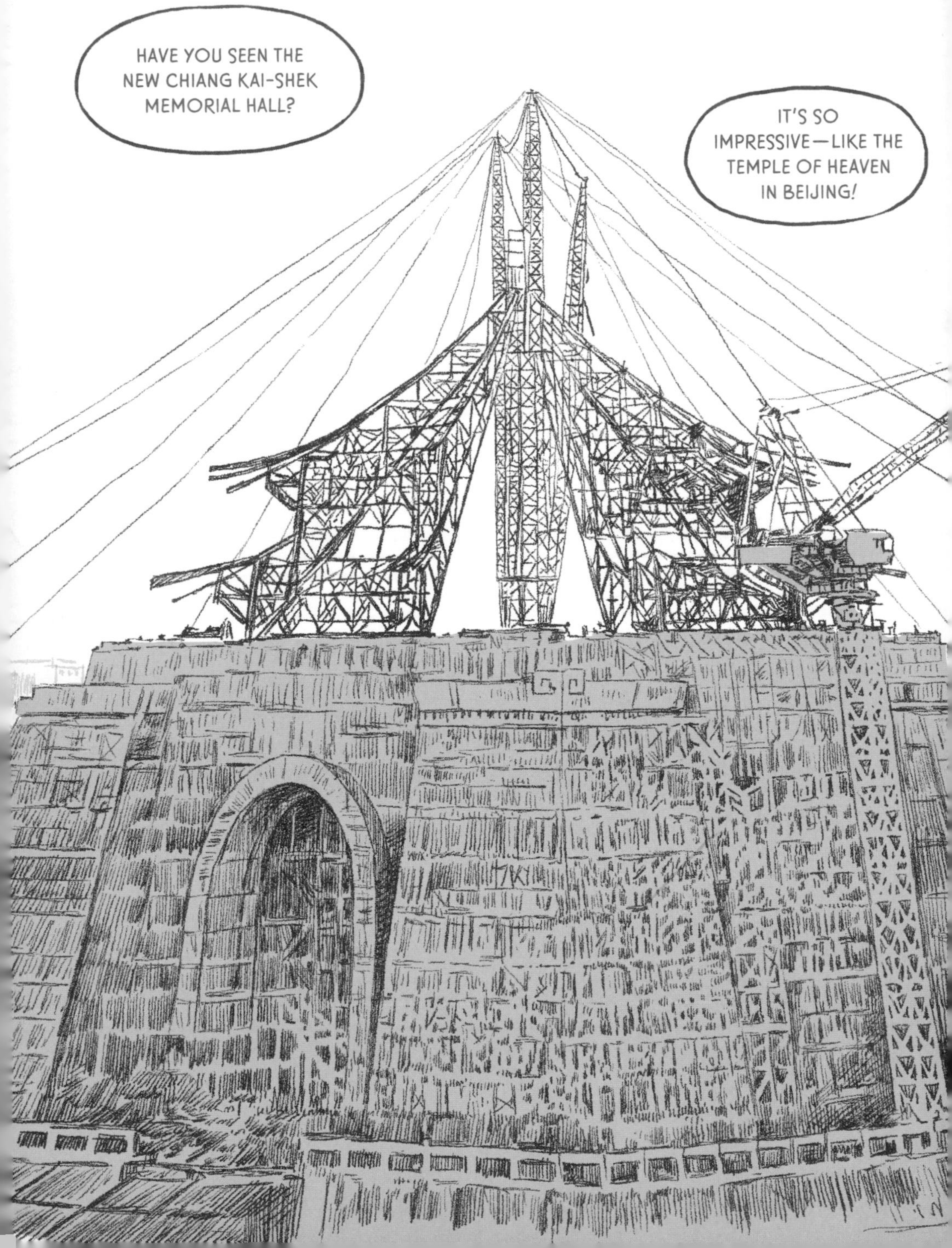
HAVE YOU SEEN THE NEW CHIANG KAI-SHEK MEMORIAL HALL?
IT'S SO IMPRESSIVE—LIKE THE TEMPLE OF HEAVEN IN BEIJING!

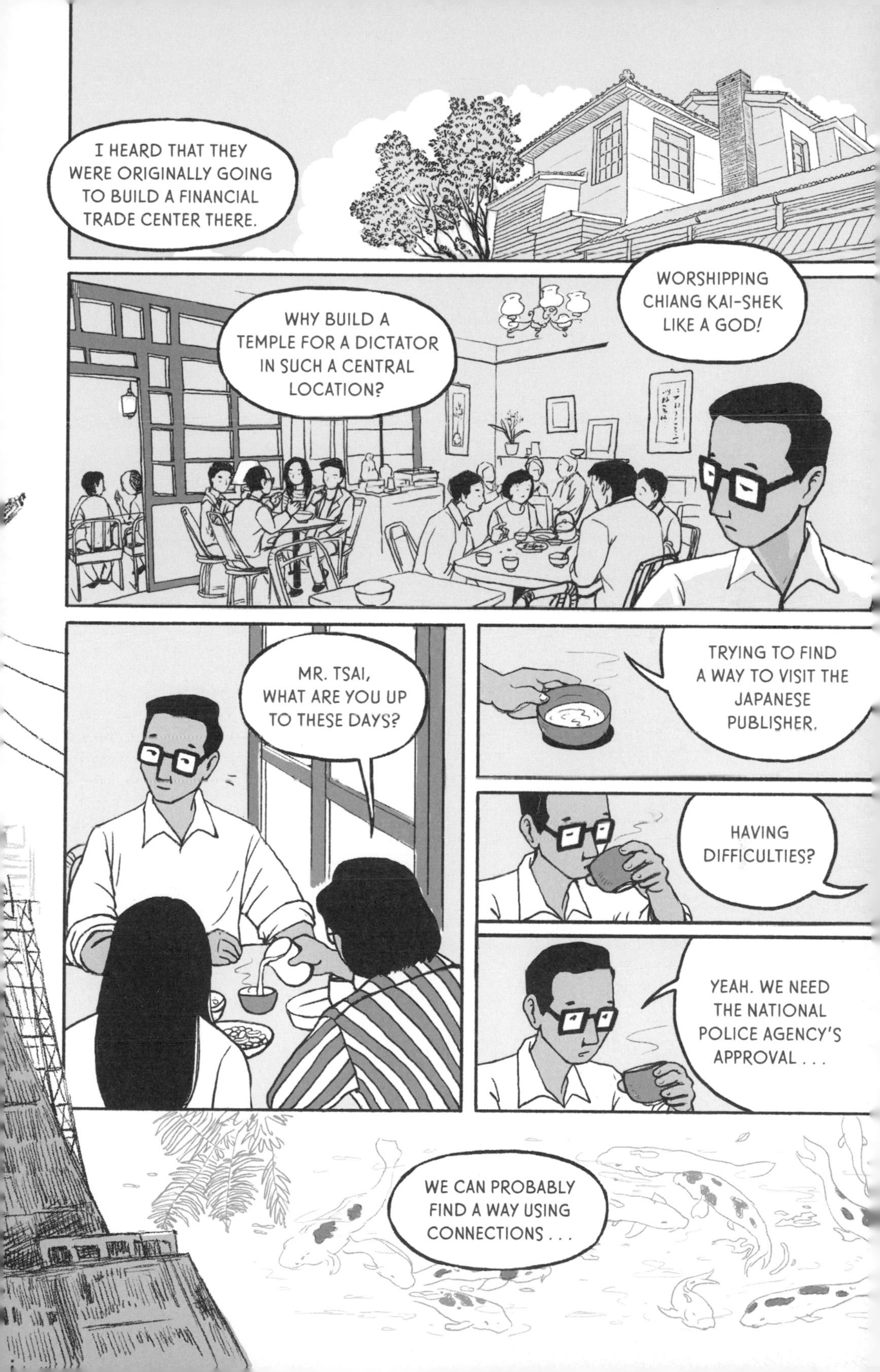
I HEARD THAT THEY WERE ORIGINALLY GOING TO BUILD A FINANCIAL TRADE CENTER THERE.
WHY BUILD A TEMPLE FOR A DICTATOR IN SUCH A CENTRAL LOCATION?
WORSHIPPING CHIANG KAI-SHEK LIKE A GOD!
MR. TSAI, WHAT ARE YOU UP TO THESE DAYS?
TRYING TO FIND A WAY TO VISIT THE JAPANESE PUBLISHER.
HAVING DIFFICULTIES?
YEAH. WE NEED THE NATIONAL POLICE AGENCY'S APPROVAL . . .
WE CAN PROBABLY FIND A WAY USING CONNECTIONS . . .

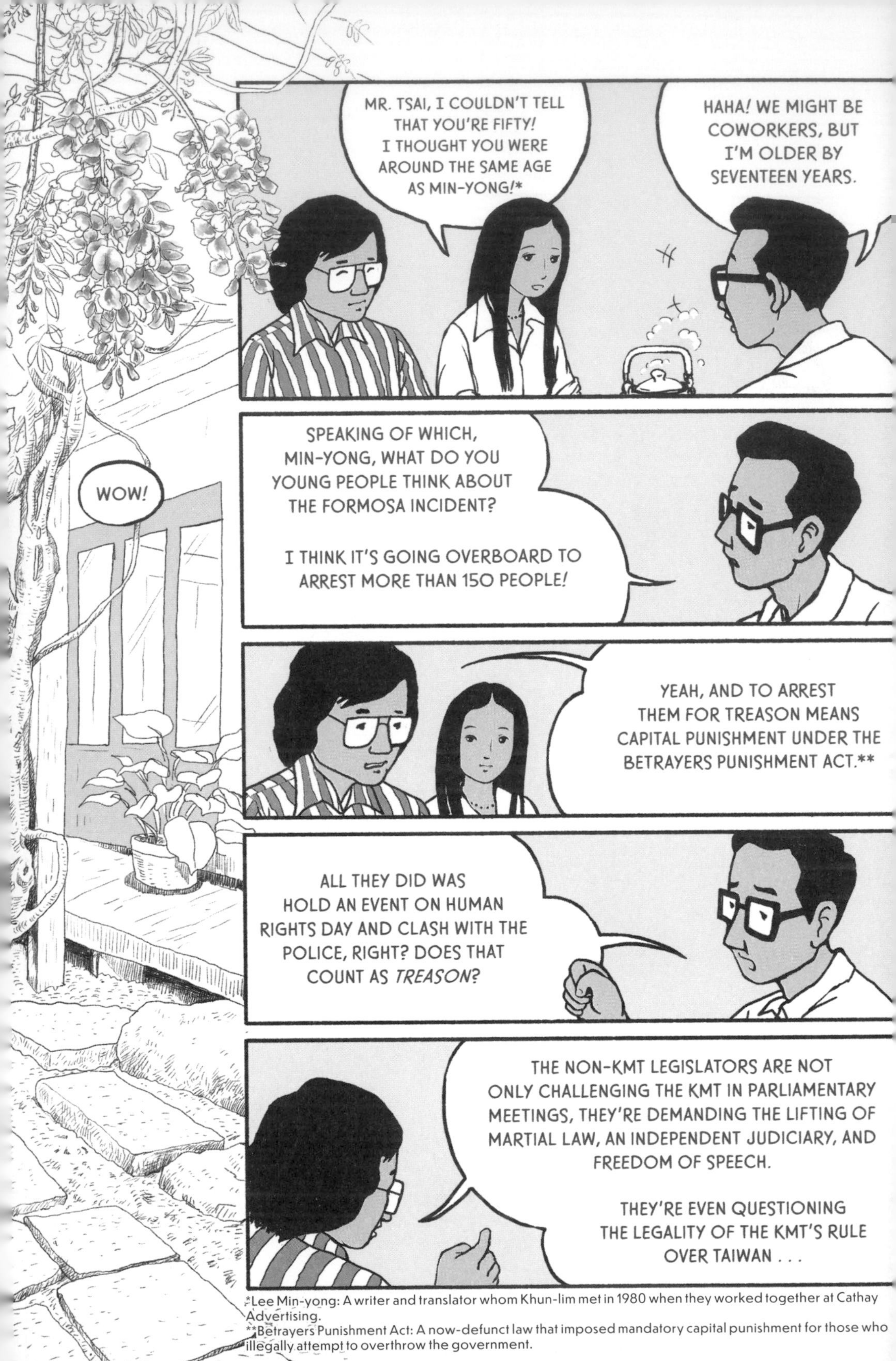
MR. TSAI, I COULDN'T TELL THAT YOU'RE FIFTY! I THOUGHT YOU WERE AROUND THE SAME AGE AS MIN-YONG!*
HAHA! WE MIGHT BE COWORKERS, BUT I'M OLDER BY SEVENTEEN YEARS.
WOW!
SPEAKING OF WHICH, MIN-YONG, WHAT DO YOU YOUNG PEOPLE THINK ABOUT THE FORMOSA INCIDENT?
I THINK IT'S GOING OVERBOARD TO ARREST MORE THAN 150 PEOPLE!
YEAH, AND TO ARREST THEM FOR TREASON MEANS CAPITAL PUNISHMENT UNDER THE BETRAYERS PUNISHMENT ACT.**
ALL THEY DID WAS HOLD AN EVENT ON HUMAN RIGHTS DAY AND CLASH WITH THE POLICE, RIGHT? DOES THAT COUNT AS *TREASON*?
THE NON-KMT LEGISLATORS ARE NOT ONLY CHALLENGING THE KMT IN PARLIAMENTARY MEETINGS, THEY'RE DEMANDING THE LIFTING OF MARTIAL LAW, AN INDEPENDENT JUDICIARY, AND FREEDOM OF SPEECH.
THEY'RE EVEN QUESTIONING THE LEGALITY OF THE KMT'S RULE OVER TAIWAN . . .

*Lee Min-yong: A writer and translator whom Khun-lim met in 1980 when they worked together at Cathay Advertising.
**Betrayers Punishment Act: A now-defunct law that imposed mandatory capital punishment for those who illegally attempt to overthrow the government.

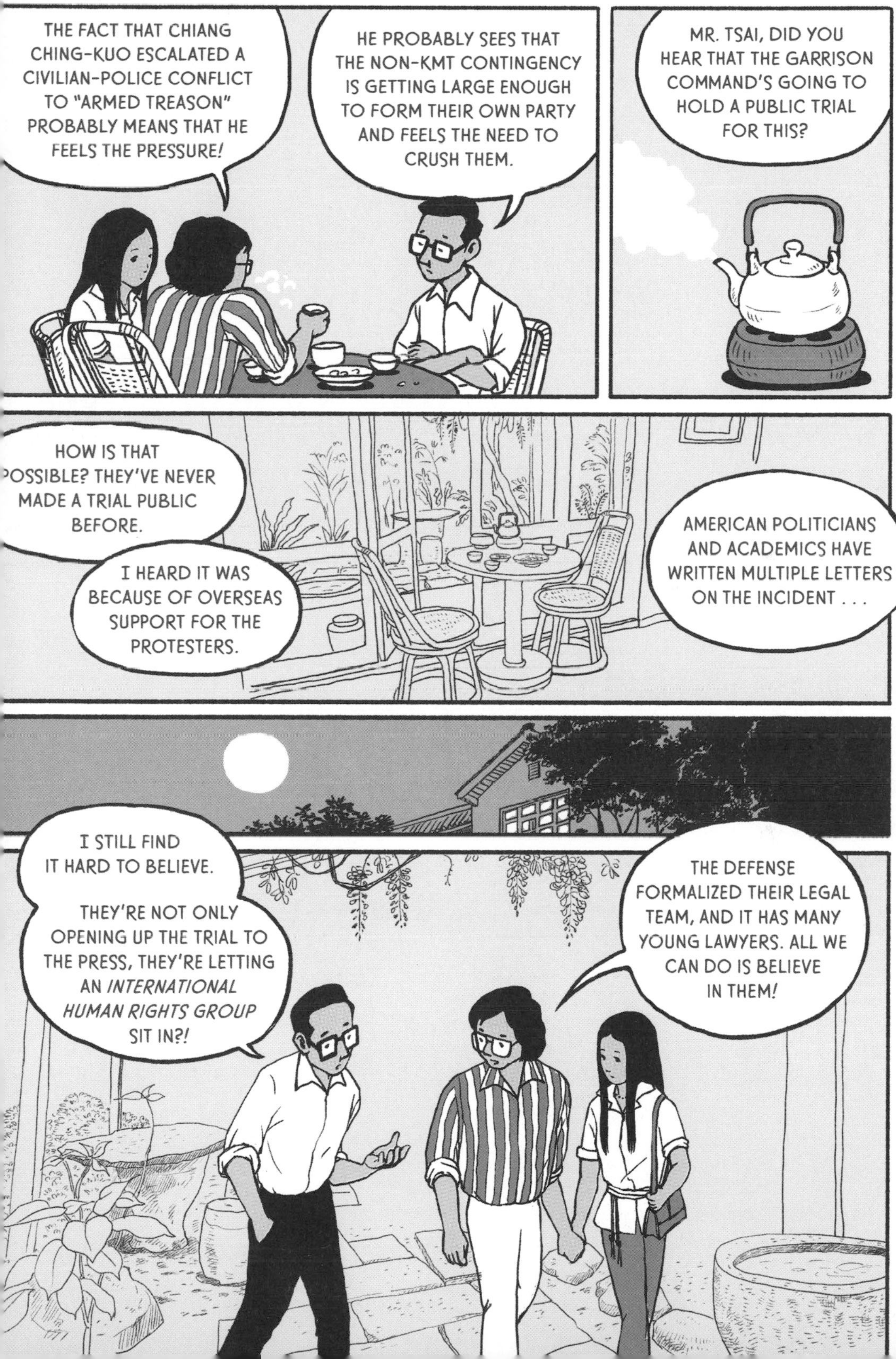
THE FACT THAT CHIANG CHING-KUO ESCALATED A CIVILIAN-POLICE CONFLICT TO "ARMED TREASON" PROBABLY MEANS THAT HE FEELS THE PRESSURE!
HE PROBABLY SEES THAT THE NON-KMT CONTINGENCY IS GETTING LARGE ENOUGH TO FORM THEIR OWN PARTY AND FEELS THE NEED TO CRUSH THEM.
MR. TSAI, DID YOU HEAR THAT THE GARRISON COMMAND'S GOING TO HOLD A PUBLIC TRIAL FOR THIS?
HOW IS THAT POSSIBLE? THEY'VE NEVER MADE A TRIAL PUBLIC BEFORE.
I HEARD IT WAS BECAUSE OF OVERSEAS SUPPORT FOR THE PROTESTERS.
AMERICAN POLITICIANS AND ACADEMICS HAVE WRITTEN MULTIPLE LETTERS ON THE INCIDENT . . .
I STILL FIND IT HARD TO BELIEVE.
THEY'RE NOT ONLY OPENING UP THE TRIAL TO THE PRESS, THEY'RE LETTING AN *INTERNATIONAL HUMAN RIGHTS GROUP* SIT IN?!
THE DEFENSE FORMALIZED THEIR LEGAL TEAM, AND IT HAS MANY YOUNG LAWYERS. ALL WE CAN DO IS BELIEVE IN THEM!

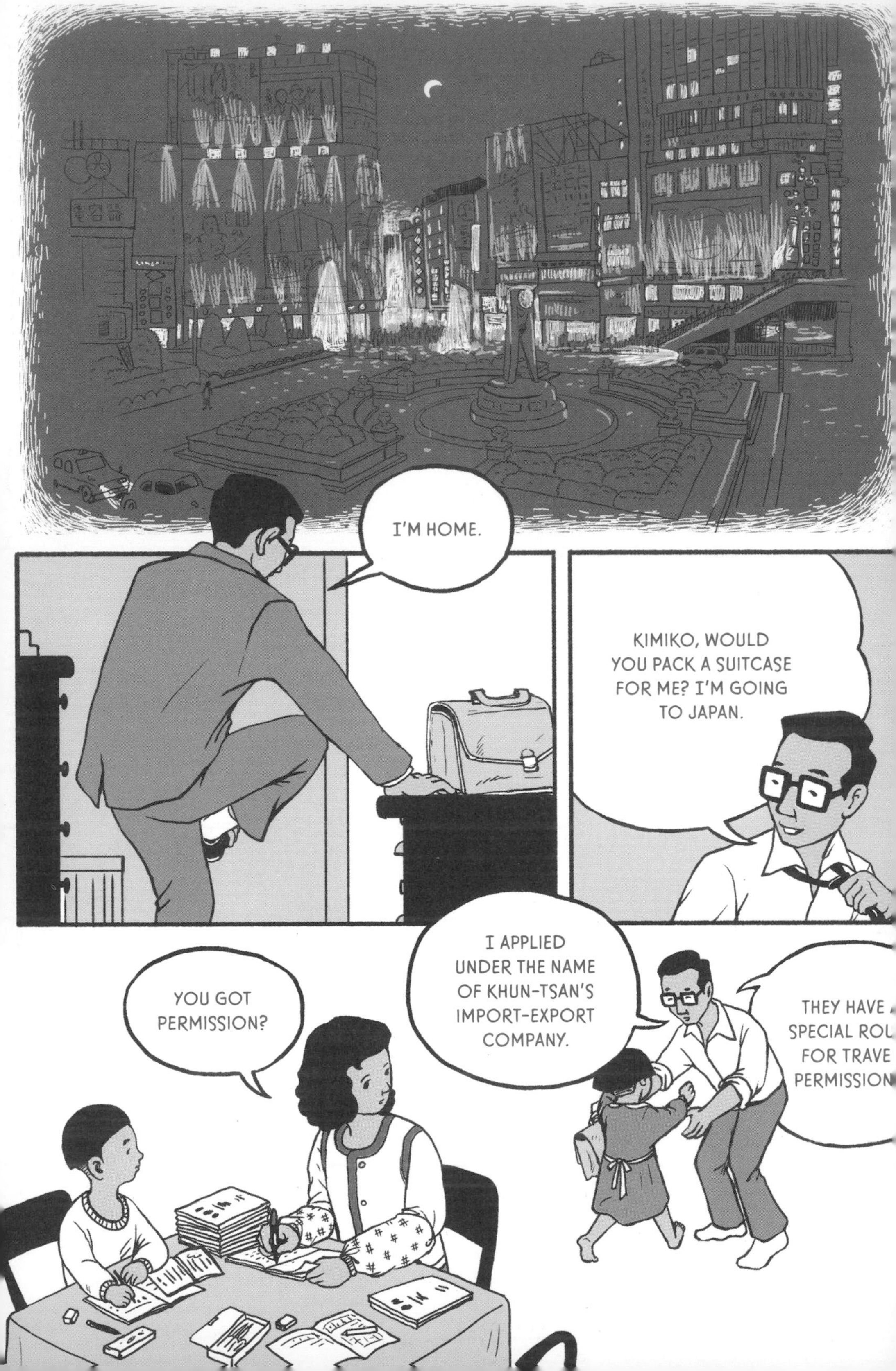
I'M HOME.
KIMIKO, WOULD YOU PACK A SUITCASE FOR ME? I'M GOING TO JAPAN.
YOU GOT PERMISSION?
I APPLIED UNDER THE NAME OF KHUN-TSAN'S IMPORT-EXPORT COMPANY.
THEY HAVE A SPECIAL ROL FOR TRAVE PERMISSION

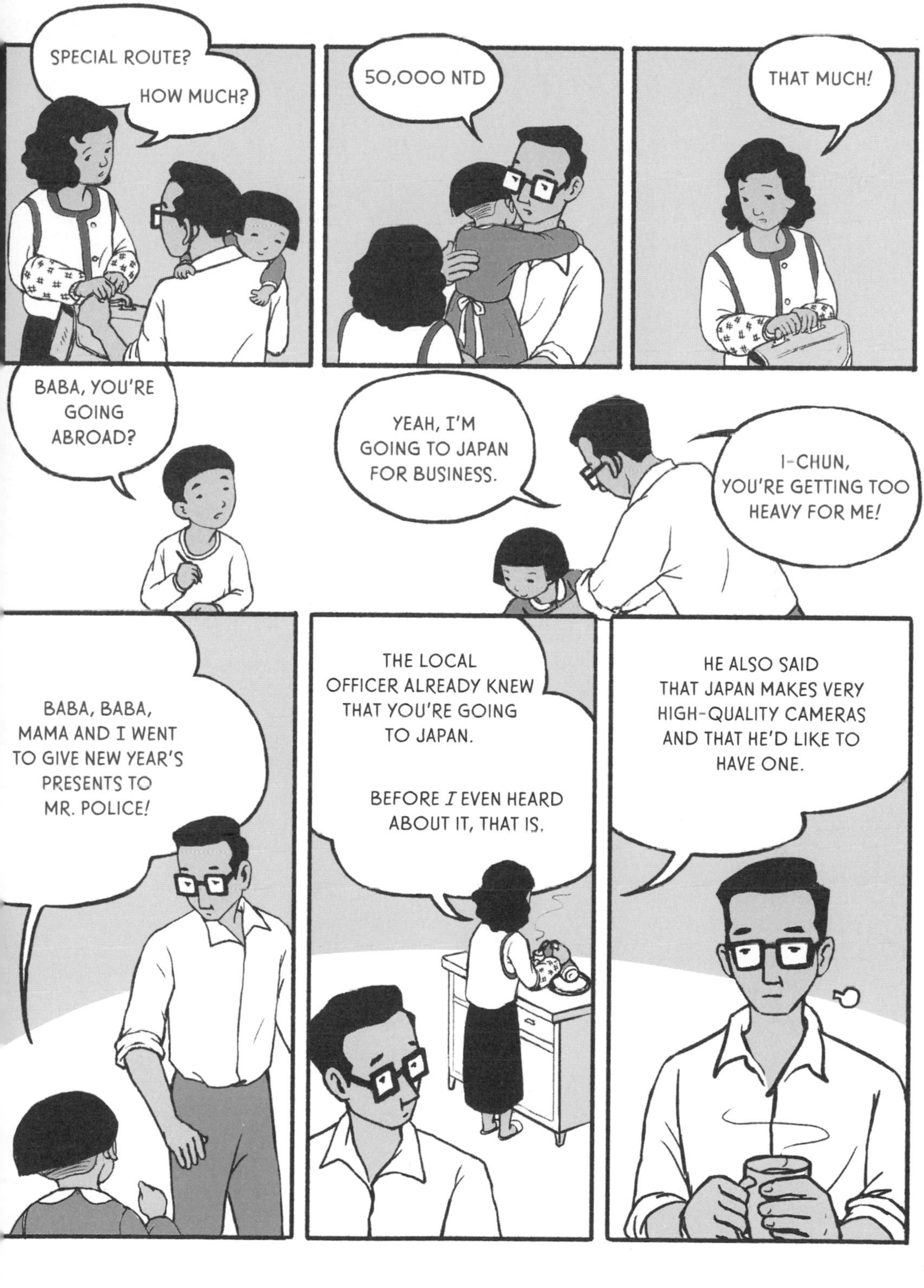
SPECIAL ROUTE?
HOW MUCH?
50,000 NTD
THAT MUCH!
BABA, YOU'RE GOING ABROAD?
YEAH, I'M GOING TO JAPAN FOR BUSINESS.
I-CHUN, YOU'RE GETTING TOO HEAVY FOR ME!
BABA, BABA, MAMA AND I WENT TO GIVE NEW YEAR'S PRESENTS TO MR. POLICE!
THE LOCAL OFFICER ALREADY KNEW THAT YOU'RE GOING TO JAPAN.
BEFORE *I* EVEN HEARD ABOUT IT, THAT IS.
HE ALSO SAID THAT JAPAN MAKES VERY HIGH-QUALITY CAMERAS AND THAT HE'D LIKE TO HAVE ONE.

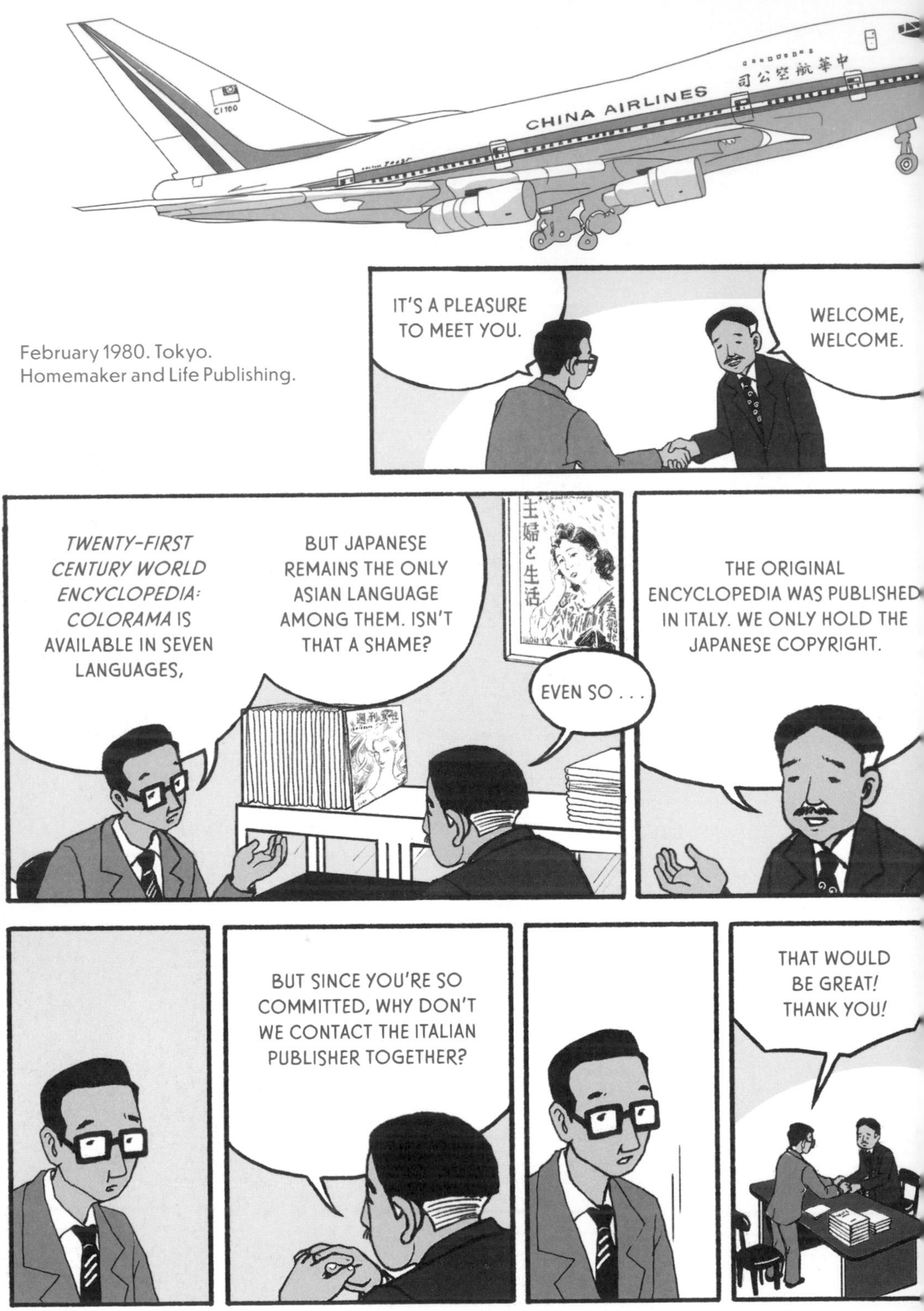
中華航空公司
CHINA AIRLINES
February 1980. Tokyo.
Homemaker and Life Publishing.
IT'S A PLEASURE TO MEET YOU.
WELCOME, WELCOME.
TWENTY-FIRST CENTURY WORLD ENCYCLOPEDIA: COLORAMA IS AVAILABLE IN SEVEN LANGUAGES,
BUT JAPANESE REMAINS THE ONLY ASIAN LANGUAGE AMONG THEM. ISN'T THAT A SHAME?
主婦と生活
EVEN SO . . .
THE ORIGINAL ENCYCLOPEDIA WAS PUBLISHED IN ITALY. WE ONLY HOLD THE JAPANESE COPYRIGHT.
BUT SINCE YOU'RE SO COMMITTED, WHY DON'T WE CONTACT THE ITALIAN PUBLISHER TOGETHER?
THAT WOULD BE GREAT! THANK YOU!

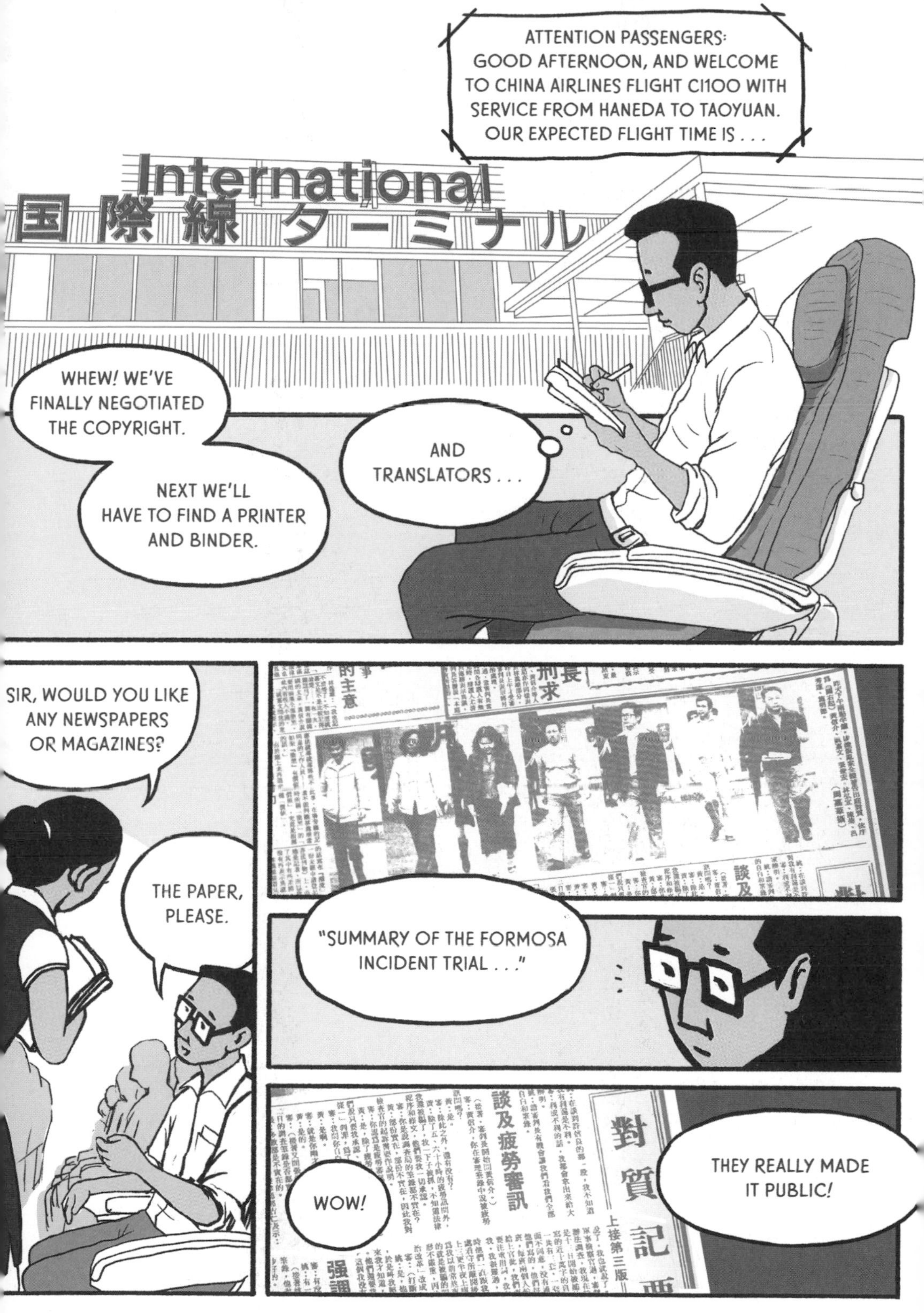
ATTENTION PASSENGERS: GOOD AFTERNOON, AND WELCOME TO CHINA AIRLINES FLIGHT CI100 WITH SERVICE FROM HANEDA TO TAOYUAN. OUR EXPECTED FLIGHT TIME IS . . .
International
国際線ターミナル
WHEW! WE'VE FINALLY NEGOTIATED THE COPYRIGHT.
NEXT WE'LL HAVE TO FIND A PRINTER AND BINDER.
AND TRANSLATORS . . .
SIR, WOULD YOU LIKE ANY NEWSPAPERS OR MAGAZINES?
THE PAPER, PLEASE.
"SUMMARY OF THE FORMOSA INCIDENT TRIAL . . ."
談及疲勞審訊
對質記
上接第三版
WOW!
THEY REALLY MADE IT PUBLIC!

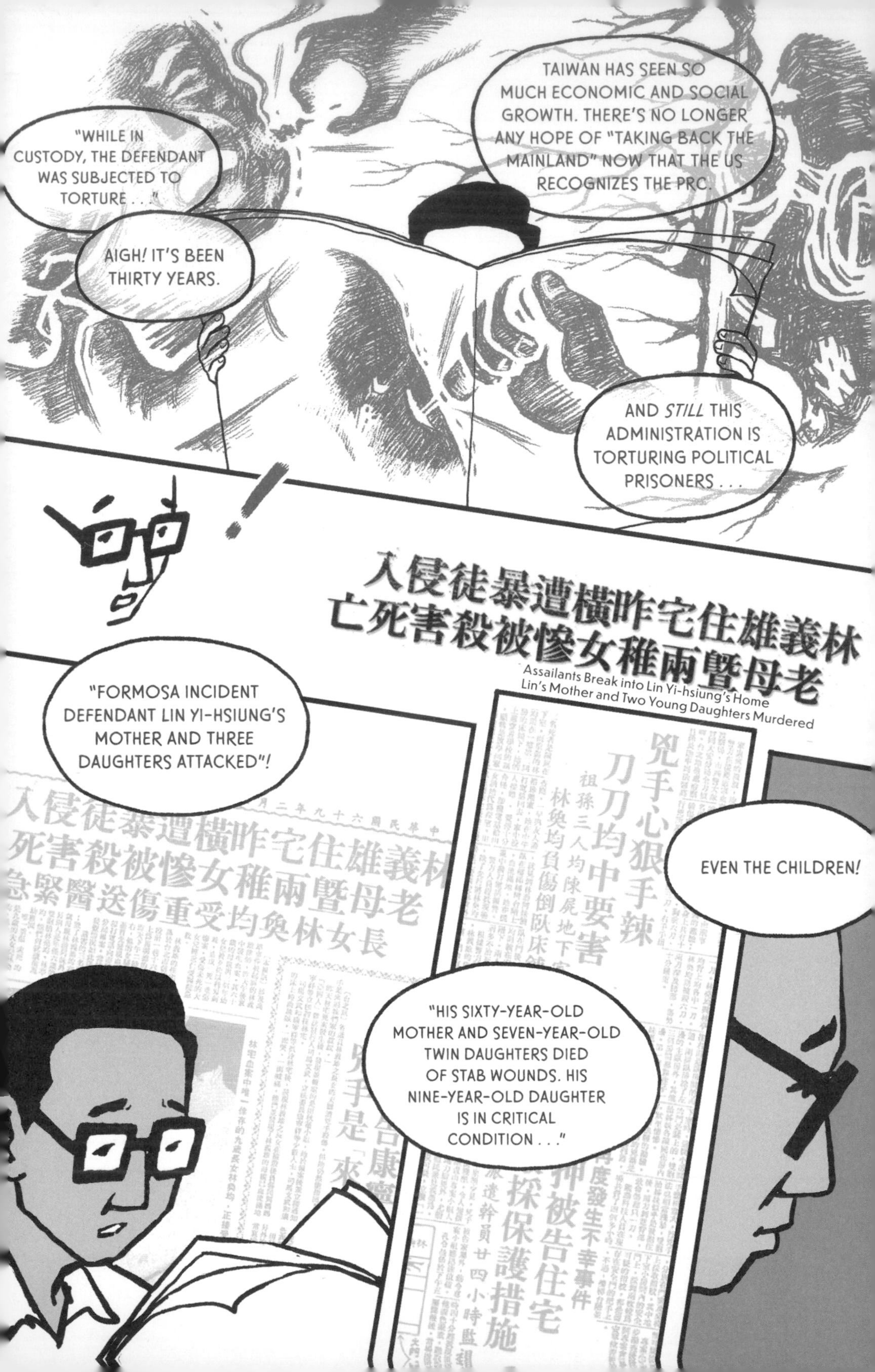
TAIWAN HAS SEEN SO MUCH ECONOMIC AND SOCIAL GROWTH. THERE'S NO LONGER ANY HOPE OF "TAKING BACK THE MAINLAND" NOW THAT THE US RECOGNIZES THE PRC.
"WHILE IN CUSTODY, THE DEFENDANT WAS SUBJECTED TO TORTURE . . ."
AIGH! IT'S BEEN THIRTY YEARS.
AND STILL THIS ADMINISTRATION IS TORTURING POLITICAL PRISONERS . . .
!
林義雄住宅昨遭橫暴徒入侵
老母暨兩稚女慘被殺害死亡
Assailants Break into Lin Yi-hsiung's Home
Lin's Mother and Two Young Daughters Murdered
"FORMOSA INCIDENT DEFENDANT LIN YI-HSIUNG'S MOTHER AND THREE DAUGHTERS ATTACKED"!
EVEN THE CHILDREN!
"HIS SIXTY-YEAR-OLD MOTHER AND SEVEN-YEAR-OLD TWIN DAUGHTERS DIED OF STAB WOUNDS. HIS NINE-YEAR-OLD DAUGHTER IS IN CRITICAL CONDITION . . ."

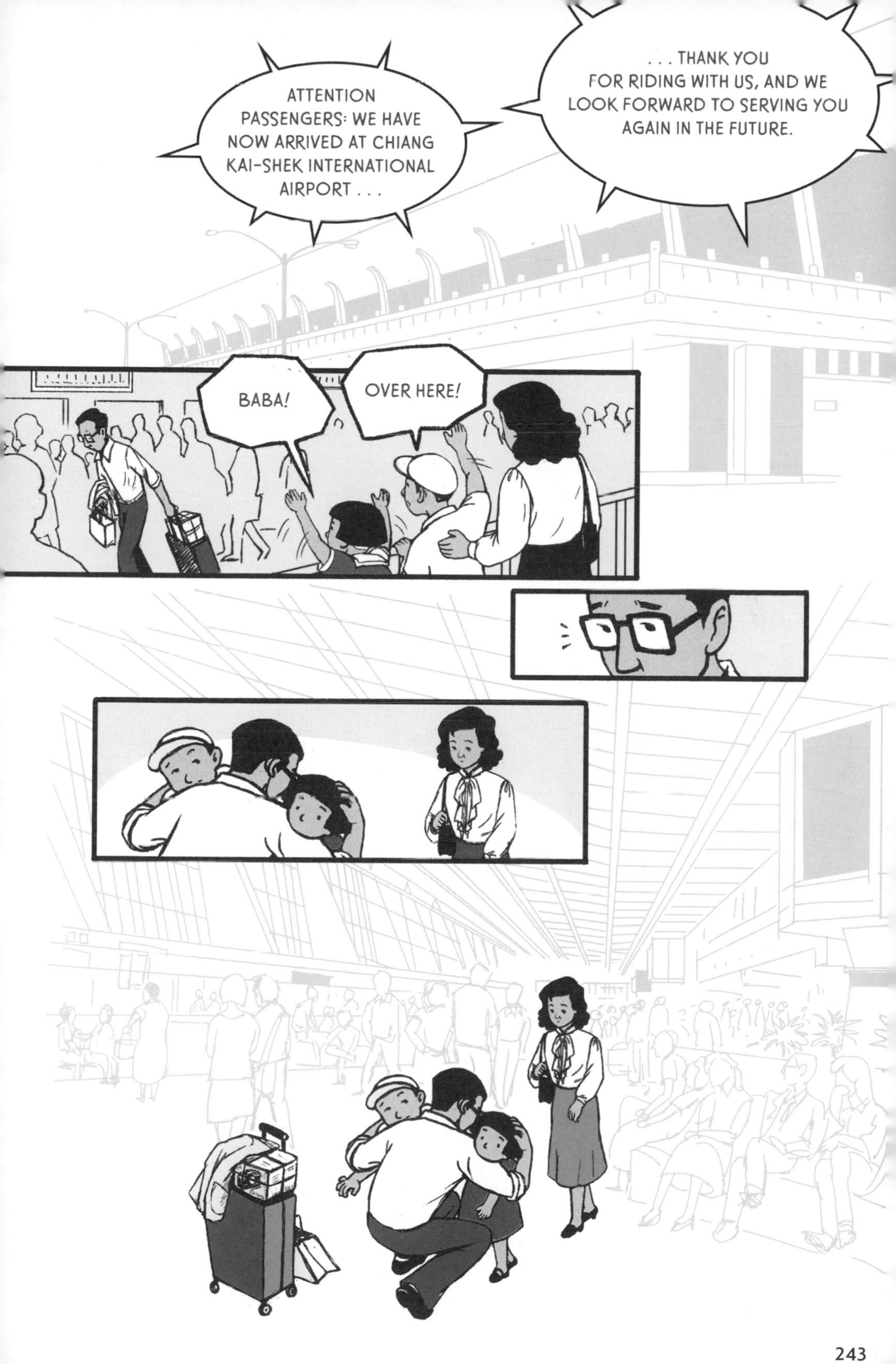
ATTENTION PASSENGERS: WE HAVE NOW ARRIVED AT CHIANG KAI-SHEK INTERNATIONAL AIRPORT . . .
. . . THANK YOU FOR RIDING WITH US, AND WE LOOK FORWARD TO SERVING YOU AGAIN IN THE FUTURE.
BABA!
OVER HERE!

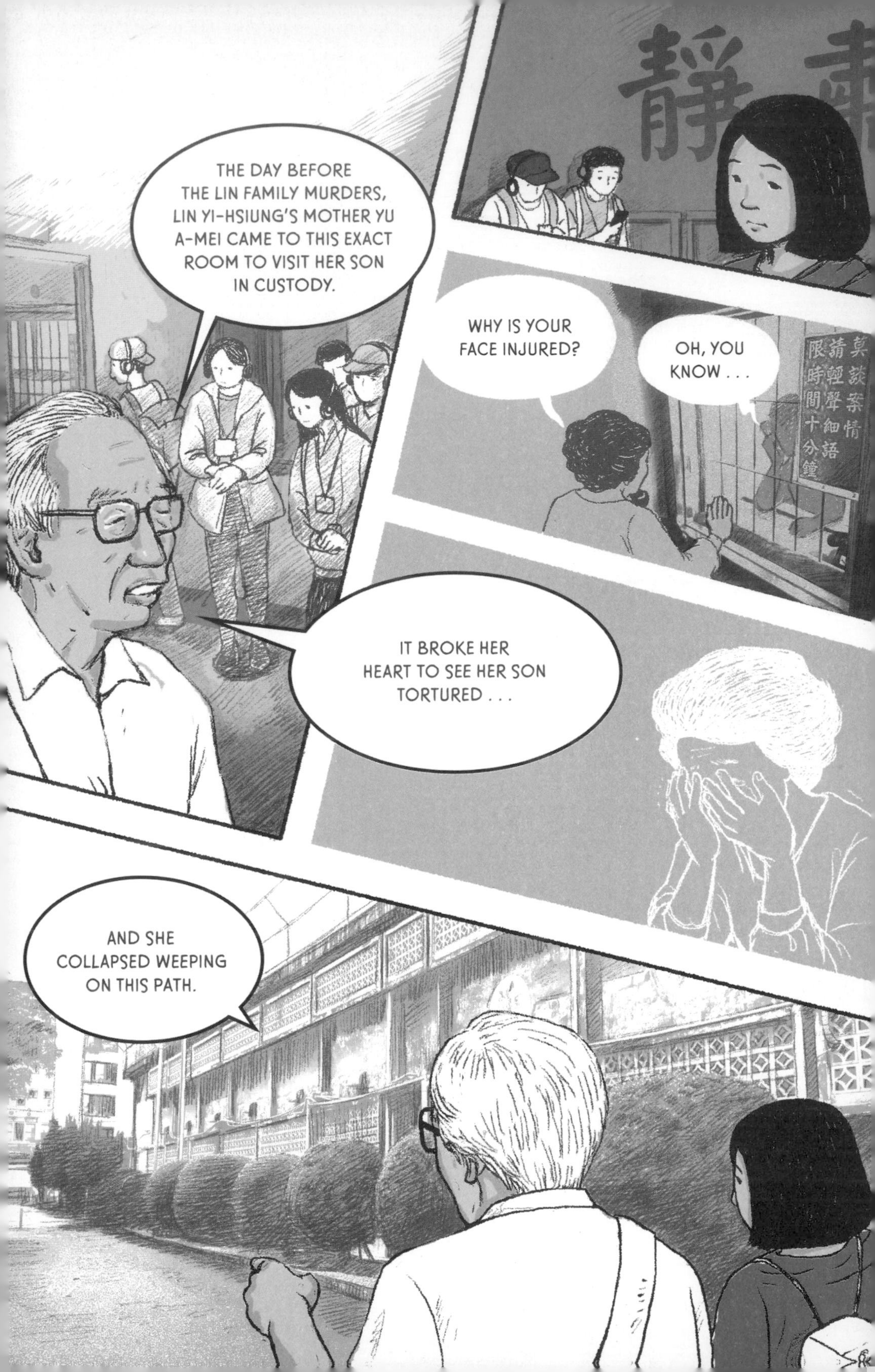
靜
THE DAY BEFORE THE LIN FAMILY MURDERS, LIN YI-HSIUNG'S MOTHER YU A-MEI CAME TO THIS EXACT ROOM TO VISIT HER SON IN CUSTODY.
WHY IS YOUR FACE INJURED?
OH, YOU KNOW . . .
莫談案情
請輕聲細語
限時間十分鐘
IT BROKE HER HEART TO SEE HER SON TORTURED . . .
AND SHE COLLAPSED WEEPING ON THIS PATH.

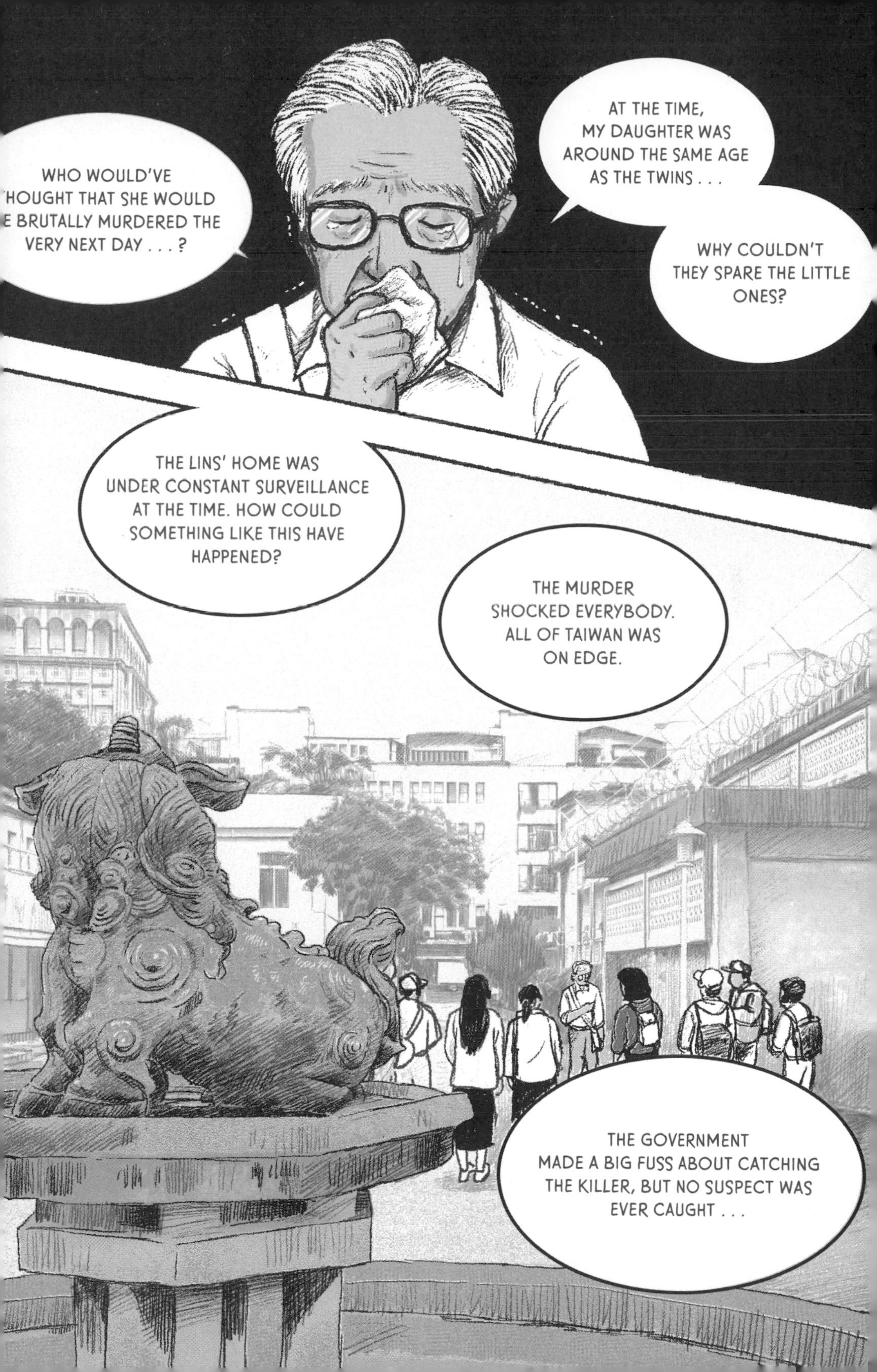
WHO WOULD'VE
HOUGHT THAT SHE WOULD
E BRUTALLY MURDERED THE
VERY NEXT DAY . . . ?
AT THE TIME, MY DAUGHTER WAS AROUND THE SAME AGE AS THE TWINS . . .
WHY COULDN'T THEY SPARE THE LITTLE ONES?
THE LINS' HOME WAS UNDER CONSTANT SURVEILLANCE AT THE TIME. HOW COULD SOMETHING LIKE THIS HAVE HAPPENED?
THE MURDER SHOCKED EVERYBODY. ALL OF TAIWAN WAS ON EDGE.
THE GOVERNMENT MADE A BIG FUSS ABOUT CATCHING THE KILLER, BUT NO SUSPECT WAS EVER CAUGHT . . .

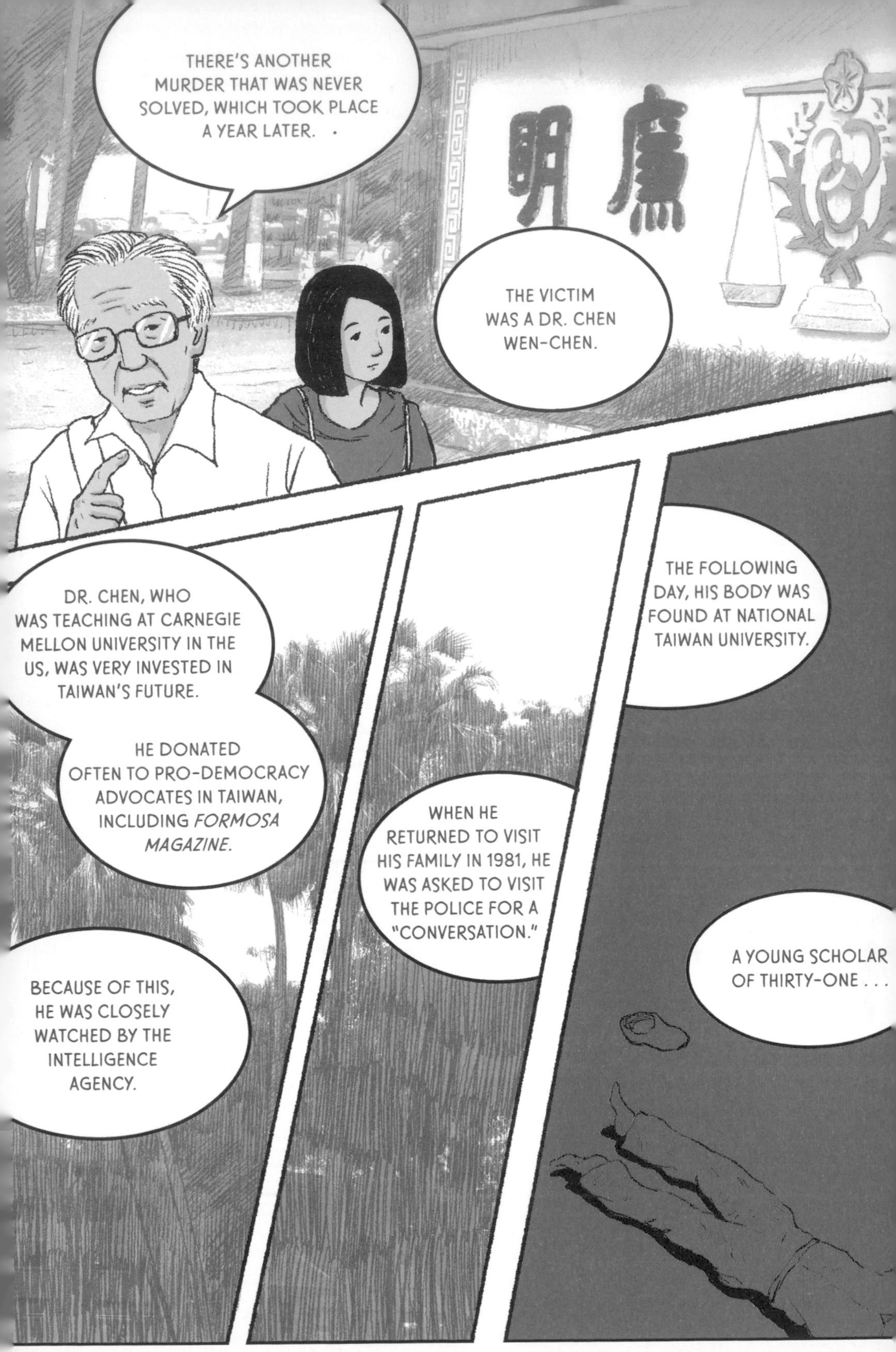
THERE'S ANOTHER MURDER THAT WAS NEVER SOLVED, WHICH TOOK PLACE A YEAR LATER. . .
THE VICTIM WAS A DR. CHEN WEN-CHEN.
DR. CHEN, WHO WAS TEACHING AT CARNEGIE MELLON UNIVERSITY IN THE US, WAS VERY INVESTED IN TAIWAN'S FUTURE.
HE DONATED OFTEN TO PRO-DEMOCRACY ADVOCATES IN TAIWAN, INCLUDING *FORMOSA MAGAZINE*.
BECAUSE OF THIS, HE WAS CLOSELY WATCHED BY THE INTELLIGENCE AGENCY.
WHEN HE RETURNED TO VISIT HIS FAMILY IN 1981, HE WAS ASKED TO VISIT THE POLICE FOR A "CONVERSATION."
THE FOLLOWING DAY, HIS BODY WAS FOUND AT NATIONAL TAIWAN UNIVERSITY.
A YOUNG SCHOLAR OF THIRTY-ONE . . .

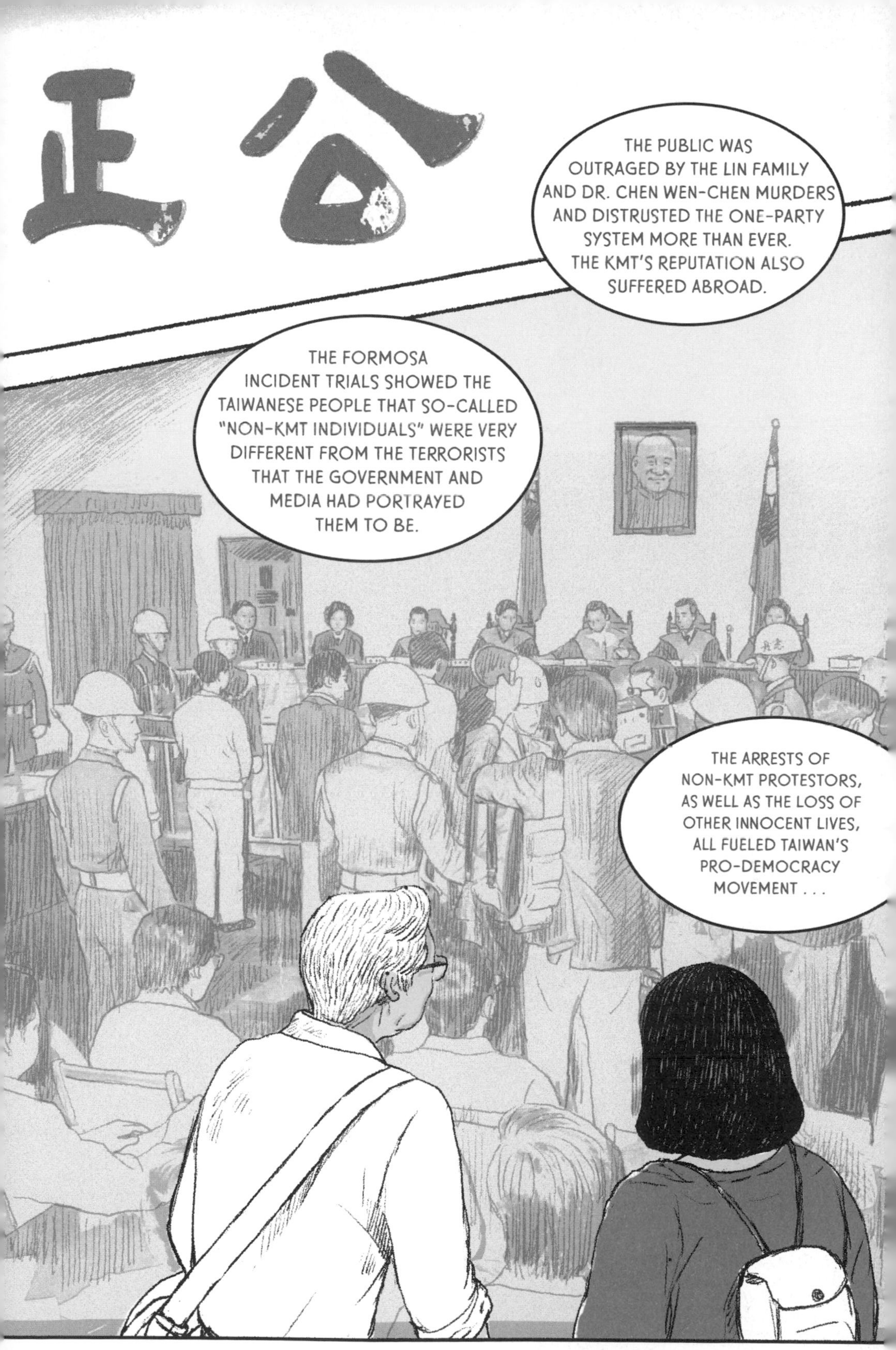

正公
THE PUBLIC WAS OUTRAGED BY THE LIN FAMILY AND DR. CHEN WEN-CHEN MURDERS AND DISTRUSTED THE ONE-PARTY SYSTEM MORE THAN EVER. THE KMT'S REPUTATION ALSO SUFFERED ABROAD.
THE FORMOSA INCIDENT TRIALS SHOWED THE TAIWANESE PEOPLE THAT SO-CALLED "NON-KMT INDIVIDUALS" WERE VERY DIFFERENT FROM THE TERRORISTS THAT THE GOVERNMENT AND MEDIA HAD PORTRAYED THEM TO BE.
THE ARRESTS OF NON-KMT PROTESTORS, AS WELL AS THE LOSS OF OTHER INNOCENT LIVES, ALL FUELED TAIWAN'S PRO-DEMOCRACY MOVEMENT . . .

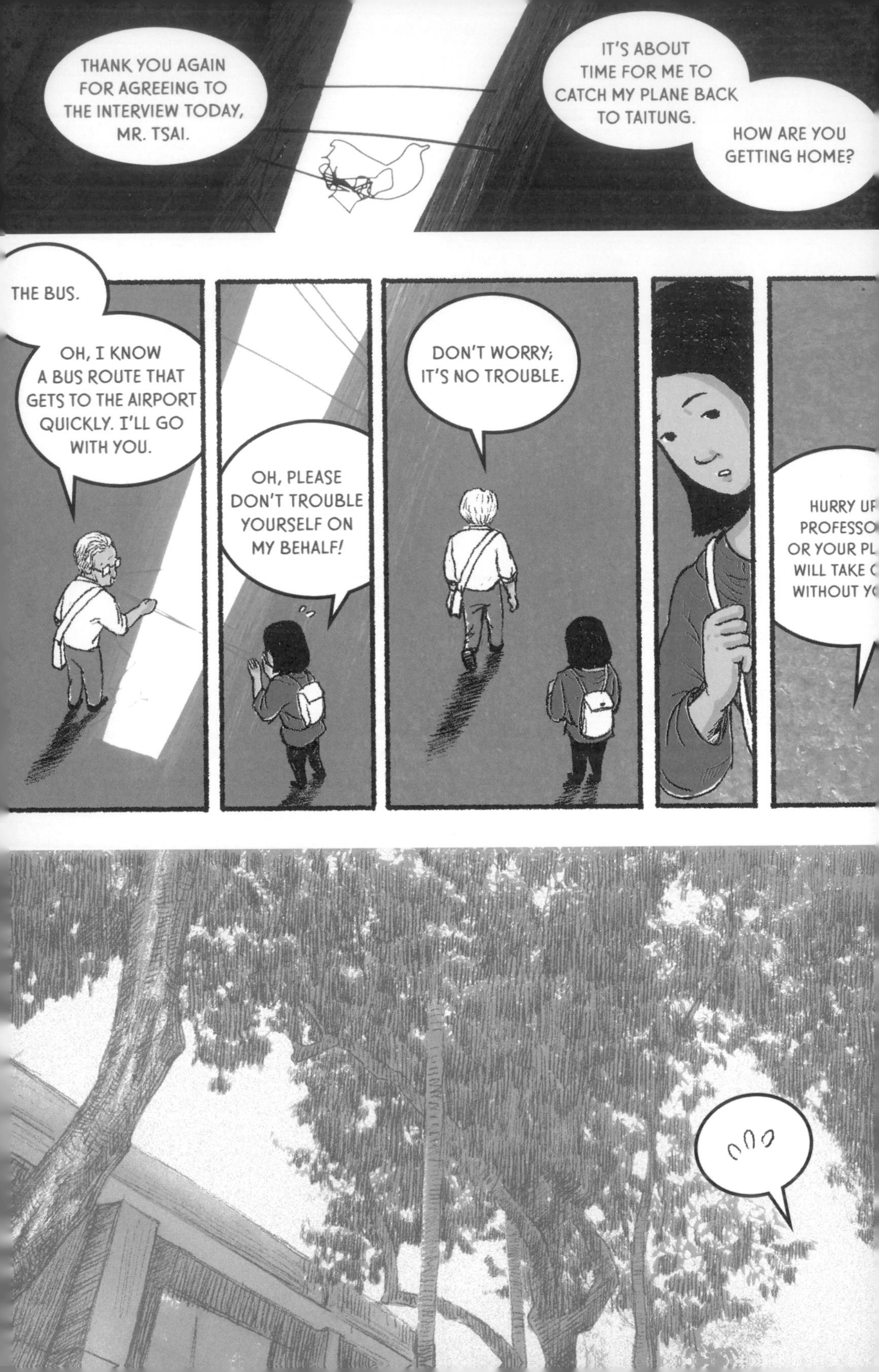
THANK YOU AGAIN FOR AGREEING TO THE INTERVIEW TODAY, MR. TSAI.
IT'S ABOUT TIME FOR ME TO CATCH MY PLANE BACK TO TAITUNG.
HOW ARE YOU GETTING HOME?
THE BUS.
OH, I KNOW A BUS ROUTE THAT GETS TO THE AIRPORT QUICKLY. I'LL GO WITH YOU.
OH, PLEASE DON'T TROUBLE YOURSELF ON MY BEHALF!
DON'T WORRY; IT'S NO TROUBLE.

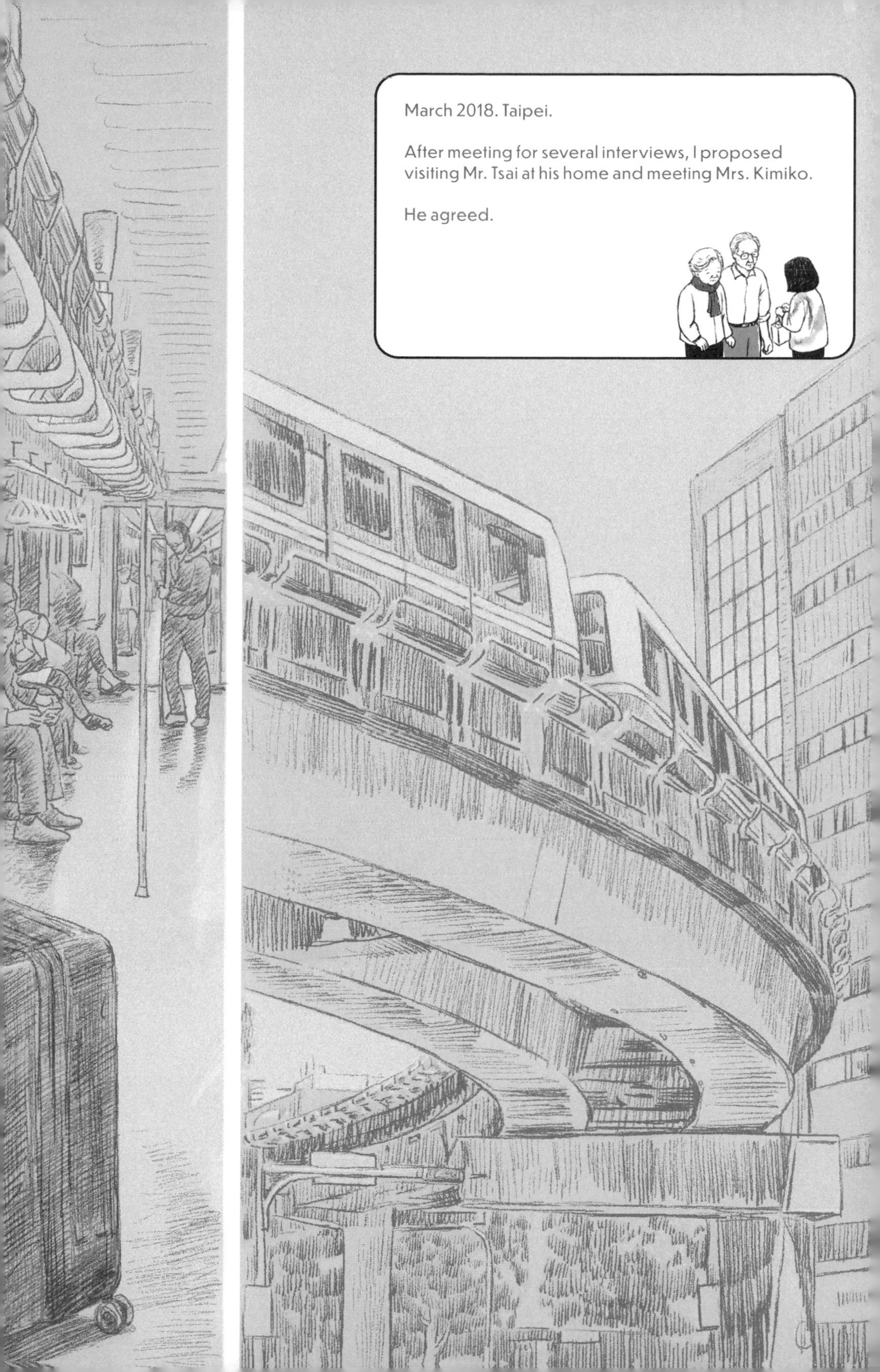
March 2018. Taipei.
After meeting for several interviews, I proposed visiting Mr. Tsai at his home and meeting Mrs. Kimiko.
He agreed.

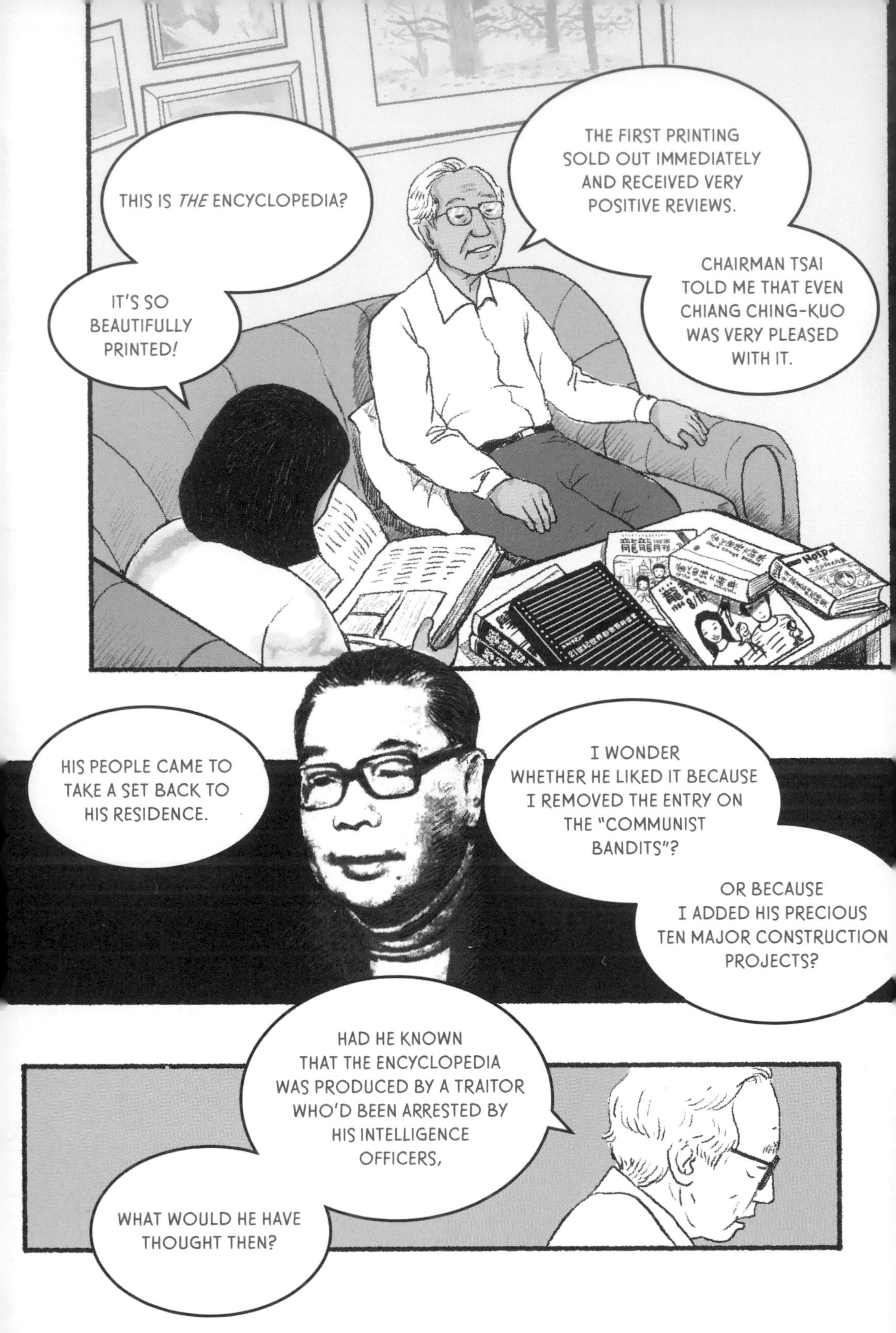
THIS IS *THE* ENCYCLOPEDIA?
IT'S SO BEAUTIFULLY PRINTED!
THE FIRST PRINTING SOLD OUT IMMEDIATELY AND RECEIVED VERY POSITIVE REVIEWS.
CHAIRMAN TSAI TOLD ME THAT EVEN CHIANG CHING-KUO WAS VERY PLEASED WITH IT.
HIS PEOPLE CAME TO TAKE A SET BACK TO HIS RESIDENCE.
I WONDER WHETHER HE LIKED IT BECAUSE I REMOVED THE ENTRY ON THE "COMMUNIST BANDITS"?
OR BECAUSE I ADDED HIS PRECIOUS TEN MAJOR CONSTRUCTION PROJECTS?
HAD HE KNOWN THAT THE ENCYCLOPEDIA WAS PRODUCED BY A TRAITOR WHO'D BEEN ARRESTED BY HIS INTELLIGENCE OFFICERS,
WHAT WOULD HE HAVE THOUGHT THEN?

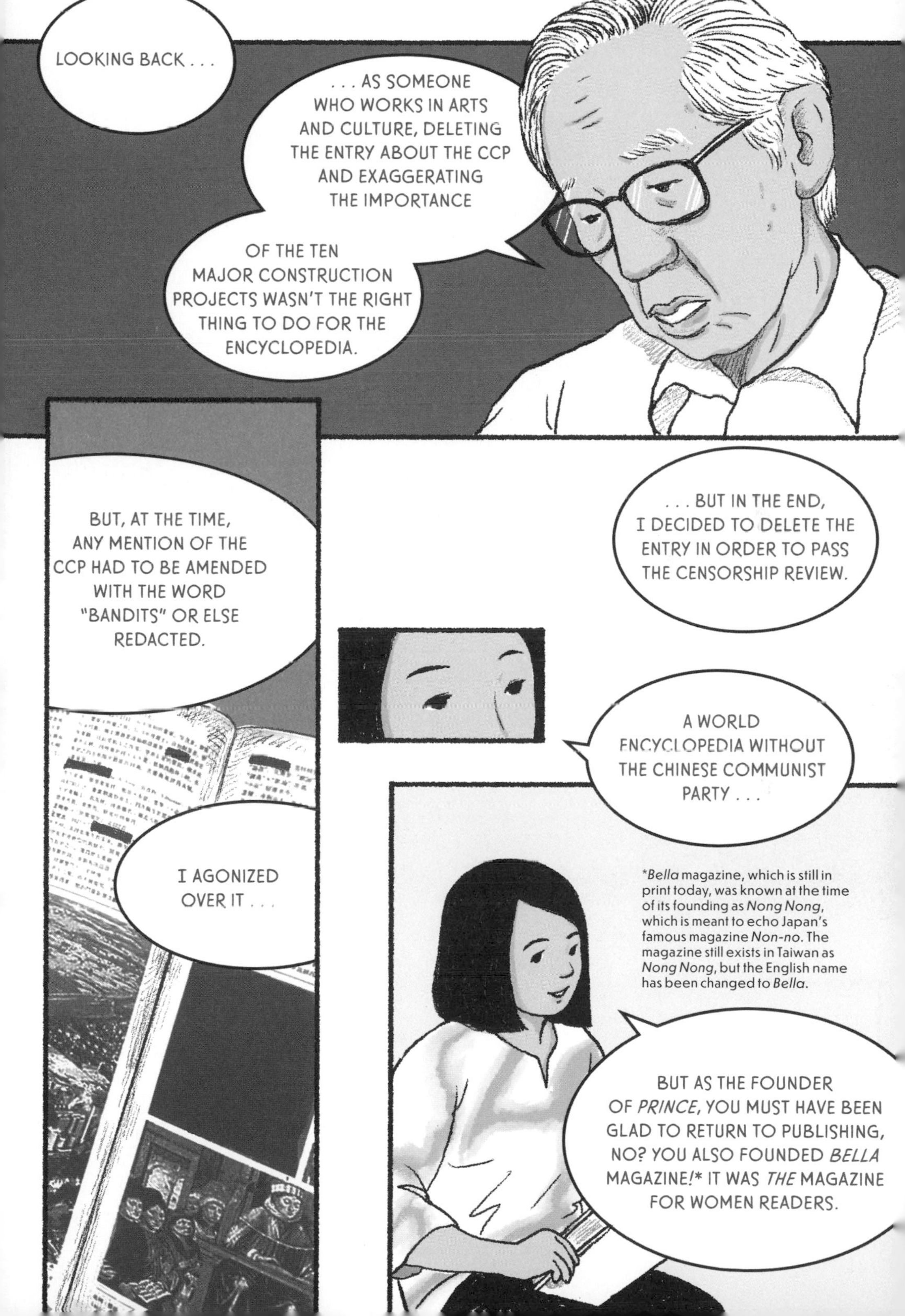
LOOKING BACK . . .
. . . AS SOMEONE WHO WORKS IN ARTS AND CULTURE, DELETING THE ENTRY ABOUT THE CCP AND EXAGGERATING THE IMPORTANCE
OF THE TEN MAJOR CONSTRUCTION PROJECTS WASN'T THE RIGHT THING TO DO FOR THE ENCYCLOPEDIA.
BUT, AT THE TIME, ANY MENTION OF THE CCP HAD TO BE AMENDED WITH THE WORD "BANDITS" OR ELSE REDACTED.
I AGONIZED OVER IT . . .
. . . BUT IN THE END, I DECIDED TO DELETE THE ENTRY IN ORDER TO PASS THE CENSORSHIP REVIEW.
A WORLD ENCYCLOPEDIA WITHOUT THE CHINESE COMMUNIST PARTY . . .
BUT AS THE FOUNDER OF *PRINCE*, YOU MUST HAVE BEEN GLAD TO RETURN TO PUBLISHING, NO? YOU ALSO FOUNDED *BELLA* MAGAZINE!* IT WAS *THE* MAGAZINE FOR WOMEN READERS.

**Bella* magazine, which is still in print today, was known at the time of its founding as *Nong Nong*, which is meant to echo Japan's famous magazine *Non-no*. The magazine still exists in Taiwan as *Nong Nong*, but the English name has been changed to *Bella*.

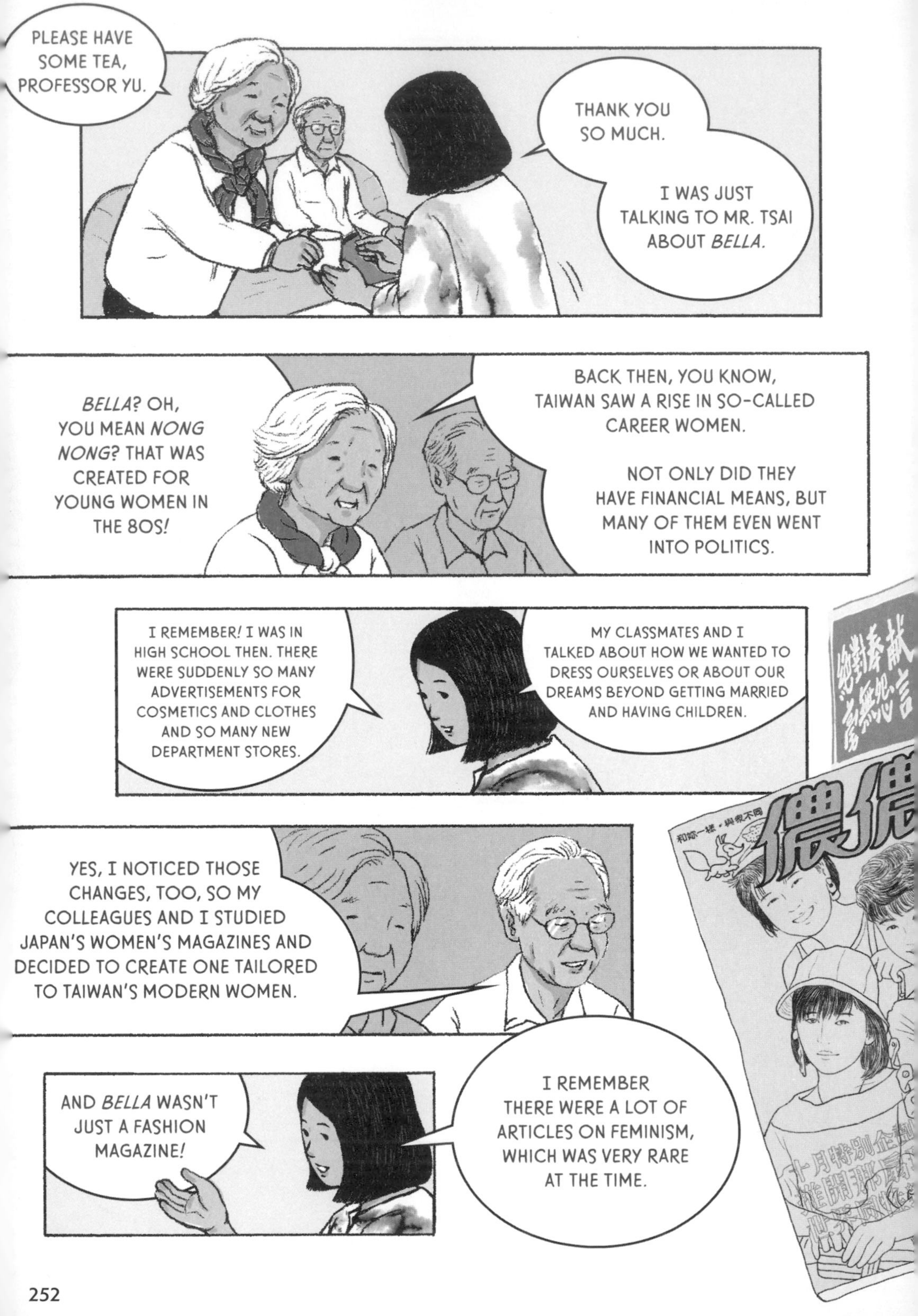
PLEASE HAVE SOME TEA, PROFESSOR YU.
THANK YOU SO MUCH.
I WAS JUST TALKING TO MR. TSAI ABOUT *BELLA*.
BELLA? OH, YOU MEAN *NONG NONG*? THAT WAS CREATED FOR YOUNG WOMEN IN THE 80S!
BACK THEN, YOU KNOW, TAIWAN SAW A RISE IN SO-CALLED CAREER WOMEN.
NOT ONLY DID THEY HAVE FINANCIAL MEANS, BUT MANY OF THEM EVEN WENT INTO POLITICS.
I REMEMBER! I WAS IN HIGH SCHOOL THEN. THERE WERE SUDDENLY SO MANY ADVERTISEMENTS FOR COSMETICS AND CLOTHES AND SO MANY NEW DEPARTMENT STORES.
MY CLASSMATES AND I TALKED ABOUT HOW WE WANTED TO DRESS OURSELVES OR ABOUT OUR DREAMS BEYOND GETTING MARRIED AND HAVING CHILDREN.
YES, I NOTICED THOSE CHANGES, TOO, SO MY COLLEAGUES AND I STUDIED JAPAN'S WOMEN'S MAGAZINES AND DECIDED TO CREATE ONE TAILORED TO TAIWAN'S MODERN WOMEN.
AND *BELLA* WASN'T JUST A FASHION MAGAZINE!
I REMEMBER THERE WERE A LOT OF ARTICLES ON FEMINISM, WHICH WAS VERY RARE AT THE TIME.
儂儂

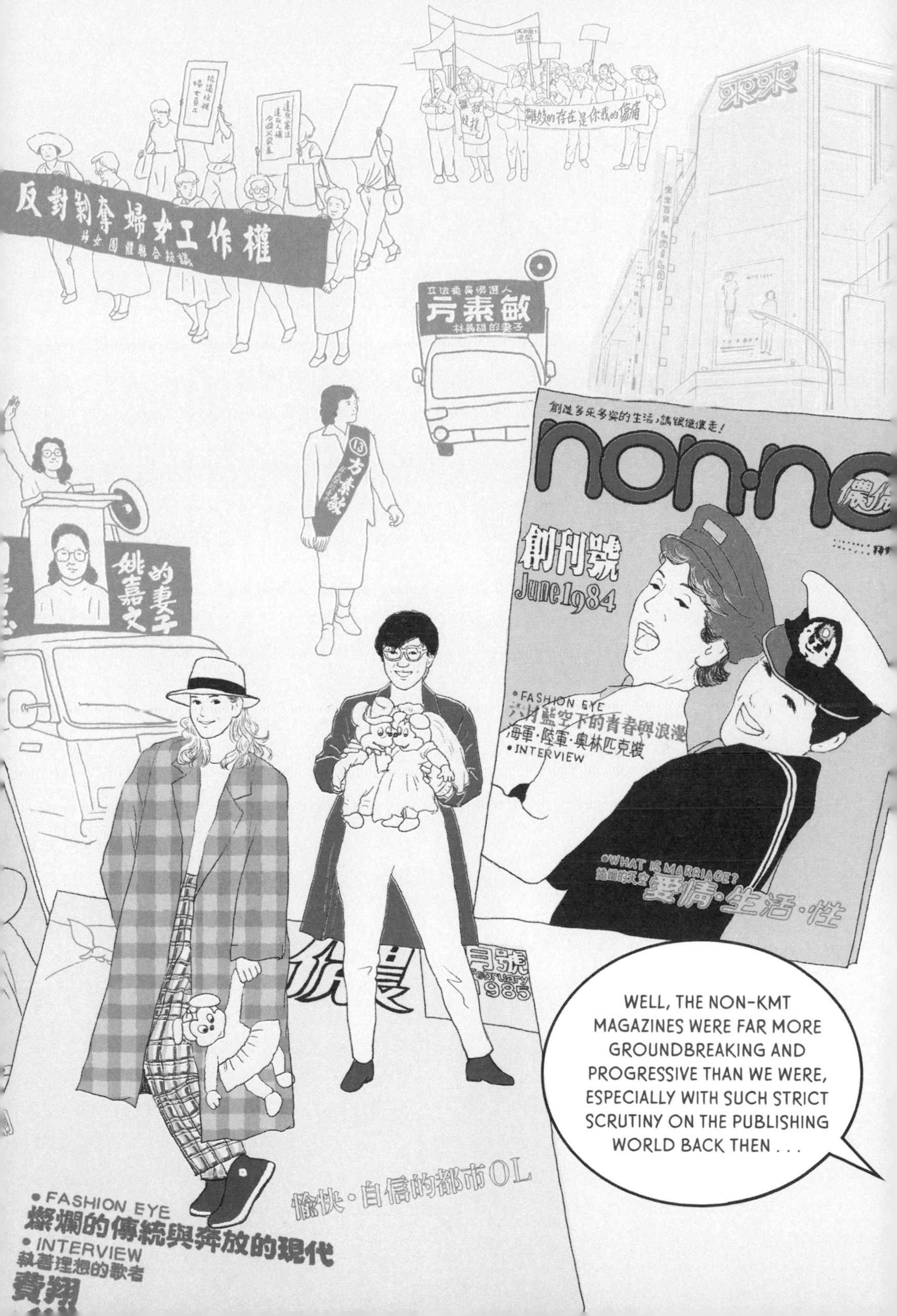

反對剝奪婦女工作權
婦女團體聯合抗議
雛妓的存在是你我的傷痛
來來
立法委員候選人
方素敏
林義雄的妻子
姚嘉文的妻子
創造多采多姿的生活，請跟儂儂走！
non-no
創刊號
June 1984
• FASHION EYE
八月藍空下的青春與浪漫
海軍·陸軍·奧林匹克裝
• INTERVIEW
• WHAT IS MARRIAGE?
婚姻的天空
愛情·生活·性
月號
February
1985
愉快·自信的都市OL
• FASHION EYE
燦爛的傳統與奔放的現代
• INTERVIEW
執著理想的歌者
費翔
WELL, THE NON-KMT MAGAZINES WERE FAR MORE GROUNDBREAKING AND PROGRESSIVE THAN WE WERE, ESPECIALLY WITH SUCH STRICT SCRUTINY ON THE PUBLISHING WORLD BACK THEN . . .

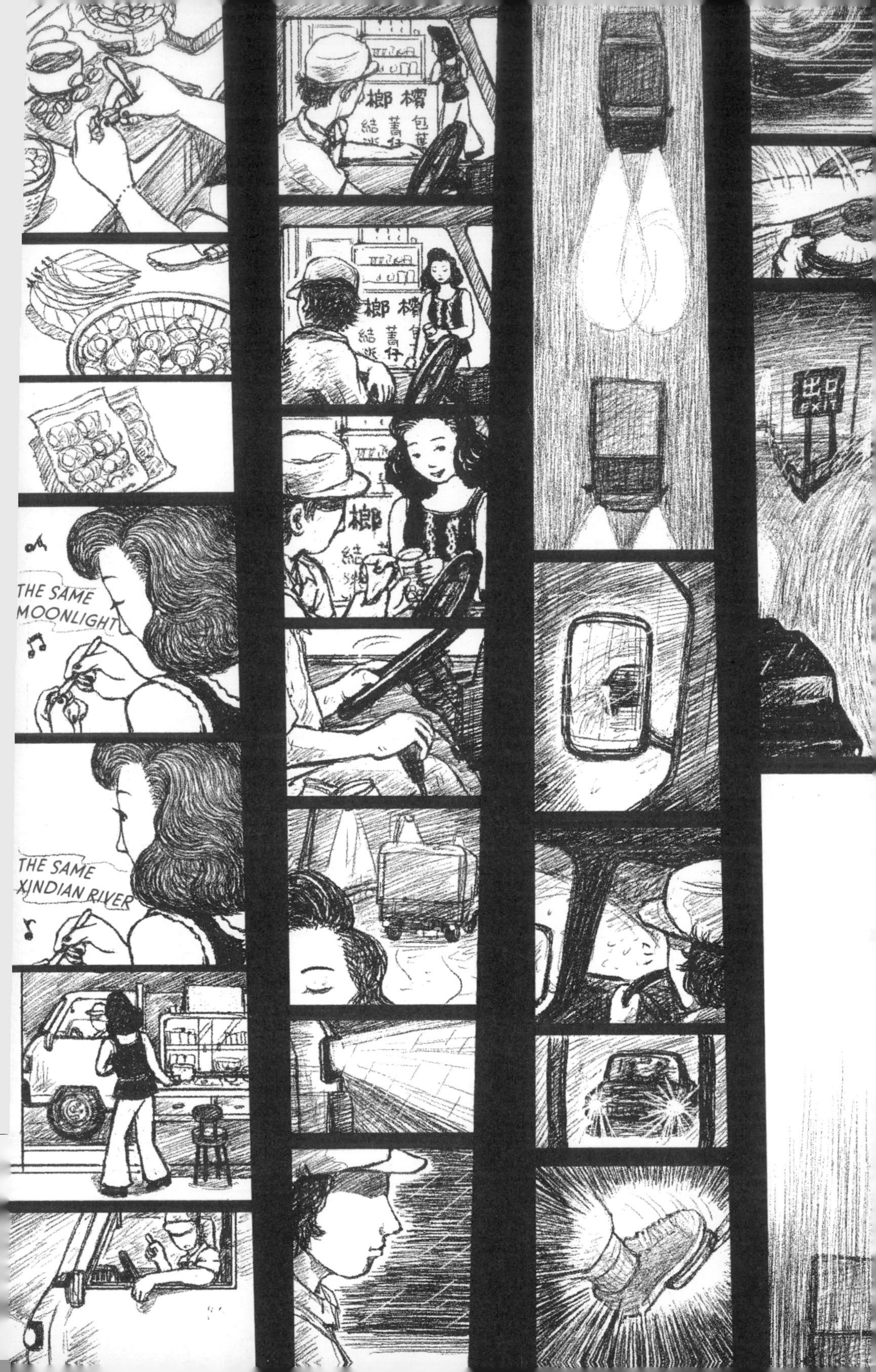
檳榔
THE SAME MOONLIGHT
THE SAME XINDIAN RIVER
出口
EXIT

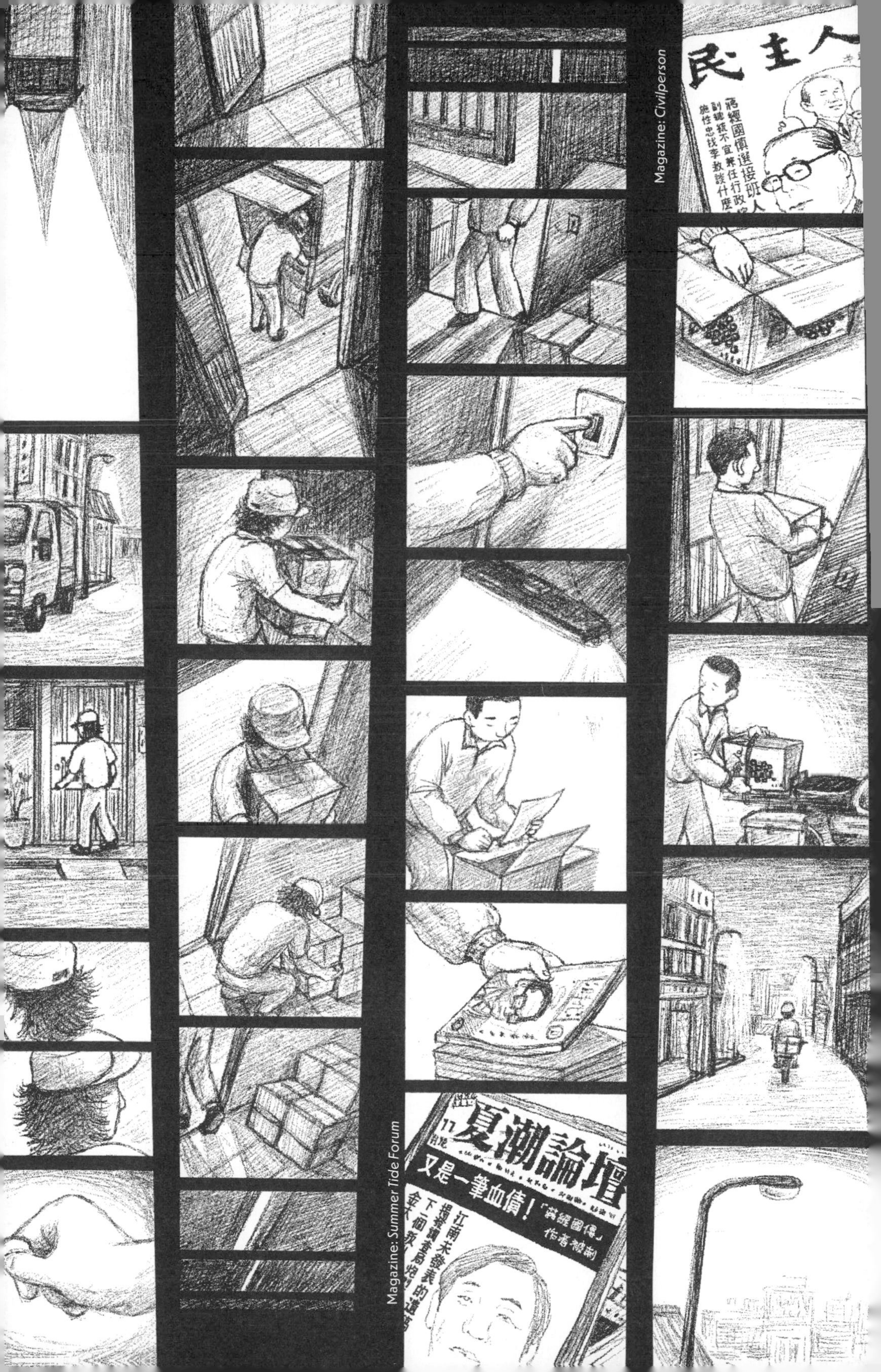
Magazine: Civilperson
民主人
蔣經國慎選接班人
副總統不宜兼任行政
施性忠找李敖談什麼
Magazine: Summer Tide Forum
夏潮論壇
又是一筆血債！
「蔣經國傳」作者被刺
江南未發表的
揭發調查局的
下一個

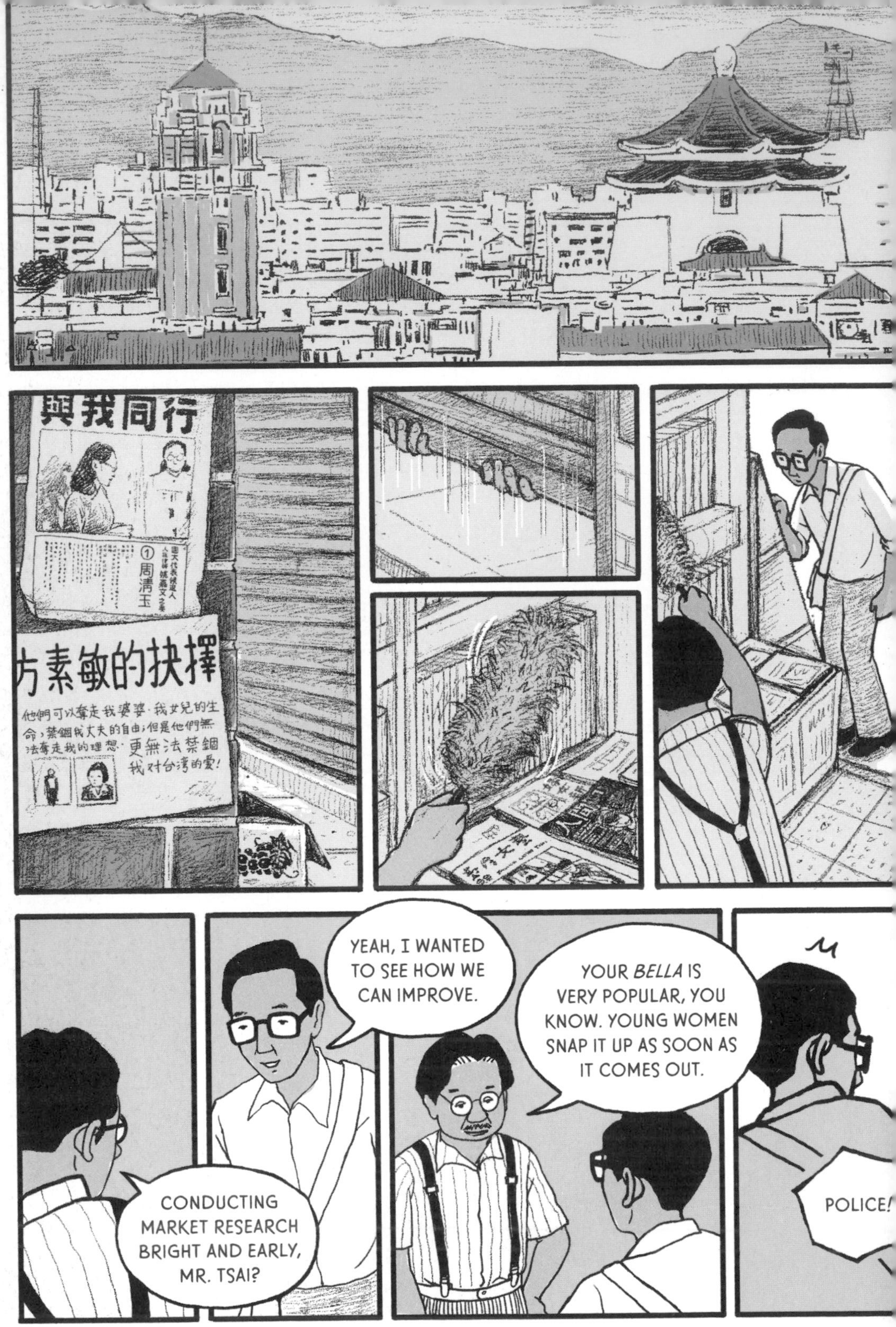
與我同行
周清玉
方素敏的抉擇
他們可以奪走我婆婆、我女兒的生命，禁錮我丈夫的自由；但是他們無法奪走我的理想，更無法禁錮我对台湾的愛!
CONDUCTING MARKET RESEARCH BRIGHT AND EARLY, MR. TSAI?
YEAH, I WANTED TO SEE HOW WE CAN IMPROVE.
YOUR *BELLA* IS VERY POPULAR, YOU KNOW. YOUNG WOMEN SNAP IT UP AS SOON AS IT COMES OUT.
POLICE!

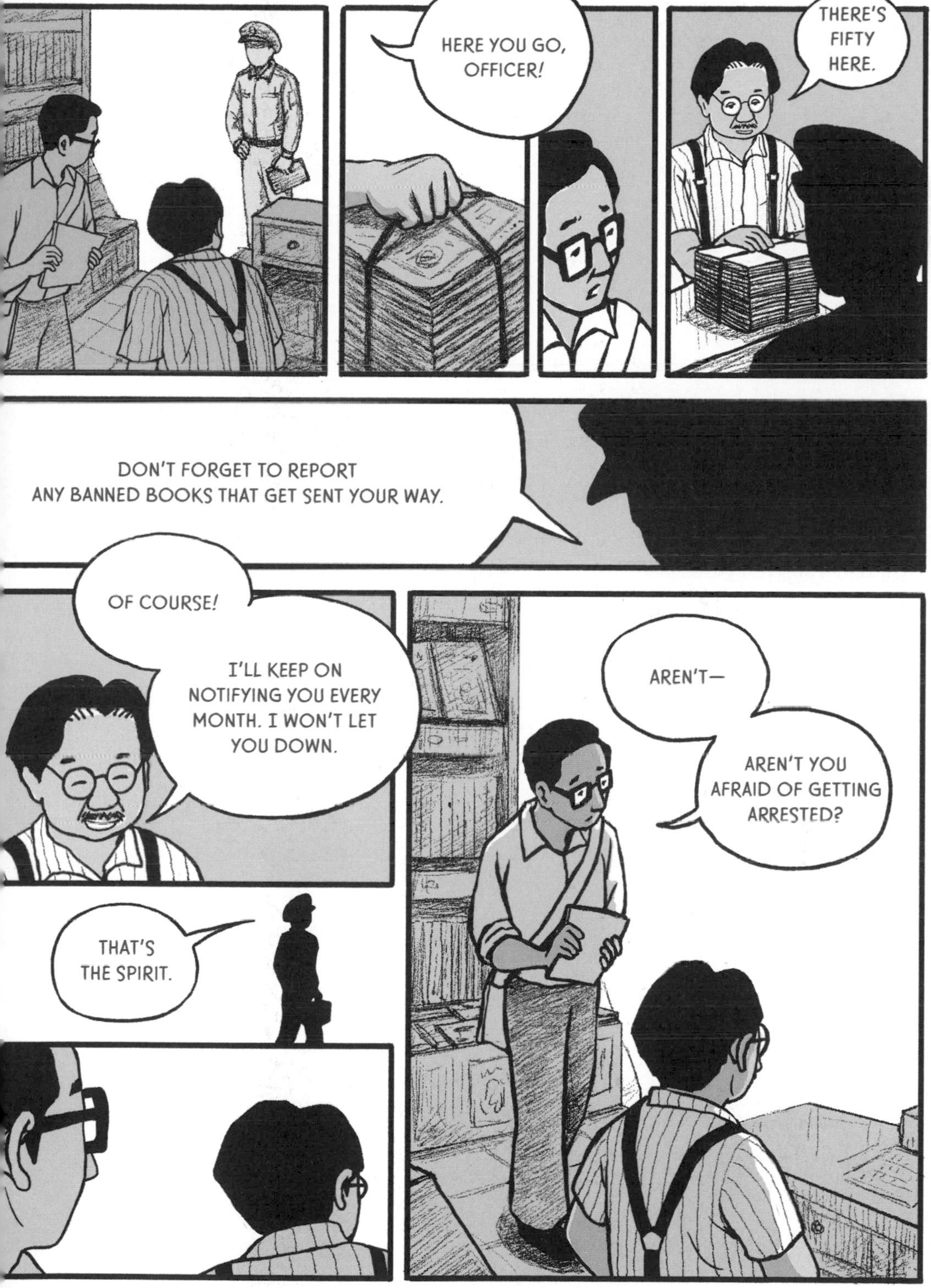
HERE YOU GO, OFFICER!
THERE'S FIFTY HERE.
DON'T FORGET TO REPORT ANY BANNED BOOKS THAT GET SENT YOUR WAY.
OF COURSE!
I'LL KEEP ON NOTIFYING YOU EVERY MONTH. I WON'T LET YOU DOWN.
THAT'S THE SPIRIT.
AREN'T—
AREN'T YOU AFRAID OF GETTING ARRESTED?

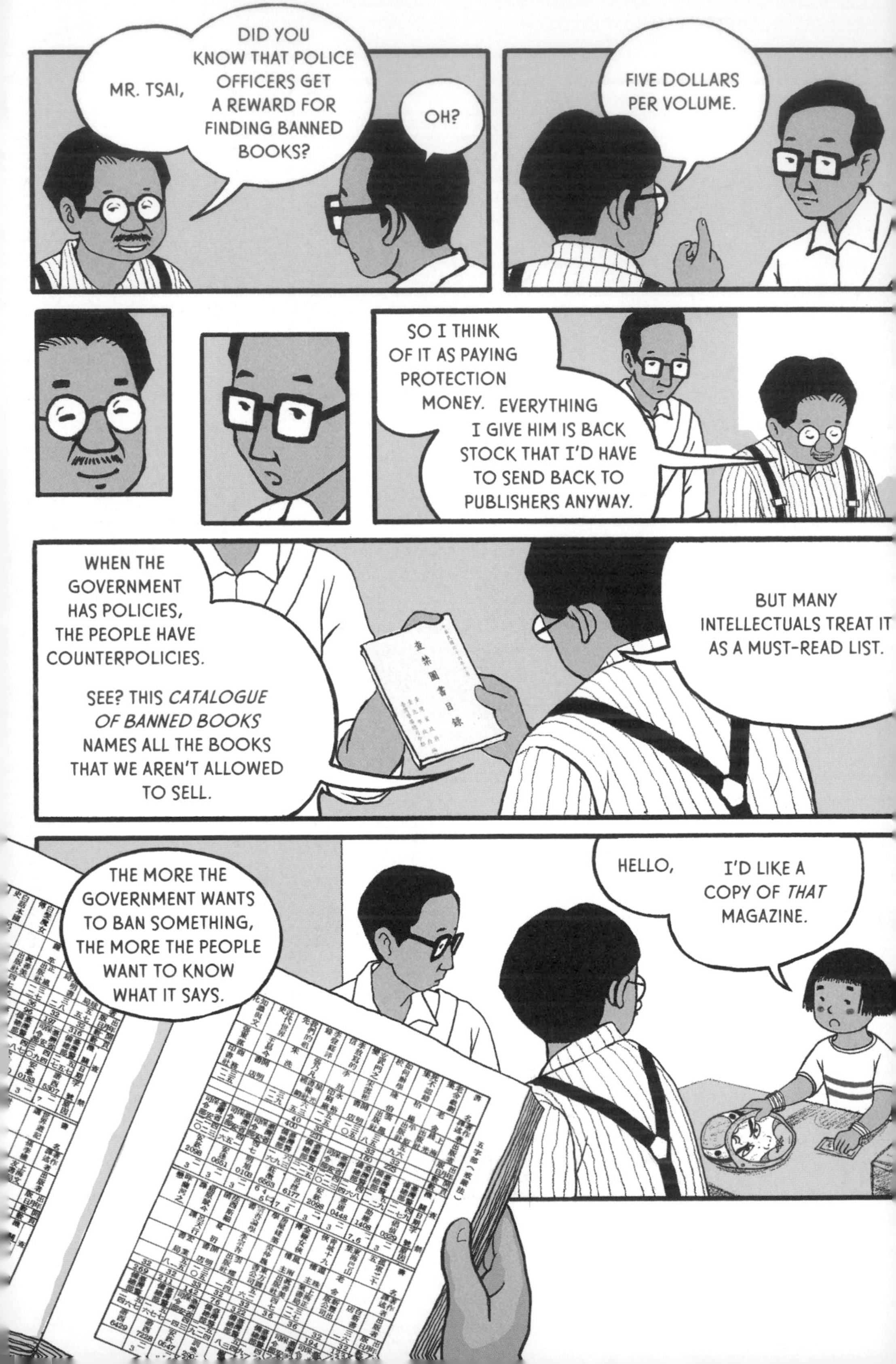
MR. TSAI,
DID YOU KNOW THAT POLICE OFFICERS GET A REWARD FOR FINDING BANNED BOOKS?
OH?
FIVE DOLLARS PER VOLUME.
SO I THINK OF IT AS PAYING PROTECTION MONEY.
EVERYTHING I GIVE HIM IS BACK STOCK THAT I'D HAVE TO SEND BACK TO PUBLISHERS ANYWAY.
WHEN THE GOVERNMENT HAS POLICIES, THE PEOPLE HAVE COUNTERPOLICIES.
SEE? THIS *CATALOGUE OF BANNED BOOKS* NAMES ALL THE BOOKS THAT WE AREN'T ALLOWED TO SELL.
查禁圖書目錄
BUT MANY INTELLECTUALS TREAT IT AS A MUST-READ LIST.
THE MORE THE GOVERNMENT WANTS TO BAN SOMETHING, THE MORE THE PEOPLE WANT TO KNOW WHAT IT SAYS.
HELLO,
I'D LIKE A COPY OF *THAT* MAGAZINE.

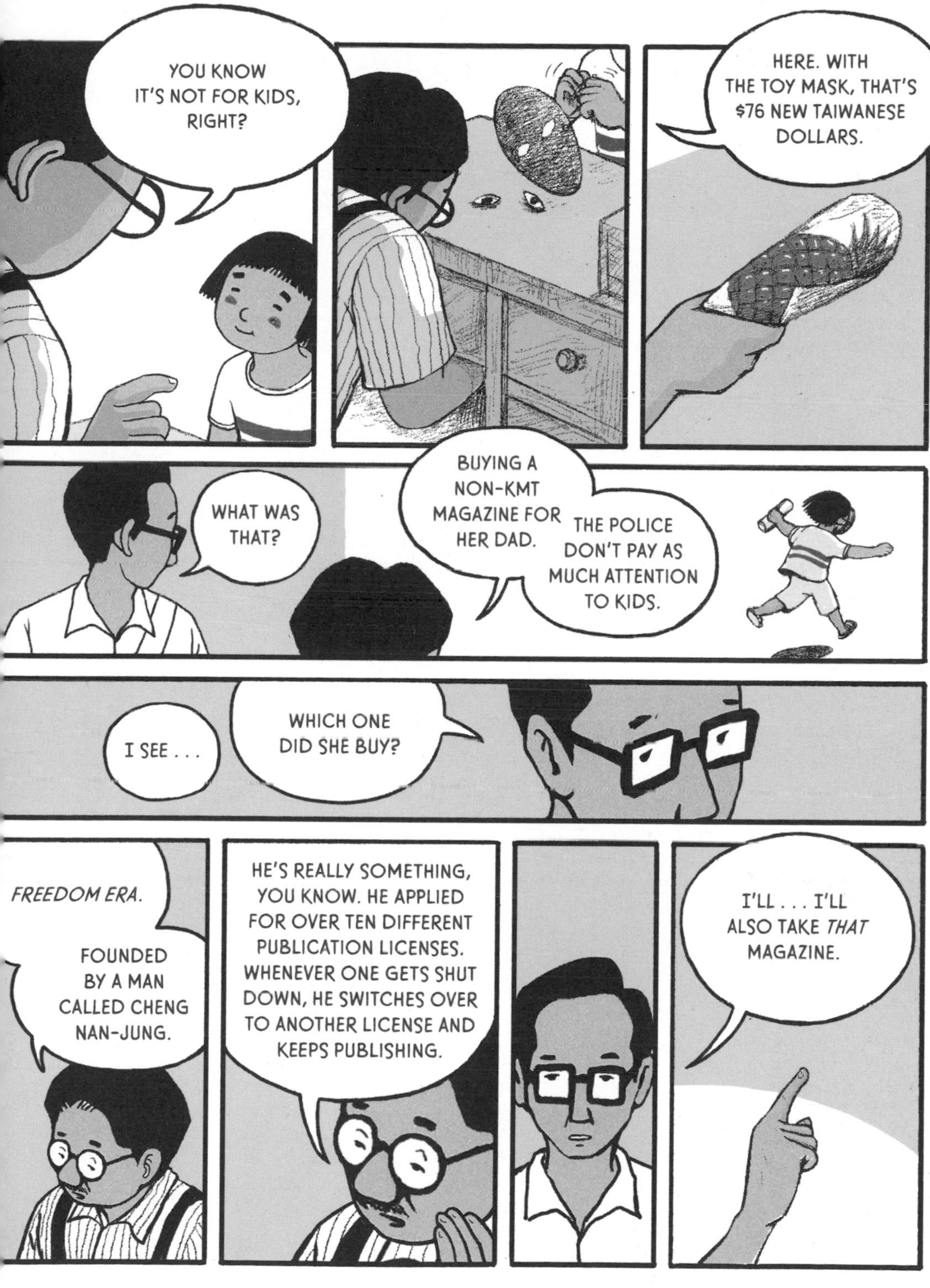
YOU KNOW IT'S NOT FOR KIDS, RIGHT?
HERE. WITH THE TOY MASK, THAT'S $76 NEW TAIWANESE DOLLARS.
WHAT WAS THAT?
BUYING A NON-KMT MAGAZINE FOR HER DAD.
THE POLICE DON'T PAY AS MUCH ATTENTION TO KIDS.
I SEE . . .
WHICH ONE DID SHE BUY?
FREEDOM ERA.
FOUNDED BY A MAN CALLED CHENG NAN-JUNG.
HE'S REALLY SOMETHING, YOU KNOW. HE APPLIED FOR OVER TEN DIFFERENT PUBLICATION LICENSES. WHENEVER ONE GETS SHUT DOWN, HE SWITCHES OVER TO ANOTHER LICENSE AND KEEPS PUBLISHING.
I'LL . . . I'LL ALSO TAKE *THAT* MAGAZINE.

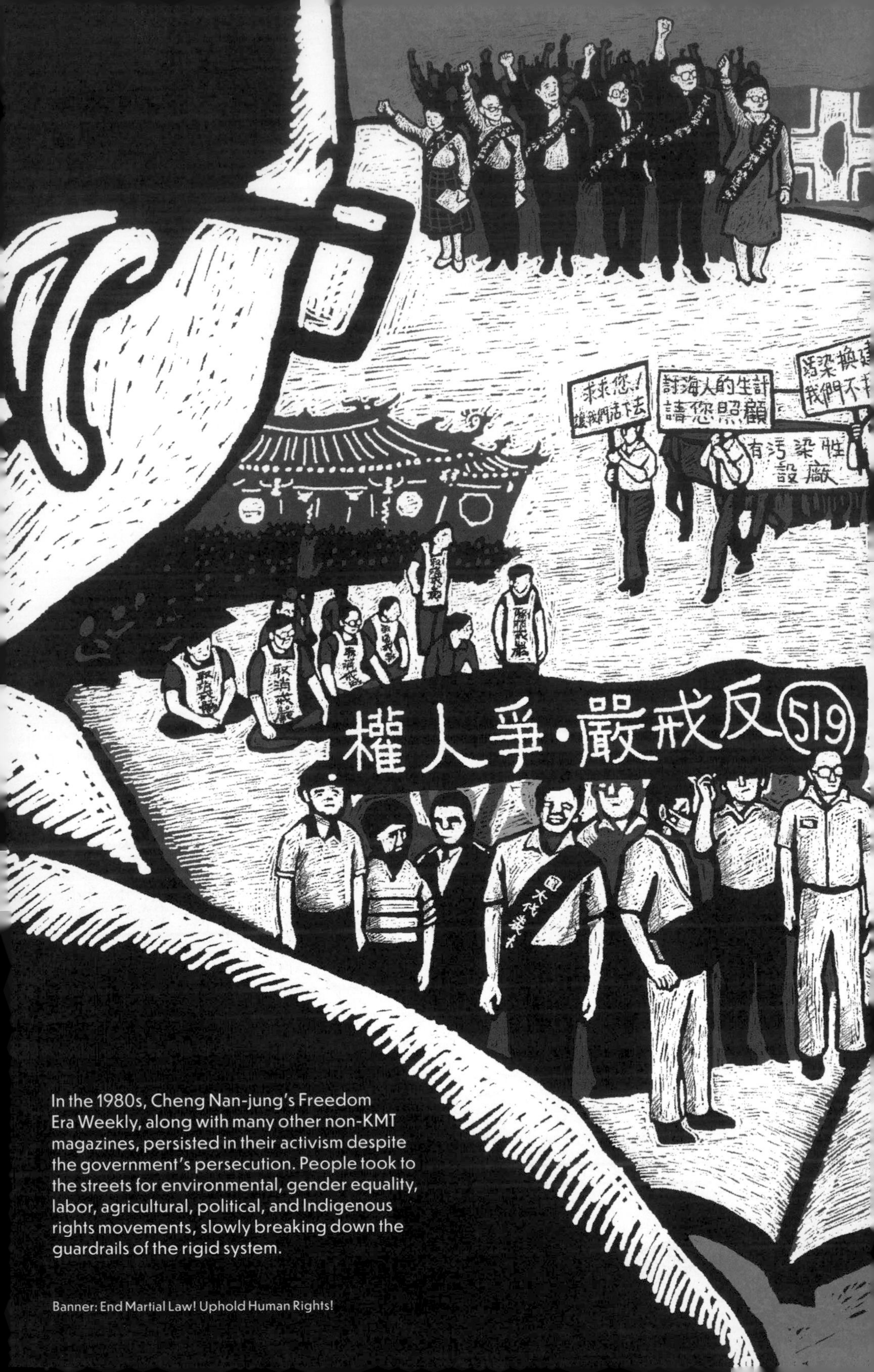
求求您！讓我們活下去
討海人的生計 請您照顧
取消戒嚴
519 反戒嚴・爭人權

In the 1980s, Cheng Nan-jung's Freedom Era Weekly, along with many other non-KMT magazines, persisted in their activism despite the government's persecution. People took to the streets for environmental, gender equality, labor, agricultural, political, and Indigenous rights movements, slowly breaking down the guardrails of the rigid system.

Banner: End Martial Law! Uphold Human Rights!

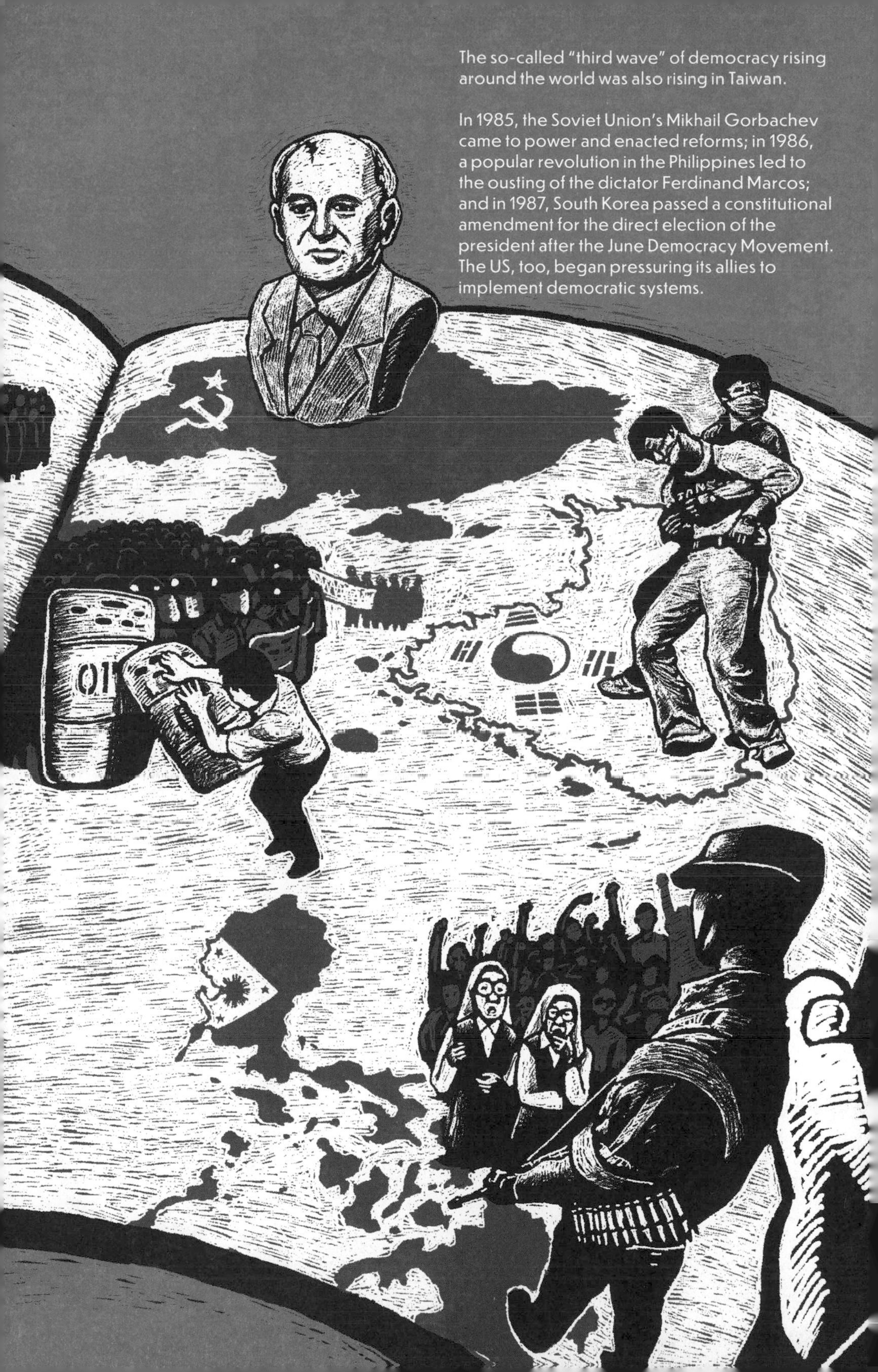
The so-called "third wave" of democracy rising around the world was also rising in Taiwan.
In 1985, the Soviet Union's Mikhail Gorbachev came to power and enacted reforms; in 1986, a popular revolution in the Philippines led to the ousting of the dictator Ferdinand Marcos; and in 1987, South Korea passed a constitutional amendment for the direct election of the president after the June Democracy Movement. The US, too, began pressuring its allies to implement democratic systems.

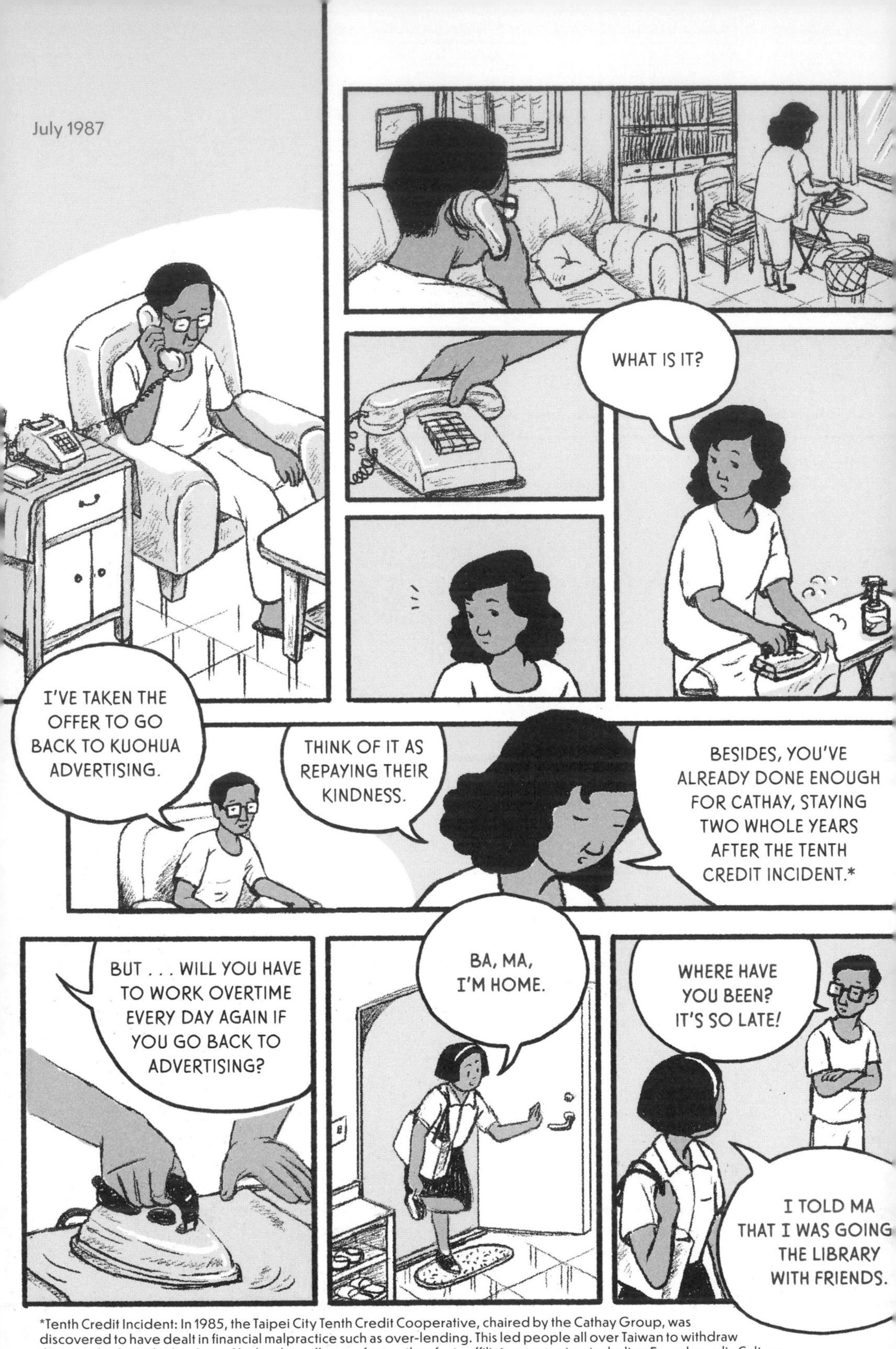
July 1987
WHAT IS IT?
I'VE TAKEN THE OFFER TO GO BACK TO KUOHUA ADVERTISING.
THINK OF IT AS REPAYING THEIR KINDNESS.
BESIDES, YOU'VE ALREADY DONE ENOUGH FOR CATHAY, STAYING TWO WHOLE YEARS AFTER THE TENTH CREDIT INCIDENT.*
BUT . . . WILL YOU HAVE TO WORK OVERTIME EVERY DAY AGAIN IF YOU GO BACK TO ADVERTISING?
BA, MA, I'M HOME.
WHERE HAVE YOU BEEN? IT'S SO LATE!
I TOLD MA THAT I WAS GOING THE LIBRARY WITH FRIENDS.

*Tenth Credit Incident: In 1985, the Taipei City Tenth Credit Cooperative, chaired by the Cathay Group, was discovered to have dealt in financial malpractice such as over-lending. This led people all over Taiwan to withdraw their money from the banks and led to the collapse of more than forty affiliate companies, including Encyclopedia Culture.

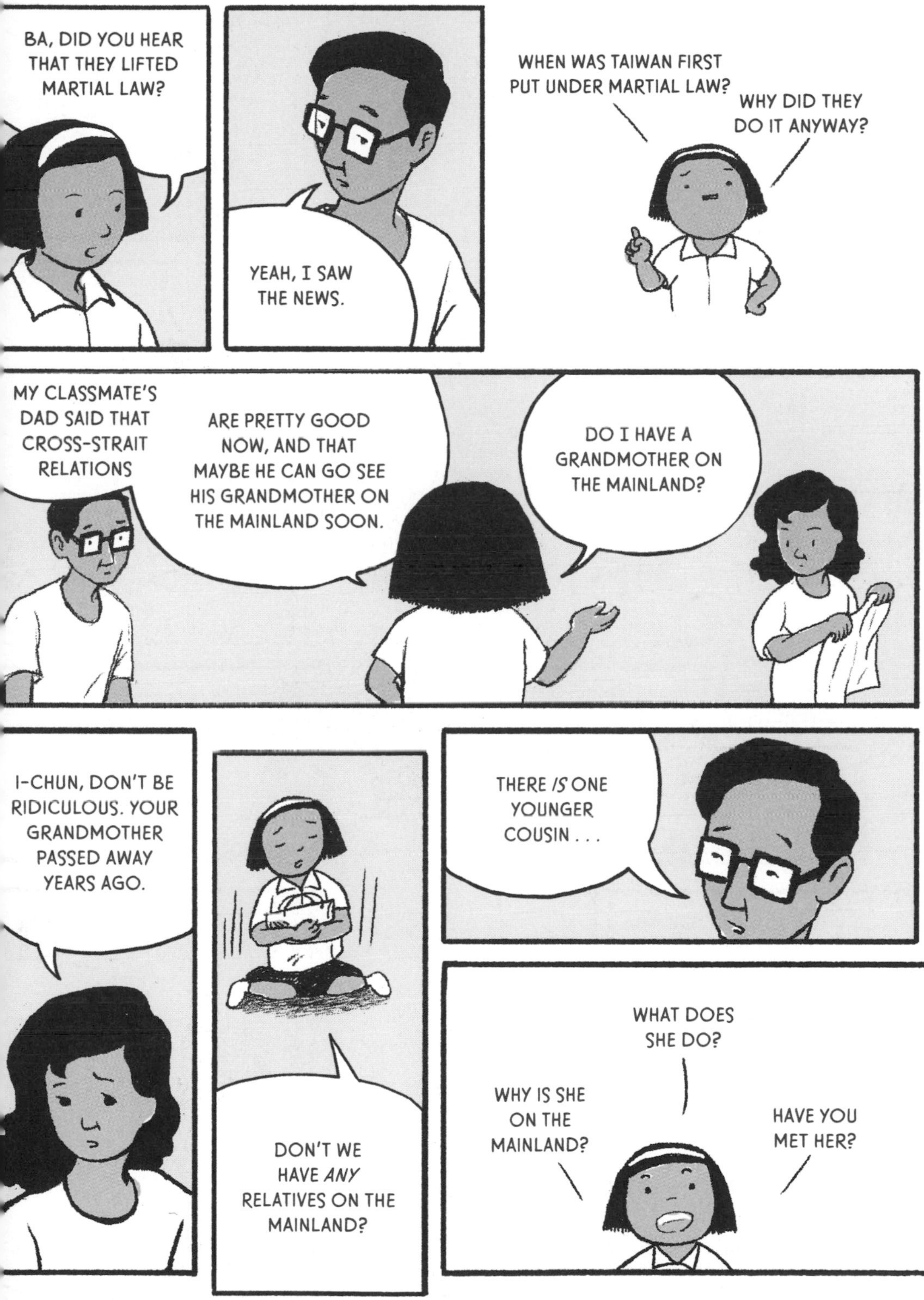
BA, DID YOU HEAR THAT THEY LIFTED MARTIAL LAW?
YEAH, I SAW THE NEWS.
WHEN WAS TAIWAN FIRST PUT UNDER MARTIAL LAW?
WHY DID THEY DO IT ANYWAY?
MY CLASSMATE'S DAD SAID THAT CROSS-STRAIT RELATIONS
ARE PRETTY GOOD NOW, AND THAT MAYBE HE CAN GO SEE HIS GRANDMOTHER ON THE MAINLAND SOON.
DO I HAVE A GRANDMOTHER ON THE MAINLAND?
I-CHUN, DON'T BE RIDICULOUS. YOUR GRANDMOTHER PASSED AWAY YEARS AGO.
DON'T WE HAVE *ANY* RELATIVES ON THE MAINLAND?
THERE *IS* ONE YOUNGER COUSIN . . .
WHAT DOES SHE DO?
WHY IS SHE ON THE MAINLAND?
HAVE YOU MET HER?

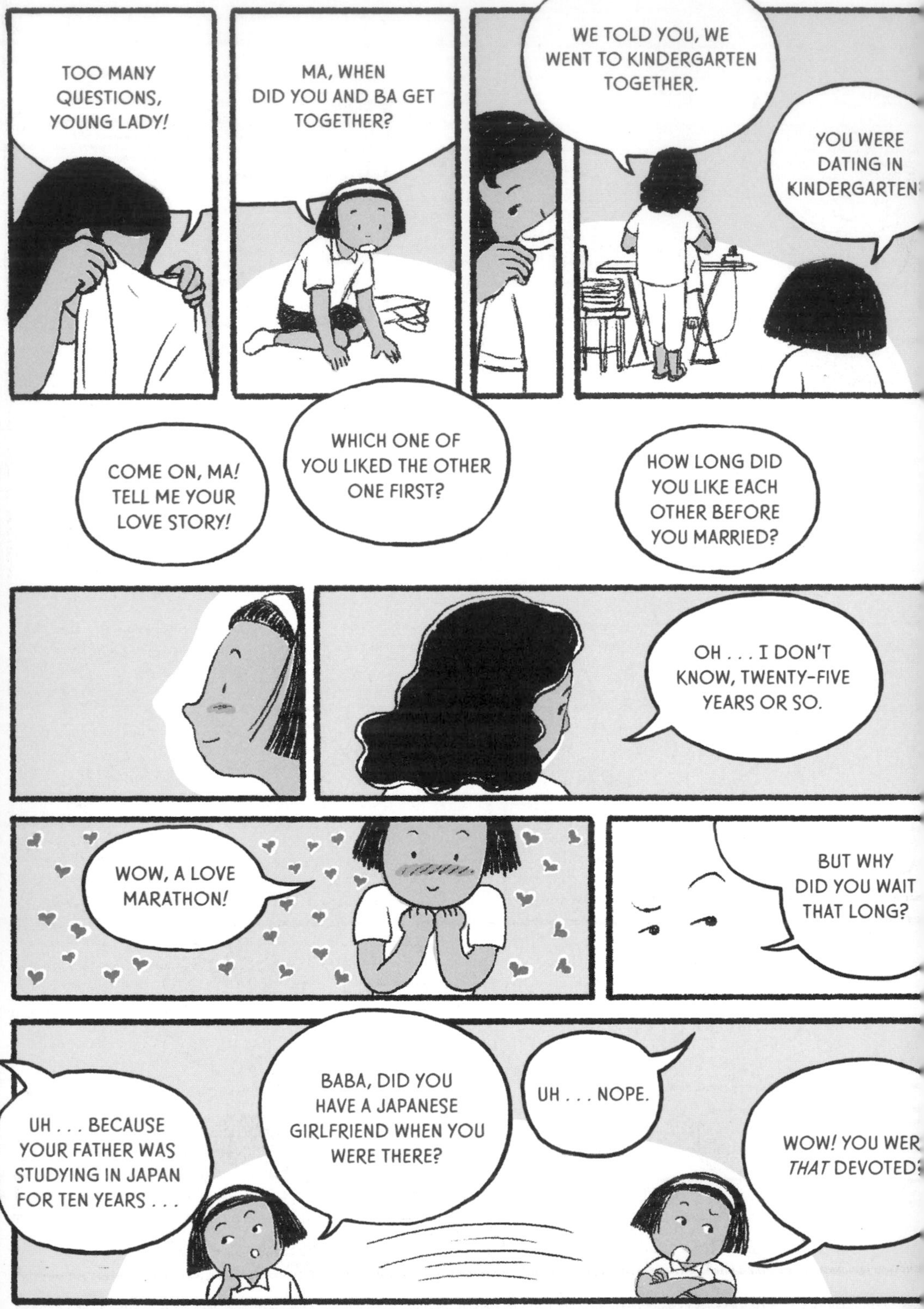

TOO MANY QUESTIONS, YOUNG LADY!
MA, WHEN DID YOU AND BA GET TOGETHER?
WE TOLD YOU, WE WENT TO KINDERGARTEN TOGETHER.
YOU WERE DATING IN KINDERGARTEN
COME ON, MA! TELL ME YOUR LOVE STORY!
WHICH ONE OF YOU LIKED THE OTHER ONE FIRST?
HOW LONG DID YOU LIKE EACH OTHER BEFORE YOU MARRIED?
OH . . . I DON'T KNOW, TWENTY-FIVE YEARS OR SO.
WOW, A LOVE MARATHON!
BUT WHY DID YOU WAIT THAT LONG?
UH . . . BECAUSE YOUR FATHER WAS STUDYING IN JAPAN FOR TEN YEARS . . .
BABA, DID YOU HAVE A JAPANESE GIRLFRIEND WHEN YOU WERE THERE?
UH . . . NOPE.
WOW! YOU WER *THAT* DEVOTED

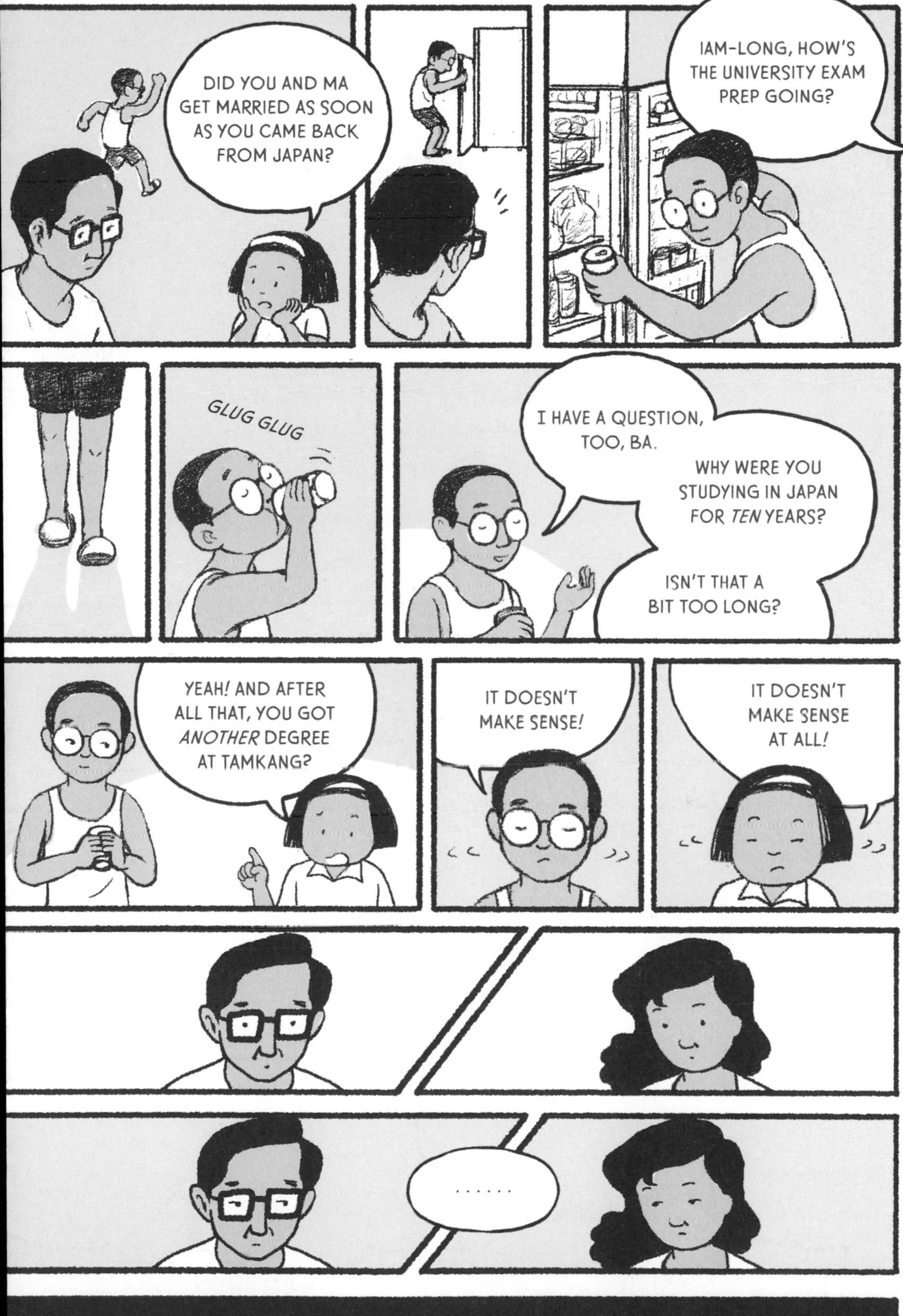
DID YOU AND MA GET MARRIED AS SOON AS YOU CAME BACK FROM JAPAN?
IAM-LONG, HOW'S THE UNIVERSITY EXAM PREP GOING?
GLUG GLUG
I HAVE A QUESTION, TOO, BA.
WHY WERE YOU STUDYING IN JAPAN FOR TEN YEARS?
ISN'T THAT A BIT TOO LONG?
YEAH! AND AFTER ALL THAT, YOU GOT ANOTHER DEGREE AT TAMKANG?
IT DOESN'T MAKE SENSE!
IT DOESN'T MAKE SENSE AT ALL!
......

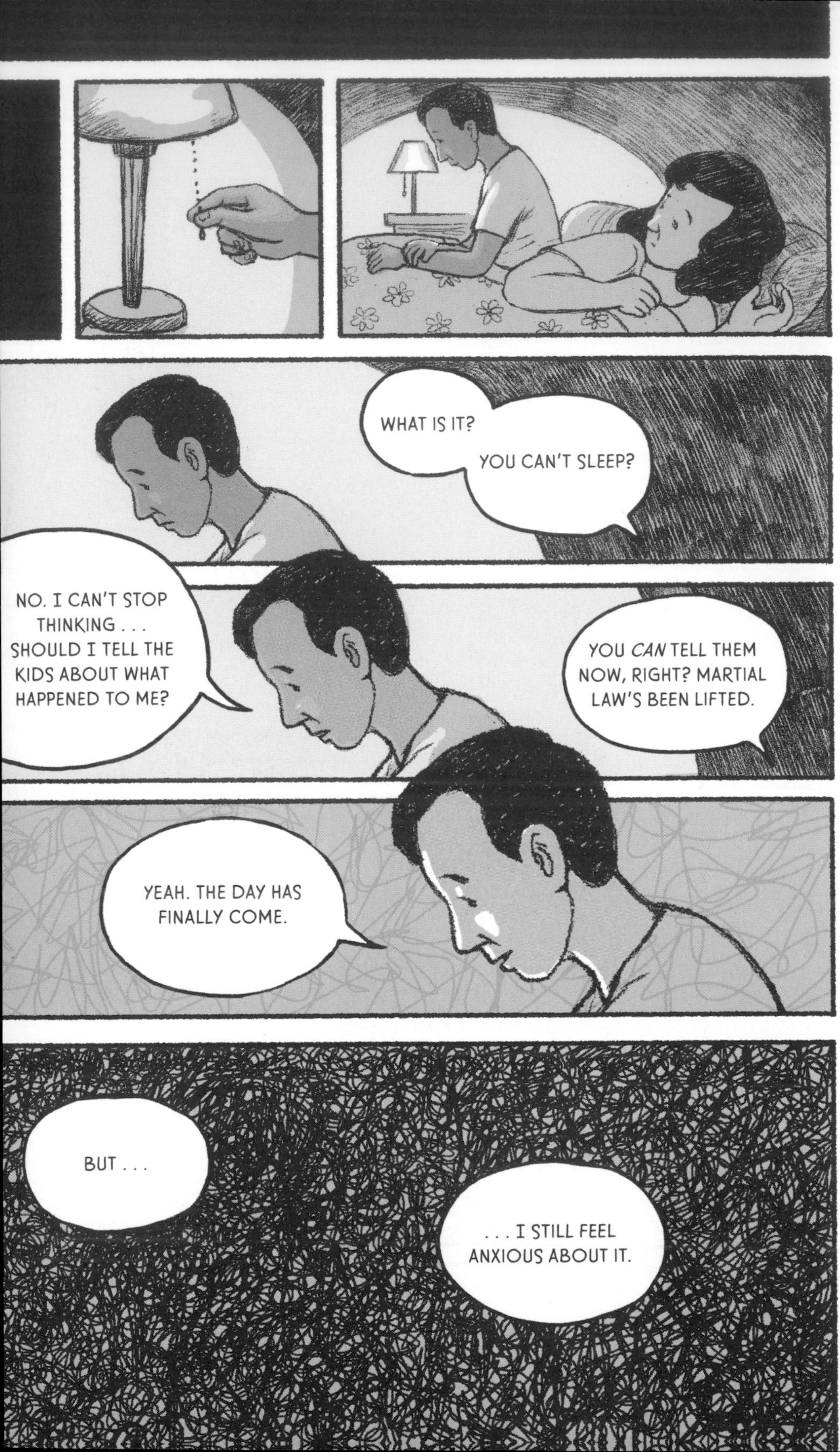
WHAT IS IT?
YOU CAN'T SLEEP?
NO. I CAN'T STOP THINKING . . . SHOULD I TELL THE KIDS ABOUT WHAT HAPPENED TO ME?
YOU *CAN* TELL THEM NOW, RIGHT? MARTIAL LAW'S BEEN LIFTED.
YEAH. THE DAY HAS FINALLY COME.
BUT . . .
. . . I STILL FEEL ANXIOUS ABOUT IT.

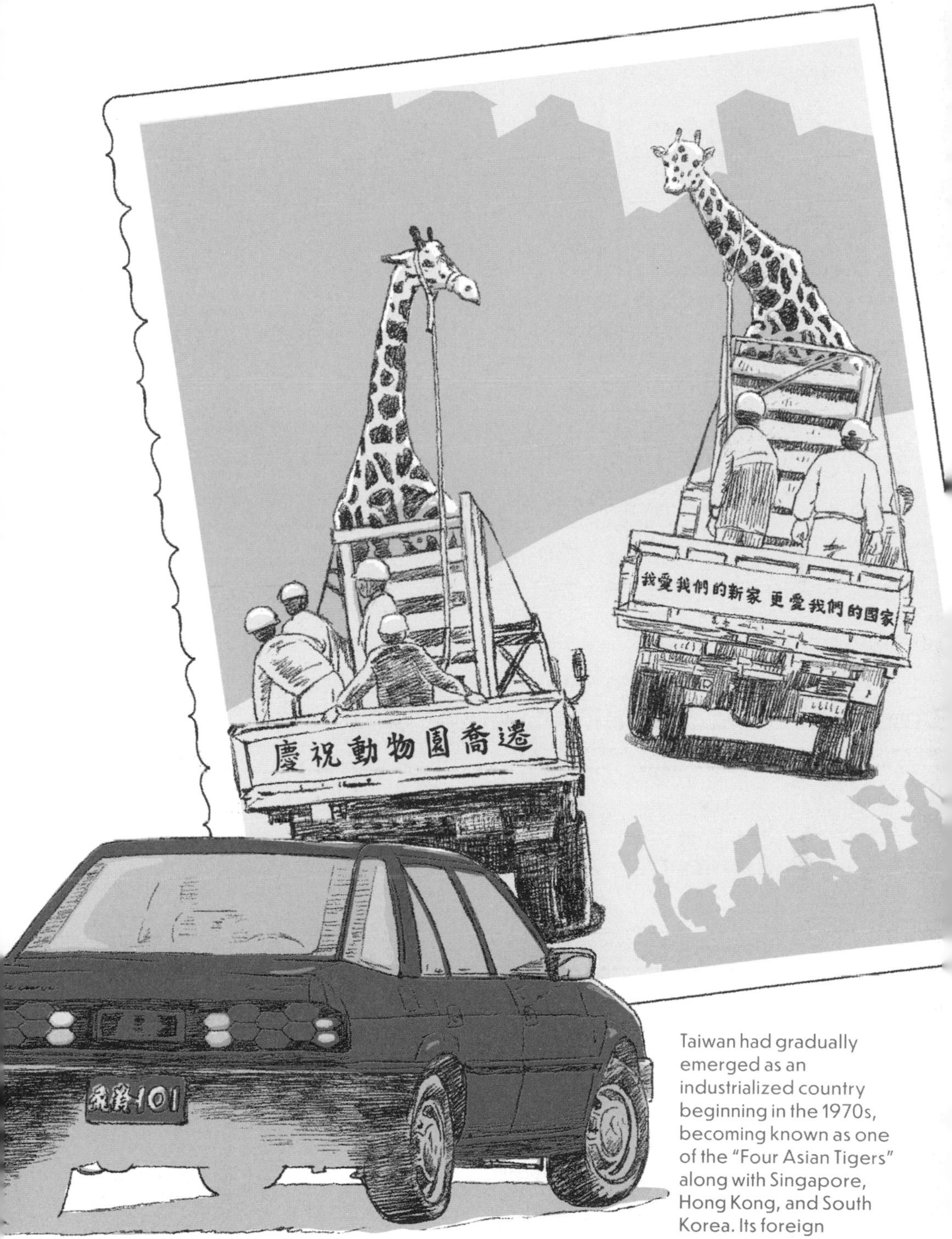
慶祝動物園喬遷
我愛我們的新家 更愛我們的國家
101

Taiwan had gradually emerged as an industrialized country beginning in the 1970s, becoming known as one of the "Four Asian Tigers" along with Singapore, Hong Kong, and South Korea. Its foreign exchange reserves soared, and it produced its first domestically made car, named the Feeling 101, in 1986.

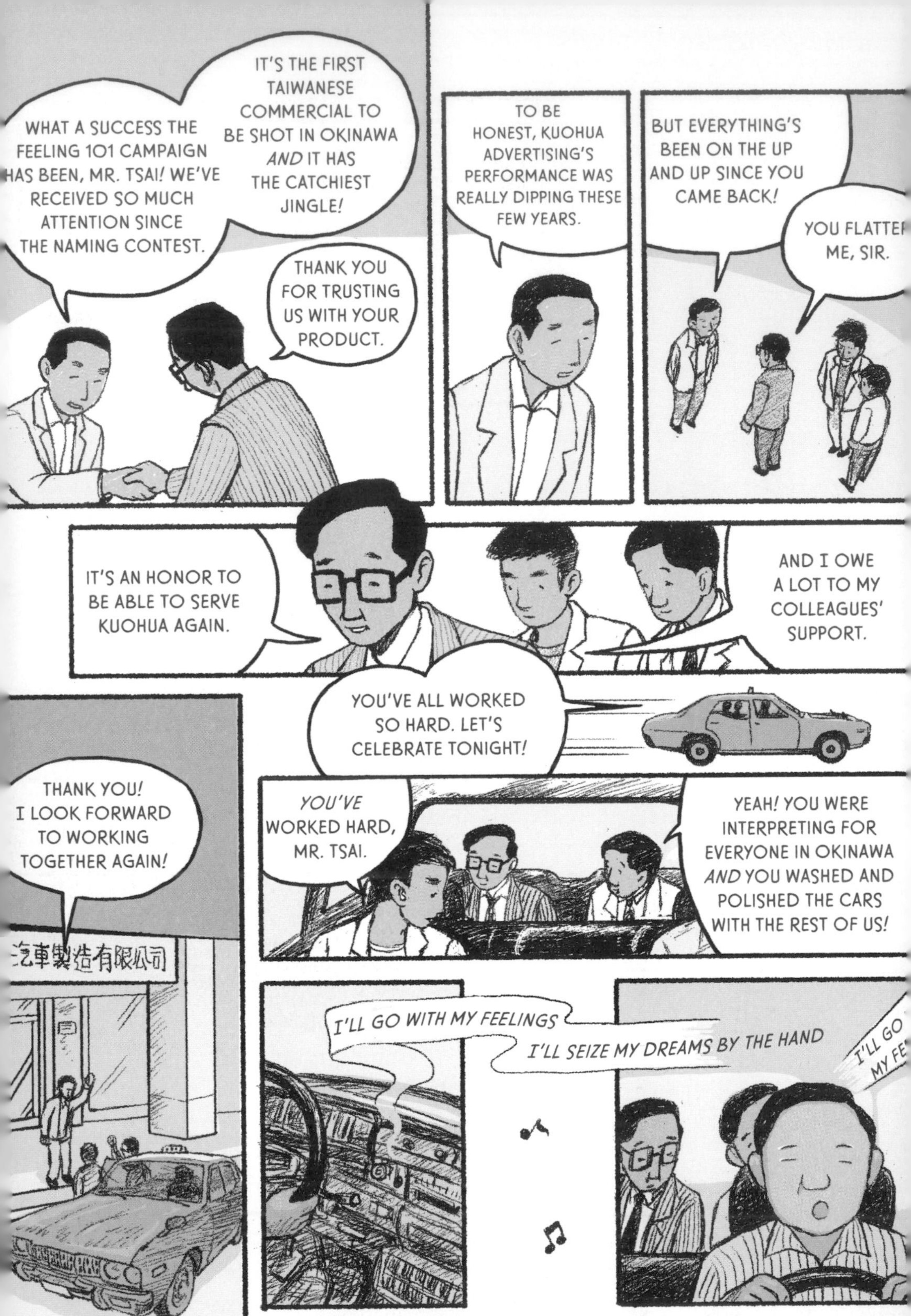
WHAT A SUCCESS THE FEELING 101 CAMPAIGN HAS BEEN, MR. TSAI! WE'VE RECEIVED SO MUCH ATTENTION SINCE THE NAMING CONTEST.
IT'S THE FIRST TAIWANESE COMMERCIAL TO BE SHOT IN OKINAWA *AND* IT HAS THE CATCHIEST JINGLE!
THANK YOU FOR TRUSTING US WITH YOUR PRODUCT.
TO BE HONEST, KUOHUA ADVERTISING'S PERFORMANCE WAS REALLY DIPPING THESE FEW YEARS.
BUT EVERYTHING'S BEEN ON THE UP AND UP SINCE YOU CAME BACK!
YOU FLATTER ME, SIR.
IT'S AN HONOR TO BE ABLE TO SERVE KUOHUA AGAIN.
AND I OWE A LOT TO MY COLLEAGUES' SUPPORT.
THANK YOU! I LOOK FORWARD TO WORKING TOGETHER AGAIN!
汽車製造有限公司
YOU'VE ALL WORKED SO HARD. LET'S CELEBRATE TONIGHT!
YOU'VE WORKED HARD, MR. TSAI.
YEAH! YOU WERE INTERPRETING FOR EVERYONE IN OKINAWA *AND* YOU WASHED AND POLISHED THE CARS WITH THE REST OF US!
I'LL GO WITH MY FEELINGS
I'LL SEIZE MY DREAMS BY THE HAND

"Follow Your Feelings," music by Chen Chi-yuan, lyrics by Che
Chia-li, performed by Su Ping.

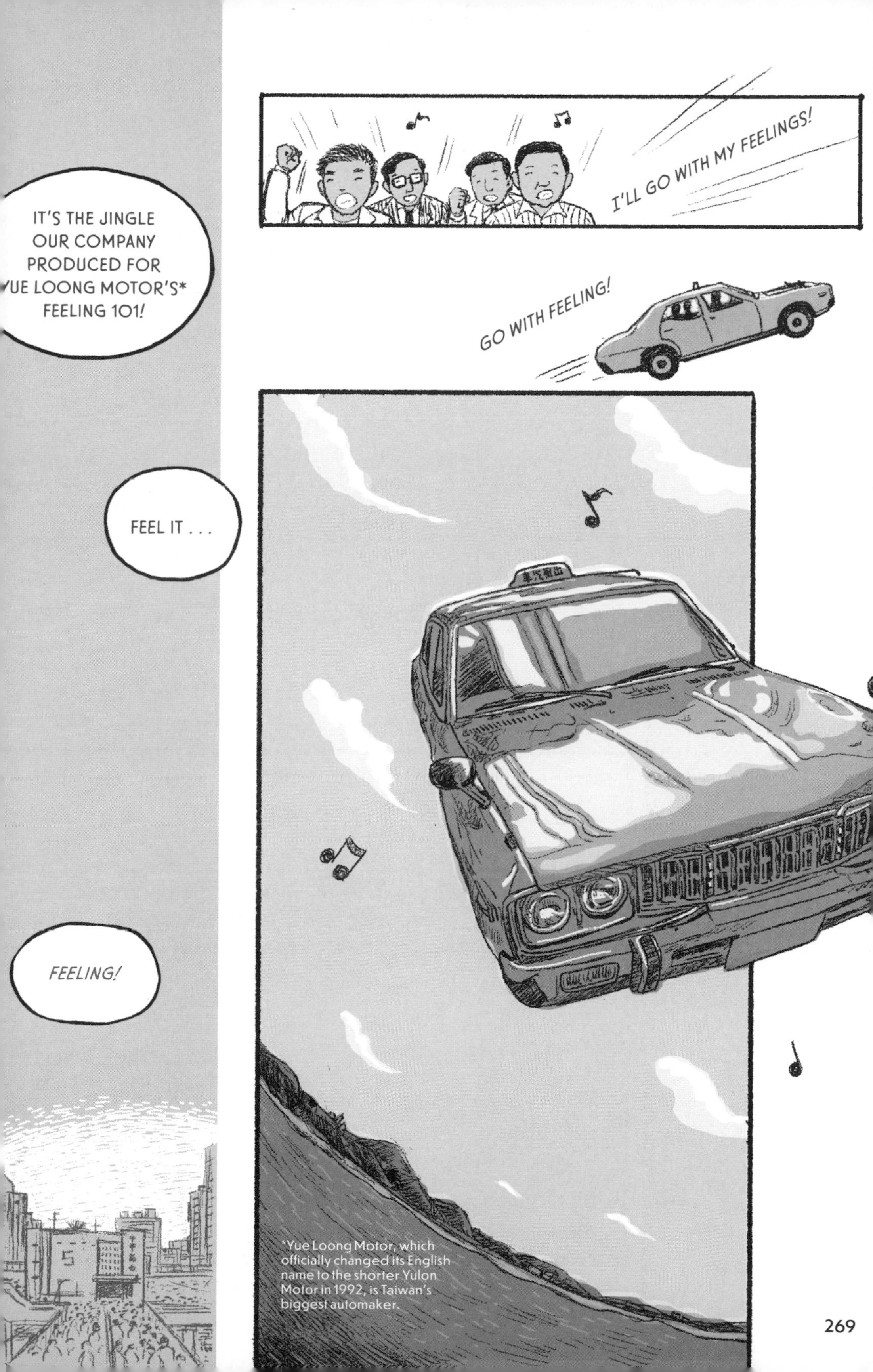
I'LL GO WITH MY FEELINGS!
IT'S THE JINGLE OUR COMPANY PRODUCED FOR UE LOONG MOTOR'S* FEELING 101!
GO WITH FEELING!
FEEL IT . . .
FEELING!

*Yue Loong Motor, which officially changed its English name to the shorter Yulon Motor in 1992, is Taiwan's biggest automaker.

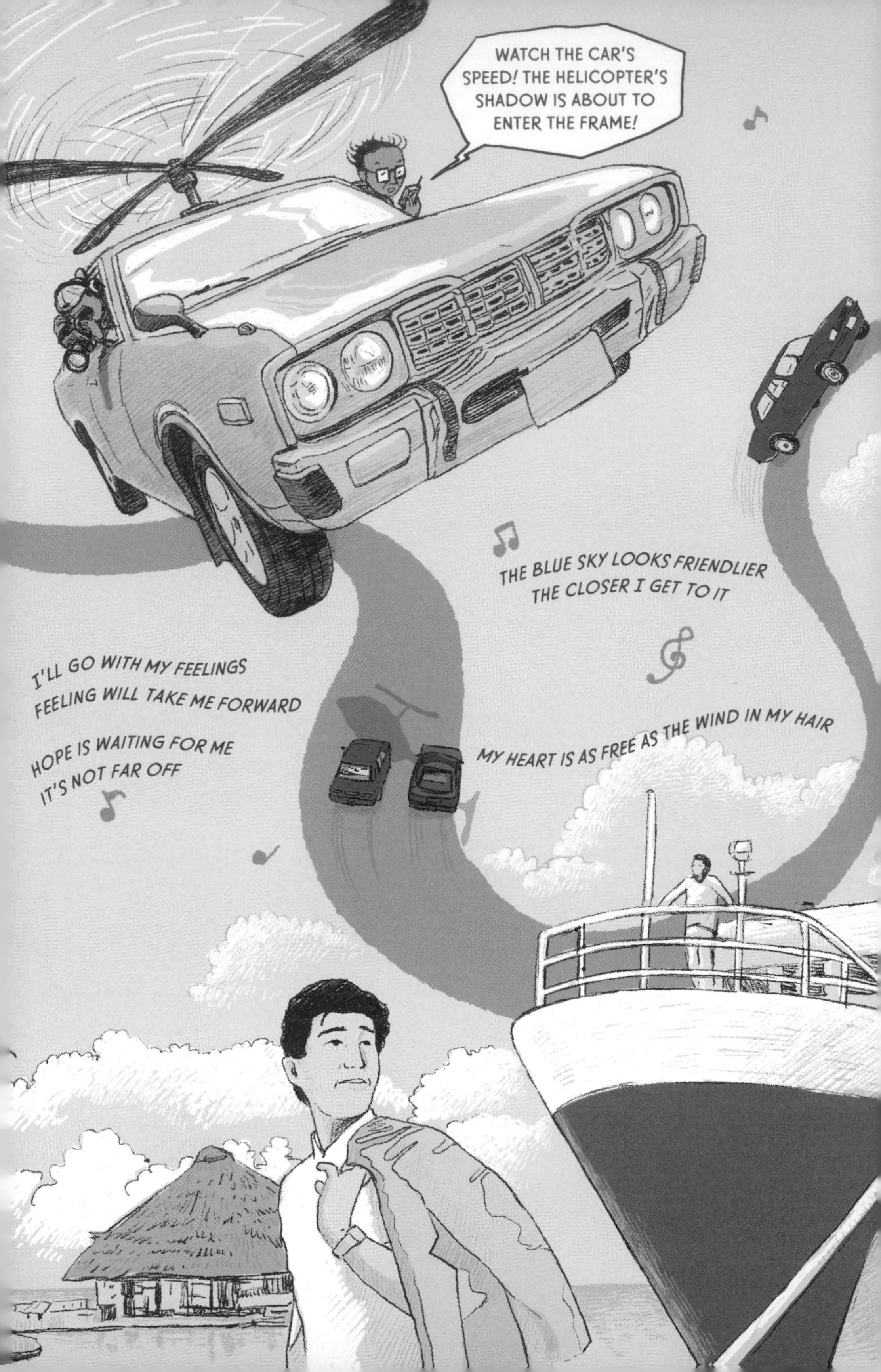
WATCH THE CAR'S SPEED! THE HELICOPTER'S SHADOW IS ABOUT TO ENTER THE FRAME!
THE BLUE SKY LOOKS FRIENDLIER THE CLOSER I GET TO IT
I'LL GO WITH MY FEELINGS FEELING WILL TAKE ME FORWARD
MY HEART IS AS FREE AS THE WIND IN MY HAIR
HOPE IS WAITING FOR ME IT'S NOT FAR OFF

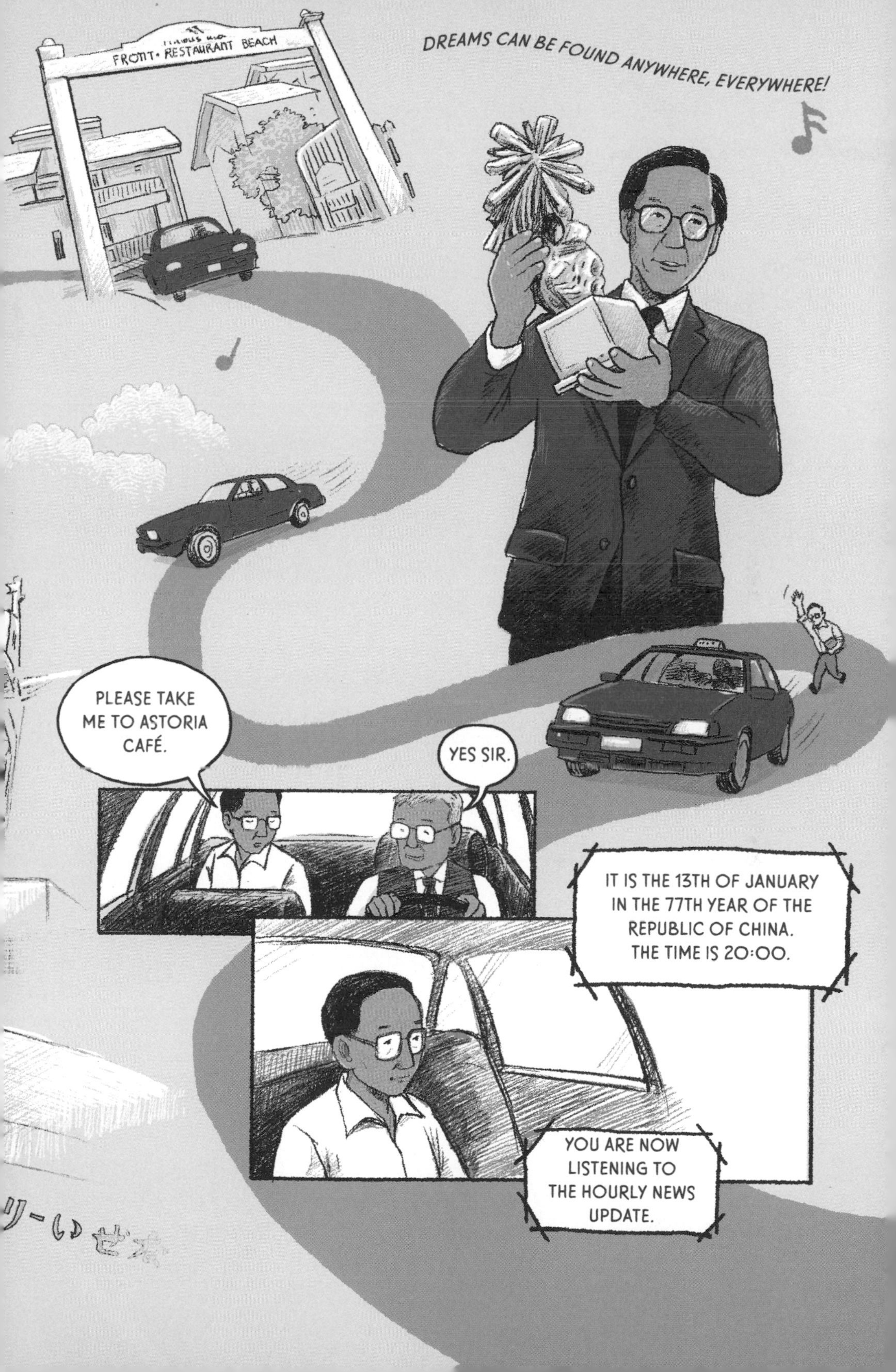

FRONT • RESTAURANT BEACH
DREAMS CAN BE FOUND ANYWHERE, EVERYWHERE!
PLEASE TAKE ME TO ASTORIA CAFÉ.
YES SIR.
IT IS THE 13TH OF JANUARY IN THE 77TH YEAR OF THE REPUBLIC OF CHINA. THE TIME IS 20:00.
YOU ARE NOW LISTENING TO THE HOURLY NEWS UPDATE.

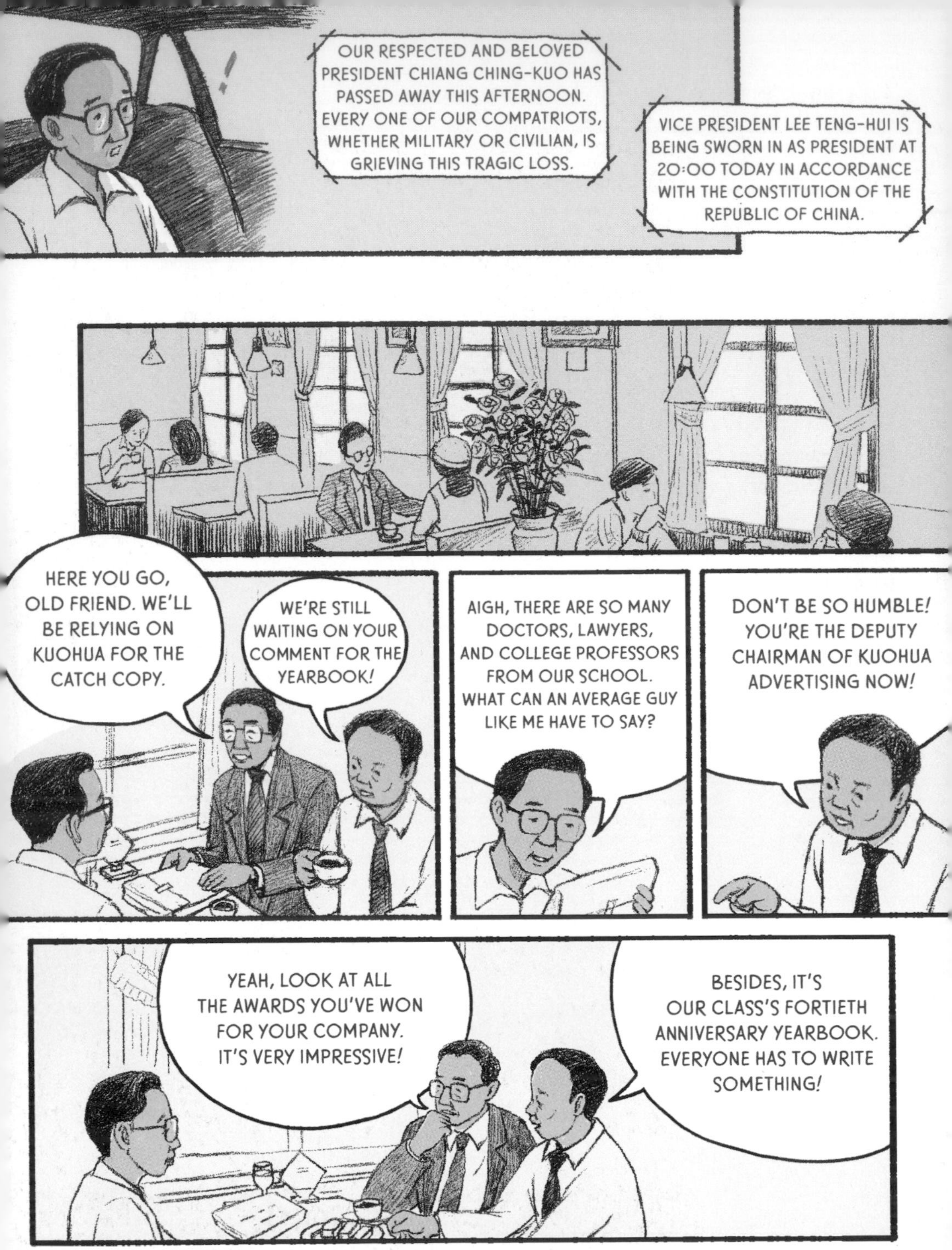

!
OUR RESPECTED AND BELOVED PRESIDENT CHIANG CHING-KUO HAS PASSED AWAY THIS AFTERNOON. EVERY ONE OF OUR COMPATRIOTS, WHETHER MILITARY OR CIVILIAN, IS GRIEVING THIS TRAGIC LOSS.
VICE PRESIDENT LEE TENG-HUI IS BEING SWORN IN AS PRESIDENT AT 20:00 TODAY IN ACCORDANCE WITH THE CONSTITUTION OF THE REPUBLIC OF CHINA.
HERE YOU GO, OLD FRIEND. WE'LL BE RELYING ON KUOHUA FOR THE CATCH COPY.
WE'RE STILL WAITING ON YOUR COMMENT FOR THE YEARBOOK!
AIGH, THERE ARE SO MANY DOCTORS, LAWYERS, AND COLLEGE PROFESSORS FROM OUR SCHOOL. WHAT CAN AN AVERAGE GUY LIKE ME HAVE TO SAY?
DON'T BE SO HUMBLE! YOU'RE THE DEPUTY CHAIRMAN OF KUOHUA ADVERTISING NOW!
YEAH, LOOK AT ALL THE AWARDS YOU'VE WON FOR YOUR COMPANY. IT'S VERY IMPRESSIVE!
BESIDES, IT'S OUR CLASS'S FORTIETH ANNIVERSARY YEARBOOK. EVERYONE HAS TO WRITE SOMETHING!

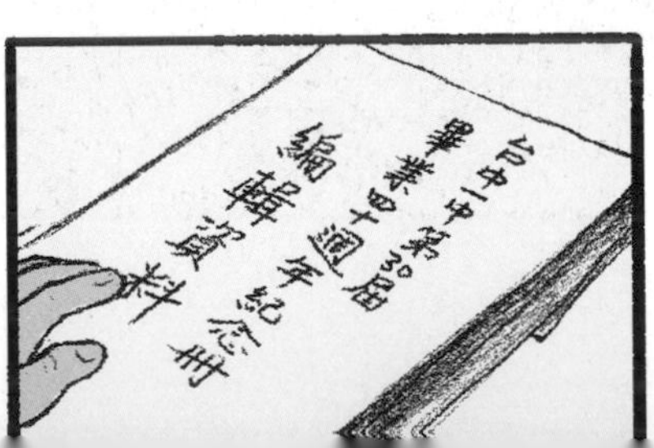

台中一中第30屆
畢業四十週年紀念冊
編輯資料

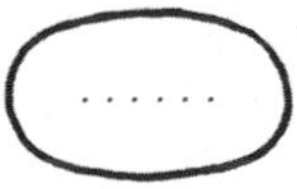

......

Front of envelope: Taichung First High School 30th Graduating Class
40th Graduation Anniversary Yearbook Materials

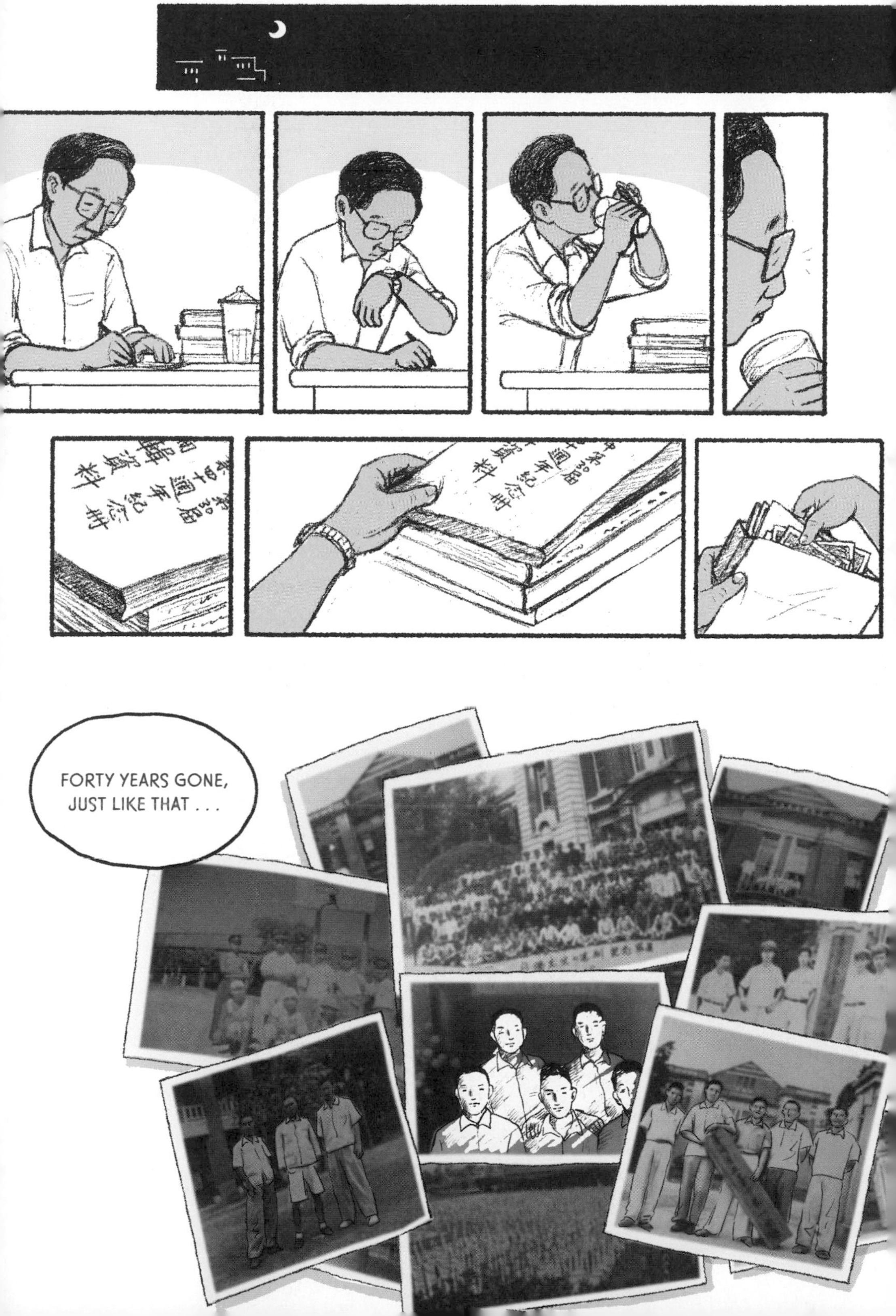
FORTY YEARS GONE, JUST LIKE THAT . . .

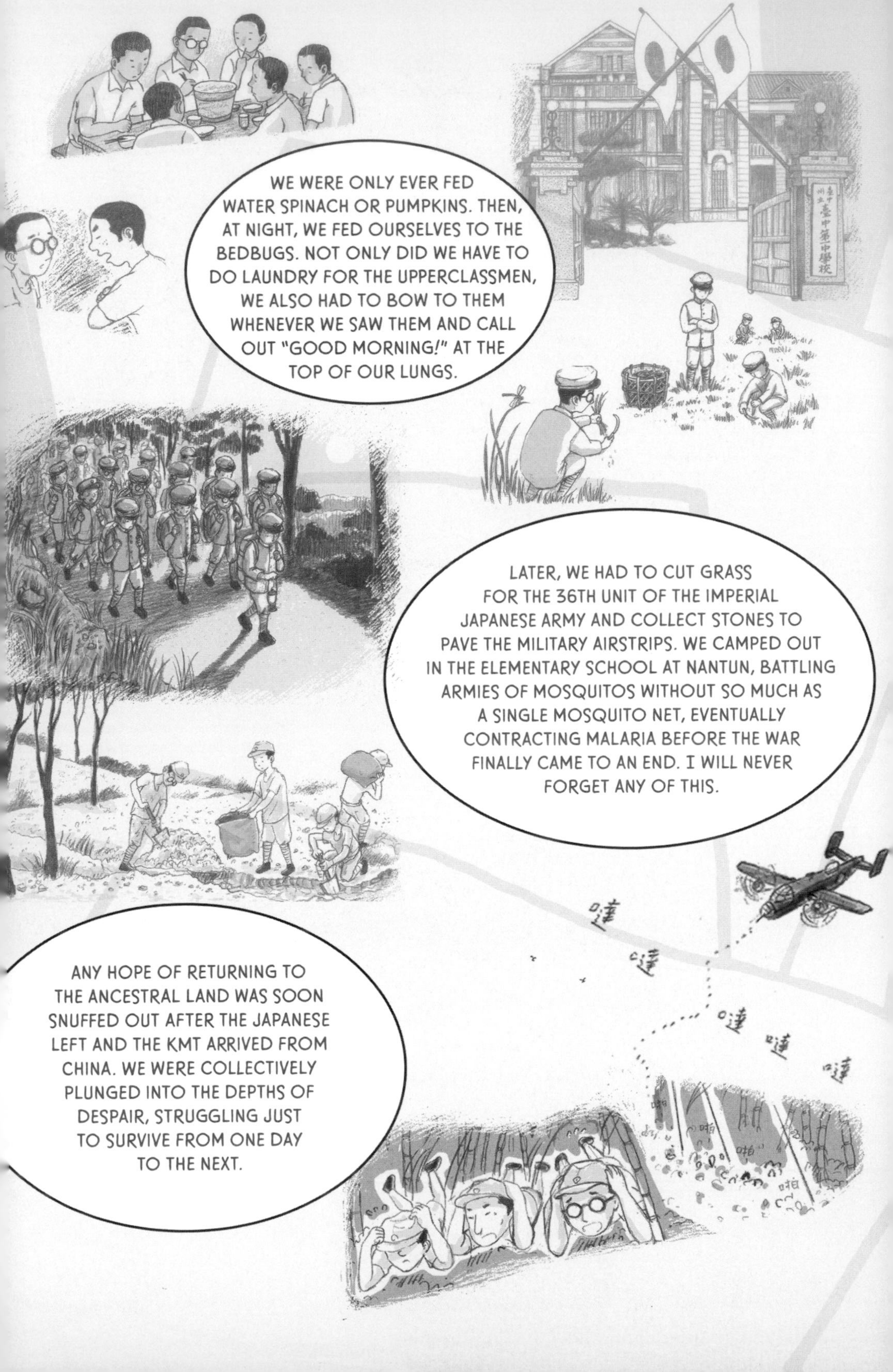
臺中州立臺中第一中學校
WE WERE ONLY EVER FED WATER SPINACH OR PUMPKINS. THEN, AT NIGHT, WE FED OURSELVES TO THE BEDBUGS. NOT ONLY DID WE HAVE TO DO LAUNDRY FOR THE UPPERCLASSMEN, WE ALSO HAD TO BOW TO THEM WHENEVER WE SAW THEM AND CALL OUT "GOOD MORNING!" AT THE TOP OF OUR LUNGS.
LATER, WE HAD TO CUT GRASS FOR THE 36TH UNIT OF THE IMPERIAL JAPANESE ARMY AND COLLECT STONES TO PAVE THE MILITARY AIRSTRIPS. WE CAMPED OUT IN THE ELEMENTARY SCHOOL AT NANTUN, BATTLING ARMIES OF MOSQUITOS WITHOUT SO MUCH AS A SINGLE MOSQUITO NET, EVENTUALLY CONTRACTING MALARIA BEFORE THE WAR FINALLY CAME TO AN END. I WILL NEVER FORGET ANY OF THIS.
噠
噠
噠
噠
噠
ANY HOPE OF RETURNING TO THE ANCESTRAL LAND WAS SOON SNUFFED OUT AFTER THE JAPANESE LEFT AND THE KMT ARRIVED FROM CHINA. WE WERE COLLECTIVELY PLUNGED INTO THE DEPTHS OF DESPAIR, STRUGGLING JUST TO SURVIVE FROM ONE DAY TO THE NEXT.
啪
啪
啪
啪

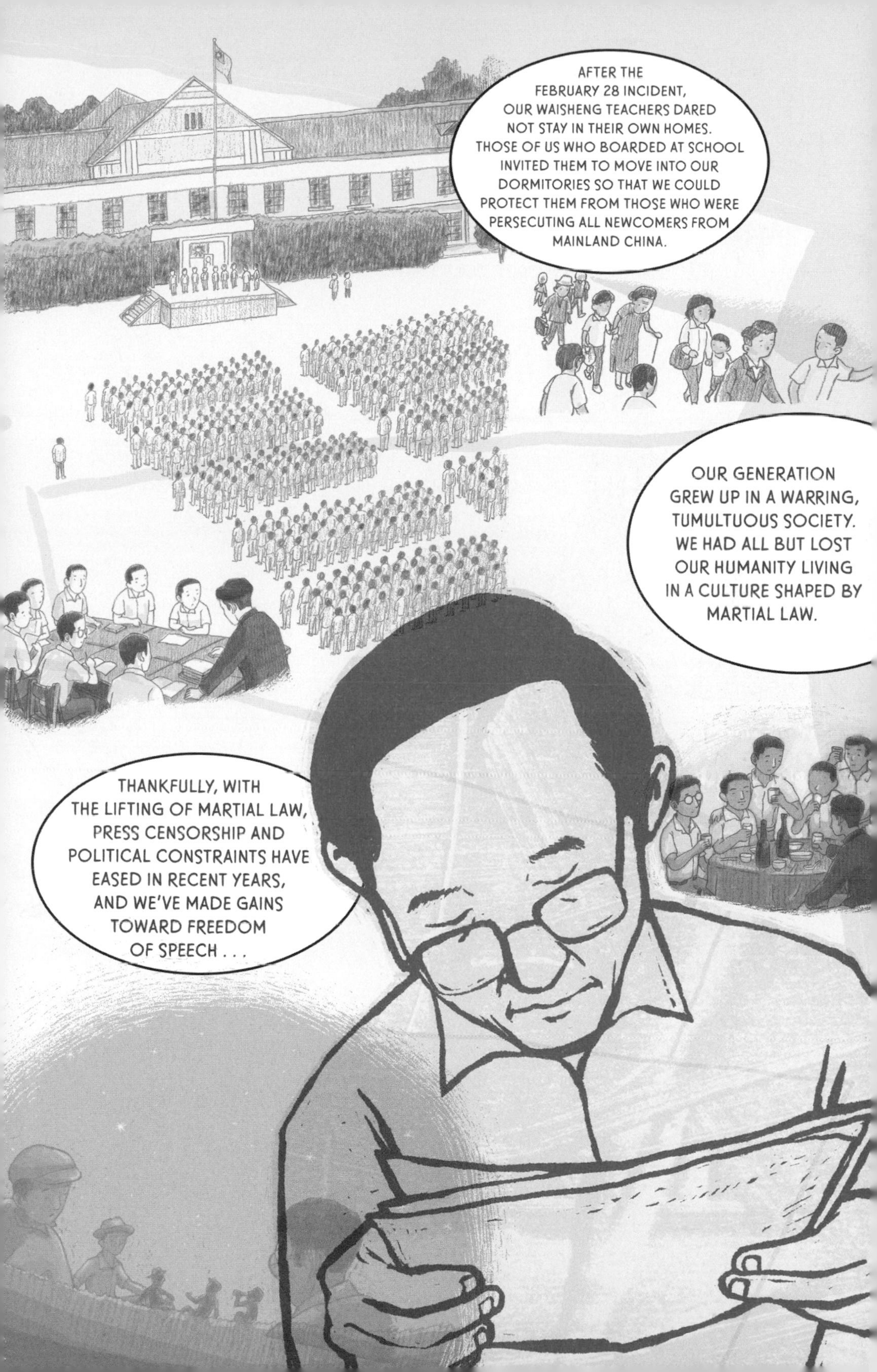
AFTER THE FEBRUARY 28 INCIDENT, OUR WAISHENG TEACHERS DARED NOT STAY IN THEIR OWN HOMES. THOSE OF US WHO BOARDED AT SCHOOL INVITED THEM TO MOVE INTO OUR DORMITORIES SO THAT WE COULD PROTECT THEM FROM THOSE WHO WERE PERSECUTING ALL NEWCOMERS FROM MAINLAND CHINA.
OUR GENERATION GREW UP IN A WARRING, TUMULTUOUS SOCIETY. WE HAD ALL BUT LOST OUR HUMANITY LIVING IN A CULTURE SHAPED BY MARTIAL LAW.
THANKFULLY, WITH THE LIFTING OF MARTIAL LAW, PRESS CENSORSHIP AND POLITICAL CONSTRAINTS HAVE EASED IN RECENT YEARS, AND WE'VE MADE GAINS TOWARD FREEDOM OF SPEECH . . .

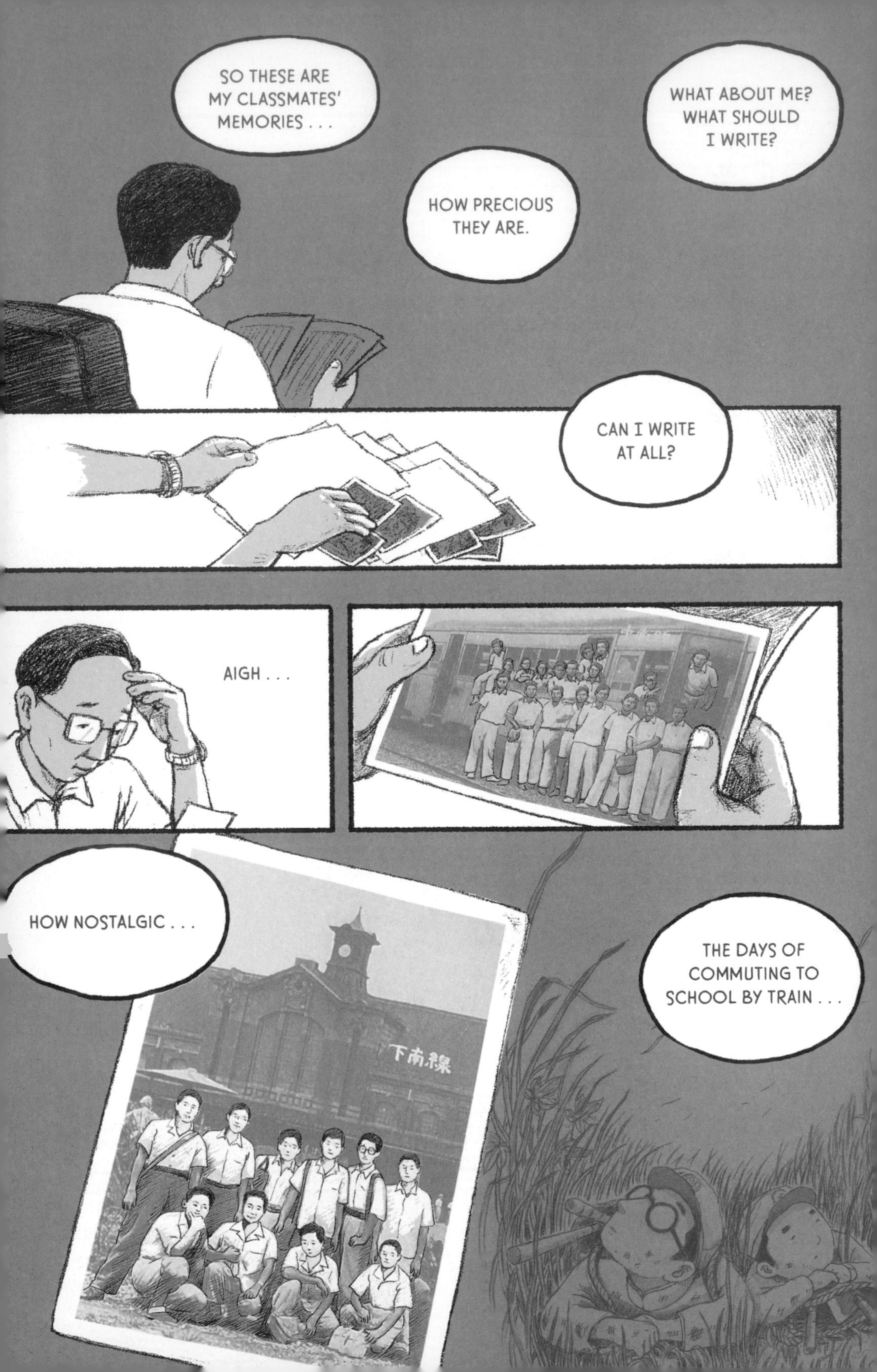
SO THESE ARE MY CLASSMATES' MEMORIES . . .
HOW PRECIOUS THEY ARE.
WHAT ABOUT ME? WHAT SHOULD I WRITE?
CAN I WRITE AT ALL?
AIGH . . .
HOW NOSTALGIC . . .
THE DAYS OF COMMUTING TO SCHOOL BY TRAIN . . .

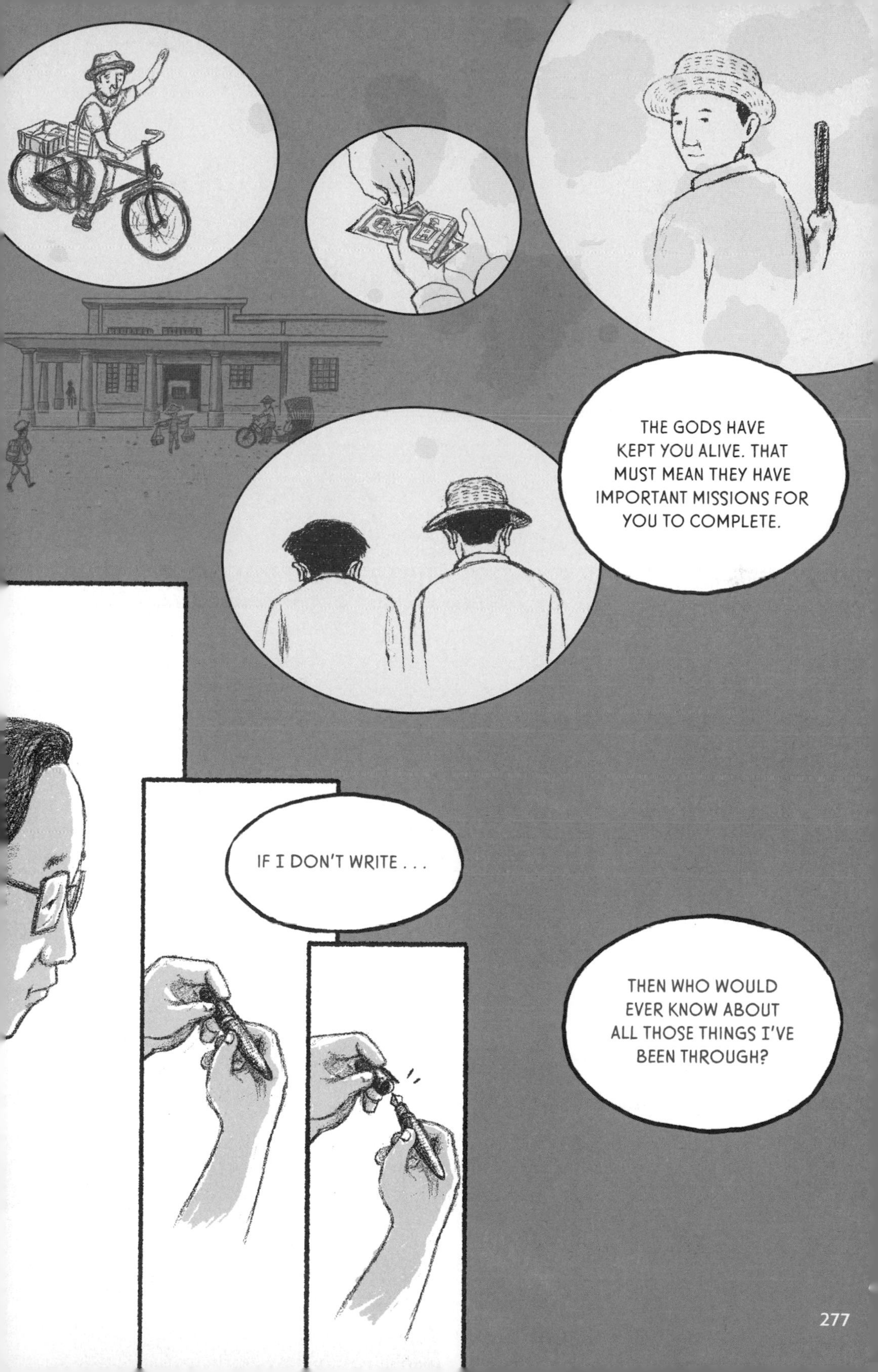
THE GODS HAVE KEPT YOU ALIVE. THAT MUST MEAN THEY HAVE IMPORTANT MISSIONS FOR YOU TO COMPLETE.
IF I DON'T WRITE . . .
THEN WHO WOULD EVER KNOW ABOUT ALL THOSE THINGS I'VE BEEN THROUGH?

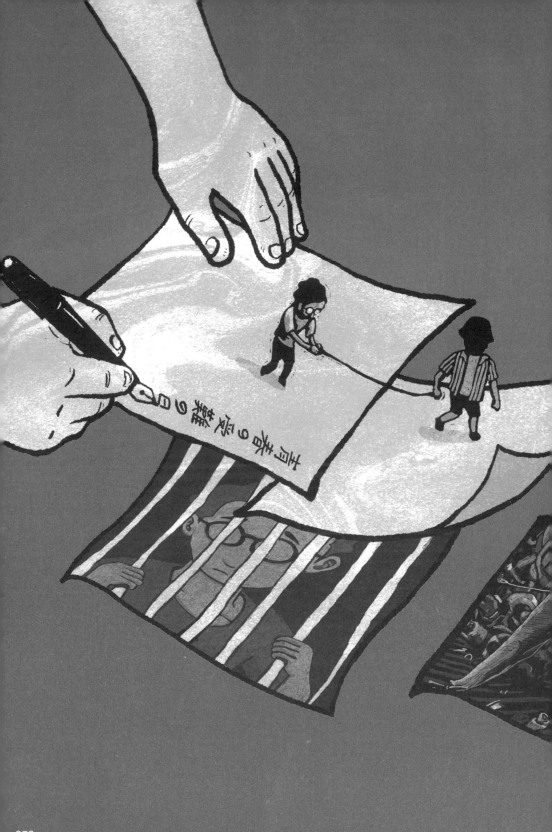

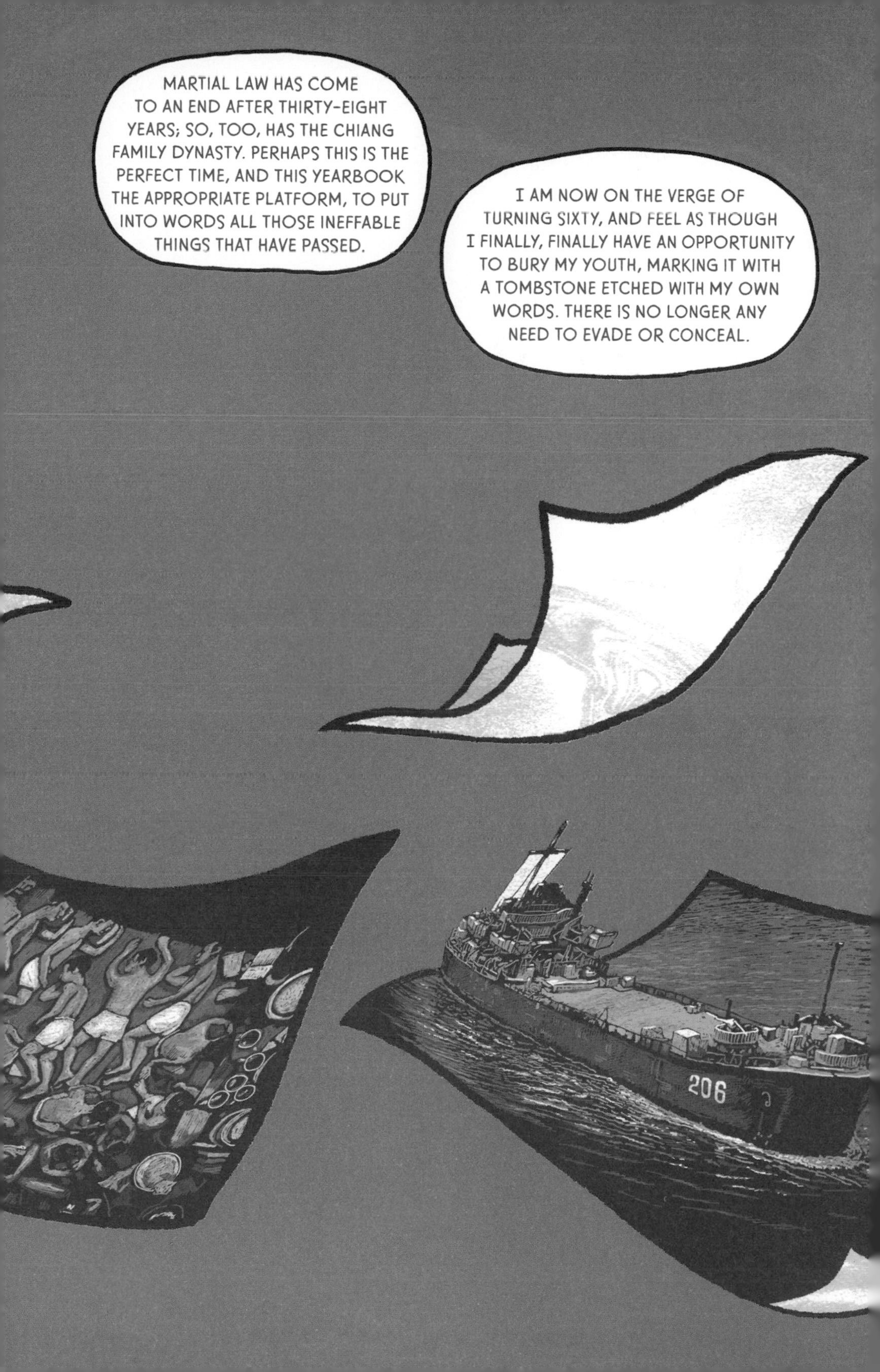
MARTIAL LAW HAS COME TO AN END AFTER THIRTY-EIGHT YEARS; SO, TOO, HAS THE CHIANG FAMILY DYNASTY. PERHAPS THIS IS THE PERFECT TIME, AND THIS YEARBOOK THE APPROPRIATE PLATFORM, TO PUT INTO WORDS ALL THOSE INEFFABLE THINGS THAT HAVE PASSED.
I AM NOW ON THE VERGE OF TURNING SIXTY, AND FEEL AS THOUGH I FINALLY, FINALLY HAVE AN OPPORTUNITY TO BURY MY YOUTH, MARKING IT WITH A TOMBSTONE ETCHED WITH MY OWN WORDS. THERE IS NO LONGER ANY NEED TO EVADE OR CONCEAL.
206

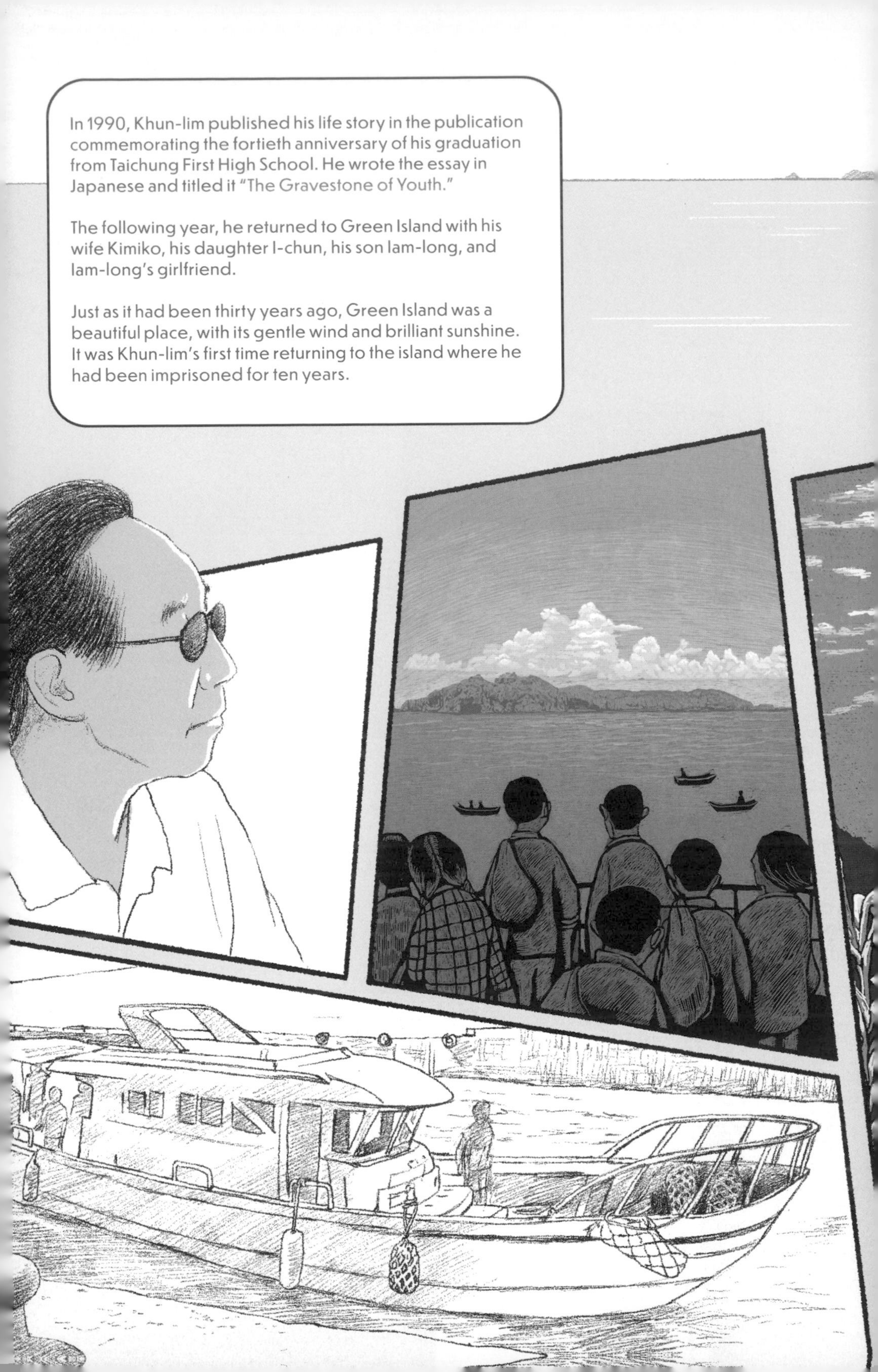
In 1990, Khun-lim published his life story in the publication commemorating the fortieth anniversary of his graduation from Taichung First High School. He wrote the essay in Japanese and titled it "The Gravestone of Youth."
The following year, he returned to Green Island with his wife Kimiko, his daughter I-chun, his son Iam-long, and Iam-long's girlfriend.
Just as it had been thirty years ago, Green Island was a beautiful place, with its gentle wind and brilliant sunshine. It was Khun-lim's first time returning to the island where he had been imprisoned for ten years.

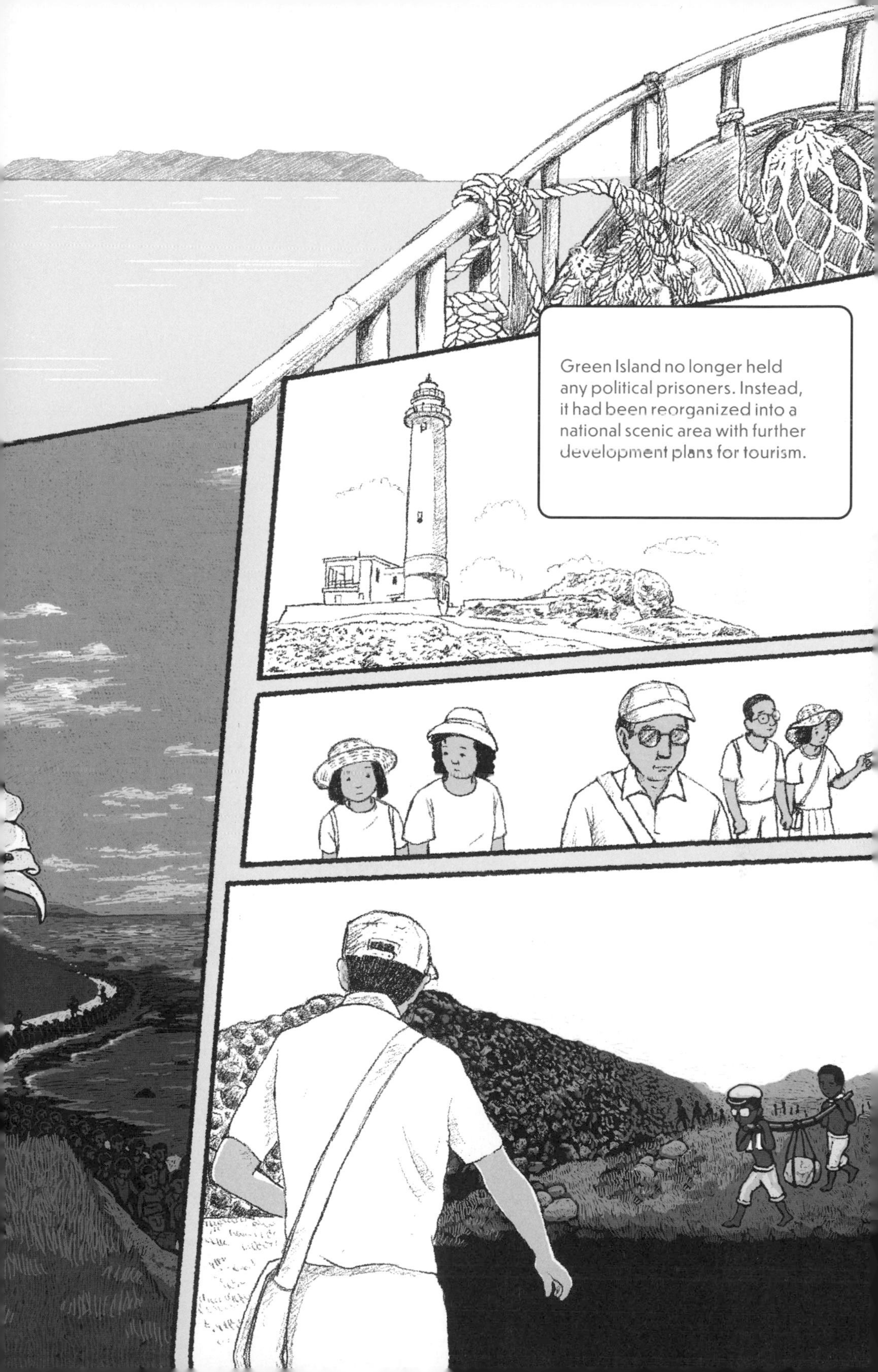
Green Island no longer held any political prisoners. Instead, it had been reorganized into a national scenic area with further development plans for tourism.

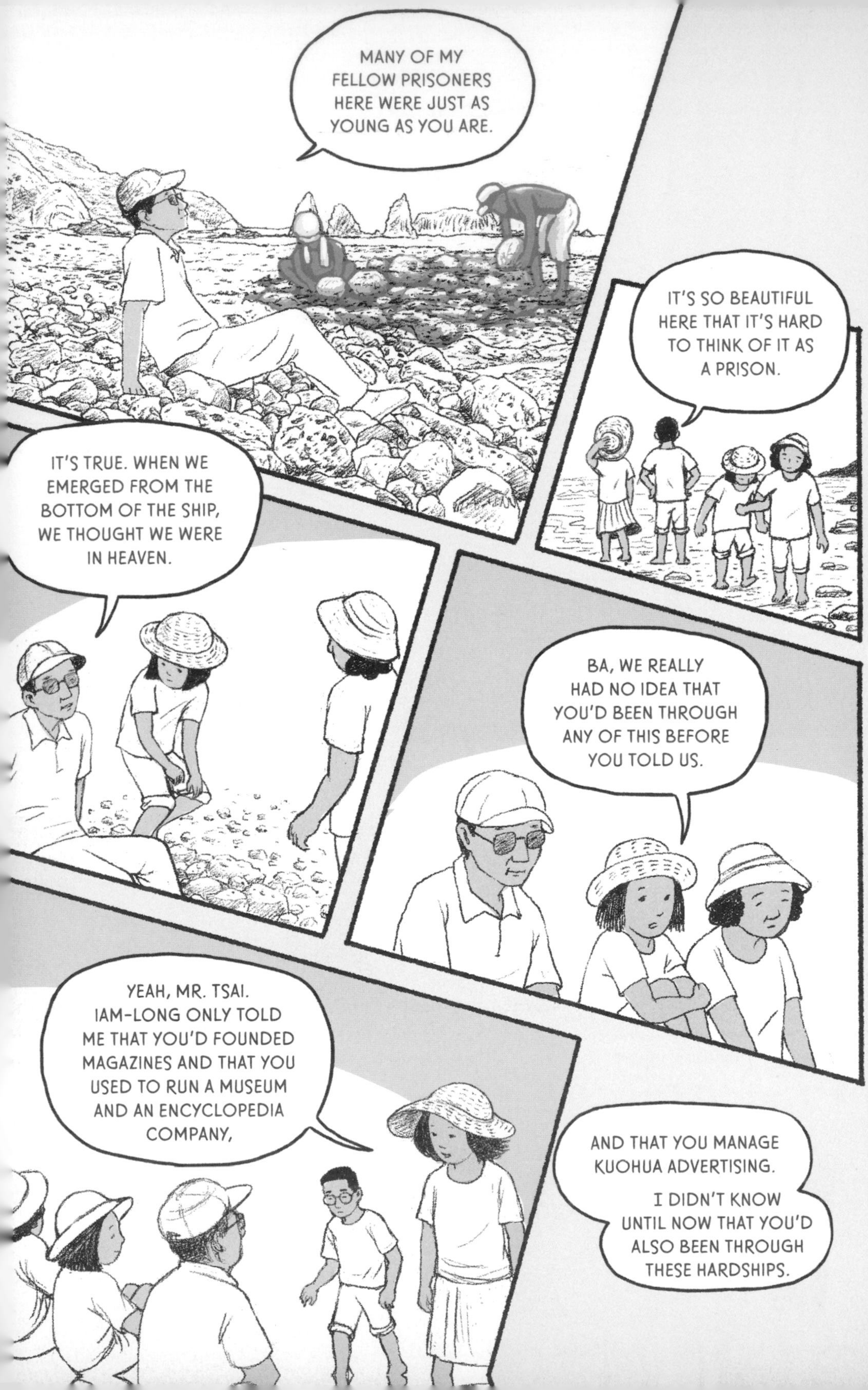
MANY OF MY FELLOW PRISONERS HERE WERE JUST AS YOUNG AS YOU ARE.
IT'S SO BEAUTIFUL HERE THAT IT'S HARD TO THINK OF IT AS A PRISON.
IT'S TRUE. WHEN WE EMERGED FROM THE BOTTOM OF THE SHIP, WE THOUGHT WE WERE IN HEAVEN.
BA, WE REALLY HAD NO IDEA THAT YOU'D BEEN THROUGH ANY OF THIS BEFORE YOU TOLD US.
YEAH, MR. TSAI. IAM-LONG ONLY TOLD ME THAT YOU'D FOUNDED MAGAZINES AND THAT YOU USED TO RUN A MUSEUM AND AN ENCYCLOPEDIA COMPANY,
AND THAT YOU MANAGE KUOHUA ADVERTISING.
I DIDN'T KNOW UNTIL NOW THAT YOU'D ALSO BEEN THROUGH THESE HARDSHIPS.

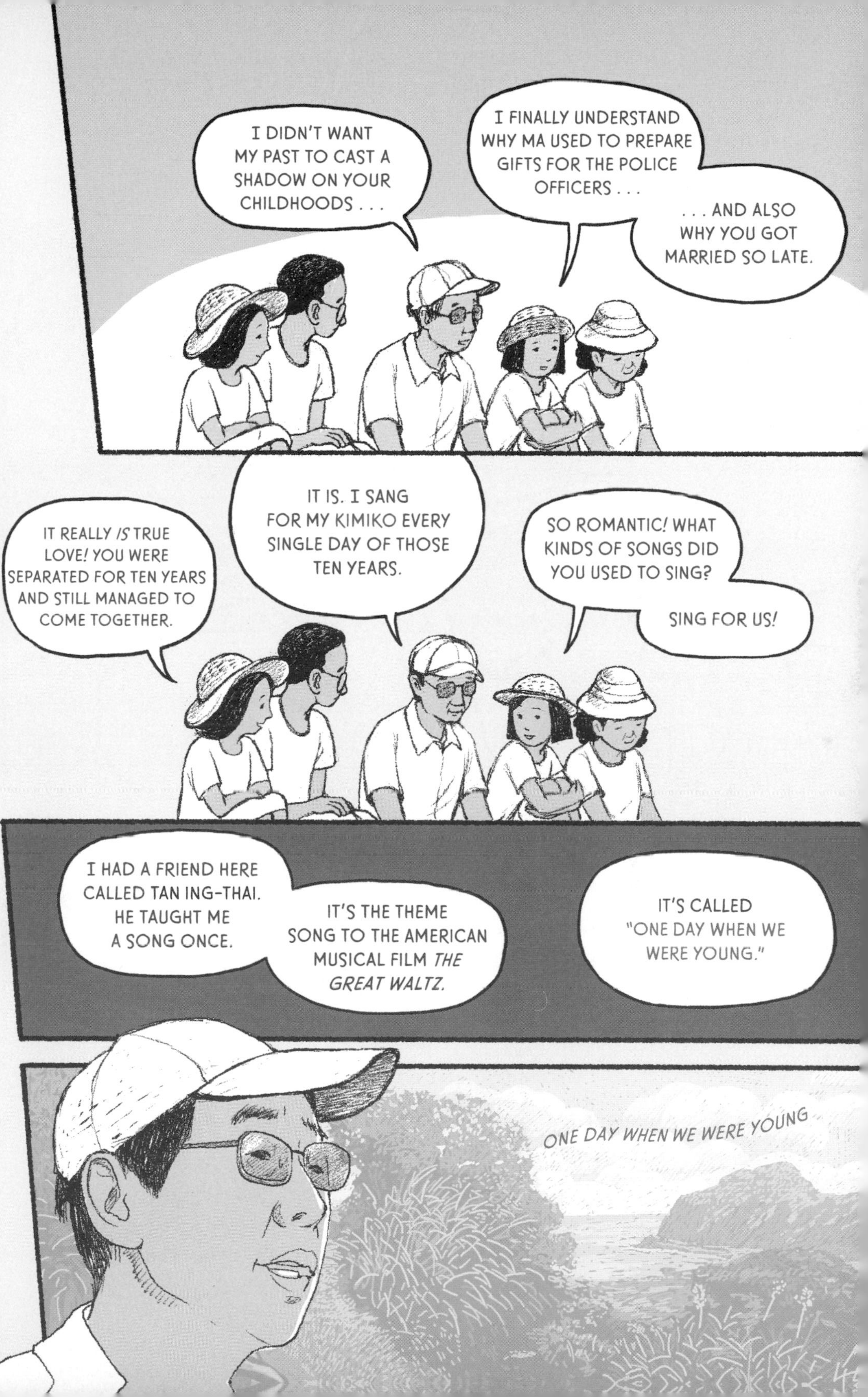
I DIDN'T WANT MY PAST TO CAST A SHADOW ON YOUR CHILDHOODS . . .
I FINALLY UNDERSTAND WHY MA USED TO PREPARE GIFTS FOR THE POLICE OFFICERS . . .
. . . AND ALSO WHY YOU GOT MARRIED SO LATE.
IT REALLY *IS* TRUE LOVE! YOU WERE SEPARATED FOR TEN YEARS AND STILL MANAGED TO COME TOGETHER.
IT IS. I SANG FOR MY KIMIKO EVERY SINGLE DAY OF THOSE TEN YEARS.
SO ROMANTIC! WHAT KINDS OF SONGS DID YOU USED TO SING?
SING FOR US!
I HAD A FRIEND HERE CALLED TAN ING-THAI. HE TAUGHT ME A SONG ONCE.
IT'S THE THEME SONG TO THE AMERICAN MUSICAL FILM *THE GREAT WALTZ.*
IT'S CALLED "ONE DAY WHEN WE WERE YOUNG."
ONE DAY WHEN WE WERE YOUNG

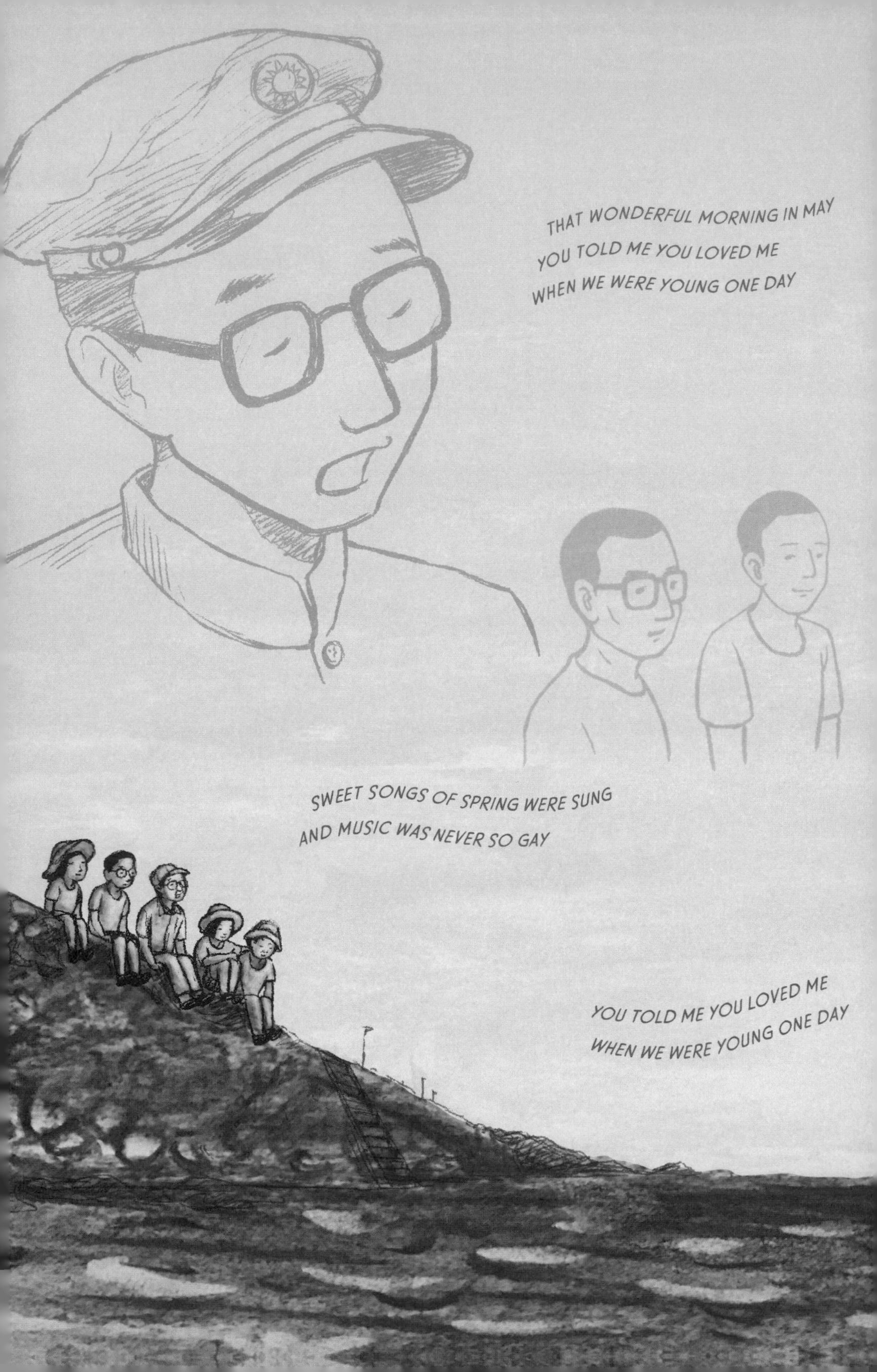
THAT WONDERFUL MORNING IN MAY
YOU TOLD ME YOU LOVED ME
WHEN WE WERE YOUNG ONE DAY
SWEET SONGS OF SPRING WERE SUNG
AND MUSIC WAS NEVER SO GAY
YOU TOLD ME YOU LOVED ME
WHEN WE WERE YOUNG ONE DAY

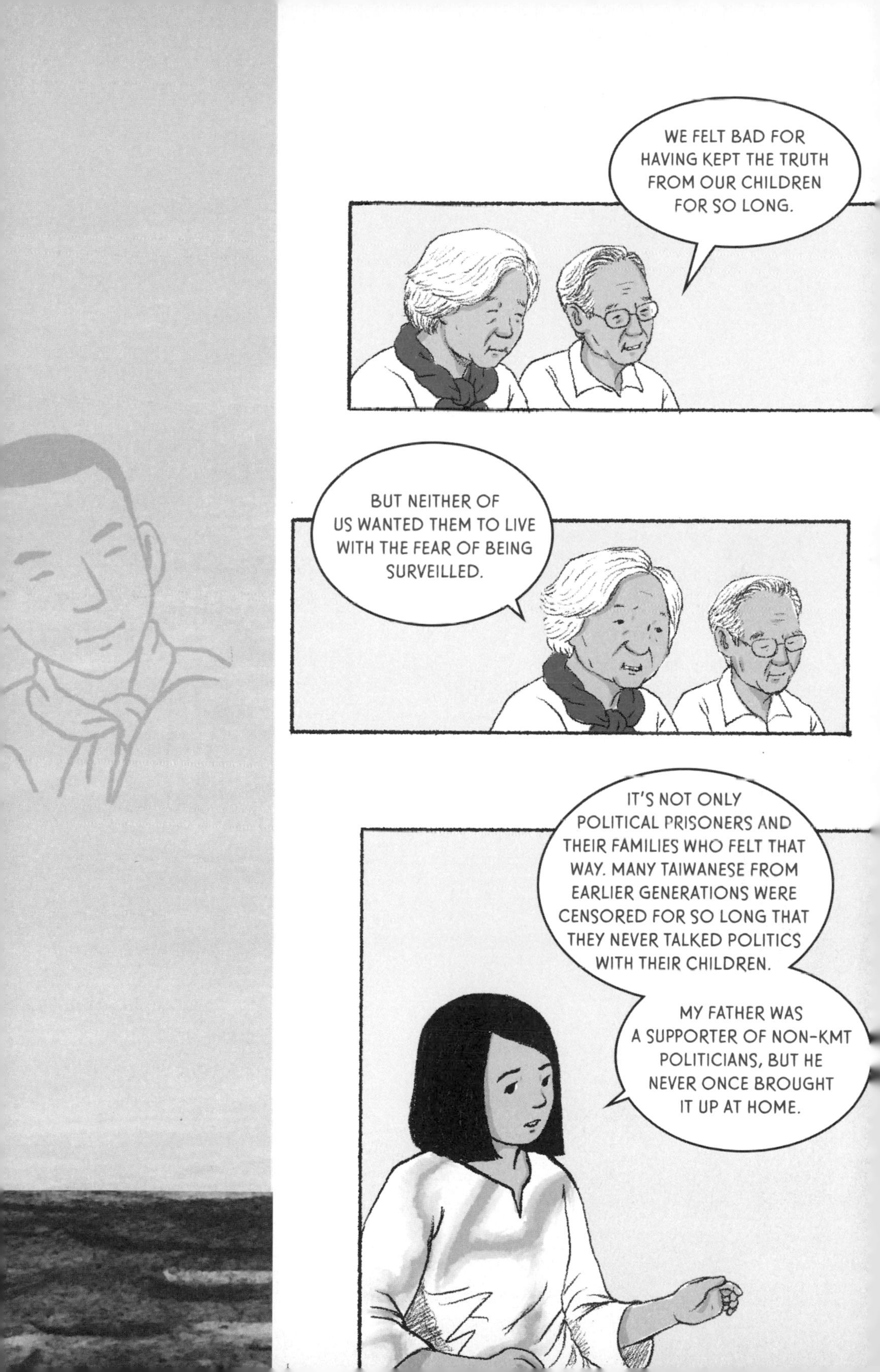
WE FELT BAD FOR HAVING KEPT THE TRUTH FROM OUR CHILDREN FOR SO LONG.
BUT NEITHER OF US WANTED THEM TO LIVE WITH THE FEAR OF BEING SURVEILLED.
IT'S NOT ONLY POLITICAL PRISONERS AND THEIR FAMILIES WHO FELT THAT WAY. MANY TAIWANESE FROM EARLIER GENERATIONS WERE CENSORED FOR SO LONG THAT THEY NEVER TALKED POLITICS WITH THEIR CHILDREN.
MY FATHER WAS A SUPPORTER OF NON-KMT POLITICIANS, BUT HE NEVER ONCE BROUGHT IT UP AT HOME.

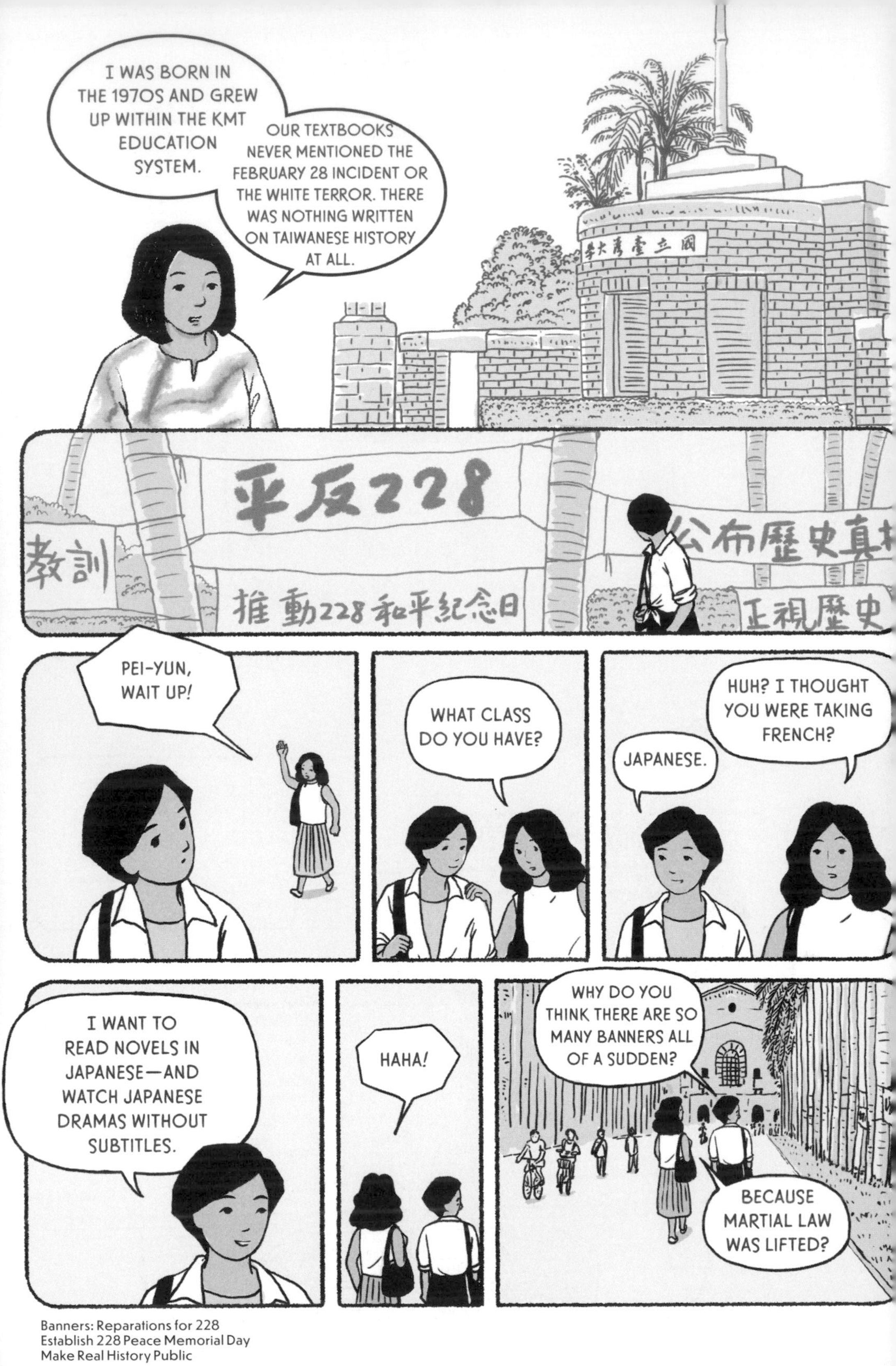
I WAS BORN IN THE 1970S AND GREW UP WITHIN THE KMT EDUCATION SYSTEM.
OUR TEXTBOOKS NEVER MENTIONED THE FEBRUARY 28 INCIDENT OR THE WHITE TERROR. THERE WAS NOTHING WRITTEN ON TAIWANESE HISTORY AT ALL.
國立臺灣大學
平反228
教訓
推動228和平紀念日
公布歷史真相
正視歷史
PEI-YUN, WAIT UP!
WHAT CLASS DO YOU HAVE?
JAPANESE.
HUH? I THOUGHT YOU WERE TAKING FRENCH?
I WANT TO READ NOVELS IN JAPANESE—AND WATCH JAPANESE DRAMAS WITHOUT SUBTITLES.
HAHA!
WHY DO YOU THINK THERE ARE SO MANY BANNERS ALL OF A SUDDEN?
BECAUSE MARTIAL LAW WAS LIFTED?

Banners: Reparations for 228
Establish 228 Peace Memorial Day
Make Real History Public

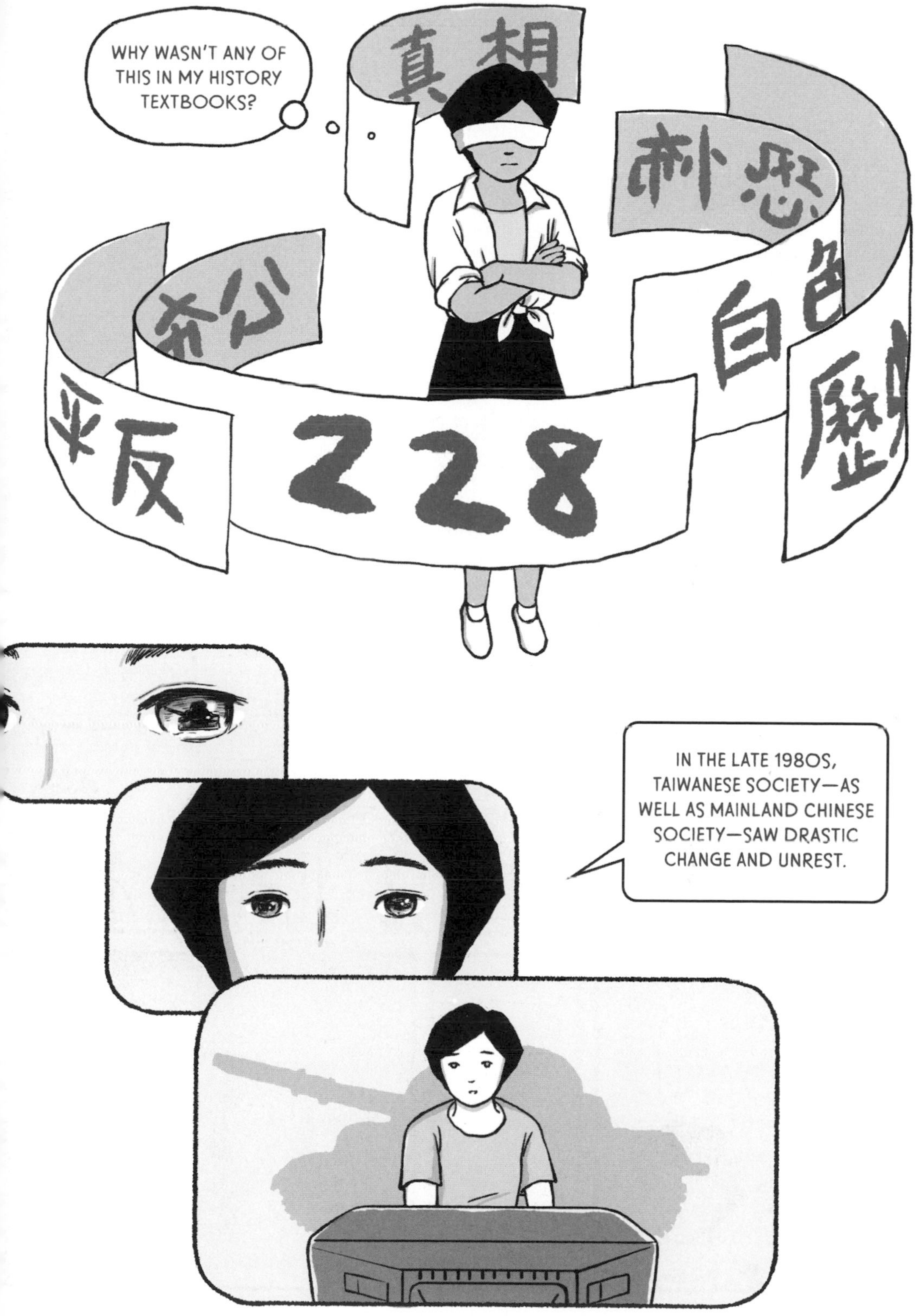
WHY WASN'T ANY OF THIS IN MY HISTORY TEXTBOOKS?
真相
228
IN THE LATE 1980S, TAIWANESE SOCIETY—AS WELL AS MAINLAND CHINESE SOCIETY—SAW DRASTIC CHANGE AND UNREST.

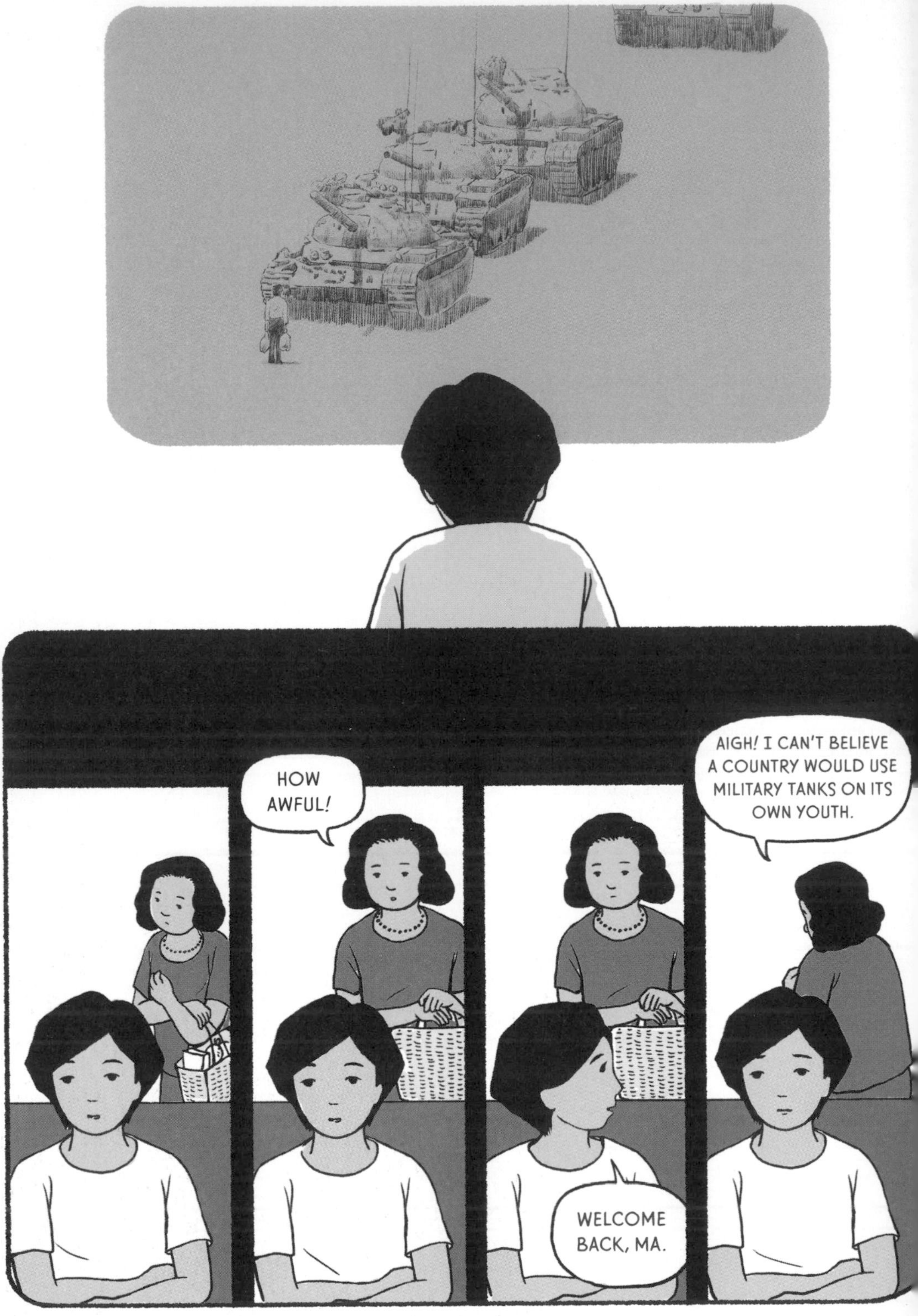
HOW AWFUL!
WELCOME BACK, MA.
AIGH! I CAN'T BELIEVE A COUNTRY WOULD USE MILITARY TANKS ON ITS OWN YOUTH.

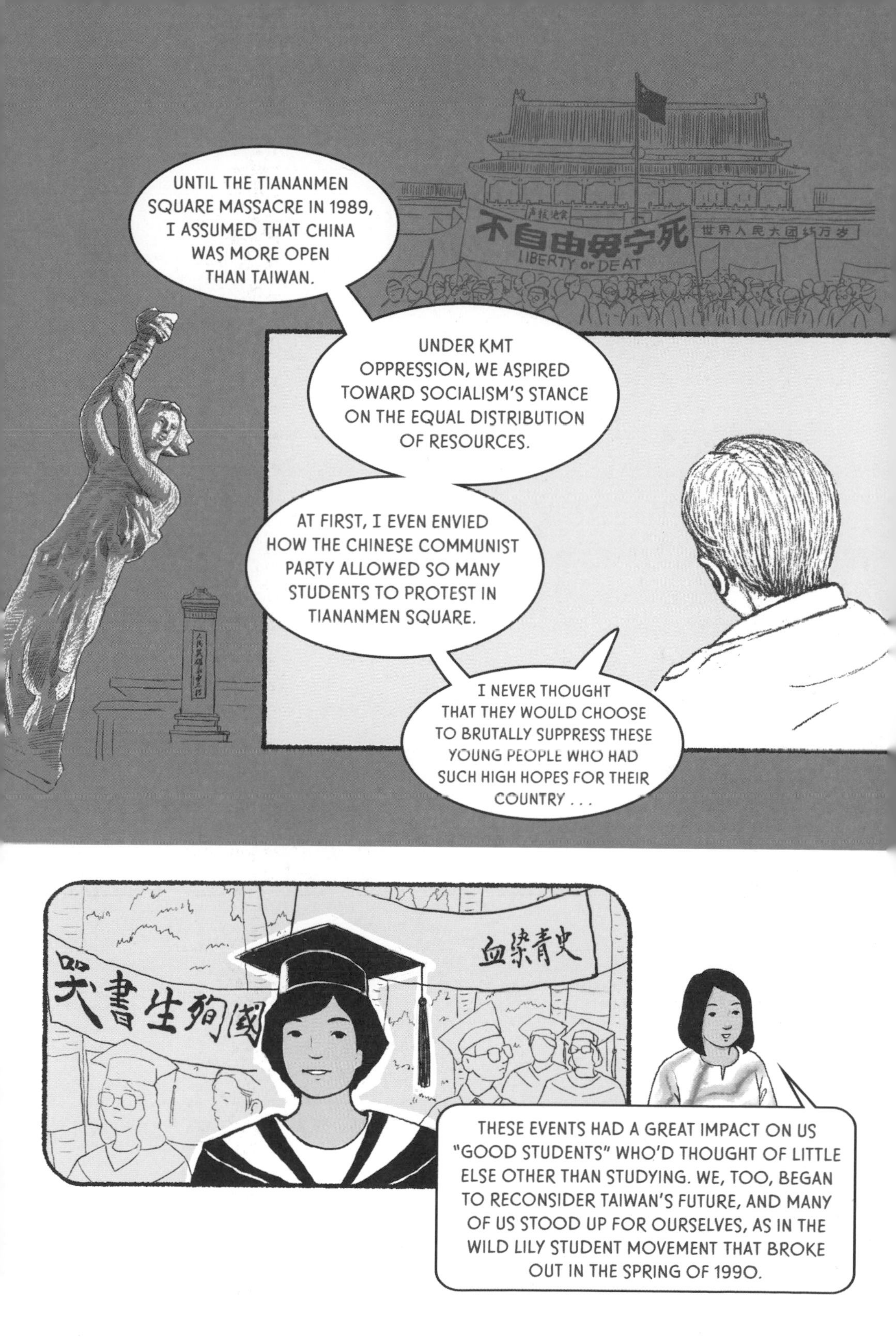
不自由毋宁死
LIBERTY or DEAT
UNTIL THE TIANANMEN SQUARE MASSACRE IN 1989, I ASSUMED THAT CHINA WAS MORE OPEN THAN TAIWAN.
UNDER KMT OPPRESSION, WE ASPIRED TOWARD SOCIALISM'S STANCE ON THE EQUAL DISTRIBUTION OF RESOURCES.
AT FIRST, I EVEN ENVIED HOW THE CHINESE COMMUNIST PARTY ALLOWED SO MANY STUDENTS TO PROTEST IN TIANANMEN SQUARE.
I NEVER THOUGHT THAT THEY WOULD CHOOSE TO BRUTALLY SUPPRESS THESE YOUNG PEOPLE WHO HAD SUCH HIGH HOPES FOR THEIR COUNTRY . . .
哭書生殉國
血染青史
THESE EVENTS HAD A GREAT IMPACT ON US "GOOD STUDENTS" WHO'D THOUGHT OF LITTLE ELSE OTHER THAN STUDYING. WE, TOO, BEGAN TO RECONSIDER TAIWAN'S FUTURE, AND MANY OF US STOOD UP FOR OURSELVES, AS IN THE WILD LILY STUDENT MOVEMENT THAT BROKE OUT IN THE SPRING OF 1990.

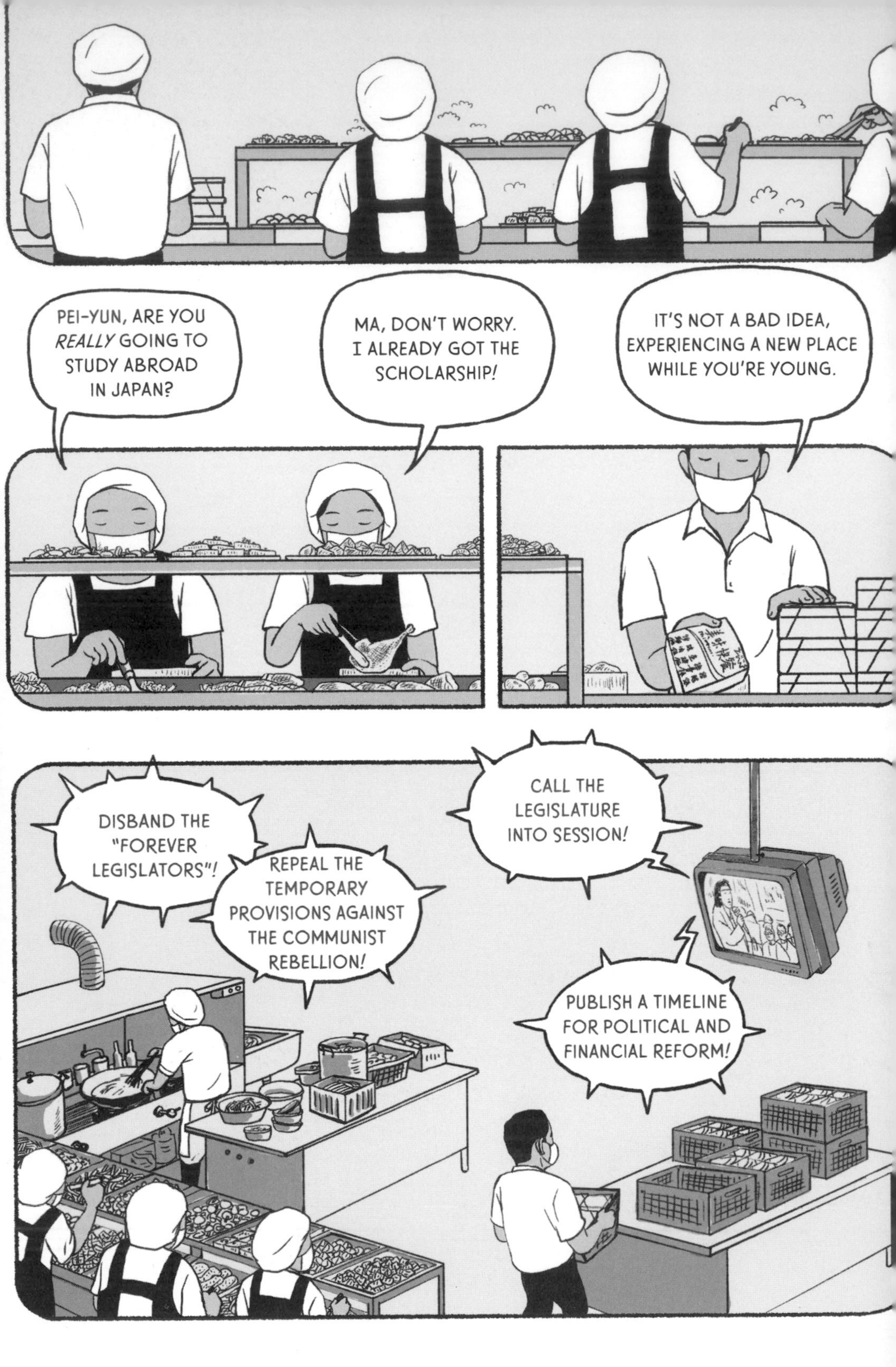
PEI-YUN, ARE YOU *REALLY* GOING TO STUDY ABROAD IN JAPAN?
MA, DON'T WORRY. I ALREADY GOT THE SCHOLARSHIP!
IT'S NOT A BAD IDEA, EXPERIENCING A NEW PLACE WHILE YOU'RE YOUNG.
DISBAND THE "FOREVER LEGISLATORS"!
REPEAL THE TEMPORARY PROVISIONS AGAINST THE COMMUNIST REBELLION!
CALL THE LEGISLATURE INTO SESSION!
PUBLISH A TIMELINE FOR POLITICAL AND FINANCIAL REFORM!

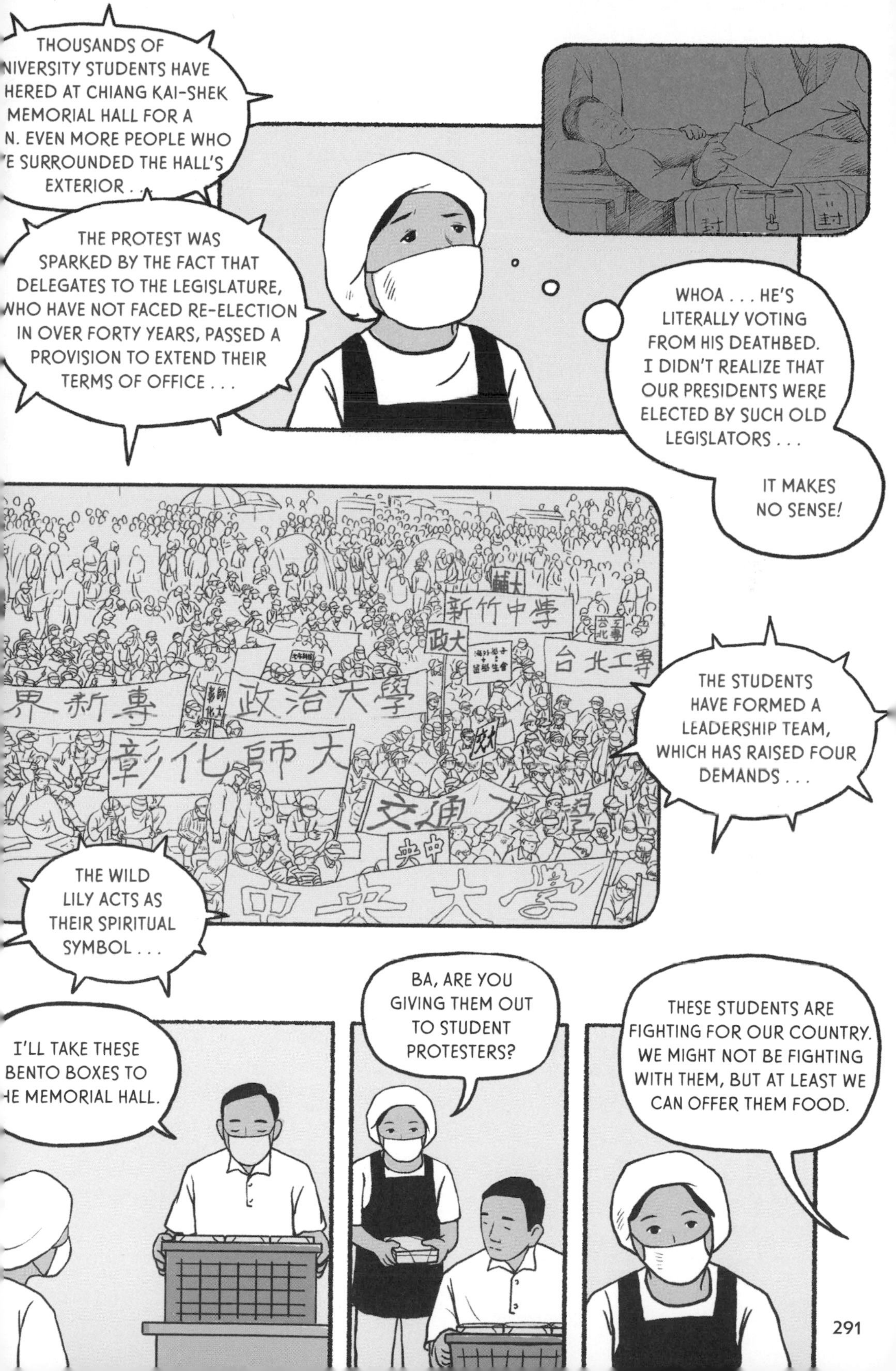

THOUSANDS OF NIVERSITY STUDENTS HAVE HERED AT CHIANG KAI-SHEK MEMORIAL HALL FOR A N. EVEN MORE PEOPLE WHO 'E SURROUNDED THE HALL'S EXTERIOR . . .
THE PROTEST WAS SPARKED BY THE FACT THAT DELEGATES TO THE LEGISLATURE, WHO HAVE NOT FACED RE-ELECTION IN OVER FORTY YEARS, PASSED A PROVISION TO EXTEND THEIR TERMS OF OFFICE . . .
WHOA . . . HE'S LITERALLY VOTING FROM HIS DEATHBED. I DIDN'T REALIZE THAT OUR PRESIDENTS WERE ELECTED BY SUCH OLD LEGISLATORS . . .
IT MAKES NO SENSE!
新竹中學
政大
台北工專
界新專
政治大學
彰化師大
中央大學
THE STUDENTS HAVE FORMED A LEADERSHIP TEAM, WHICH HAS RAISED FOUR DEMANDS . . .
THE WILD LILY ACTS AS THEIR SPIRITUAL SYMBOL . . .
I'LL TAKE THESE BENTO BOXES TO HE MEMORIAL HALL.
BA, ARE YOU GIVING THEM OUT TO STUDENT PROTESTERS?
THESE STUDENTS ARE FIGHTING FOR OUR COUNTRY. WE MIGHT NOT BE FIGHTING WITH THEM, BUT AT LEAST WE CAN OFFER THEM FOOD.

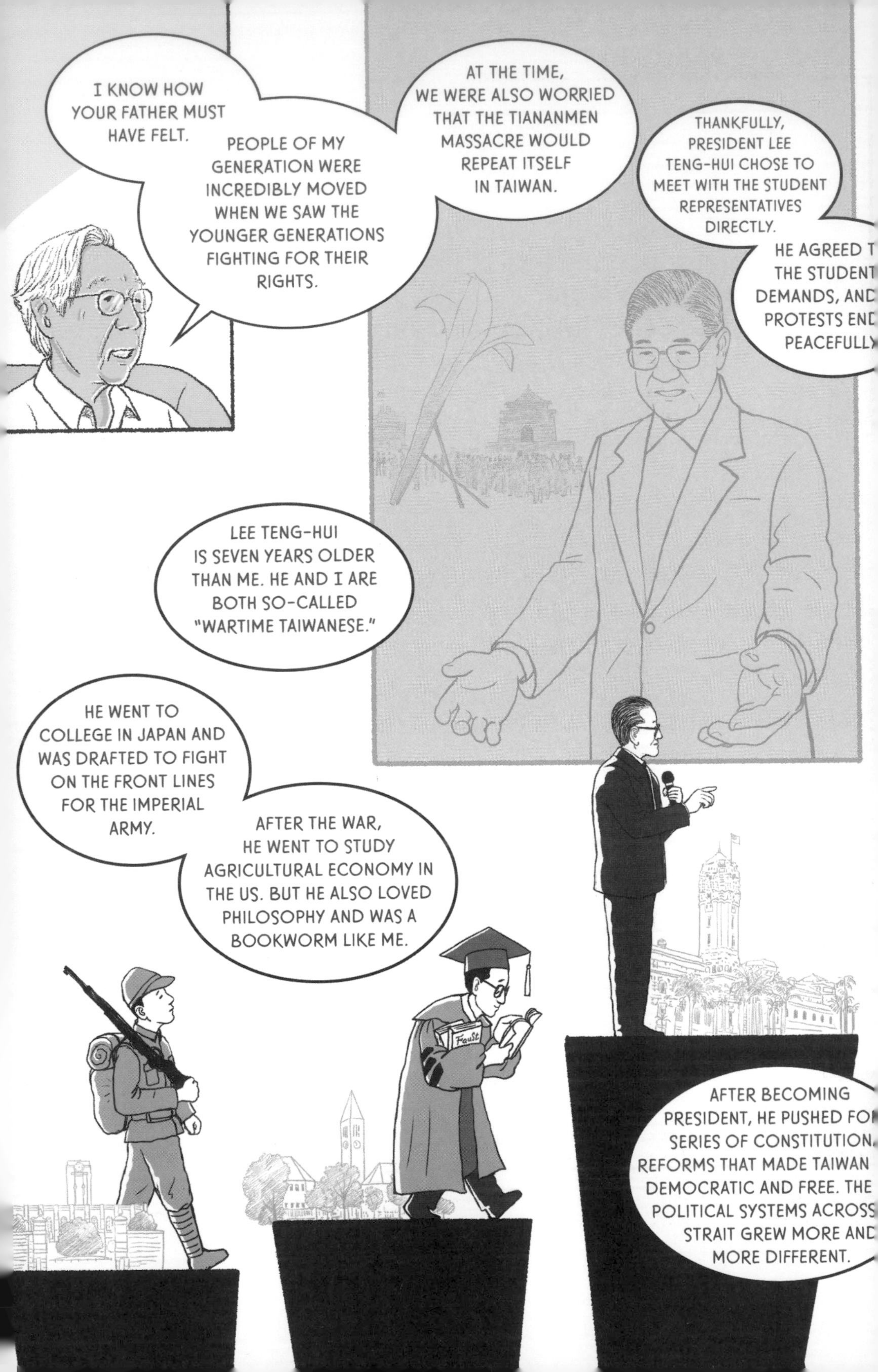
I KNOW HOW YOUR FATHER MUST HAVE FELT.
PEOPLE OF MY GENERATION WERE INCREDIBLY MOVED WHEN WE SAW THE YOUNGER GENERATIONS FIGHTING FOR THEIR RIGHTS.
AT THE TIME, WE WERE ALSO WORRIED THAT THE TIANANMEN MASSACRE WOULD REPEAT ITSELF IN TAIWAN.
THANKFULLY, PRESIDENT LEE TENG-HUI CHOSE TO MEET WITH THE STUDENT REPRESENTATIVES DIRECTLY.
HE AGREED T THE STUDENT DEMANDS, AND PROTESTS END PEACEFULLY
LEE TENG-HUI IS SEVEN YEARS OLDER THAN ME. HE AND I ARE BOTH SO-CALLED "WARTIME TAIWANESE."
HE WENT TO COLLEGE IN JAPAN AND WAS DRAFTED TO FIGHT ON THE FRONT LINES FOR THE IMPERIAL ARMY.
AFTER THE WAR, HE WENT TO STUDY AGRICULTURAL ECONOMY IN THE US. BUT HE ALSO LOVED PHILOSOPHY AND WAS A BOOKWORM LIKE ME.
Faust
AFTER BECOMING PRESIDENT, HE PUSHED FO SERIES OF CONSTITUTION REFORMS THAT MADE TAIWAN DEMOCRATIC AND FREE. THE POLITICAL SYSTEMS ACROSS STRAIT GREW MORE AND MORE DIFFERENT.

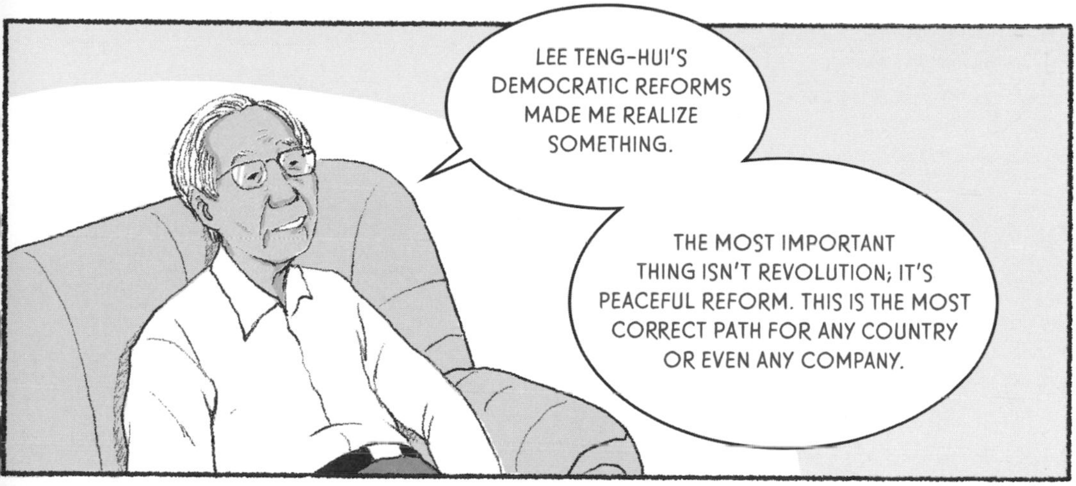
LEE TENG-HUI'S DEMOCRATIC REFORMS MADE ME REALIZE SOMETHING.
THE MOST IMPORTANT THING ISN'T REVOLUTION; IT'S PEACEFUL REFORM. THIS IS THE MOST CORRECT PATH FOR ANY COUNTRY OR EVEN ANY COMPANY.

1996. Taipei. Kuohua Advertising.

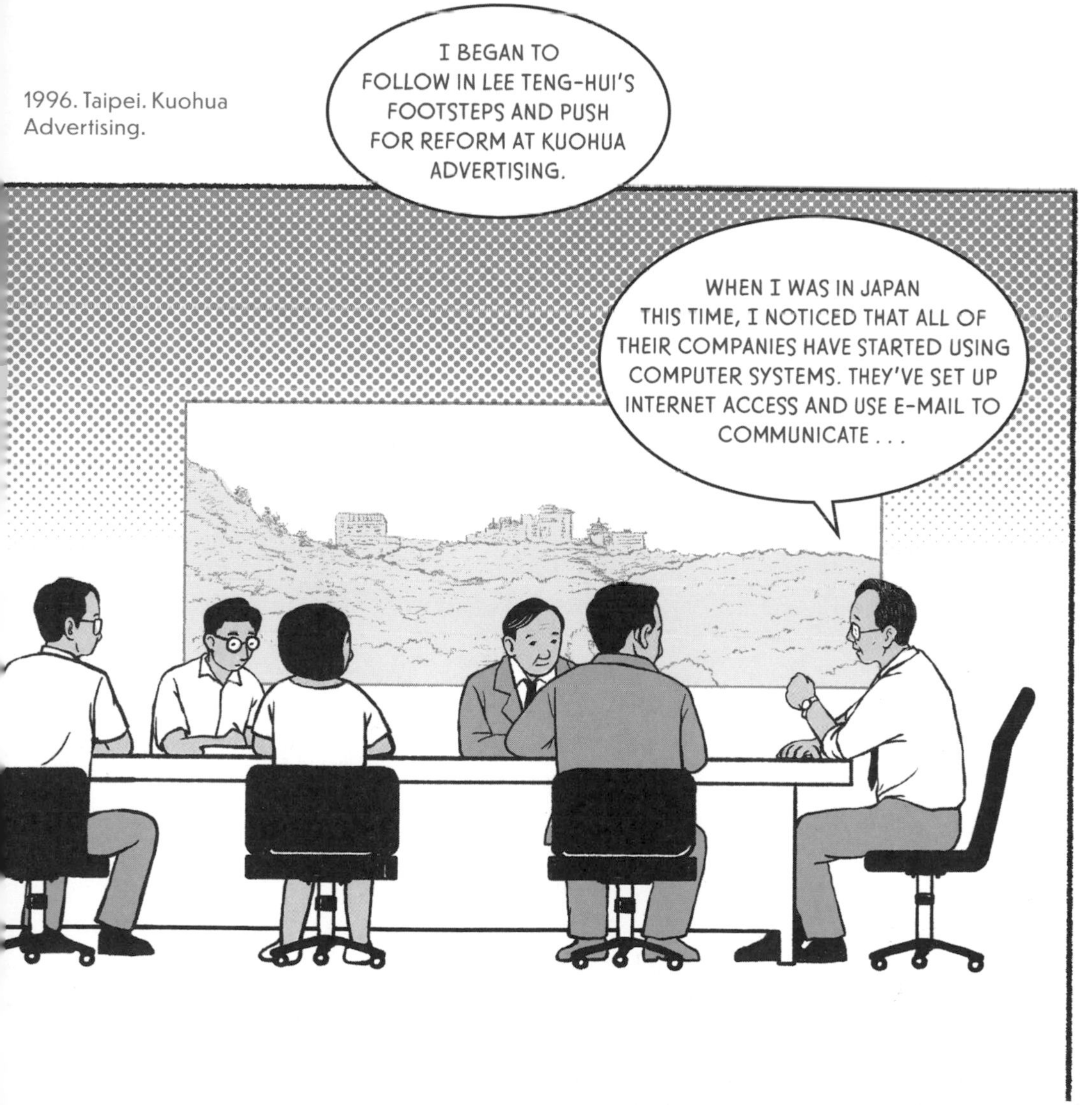
I BEGAN TO FOLLOW IN LEE TENG-HUI'S FOOTSTEPS AND PUSH FOR REFORM AT KUOHUA ADVERTISING.
WHEN I WAS IN JAPAN THIS TIME, I NOTICED THAT ALL OF THEIR COMPANIES HAVE STARTED USING COMPUTER SYSTEMS. THEY'VE SET UP INTERNET ACCESS AND USE E-MAIL TO COMMUNICATE . . .

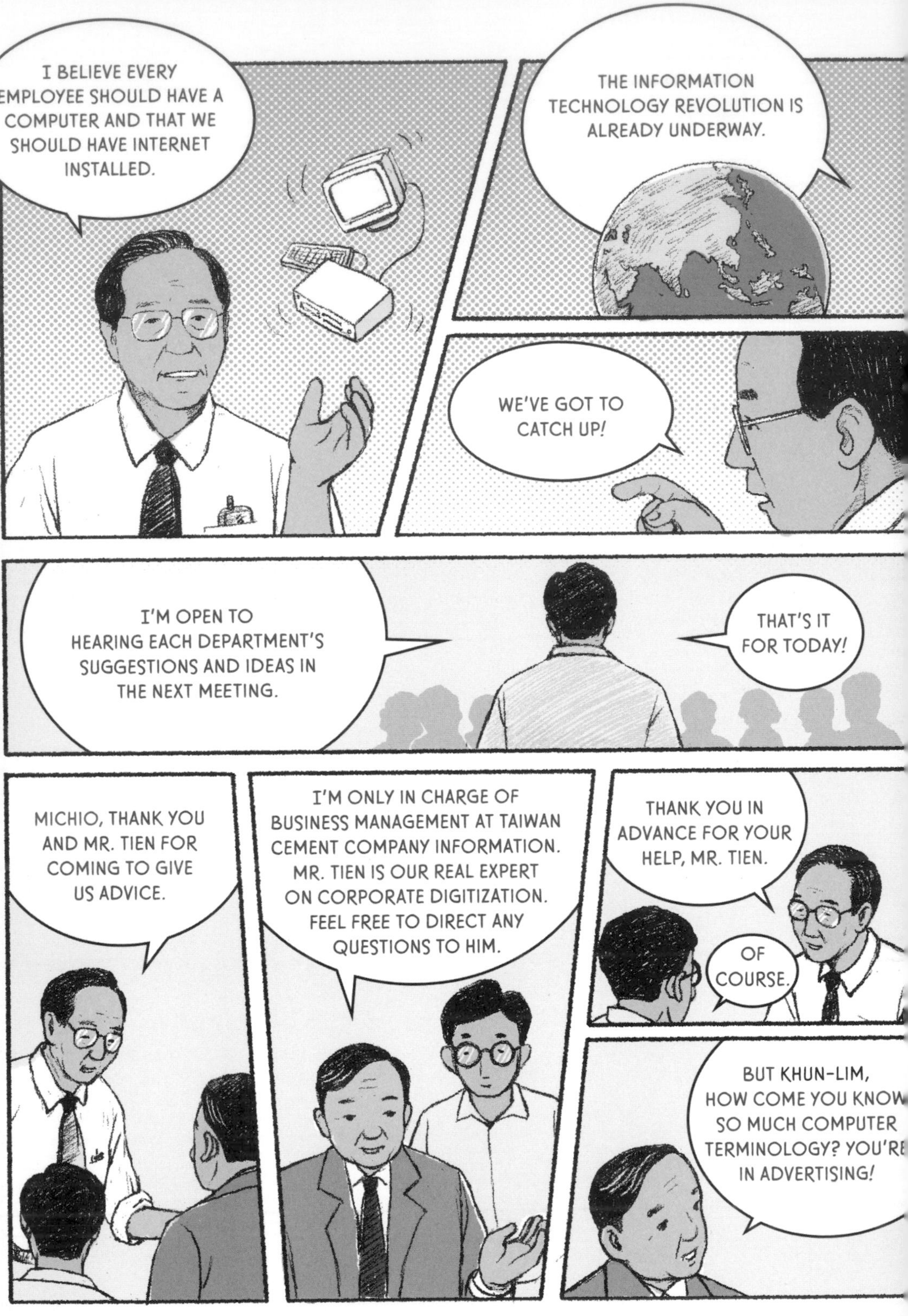
I BELIEVE EVERY EMPLOYEE SHOULD HAVE A COMPUTER AND THAT WE SHOULD HAVE INTERNET INSTALLED.
THE INFORMATION TECHNOLOGY REVOLUTION IS ALREADY UNDERWAY.
WE'VE GOT TO CATCH UP!
I'M OPEN TO HEARING EACH DEPARTMENT'S SUGGESTIONS AND IDEAS IN THE NEXT MEETING.
THAT'S IT FOR TODAY!
MICHIO, THANK YOU AND MR. TIEN FOR COMING TO GIVE US ADVICE.
I'M ONLY IN CHARGE OF BUSINESS MANAGEMENT AT TAIWAN CEMENT COMPANY INFORMATION. MR. TIEN IS OUR REAL EXPERT ON CORPORATE DIGITIZATION. FEEL FREE TO DIRECT ANY QUESTIONS TO HIM.
THANK YOU IN ADVANCE FOR YOUR HELP, MR. TIEN.
OF COURSE.
BUT KHUN-LIM, HOW COME YOU KNOW SO MUCH COMPUTER TERMINOLOGY? YOU'RE IN ADVERTISING!

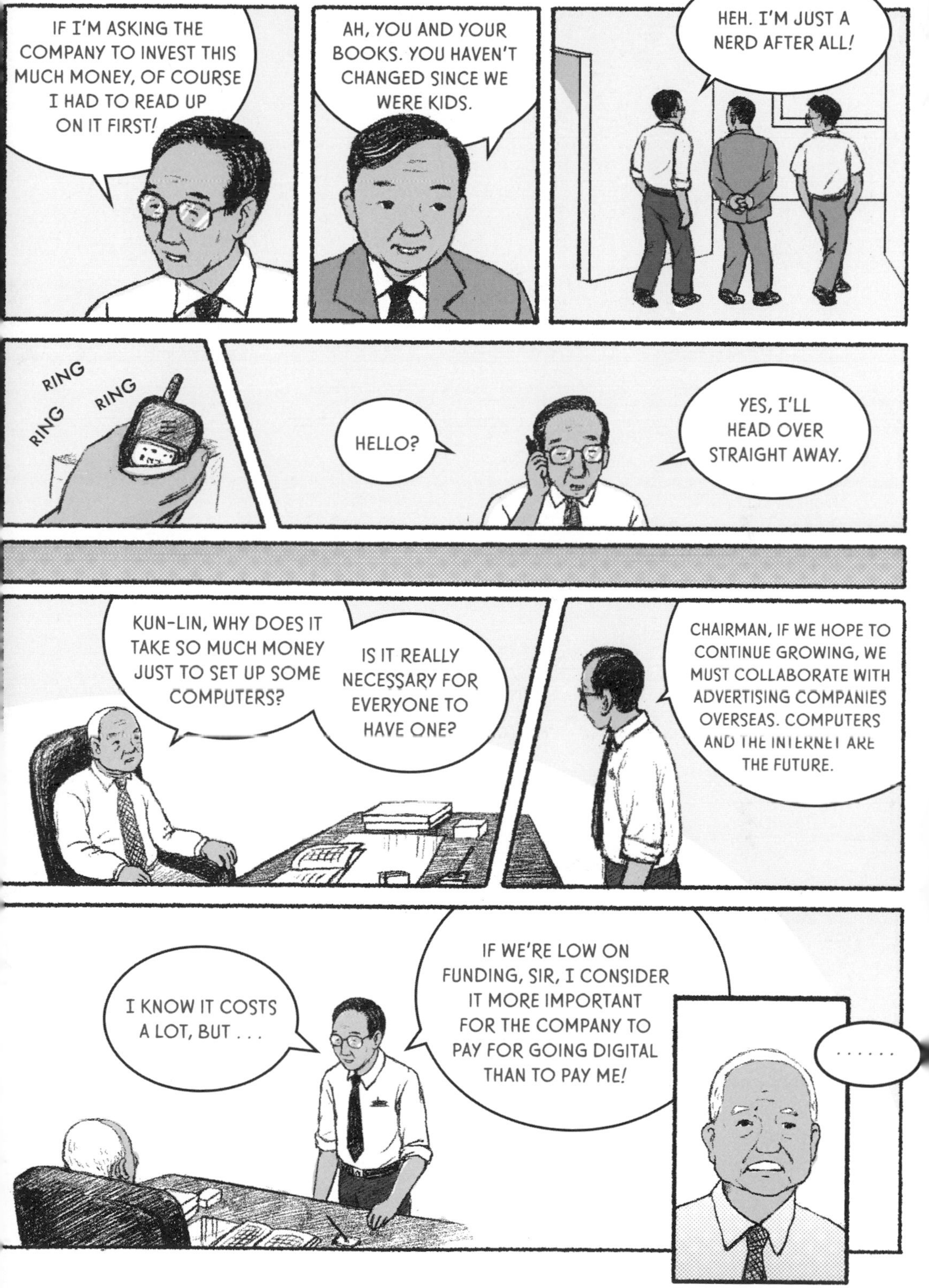
IF I'M ASKING THE COMPANY TO INVEST THIS MUCH MONEY, OF COURSE I HAD TO READ UP ON IT FIRST!
AH, YOU AND YOUR BOOKS. YOU HAVEN'T CHANGED SINCE WE WERE KIDS.
HEH. I'M JUST A NERD AFTER ALL!
RING
RING
RING
HELLO?
YES, I'LL HEAD OVER STRAIGHT AWAY.
KUN-LIN, WHY DOES IT TAKE SO MUCH MONEY JUST TO SET UP SOME COMPUTERS?
IS IT REALLY NECESSARY FOR EVERYONE TO HAVE ONE?
CHAIRMAN, IF WE HOPE TO CONTINUE GROWING, WE MUST COLLABORATE WITH ADVERTISING COMPANIES OVERSEAS. COMPUTERS AND THE INTERNET ARE THE FUTURE.
I KNOW IT COSTS A LOT, BUT . . .
IF WE'RE LOW ON FUNDING, SIR, I CONSIDER IT MORE IMPORTANT FOR THE COMPANY TO PAY FOR GOING DIGITAL THAN TO PAY ME!
. . . . . .

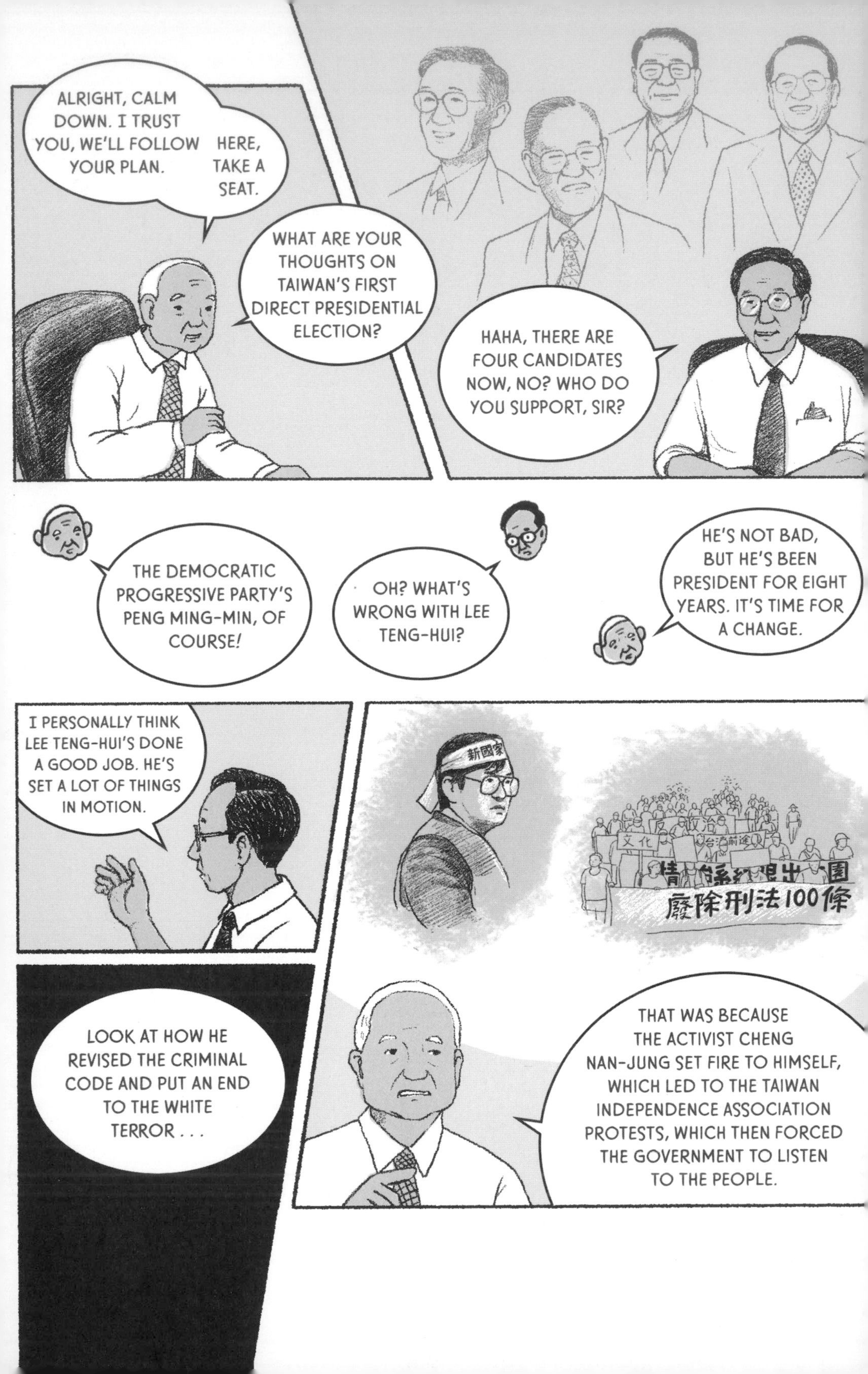
ALRIGHT, CALM DOWN. I TRUST YOU, WE'LL FOLLOW YOUR PLAN.
HERE, TAKE A SEAT.
WHAT ARE YOUR THOUGHTS ON TAIWAN'S FIRST DIRECT PRESIDENTIAL ELECTION?
HAHA, THERE ARE FOUR CANDIDATES NOW, NO? WHO DO YOU SUPPORT, SIR?
THE DEMOCRATIC PROGRESSIVE PARTY'S PENG MING-MIN, OF COURSE!
OH? WHAT'S WRONG WITH LEE TENG-HUI?
HE'S NOT BAD, BUT HE'S BEEN PRESIDENT FOR EIGHT YEARS. IT'S TIME FOR A CHANGE.
I PERSONALLY THINK LEE TENG-HUI'S DONE A GOOD JOB. HE'S SET A LOT OF THINGS IN MOTION.
新國家
文化
台灣前途
廢除刑法100條
LOOK AT HOW HE REVISED THE CRIMINAL CODE AND PUT AN END TO THE WHITE TERROR . . .
THAT WAS BECAUSE THE ACTIVIST CHENG NAN-JUNG SET FIRE TO HIMSELF, WHICH LED TO THE TAIWAN INDEPENDENCE ASSOCIATION PROTESTS, WHICH THEN FORCED THE GOVERNMENT TO LISTEN TO THE PEOPLE.

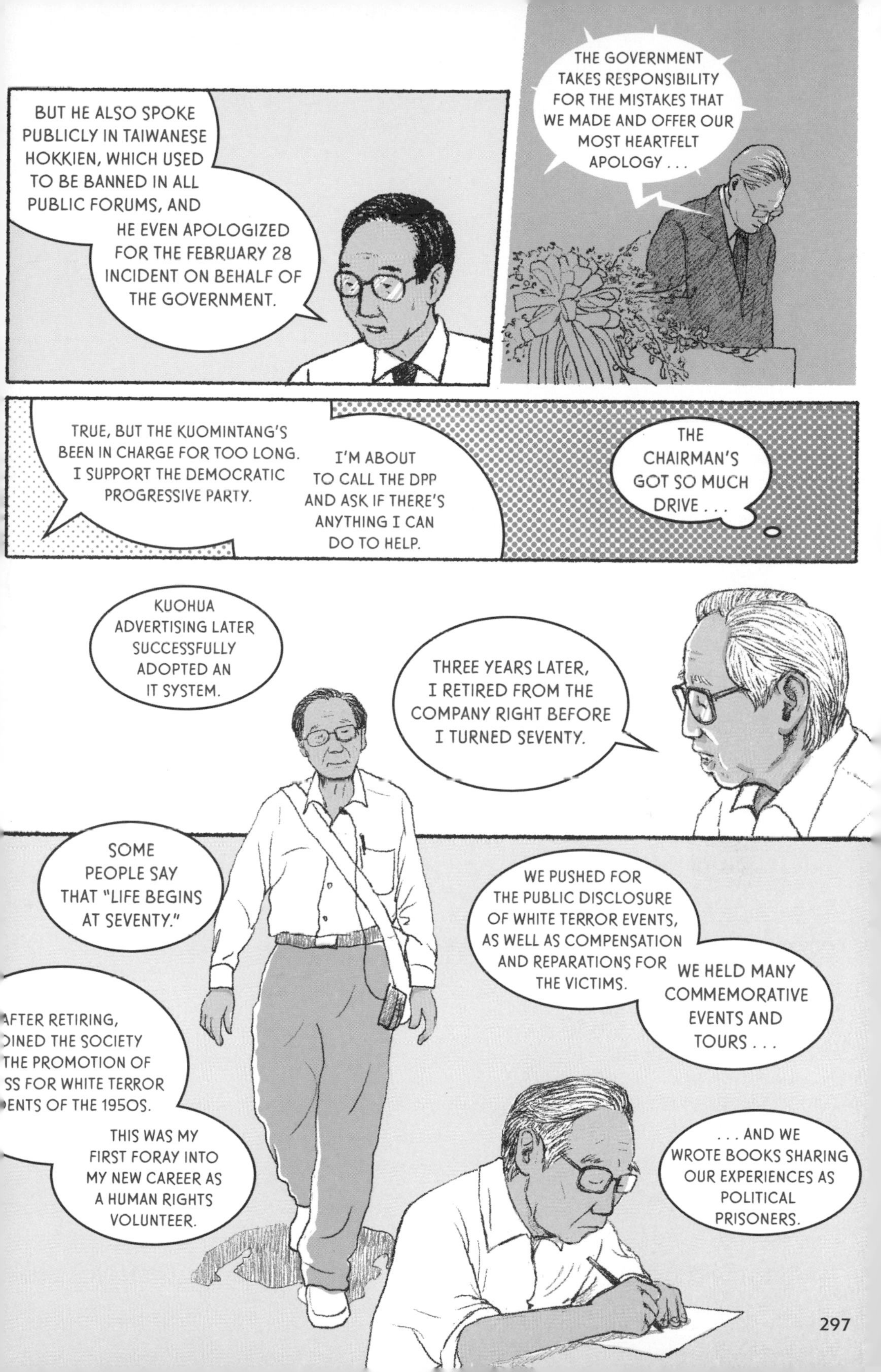
BUT HE ALSO SPOKE PUBLICLY IN TAIWANESE HOKKIEN, WHICH USED TO BE BANNED IN ALL PUBLIC FORUMS, AND
HE EVEN APOLOGIZED FOR THE FEBRUARY 28 INCIDENT ON BEHALF OF THE GOVERNMENT.
THE GOVERNMENT TAKES RESPONSIBILITY FOR THE MISTAKES THAT WE MADE AND OFFER OUR MOST HEARTFELT APOLOGY . . .
TRUE, BUT THE KUOMINTANG'S BEEN IN CHARGE FOR TOO LONG. I SUPPORT THE DEMOCRATIC PROGRESSIVE PARTY.
I'M ABOUT TO CALL THE DPP AND ASK IF THERE'S ANYTHING I CAN DO TO HELP.
THE CHAIRMAN'S GOT SO MUCH DRIVE . . .
KUOHUA ADVERTISING LATER SUCCESSFULLY ADOPTED AN IT SYSTEM.
THREE YEARS LATER, I RETIRED FROM THE COMPANY RIGHT BEFORE I TURNED SEVENTY.
SOME PEOPLE SAY THAT "LIFE BEGINS AT SEVENTY."
AFTER RETIRING, OINED THE SOCIETY THE PROMOTION OF SS FOR WHITE TERROR ENTS OF THE 1950S.
THIS WAS MY FIRST FORAY INTO MY NEW CAREER AS A HUMAN RIGHTS VOLUNTEER.
WE PUSHED FOR THE PUBLIC DISCLOSURE OF WHITE TERROR EVENTS, AS WELL AS COMPENSATION AND REPARATIONS FOR THE VICTIMS.
WE HELD MANY COMMEMORATIVE EVENTS AND TOURS . . .
. . . AND WE WROTE BOOKS SHARING OUR EXPERIENCES AS POLITICAL PRISONERS.

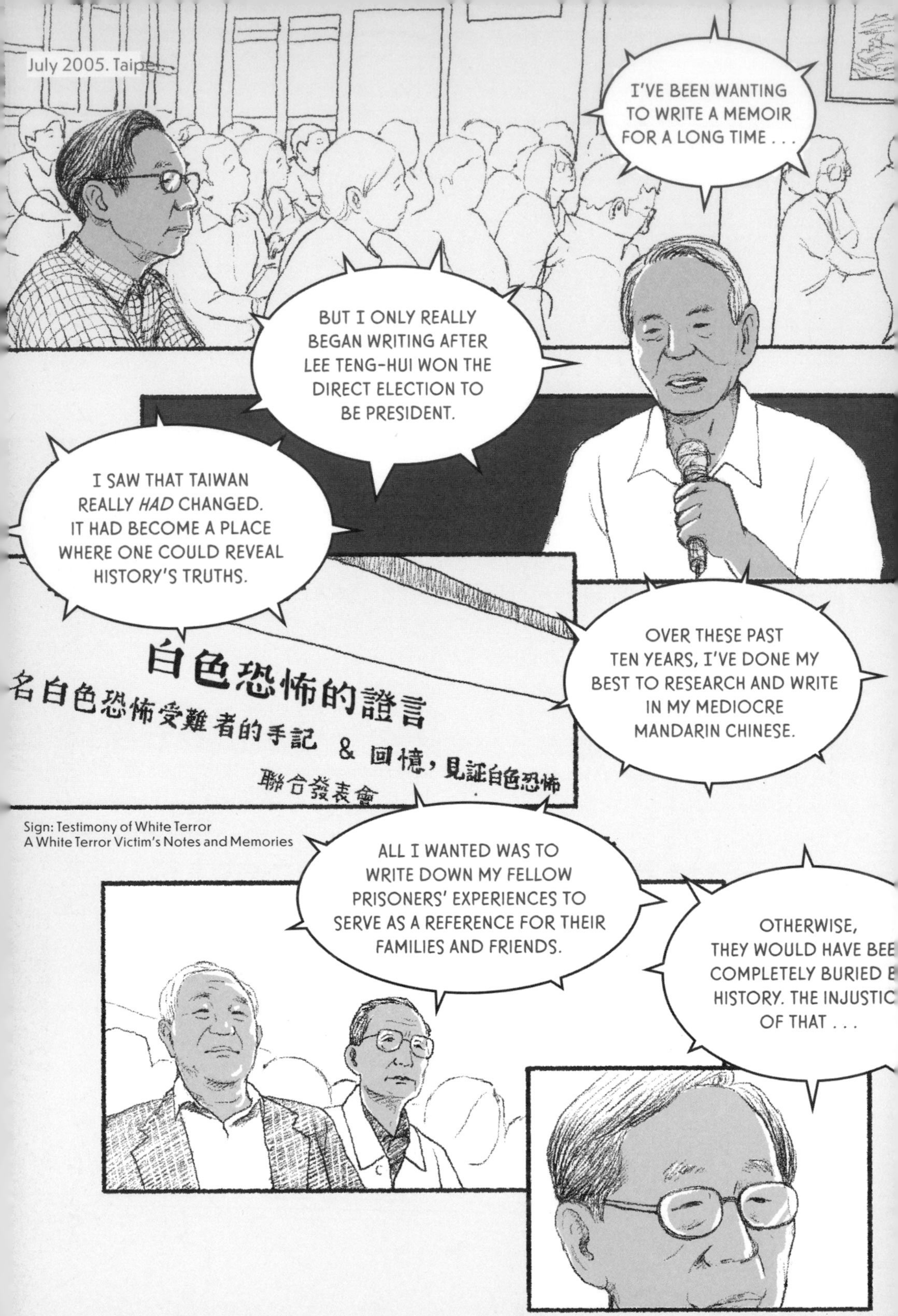
July 2005. Taipei.
I'VE BEEN WANTING TO WRITE A MEMOIR FOR A LONG TIME . . .
BUT I ONLY REALLY BEGAN WRITING AFTER LEE TENG-HUI WON THE DIRECT ELECTION TO BE PRESIDENT.
I SAW THAT TAIWAN REALLY *HAD* CHANGED. IT HAD BECOME A PLACE WHERE ONE COULD REVEAL HISTORY'S TRUTHS.
OVER THESE PAST TEN YEARS, I'VE DONE MY BEST TO RESEARCH AND WRITE IN MY MEDIOCRE MANDARIN CHINESE.
自色恐怖的證言
名自色恐怖受難者的手記 & 回憶，見証自色恐怖
聯合發表會
Sign: Testimony of White Terror
A White Terror Victim's Notes and Memories
ALL I WANTED WAS TO WRITE DOWN MY FELLOW PRISONERS' EXPERIENCES TO SERVE AS A REFERENCE FOR THEIR FAMILIES AND FRIENDS.
OTHERWISE, THEY WOULD HAVE BEE COMPLETELY BURIED E HISTORY. THE INJUSTIC OF THAT . . .

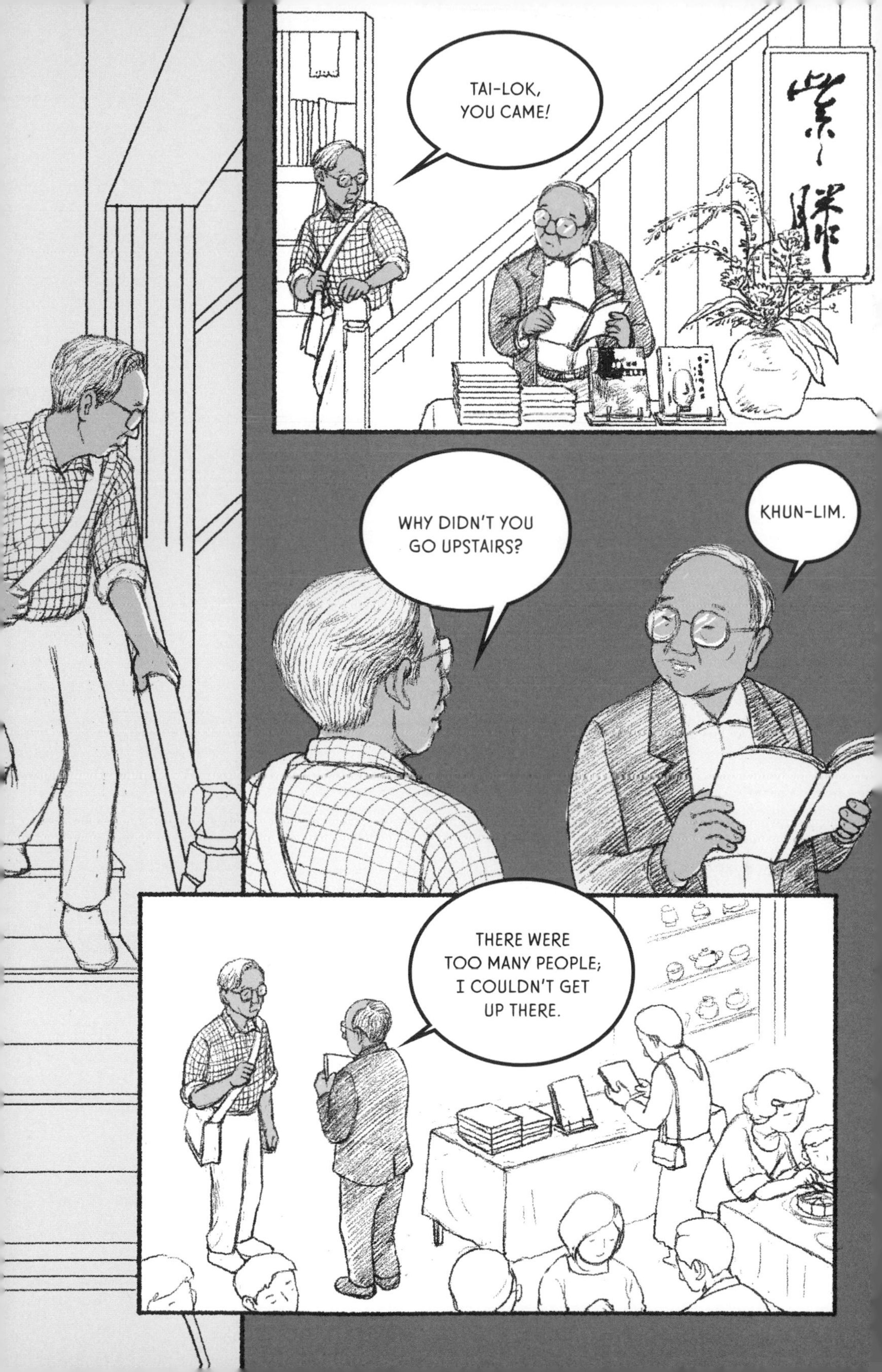
TAI-LOK, YOU CAME!
WHY DIDN'T YOU GO UPSTAIRS?
KHUN-LIM.
THERE WERE TOO MANY PEOPLE; I COULDN'T GET UP THERE.

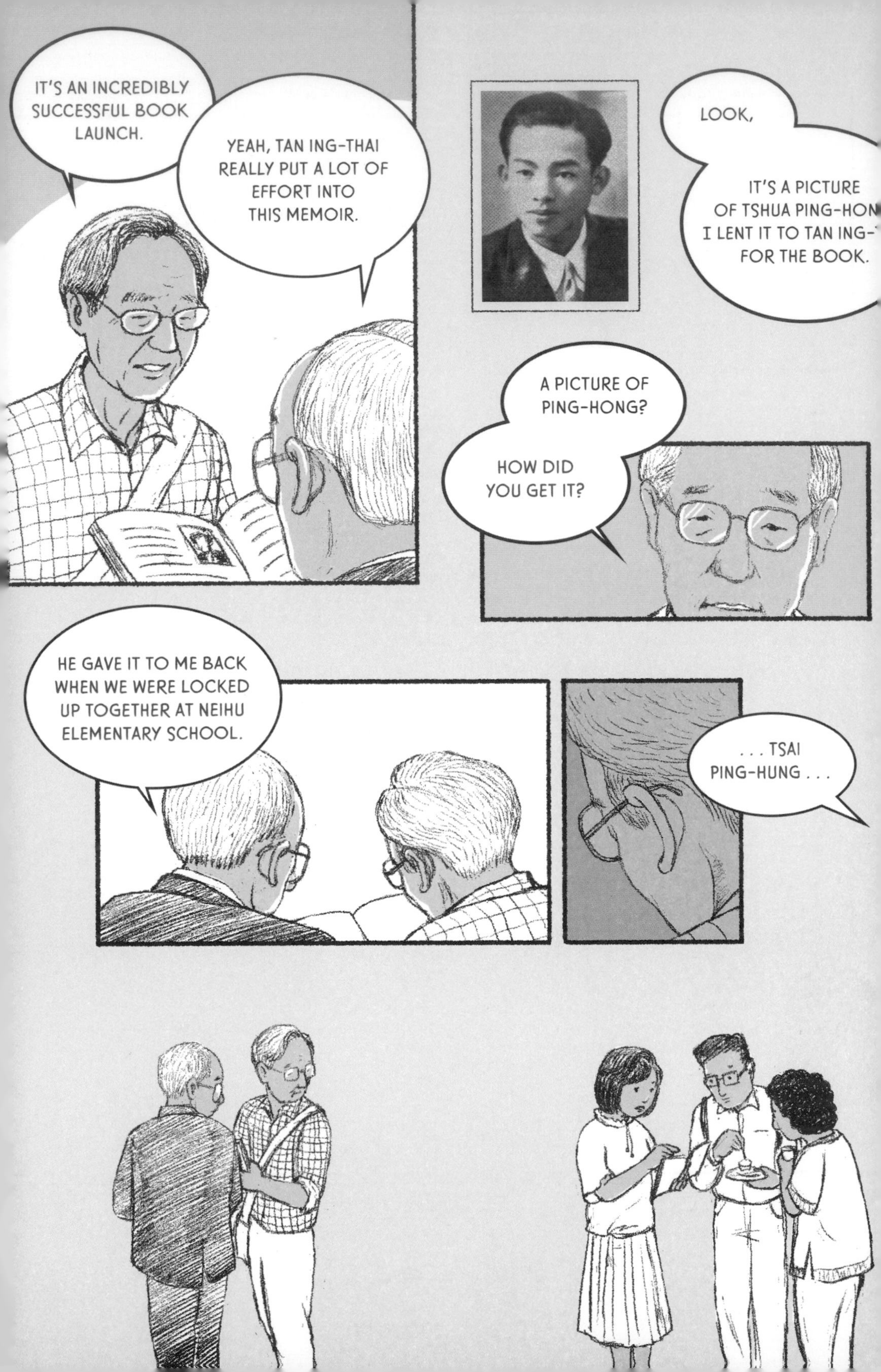
IT'S AN INCREDIBLY SUCCESSFUL BOOK LAUNCH.
YEAH, TAN ING-THAI REALLY PUT A LOT OF EFFORT INTO THIS MEMOIR.
LOOK,
IT'S A PICTURE OF TSHUA PING-HON
I LENT IT TO TAN ING-
FOR THE BOOK.
A PICTURE OF PING-HONG?
HOW DID YOU GET IT?
HE GAVE IT TO ME BACK WHEN WE WERE LOCKED UP TOGETHER AT NEIHU ELEMENTARY SCHOOL.
. . . TSAI PING-HUNG . . .

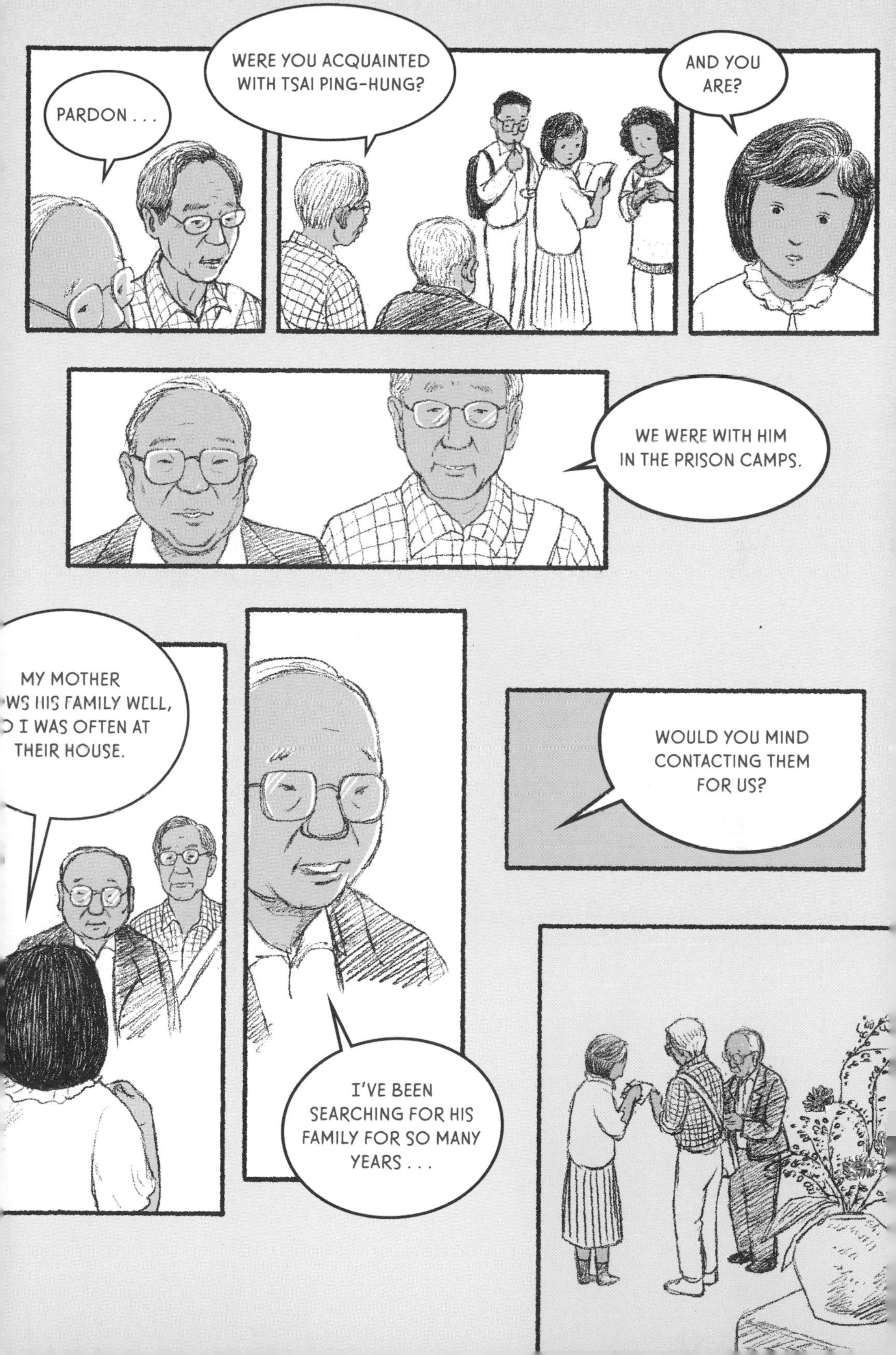

PARDON . . .
WERE YOU ACQUAINTED WITH TSAI PING-HUNG?
AND YOU ARE?
WE WERE WITH HIM IN THE PRISON CAMPS.
MY MOTHER WS HIS FAMILY WELL, I WAS OFTEN AT THEIR HOUSE.
I'VE BEEN SEARCHING FOR HIS FAMILY FOR SO MANY YEARS . . .
WOULD YOU MIND CONTACTING THEM FOR US?

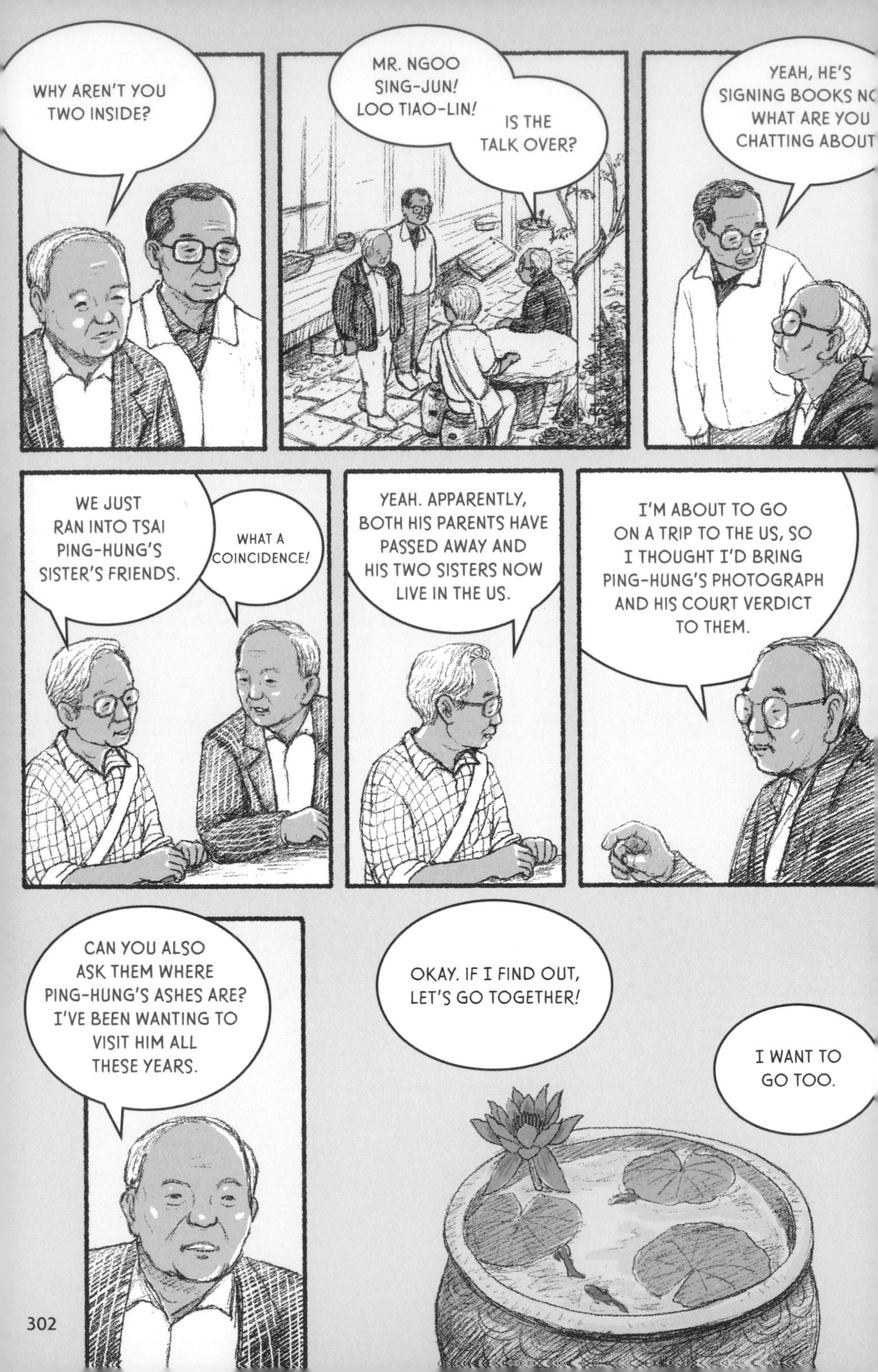
WHY AREN'T YOU TWO INSIDE?
MR. NGOO SING-JUN! LOO TIAO-LIN!
IS THE TALK OVER?
YEAH, HE'S SIGNING BOOKS NO
WHAT ARE YOU CHATTING ABOUT
WE JUST RAN INTO TSAI PING-HUNG'S SISTER'S FRIENDS.
WHAT A COINCIDENCE!
YEAH. APPARENTLY, BOTH HIS PARENTS HAVE PASSED AWAY AND HIS TWO SISTERS NOW LIVE IN THE US.
I'M ABOUT TO GO ON A TRIP TO THE US, SO I THOUGHT I'D BRING PING-HUNG'S PHOTOGRAPH AND HIS COURT VERDICT TO THEM.
CAN YOU ALSO ASK THEM WHERE PING-HUNG'S ASHES ARE? I'VE BEEN WANTING TO VISIT HIM ALL THESE YEARS.
OKAY. IF I FIND OUT, LET'S GO TOGETHER!
I WANT TO GO TOO.

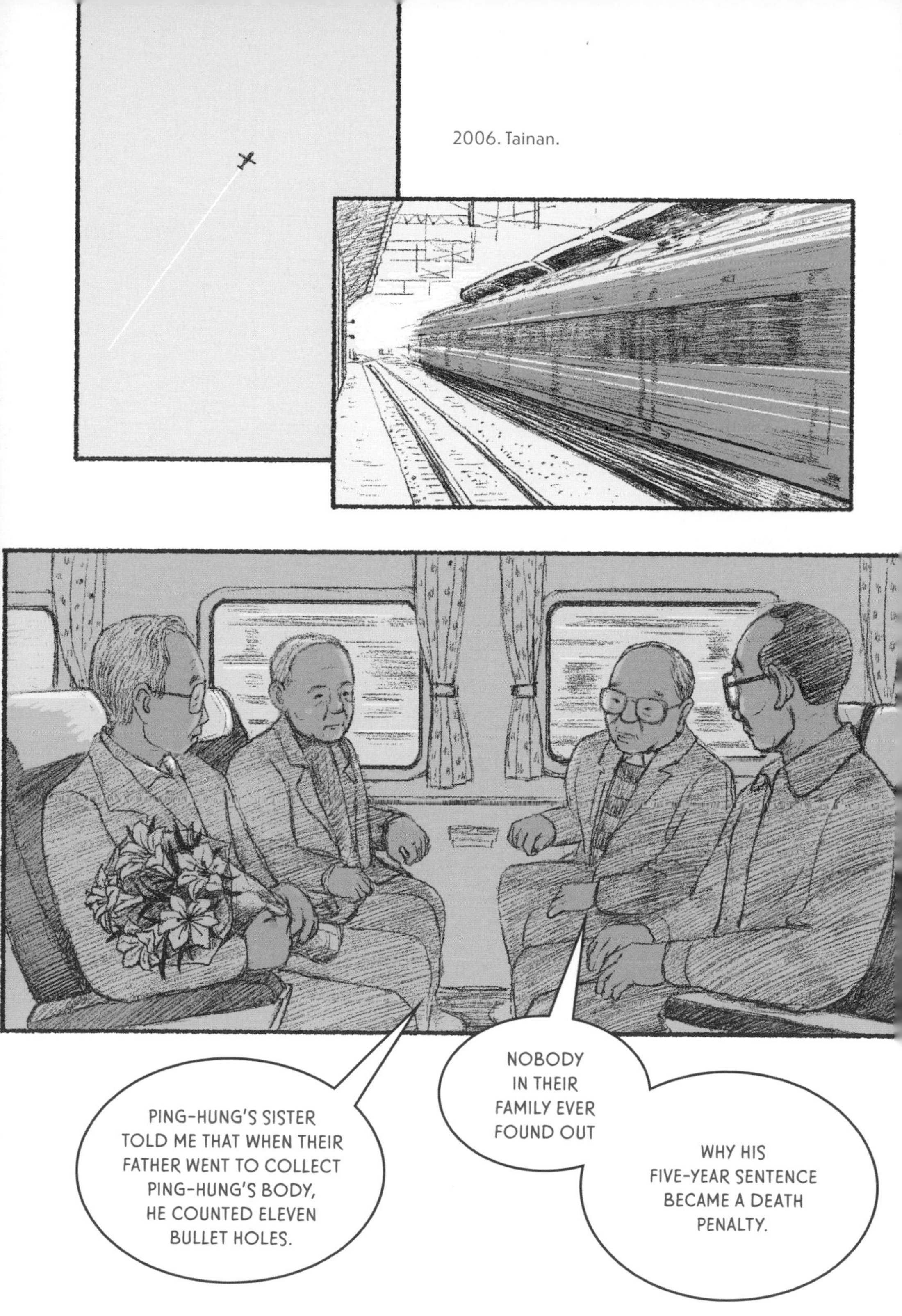
2006. Tainan.
PING-HUNG'S SISTER TOLD ME THAT WHEN THEIR FATHER WENT TO COLLECT PING-HUNG'S BODY, HE COUNTED ELEVEN BULLET HOLES.
NOBODY IN THEIR FAMILY EVER FOUND OUT
WHY HIS FIVE-YEAR SENTENCE BECAME A DEATH PENALTY.

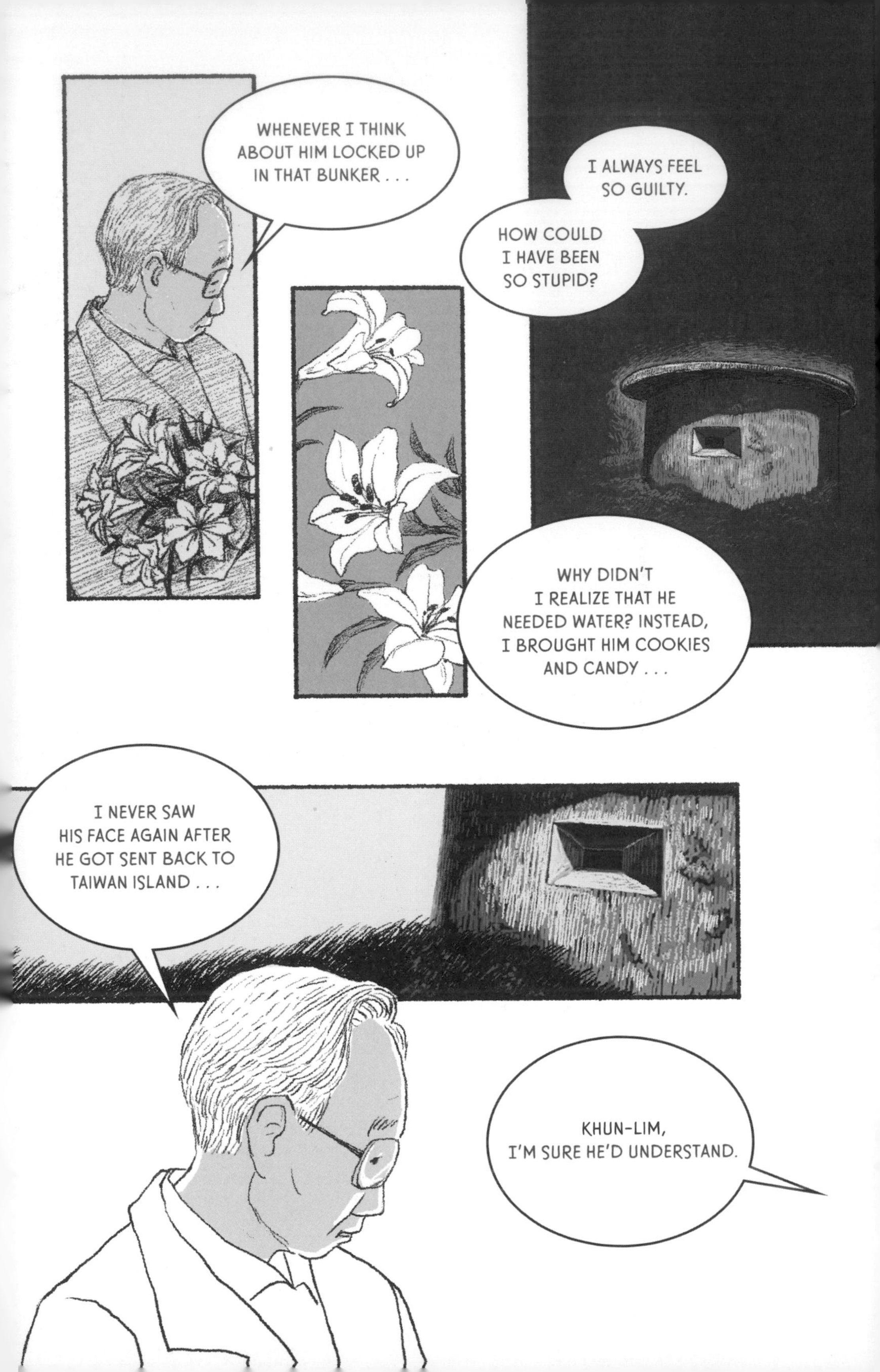
WHENEVER I THINK ABOUT HIM LOCKED UP IN THAT BUNKER . . .
I ALWAYS FEEL SO GUILTY.
HOW COULD I HAVE BEEN SO STUPID?
WHY DIDN'T I REALIZE THAT HE NEEDED WATER? INSTEAD, I BROUGHT HIM COOKIES AND CANDY . . .
I NEVER SAW HIS FACE AGAIN AFTER HE GOT SENT BACK TO TAIWAN ISLAND . . .
KHUN-LIM, I'M SURE HE'D UNDERSTAND.

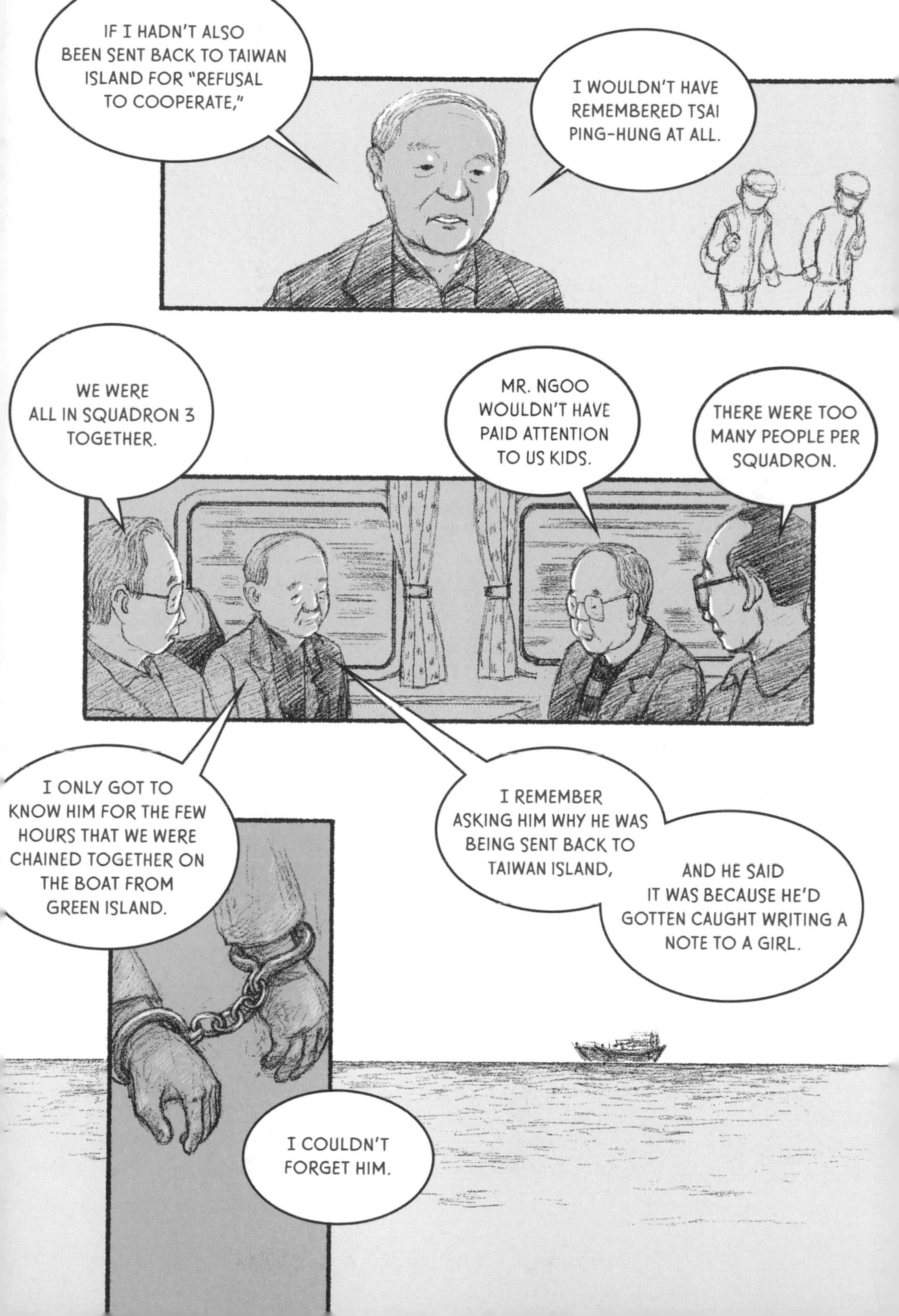
IF I HADN'T ALSO BEEN SENT BACK TO TAIWAN ISLAND FOR "REFUSAL TO COOPERATE,"
I WOULDN'T HAVE REMEMBERED TSAI PING-HUNG AT ALL.
WE WERE ALL IN SQUADRON 3 TOGETHER.
MR. NGOO WOULDN'T HAVE PAID ATTENTION TO US KIDS.
THERE WERE TOO MANY PEOPLE PER SQUADRON.
I ONLY GOT TO KNOW HIM FOR THE FEW HOURS THAT WE WERE CHAINED TOGETHER ON THE BOAT FROM GREEN ISLAND.
I REMEMBER ASKING HIM WHY HE WAS BEING SENT BACK TO TAIWAN ISLAND,
AND HE SAID IT WAS BECAUSE HE'D GOTTEN CAUGHT WRITING A NOTE TO A GIRL.
I COULDN'T FORGET HIM.

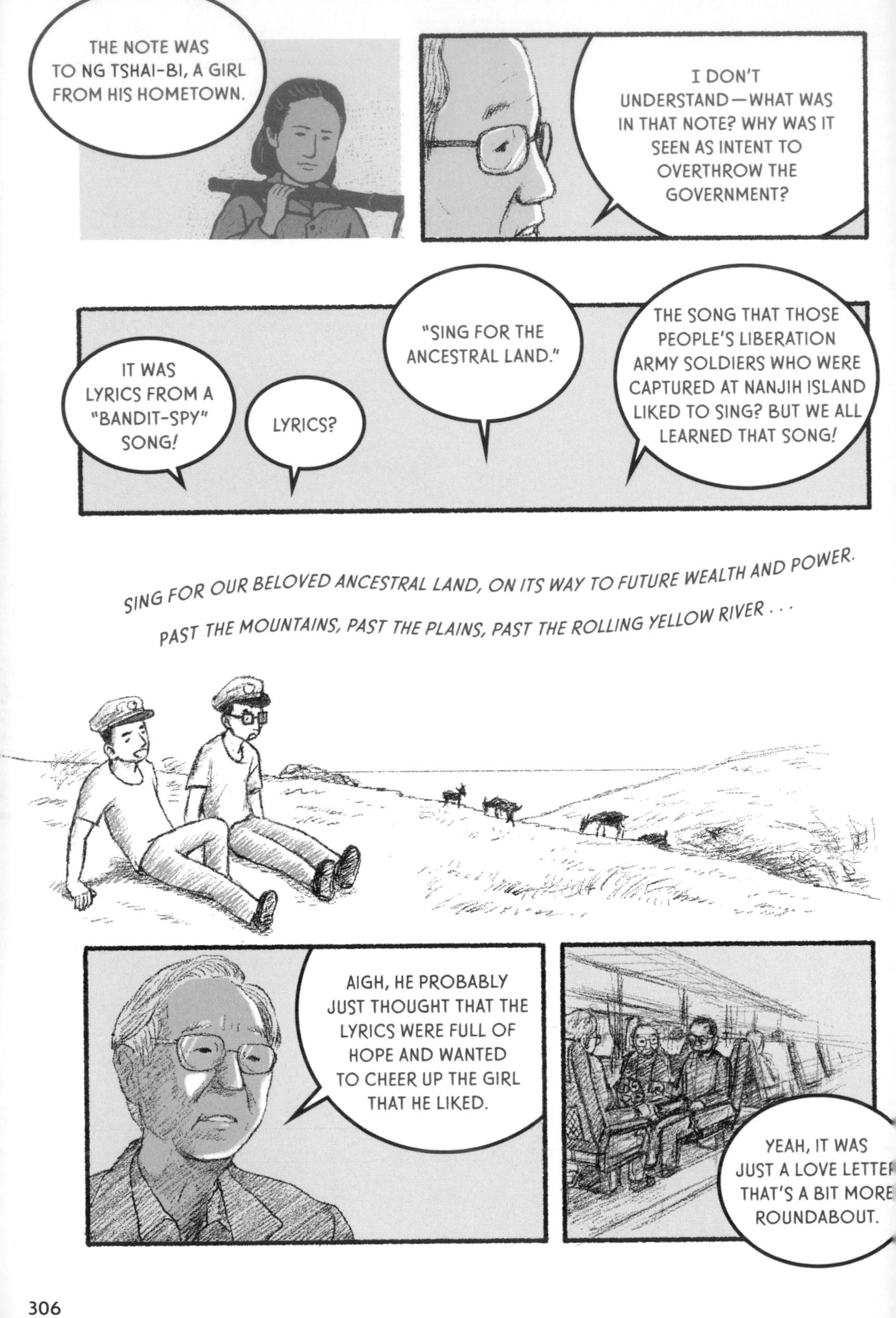
THE NOTE WAS TO NG TSHAI-BI, A GIRL FROM HIS HOMETOWN.
I DON'T UNDERSTAND—WHAT WAS IN THAT NOTE? WHY WAS IT SEEN AS INTENT TO OVERTHROW THE GOVERNMENT?
IT WAS LYRICS FROM A "BANDIT-SPY" SONG!
LYRICS?
"SING FOR THE ANCESTRAL LAND."
THE SONG THAT THOSE PEOPLE'S LIBERATION ARMY SOLDIERS WHO WERE CAPTURED AT NANJIH ISLAND LIKED TO SING? BUT WE ALL LEARNED THAT SONG!
SING FOR OUR BELOVED ANCESTRAL LAND, ON ITS WAY TO FUTURE WEALTH AND POWER.
PAST THE MOUNTAINS, PAST THE PLAINS, PAST THE ROLLING YELLOW RIVER . . .
AIGH, HE PROBABLY JUST THOUGHT THAT THE LYRICS WERE FULL OF HOPE AND WANTED TO CHEER UP THE GIRL THAT HE LIKED.
YEAH, IT WAS JUST A LOVE LETTER THAT'S A BIT MORE ROUNDABOUT.

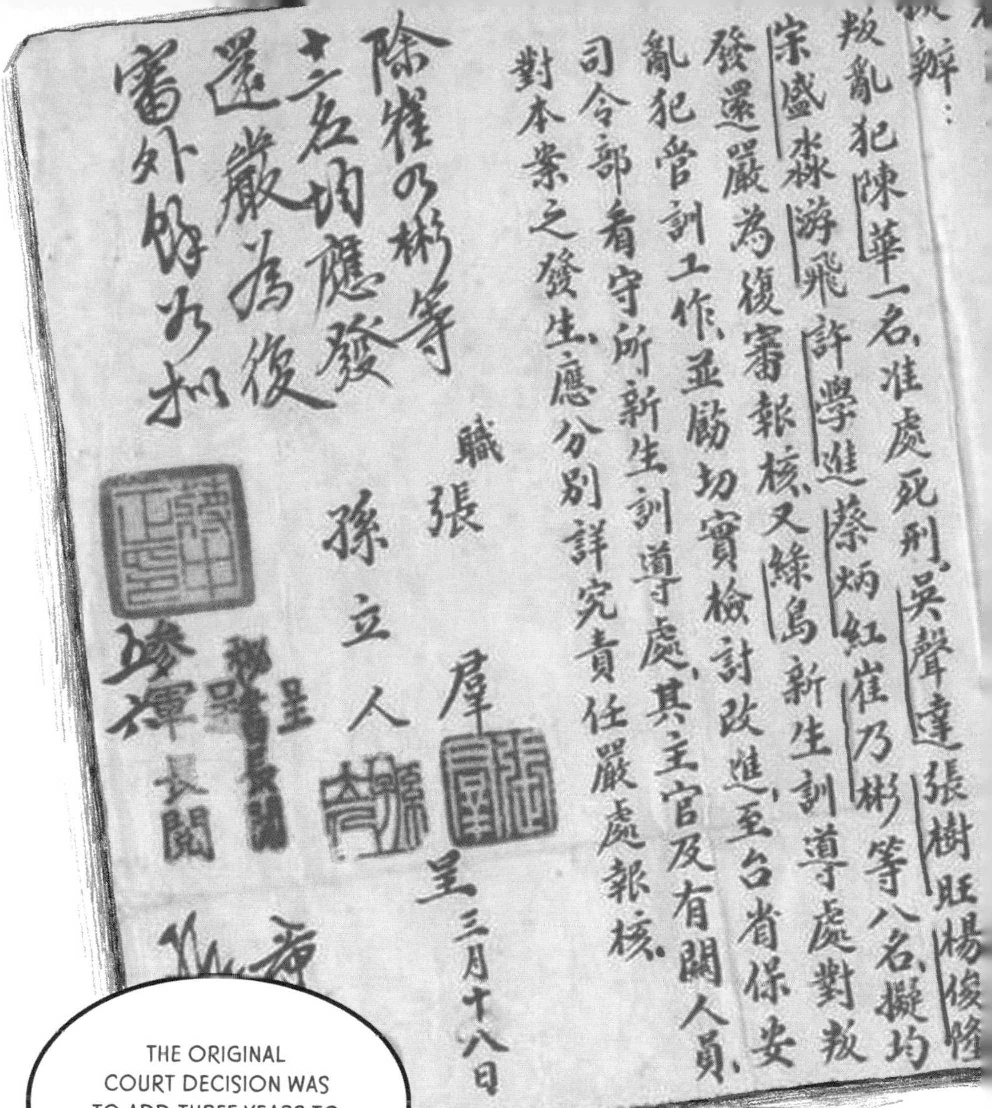

辦：
叛亂犯陳華一名，准處死刑，吳聲達、張樹旺、楊俊隆
宗盛、森游飛、許學進、蔡炳紅、崔乃彬等八名，擬均
發還嚴為復審報核，又綠島新生訓導處對叛
亂犯管訓工作，並勵切實檢討改進，至台省保安
司令部看守所新生訓導處，其主官及有關人員，
對本案之發生，應分別詳究責任，嚴處報核。

職 張羣
孫立人 呈
三月十八日

除崔乃彬等
十二名均應發
還嚴為復
審外餘如擬

THE ORIGINAL COURT DECISION WAS TO ADD THREE YEARS TO HIS SENTENCE.

IT'S REALLY JUST ATROCIOUS THAT ONE PERSON CAN DECIDE ON ANOTHER'S LIFE AND DEATH LIKE THAT!

WHO WOULD'VE THOUGHT THAT WHEN THEY SENT IN THE PAPERS FOR APPROVAL, CHIANG KAI-SHEK WOULD CALL FOR A MAJOR RETRIAL, AND PING-HUNG AS WELL AS THIRTEEN OTHERS WOULD BE GIVEN CAPITAL PUNISHMENT.

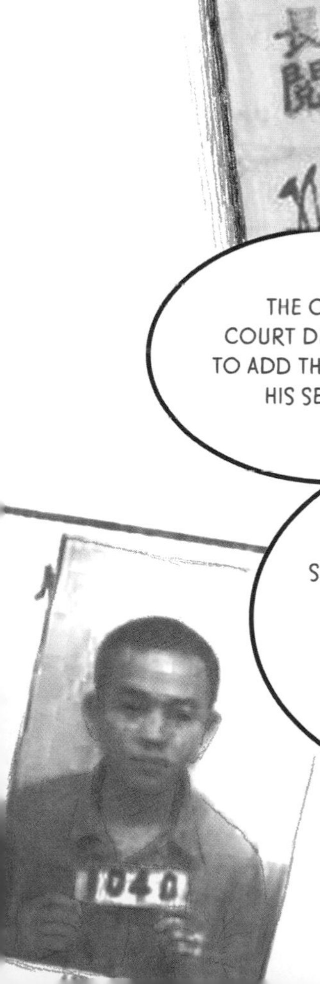
1045

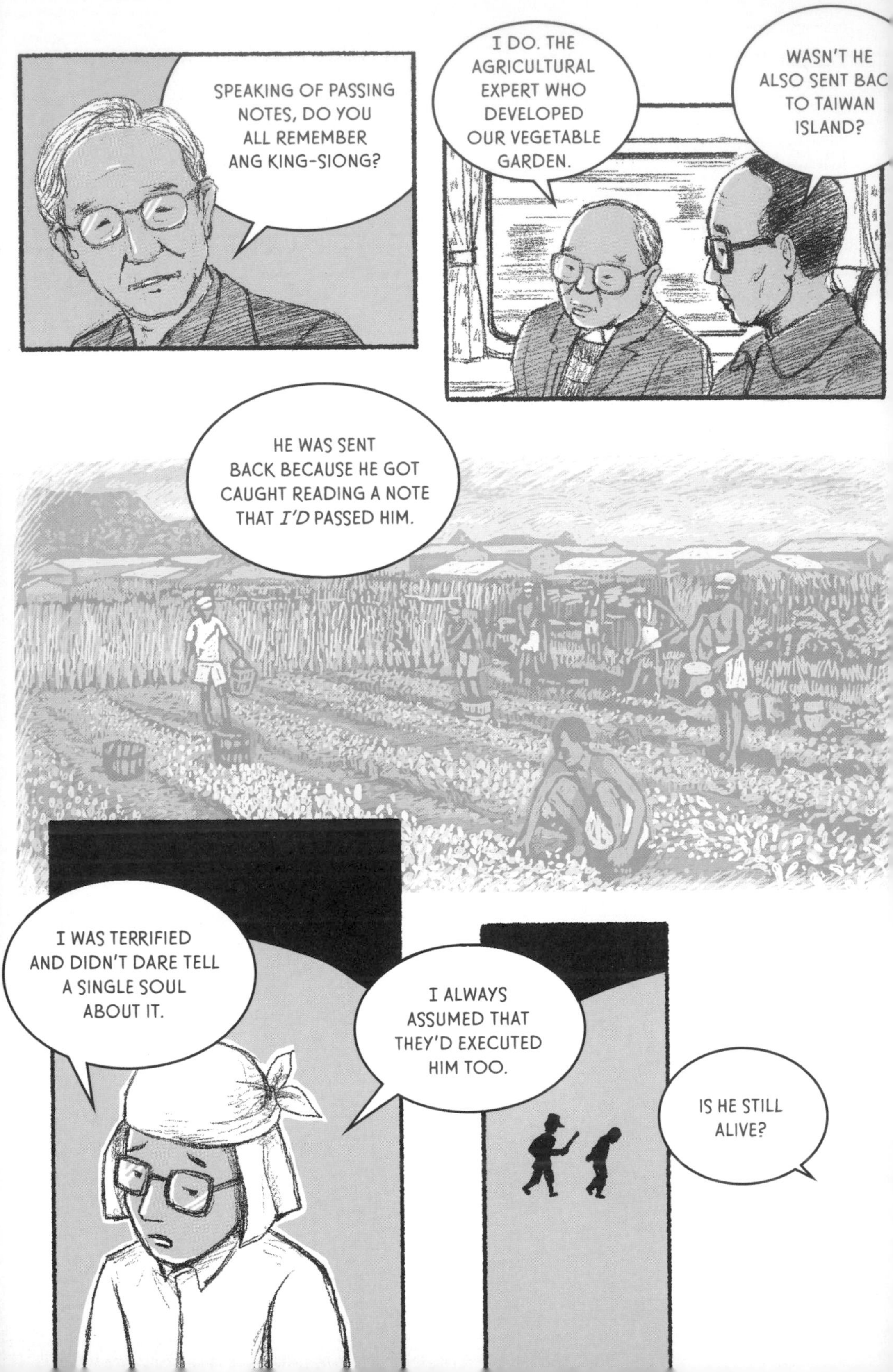
SPEAKING OF PASSING NOTES, DO YOU ALL REMEMBER ANG KING-SIONG?
I DO. THE AGRICULTURAL EXPERT WHO DEVELOPED OUR VEGETABLE GARDEN.
WASN'T HE ALSO SENT BAC TO TAIWAN ISLAND?
HE WAS SENT BACK BECAUSE HE GOT CAUGHT READING A NOTE THAT *I'D* PASSED HIM.
I WAS TERRIFIED AND DIDN'T DARE TELL A SINGLE SOUL ABOUT IT.
I ALWAYS ASSUMED THAT THEY'D EXECUTED HIM TOO.
IS HE STILL ALIVE?

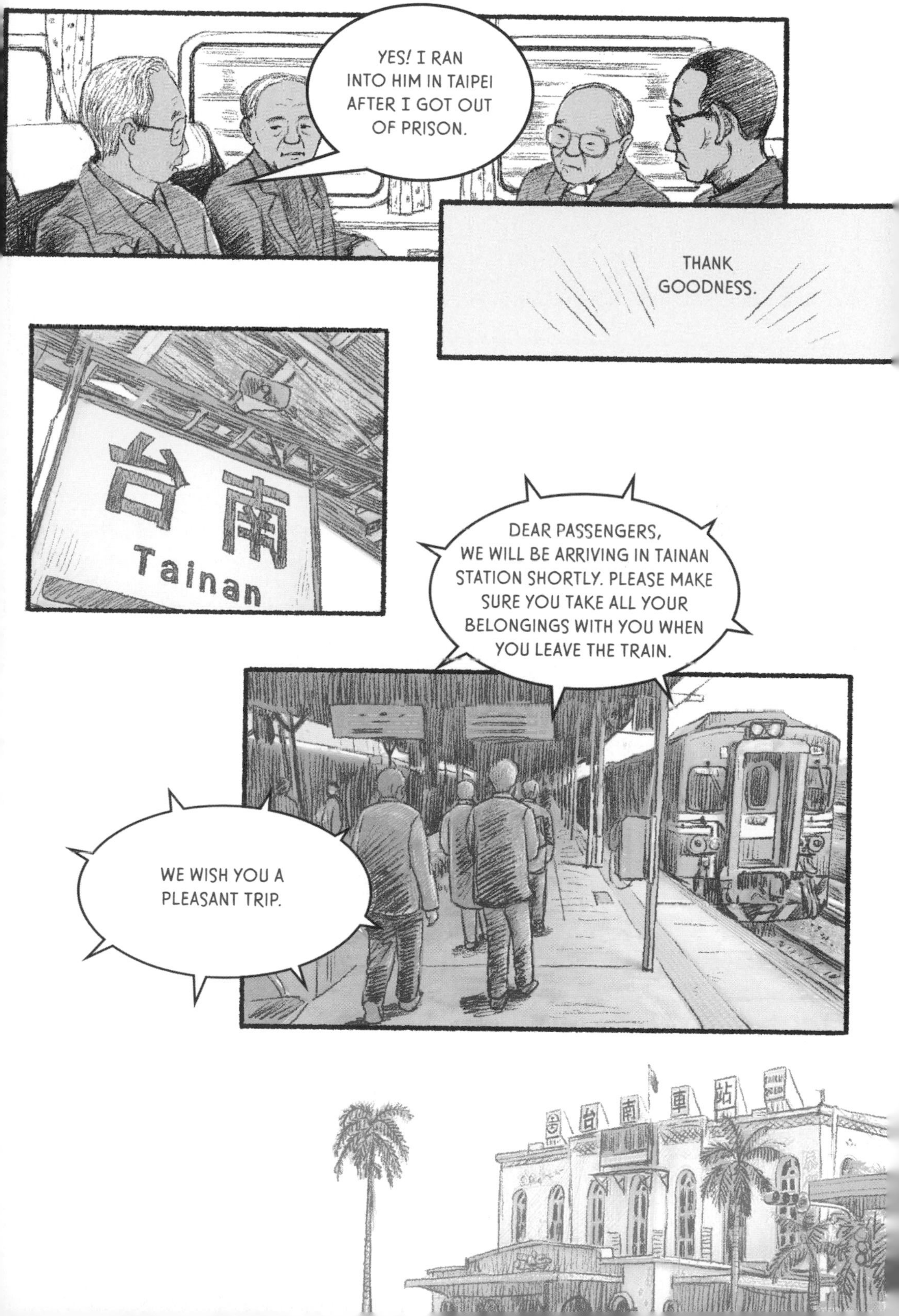
YES! I RAN INTO HIM IN TAIPEI AFTER I GOT OUT OF PRISON.
THANK GOODNESS.
台南
Tainan
DEAR PASSENGERS, WE WILL BE ARRIVING IN TAINAN STATION SHORTLY. PLEASE MAKE SURE YOU TAKE ALL YOUR BELONGINGS WITH YOU WHEN YOU LEAVE THE TRAIN.
WE WISH YOU A PLEASANT TRIP.
台南車站

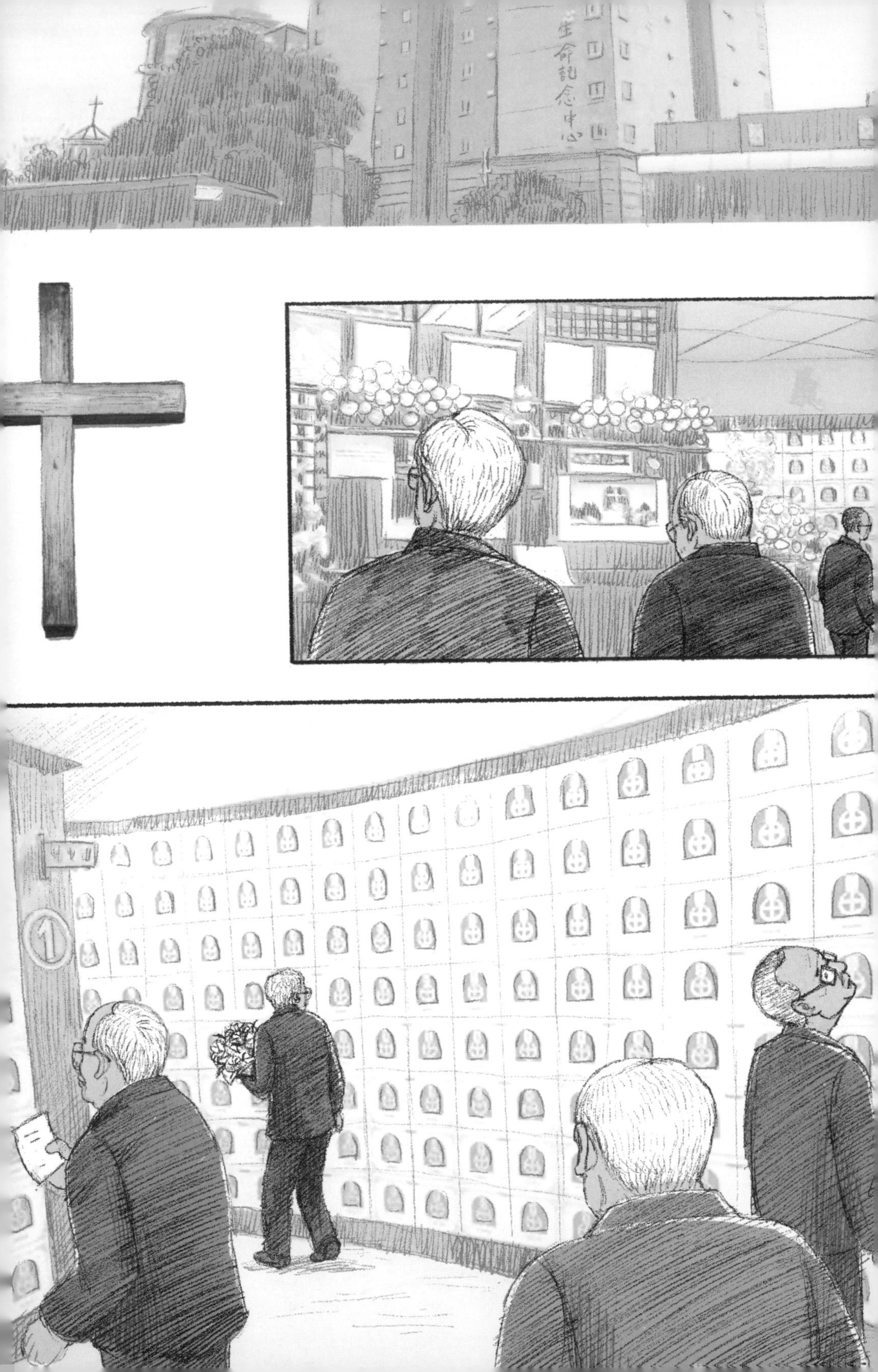

生命記念中心
1

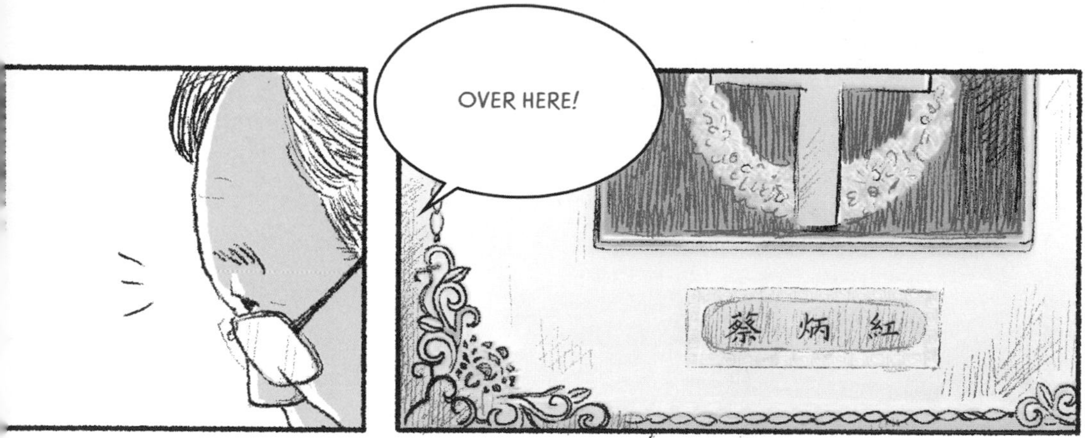
OVER HERE!
蔡 炳 紅

Legend: Tsai Ping-hung

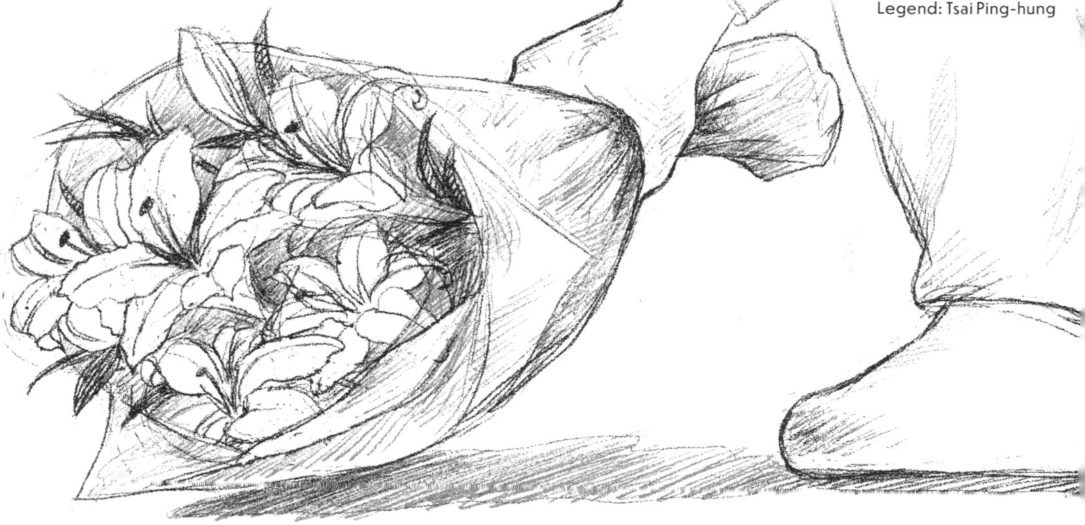

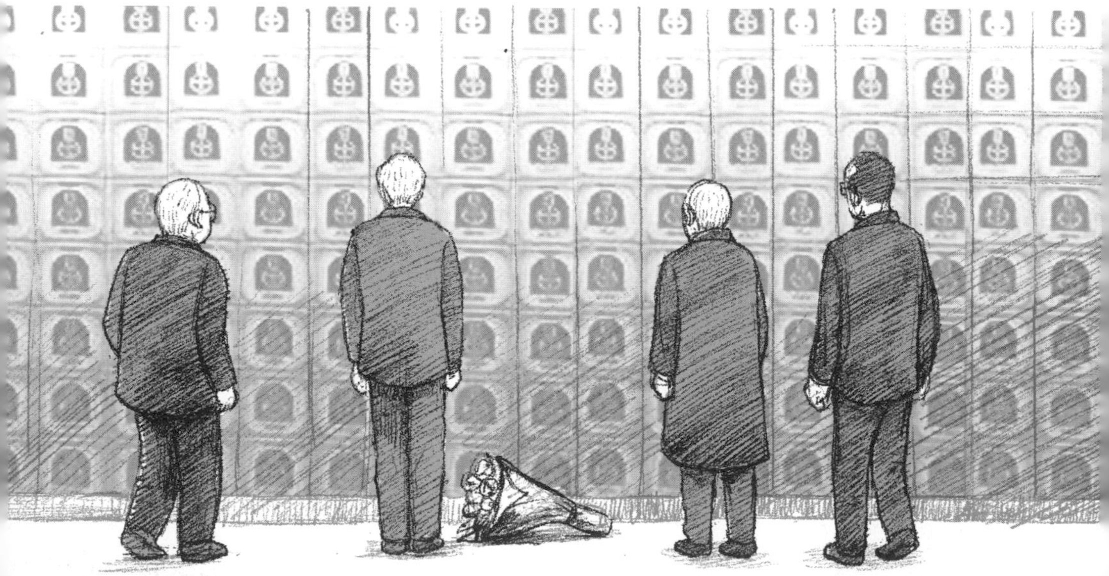

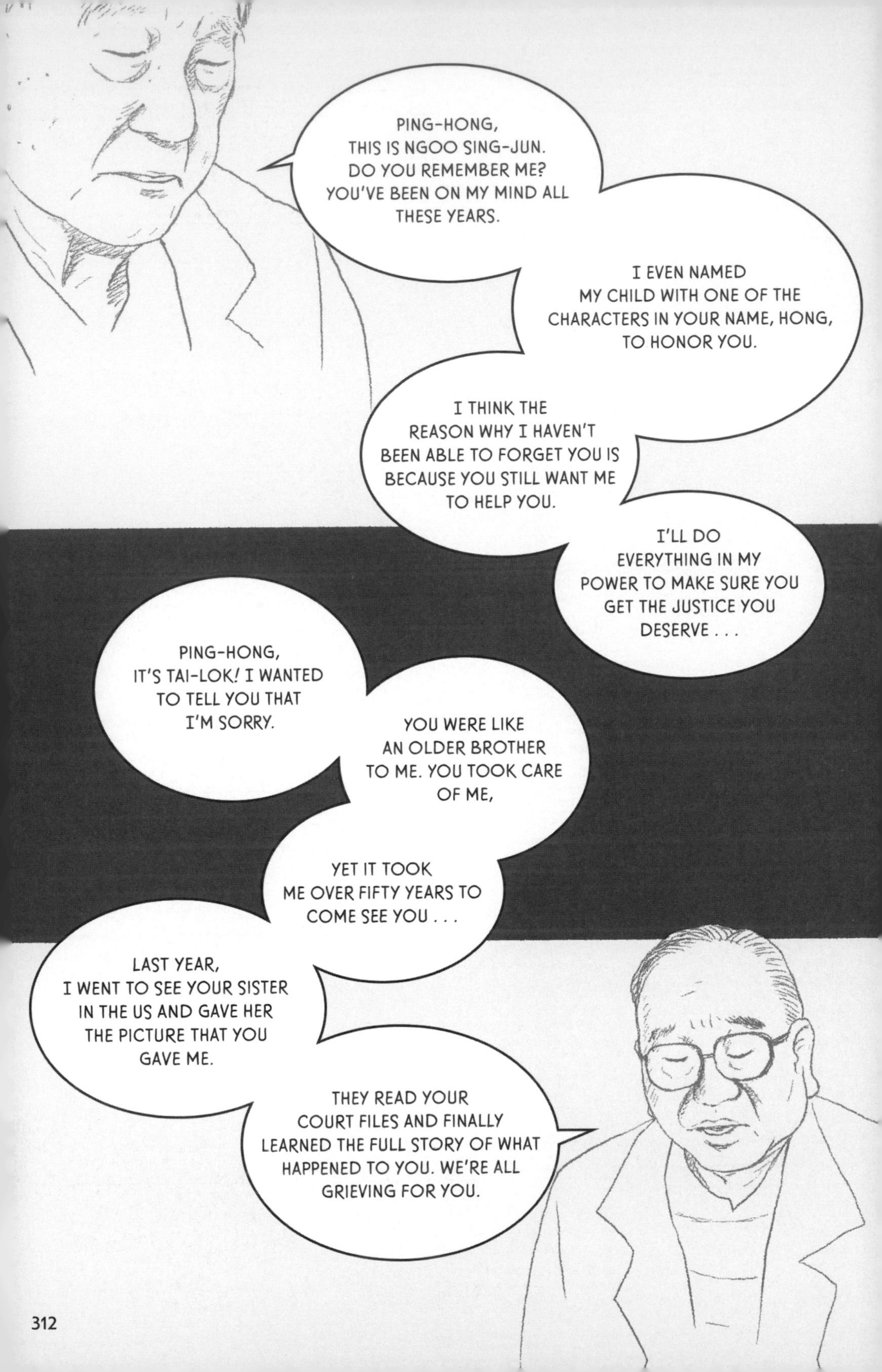
PING-HONG, THIS IS NGOO SING-JUN. DO YOU REMEMBER ME? YOU'VE BEEN ON MY MIND ALL THESE YEARS.
I EVEN NAMED MY CHILD WITH ONE OF THE CHARACTERS IN YOUR NAME, HONG, TO HONOR YOU.
I THINK THE REASON WHY I HAVEN'T BEEN ABLE TO FORGET YOU IS BECAUSE YOU STILL WANT ME TO HELP YOU.
I'LL DO EVERYTHING IN MY POWER TO MAKE SURE YOU GET THE JUSTICE YOU DESERVE . . .
PING-HONG, IT'S TAI-LOK! I WANTED TO TELL YOU THAT I'M SORRY.
YOU WERE LIKE AN OLDER BROTHER TO ME. YOU TOOK CARE OF ME,
YET IT TOOK ME OVER FIFTY YEARS TO COME SEE YOU . . .
LAST YEAR, I WENT TO SEE YOUR SISTER IN THE US AND GAVE HER THE PICTURE THAT YOU GAVE ME.
THEY READ YOUR COURT FILES AND FINALLY LEARNED THE FULL STORY OF WHAT HAPPENED TO YOU. WE'RE ALL GRIEVING FOR YOU.

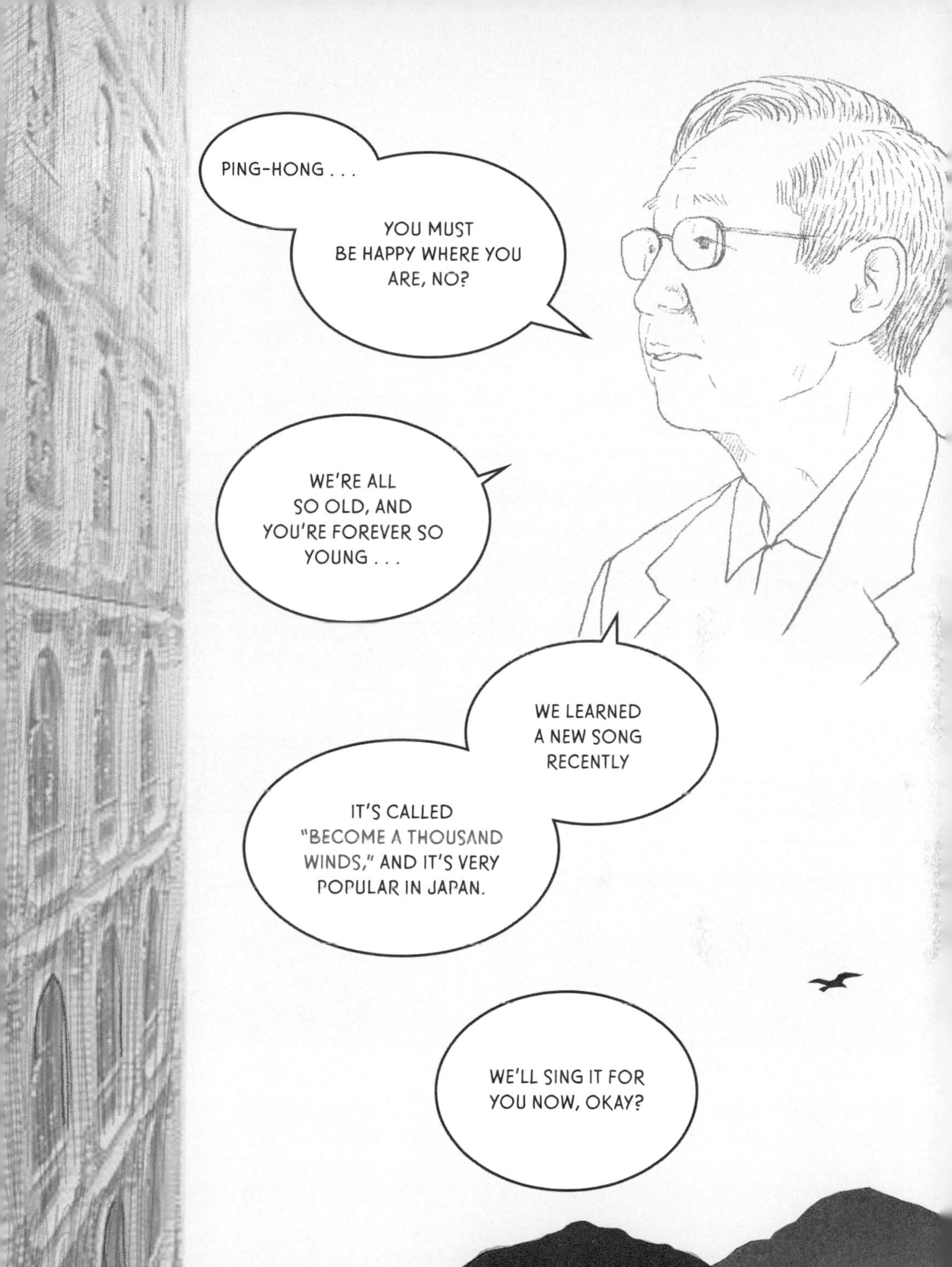
PING-HONG . . .
YOU MUST BE HAPPY WHERE YOU ARE, NO?
WE'RE ALL SO OLD, AND YOU'RE FOREVER SO YOUNG . . .
WE LEARNED A NEW SONG RECENTLY
IT'S CALLED "BECOME A THOUSAND WINDS," AND IT'S VERY POPULAR IN JAPAN.
WE'LL SING IT FOR YOU NOW, OKAY?

"Become a Thousand Winds": Arai Man, a Japanese singer, translated the English poem "Immortality" by Clare Harner (often known by its first line "Do not stand at my grave and weep") into Japanese under the title "Become a Thousand Winds," which was set to a song and released in 2003.

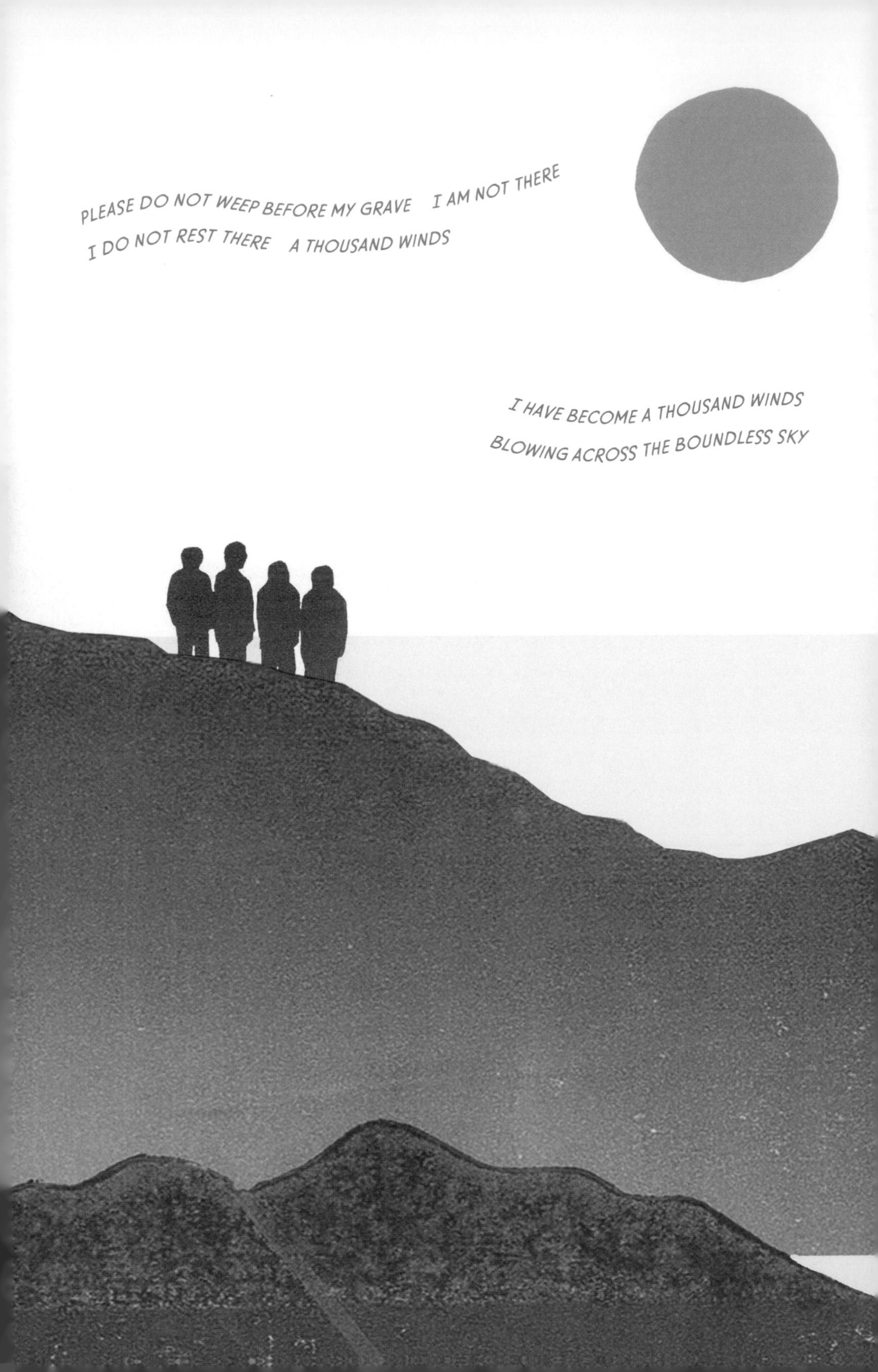
PLEASE DO NOT WEEP BEFORE MY GRAVE I AM NOT THERE
I DO NOT REST THERE A THOUSAND WINDS
I HAVE BECOME A THOUSAND WINDS
BLOWING ACROSS THE BOUNDLESS SKY

IN THE AUTUMN, I BECOME THE LIGHT SHINING DOWN ON THE FIELDS

IN THE WINTER, I BECOME THE SNOW SHIMMERING LIKE DIAMONDS

IN THE MORNINGS, I BECOME THE BIRDS ROUSING YOU FROM SLEEP

IN THE EVENINGS, I BECOME THE STARS WATCHING OVER YOU

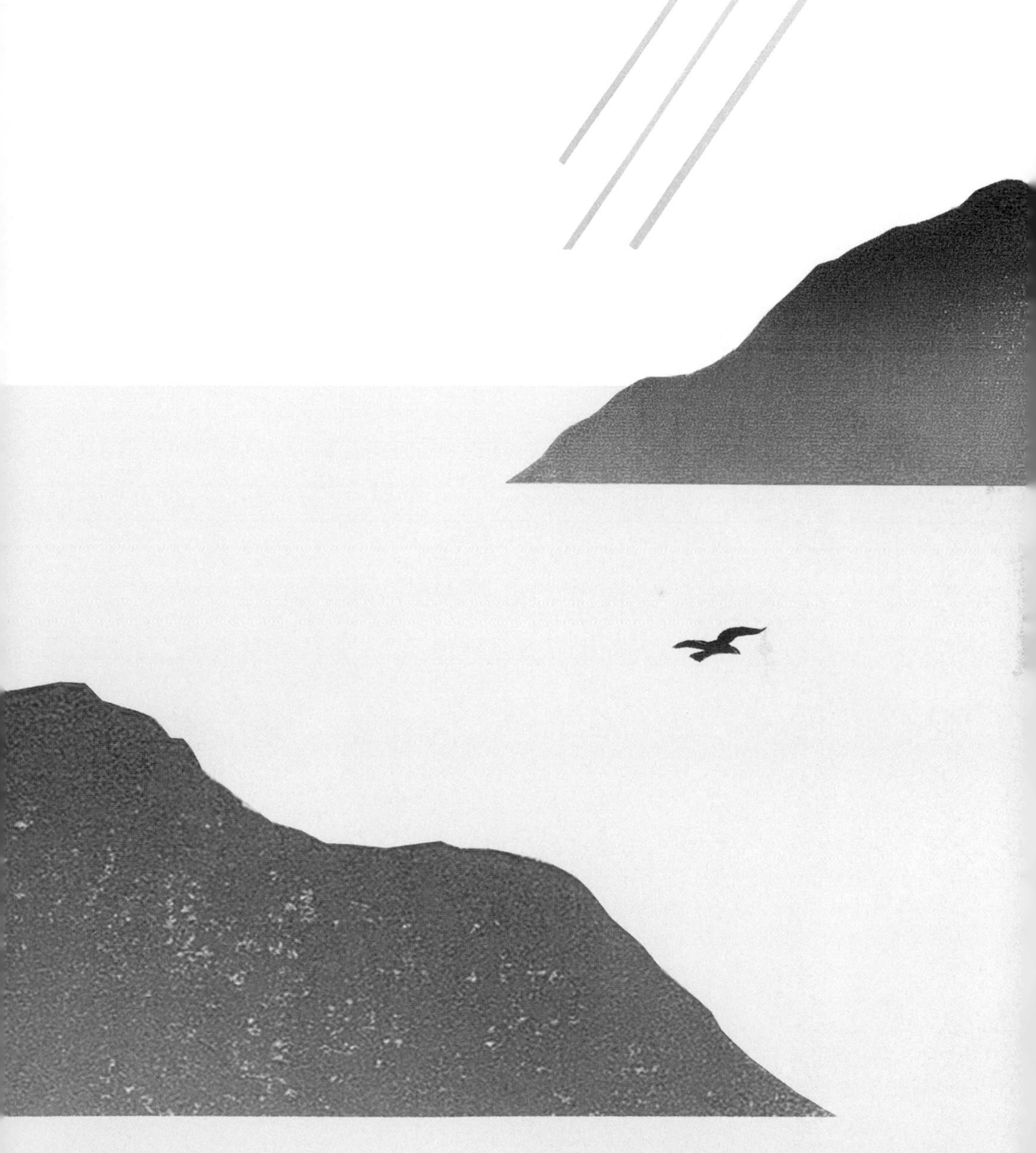

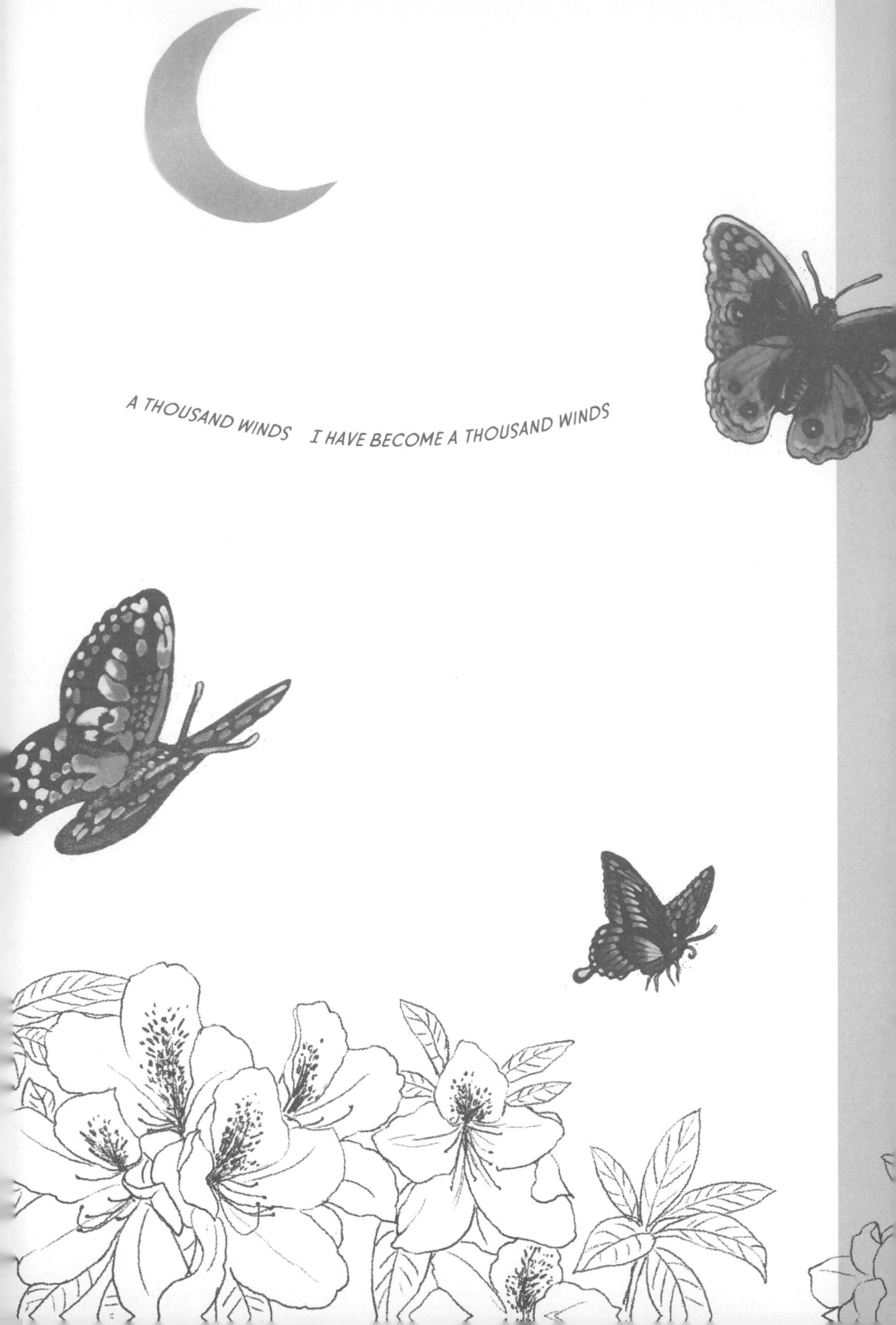
A THOUSAND WINDS I HAVE BECOME A THOUSAND WINDS

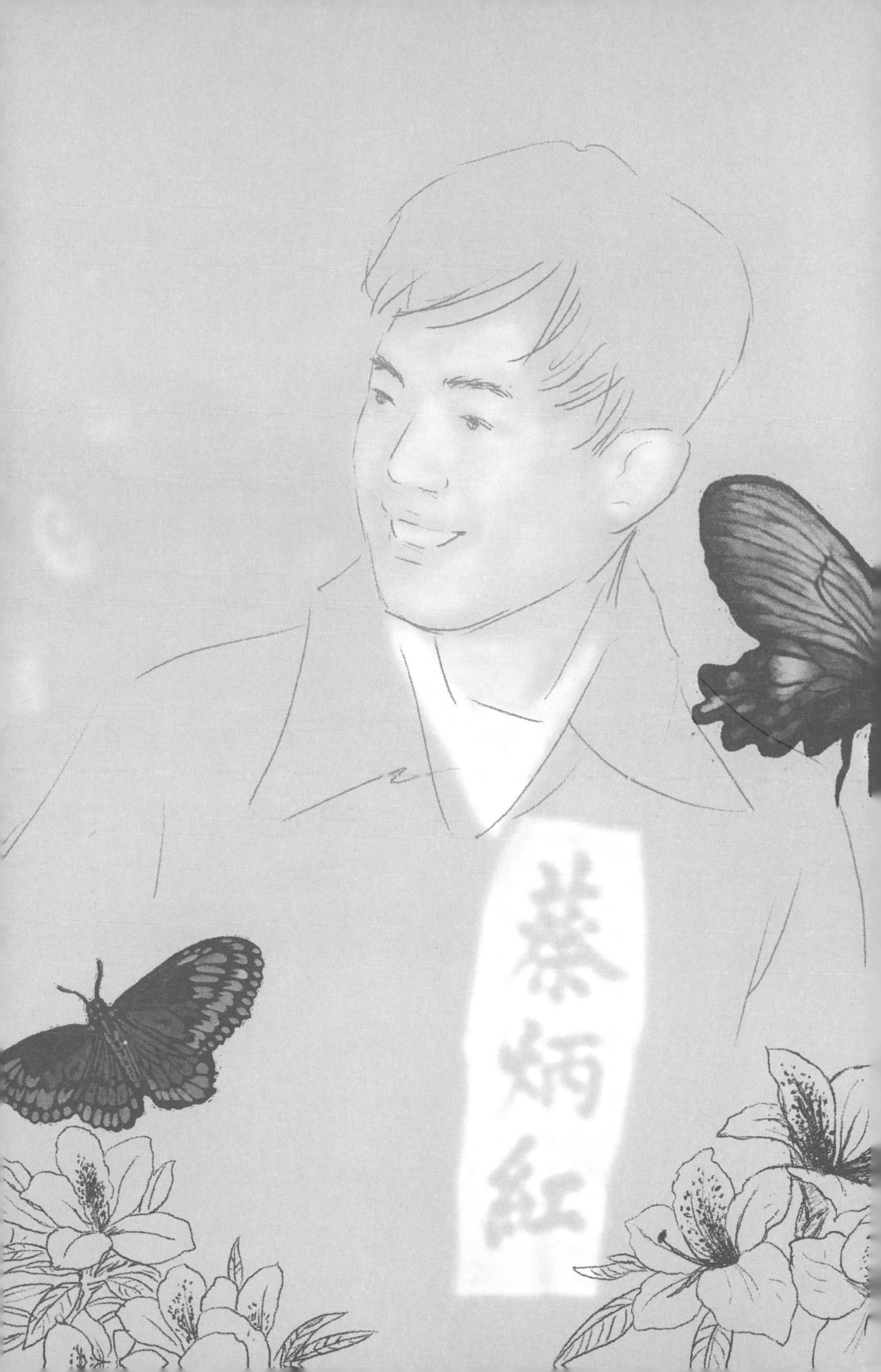
蔡炳紅

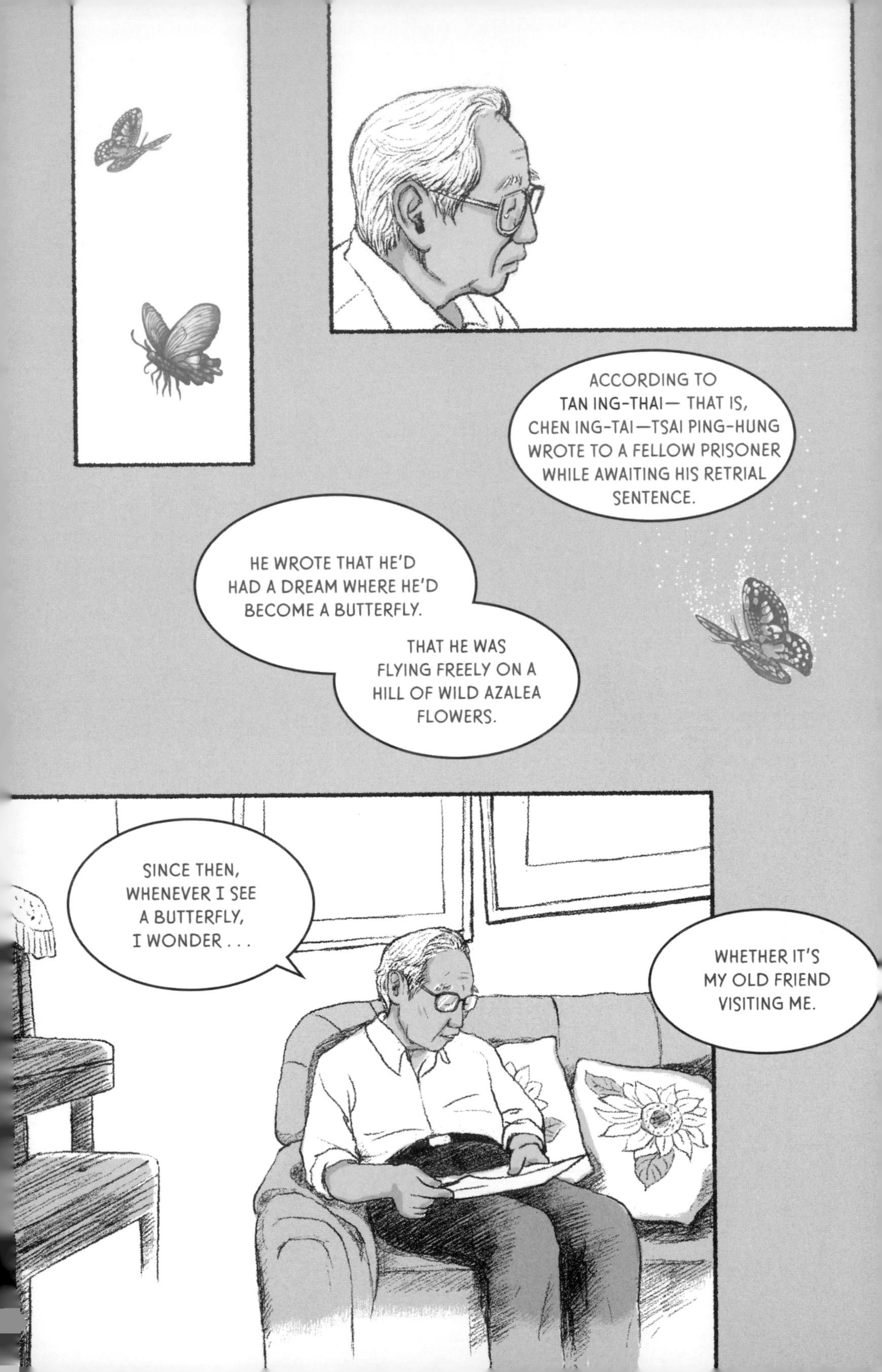
ACCORDING TO TAN ING-THAI— THAT IS, CHEN ING-TAI—TSAI PING-HUNG WROTE TO A FELLOW PRISONER WHILE AWAITING HIS RETRIAL SENTENCE.
HE WROTE THAT HE'D HAD A DREAM WHERE HE'D BECOME A BUTTERFLY.
THAT HE WAS FLYING FREELY ON A HILL OF WILD AZALEA FLOWERS.
SINCE THEN, WHENEVER I SEE A BUTTERFLY, I WONDER . . .
WHETHER IT'S MY OLD FRIEND VISITING ME.

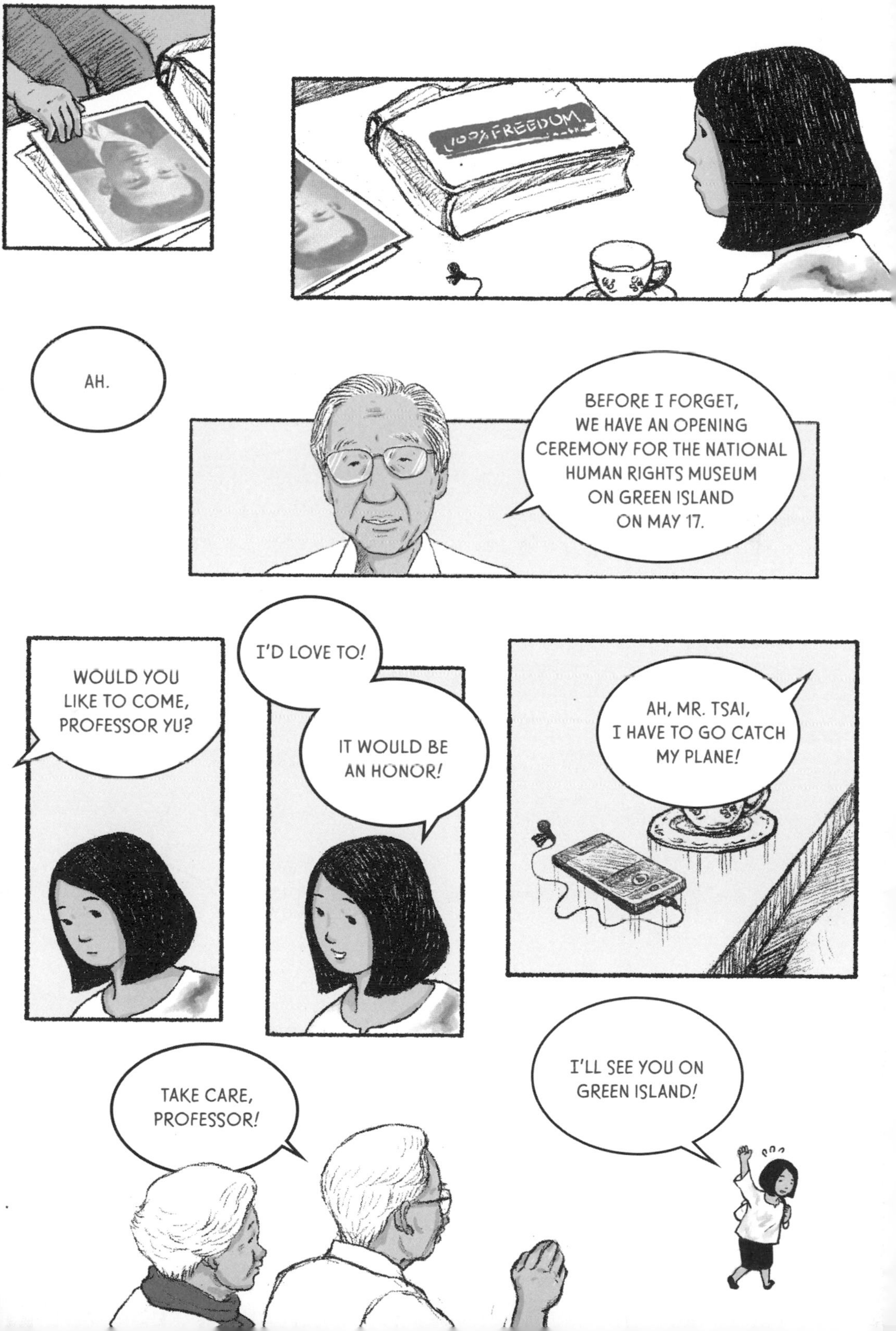
100% FREEDOM.
AH.
BEFORE I FORGET, WE HAVE AN OPENING CEREMONY FOR THE NATIONAL HUMAN RIGHTS MUSEUM ON GREEN ISLAND ON MAY 17.
WOULD YOU LIKE TO COME, PROFESSOR YU?
I'D LOVE TO!
IT WOULD BE AN HONOR!
AH, MR. TSAI, I HAVE TO GO CATCH MY PLANE!
TAKE CARE, PROFESSOR!
I'LL SEE YOU ON GREEN ISLAND!

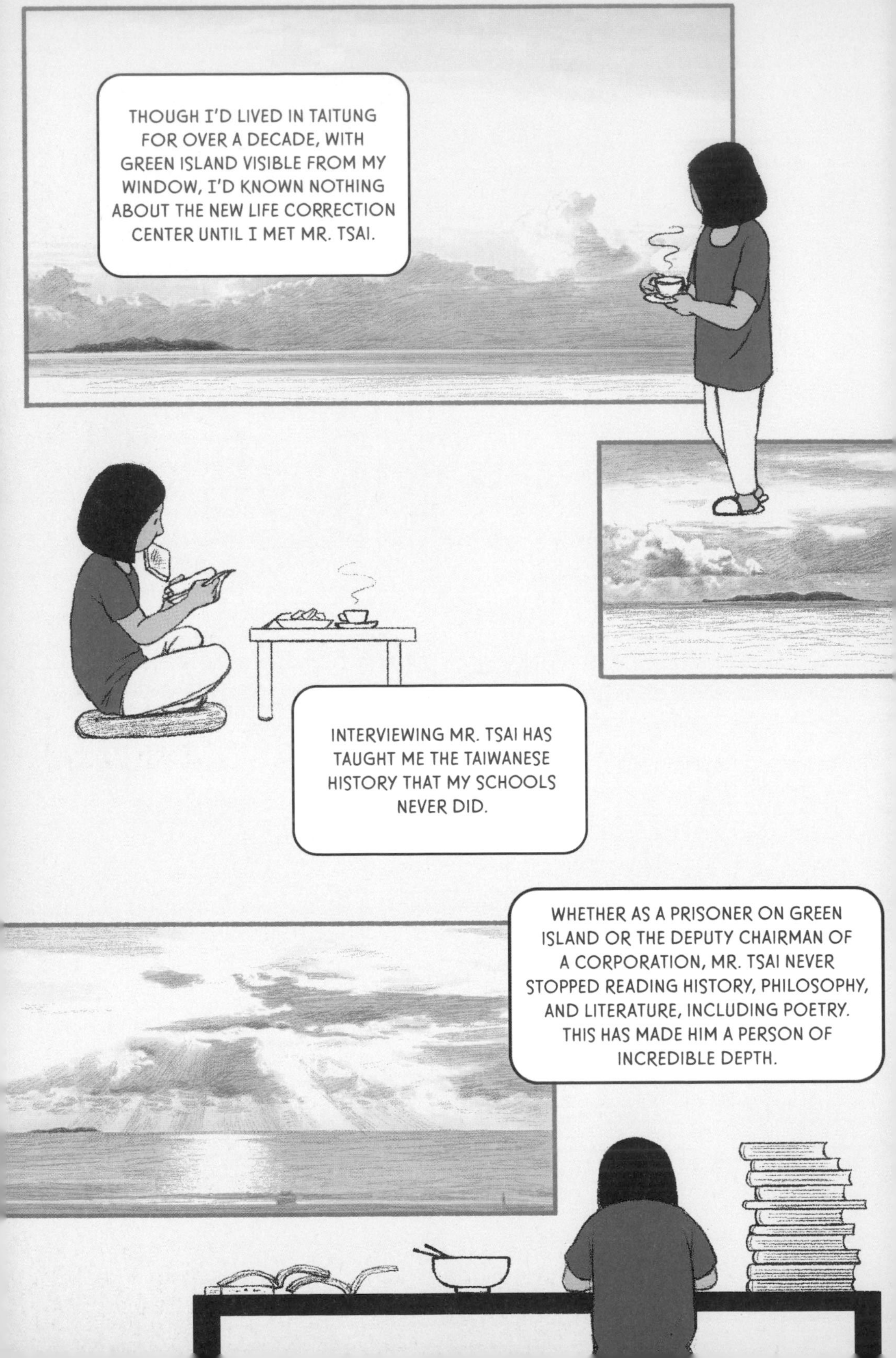
THOUGH I'D LIVED IN TAITUNG FOR OVER A DECADE, WITH GREEN ISLAND VISIBLE FROM MY WINDOW, I'D KNOWN NOTHING ABOUT THE NEW LIFE CORRECTION CENTER UNTIL I MET MR. TSAI.
INTERVIEWING MR. TSAI HAS TAUGHT ME THE TAIWANESE HISTORY THAT MY SCHOOLS NEVER DID.
WHETHER AS A PRISONER ON GREEN ISLAND OR THE DEPUTY CHAIRMAN OF A CORPORATION, MR. TSAI NEVER STOPPED READING HISTORY, PHILOSOPHY, AND LITERATURE, INCLUDING POETRY. THIS HAS MADE HIM A PERSON OF INCREDIBLE DEPTH.

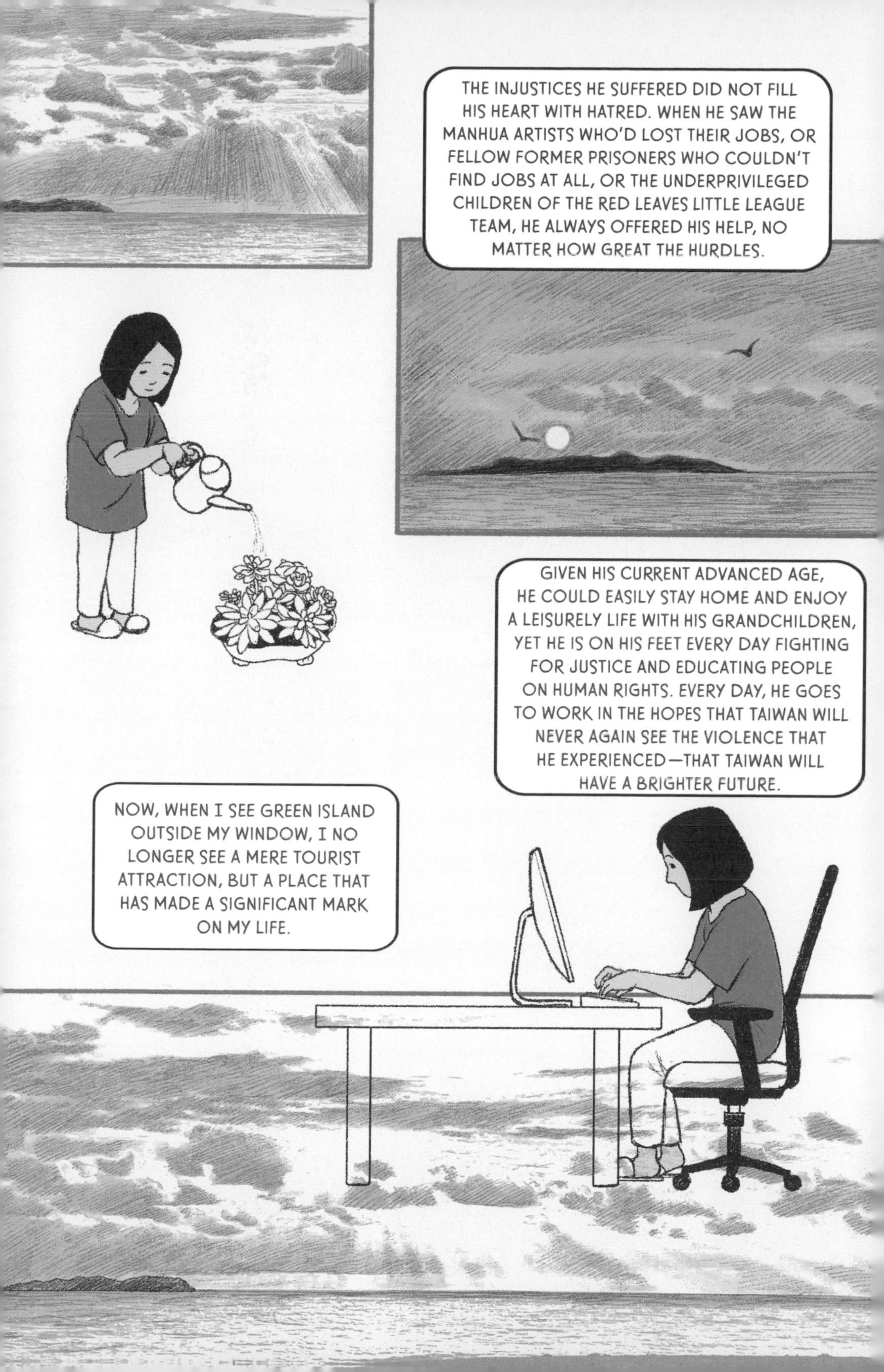
THE INJUSTICES HE SUFFERED DID NOT FILL HIS HEART WITH HATRED. WHEN HE SAW THE MANHUA ARTISTS WHO'D LOST THEIR JOBS, OR FELLOW FORMER PRISONERS WHO COULDN'T FIND JOBS AT ALL, OR THE UNDERPRIVILEGED CHILDREN OF THE RED LEAVES LITTLE LEAGUE TEAM, HE ALWAYS OFFERED HIS HELP, NO MATTER HOW GREAT THE HURDLES.
GIVEN HIS CURRENT ADVANCED AGE, HE COULD EASILY STAY HOME AND ENJOY A LEISURELY LIFE WITH HIS GRANDCHILDREN, YET HE IS ON HIS FEET EVERY DAY FIGHTING FOR JUSTICE AND EDUCATING PEOPLE ON HUMAN RIGHTS. EVERY DAY, HE GOES TO WORK IN THE HOPES THAT TAIWAN WILL NEVER AGAIN SEE THE VIOLENCE THAT HE EXPERIENCED—THAT TAIWAN WILL HAVE A BRIGHTER FUTURE.
NOW, WHEN I SEE GREEN ISLAND OUTSIDE MY WINDOW, I NO LONGER SEE A MERE TOURIST ATTRACTION, BUT A PLACE THAT HAS MADE A SIGNIFICANT MARK ON MY LIFE.

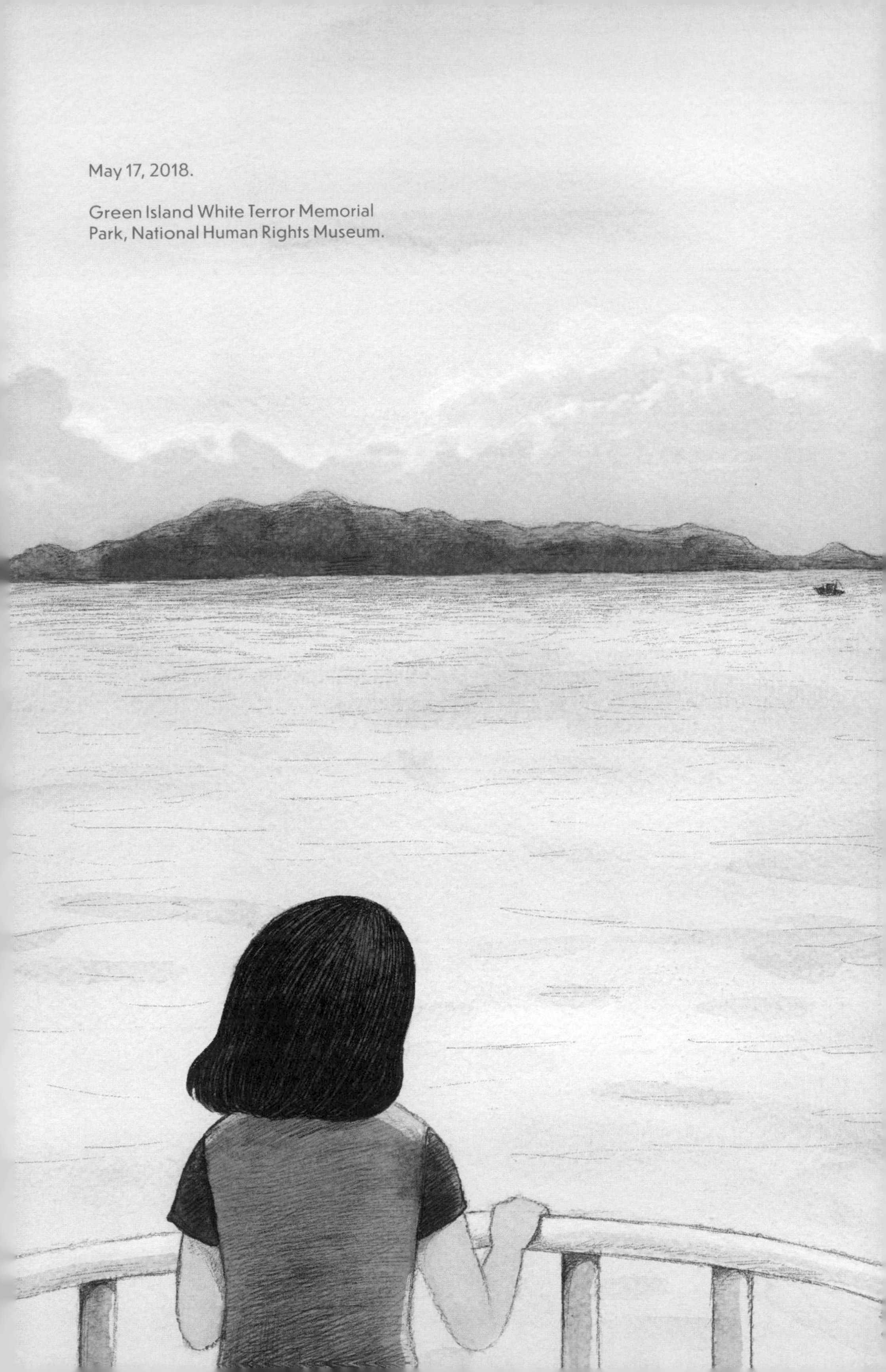
May 17, 2018.
Green Island White Terror Memorial Park, National Human Rights Museum.

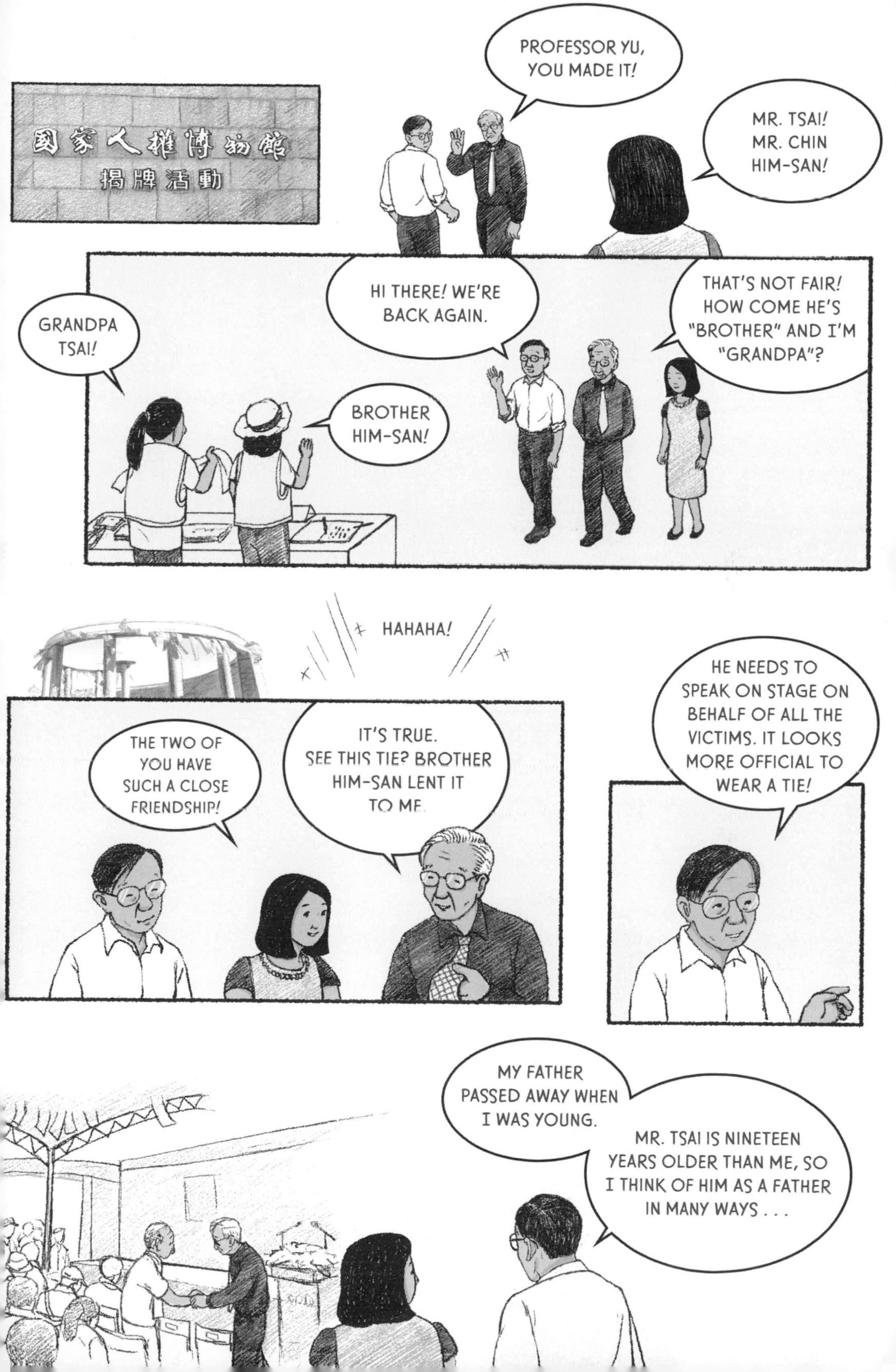

國家人權博物館
揭牌活動
PROFESSOR YU, YOU MADE IT!
MR. TSAI! MR. CHIN HIM-SAN!
GRANDPA TSAI!
HI THERE! WE'RE BACK AGAIN.
THAT'S NOT FAIR! HOW COME HE'S "BROTHER" AND I'M "GRANDPA"?
BROTHER HIM-SAN!
HAHAHA!
THE TWO OF YOU HAVE SUCH A CLOSE FRIENDSHIP!
IT'S TRUE. SEE THIS TIE? BROTHER HIM-SAN LENT IT TO ME.
HE NEEDS TO SPEAK ON STAGE ON BEHALF OF ALL THE VICTIMS. IT LOOKS MORE OFFICIAL TO WEAR A TIE!
MY FATHER PASSED AWAY WHEN I WAS YOUNG.
MR. TSAI IS NINETEEN YEARS OLDER THAN ME, SO I THINK OF HIM AS A FATHER IN MANY WAYS . . .

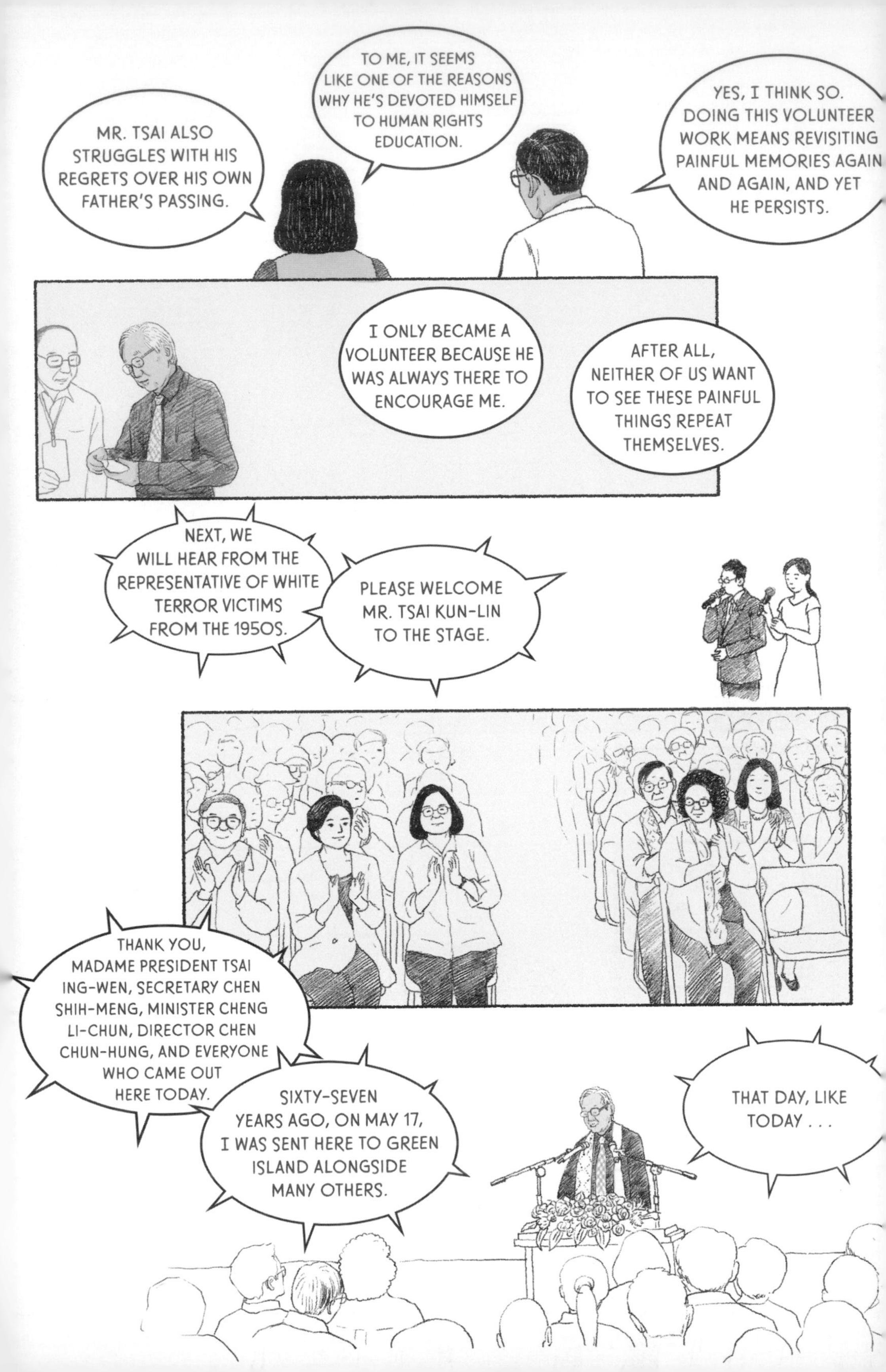
MR. TSAI ALSO STRUGGLES WITH HIS REGRETS OVER HIS OWN FATHER'S PASSING.
TO ME, IT SEEMS LIKE ONE OF THE REASONS WHY HE'S DEVOTED HIMSELF TO HUMAN RIGHTS EDUCATION.
YES, I THINK SO. DOING THIS VOLUNTEER WORK MEANS REVISITING PAINFUL MEMORIES AGAIN AND AGAIN, AND YET HE PERSISTS.
I ONLY BECAME A VOLUNTEER BECAUSE HE WAS ALWAYS THERE TO ENCOURAGE ME.
AFTER ALL, NEITHER OF US WANT TO SEE THESE PAINFUL THINGS REPEAT THEMSELVES.
NEXT, WE WILL HEAR FROM THE REPRESENTATIVE OF WHITE TERROR VICTIMS FROM THE 1950S.
PLEASE WELCOME MR. TSAI KUN-LIN TO THE STAGE.
THANK YOU, MADAME PRESIDENT TSAI ING-WEN, SECRETARY CHEN SHIH-MENG, MINISTER CHENG LI-CHUN, DIRECTOR CHEN CHUN-HUNG, AND EVERYONE WHO CAME OUT HERE TODAY.
SIXTY-SEVEN YEARS AGO, ON MAY 17, I WAS SENT HERE TO GREEN ISLAND ALONGSIDE MANY OTHERS.
THAT DAY, LIKE TODAY . . .

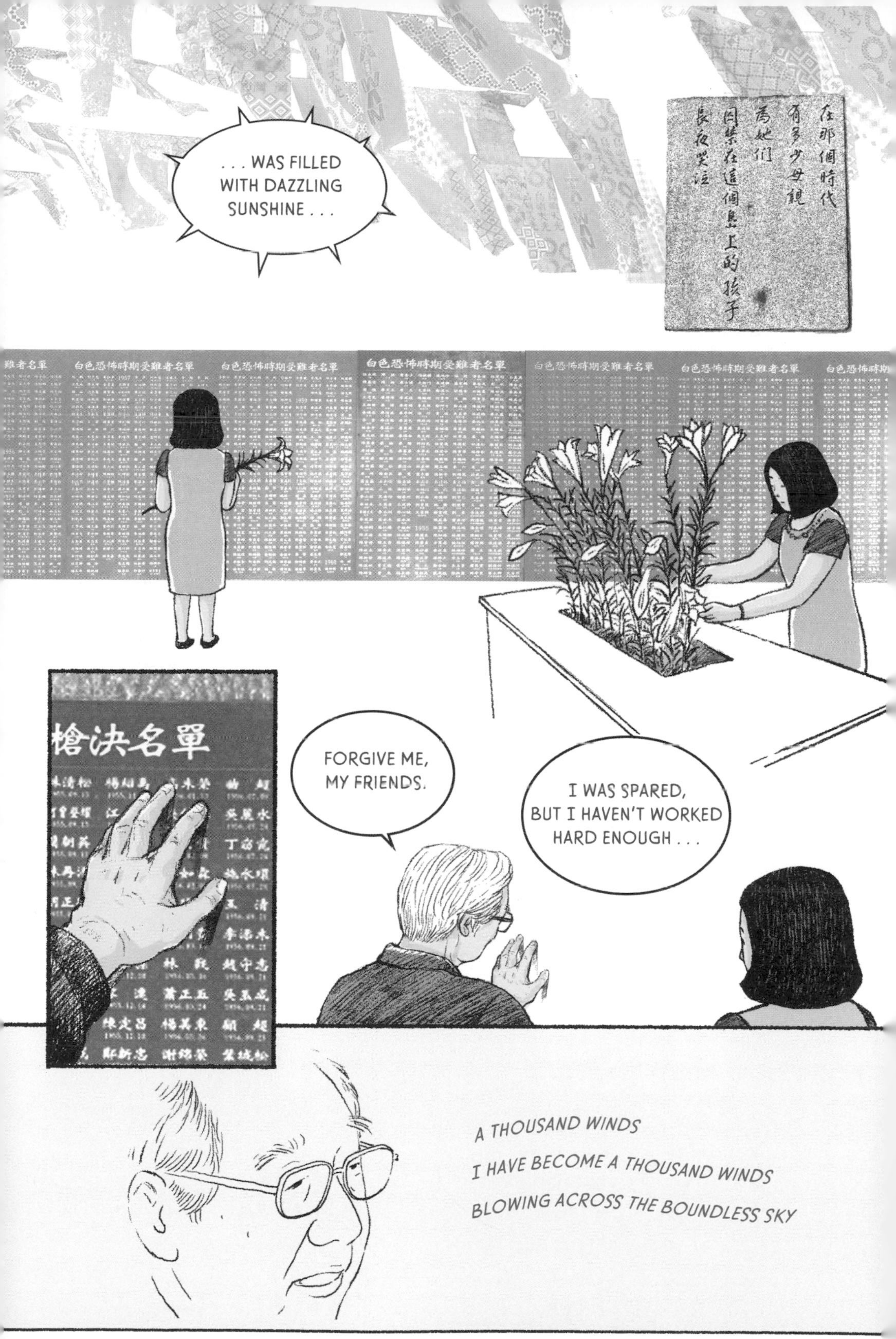

. . . WAS FILLED WITH DAZZLING SUNSHINE . . .
在那個時代
有多少母親
為她們
囚禁在這個島上的孩子
長夜哭泣
白色恐怖時期受難者名單
槍決名單
FORGIVE ME, MY FRIENDS.
I WAS SPARED, BUT I HAVEN'T WORKED HARD ENOUGH . . .
A THOUSAND WINDS
I HAVE BECOME A THOUSAND WINDS
BLOWING ACROSS THE BOUNDLESS SKY

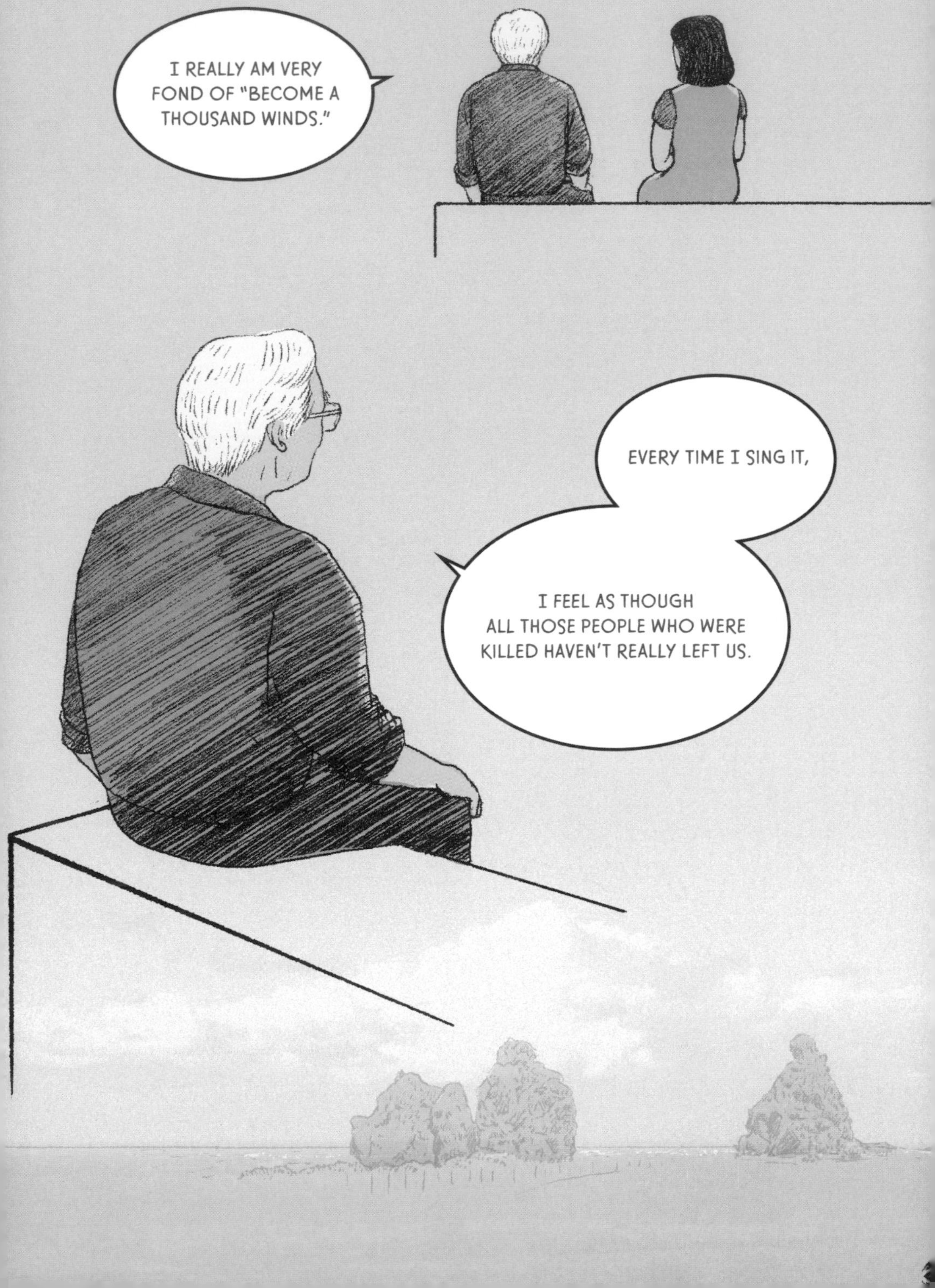
I REALLY AM VERY FOND OF "BECOME A THOUSAND WINDS."
EVERY TIME I SING IT,
I FEEL AS THOUGH ALL THOSE PEOPLE WHO WERE KILLED HAVEN'T REALLY LEFT US.

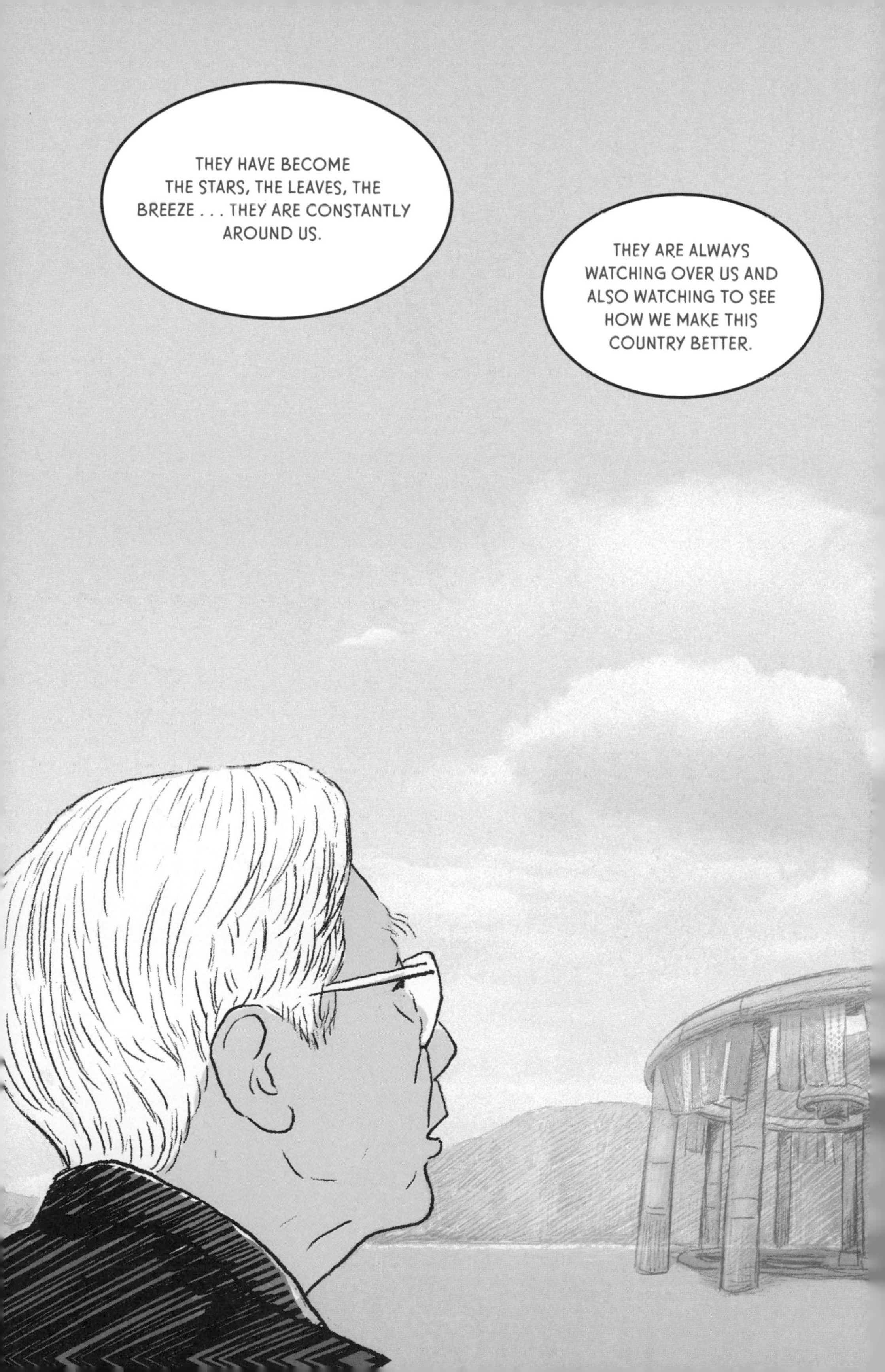
THEY HAVE BECOME THE STARS, THE LEAVES, THE BREEZE . . . THEY ARE CONSTANTLY AROUND US.
THEY ARE ALWAYS WATCHING OVER US AND ALSO WATCHING TO SEE HOW WE MAKE THIS COUNTRY BETTER.

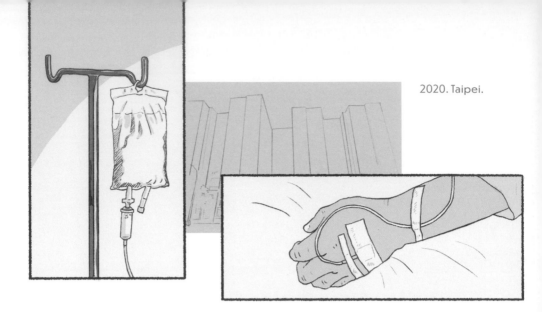

2020. Taipei.

BA, THE DOCTOR SAYS THE SURGERY WENT REALLY WELL.

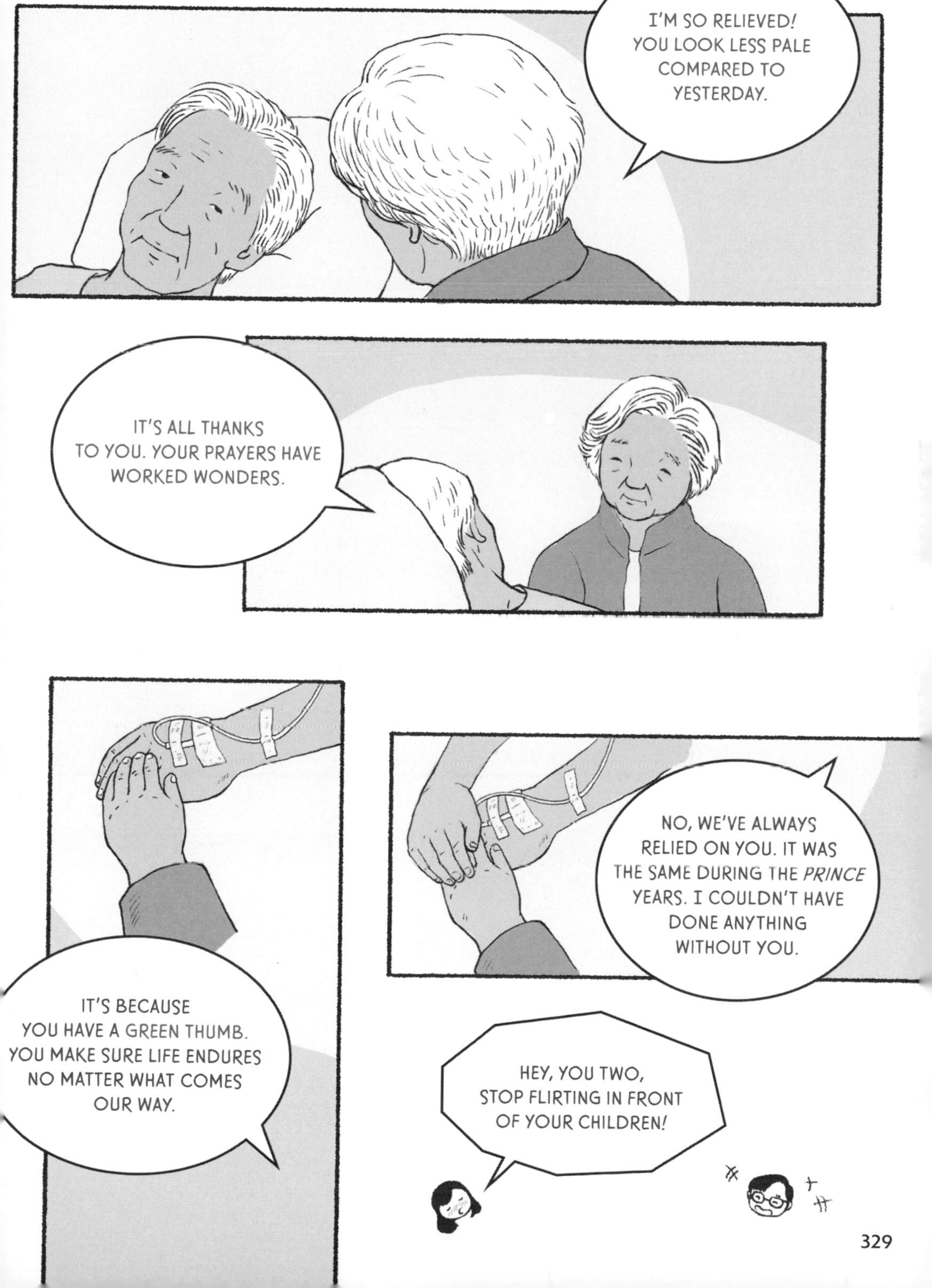
I'M SO RELIEVED! YOU LOOK LESS PALE COMPARED TO YESTERDAY.
IT'S ALL THANKS TO YOU. YOUR PRAYERS HAVE WORKED WONDERS.
IT'S BECAUSE YOU HAVE A GREEN THUMB. YOU MAKE SURE LIFE ENDURES NO MATTER WHAT COMES OUR WAY.
NO, WE'VE ALWAYS RELIED ON YOU. IT WAS THE SAME DURING THE *PRINCE* YEARS. I COULDN'T HAVE DONE ANYTHING WITHOUT YOU.
HEY, YOU TWO, STOP FLIRTING IN FRONT OF YOUR CHILDREN!

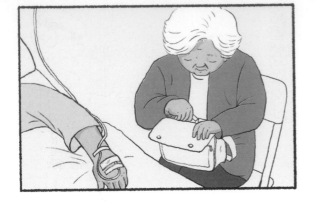

I'LL WHISPER, THEN.
LET ME READ YOU A STORY.

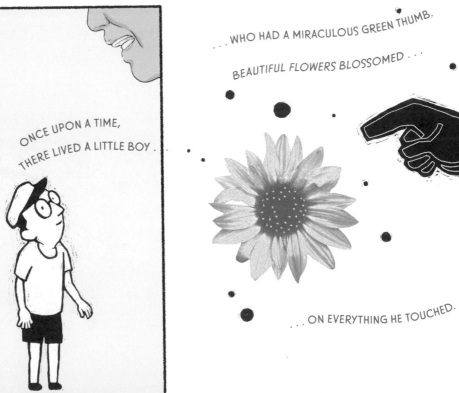

ONCE UPON A TIME,
THERE LIVED A LITTLE BOY . . .

. . . WHO HAD A MIRACULOUS GREEN THUMB.

BEAUTIFUL FLOWERS BLOSSOMED . . .

. . . ON EVERYTHING HE TOUCHED.

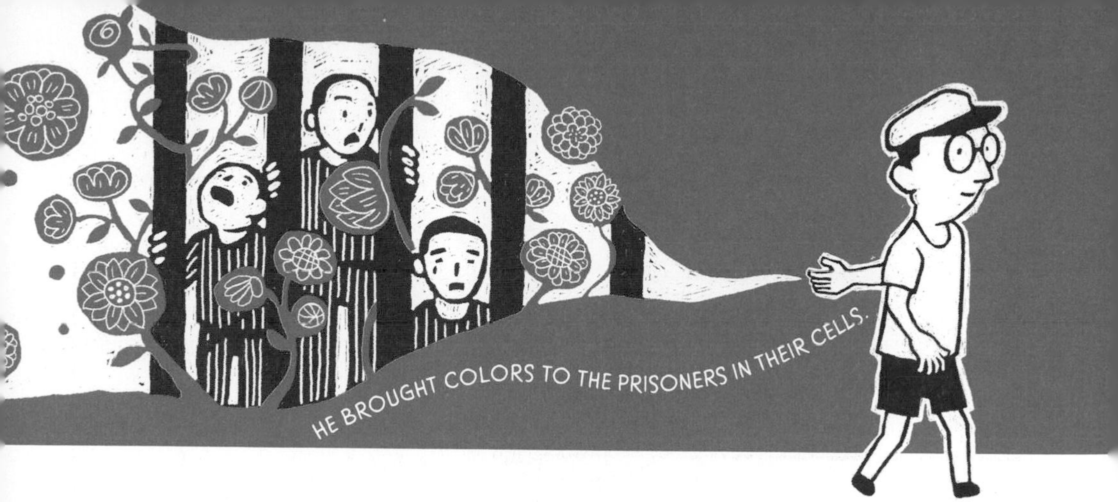
HE BROUGHT COLORS TO THE PRISONERS IN THEIR CELLS.

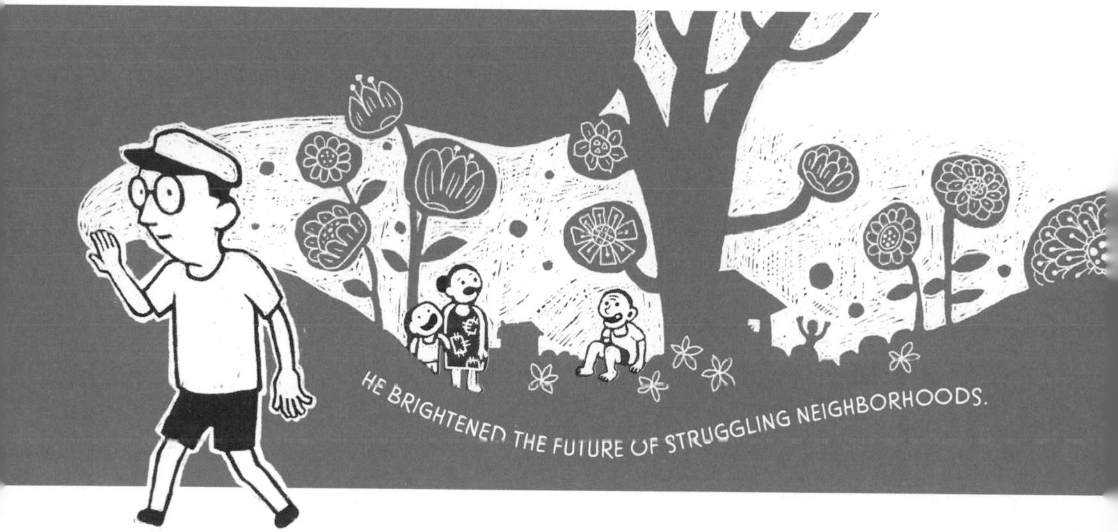
HE BRIGHTENED THE FUTURE OF STRUGGLING NEIGHBORHOODS.

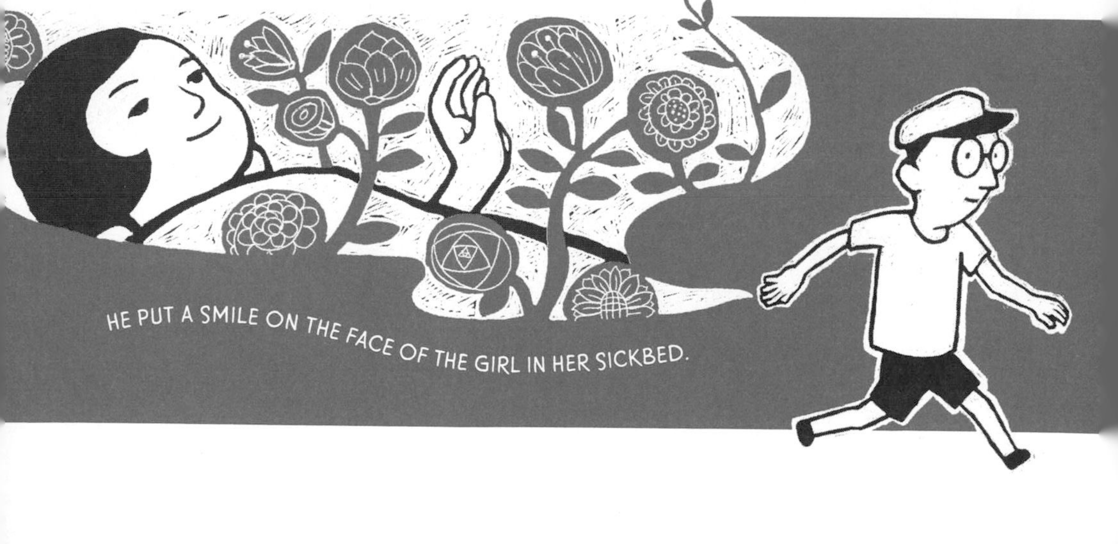
HE PUT A SMILE ON THE FACE OF THE GIRL IN HER SICKBED.

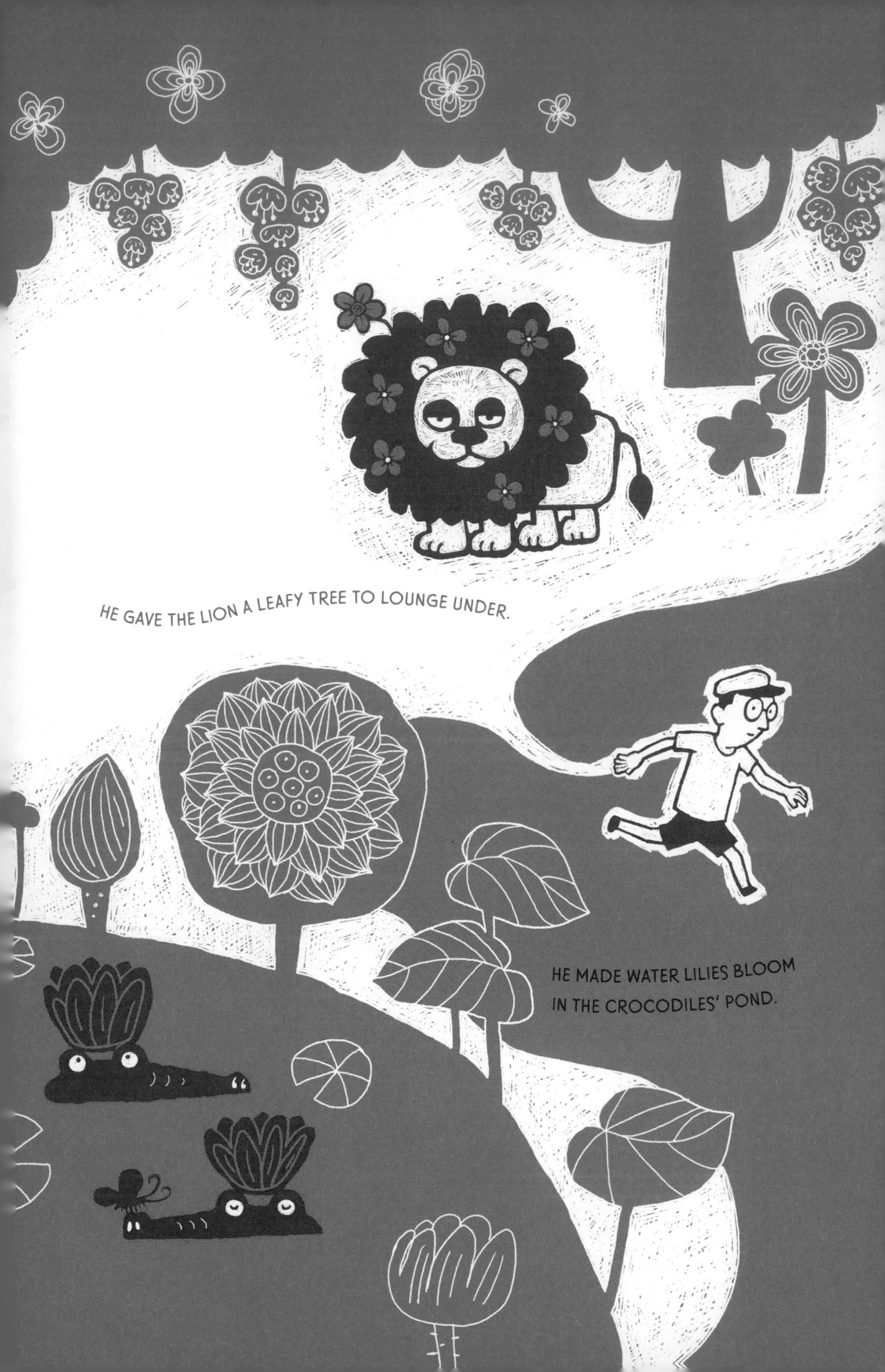

HE GAVE THE LION A LEAFY TREE TO LOUNGE UNDER.

HE MADE WATER LILIES BLOOM
IN THE CROCODILES' POND.

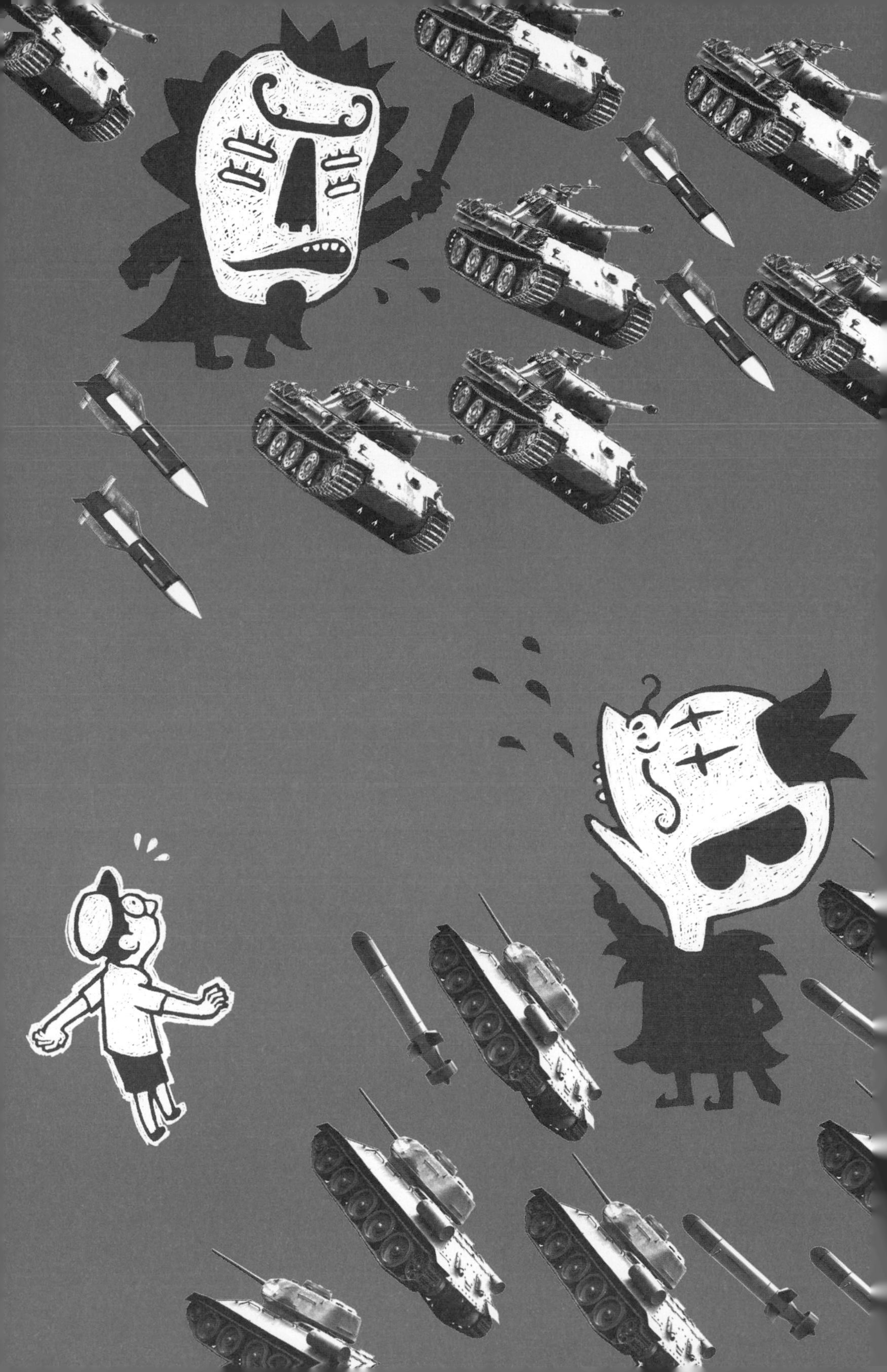

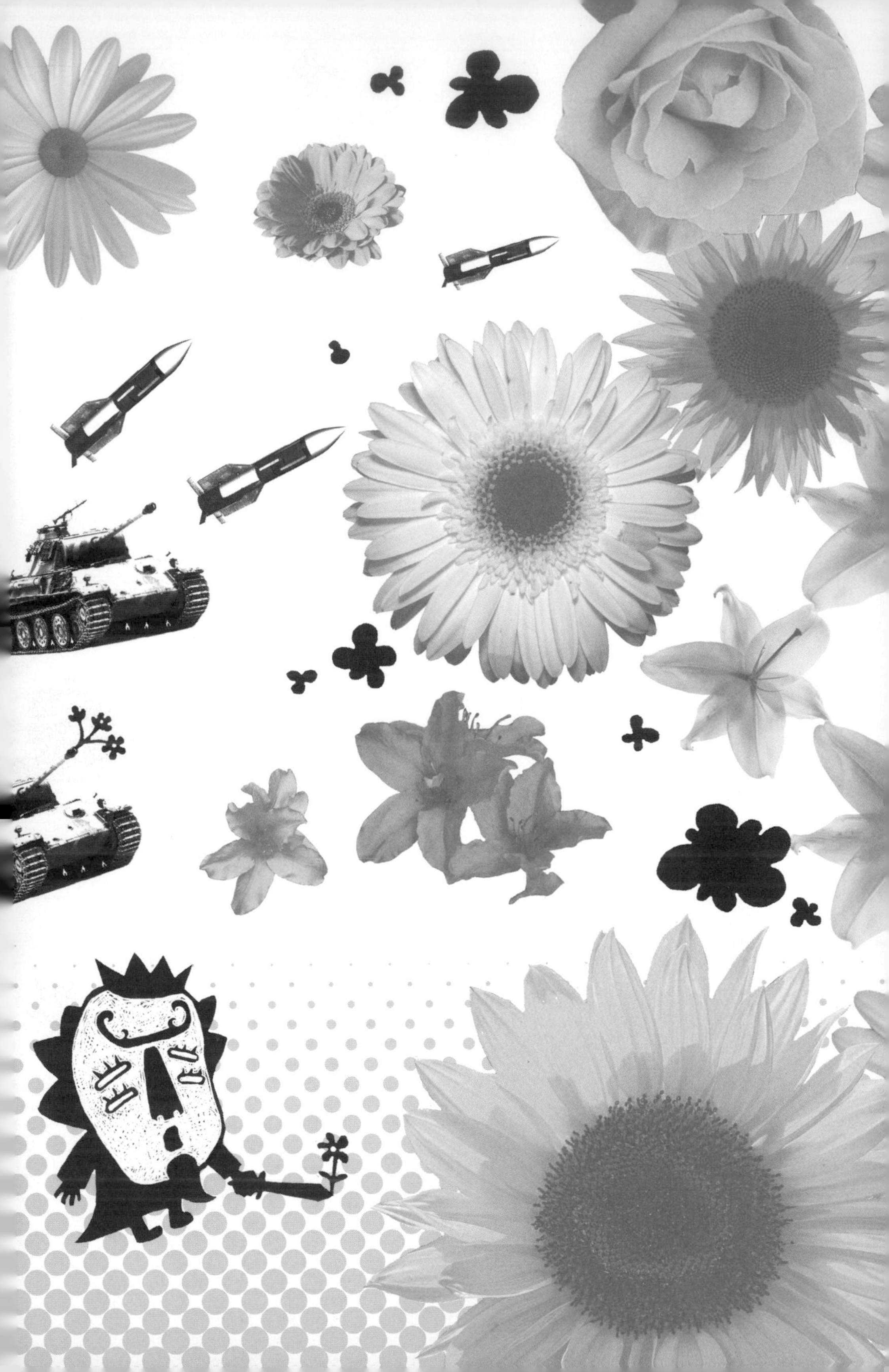

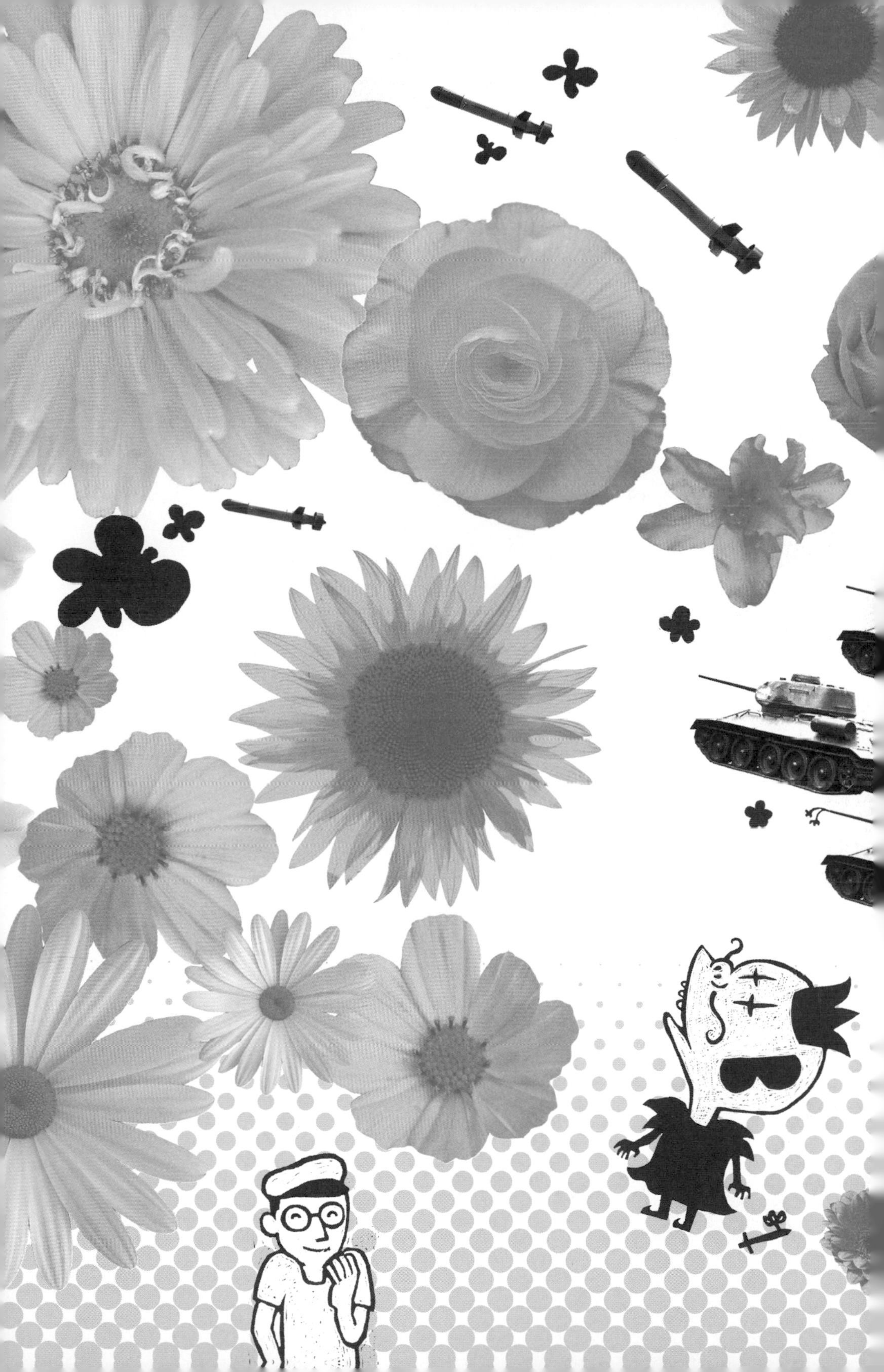

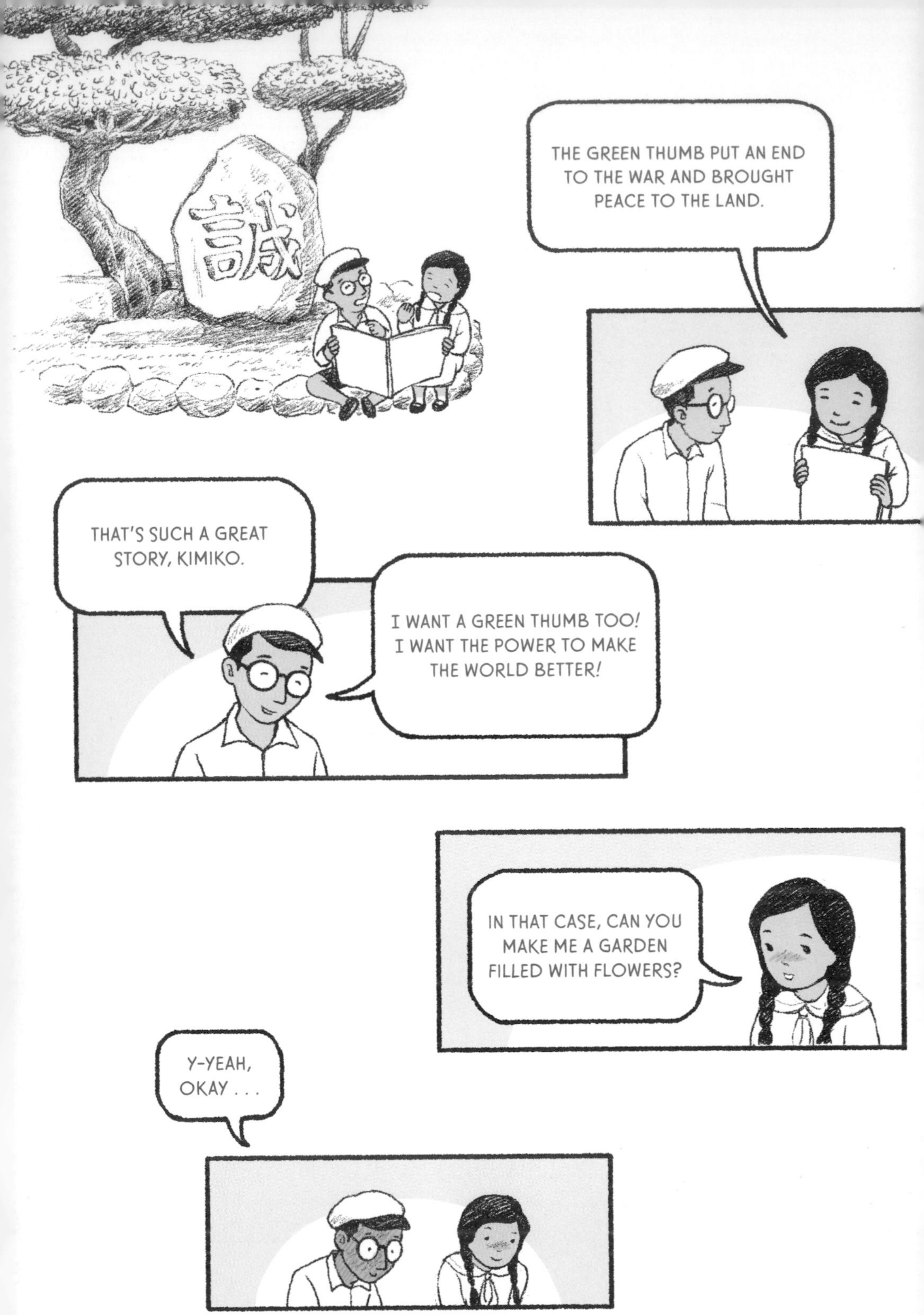
THE GREEN THUMB PUT AN END TO THE WAR AND BROUGHT PEACE TO THE LAND.
THAT'S SUCH A GREAT STORY, KIMIKO.
I WANT A GREEN THUMB TOO! I WANT THE POWER TO MAKE THE WORLD BETTER!
IN THAT CASE, CAN YOU MAKE ME A GARDEN FILLED WITH FLOWERS?
Y-YEAH, OKAY . . .

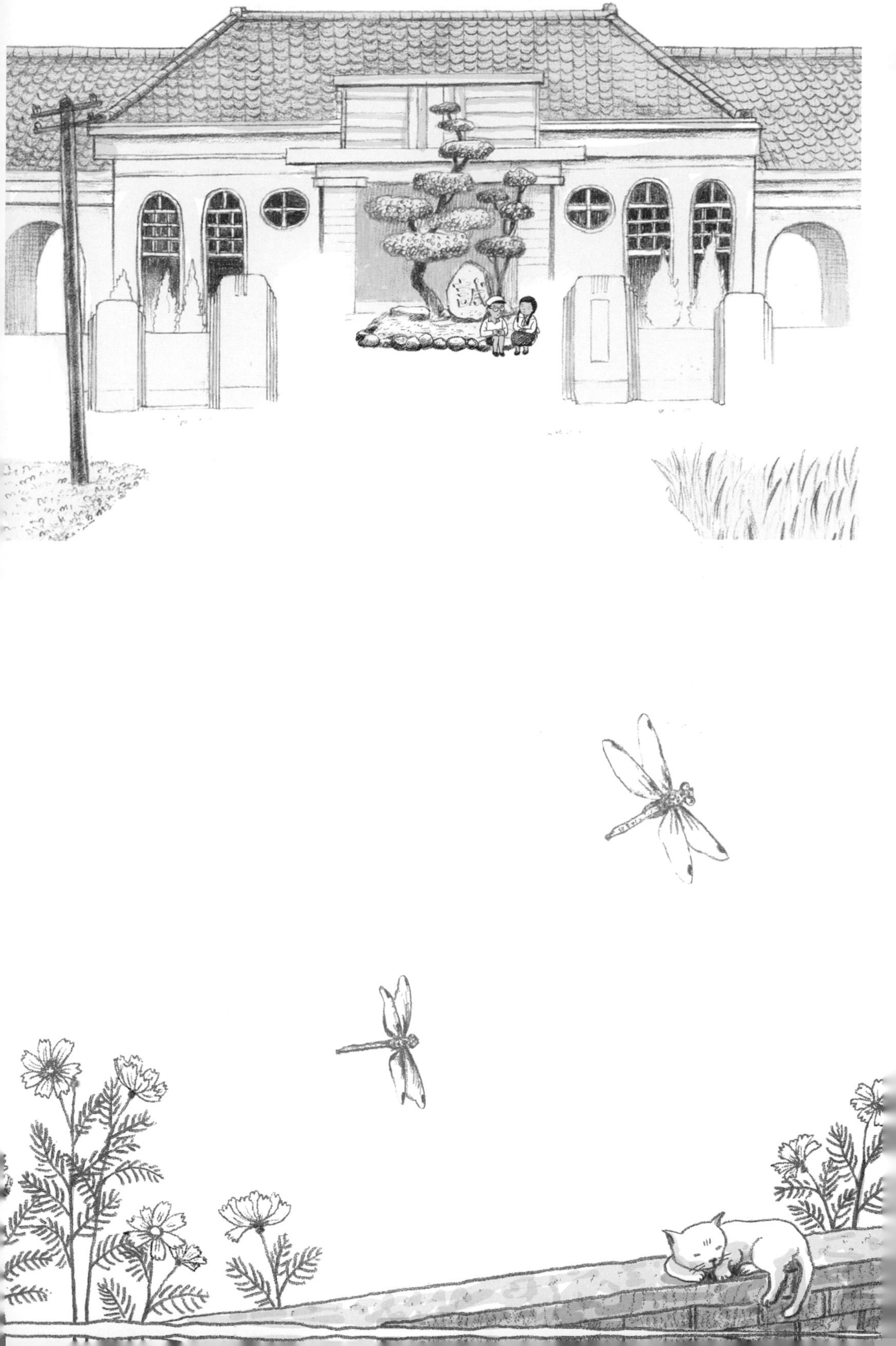

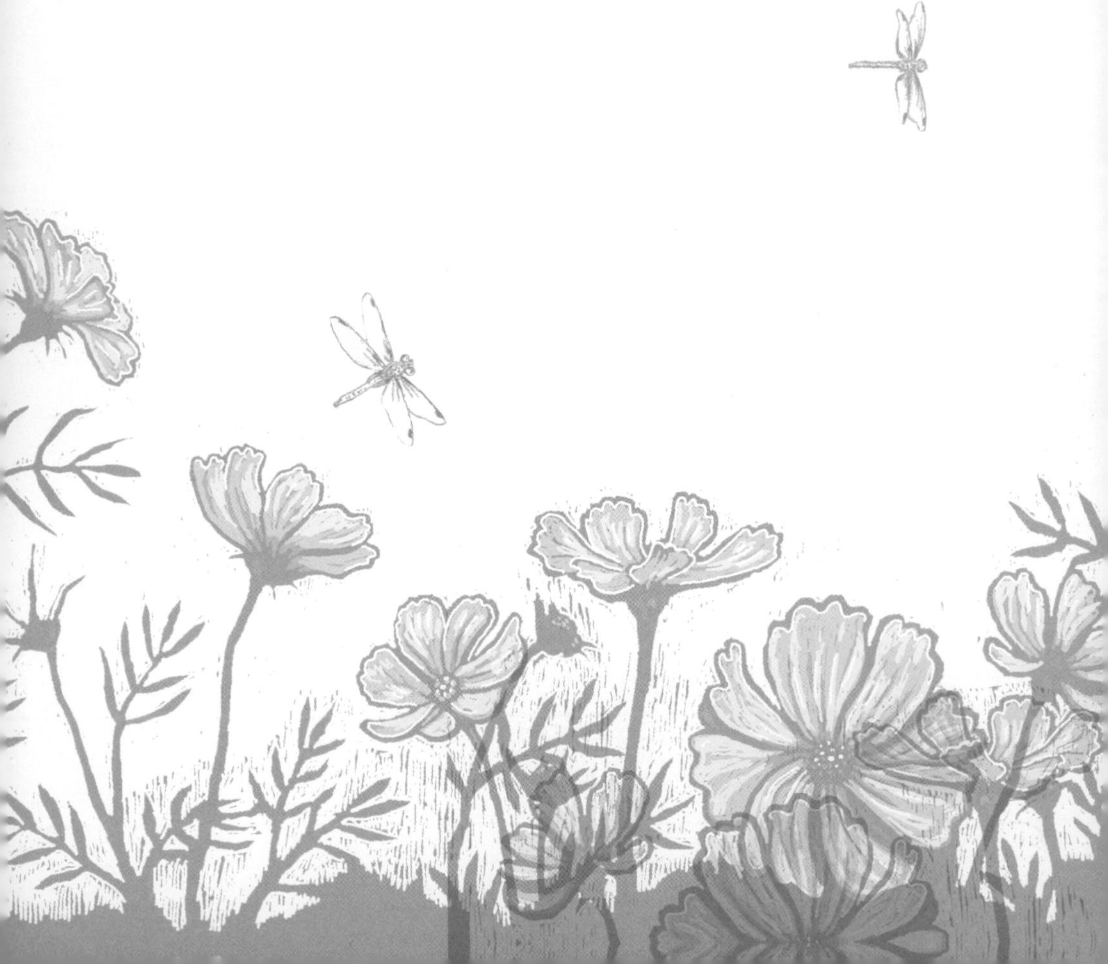

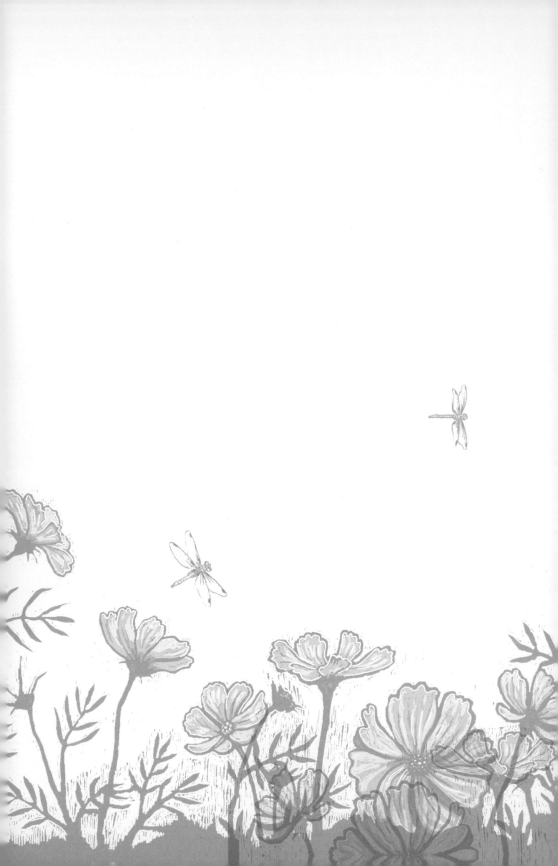

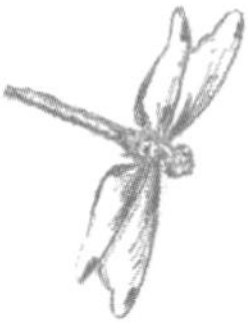

In October 2018, Taiwan's Transitional Justice Commission announced the exoneration of White Terror Era prisoners. In this first wave, 1,270 people convicted of political crimes—including Tshua Khun-lim—were exonerated.

In December of the same year, Khun-lim, Ngoo Sing-jun, and Ngoo Tai-lok pushed to have Tshua Ping-hong absolved of any crimes in the second wave of exonerations.

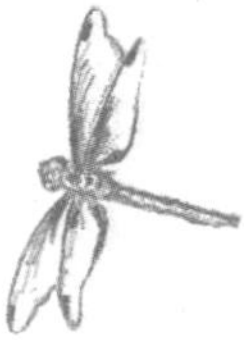

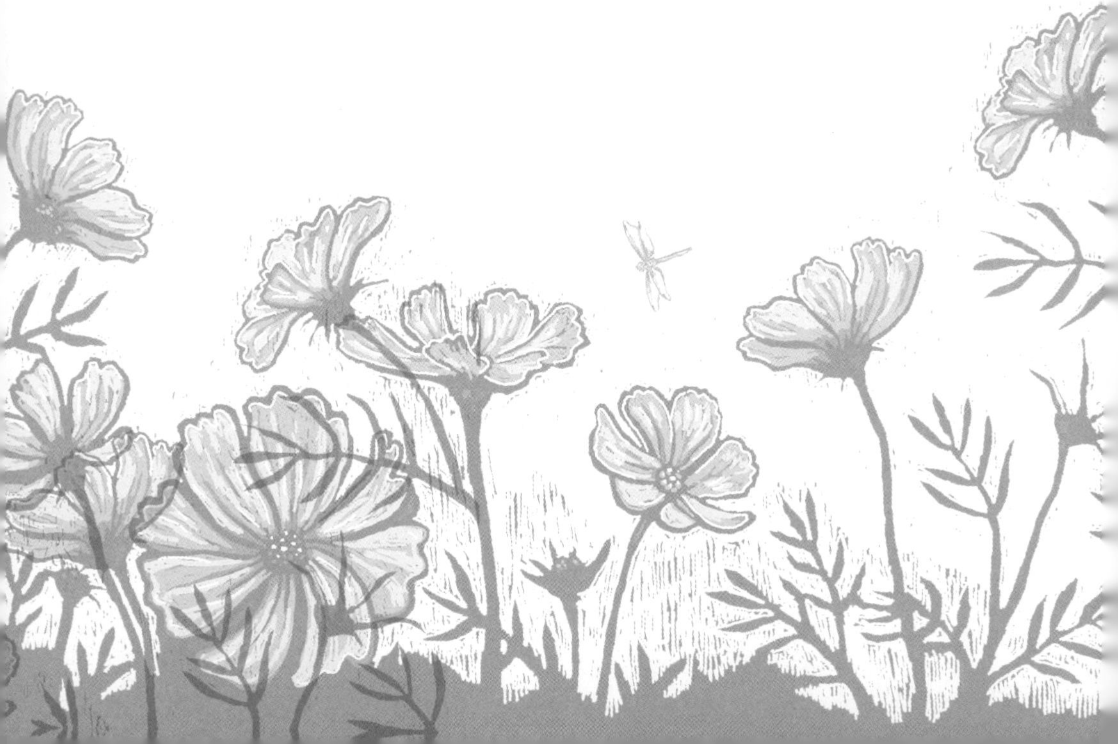

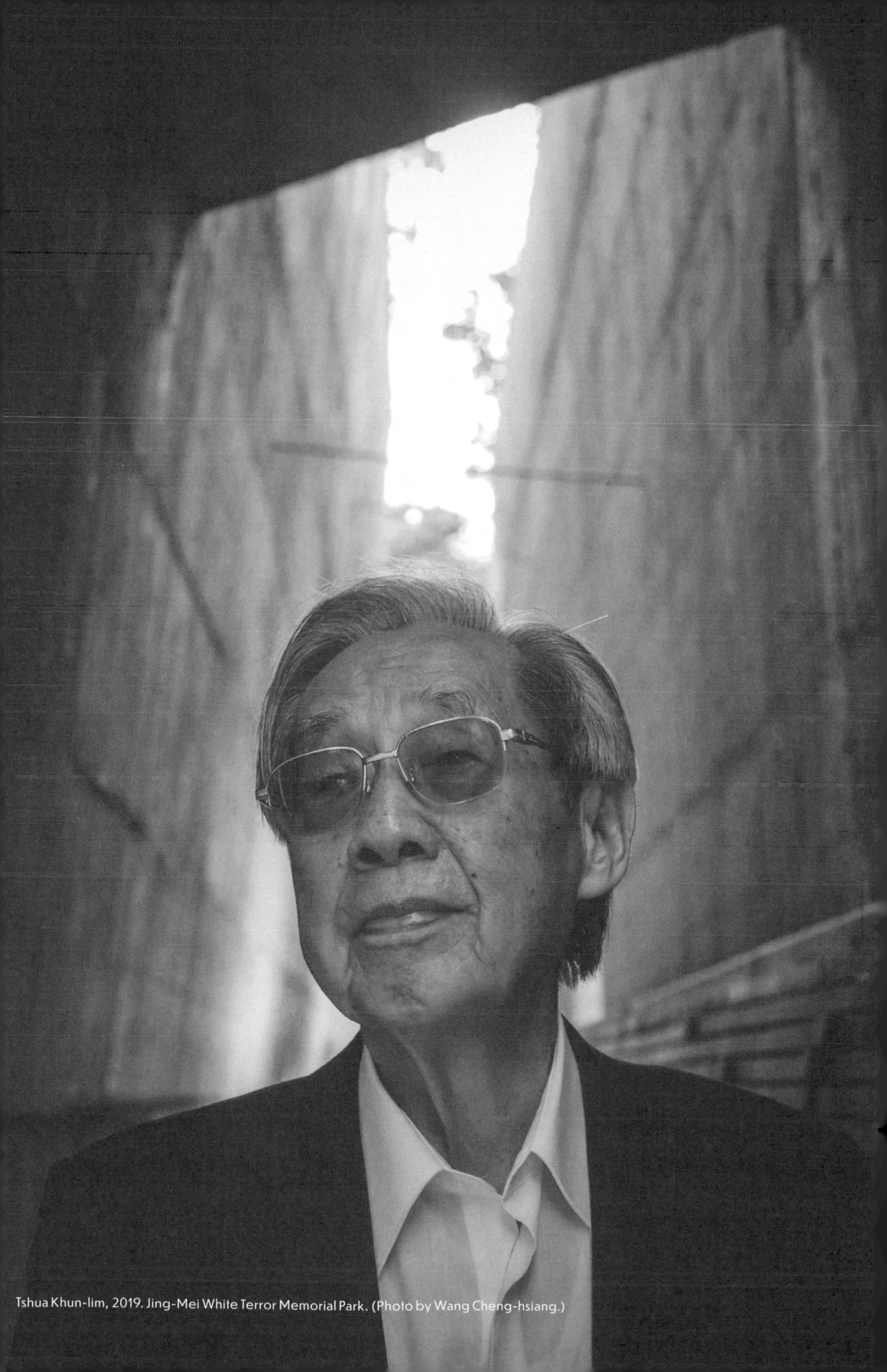

Tshua Khun-lim, 2019. Jing-Mei White Terror Memorial Park. (Photo by Wang Cheng-hsiang.)

FURTHER READING

THE BOY FROM CLEARWATER
TIMELINE—PART 3

Year	KL's Age	Events
1960	30	*September 10: Khun-lim completes his ten-year sentence and returns to Taiwan from Green Island.*
1961	31	*Due to his record as a "bandit-spy criminal," Khun-lim is forced to leave his brief tenure at* Financial Credit News *to become a translator at Jewel Press; later in the same year, he becomes an editor at Eastern Youth.* January 20: John F. Kennedy becomes president of the United States and prioritizes American military aid to South Vietnam. The Vietnam War continues to escalate. *March 18: Khun-lim and Pik-ju are engaged to be married.* *Khun-lim invests in and co-founds Wenchang Press with his former colleague at* Eastern Youth *magazine, Liao Wen-mu, and serves as the editor-in-chief. The new press collaborates with young Taiwanese manhua artists including Hong I-lan, Chen Wen-fu, Fang I-nan, Chen I-nan, and Tsai Chi-chong.* *September: Khun-lim successfully tests into Taipei Teachers' College but is forced to withdraw two months later due to his criminal record.*
1962	32	*July 29: Khun-lim and Pik-ju marry.* August 23: Indonesia refuses to let the Republic of China (Taiwan) participate in the Asian Games. *September: Khun-lim enrolls in Tamkang College of Arts and Sciences' Department of Western Literature night school to study French literature.* October 10: Taiwan Television Enterprise goes on air, launching Taiwan's first television programming. October 16-29: The Cuban Missile Crisis becomes the most dire political and military conflict between the United States and the Soviet Union during the Cold War.
1963	33	*Khun-lim becomes a copywriter at Kuohua Advertising.* December 16: Yen Chia-kan is named Premier of the Republic of China. Chiang Ching-kuo is named Minister of Defense.

Year	KL's Age	Events
1964	34	February 29: Prime Minister of Japan Ikeda Hayato publishes "Theory of the Undetermined Status of Taiwan."
		September 20: Democracy advocates Peng Ming-min and Roger Tsung-min Hsieh are arrested for publishing "Declaration of the Self-Salvation of Taiwanese People."
		Khun-lim is promoted to manager of the Matsushita Taiwan Special Account at Kuohua Advertising.
1966	36	March 21: Chiang Kai-shek is elected to his fourth term as President of the Republic of China.
		April: The government implements the Regulations for Editing and Printing Comic Books, heavily censoring manhua and causing the manhua market to quickly decline.
		December 3: Kaohsiung Export Processing Zone opens, becoming the world's first export processing zone (EPZ) where import, processing, and export can take place without payment of duties as an incentive for foreign investors. This defines and sets up the development for Taiwan's approach to manufacturing and export for decades to come.
		December 15: Prince magazine launches its inaugural issue.
1967	37	*April: Childhood magazine, designed for a younger readership than Prince's, launches its inaugural issue.*
		Khun-lim hires many of his fellow political prisoners who have returned from Green Island, drawing frequent visits from the local police to Prince Press.
1968	38	*March: Pik-ju interviews Oh Sadaharu (Mandarin Chinese: Wang Chen-chih), the famed baseball player, during the Tokyo Giants' team's preseason training in Taiwan.*
		April 4: After seeing an article on the youth baseball team Taitung Red Leaves, Khun-lim decides to sponsor the team's travel expenses so that they can compete in the 20th Taiwan Little League national championship series.
		May 21: The Red Leaves win the national championship.
		August 25: The Red Leaves defeat Japan's Little League Kansai team in an exhibition match held in Taiwan.
		Princess magazine, designed for girl readers, launches its inaugural issue.

Year	KL's Age	Events
1969	39	*December 15: Khun-lim and Pik-ju's first child, Tshua Iam-long (Mandarin Chinese: Tsai Ien-lung), is born.* July 20: Apollo 11 lands on the moon. August 23: Taichung's youth baseball team Golden Dragons defeat the team from California to win the 23rd Little League World Series. October 15: Typhoons Elsie and Flossie cause tremendous damage in Taiwan, flooding all of Prince Press's production machinery and inventory. The company's checks bounced; it is blacklisted by banks and eventually forced to declare bankruptcy.

THE BOY FROM CLEARWATER
TIMELINE—PART 4

Year	KL's Age	Events
1970	40	*Khun-lim passes the exam to teach and edit educational materials for Cathay Life Insurance's Tamsui Education Center.* April 24: Chiang Ching-kuo visits the US, where World United Formosans for Independence members Cheng Tzu-tsai and Peter Wen-hsiung Huang attempt and fail to assassinate him. October 25, 1971: The United Nations General Assembly passes Resolution 2758, officially recognizing the People's Republic of China as the only representative of China, thereby removing the Republic of China (Taiwan) from the UN.
1972	42	*Khun-lim is asked last-minute to interpret for Hara Ippei, known as "the god of sales," on a lecture tour in Taiwan. Immediately following this, he is arrested for a second time due to his earlier violation of the Law of Negotiable Instruments. With help from Cathay Life Insurance's chairman, Tsai Wan-chun, he is able to pay the NTD$200,000 bail.* *Khun-lim and Pik-ju have a second child, Tshua Gi-kun (Mandarin: Tsai I-chun).* *Khun-lim is transferred to Cathay Advertising, then again transferred to act as executive assistant to Cathay Group's deputy chairman, Tsai Chen-nan.* February 21 - February 28: US President Richard Nixon visits the PRC. May 29: Chiang Ching-kuo is named president of the Executive Yuan and premier of the ROC. September 25 - September 30: Japanese Prime Minister Tanaka Kakuei visits and establishes diplomatic relations with the PRC, ending relations with the ROC.
1973	43	September 11 : The Chilean coup places the country under the military dictatorship of Augusto Pinochet, which lasts until 1990. The military coup is regarded as a manifestation of the US-Soviet Cold War power struggle in Chile.
1974	44	Chiang Ching-kuo proposes the Ten Major Construction Projects to improve Taiwan's infrastructure and further industrialization.
1975	45	April 5: Chiang Kai-shek dies; Vice President Yen Chia-kan becomes President of the ROC. Chiang Ching-kuo becomes Chairman of the Kuomintang (KMT).

Year	KL's Age	Events
		April 23: US President Gerald Ford announces that the war is "finished" for America, and the US will pull out of Vietnam. On April 30, Communist North Vietnam and the National Liberation Front of South Vietnam take over Saigon in South Vietnam. The Vietnam War ends.
1976	46	September 9: Mao Zedong dies. On October 6, the Gang of Four—CCP leaders led by Mao's last wife Jiang Qing—are arrested for treason. This is regarded as the end of the Cultural Revolution.
1977	47	*The Cathay Museum, which Khun-lim helped plan from scratch, opens. Khun-lim serves as the inaugural museum director.*
		November 19: For the first time in Taiwanese history, civilians spontaneously break out in protest against the KMT's election fraud; later known as the Chungli Incident.
1978	48	*Khun-lim produces the exhibition* Paintings of 20th Century Spain *in collaboration with the painter Lin Hsing-yu and the founder of Artist Magazine, Ho Cheng-kuang. The exhibition is a great hit.*
		March: Chiang Ching-kuo is elected president of the ROC.
		December 15: The US and the PRC announce the Three Joint Communiqués, stating that they will establish diplomatic relations on January 1, 1979, and end diplomatic relations between the US and the ROC.
1979	49	*Khun-lim is asked by Cathay Chairman Tsai Chen-nan to found the company Encyclopedia Culture and serve as its editor-in-chief, with the objective of publishing an encyclopedia for Taiwan's readership.*
		December 10: The Formosa Incident breaks out in Kaohsiung, with physical confrontation between pro-democracy advocates affiliated with *Formosa Magazine* and the military police.
1980	50	*Khun-lim produces and publishes* An Encyclopedia of Music for Students, *which won the Golden Tripod Award, one of the highest honors in Taiwan's publishing industry.*
		February 28: Democracy activist Lin Yi-hsiung's mother and children are murdered in what becomes known as the "Lin family massacre."
		March 18 to March 27: Court-martial is held for the Formosa Incident. Verdicts are announced on April 18.
1981	51	July 2: The scientist Dr. Chen Wen-chen is forcibly taken from his home by the military police. The following day, his body is found at Taiwan National University.

Year	KL's Age	Events
1982	52	*Khun-lim acquires the rights from the Italian publisher Arnoldo Mondadori Editore to translate their encyclopedia from Japanese to Mandarin Chinese, which is then edited to become* The Full-Color World Encyclopedia of the 21st Century.
1983	53	*Khun-lim founds the bimonthly children's magazine* Long Long *and a magazine targeting young women readers called* Nong Nong.
1984	54	October 15: Henry Liu (also known by his pen name Chiang Nan), a Taiwanese-American writer, KMT critic, and author of a famous unauthorized biography of Chiang Ching-kuo, is assassinated in California by Taiwanese gang members affiliated with the ROC's Intelligence Agency.
		June 26: Deng Xiaoping, leader of the PRC, once again proposes the concept of "one country, two systems" in relation to Hong Kong, Macau, and Taiwan.
1985	55	February 18: In what will become known as the Tenth Credit Incident, ten credit unions, including the Cathay Group, are found to have engaged in serious financial malpractice. Over forty subsidiary companies, including Encyclopedia Culture, suffer severe damages.
		March 11: Mikhail Gorbachev becomes general secretary of the Soviet Union and the youngest member of Soviet leadership.
1986	56	February 25-26: The People Power Revolution in the Philippines succeeds; Corazon Aquino becomes President of the Philippines; the former president, Ferdinand Marcos, escapes to Hawaii.
		April 26: The Chernobyl disaster becomes the most severe nuclear power plant disaster in history.
		May 19: Non-KMT politicians, including the pro-democracy activist Cheng Nan-jung, start the May 19 Green Movement march, demanding the end of martial law.
		September 28: The Democratic Progressive Party is founded at Grand Hotel Taipei.
		February 28: The 228 Peace Memorial Day Association starts the 228 Truth and Peace Movement, demanding that the government make public the truth of events surrounding the incident and offering redress to victims.
1987	57	*Khun-lim returns to Kuohua Advertising and is later promoted to deputy director.*
		An advertising campaign for Taiwan's first domestically manufactured car, Feeling 101, along with the jingle "Go with My Feelings" performed by Su Ping, becomes a major hit and wins Taiwan's top award for advertising design.
		July 15: President Chiang Ching-kuo announces the lifting of martial law in the ROC, ending an era that lasted thirty-eight years.

Year	KL's Age	Events
1988	58	November 1: The PRC and ROC announces that their citizens are now allowed to visit relatives across the Taiwan Strait.
		December 16: South Korea holds its first direct presidential election and begins the process of democratization. Roh Tae-woo of the governing Democratic Justice Party wins.
		January 13: Chiang Ching-kuo dies; Vice President Lee Teng-hui becomes president.
		Khun-lim is promoted to director of Kuohua Advertising.
		August 30: The Taiwan Society for Victims of Political Persecution formed.
		October 5: The Chilean dictator Augusto Pinochet loses the presidency in an election and is forced to step down in 1990. This proves a symbolic moment for the decline of military dictatorships and the growing trend of democratization.
1989	59	*With the aim of keeping up with globalization, Khun-lim pushes for the design of "corporate identity systems" for major corporate clients from Cathay, including Taiwan Television and Chunghwa Telecom. He also establishes a market research department in accordance with the new concepts of "integrated marketing communications," transitioning Kuohua into a full-service advertising agency.*
		April 7: The PRC reaches an agreement with the International Olympic Committee for the ROC team to compete in the Olympic Games under the name "Chinese Taipei."
		April 7: Cheng Nan-jung, founder of *Freedom Era* magazine, sets himself on fire after locking himself in the magazine's offices for seventy-one days as part of his battle for absolute freedom of speech.
		June 4: At dawn, the People's Liberation Army uses military tanks to forcibly suppress pro-democracy protesters in Beijing. This bloody conclusion to the 1989 Democracy Movement is now known as the Tiananmen Square Massacre.
		August 23: Approximately 2 million people from Estonia, Latvia, and Lithuania hold hands in a human chain that stretches over 600 kilometers long to protest nearly fifty years of occupation by the Soviet Union.
		November 9: The Berlin Wall falls.
		November 17: The Velvet Revolution breaks out in Prague, the capital of the country then known as Czechoslovakia, with large-scale student protests. On December 29, the anti-communist dissident and writer Václav Havel is elected president.
1990	60	*Khun-lim pushes for the reorganization of Kuohua Advertising by bringing in young talent; he is promoted to deputy chairman.*
		February 28: For the first time, the Legislative Yuan dedicates a moment of silence to victims of the February 28 Incident and new editions of high school history textbooks are revised to include the Incident.

Year	KL's Age	Events
		Khun-lim publishes an essay written in Japanese, titled "The Gravestone of Youth," in a publication for his Taichung First High School class's fortieth graduation anniversary.
		March 16: The Wild Lily Student Movement breaks out across Taiwan. Students demand the breaking up of the legislature, the abolition of the Temporary Provisions Against the Communist Rebellion, calling the legislature into session, and a public timeline by the government for political and economic reform.
		May 30-June 1: Leader of the Soviet Union Mikhail Gorbachev and US President George H.W. Bush hold a summit in Washington, DC, signaling the end of the Cold War.
1991	61	January: The Gulf War begins.
		May 1: Lee Teng-hui repeals the Temporary Provisions, dissolving federal organizations created to enforce martial law and reinstating a two-term office limit for the presidency.
		May 9: Several people are arrested for joining the Taiwan Independence Association. On May 20, large-scale protests break out, with protesters demanding the abolition of thought police and an absolute end to White Terror. Within a week, the Legislative Yuan abolishes the Betrayers Punishment Act and the Statues for the Detection and Eradication of Spies.
		December 25: The Soviet Union—the world's first Socialist country—is dissolved.
1992	62	May 15: The Legislative Yuan passes an amendment to Article 100 of the ROC Criminal Code, removing the crime and punishment for conspiracy to commit rebellion and effectively putting an end to the White Terror era.
		December 19: After the Legislative Yuan members with extended terms are forced to retire, Taiwanese citizens are able to vote for and elect members of the Legislative Yuan for the first time.
1993	63	April 27-29: The first of the "Wang-Koo talks" is held in Singapore between Taiwan's Straits Exchange Foundation (SEF) chairman Koo Chen-fu and the PRC's Association for Relations Across the Taiwan Straits (ARATS) chairman Wang Daohan.
		July 25: The Taiwan Society for Victims of Political Persecution establishes the White Terror Victims Redress and Rights Committee.
1995	65	February 28: The government completes construction of a February 28 Incident Memorial. At the opening ceremony, President Lee Teng-hui publicly apologizes to the political prisoners and their families on behalf of the government.
		October 21: The 228 Memorial Foundation is founded. On December 18, it begins accepting cases for victims applying for reparations.

Year	KL's Age	Events
1996	66	*Khun-lim pushes for the adoption of an IT system at Kuohua Advertising, installing internet in the office and assigning a computer to each employee.* March 18: On the eve of Taiwan's first direct presidential election, the PRC's People's Liberation Army holds military exercises in the Taiwan Strait, leading to the Taiwan Strait Missile Crisis. March 23: Kuomintang candidate and incumbent Lee Teng-hui wins the presidency with 54% of the popular vote. On May 20, Lee Teng-hui is sworn in as the ROC's first democratically elected president.
1997	67	*Khun-lim joins the newly-formed Society for the Promotion of Redress for White Terror Incidents of the 1950s.* July 1: The handover of Hong Kong from the UK to the PRC ends 156 years of British rule in the former colony. Hong Kong is established as a special administrative region (SAR) of China. July - October: The 1997 Asian financial crisis affects much of East and Southeast Asia.
1998	68	*Khun-lim pushes for the merger between Nippon Dentsu, a big communications company in Japan, and Kuohua Advertising.* June 17: Lee Teng-hui announces the Compensation Act for Wrongful Trials on Charges of Sedition and Espionage during the Martial Law Period. The government begins reprocessing trials from the White Terror era.
1999	69	*March: Khun-lim retires from Kuohua Advertising.* April 1: The Legislative Yuan establishes the Foundation of Compensation for Wrongful Trials on Charges of Sedition and Espionage. The foundation processes reparations for victims of wrongful trials and certificates for "restoring reputations" damaged by false charges and verdicts. *"The Gravestone of Youth" is translated into Mandarin Chinese and serialized in the* United Daily News Supplement *over the course of eight days. It is Khun-lim's first time sharing his White Terror experiences with the general public.* September 21: An earthquake of magnitude 7.3 occurs in Nantou County in central Taiwan in the night. It is Taiwan's deadliest natural disaster since World War II.
2000	70	November 17: The Taiwan Martial Law Era Political Victims Society is founded; most new members were originally members of the Taiwan Society for Victims of Political Persecution. *Khun-lim and Loo Tiao-lin (Mandarin: Lu Chao-lin) begin running operations for the Society for the Promotion of Redress for White Terror Incidents of the 1950s.*

Year	KL's Age	Events
2001	71	In the ROC presidential election of 2000, Democratic Progressive Party candidate Chen Shui-bian wins the presidency with 39.3% of the popular vote. This marks the first transfer of power between political parties in Taiwanese history. February 23: The Legislative Yuan passes a motion for the former New Life Correction Center to become the Green Island Human Rights Memorial Park.
2002	72	December 10: On Human Rights Day, the Green Island Human Rights Memorial Park and the Jing-Mei Human Rights Memorial Park officially open.
2005	75	*At the invitation of the Professor Chen Wen-Chen Memorial Foundation, Khun-lim and Loo Tiao-lin translate the book* The Road to Freedom—Taiwan's Postwar Human Rights Movement *into Japanese. Khun-lim begins volunteering at the Foundation to translate between Mandarin and Japanese and serve as a lecturer at the Green Island Human Rights Youth Camp.*
2008	78	*February 5-28, Khun-lim carries photographs of deceased pro-democracy activists Yang Chun-long and Dr. Chen Wen-chen on the Walk against the Wind from Changhua to Taichung.* March 22: Kuomintang candidate Ma Ying-jeou wins the presidential election. Taiwan ROC sees another peaceful transfer of power when he is inaugurated on May 20.
2010	80	*Khun-lim facilitates mutual visits and cultural exchanges between the Green Island Human Rights Culture Park (formerly the Human Rights Memorial Park) and three human rights-related museums in Okinawa.* December: The Jasmine Revolution breaks out in Tunisia, heralding the Arab Spring anti-government protests.
2011	81	March 11: The 2011 Tōhoku earthquake and tsunami occurs, leading to the Fukushima nuclear disaster. *December: The National Human Rights Museum Planning Office is established; the Museum is to take over ownership and management of both the Green Island and Jing-Mei Human Rights Culture Parks. Khun-lim joins the advisory board.* *Khun-lim's autobiographical essay "A Young Bookworm's Prison Song" is collected in the first volume of a series of books on the life stories of political persecution victims,* Walking Through the Long Night, Volume 1: Lament of the Autumn Cicada.
2012	82	September 1: The Anti-Media-Monopoly March takes place, protesting PRC businesses and Taiwanese corporations that interfere with the Taiwanese media's freedoms.

Year	KL's Age	Events
2014	84	*March 18: Khun-lim, carrying the photographs of political persecution victims Yang Chun-lung and Tshua Ping-hong (Mandarin: Tsai Bing-hung), cheers on students of the Sunflower Student Movement protesting against a trade pact with the PRC.* September 26 - December 15: The pro-democracy Umbrella Movement breaks out in Hong Kong.
2015	85	*May 24: Khun-lim participates in the Anti-Black Box Curriculum Movement of students protesting at the Ministry of Education against changes to high school history curricula and other education norms in Taiwan.*
2016	86	January 16: Democratic Progressive Party candidate Tsai Ing-wen wins the presidential election. Taiwan sees another peaceful transfer of power.
2017	87	December 5: The Legislative Yuan passes the Act on Promoting Transitional Justice to publicize the truth behind martial-law-era events and to bring justice to those who suffered under the government's unjust behavior. March 15: The National Human Rights Museum officially opens. It includes two sites, the Green Island White Terror Memorial Park and the Jing-Mei White Terror Memorial Park.
2018	88	*May 17: Khun-lim gives a speech on behalf of all White Terror victims from the 1950s at the opening ceremony of the Green Island White Terror Memorial Park.* May 31: The Transitional Justice Commission is officially established. *Khun-lim wins a Special Contributions Award at the ninth annual Golden Comic Awards.* *October 5: 1,270 victims of political persecution, including Khun-lim, are exonerated of all charges.*
2019	89	March 15: The Anti-Extradition Law Amendment Bill Movement breaks out in Hong Kong, protesting against an amendment that would allow extraditions from Hong Kong to any place outside of Hong Kong, including to Taiwan and Mainland China.
2020	90	COVID-19 breaks out around the world.
2021	91	*September: Khun-lim is inducted into the Order of the Rising Sun for meritorious services to Japan.*

SOME NOTES ON THIS BOOK'S PRODUCTION

The art for the jacket and interiors was created by Zhou Jian-Xin using a manhua-inspired style illustrations in yellow tones for part three and a more realistic, documentary-inspired technique with a background color of red for part four. The text was set in Sequentialist BB, a comic book lettering font family inspired by crime noir, and the far-flung future as imagined in the 1950s. It has clean, legible lines and a deco feel. It was composed by Westchester Publishing Services in Danbury, CT.
The book was printed on 120 gsm, FSC-certified paper and bound in India.

Production was supervised by Freesia Blizard
Book design by Andrea Miller
Managing Editor: Danielle Maldonado
Edited by Arely Guzmán

LQ
LEVINE QUERIDO